Unreliable Narration and Trustworthiness

Narratologia

Contributions to Narrative Theory

Edited by
Fotis Jannidis, Matías Martínez, John Pier
Wolf Schmid (executive editor)

Editorial Board
Catherine Emmott, Monika Fludernik
José Ángel García Landa, Inke Gunia, Peter Hühn
Manfred Jahn, Markus Kuhn, Uri Margolin
Jan Christoph Meister, Ansgar Nünning
Marie-Laure Ryan, Jean-Marie Schaeffer
Michael Scheffel, Sabine Schlickers, Jörg Schönert

44

De Gruyter

Unreliable Narration and Trustworthiness

Intermedial and Interdisciplinary Perspectives

Edited by
Vera Nünning

De Gruyter

ISBN 978-3-11-055309-3
e-ISBN (PDF) 978-3-11-040826-3
e-ISBN (EPUB) 978-3-11-040841-6
ISSN 1612-8427

Library of Congress Cataloging-in-Publication Data
A CIP catalog record for this book has been applied for at the Library of Congress.

Bibliographic information published by the Deutsche Nationalbibliothek

The Deutsche Nationalbibliothek lists this publication in the Deutsche Nationalbibliografie; detailed bibliographic data are available on the Internet at http://dnb.dnb.de.

© 2017 Walter de Gruyter GmbH, Berlin/Munich/Boston

This volume is text- and page-identical with the hardback published in 2015.

Printing and binding: CPI books GmbH, Leck

♾ Printed on acid-free paper

Printed in Germany

www.degruyter.com

Preface and Acknowledgements

Though the phenomenon known as "unreliable narration" or "narrative unreliability" has received quite a lot of attention during the last two decades, narratological research has mainly focused on its manifestations in narrative fiction, particularly in homodiegetic or first-person narration. Except for narrative unreliability in film, forms and functions of unreliable narration in other genres, media and disciplines have so far been relatively neglected.

The present volume attempts to redress the balance by directing scholarly attention to those disciplines and domains that narratology has so far largely ignored. It aims at initiating an interdisciplinary approach to, and debate on, narrative unreliability and to explore unreliable narration in a broad range of literary genres, other media and non-fictional text-types, contexts and disciplines beyond literary studies. Crossing the boundaries not only between genres and media, but also between disciplines, the present volume acknowledges that the question of whether or not to believe or trust a narrator transcends the field of literature: The issues of (un)reliability and (un)trustworthiness play a crucial role in many areas of human life as well as a wide spectrum of academic fields ranging from law to history, and from psychology to the study of culture.

More specifically, the volume pursues three main aims: First, it is meant to stimulate an interdisciplinary dialogue on the concept of (un)reliability by exploring how the phenomenon has been conceptualised and analysed in a broad range of disciplines. Secondly, this volume offers suggestions for a re-conceptualisation of (un)reliability and related terms, not only from the vantage point of literary narratology but also from an intermedial and interdisciplinary perspective. The third goal consists in a transgeneric, intermedial and interdisciplinary investigation of (un)reliable narration, including e.g. non-fictional unreliable narrators on YouTube, in news broadcasting, journalism, politics and other areas such as law, medicine, psychology, and history.

During the preparation of this volume and the conference in Mainz in January 2013 from which it has originated I have incurred many debts, and it is a great pleasure to acknowledge them and to thank those institutions and colleagues who have been helpful in various ways. Though it may go without saying, such a daunting task as trying to examine unreliable narration from a broad range of disciplines requires the joined effort of adventurous and knowledgeable colleagues prepared to rush in where more sober-minded narratologists have so far apparently feared to tread. The biggest thank you, of course, goes to the colleagues who have kindly agreed to contribute original articles to this volume and who not only just build upon, but also question, enrich and modify widely accepted definitions of fictional unreliable narration. Their willingness to critically engage with assumptions and theories from research on other genres and media as well as from a variety of disciplines turned the conference into a rewarding experience.

The publication of this volume was only made possible through the generous support of a number of institutions and helpful colleagues. First and foremost, I would like to thank the director of the Gutenberg Research College of Mainz University, Prof. Dr. Matthias Neubert, and Prof. Dr. Jörg Rogge, who is the head of the research area "Historical Cultural Studies" and who kindly invited me to become a fellow at this renowned institute of advanced study. The Gutenberg Research College not only provided very generous funding for the conference but also supported me and the other fellows in various ways. They and other colleagues from the university and the Gutenberg Research College were excellent hosts, who made any number of valuable suggestions concerning my research project. Many thanks are also due to the colleagues who attended the conference, patiently answered the many questions that came up during the revision of the articles and delivered the manuscripts in time. The fact that the conference ran so smoothly is largely due to the dedicated support provided by Davina Brückner. I am particularly grateful to Daniela Vasiloiu, who spent days and even nights correcting and unifying the format of the bibliographies, admirably meeting the many challenges involved in the production of the final manuscript. I also received invaluable help from Sebastian Beckmann, who checked countless quotes and bibliographical data, and Miki Gallash as well as Martin Zettersten, who worked as our "native speakers" and made many suggestions concerning the style. I am also grateful to Corinna Assmann, Stephanie Frink and Jan Rupp for their generous support in the copyediting. In addition, I would like to thank the editors of "Narratologia" for their decision to publish the volume in their renowned book series. Last but not least, my biggest thanks go, for many reasons, to my husband Ansgar.

Heidelberg, July 2014   Vera Nünning

Contents

Preface and Acknowledgements... v

VERA NÜNNING
Conceptualising (Un)reliable Narration and (Un)trustworthiness........ 1

THEORETICAL ISSUES AND NEW DIRECTIONS

URI MARGOLIN
Theorising Narrative (Un)reliability: A Tentative Roadmap................. 31

LIESBETH KORTHALS ALTES
What about the Default, or Interpretive Diversity?
Some Reflections on Narrative (Un)reliability... 59

VERA NÜNNING
Reconceptualising Fictional (Un)reliability and
(Un)trustworthiness from a Multidisciplinary Perspective:
Categories, Typology and Functions... 83

BO PETTERSSON
Kinds of Unreliability in Fiction:
Narratorial, Focal, Expositional and Combined..................................... 109

ROBERT VOGT
Combining Possible-Worlds Theory and Cognitive Theory:
Towards an Explanatory Model for Ironic-Unreliable Narration,
Ironic-Unreliable Focalization, Ambiguous-Unreliable and
Alterated-Unreliable Narration in Literary Fiction................................ 131

GUNTHER MARTENS
Unreliability in Non-Fiction: The Case of the Unreliable Addressee... 155

TRANSGENERIC AND INTERMEDIAL APPROACHES

PETER HÜHN
Unreliability in Lyric Poetry... 173

ANSGAR NÜNNING & CHRISTINE SCHWANECKE
The Performative Power of Unreliable Narration and
Focalisation in Drama and Theatre: Conceptualising the
Specificity of Dramatic Unreliability.. 189

MATTHIAS BRÜTSCH
Irony, Retroactivity, and Ambiguity: Three Kinds of "Unreliable
Narration" in Literature and Film 221

MARKUS KUHN
(Un)reliability in Fictional and Factual Audiovisual Narratives
on YouTube 245

CHRISTOPH BIETZ
Tracing Televised 'Truth': Reality Effect and Unreliable
Narration in TV News 273

INTERDISCIPLINARY PERSPECTIVES ON (UN)RELIABILITY

BEATRICE DERNBACH
(Un)reliable Narration in Journalism:
The Fine Line between Fact and Fiction 305

ANDREAS ELTER
Unreliable Narratives in the US Elections:
How Much Reliability Can a Campaign Take? 329

ANDREAS VON ARNAULD & STEFAN MARTINI
Unreliable Narration in Law Courts 347

STEPHAN JAEGER
Unreliable Narration in Historical Studies 371

JARMILA MILDORF
Unreliability in Patient Narratives:
From Clinical Assessment to Narrative Practice 395

BRIGITTE BOOTHE & DRAGICA STOJKOVIĆ
Communicating Dreams: On the Struggle for
Reliable Dream Reporting and the Unreliability of Dream Reports 415

Notes on Contributors 429

Index 435

VERA NÜNNING

(Heidelberg)

Conceptualising (Un)reliable Narration and (Un)trustworthiness

Unreliable narrators abound not only in fiction and film, but, unfortunately, in real life, too. From little children to leading politicians, unreliable narrators can be found everywhere. Since it is in the interest of human beings to manipulate others to make them behave in a way that ensures their own well-being and survival, miscommunication has even been called a part "of the proper functioning of social communication" (Sperber 2006: 177). According to this worldview, deception and manipulation are ingrained in human interactions. On the other hand, sociologists have emphasised the crucial importance of reliability and trust "as a basic fact of social life [...]. [A] complete absence of trust would prevent [man] even from getting up in the morning" (Luhmann [1968] 1979: 4). Social interactions run more smoothly, and time and cognitive effort are saved when people who communicate with one another do not have to ask themselves in what possible ways and to what ends the narrator might be trying to deceive them. Trust is therefore the starting point for defining the rules of proper conduct; its function is the reduction of complexity (cf. ibid.: 8, 21). Following Niklas Luhmann, researchers in different disciplines proceed from the premise that, as a necessary condition (and result) of human interaction, trust is the basis of social life.[1] Unfortunately, however, trust has to be distinguished from knowledge. The decision to believe in the reliability of a person always involves a risk and may be misguided and entail radical consequences for the future behaviour of both speaker and listener.

We are therefore faced with a situation fraught with contradictions: As narrators, we may profit from telling unreliable tales; as listeners, we need reliable information. It has even been claimed that human beings have

---

1 Trust has a number of positive consequences in that it "enables cooperative behavior; [...] reduces harmful conflict [...] promotes effective responses to crisis" (Rousseau/Sitkin/Burt et al. 1998: 394). Even the economy depends on the trust of buyers both in material goods and shares.

developed particular skills for "cheater detection"² during the course of our evolution in order to distinguish trustworthy from untrustworthy communicators. Whether we adopt the sceptical view of human nature voiced by Dan Sperber and others or whether we regard trust as the basis of human interactions,³ the identification of untrustworthy stories is certainly of great importance in many areas of human life. The question of whether to believe a narrator or not transcends the field of literature. It is crucial in daily life as well as in social and economic interactions. The exploration of (un)reliability is conducted across a broad gamut of academic fields ranging from law to history, and from psychology to the study of culture. Each discipline has developed its own elaborate research traditions, methods, and approaches to analyse this phenomenon. The growing wealth of studies on (un)reliability in many fields, particularly in literary studies, at the same time raises the question of why one should read yet another volume on this topic; surely nothing new can be said about it. Looked at more closely, however, this statement itself turns out to be unreliable.

There are at least three reasons for the kind of research presented in this volume. First, though unreliable narrations have been the focus of a host of literary analyses, these have so far been mainly concerned with one specific type of unreliability: the phenomenon of unreliable homodiegetic (character) narrators. Even though there are a few articles on heterodiegetic ('omniscient') narrators, much unmapped terrain remains in this field. Perhaps more importantly, literary interpretations of unreliable narration have so far concentrated on a particular kind of narrator who, according to Wayne C. Booth (1961: 304), becomes the object of dramatic irony while a story is told "behind his back" in a communication between implied author and reader. However, there are quite a number of other unreliable narrators who should be taken into consideration, too. Moreover, even within literary studies, the discussion of this phenomenon has so far been largely confined to the study of fiction, novels and short stories. There are a few pioneering works in other fields, especially film studies, but though it has long been acknowledged that it would be rather naïve to trust all the stories that narrators tell in literary ballads, dramatic monologues, memory plays or even lyric poems, the analysis of unreliability in drama and in poetry has been neglected. A consideration of the

---

2   Cosmides/Tooby (1992: 198). These two authors have reviewed the relevant empirical studies and concluded that "people have inference procedures specialized for detecting cheaters: individuals who have illicitly taken benefits" (1992: 199).

3   Tomasello/Carpenter/Call et al. (2005) have shown that children tend to be trusting in social communication till the age of four; ontogenetically, distrust is developed later than trust.

particularities of these forms of unreliability can be the starting point in closing a gap in the existing research; it can also highlight specific features or characteristics that might then be transferred to the study of fiction and to other academic fields.[4]

Second, the literary study of unreliable narration has been pursued more or less in splendid isolation, with a rather narrow research orientation geared towards the analysis of a specific type of homodiegetic narrator in fiction published from the late eighteenth century onwards. Wayne C. Booth set this track of inquiry in his famous definition, the importance of which will briefly be considered below. By choosing this focus, the literary discussion has closed itself off against the insights that other disciplines have achieved in their studies of unreliability. Given the basic similarities between (un)reliable narrators in daily life and those featured in fictional stories, there is much to gain from looking at the way other research traditions conceptualise the phenomenon. In order to connect the literary study of unreliability with other disciplines, however, one should also consider related terms which are closely linked to the discussion of reliability. The concept of trust or trustworthiness, for instance, is an object of debate in a large number of disciplines ranging from psychology and philosophy to sociology, which have explicated trust and related terms to achieve insights we ignore at our own peril.[5] A comparison between the approaches, methods and criteria for exploring unreliability can highlight gaps in our own discipline, open up new perspectives and make it possible to modify and elaborate existing categories.

Third, the research on (un)reliability and trust has so far mainly been conducted within disciplinary boundaries, too. Even within a field like economics, the joint consideration and discussion of the concept of 'trust' that had previously been analysed separately in different approaches within economics was considered a milestone in the field (cf. Rousseau/Sitkin/Burt et al. 1998). The tendency to stay within disciplinary boundaries therefore seems not only to pertain to literary studies—other fields con-

---

[4] The research on unreliability in films is quite substantial by now; for a brief overview see Sulzbacher/Socha (2009). There is as yet next to no exploration of unreliability both in drama and in poetry, however, although the untrustworthiness of narrators in dramatic monologues has been studied by Rohwer-Happe (2011).

[5] Even though the terms '(un)trustworthiness' and '(un)reliability' cover any number of aspects that are not applicable to untrustworthy narrators or unreliable narrations, they will sometimes be used as a shorthand for the reference to the respective narrators or narrations both in this introduction as well as in the other chapters. Other usages of the word (for instance unreliable utterances in general in contrast to unreliable narrations in particular) will be made explicit. Moreover, the terms narrators and narrations will be used indiscriminately in those cases where both a narrator and a narration is unreliable. When only one or the other is unreliable, the distinction will be made explicit by the respective use of terms.

cerned with the exploration of (un)reliability adhere to the same kind of policy. A multidisciplinary analysis of (un)reliability and (un)trustworthiness, concepts which are arguably at the core of social life, promises new insights. Moreover, it seems that narratological methods and concepts can fruitfully be used in the study of non-fictional narratives, too.

The contributors to this volume attempt to close the gaps outlined above and to broaden the horizon of the discussion of unreliable narrators. There are three major aims: First, this volume is meant to initiate an interdisciplinary dialogue on the concept of (un)reliability—a dialogue that will hopefully be pursued further in the future. Second, several contributions offer suggestions for a re-conceptualisation of (un)reliability and related terms. These suggestions are mainly found in the theory section of this volume, but many of the contributions that focus on intermedial or interdisciplinary approaches to unreliability contain valuable insights concerning the conceptualisation of unreliability, too. The third goal consists of a transgeneric and intermedial consideration of (un)reliable narrators; instead of focussing on literary prose, there will be pioneering chapters on lyric poems and drama. In keeping with the broad scope of this volume, non-fictional unreliable narrators on YouTube, as well as in news broadcasting, journalism, politics and other areas such as law, medicine, psychology, and history will also be considered.[6]

In order to provide a framework that will be referred to in the following chapters, this introduction will differentiate between five aspects that are involved in the transfer of a concept like unreliability between disciplines. What is more, the framework will make it easier to compare the results. First of all, it seems necessary to clarify the terminology and explicate the key terms for characterising a given phenomenon. As far as this volume is concerned, these terms centre around (un)reliability and (un)trustworthiness, but a host of other related terms like authenticity are taken into consideration as well. The brackets surrounding 'un' indicate that it is helpful to focus not only on unreliability but also to consider reliability; this is after all the unmarked case, which serves as the default and measure of unreliability. A second aspect involves the theoretical

---

[6] One might object that fictional unreliable narrators are fundamentally different from factual ones, since, in fiction, there is the literary (or implied) author who uses the unreliable narrator for specific ends. However, this difference is not as fundamental as one might think: First, more complex factual narrations include three narrative levels (and thus the 'implied author'), too, and James Phelan (2005: 66–97) also discussed a factual memoir in his exploration of unreliable narration. Second, Richard Gerrig argued that "in cases of unreliability readers [of fiction] generally treat the narrator as the sole originator of the misinformation" (2013: 31; see also ibid.: 32–25). Besides, the boundaries between factual and fictional narrations are blurring; with regard to many genres, particularly in television or the new media, it is often impossible to decide whether they are factual or fictional.

framework in which the terms are embedded; for without this framework, it would be impossible to fully gauge their meaning. Third, the methodology—in particular, the criteria for identifying (un)trustworthy narrators—should be explored in an interdisciplinary framework. Both this third aspect and a fourth one, creating a typology of unreliable narrators, are concerned with issues common to most interpretations of particular fictional works; so far, however, they have not incorporated perspectives gained from other fields. The last aspect focuses on the question of which functions unreliable narrators can fulfil. The second part of this introduction provides a brief overview of the contributions to this volume.

1. Sets of Criteria for the Intermedial and Interdisciplinary Discussion of (Un)Reliable Narration and (Un)Trustworthiness Terminology: Explication of Terms

Conceptual transfer between literary studies and other disciplines is impeded by the fact that unreliability was first—and decisively—defined by an academic working within a rhetorical approach to literature. Wayne C. Booth, the renowned scholar who introduced the term in 1961, wanted to come to terms with a specific type of narrator whom he conceptualised within the theoretical framework of the Chicago school—that is, within rhetorical and ethical narrative theory. For him, literary works are part of a dialogue between an author and reader in general, and between the implied author located within the text and the individual reader in particular. Moreover, he was interested in ethics and morals and concerned with the distinction between the often highly questionable values of the narrator and those of the work as a whole or, in his terminology, of the implied author. These concerns shape his approach to the topic and his definition: "I have called a narrator reliable when he speaks for or acts in accordance with the norms of the work (which is to say the implied author's norms), unreliable when he does not" (Booth 1961: 158–159). This definition makes clear that the implied author does not communicate questionable morals to the reader; instead, implied author and reader are "in secret collusion, behind the speaker's back" (ibid.: 304). The narrator therefore becomes the "butt of the ironic point" (ibid.: 304); unreliable narration is a kind of dramatic irony in which a narrator tells a story while the reader recognises the unreliability of the story as well as the faults and flaws of the narrator. Author and reader agree upon "the standard by which [the narrator] is found wanting" (ibid.).

Within the context of literary studies, this definition seems perfectly reasonable. Some scholars have questioned the role of the implied author and established other criteria for the identification of unreliable narrators, but the basic thrust of Booth's definition is more or less taken for granted in the field. This has led to two problems: First of all, literary scholars have for quite a long while neglected to ask whether there might be other kinds of unreliable narrators, for instance overt—or even covert—heterodiegetic ones. And second, with one worthy exception, Liesbeth Korthals Altes, who is among the contributors to this volume, there has been no attempt to relate the concept of unreliability to that of reliability (cf. Korthals Altes 2008).[7] One of the reasons for this neglect is probably the fact that literary scholars are aware that there is no reliable narration in the sense of an objective rendering or mirroring of the events that are told. Instead, narrative is a way of attributing meaning to occurrences, a process governed, among other things, by selection, perspectivisation, moral positioning, and genre conventions.

However, the correspondence between the content of the story and the events that are told only plays a minor role in many considerations of reliability, for instance in sociology or psychology. In these fields, different aspects are foregrounded in order to explore the reliability of a speaker. Reliability is linked to the concept of trust, which is held to be a necessary precondition as well as a result of human interaction both in personal relationships and in institutions. A preliminary overview of some major publications in the multidisciplinary discussion of trust yields a number of insights, which are further elaborated on in this volume. Reliability and trust can be understood as aspects of communication; they are constructs that arise out of the interaction between a set of given partners.[8] Therefore, a number of structural as well as performative aspects pertaining to the specific situation should be taken into account as well. The situation in which a story is told is, moreover, influenced by a host of factors such as the previous encounters between narrators and listeners and the relations of dominance and power between them. Aspects such as these influence listeners' opinions that it is worthwhile to act 'as if' the person trusted were sincere, open, and moral as well as competent to act in a way that is beneficial—or at least not detrimental—to the truster.[9] Dispositional

---

[7] For the human disposition to first accept and believe information, and only critically question it later on, see the path-breaking essay by Gilbert (1991).

[8] Dernbach/Meyer state in their introduction to the volume *Vertrauen und Glaubwürdigkeit* [i.e. trust and reliability] that all of the interdisciplinary contributions gathered in the volume start from the assumption that trust and reliability emerge in communication processes (cf. 2005: 19); see also Möllering/Sydow (2005: 87).

[9] There are many interesting aspects explored in the interdisciplinary debate that cannot easily be related to the understanding of unreliable narrations in literature. A widely

aspects such as the sincerity, consistency, competence, and morality of a narrator are therefore held to be of paramount importance. The attribution of trust is part of the dynamics of communication or of the distribution of information throughout a story.

In this context, sincerity and reliability can be understood as dispositions and personality traits indicative of the trustworthiness of a speaker.[10] Trust can function as a cover term for at least three characteristics attributed to the person one trusts:

- Reliability—'engagement' (the expectation that speakers will act according to their words and manifest intentions)[11]
- Sincerity—the belief that someone is giving a truthful account of his or her beliefs, knowledge, feelings and motives
- Competence—the belief in the ability of the speaker to do what he or she intends.[12]

In defining fictional (un)reliable narrators, therefore, there are several aspects to consider; in addition to those already noted, consistency, expertise, morals, and ethics play a role.[13] These terms are defined in different ways, and it seems promising to look more closely at the prevailing definitions of both trustworthiness and reliability in order to establish a common ground. The contributions to this volume not only raise the question about the meaning of the term (un)reliability but also consider the relation between this phenomenon and other related concepts.

---

accepted definition of trust is "a psychological state comprising the intention to accept vulnerability based upon positive expectations of the intentions or behaviour of another" Quoted after Rousseau/Sitkin/Burt et al. (1998: 395); see also Möllering (2009: 140); Möllering/Sydow (2005). Economics places significant emphasis on the role of institutions and sanctions for breaking rules.

10 Reliability, then, is regarded as one of several dispositions that people ascribe to those narrators whom they decide to trust. In such definitions, reliability is a sub-category of trust (see Schweer/Thies 2005: 56). The three aspects listed here are further differentiated and expanded in a list of 18 categories that Laucken elaborates in his brilliant article (2005: 99–109).

11 However, different scholars define reliability in different ways; Habermas (1976: 435) also connects it to sincerity since this is the disposition which will guarantee that the speaker will do as he says. In medicine, unreliability serves as the cover term for all kinds of aspects that raise "questions about the accuracy of reported information" (see the contribution by Jarmila Mildorf in this volume). For a conceptualisation that refers to the future action of the partner, see Schipper/Petermann (2011: 246).

12 Cf. Schweer/Thies (2005: 57); Möllering (2001: 413).

13 In social psychology, trustworthiness is closely linked to (source) credibility, which has been connected to a number of factors like expertise, attractiveness, power and dynamism. The results of a large number of empirical studies are, however, ambivalent. For a review of pertinent studies see Pornpitakpan (2004).

1.1 Theoretical Frames of Reference

Any transfer of a concept from one discipline to another requires a consideration of the theoretical frame of reference. Terms cannot simply be singled out and incorporated into new frameworks in isolation; their meaning is also determined by the theory in which they fulfil a specific function and by their position in a network of related terms. In the following, I will briefly refer to the frames of reference used within literary studies; the articles in this volume will take into consideration a wide range of additional theoretical frameworks. In literary studies, the most predominant frame of reference has long been that of rhetorical narratology, which was briefly described earlier. However, the articles in this volume take into consideration a wide range of theoretical frameworks.

A second promising approach is opened up by structural and cognitive narratology. The toolkit of structural narratology makes it possible to provide text-internal signals for the identification of unreliable narrators. Cognitive narratology considers the cognitive rules, frames and schemata that readers apply when they process textual information. Instead of relying on the identification of textual clues alone, cognitive narratology stresses the reciprocal process between bottom-up and top-down operations on the part of readers, who apply preference rules and their knowledge of the world in order to understand a narrative text. For cognitive narratologists, the decision to call a narrator untrustworthy is a kind of naturalisation strategy that is used in order to reconcile and explain text-internal as well as -external discrepancies. When such inconsistencies become so pronounced that it is not possible to establish a coherent mental model of the narrative world, readers check whether identifying a narrator as unreliable can serve to eliminate major discrepancies; the aim is to establish a new interpretative hypothesis that can explain the most significant textual data. The importance of readers' knowledge and experiences therefore requires not only the consideration of textual features and cognitive processes but also the implicit cultural knowledge in a given period and culture.

Recently there has been an attempt to reconceptualise unreliable narration within the framework of pragmatics as a violation of the conversational maxims put forth by Paul Grice (cf. Heyd: 2011). This is compatible with the major premises of cognitive narratology, since the theoretical framework of Grice's approach within pragmatic linguistics also stresses the role of inferences on the part of readers. According to Grice, there are a number of rules that speakers are expected to adhere to in successful communication, and these are governed by the overarching 'Cooperative Principle' which requires speakers to adjust their utterances to the given communicative situation. Grice specifies four conversational maxims that speakers are expected to adhere to: the maxims of Quality (truthfulness), Quantity (informativeness), Relation (relevance), and Manner (clarity, which concerns matters of style and wording).[14] However, there are a number of problems for a new conceptualisation of unreliable narration as a violation "of the Cooperative Principle without the intention of an implicature" (Heyd 2011: 7). Dan Sperber and Deirdre Wilson highlight, for instance, that Grice is concerned with intentional, overt breaches of implicatures such as joking or irony. Moreover, he does not distinguish between the ability and the willingness of a speaker to conform to these rules.[15] Both of these aspects impede the application of Grice's conversational maxims to the study of unreliable narrators.

1.2 Methodology: Criteria for Identifying Untrustworthy Narrators

In this section, I will briefly explore some criteria for identifying unreliable narrators put forward within the field of literary studies, which are, of course, geared towards the interpretation of fictional narratives; they do not cover many of the criteria that have been developed in other disciplines but which might be useful for analysing narratives. The schematic outline may also prove helpful for other fields, just as I hope that literary studies will profit from the criteria applied in other disciplines.

Since the criteria for detecting unreliability in narratives are situated within, and cannot be understood apart from, the theoretical frameworks in which they are embedded, the respective theory will serve as a reference point of this outline. Within rhetorical narratology, the "degree and kind of distance" (Booth 1961: 155) between the implied author and the narrator serves as one criterion; but though there are very lucid and convincing interpretations of particular literary works that feature unreliable narrators, it is not entirely clear how one can measure this degree and kind

---

14 Cf. Grice (1989: 368–372). In light of the first maxim, the question of truthfulness, it seems necessary to consider what Geoffrey Leech has termed the 'Politeness Principle' as well, since general rules of conversation often prohibit telling true stories which might be embarrassing or otherwise inappropriate. Leech distinguishes between the tact maxim, the generosity maxim, the approbation maxim, the modesty maxim, the agreement maxim and the sympathy maxim.

15 See Sperber/Wilson (2002: 6–9); Wilson/Sperber (2004: 608, 611, 613). This makes it impossible to consider deliberate liars as part of "[u]nreliable narratives [which] 'quietly and unostentatiously violate a maxim' (Grice 1975)" (Heyd 2011: 7). Both lying on the part of narrators, and the intention of making the narrator the butt of the dramatic joke by (implied) authors cannot be covered by Grice's approach.

of distance.¹⁶ The criteria employed in structural and cognitive narratology are more explicit. Basically, this approach distinguishes between three types of clues: text-internal, text-external and paratextual clues (such as signals in the title or foreword).

The text-internal clues consist of inconsistencies concerning the story and/or discourse level as well as stylistic features. Since fictional homodiegetic unreliable narrators are often deeply emotionally involved, obsessed or disturbed monologists, they can frequently be recognised by features like exclamations, ellipses, rhetorical questions, any number of repetitions and the tempo of their narration. In trying to convince readers of the truth of their story, they often appeal to the reader by direct address and explanations. A third group of criteria in the field of cognitive narratology can be applied to those narrators who are untrustworthy not mainly because of their incorrect account of the facts within the fictional world but rather because of their faulty interpretations, evaluations and morals.¹⁷ A murderer may gleefully and consistently tell the story of how much he enjoyed torturing and killing his victims; a paedophile may tell the story of his love for a young girl realistically and truthfully—but they would both still have to be considered untrustworthy. It is possible, of course, that individual readers who enjoy torturing young girls may think of these narrators as perfectly reliable, but by having recourse to the prevalent cultural norms and values one can point out their untrustworthiness. Thus aspects such as the general knowledge, personality theories and values of a given culture have to be taken into account. This also applies to the values dominant in subcultures or those characteristics that are deemed normal or natural with regard to different kinds of people. Children, for instance, are regarded as untrustworthy according to different criteria than adults; in certain cultures, women may be expected to display different kinds or degrees of emotion than men, etc. Literary frames of reference and genre conventions should be considered too. In fantastic novels, trustworthy narrators may talk about rides on broomsticks, and in realistic 'authorial' novels a narrator may have insight into the consciousness of all of the characters within the fictional world.

While most of these criteria are taken for granted in the contributions to this volume just as they were during the lectures of the conference preceding it, there has been some controversy in the discussion of whether pragmatics and, in particular, breaches of the conversational rules put forward by Grice can be used for the identification and typology of signals for unreliability. Some contributors to the current volume are in favour of

---

16   James Phelan (2007) has convincingly argued that there are also cases in which the distance between narrator and reader is minimized, a process which he calls 'bonding unreliability'.
17   See Ansgar Nünning (1997, 2005) for a more elaborate discussion of these signals.

such an integration of Grice's conversational maxims, which they combine with other theoretical frames of reference. In the debate following the lectures, others were more sceptical, citing unresolved theoretical problems concerning the difference between intentional and unintentional implicatures, the incompatibility between speech acts (as studied in pragmatics) and narratives as well as the particularities of aesthetic fictional works, which employ language that cannot simply be equated with everyday speech. Apart from the theories sketched above, the chapters of this book will take further criteria into account which are important in face-to-face communications and can enrich the more or less text-related features that usually dominate the analyses of unreliable narrators in literary studies.

1.3 Typology

The most striking difference between the types of motives (and persons) involved in untrustworthy narrations is that between people who set out to deceive others and try to profit from their misconceptions and people who want to tell the truth but are unable to do so. The reasons behind this incompetence can be manifold: it might be due to a lack of insight into the facts, some kind of emotional involvement or even obsession that leads the narrators to distort events, a more general inability to interpret and evaluate what is going on, the application of an inadequate pattern of explanation or evaluation, or sheer incapability as far as social and narrative conventions are concerned. In spite of this wealth of reasons which may cause the involuntary self-delusion of narrators, the underlying similarities between these various reasons deserve to be stressed as well as the radical differences to those of the other type of storyteller who deliberately misleads his or her audience. In line with these observations, the category of intentionality plays a large role in several contributions to this volume. Schematically, one might refer to the two basic types as the liar and the fool—though admittedly there can be complex combinations such as the case of a deliberate liar who at the same time fools himself.

Within literary studies, the typology of untrustworthy narrators is a matter of contention. At first the research was concerned with identifying different character types such as the madman, the picaro, the naïf, or the clown; but these kinds of detailed and not very fruitful distinctions soon gave way to another discussion which centred on the question of whether only a homodiegetic narrator (i.e. a narrator who is part of the story world and tells about his or her own experiences) can be called untrustworthy, or whether 'authorial', heterodiegetic narrators can be called unreliable too. This discussion made perfect sense for two reasons: First, omniscient, heterodiegetic narrators were held to be trustworthy by way of definition; they are often thought to establish the facts which make up the story world. Second, within the tradition initiated by Booth, it is part of the preconditions for untrustworthiness that there is a human or humanlike character who becomes visible as a person; otherwise, one cannot attribute untrustworthiness to him or her. Though it is futile to ascribe unreliability to the narrators of fantasies, fairy tales, or postmodern fiction merely because they conform to genre conventions by telling unrealistic or impossible stories, one still has to be able to identify a human-like narrator who can become the butt of the joke and unwittingly reveal him- or herself.

Recently, however, new insights have been achieved—insights which will be pursued further in this volume. First, it is possible for omniscient, heterodiegetic narrators to become visible as personalities. Such overt narrators comment on the story, voice value judgements and generalisations. Their interpretations and evaluations can become suspect to the reader, who may arrive at the conclusion that they are untrustworthy not because of their rendering of the facts but rather on account of their interpretations and evaluations. Gunther Martens has been one of the first to draw attention to these narrators; his analyses (see Martens 2008) also integrate insights from other scholars. Such narrators are rare, but they existed both in the eighteenth and the twentieth century; and they may become more popular in the twenty-first. Second, the precondition of becoming visible as a person only pertains to the kind of narrators that Booth was interested in—those that unwittingly expose their delusions.

There seems to be another kind of narrator, however, that misleads the reader by leaving out crucial information or by presenting the data in a way that makes it very likely that it is misunderstood. Building on the work of Fabienne Liptay (2005) and Britta Hartmann (2007), Robert Vogt (2009) has introduced this second type into narratological theory. According to him, examples of this type of narrator run across the homodiegetic—heterodiegetic divide. In Agatha Christie's *The Murder of Roger Ackroyd*, for instance, the narrator tells the story of his involvement in a 'murder hunt', even though it turns out that he himself committed the murder but skilfully left out those ten minutes in which he killed his victim. In Ambrose Bierce's short story "An Occurrence at Owl Creek Bridge", in contrast, a covert, heterodiegetic narrator narrates a tale that seems to show that a man about to be executed at the beginning of the story can escape and reach his home. At the end, however, it becomes obvious that this is just the final fantasy of the man before he is hanged. Such homo- as well as heterodiegetic narrators differ from those defined by Booth, since none of them unwittingly reveals the flaws of his or her own story or becomes the butt of the irony. The contributions in this volume start from these distinctions between different kinds of unreliable narration and further explore their distinctive features.

1.4 Functions

There are many functions that unreliable narrations may fulfill. They can damage relationships, destroy trust, make listeners buy goods they never wanted in the first place or, if recognised as unreliable, make them aware of personality traits of the speaker. In different social contexts, the detection of unreliable narrators can evoke pity just as well as hatred; it can do damage just as well as good. The functions that unreliable narrations can serve differ quite substantially in different disciplines; they depend on the main research questions, the theoretical frame, and the methodology employed.

From the narrators' point of view, the most important function is to convince others of the truth of their stories. As far as storytelling is concerned, there are other aims involved, too, such as the interest to amuse or entertain, to show what a good guy one is, to establish common ground or a common identity, to become accepted by others, to break the ice, or simply to pass the time. However, nearly all of these additional functions in some way involve an interest in being believed; if the narrator is suspected to be a fraud or a liar, he or she will have difficulty realising his communicative intentions. We must also differentiate between the aims and intentions of those who willfully misrepresent the truth and those who unwittingly and naïvely want to share their misguided view of the events.

The same difference between liars and fools should be noticed when one explores the consequences that unreliable narrations have for those people who are exposed to them. One might posit that a narrator who deliberately distorts the events in face-to-face communication probably causes some kind of damage to those listeners who believe him or her since they act upon mistaken beliefs and probably suffer from the results of these actions. While the liar often profits from misrepresentations, the opposite seems to be the case with regard to unwitting but sincere narrators. Since the latter are likely to involuntarily provide signals that make it possible to detect their untrustworthiness, they cause damage primarily to themselves. If they are recognised as untrustworthy, listeners will arrive at less than favourable conclusions about the personality traits, competence or ethics of the narrator in question. Moreover, narrators who unwittingly provide insight into their ways of thinking make it possible to recognise their aims, delusions, dispositions, or personality traits. It becomes possible to characterise and know them in a more profound way, since the knowledge gained about them is derived from signals that the narrators did not intend to send.

From the perspective of the anthropologist, sociologist, and (literary) historian, unreliable narrations can be a means of gaining insights into a given (sub)culture. What is perceived as unreliable at a particular time and place is marked as beyond the pale. Judgements concerning unreliability thus highlight the borderline between the normal and the deviant; they show those implicit norms, values, and personality theories that are part of the implicit cultural knowledge but rarely expressed in explicit terms. The treatment of untrustworthy persons in a given society is highly interesting too; how unreliable narrators are dealt with allows one to recognise what is unreliable but tolerable and just within the limits of the acceptable, what is considered as scandalous and criticised, and what is mad or deceitful to such an extent that it is deemed necessary to send the narrators to closed psychiatric wards or commit them to prison. The central values of a culture, the fuzzy borderlines between normal and abnormal, between adequate and dangerous, become visible in a culture's treatment of different kinds of unreliable narrators.

Since the functions of unreliable narrations depend on the social context in which they are told and upon the disciplinary approach to their analysis, the contributions in this volume explore a number of different functions which have not been mentioned in this brief sketch. In Jarmila Mildorf's chapter on unreliability in patients' narratives, for instance, the great divide between intentional and unintentional unreliability becomes obvious: On the one hand, there are millions of Euros lost because healthy people pretend to be sick and consequently do not work; on the other hand, many patients are not treated in the way they should because they do not manage to give an appropriate description of their symptoms to their physicians. Even within literary studies, the functions that are highlighted in different chapters differ not only according to the theoretical approach but also according to the type of character and the genre that is the focus of the discussion.

2. Overview of the Chapters in This Volume

This short outline of the main aspects which are discussed in this volume shows that there is a lot of ground to be covered. At the same time, there are many noteworthy studies which have provided valuable insights into the topics of (un)reliability and (un)trustworthiness. An important work on the study of unreliable narration in fiction, edited by Elke D'hoker and Gunther Martens, was published a few years ago and put forth a number of new theoretical insights as well as broadened the scope of fictional texts. Whereas most book-length studies of fictional unreliable narration had, up to that time, been restricted to British and North American literature, the volume by D'hoker and Martens is transnational and includes texts from many European and Latin American cultures. As the title indicates, however, the volume focused on "First-Person Novel[s]" of the twentieth century, which arguably excludes a host of interesting texts and issues worthy of exploration.[18]

The present volume builds on previous research, but at the same time extends its range in several ways. In the first section, "Theoretical Issues and New Directions", new frameworks and categories for the study of unreliability in fictional as well as factual texts are developed. The chapters in this part build on existing (interdisciplinary) research and consider presuppositions as well as criteria for the analysis of homo- and heterodiegetic narrators and focalizers. In the following sections, the scope is enlarged in ever-widening circles beginning with literary genres in which the potential unreliability of narrators or focalizers has yet to be explored. The section on transgeneric and intermedial issues begins with the consideration of lyrical and dramatic texts, which is followed by an intermedial application of the concept of unreliable narration, including new forms of storytelling on the Internet. Especially with regard to narratives on YouTube, the distinction between factual and fictional storytelling becomes a contentious issue. The last and largest section comprises interdisciplinary approaches to factual unreliable narration which—with the exception of the article on unreliability in several legal discourses—concentrate on individual (homodiegetic) narrators. In these chapters, the focus lies on the particular features of unreliable narration in non-fictional discourses in which the detection of (un)reliability can have important social and economic consequences; for instance, the sentencing and imprisonment of people whose guilt is questionable or the inadequate and detrimental treatment of patients who may or may not pretend to be sick.

The first section, which deals with theoretical aspects of the definition of and approaches to (un)reliability and (un)trustworthiness, consists of six chapters. It begins with Uri Margolin's wide-ranging, cogently argued,

---

18 A special issue of the *Journal of Literary Theory* (2011), edited by Tom Kindt and Tilmann Köppe, also provides a host of noteworthy insights into the phenomenon of unreliable narration; citations of articles in this issue crop up in many of the chapters in the theory section of this volume. While many of its contributions in the *Journal of Literary Theory* concern issues also discussed in D'hoker/Martens, the explorations of Theresa Heyd, Tilmann Köppe/Tom Kindt and Frank Zipfel are closely related to issues explored here.

and innovative reconceptualisation of unreliable narration. Straddling the fact/fiction divide, Margolin differentiates between three areas of unreliable narration, viz. between the product (the narrated text), the production (the process of narration), and the producer (the narrator). These three areas are different in kind; the narrated product, for instance, belongs to semantics, while the process itself is pragmatic in nature. Moreover, the existence and degree of (un)reliability have to be explored by applying specific criteria which are aimed at the differences between these three components. Starting from these premises, Margolin provides an overview of the different units and status of the three areas. At the same time he distinguishes between the three basic modalities of the "alethic (what there is), the epistemic, and the axiological" (40), thus incorporating the three functions of communication introduced by James Phelan and Patricia Martin (1999), which concern facts (report), interpretation ("regarding") and evaluation. The (un)reliability of these three modalities must be judged by different criteria. Concentrating on the question of the (un)reliability of narratives with regard to their correspondence to what is believed to be true in a given society, Margolin also considers aspects such as coherence and completeness. He also discusses the process of narration, suggesting that in some instances, in which a narrator occupies the role of "fabulator or spinner of tales" (47), the correspondence to facts and beliefs is irrelevant, while aesthetic and emotive aspects concerning skilfulness or inventive power become more important. Most of the contributors to this volume were not only impressed with this feat of scholarship, they also use Margolin's distinction between the three areas of narrated texts, processes of narration, and narrator in their own chapters.

Equally wide-ranging and innovative, the second chapter, "What about the Default, or Interpretive Diversity?" by Liesbeth Korthals Altes, explores narratology's potential for theorising and identifying unreliable narrators by comparing different narratological approaches and developing a new, encompassing framework for the analysis of unreliability. Skilfully and subtly teasing out the main differences between these approaches, Korthals Altes shows the cognitive and heuristic value of each of them while also drawing attention to their limits. She employs a metahermeneutic approach, integrating rhetorical, structural, cognitive and pragmatic conceptualisations of unreliability and elaborates "on some of the factors that, arguably, combine into an over-arching, dynamically synthetic *framing* assumed to play a steering role in readers' interpretive decisions regarding a narrator's or author's (un)reliability" (60). Some of these framing acts—which she relates to Ervin Goffman's and Gregory Bateson's definition of frames—are connected, and the chapter focuses on how these can be conceptualised in order to gain insight into readers' interpretative strategies. Such activities include framing effects that pertain to the construction of the overall intention of the work—for instance, the decision to read a text as meta-fictional or autobiographical, to read in terms of psychology or morality instead of aesthetics, or to create an image of the author's ethos. By discussing key issues arising in an interpretation of Christine Angot's *Sujet Angot* (1998), Korthals Altes convincingly points out the importance of the readers' choice of communicational and generic conventions, which provide the basis for readers' and scholars' interpretative activities, and prompt them to identify particular textual elements as signals for unreliability. She acknowledges the potential of fields like discourse-analysis and sociology to back up and concretise some of the issues discussed in the chapter, but nonetheless confirms the importance of hermeneutics and interpretation.

In my own contribution, I attempt to re-conceptualise (un)reliability and (un)trustworthiness by drawing on definitions from several disciplines, particularly from psychology, communication theory, and sociology. I adapt three major categories in order to identify and typologise (un)reliability: the (un)reliability of narrations, which concerns the correspondence between the content of the narrative and the facts within the story world; the (in)sincerity of narrators, which is closely connected to the category of intentionality and concerned with the relation between the narrators' knowledge and the facts that are told throughout the major part of the story; and the (in)competence of narrators, which refers to the narrator's ability to present, interpret and evaluate the events as well as his or her competence with regard to conversation rules and narrative conventions of a particular situation. While these criteria can serve to analyse fictional as well as factual (and oral) stories, the study of literary narratives should additionally take into account another set of criteria: the communicative level on which the narrators tell their tales (i.e. embedded narrators or homodiegetic narrators) and the question of multi-perspectivity along with the related issue of the scope or extension of unreliability with regard to the story as a whole. An over-arching framework that combines these categories makes it possible to show the particularities of unreliable focalization and to consider kinds of narrations which have not been discussed in the debate on unreliable narration so far. In addition, I consider the presuppositions that have to be met in order to judge the (un)reliability of a tale, relate certain criteria for (un)reliability with Grice's conversational maxims and distinguish between different functions of fictional unreliable narration. I also draw attention to the as yet unexplored field of identifying and evaluating unreliable narrators in factual texts, particularly in those which were told before the eighteenth century.

Bo Pettersson adds a number of salient aspects to the theoretical debate. In the first part of his chapter, he takes a closer look at the typology of unreliability. Building on his previous studies of unreliability, Pettersson considers both unreliable narration and focalization; he also includes different markers of unreliability. Moreover, he integrates a scale of intentionality into his theoretical framework. This scale has as its two opposing poles fallibility (that is, unintentional under- or misrepresentation) and intentional deception, with a variety of forms of (self-)delusion in between. Elaborating on the importance of intentionality, Pettersson not only takes up a criterion that is often mentioned in passing in other studies; his suggestions also fit in well with the interdisciplinary discussion on the relevance of narrators' competence for gauging their reliability. Furthermore, Pettersson draws attention to the importance of the reading process's dynamic nature, which he explores under the heading "expositional manipulation" in the second part of his chapter. Starting from Menakhem Perry's insight that "the reader maintains the rejected meanings as a system of 'hovering' meanings" (Perry 1979: 356) and that discarded interpretations are part of the meaning of a fictional text, Pettersson distinguishes between different *"techniques and features of fictional unreliability by expositional manipulation"* (117) and illustrates how devices such as 'speculation' or 'partiality' serve to mislead the reader.

The theoretical discussion of unreliable narration continues with Robert Vogt, who distinguishes between three major types of unreliability: first, ironic-unreliable narrators, the type of narrator focused on by Booth and others; second, ambiguous-unreliable narration (i.e. narrations in which readers are unable to decide whether the narrator is unreliable or not); and, third, alterated-unreliable narration, which refers to tales in which readers are led to believe in one version of the story throughout the major part of the text, with the 'true' story only becoming apparent at the end of the tale. He also considers unreliable focalizers and stresses their close resemblance to ironic-unreliable narrators. In order to further explore the features of these three types of unreliability, Vogt employs insights from literary possible-worlds theory and analyses which kinds of internal inconsistencies can serve as indications of unreliability. He distinguishes, for instance, between conflicts within a narrator's world and those between a narrator's world and a focalizer's world. In a final step, he draws upon insights from cognitive narratology, particularly on the concept of decoupling, i.e. of 'tagging' particular propositions and bearing in mind that they are believed by specific characters. This perspective stresses that it is necessary to remember which character holds particular beliefs and then to construct the character's mental world as well as comparing this to the worlds of others. Vogt's insights highlight some cognitive practices that readers employ in order to make sense of unreliable narrations.

Gunther Martens' contribution on unreliability in nonfiction provides an interesting link between the issues highlighted in the theoretical section and those which are discussed in the intermedial and interdisciplinary parts of this volume. Addressing unreliability in interdisciplinary settings and in terms of a more general competence beyond understanding fictional stories, Martens discusses narrative unreliability in relation to nonfiction. He does so in the context of a specific approach to rhetorical narratology which aims to draw attention to the unreliability of the addressee rather than to that of the narrator. Martens focuses on narrative situations and narratorial profiles which provide corrective information contradicting an obsessively monologistic account and which make it possible to detect unreliability. In this way, he shows that this possibility does not imply that actual addressees take advantage of it. According to Martens, this reluctance or inability is due to increasingly hybridized multicultural contexts and memory communities, but also to the fact that seemingly reliable narratorial profiles (such as the documentary voice-over) can be re-appropriated and rendered unreliable by rhetorical means. His examples of unreliable narration focus on genres that obscure the divide between fiction and nonfiction and include gonzo journalism, fake manuals and news reports as well as subversive corporate storytelling, but also the ambiguous trend of New Sincerity in docu-fiction. Showing that, to some extent, unreliability has become a new norm in several formats, Martens argues that addressees are, on the one hand, held to be able to decode unreliability, while they are at the same time denied markers of irony which would allow them to form a communicative bond 'behind the back of the speaker'. The exploration of hybrid forms which straddle the fact/fiction divide in several media formats relates this chapter to Beatrice Dernbach's discussion of new forms of journalism and to Markus Kuhn's concern with questions of authenticity in narratives on YouTube.

The transgeneric and intermedial section of this volume, which considers the importance of unreliable narrations in literary genres other than short stories or novels and in several media, begins with Peter Hühn's exploration of unreliability in poetry. After a brief glance at dramatic monologues, the most likely candidates for an analysis of unreliability in poems because of their narrative structure and the often pronounced unreliability of their narrators, Hühn takes up the more difficult task of examining the potential and functions of unreliability in lyric poems. Even though such poems are usually held to be non-narrative, Hühn argues that quite a number of at first glance unlikely poems do contain narrative structures, particularly with regard to conveying experiences. Concentrating on poems in which narrators do not address a narratee but speak to themselves, he introduces the concept of 'self-intransparency' for those speakers who are not aware of important blind spots, which distort their narrative as well as judgement, and highlights two different functions that unreliable narration in lyric poems can fulfil.

In a pathbreaking attempt to conceptualise the forms and types of unreliable narration in plays, Ansgar Nünning and Christine Schwanecke show how fruitful it can be to transfer terms and categories from narratology to the study of plays. They proceed from the assumption that a transgeneric conceptualisation of unreliable narration can highlight gaps and blind spots in narrative theory, too: after all, most studies have concerned themselves with fiction and foregrounded the presence of an anthropomorphic narrator. Starting from a model of narrative communication fitted to the analysis of plays, they locate unreliability on three levels of communication: First, the level of action in which characters can serve as 'embedded narrators' and can turn out to be unreliable; second, on the level of narrative mediation, narrators can present the scene and comment on the action, sometimes revealing their highly untrustworthy memory and interpretation of the events. In addition, Ansgar Nünning and Christine Schwanecke propose a third, more abstract level of communication that determines the selection, perspectivisation and staging of the events, which they call 'focalisation', and which can be exposed as unreliable at the end of a play when the 'true' course of happenings is revealed. They further differentiate between different types of unreliability on these communicative levels. A brief discussion of examples demonstrates that there are more instances of unreliability in plays than has been supposed hitherto; it also highlights some of the possible combinations of the three basic types of unreliability.

The intermedial analysis of unreliability begins with Matthias Brütsch's exploration of unreliable narration in fiction and in film. As the title of the chapter indicates, Brütsch differentiates between three types of unreliability, "Irony, Retroactivity, and Ambiguity". While this distinction is compatible with Robert Vogt's contribution to this volume, Brütsch's perspective is informed by film studies. He chooses the fact that readers and viewers of fiction and films as a rule are only able to detect the unreliability of the second kind of narration in retrospect at the end of the story as its most significant feature, and stresses the differences between the three types. Moreover, he relates his discussion of the third kind of unreliable narration to Todorov's study on the features of fantasy and to the latter's concept of "fantastic hesitation" (221). Brütsch's discussion of examples of short stories, novels and films shows that the three kinds of unreliability can be found in verbally told stories and in films, but that there are media specific ways of establishing unreliability. His probing into signs of unreliability leads him to conclude that, in particular constellations, "partiality are signs of narrative *reliability* rather than of narrative unreliability" (235), an insight that is, in slightly different form, also stressed by Stephan Jaeger in his analysis of unreliable narration in historical studies. Moreover, Brütsch agrees with other contributors to this volume that there is no fixed relation between the type of narrative situation (i.e. homo- or heterodiegetic narrators) on the one hand, and the three kinds of unreliability on the other.

Markus Kuhn's exploration of "(Un)reliability in Fictional and Factual Audiovisual Narratives on YouTube" adds another facet to the study of intermedial issues by discussing key topics concerning the identification of (un)reliability in narratives across new media. Concentrating on several narrative formats of audiovisual storytelling on YouTube, Kuhn differentiates several concepts and criteria that impinge upon reliability-judgements of users. He develops a theoretical framework in which he stresses the impact of "*intermedial and other media- and genre-specific* contextual frames of reference" (248). He refers back to Ansgar Nünning's exploration of generic and contextual frames of reference, but his discussion at the same time provides further substantiation of the importance of interpretative frames explored by Liesbeth Korthals Altes in this volume. In particular, Kuhn draws attention to the alleged factuality of the tale and its correspondence to events in the real world and uses Manfred Hattendorf's definition of authenticity in order to highlight the importance of the believability of the media-specific narrative mediation of the events. This appearance of trustworthiness is linked to the effect of filmic strategies creating the impression of authenticity, i.e. stylistic patterns serving as "signposts of authenticity". Paying close attention to the rapid changes in genre conventions and authenticity markers in several kinds of audiovisual storytelling on YouTube, Kuhn singles out some combinations of devices such as the hand-held camera or breaking the fourth wall by directly talking to the camera. At the same time, however, he emphasises the rapidity and simultaneity of counteractive processes: conventions are subverted more or less at the same time at which they are established. The study of (un)reliability on YouTube therefore has to be highly aware of the particular context, of intermedial references, of the use (and possible manipulation and functionalisation) of media-specific "signposts of authenticity", and of negotiation processes and commentaries by the users. Though many of Kuhn's insights can be transferred to other modes of storytelling on the Internet, the example of unreliability in particular forms of audiovisual narrative on YouTube points to a broad range of (un)reliability in narratives across new or digital media waiting to be explored by future scholars.

Christoph Bietz' chapter on "Reality Effect and Unreliable Narration in TV News" provides a link between the intermedial contributions and the interdisciplinary section. In his wide-ranging article, which considers several basic aspects concerning the discourse on unreliability, Bietz inspects TV news both from the point of view of intermediality as well as from the point of view of journalism. Criticising the stance that journalism cannot be truthful because of the "added" narrativity of the news story, Bietz demonstrates that the consideration of narratological categories can help to avoid some problems which are inherent in standard approaches to the analysis of news, particularly news value theory. Additionally, he develops the stepping stones for an intermedial narratology specifically geared at the study of TV news. In order to delineate criteria for judging the reliability of TV news, Bietz concentrates on the level of discourse and on categories which can be used to explore the reliability of this level of narration as well as possible world theory (thus providing a link to Robert Vogt's chapter). Interestingly, Bietz distinguishes between several levels of narration, defining the "filmic composition device" as well as the "televisionary composition device (TCD)", which enables him to explore unreliability on different levels. Positing that journalists have to try to appear trustworthy by their job's virtue, Bietz explores the importance of verisimilitude and the "effet de réel", which enhance the credibility, though not the reliability, of a narrative. The last part of the chapter distinguishes between different forms and levels of unreliability in TV news by analysing two exemplary news stories from German public television. Similarly to Stephan Jaeger, Bietz concludes that one form of admitting unreliability increases the credibility as well as reliability of the story.

The third part of the volume, "Interdisciplinary Perspectives to (Un)reliability", begins with Beatrice Dernbach's chapter on unreliability in journalism. In her contribution, Dernbach questions the role that reliability plays in a discourse the very function of which is to provide accurate information. At the same time, readers often know better than to expect precise and correct information in some media formats. The potential unreliability of journalistic texts is therefore closely linked to their usefulness as well as legitimacy. Journalism is subject both to internal changes and to external circumstances, which may lead readers to doubt the reliability of the stories. Distinguishing between the media (the main function of which, according to experts, is entertainment) and journalism (which is supposed to offer truthful accounts of real events), Dernbach looks at three levels on which reliability is important within journalism: the macro level of media and journalism, the meso-level of institutional organisations, and the micro-level of individual actors and journalists. She provides useful data about journalists' self-image and reader responses while exploring the "fine line" between fact and fiction as well as that between unreliable and reliable journalism. The main theses of the chapter are illustrated by the discussion of some examples in which journalists were heavily criticised because they wrote stories that infringed upon different criteria of journalistic reliability.

Closely connected to Dernbach's topic, Andreas Elter's contribution explores the importance of narratives and their (un)reliability in the field of politics, with a particular focus on American election campaigns. Starting from sociological and psychological definitions of trust as well as the relevance of the need for a certain degree of plausibility and trustworthiness in order to motivate citizens to vote, Elter goes on to analyse these requirements in the context of American elections. He also takes the importance of the media and the move towards staging, marketing and personalising political issues into account, while he stresses that candidates' stories have to match the goals of the party as well as the attitudes, self-images and aims of voters who have to be able to identify with the candidate. These narratives have to refer back to well-known myths, to stories that invite voters to become a part of the common (national) identity that is conjured up and shaped by such mythic narratives. Identifying four main American myths which have proved to be successful over the past few centuries, Elter distinguishes between (un)reliable (factual) narratives, which can be verified or falsified with recourse to facts, and (un)reliable mythic narratives, the plausibility of which lies in their consistency with the main American myths as well as with the concordance between the narrators' self-image (as projected in the stories) and the goals of the respective party. Comparing Barack Obama's and Mitt Romney's key election speeches, Elter shows that Obama refrains from appearing to be an egotistic, potentially unreliable narrator by saying little about himself, but rather he casts himself as the witness and mediator of personal stories of selected 'common people', while Romney sometimes succumbs to the temptation of self-heroisation—and, therefore, to the creation of unreliable (factual) stories.

In their article "Unreliable Narration in Law Courts", Andreas von Arnauld and Stefan Martini also refer to American politics, using quotes from the American Declaration of Independence as an example of one of those—factually unreliable—stories that are told in legal documents. In their poignant survey of legal discourses in which unreliable narration may play a role, they show how unreliability is identified, especially in law courts. However, they do not confine themselves to the consideration of predictably unreliable texts—such as witness narratives in court. Rather, they begin by explaining how various kinds of legal discourse narrate and differentiate between binding (prescriptive) and non-binding (empirical) texts. In addition, they unravel the implications of the setting of norms, which are backed up by prototypical (though culturally variable) stories—and which, in turn, can influence the interpretation of facts and the way in which they are related to the law in question. Interestingly, von Arnauld and Martini do not exclude binding legal texts and judgements from their analysis. Narratives play a role in the decision finding process, too, since the statements of witnesses are directed by questions concerning what is relevant to the (breaking of the) law in question, and the judge selects and integrates those parts of the stories that seem to be both pertinent and reliable "into her own version of legal and factual reality—eventually, she creates a legally valid and enforceable master narrative laid down in the opinion of the court" (357). The criteria that von Arnauld and Martini list for establishing the unreliability of a narrator are similar to, but also different from those used in narratology: internal consistency; the provision of details and the expression of an adequate degree of emotionality on the part of the narrator; external consistency (including the relation to other stories and a 'hegemonic' narrative) and plausibility with regard to culturally accepted notions of 'normality'. The authors stress that, on the one hand, the "ruling establishes the facts of the case; it determines the law because it is legally entitled to do so" (361), and thus, by definition, cannot be illegal. However, they also emphasise that the judgement may be illegitimate and unreliable. This is demonstrated by their analysis of a legal case study, the decision of the German Federal Constitutional Court on the penalisation of sibling incest from 2008, which was finally upheld by the European Court of Human Rights in 2012.

Stephan Jaeger's exploration of "Unreliable Narration in Historical Studies" also deals with the (un)reliability of the narratives of witnesses, but he adds another dimension to the discussion in that he focuses on historical studies. Three quotes from historical texts, placed at the beginning of his chapter, highlight the importance of as well as the difficulty in determining unreliability in different types of historical works. On the one hand, similar to a judge, a historian is held to give an unbiased, correct account of what happened; on the other hand, objectivity is unattainable. In the first part of the chapter, Jaeger explores the conceptualisations of unreliability in historical studies as well as the critical methods which are developed to deal with the problem. 'Source criticism', that is the critical evaluation of the historical text which is studied in order to get insight into past events, is differentiated from the possible bias as well as value judgements of historians, which Jaeger relates to the discussion of objectivity and partiality. After an analysis of three different approaches to the narration of past events, all of which have to face the problem that all that is left are traces of a past, which at best add up to incomplete narrations, the second part of the chapter deals with three narrative levels of (un)reliability and (un)trustworthiness: primary narration, which consists of the sources and the narratives of witnesses, and a secondary level, on which Jaeger locates the (un)reliability of the historian's discourse and the reliability of the historian; and a third level, which also concerns the potential unreliability of the historian's narration; but in contrast to the use of unreliability in the other articles of this volume, this kind of unreliability turns out to be both correct and sincere on a higher level: It concerns an "unreliable narration [which] consciously undermines the supposedly reliable narrative" (380). In this mode of writing, historians do not fill the infinite gaps of history or smooth over and synthesise contrastive sources by integrating them into a seamless narrative. Instead, they use metanarration or provide multiple points of view to highlight the gaps and contradictions. According to Jaeger, this reveals the unreliability of the account and makes it more reliable at the same time.

Jarmila Mildorf's investigation of the different types and consequences of unreliability in patients' narratives demonstrates not only the overlap between the questions that are asked in medicine and in narratology but also supplies cogent arguments for a dialogue between the two fields. Mildorf begins with a brief sketch of the two different approaches to patients' unreliability in medicine, clinical approaches on the one hand, and narrative medicine and the medical humanities on the other, which attempt to detect and deal with patients' unreliability in completely different ways. She also differentiates between various terms used for the description of those narratives that do not conform to physicians' data; her definitions of unreliability, nondisclosure, self-disclosure, deception and dissimulation highlight both the correspondences between and the differences to narratological conceptualisations of different types of unreliability. Revealing the grave repercussions that both the deliberate feigning of symptoms and the unintended distortion of facts (or the incongruity between the terms and language of the patients and those of the physicians) can have, she calls attention to the possible damage an insufficient understanding of unreliable narratives can cause. Mildorf succeeds decisively in showing the potential importance of applying (and developing) narratological categories for the analysis of patients' narratives.

The section comprising different disciplinary approaches to (un)reliable narration and (un)trustworthiness closes with Brigitte Boothe's and Dragica Stojković's exploration of unreliability in dream reports. This is related to Mildorf's chapter as such narratives are often recorded during sessions in which patients tell their dreams. Boothe's and Stojković's contribution provides a fitting conclusion to this part of the volume since it underlines the complexity of the issues involved in the study of unreliability. Though the sincerity of the tellers of dreams is usually as pronounced as their attempt to understand and interpret their dreams in retrospect through the act of narration, the reliability of their narratives is impaired by the crucial differences between the experiencer and the narrator: lapses of memory as well as the obscurity and intransparency of dreams render understanding precarious. In addition, the act of developing a fully-fledged account following a narrative logic, which contrasts sharply to the passivity of the experiencer of dreams, is often shared by a listener, who participates in the process of narration and interpretation. The implications of embedding (un)reliable narratives in an act of communication, which are considered in a number of contributions, are taken up from a different perspective: on the one hand, the privacy of dreams is paramount, on the other, people feel the urge to communicate, which often leads eventually to a retrospective sharing of a less than reliable narration.

Works Cited

Booth, Wayne C. 1961. *The Rhetoric of Fiction*. Chicago, IL: University of Chicago Press.

Cosmides, Leda & John Tooby. 1992. "Cognitive Adaptions for Social Exchange." In: Jerome H. Barkow, Leda Cosmides & John Tooby (eds.). *The Adapted Mind. Evolutionary Psychology and the Generation of Culture*. Oxford/New York, NY: Oxford University Press. 163–228.

Dernbach, Beatrice & Michael Meyer. 2005. "Einleitung." In: Beatrice Dernbach & Michael Meyer (eds.). *Vertrauen und Glaubwürdigkeit. Interdisziplinäre Perspektiven*. Wiesbaden: VS Verlag für Sozialwissenschaften. 11–26.

Dernbach, Beatrice & Michael Meyer (eds.). 2005. *Vertrauen und Glaubwürdigkeit. Interdisziplinäre Perspektiven*. Wiesbaden: VS Verlag für Sozialwissenschaften.

D'hoker, Elke & Gunther Martens (eds.). 2008. *Narrative Unreliability in the Twentieth-Century First-Person Novel*. Narratologia 14. Berlin/New York, NY: De Gruyter.

Gerrig, Richard J. 2010. "Readers' Experiences of Narrative Gaps." *Storyworlds: A Journal of Narrative Studies* 2.1: 19–37.

Gilbert, Daniel S. 1991. "How Mental Systems Believe." *American Psychologist* 46.2: 107–119.

Grice, H. Paul H. 1989. *Studies in the Way of Words*. Cambridge, MA: Harvard University Press.

Hartmann, Britta. 2007. "Von roten Heringen und blinden Motiven: Spielarten Falscher Fährten im Film." In: Patric Blaser (ed.). *Falsche Fährten in Film und Fernsehen*. Wien/Köln: Böhlau. 33–54.

Heyd, Theresa. 2011. "Unreliability. The Pragmatic Perspective Revisited." *Journal of Literary Theory* 5.1: 3–17.

Kindt, Tom & Tilmann Köppe (eds.). 2011. *Unreliable Narration. Special Issue of Journal of Literary Theory* 5.1.

Korthals Altes, Liesbeth. 2008. "Sincerity, Reliability and Other Ironies—Notes on Dave Eggers' *A Heartbreaking Work of Staggering Genius*." In: D'hoker & Martens 2008: 107–128.

Laucken, Uwe. 2005. "Explikation der umgangssprachlichen Bedeutung des Begriffs Vertrauen und ihre lebenspraktische Verwendung als semantisches Ordnungspotenzial." In: Dernbach & Meyer 2005: 94–120.

Liptay, Fabienne. 2005. "Spinn' es noch einmal, Spider! Ambiguität als Voraussetzung für die doppelte Filmlektüre am Beispiel von David Cronenbergs *Spider*." In: Jörg Helbig (ed.). *Camera doesn't lie: Spielarten erzählerischer Unzuverlässigkeit im Film*. Trier: WVT. 189–223.

Luhmann, Niklas. 1979 [1968] *Trust and Power*. [Includes a translation of *Vertrauen: Ein Mechanismus zur Reduktion sozialer Komplexität*. 1968. Transl. Howard Davis, John Raffan & Kathryn Rooney. Chichester/New York, NY: John Wiley.

Martens, Gunther. 2008. "Revising and Extending the Scope of the Rhetorical Approach to Unreliable Narration." In: D'hoker & Martens 2008: 77–106.

Möllering, Guido & Jörg Sydow. 2005. "Kollektiv, kooperativ, reflexiv: Vertrauen und Glaubwürdigkeit in Unternehmungen und Unternehmungsnetzwerken." In: Dernbach & Meyer 2005: 64–93.

Nünning, Ansgar. 1997. "'But why *will* you say that I am mad?' On the Theory, History, and Signals of Unreliable Narration in British Fiction." *Arbeiten aus Anglistik und Amerikanistik* 22.1: 83–105.

Nünning, Ansgar. 2005. "Reconceptualizing Unreliable Narration: Synthesizing Cognitive and Rhetorical Approaches." In: James Phelan & Peter J. Rabinowitz (eds.). *A Companion to Narrative Theory*. Oxford: Blackwell. 89–107.

Perry, Menakhem. 1979. "Literary Dynamics. How the Order of a Text Creates its Meanings [With an Analysis of Faulkner's 'A Rose for Emily']." *Poetics Today* 1.1–2: 35–64; 311–361.

Phelan, James & Mary P. Martin. 1999. "The Lessons of 'Weymouth': Homodiegesis, Unreliability, Ethics and *The Remains of the Day*." In:

David Herman (ed.). *Narratologies. New Perspectives on Narrative Analysis.* Columbus, OH: Ohio State University Press. 88–109.

Phelan, James. 2005. *Living to Tell About It. A Rhetoric and Ethics of Character Narration.* Ithaca, NY: Cornell University Press.

Phelan, James. 2007. "Estranging Unreliability, Bonding Unreliability, and the Ethics of Lolita." *Narrative* 15.2: 222–238.

Pornpitakpan, Chanthika. 2004. "The Persuasiveness of Source Credibility: A Critical Review of Five Decades' Evidence." *Journal of Applied Social Psychology* 34.2: 243–281.

Rohwer-Happe, Gislind. 2011. *Unreliable Narration im dramatischen Monolog des Viktorianismus. Konzepte und Funktionen.* Göttingen: V&R unipress GmbH.

Rousseau, Denise M., Sim B. Sitkin, Ronald S. Burt & Colin Camerer. 1998. "Not so Different after All: A Cross-Discipline View of Trust." *Academy of Management Review* 23.3: 393–404.

Schweer, Martin K. W. & Barbara Thies. 2005. "Vertrauen durch Glaubwürdigkeit—Möglichkeiten der (Wieder-)Gewinnung von Vertrauen aus psychologischer Perspektive." In: Dernbach & Meyer 2005: 47–63.

Sperber, Dan & Deirdre Wilson. 2002. "Pragmatics, Modularity and Mindreading." *Mind & Language* 17.1–2: 3–23.

Sperber, Dan. 2006. "An Evolutionary Perspective on Testimony and Argumentation." In: Riccardo Viale, Daniel Andler & Lawrence Hirschfeld (eds.). *Biological and Cultural Bases of Human Inference.* Mahwah, NJ: Lawrence Erlbaum. 177–189.

Sulzbacher, Laura & Monika Socha. 2009. "Forschungsübersicht zum unzuverlässigen, audiovisuellen und musikalischen Erzählen im Film." In: Susanne Kaul, Jean-Pierre Palmier & Timo Skrandies (eds.). *Erzählen im Film. Unzuverlässigkeit—Audiovisualität—Musik.* Bielefeld: Transcript. 255–274.

Tomasello, Michael, Malinda Carpenter, Josep Call et al. 2005. "Understanding and Sharing Intentions: The Origins of Cultural Cognition." *Behavioral and Brain Sciences* 28.5: 675–691.

Vogt, Robert. 2009. "Kann ein zuverlässiger Erzähler unzuverlässig erzählen? Zum Begriff der 'Unzuverlässigkeit' in Literatur- und Filmwissenschaft." In: Susanne Kaul, Jean-Pierre Palmier & Timo Skrandies (eds.). *Erzählen im Film. Unzuverlässigkeit—Audiovisualität—Musik.* Bielefeld: Transcript. 35–53.

Wilson, Deirdre & Dan Sperber. 2004. "Relevance Theory." In: Laurence R. Horn & Gregory Ward (eds.). *The Handbook of Pragmatics.* Oxford: Blackwell. 607–632.

Theoretical Issues and New Directions

URI MARGOLIN
(Alberta)

Theorising Narrative (Un)reliability: A Tentative Roadmap

1. Defining (Un)reliability

Assessments of the (un)reliability or dependability of something or another are an integral part of our everyday life activities. And indeed (un)reliable is an evaluative predicate which can be applied to the most diverse things: systems, objects, instruments, methods, procedures, performances, products (including data and discourses), and agents. Even our own mental activities, from perception to introspection, as well as our accounts of our internal psychological states and activities are often examined as to their reliability. Within the universe of verbal discourses, issues of reliability apply equally to all major kinds of discourse consisting of claims (semantic knowledge that): descriptions, arguments—including theories and inferences—and narratives, as well as to the deontic discourse consisting of instructions (procedural knowledge how). In terms of the major kinds of speech acts, reliability is central to constatives or assertives, directions and commissives. And of course reliability is crucial whenever assessments, predictions, projections and future scenarios are involved.

But in all of these cases reliability is not a first order or manifest property but rather a supervenient one, in the sense of being the consequence of or being dependent upon the object in question possessing some other underlying properties which serve as the basis for assessing and judging its reliability. So an object may turn out to be reliable if property A serves as the basis for this judgement and unreliable if a different property B serves in this capacity. And unreliability admits not only of kinds but also of degrees (and of variations over time, at least in so far as agents are concerned). In fact, products, processes and agents are seldom assessed as totally reliable or unreliable. Reliability is actually a gradient, as attested by our everyday assessment of all of the above as highly, mostly, by and large, fairly or marginally reliable. In technical contexts, methods (metrics) in fact exist for assigning numerical degrees of reliability to procedures or products. And in each case one obviously needs some criteria for the assessment of (for deciding) the degree of reliability with respect to a given property, and an individual or group carrying out this assessment. We end up with a strongly pragmatic general claim, to wit: *someone or something is (judged) reliable for someone to some degree, with respect to some property, and at a given point in time, according to a specific criterion or criteria employed by an individual or a group.* Change any of these factors, and the judgment of reliability will change with it. Decisions of unreliability are hence never direct or one step but a function of prior decisions regarding the nature/quality of some other properties of a producer, production or a product in the case of discourses. Any theory of (un)reliability thus presupposes other theories dealing with the properties which serve as the basis for reliability decisions, and these properties themselves are usually quite complex.

In addition to naming the relevant properties which serve as *criteria* for labelling something (un)reliable, one needs also to specify in each case the accompanying surface features of the object or process which function as initial *signals* or indicators for reliability in a given respect, and the *methods* or decision guidelines and procedures to be employed in each particular case to determine reliability vis-à-vis a given criterion. It is a moot question whether there are any universal criterial properties, signals or verification methods applicable to all kinds of discourse in the context of (un)reliability, or whether they need to be discourse or context specific, or whether a combination of both kinds best defines any individual situation. I shall return to this question later on. Finally, on a second, or meta-theoretical level one could examine critically the relevance, appropriateness and reliability of these criteria, signals and decision procedures themselves, as well as their relative strengths and limitations.

We must always beware of the *unum nomen unum nominatum* fallacy, yet one is tempted to ask whether there is anything common to the various kinds of (un)reliability. I would hazard a guess that there is, that it is once again pragmatic in nature, and that it is two pronged. (1) If someone or something is considered reliable, it means acceptance that is yet short of certainty or positive proof (Dernbach 2005: 11–27). It means that this someone or something is considered unlikely to be wrong or go wrong, to fail or to fail us. If we consider a product reliable, it means that we expect it to function successfully and to carry out its designated function. If the product is a report for example, we are fairly confident that it is at least plausible or credible, that is, well supported relative to the available evidence, and that the beliefs it gives rise to in us are hence also true or justified. If it is a procedure, we anticipate it to be effective and yield repeatedly the expected results, and if a person to be usually competent and true to his word in his relation with others.

(2) Secondly, if something or someone is reliable it means that it is warranted to build on it in the selection, planning and execution of *our own* future actions, such as further elaboration, drawing conclusions, taking or avoiding certain steps and so on. In the case of assertions, for example, relying on their truth means that we may base our actions—intellectual, social and physical—on this assumption (Williams 2002: 79). Conversely, if someone or something is deemed unreliable it is likely to be or go wrong, frustrate our expectations in specific respects [we want to know what 'really' happened, we want to achieve certain results] and be unfit (inadequate) to serve as the basis on which to plan and perform our own actions, intellectual or otherwise.

And now to a lexico-conceptual note. I feel the terms 'reliable' *strictu sensu* or 'dependable', like the German 'zuverlässig', are best applied to objects, processes and agents, while 'credible', like the German 'glaubwürdig', is best applied to claims, evidence and testimony. 'Trustworthy' on the other hand, like 'vertrauenswert', is concerned with agents only and in a more general way, namely, with the overall interpersonal or social disposition of a person, with virtue and moral quality (such as honesty and openness in dealing with others, good will and good intentions, readiness to help, having the other's best interest in mind, keeping promises and commitments), and also with predictability of desirable behaviour, and hence with justified positive expectations as regards that person's future behaviour (cf. Laucken 2005; Audi 2009). As for truthfulness ('Wahrhaftigkeit'), it is a form of trustworthiness which relates in a particular way to speech, and encompasses both accuracy and sincerity (cf. Williams 2002: 94). Moreover, in the context of verbal discourses, the terms 'reliable' and 'trustworthy', when applied to process and agent respectively, function as dispositional terms, designating a long term tendency to act in characteristic ways in communicative situations. For reliable narration, a characteristic way would thus be to fully disclose all available information and to present it in a logically organised manner, and for a reliable or trustworthy narrator it would be the abiding intention and concomitant effort to make sure that one's assertions express what one actually believes and that they would give rise to true beliefs only in the minds of one's addressees (cf. ibid.).

Another basic question is from which end should one approach the issue: the positive—reliability, or its negation—unreliability. In the first case we would ideally seek to provide a set of necessary or just sufficient conditions for some object or behaviour to be considered reliable in some respect, and whenever they are not met the object or behaviour will be considered unreliable, on the old principle *malum privatio boni est*. In the opposite case we could seek to provide a set of necessary and sufficient conditions or at least good reasons to consider something or someone unreliable, but their absence (we have no reason to consider it unreliable) may logically make the object either reliable by default or just indeterminate, not disqualified yet not necessarily endorsed, so this relation is not perfectly symmetrical. I believe that in the actual discussion of a given type of narration, it is sometimes more fruitful to focus on the positive pole and sometimes on the negative, and will try later to demonstrate this claim in action. In practical terms, it may also be easier in some cases to define when something is reliable and in others when it is unreliable.

The choice from which end to start seems also to vary according to discipline and type of discourse. In *engineering*, including computer science, defining and then maximising the reliability of a process or product is the key concern. Unreliability is simply a low degree of reliability of either. In *philosophy* one invariably discusses the conditions of reliability of a procedure or person and treats unreliability as simply the failure to satisfy one or more of them. In the assessment of both witnesses and their testimony *in court* neither aspect takes precedence prima facie, but certain criteria of credibility must govern the judicial process, leading in some cases to the rule-based exclusion of whole kinds of evidence as prima facie unreliable. Now in court the two sides have opposite interests, so that for any given witness for the prosecution, the defence lawyer will try to convince the judge of the unreliability of his account of the events, and vice versa. We may thus end up with contradictory evaluations of the reliability of the same witness and/or testimony, and it is up to the judge to decide on a second order level, following his culture's rules of epistemic logic—and/or culturally established schemata and scripts—which of these two assessments of reliability is itself the more reliable one. In *psychopathology* it is obvious from the very meaning of the term that the therapist should focus on the unreliable claims about the outside world made by the patient as he tells his story, and on the unreliable (because illogical, untenable etc.) thought processes/mechanisms giving rise to these claims. The therapist will then do repair work and suggest to the patient a different story and different thought patterns which he, the therapist, considers the correct ones. But here too one could wonder about the reliability of the procedures employed by the therapist in inferring and formulating this alternative narrative. The due diligence principle or norm in *business* dictates that whenever a company offers a narrative of its past and present performance and achievements together with a scenario, usually rosy, of its future performance, one ought to be critical and look first and foremost for any indications of the unreliability of any part of this narrative. *Caveat emptor* indeed. In *literary narrative* studies, Andreas Solbach (2005) has very eloquently defended the primacy of reliability, but he seems to be the exception, with most other narratologists going for unreliability as the salient case or the foregrounded phenomenon, treating reliability as the unmarked, backgrounded or default case.

2. (Un)reliability and Narrative

Issues of unreliability in narration arise in many types of discourse and are of concern to numerous disciplines. Some of these issues are indeed discourse and discipline specific, but our task is precisely to look at matters from an inter- or multidisciplinary perspective. Now this can be done in at least two different ways: one is to compare and contrast discipline-specific criteria and procedures for assessing the reliability of narration and narrated, and the other is to try and define some fundamental categories, components or issues which are, or at least could be, shared by all of them, thereby providing building blocks for a general model of (un)reliability in narration "Überhaupt". I know of no such model, nor can I presume to offer one. What I will try to do instead is offer some reflexions and observations which could hopefully serve as building blocks for such a future model. Being myself officially in literary narratology, I have noticed that quite often categories and distinctions developed in it for the discussion of fiction turn out to be of wider applicability both through direct application to other types of discourse and through transfer, sometimes with modification, to the theoretical languages of other disciplines; and this is indeed the route I am going to follow. To be more specific, my aim in this essay is to present in outline a general model of (un)reliability in written narratives which straddles the fact/fiction divide.

Narrative texts as semiotic objects are products, and as such presuppose both a process or procedure of their production, and an agent-producer. Let us call the product narrative, the process narration and the producer narrator. Now (un)reliability may reside in any of these components, but causally they form a hierarchical progression: one detects or identifies unreliability in the narrative with respect to one or more dimensions of the domain it is about and tries to find its presumed source in what happened in the production process: in the non-fulfillment of certain communicative norms, rules or established procedures, their replacement with procedures of a different nature or with a mere random, haphazard operation. This is akin to what is known in contemporary philosophy as 'process reliabilism', whereby justified or true beliefs are produced by a reliable process of belief formation, and unjustified ones by inappropriate ones. And going one step further back, one looks for the causes or motives of such non-compliance with established logical or cultural norms and ends up with an inferred (constructed, projected) image of the producer, his capacities, competencies, beliefs, dispositions, intentions and character traits, reflected in such pertinent attributes as ignorance, feebleness, negligence, or deceitfulness. We thus start with the semantic, move to the pragmatic and end up with the cognitive or behavioural. This sequence is followed as a matter of course for both fiction and non-fiction, whenever we have no face-to-face communication or previous knowledge of the narrator. On second reading though we may reverse the order and follow things in their causal sequence: because the narrator is thus and so he uses or fails to use certain communicative procedures or obey certain norms and therefore ends up with narrative claims we find unreliable. But the danger of circularity is inherent in this reversed direction, unless we can provide independent corroborating evidence for our characterisation of the narrator, and in fiction this is clearly impossible. Moreover, while shortcomings and devious intentions will lead to deficient communicative behaviour and will normally engender an unreliable or at least questionable narrative, this may also be the end result in the case of an honest narrator who obeys standard norms of communication when the available data are inadequate or dubious or when insurmountable difficulties prevent one from arriving at their adequate interpretation, explanation or evaluation. Consequently, a pragmatically truthful hence reliable communicative performance does not guarantee, and will not always yield a semantically true set of claims about a domain. In fiction this is so because of the biographical author's conscious decision to employ unreliable claims as an artistic strategy, while in actual world discourses such an end result may well be beyond the narrator's control, whether he is a journalist, historian or anthropologist.

Either way, a comprehensive theory of narrative unreliability will have to build upon a theory of the narrated domain and its various dimensions; of the process of production, that is, a theory of communication (or rhetoric), and on a theory of the producer, drawing on mental representations, and/or dispositions and intentions and/or personality traits, as well as socio-cultural roles. This is a tall order indeed, and it can only be approximated, and even then only in a piecemeal fashion.

One can now define the conditions of reliability for each of these three components:

(1) A narrative proposition (claim) or set of propositions is deemed reliable or *credible* if we can count on it to provide us with the kind of true or valid information regarding the narrative domain we expect from propositions of this type, and unreliable if we cannot. Propositions are deemed credible if they satisfy a set of semantic con-

ditions to be specified. In each individual case we will also have to provide specific reasons for our decision to count (or not) the narrated information as credible, and spell out the criteria employed for its credibility assessment.

(2) A narrational communicative performance (speech act) is deemed reliable or *successful* if we can count on it [or: if it is likely/conducive to] to produce reliable narrative propositions of one or more types, unreliable otherwise. Such performance is deemed successful if it obeys certain communicative norms (maxims, rules, procedures). And again, in each case specific grounds for our decision to count the performance as (un)successful will have to be supplied.

(3) A narrator as producer of the narration is deemed reliable or *dependable* if we can count on him to have the requisite mental states and to obey the communicative norms which, put together, are favourable to or the most likely to lead to the production of reliable narrative propositions, unreliable if we cannot. The mental states in question are to be specified in terms of capacities, dispositions and intentions. Here too we need to provide in each case reasons why we count the narrator dependable or not.

All this may sound very formal and abstract, but I believe it reflects correctly the interpretative steps actually taken by literary scholars when they approach the issue of unreliability, its kinds and sources in a given work.

Now while a complete picture must contain all three dimensions, one need not place equal emphasis on all components in any particular case, as one's interest may focus on one of them only. In different contexts and for different purposes, a different component (teller, telling, tale) will be the one chosen for primary or even exclusive attention. What is more, (un)reliability of told or telling is a meaningful issue in all narratives, including those containing no signs of an inscribed narrator beyond a bare speech position or deictic center (Benveniste's *histoire*). The (un)reliability of the teller, on the other hand, becomes a meaningful question only when there are enough textual signs to enable us to construct an image of a quasi-human subject (person) with an interiority and at least communicative capabilities. Obviously, in all first person narratives we have automatically such an individual in the narrated domain and by implication in the narratorial sphere as well. But the (un)reliability of narrated and narration can be dealt with separately from and independently of the availability of an inscribed narrating instance, hence even in the most impersonal of third person narratives, such as an 'objective historical account'. I would even risk the following claim: the reliability of the narrator is nothing but general human trustworthiness reduced to the communicative dimension and within it to the reporting, interpreting and evaluating functions or activities. Note however that in the total picture communicative procedures occupy a pivotal position, since one can go backward by metonymy from properties of procedure to those of producer, or forwards, using properties of the procedure as signals or indicators of the anticipated quality of the product.

Sometimes in fiction and almost always in actuality we are faced with multiple reports originating with multiple narrators and offering multiple, diverse, and sometimes alternative versions of what, on the macro level, is the 'same' course of events. The different reports may deal with different aspects of the total course of events or with the same aspect (event, situation) of it. In such cases one could try to assess the absolute degree of reliability of each version, or its relative degree of reliability (that is, relative to the others) and rank the whole lot along such a scale. One epistemic norm for deciding which report is the most reliable could be "prefer that set of claims which would figure in the best explanation of the facts in question". Another crucial question is whether or not it is possible to construct a selective composite version or master narrative of the events, which would be reliable tout court or at least the most reliable one could attain under the circumstances. In such a case, convergence of claims among several reports increases the probability that these particular claims are the more reliable ones. And this is no pure theory: Many committees of enquiry, for example, are confronted with precisely these daunting tasks. Now if we have a rationalist conception of the actual world we will inevitably assume that there is only one correct version of the events, even when it cannot be secured. Fiction, on the other hand, is allowed the privilege of ultimate subjectivity. Going back to committees of enquiry, depending on the committee's mandate or objective, the decisive issue could well be not what actually happened, but rather the general trustworthiness of the various narrators as inferred from their respective versions. And although narrators in the actual world may have reputations and past histories of (un)reliability, this is no sure indicator in a new case, as context, personal interests and motives may lead any of them to provide information they know is exaggerated or false, or at least omit/suppress some information they possess.

And, to conclude, a point about unreliability and value judgments. We feel intuitively that reliability is a good-making feature of an object or process, while unreliability is its undesirable counterpart. But is this universally so? Here *literature* may indeed be the great institutional exception. Literature presents us with display texts which do not carry out the business of the world (Pratt 1977) and in them putting on display a profoundly unreliable narrated domain (Robbe-Grillet) or narration and narrator (Zeitblom in Mann's *Doktor Faustus*), and then making us figure out their causes, residing ultimately in the actual author's artistic procedures and intentions, may be the most interesting thing, as well as being considered aesthetically more challenging and valuable than straightforward reliable narration. And while unreliability is normally undesirable in actual world situations, even here readers may occasionally derive intellectual pleasure or at least (self)satisfaction from the very detection of unreliability in any of these three areas (product, process, producer) even if unintended, but especially if it needs to be ferreted out and is deemed to be the product of an attempt at deliberate deception—and to a lesser degree of irony or role playing (pretending)—by a narrator, as such detection can save the readers from sometimes fatal errors of interpretation, judgement and subsequent action. Exposing students to unreliable narratives, especially actual world ones, such as in advertising or historiography, and having them detect and identify their unreliability, its kinds and causes, can be pedagogically beneficial in honing their critical abilities and ultimately their survival skills.

In the rest of this paper I will try to develop in greater detail the conditions of (un)reliability for each of the three components of the told, telling and teller in this order.

3. (Un)reliability and the Narrated

A verbal narrative text is at least the presentation of or an account of an interconnected series of actions or events occurring in some domain and involving one or more agents. Whether the domain is actuality related or part of a game of make-believe, we assume that it is separate from and independent of the specific propositions that present it, that certain features of it are determinate, can be known with relative certainty and correctly described, and that it is possible and worthwhile acquiring such objective knowledge (Allrath/Nünning 2005). A rejection of these basic assumptions, as in some radical postmodern contexts, renders the whole issue of narrative unreliability irrelevant if not meaningless. A narrative is thus minimally a collection of propositions or claims about a domain, each of which in isolation or any conjunction of them or their totality being reliable or unreliable regarding the information they provide. Seymour Chatman (1978: 219–253) proposed classifying these propositions into reports of facts, generalisations, interpretations and judgements. James Phelan (1999: 94) has proposed similar three basic classes of such propositions, based on their dominant function: reporting, interpreting and evaluating. This intuition can be given a solid theoretical foundation by linking it to three basic modalities: the alethic (what there is), the epistemic, and the axiological. The alethic comprises claims of what is the case in the domain, both specifics (individual facts) and generalities (cf. Martínez/Scheffel 2000 [1999]: 101–104). The epistemic in the widest sense will consist of inferences drawn from these facts, putative explanations for them, and, in the human sphere, also of the ascription of semiotic, socio-cultural significance to human doings, thereby turning them into meaningful actions. The axiological consists of evaluations of any element or action of the domain according to some criterion: ethical for sure, but also at least intellectual, utilitarian, or aesthetic.

Individual alethic claims are true, false or indeterminate. If true (in actuality or in the game of make-believe) they are credible; if false non-credible, and if indeterminate problematic or questionable. Gregory Currie has introduced a further distinction for fiction between strongly true propositions, those which are true according to every interpretation, strongly false ones, which are not true on any interpretation, and those that are both weakly true and weakly false. A strongly unreliable claim is shown to be untenable according to any interpretation, while in the case of a weakly unreliable claim we should withhold opinion (cf. Currie 2004: 149–153). Epistemic propositions, as we have seen, are either inferential or interpretative (hermeneutic) in nature and valid/invalid or plausible/implausible respectively, with the first term of each pair associated with reliability and the second with unreliability. Axiological propositions consist of evaluating a person, action or product according to some criterion, and ranking it on a scale accordingly. Such propositions are apt or appropriate or not and can be treated as tenable or not. Once again, the first term is associated with reliability and the second with its absence. In sum, narrative propositions can thus be alethically, epistemically or axiologically (un)reliable. Adopting a functionalist perspective, we could say that the overall function of a comprehensive account of a narrated domain is to provide true/valid information of all three kinds about this domain and that, if the account succeeds in doing so, it is reliable. The real task is to formulate criteria by which reliability of each kind could be measured, procedures for evaluating degree of fulfillment in individual cases and, most elusively, the minimal degree of satisfaction of the criteria in each case which would still justify a reliability stamp of approval.

The relative prominence of the three kinds of claims is very different in different types of narratives, and in fact only the alethic is indispensable for a report to exist minimally. In *court*, witnesses are enjoined to restrict themselves to the so-called facts and refrain from any interpretation or the imputation of motives or intentions to agents. In literature there are styles of restricted narration, where alethic statements are the only ones on offer. But even within a type of discourse containing all three kinds the emphasis may vary greatly. Some *historical studies* thus focus on the bare facts (*les annalistes*), some on making sense of them through narrativisation (Hayden White), some on the explanation of historical events and processes, and some on their ideological evaluation (e.g. Marxist historiography). *Anthropological* narratives, recounting the experiences and observations of a scholar in a society very different from his own, are often dominated not by pure action descriptions but rather by propositions concerning the semiotic significance of observed behaviours (according to participants and observing scholar), and offering functional explanations of these behaviours. And all *didactic* narratives, whether fictional or factual, are dominated by the axiological and attendant deontic modalities. Moreover, we, according to our own needs and interests, may focus on any one of these three strains in a given narrative, regardless of whether it functions as its dominant strain.

For each of the three dimensions, different criteria of reliability are in effect, since the decision is based in each case on different kinds of textual propositions (alethic, interpretative, evaluative). And a given work may also be judged to possess very different degrees of reliability as regards each of these three dimensions because they are semi independent variables. One could imagine finding a non-fictional narrative strong on facts and poor on their interpretation or vice versa, the way we look at some nineteenth-century historiographic works. One may also accept both the description and the explanation of a sequence of events in a history book as reliable, yet reject the evaluation of these events, as when it is heavily ideological or tendentious. Narratives of illness as relayed by patients to doctors are probably most reliable when the description/reporting of symptoms is concerned, less so when the patient seeks to interpret them and explain their causes in a self-diagnosis, and maybe still less reliable when the patient evaluates the seriousness of what ails him. But of course this assumes sincere and complete disclosure of facts by the patient as point of departure. The overall reliability of the narrative is hence some kind of weighted average of its score on each. And one more thing: as we proceed from claims about narrative facts at one end to claims about their evaluation at the other, our decisions about the reliability of the respective claims involve more complex factors, and thus become more difficult to attain and less likely to show unanimity among readers. Finally, for actual world narratives, our decisions about the reliability of all three dimension often changes radically over time as the relevant store of culturally certified knowledge, as well as models of explanation and criteria of value, change, and sometimes drastically. For fictional narratives, obviously, it is only the latter two that are capable of changing.

The next question naturally is under what conditions can we or can't we count on each of these kinds of propositions to provide us with *reliable* information. This requires in principle theories of truth and truth-in-fiction, of explanation, argumentation, inference and sense making, and of evaluation. This is ideal, but totally impractical. So what we actually do is proceed by rules of thumb and by informal reasoning. I will now proceed to make some remarks on (un)reliability on the alethic dimension only, leaving the much less developed epistemic and axiological ones to better minds, and then go on to offer some observations on narrational and narratorial (un)reliability.

Alethic propositions serve the function of reporting of what is the case in a domain. Depending on the correctness and fullness of the descriptions of the domain they provide, the report containing them will be deemed accurate and credible or not, hence reliable or not. An accurate account of a narrated domain, one consisting entirely of true propositions, is of course maximally credible and hence also maximally reliable. The key question here is what semantic features of alethic propositions will enhance the correctness of the domain description they provide, hence its overall reliability. Such *reliability* of the account as a whole is judged by at least four semantic factors.

There is first of all the question of the *truth of individual propositions in isolation*, whether singular or general, in the sense of correspondence to the actual state of affairs in the domain of reference. Now in some actual world contexts this correspondence can be verified by observation, by bringing in supporting evidence from other sources, and/or by checking for confirmation by, or at least compatibility with (or plausibility relative to) the standard world model of a community, its shared knowledge, encyclopedia etc. (van Dijk 2012). There are, curiously enough, well known cases of factually true travel accounts which were deemed unreliable by their initial, contemporary audience on the grounds of such incompatibility (Marco Polo), and of false ones deemed reliable thanks to such compatibility (Mandeville). In the case of a make-believe game, governed by say-so semantics, and not by the correspondence criterion of truth, this option is not available, and such verification can be carried out only with respect to other propositions in the same text. In other words, the decisive factor is agreement with a communal actual world model in the first case and with the textual actual world of the given Game of Make-believe, however determined, in the second (usually by a process of textual analysis and description). In fact, a principle of semantic charity dictates that for Game of Make-believe texts one should accept all factual individual and general propositions as true unless there are strong counter-indications, precisely because of the lack of alternative sources of information. For texts dealing with the actual world, in contrast, one could allow oneself to be more suspicious from the outset, at least whenever other sources of information about the domain in question are available. But now a very important caveat. In general, many of the claims about a domain, whether actual or fictional, contained in a given text, will turn out to be not completely true, but rather truthlike, that is, pretty close to the actual state of affairs (Niiniluoto 1987). In such cases, although they are technically false, it would be advisable to view such claims not as depriving the account in which they occur of reliability, but merely as reducing its extent from say highly reliable to fairly reliable. In fact, in standard practice concerned with actuality-oriented discourses we normally rank factual claims, but also explanations and interpretations, as highly reliable, mostly, reasonably or fairly so, depending on the extent of their truthlikeness.

The next issue involves the *relation of consistency*, that is compatibility and lack of contradictions, within any conjunction of alethic propositions in the given narrative. Failure of this relation is of course a matter of kinds and degrees and some leading philosophers (Rescher 1979 for actuality; David K. Lewis 1978 for fiction) have even argued that minor, well-circumscribed infringement of these requirements should be isolated and not serve as grounds for tossing out the narrative as a whole as untrue and hence unreliable. Better regard it merely as one with less than full reliability, or the price we pay may be too high, which is once again a pragmatic criterion.

A further issue is that of *overall coherence and semantic relevance*. The members of a collection of alethic propositions need to be not only individually true (or nearly true) and mutually compatible, but also hang together to provide a fairly interconnected account of a particular series of actions and events in a domain. General checks, as well as standard cases of such models of global coherence, may be provided by the scripts and scenarios of actual human behaviour current in a society/culture, or by models of literary genres for Games of Make-Believe. Both credibility and reliability are reduced if a feeling of randomness, of haphazardness, is created by the narrative text, but overall coherence itself is also a matter of degree.

And finally there is the issue of the *completeness or comprehensiveness of information* of the account/report as regards the salient features of the sequence of actions in question. Clearly, missing links in an account can never enhance its overall reliability and will often tend to reduce it for the normal recipient. And this is as crucial for both factual and fictional accounts, where once again attempts will be made to supplement or fill gaps in necessary information via world knowledge or generic models, but only after inner-textually warranted implications/inferences have been exhausted. Completeness of information is a matter of degree, and is practically impossible for any actual, vs. fictional world account, since an infinite number of claims can be made regarding any actual domain.

An alethically maximally reliable account of a sequence of events in a domain will thus be one fully satisfying four conditions:

- All claims contained in it are true
- No inconsistencies exist between any propositions contained in it
- The full account is maximally coherent
- The information is complete, at least as far as the major events/actions are considered.

As already noted, no actuality oriented account can fully satisfy these conditions, and the question is hence to what extent is each of them satisfied in a given case and what their relative importance is. Only when such a metric, general or case specific, is developed can one assign a warranted, objective degree of overall reliability to an account, whether actuality-oriented or fictional. Furthermore, as we have already seen, quite often alternative accounts of the same course of events, provided by different narrators (witnesses, historians, journalists, literary narrators) are available. In this case too the metric in question will need to be employed to determine their relative degree of reliability and rank them relative to one another.

Completeness of coverage requires that we pay some attention to non-factive narratives as well, a class containing counterfactual sequences of events, possible but non-actualised courses of events, predictions, scenarios, future oriented hypothetical or conditional action sequences of the 'if → then' type, and thought experiments. Now all of these kinds of narrative have no fact of the matter at their core, so their reliability cannot be measured by alethic criteria, based on correspondence between proposition and state of affairs or on completeness, but criteria of consistency and coherence could still be employed. In addition, in all of these cases epistemic criteria of reliability need to be centrally employed, based on both logical and substantive relations between premise and conclusion or on the overall probability of the given scenario relative to pertinent world knowledge or generic models or frames.

And now, how about semantic features giving rise to alethic *un*reliability? In essence, they boil down to two: false/wrong claims—whether invented or just exaggerated—about the narrated domain (condition 1), and the absence (omission or reduction) of pertinent items of information about it (condition 4). In either case, false beliefs about the narrated domain are engendered in the reader, at least temporarily. One could obviously just register deficiencies of one or more of these kinds in a narrative, judge the account (narrative) as consequently unreliable in some respect and to some degree and let the matter rest there. But this runs counter to our basic desire to figure out what 'really' happened, and, to do so, the reader needs to become not just a processor but a producer of information as well. In the reporting case with false information the reader becomes a co-creator of the narrative, or the creator of a modified version of it, insofar as he tries to replace false/wrong claims with true ones. The correction of false/wrong claims may be easier in actual world reports where other sources of information may be available, so that false narrative claims are replaced by different, sometimes opposite ones, and more difficult in Game of Make-Believe ones, since there are no outside alternative observations or accounts. When information is missing, the reader will seek to enhance overall completeness and/or supply the missing links. As already stated, this supplementation will once again have to follow the routes of world models or generic ones respectively. Now true propositions lead us towards the formation of justified beliefs, while false ones mislead us towards the formation of unjustified ones. In the misleading case (= false claims) reliability of the first kind, namely acceptance, is already severely damaged. Lack or omission of information, though, when coupled with truthfulness of what is supplied, is simply lack of further leads, and will normally just prevent us from proceeding to step 2: using the given report as the basis for the planning of our own further actions. As for inconsistencies and incoherencies, while they do not strictly give rise to false beliefs, they too tend to increase the resultant unreliability of the account as a whole, and may challenge the reader to resolve or reduce them respectively.

4. (Un)reliability and Narration

All claims about the narrated domain, whether reliable or not, are conveyed in an extended discourse—the narration—sometimes referred to as the narrative act, hence a performance. The next major question is accordingly what substantive norms (rules, maxims, procedures) of performance or production, both universal and discourse-type specific, will tend to enhance the perceived reliability of any such discourse (and hence by implication of the claims it contains), and which factors will tend to reduce, undermine or eliminate it altogether, giving rise obviously to a globally unreliable narrative discourse. As we have earlier seen, reliability in the context of the narrated domain is a semantic issue: one deals here with propositions (locutions) and wonders about their correctness (validity, appropriateness). For alethic claims specifically, such (in)correctness is judged by checking whether or not, or to what extent, the claims in question satisfy a specific set of truth criteria or conditions, of which I have listed four. Now in the area of narration, the issue of reliability is pragmatic in nature. One deals here with speech acts (utterances, illocutions) or verbal performances, mostly of the constative type, and wonders about their well-formedness (Kindt 2008) and communicative status. These two in their turn are judged by checking whether or not, or to what degree, they comply with (satisfy) certain basic norms of communicative cooperation. Narratorial unreliability is accordingly the product of the failure of communicative cooperation, or of communicative non-cooperation, as manifested by non-cooperative speech acts and the violation of one or more of the basic norms (Heyd 2011: 8). One extreme example of communicative failure due to norm violation is provided by schizophrenic accounts, with their incoherence of discourse and failure to follow repairs suggested by the other party (Good 2006). Good goes on to claim that in general communicative failure is easier to identify than success, and that communicative success is simply the absence of failure. If this is correct, then it also follows that unreliable narration is indeed the salient one and is easier to identify and describe than reliable one.

In the previous section we noted how answers to questions concerning the reliability of claims about the narrated domain depended on answers to more basic questions about truth, interpretation and evaluation. The same situation obtains in the context of reliability of narration. Here too much wider theories of communication, linguistic pragmatics, socio- and psycholinguistics need to serve as the foundation for the more specific discussion of narrational (un)reliability. Let me single out in brief some of the leading foundational claims in this area. Most succinctly, David K. Lewis (as qtd. in Vincent-Marrelli 2006) points out to a basic convention of speaker truthfulness and hearer trust as underlying all successful communicative cooperation. According to Jürgen Habermas (Habermas 1984) by performing a constative speech act (i.e. an assertion) a speaker makes three implicit validity claims regarding (1) the truth of what is said or presupposed, (2) the speaker's truthfulness or sincerity concerning this claim, and (3) the normative rightness of the speech act in the given context. In other words, implicit claims are made simultaneously about the domain of reference, the speaker's belief world and his interpersonal social commitment. Differently put, an assertion by A to B implies commitment and responsibility by A for having made this claim, and an invitation to B to place faith in A (Vincent-Marrelli 2006). A slightly different version of communicative truthfulness is provided by Bernard Williams (2002) who proposes accuracy and sincerity as its two pillars. Accuracy dictates that a speaker should do the best he can to acquire true beliefs and make sure the beliefs he passes to others are true, and sincerity requires that what he says should reveal what he believes (i.e. no lying or deception). In a word: take care, and don't lie (Williams 2002: 11). A constative claim having the properties of accuracy and sincerity is thus tantamount to an undertaking by the speaker that this proposition represents a state of affairs actually existing in the domain of reference.

The Gricean theory of communication whose focus in fact is on everyday, ordinary exchange seems to be the one currently preferred by many philosophers, and also by literary scholars (Pratt 1977; Heyd 2006, 2011; Kindt 2008). For Grice (1975), human communication is an essentially rational and purposeful form of interaction. Narrating a story implies as a default both truthfulness and the inclusion of all salient facts. Such truthfulness and inclusive coverage are defined by the maxims of quality and of quantity, stipulating that no statements that are deemed by the speaker as less than truthful (because the speaker has no adequate evidence for them, or because he believes them to be false) should be put forth, and that no salient items of information he is aware of should be omitted.

In a somewhat reformulated version, slanted specifically towards narration, a narrative claim is defined as quantitatively well-formed if it is as informative as the purpose of the telling and the context of utterance require, and qualitatively well-formed if it is correct, grounded and believed by its originator to be true in the narrated domain (Kindt 2008: 66–67). In addition to these universal norms, different actual-world narrative discursive practices, such as journalism, historiography, police and intelligence reporting and psychotherapy have their own more specific rules of procedure or protocols how to construct their accounts of a given series of events so as to maximise/optimise the reliability—both qualitative and quantitative—of the resultant report in relation to a given set of data. Careful assessment and analysis of the evidence (=sources) according to numerous criteria is of course key in all these cases, and internalisation of these criteria and associated procedures is an essential part of acquiring discipline-specific competence and expertise in the production of the relevant type of discourse, of becoming a professional in any of these fields. Now in all of the foregoing cases the narrator's role is that of a gatherer and purveyor of information; but in both actual world and fictional contexts a narrator may occupy the alternative role of story teller, fabulator or spinner of tales, a role very prominent in much of metafiction, from Cervantes to Post-modernism, but also in tall tales, playful talk and the like. In such cases, reliability as defined by truthfulness (accuracy and sincerity) is no longer a relevant criterion, and is replaced by aesthetic or emotive ones such as inventive power, skillfulness of performance, and the twin effects of suspense and surprise.

A narrative claim is not well-formed if it constitutes a violation of one or both of the above norms. There are of course many kinds and degrees of the possible violation of any norm, ranging from failure to observe it constantly, through persistent disregard to deliberate violation, flouting or inversion, suggesting an anti-norm such as 'seek to offer untruths', or 'don't care if a claim is true or not' or 'talk about anything you wish, regardless of what you know about it' or 'just chat on, without checking if all important information is in'. In the context of narration, such unreliability-engendering violations will typically consist of a report being repetitious, containing claims about events and experiences which are beyond the narrator's horizons of knowledge and perception, and/or contradictions, unsupported conjectures and implausibilities (Kindt 2008: 66–67). Ignoring or suppressing counter-evidence or alternative versions and omitting uncomfortable facts are related practices which render reporting unreliable, and the same goes for half truths, double talk, vagueness, ambiguity and equivocation. A slightly different, and more succinct, formulation of the violations of the maxims of quality and quantity is provided by Phelan (2012: 34) who refers to them as MIS (reporting, interpreting and evaluating) and UNDER (reporting, interpreting and evaluating) or, in other words, sins of commission and of omission, *suggestio falsi* and *suppressio veri* (traditional terms mentioned in Vincent-Marrelli 2006). In the first case the reader is being misled or given false information about what is the case in the narrated domain, while in the second relevant information is omitted or withheld. Misrepresenting, I might add, can be broken down in terms of the operations of adding unfounded information, replacing correct information with incorrect one and falsely or erroneously re-arranging the sequence of events. Under-reporting is tantamount to deleting relevant information items. Grice's maxims of quality and quantity could now be given a succinct don't formulation: when narrating, don't MIS or UNDER in any way, since otherwise the net result is going to be an unreliable description of the narrated domain. It is worth noting that in the context of the well-formedness, and hence reliability of the narration as such, the properties of the narrating agent which cause such under or misreporting are irrelevant, be it that the narrator cannot do better, does not know how to do better or won't do better even though he can.

In the case of fictional narratives, and ONLY in this case, it is a constitutive convention of this type of discourse that all assertions about the narrated domain contained in a fictive discourse written in the third person, past tense impersonal or 'objective' style are self-authenticating and to be taken as absolutely authoritative, hence fully reliable, (except in cases of internal contradictions between them). Issues of the potential epistemic limitations of the instance with whom the narration originates are simply bracketed. Conversely, in first person autodiegetic narration with rich subjective semantics these issues are front and center. In such a case too the claims about the narrated domain may end up being judged as reliable, but issues of epistemic competence, intentions and motivations or psychological traits, all tending to cast potential doubt on the reliability of the telling, may always be legitimately raised.

A related yet different question concerns the nature of the rhetorical strategies and surface expressive devices (micro-stylistic features) which would tend to increase the *impression* of reliability of a given communicative act, lending it initial credence irrespective of the truth or validity of the claims contained in it. One may call such strategies and devices certifying or reliability enhancing signals/indicators/markers, and the question of their nature has already been raised and amply discussed in classical rhetoric, followed by modern studies of propaganda and advertising techniques. One could also conversely seek to define kinds of procedures and elements tending to weaken the impression of discourse reliability, hence strengthen the impression of unreliability, once again regardless of the actual situation. Grice provides two maxims, relevance and modality, concerned with the manner of communication, both enjoining the speaker to avoid irrelevancies, unclarity, disorderliness and ambiguity. As I have just said, there is no direct or 1–1 correlation between fulfilling or violating these norms and the correctness, hence reliability of what is claimed, but at least in actual-world contexts the marked occurrence of irrelevancies, ambiguities, and of vague and underdetermined claims will usually tend to arouse suspicion about the reliability of the told, while their absence will tend to enhance its assumed reliability. But the (de)certifying status of any stylistic marker is ultimately context dependent. For example: it has been empirically established that in the context of legal evidence given by children, irrelevant detail is an indicator of reliability, while neat organisation is an indicator of coaching by an adult (see Steller 1989). The same strategies and stylistic markers described in rhetorical studies tend to occur in the lists of (un)reliability indicators put forward by literary narratologists as well, at least as long as they operate within the mimetic, broadly realistic framework (Allrath 1998: 70–72; Nünning 1999: 64–65).

In general, such strategies and markers may concern the narrator's attitude to the content and the truth-value of his claims, or to his current activity of narration and its illocutionary status and force with respect to its receiver. To give just a few examples, stylistic and rhetorical features likely to foster the impression of reliability include authoritative language, impersonal, objective manner of presentation (voice of truth), apodictic style, impersonal, nominal and passive constructions, professional and technical terms and modalising particles such as: 'it is clear', 'it is evident', 'obviously', 'doubtlessly', 'as is well known', and so on. Reliability reducing procedures, of which Dostoevski's "Notes from Underground" provides one of the fullest and most striking examples, include a defensive and apologetic style full of obfuscations, hedges, retractions, restrictions, self-corrections, escape clauses, forestalling of anticipated objections, repeated assertions of the truthfulness of one's report, subjective modalities such as 'as far as I can tell' or 'if I am not mistaken', or such qualifiers as 'it seems', 'apparently', 'maybe' 'one could say', 'some say' and so on. But one should not forget that in fiction the author can match any narration style with any type of events, while in actual-world discourses the use of reliability reducing expressions is usually dictated by the epistemic situation itself, and becomes inevitable when not enough good quality information, and especially documentation (or conflicting, undecidable versions) is available for the construction of a full and adequate factual narrative. Such is the case with much of ancient history, chronicles of espionage and secret operations where information is inaccessible or has been destroyed, biographies of reticent personalities and the like. In fact, in such cases the employment by the writer of the authoritative and apodictic manner of writing may be, or at least seem to be, an attempt to disguise or gloss over the (inevitably) radically incomplete and purely hypothetical (conjectural) and hence marginally reliable nature of the narrative he is offering, and as such constitutes a blatant case of communicative non-cooperation.

An additional related area where issues of (un)reliability occur is that of the relation between metanarrative utterances and the narrative discourse they are about (and in which they occur). Metanarrative claims are para- or intratextual assertions or second order speech acts referring to and commenting upon the act/process of production of the current discourse, as well as on the constructedness of this discourse as it unfolds or comes into being (Nünning 2001). Such comments may range from assurances about the authenticity and reliability of specific claims made in the discourse about the narrated domain to comments about the discourse's language, organisation, progression and manner of presentation of the relevant sequence of events. In general, the purpose of such metanarrative comments is to set the stage for (prime), regulate and steer the reader's reception of the textual product in which they occur both as a source of information, interpretation and explanation of certain events and as a writerly project or performance. Almost any historical or biographical study, piece of investigative journalism or extended political chronicle contains a metanarrative component, which is normally taken very seriously by its author, since its perceived validity may greatly influence our judgment of the credibility of both product and producer.

What is special about metanarrative comments is that their validity can often be judged directly, by confronting the claims they make about some property of the text before us with our own judgment of this property. Paratextual commissives promising an objective and non-judgmental description of certain events or an orderly and detailed manner of their presentation can thus be directly assessed and found to be fulfilled or sadly wanting, and the same goes for intradiegetic claims as to what has been accomplished up to a given point in the text sequence and in what way. A discrepancy between such claims and the reader's judgment of the issue will reduce or negate the perceived reliability of the meta-textual claim and by contagion, even though this does NOT follow logically, of the narrational process itself and ultimately of the claims made in it about the narrated domain. Oddly enough, metanarrative comments warning about the imperfect quality of the narration/presentation and the merely conjectural nature of some of the claims raised in the text about the narrated (facts, interpretations, evaluations) serve to forestall potential readerly objections, and thus ultimately to increase the overall impression of reliability of the telling and told alike, because the originator of the discourse is now deemed honest or sincere, self-aware and the like. Speaking of the originator of the discourse, whether fictional narrator in literature or actual author otherwise, one should note that metanarrative claims may be self-referential not just with respect to the discourse itself, but also with regard to its originator, constituting an at least rudimentary self presentation or self image (persona) of the narrator, his features, role and performance *qua* originator of the current discourse (which clearly need not be about this narrator at all). Currie (2010: 70) notes that historians sometimes project in their works a persona specific to the project at hand, which may be quite different from their actual personality. Since the personal qualities mentioned in such a self presentation are supposedly manifested in corresponding, resultant features of the discourse ('I have thought long and hard about X' → a thorough, well-reasoned interpretation or evaluation of certain events), such speaker self-characterisation is once again open to direct assessment of reliability through the examination of the relevant discourse features.

5. (Un)reliability and the Narrator

Issues of the narrator's (un)reliability as information gatherer, processor/interpreter and transmitter are of major concern to a variety of disciplines such as medicine (patient error or malingering), organisational research (deception and false representations in business and institutional contexts), psychotherapy (delusional syndromes) and law (witness credibility). In so far as the transition from a reporting discourse to the personality of the reporter behind it is concerned, contemporary narratology has managed to provide an extensive, maybe even exhaustive, picture, which needs only to be briefly recapitulated here.

I have claimed repeatedly that, for a given written discourse, the reliability of the narrated and the narration alike can be examined and meaningfully judged without recourse to the discourse's originator-narrator, whether an actual world individual or an inner-textual fictional one. In fact, our judgment of the (un)reliability of the narrator of a written discourse is a function of our prior judgment of the (un)reliability of the discourse itself. When the discourse is deemed unreliable, it becomes meaningful or warranted to look for the causes of this unreliability and to anchor the unreliability-engendering properties of the discourse in some mental or social features of its originator, whether actual or fictional, and to label this originator 'unreliable narrator'. Observed or accessible properties of the written discourse will accordingly give rise to readerly hypotheses about the corresponding non-observable mental or social properties or state of mind of the actual or fictional originator of the discourse (on the general logic of this procedure, see Margolin 1986). Such hypothesised properties or states of mind could in their turn function as causal explanations of the occurrence and specific nature of the unreliability-engendering discursive properties. The discursive properties are now 'naturalised' as manifestations or consequences of the unreliable narrator's mental make-up (Yacobi 1981). Emphasis is accordingly shifted from the discourse per se to speculation about the kind of mind that could have given rise to it, and in case of psychopathology and psychotherapy, for example, such procedure is not just warranted but essential for therapy to even begin. One should not forget though that all personality modeling based on backward inference or reasoning from effects to causes is not only purely hypothetical and probabilistic, but also of the one-to-many variety, being fully dependent on the specific nature of the rules of inference employed. As both these rules and the available repertoire of personality models greatly vary between periods and cultures, the same textual features may lead in individual cases to the formulation of greatly different underlying personality models.

For actuality-oriented discourses, the transition from discourse to actual-world producer is always meaningful, but may remain purely conjectural if no independent information about the author is available. In the context of fiction and fictional narrators there obviously cannot be any independent information about or independent access to the narrator, and the very transition from product to producer is meaningful if and only if a personalised situation of narration (Benveniste's *discours*) exists in the text, with clear linguistic indications of a subjectivity or individuated human-like speaker behind narration and narrated. If the fictive narrative transmission is in the impersonal mode, the very concept of unreliable narrator, as distinct from narration and narrated, becomes inoperative, no matter how inconsistent or incoherent the narrated domain (Robbe-Grillet).

All cases of narratorial unreliability may be divided into intentional and unintentional, according to the narrator's awareness (or lack of it) of the unreliable nature of his performance, with the intentional being further divided into the playful and the deceptive. In the intentional cum playful case we are confronted with unreliability engendered by untruthfulness rooted in the misrepresentation of the literal case. But the misrepresentation is employed not to deceive, but rather to be identified and deciphered for its reliable indirect message. Detection of the unreliability of the process/product is thus often hoped for (kidding, tall tales, joking), and the same goes for some cases of ludic behaviour (pretend, role-playing). At least in the case of irony and sarcasm, an intended implicit serious and reliable message may be inferred by the receiver from the unreliable explicit literal one through a process similar to Grice's implicature, once the ironic or playful attitude is recognised or postulated. Insincerity or dishonesty lie at the heart of the verbal performance associated with the second kind of intentional unreliability, namely deception, together with a deliberate, conscious intent to misrepresent information and thereby deceive the receiver. The narrator-deceiver wants his addressee to believe as true (or false, respectively) claims which he, the deceiver, believes to be false (or true, respectively), and also to believe that he, the narrator, entertains certain beliefs which in fact he does not, or vice versa. The narrator's goal is thus to create false beliefs in the addressee's mind concerning both the state of affairs in a given domain and the narrator's own beliefs in this regard. Such false beliefs may be engendered by outright lies, half-truths, suggestions of false inferences and so on. The narrator aims to be taken seriously and literally and to keep his deceit covert, since his game is up as soon as the unreliability is detected. The deceiver's motive is often, but not always, self interest, and acts of deception are not necessarily morally reprehensible, as when a deliberate misrepresentation is undertaken in order to spare the addressee some painful knowledge, shock, public embarrassment or the like.

Unintentional unreliability is a blanket term covering a wide range of factors, all rooted in the narrator's limitations (deficiencies, inadequacies, shortcomings) or failings as regards his information basis, or his cognitive processing of the information at his disposal, or his articulation of this information. Under the first subdivision, ignorance due to age, naiveté, lack of education or cultural differences is often mentioned. Processing shortcomings or failures are associated with the narrator's mental capabilities, traits and dispositions, degree of self-awareness, and particular mental/cognitive operations. In this context, delusion and self-delusion, foolishness, mental weakness, fallibility, confusion, selective memory and forgetfulness are prominent, as well as lack of critical sense and errors of reasoning and judgment, sometimes due to emotional factors. Finally, inability to articulate and convey one's claims in a comprehensible manner is obviously bound to lead to communicative failure and the resultant ascription of unreliability to the narrator-communicator.

Any discussion of narrator's unreliability, like that of narrated and narration, is ultimately based upon wider theoretical perspectives or frameworks. I am convinced that, once again, the four that have been employed in the study of fictive narrators are equally fruitful for the study of actual ones, and here they are:

- Philosophy of mind, focusing on propositional attitudes, that is beliefs, right or wrong, and on intentions, sincere or deceitful, as determining what kinds of assertions a narrator will make. Attributing intentions to a narrator is essentially a particular kind of mental state attribution, drawing upon a general theory of mind or on case-specific simulation.
- Cognitive *cum* possible worlds models, explaining unreliability as stemming from the lack of overlap between the situation in the actual or make-believe world and its situation model or mental representation in the narrator's mind, with the discrepancy stemming from error, lack of knowledge or an inability to separate one's beliefs and wishes from facts.
- Personality models singling out individual character traits or syndromes, including mental abnormality, as the cause of unreliability.
- Socio-cultural theories where an individual's role, position and interpersonal situation are seen as the causes of the unreliability of narration or narrated.

***

In this paper I have sought to provide a brief systematic description of what I see as the main issues involved in theorising (un)reliability in written narrative—be it actuality-oriented or fiction—by proceeding from product (what) to production or performance (how), and ending with the narrator (who). Let me now recapitulate in brief the main features of my model.

The NARRATED consists of a set of claims (propositions) about one or more domains of reference, with the crucial dimension for their assessment being the *semantic* one. Individual claims or reports as collections/conjunctions of claims are deemed reliable if they are *credible*, with credible meaning at least *plausible*, the receiver having more reasons to accept the claim(s) in question than to reject them. Claims can be assigned degrees of plausibility, since this is a scalar feature. A claim or report is unreliable, hence non-credible, if it is by and large not plausible, if we have more reasons to reject or at least modify it than to accept it as is. The credibility of claims is assessed according to the degree to which they satisfy/fulfil semantic conditions/criteria of three kinds: alethic (concerning both individual factual claims and generalisations), epistemic (concerning inference, explanation and interpretation or sense making), and axiological (evaluative). For the alethic dimension, four conditions can be formulated: truth by correspondence (vs. errors and inaccuracies), consistency (vs. internal discrepancies), coherence (vs. dissociation), and completeness (vs. key lacunae). For inference and explanation the minimum requirements are being logically valid and factually supported, while for interpretation the basic requirement is that of being motivated by an explicit semiotic code and its rules of sense making. For an evaluation to be reliable, it must choose pertinent general criteria and apply them correctly in the given case. All rules and criteria beyond the purely formal ones are conventional, hence culture, period and genre dependent, and the relative weight attached to the fulfillment of each of them in a given case is user dependent.

NARRATION (telling, reporting) consists of the process or activity of formulating and transmitting claims about one or more domains of reference. The crucial dimension for the assessment of this verbal activity is the *pragmatic*. The building blocks of the communicative performance concerned with the formulation and transmission of narrative claims are speech acts. A reporting performance is deemed reliable if it is *successful*, with successful being equivalent to *confirming to* or obeying *a set of communicative norms* (maxims, rules of procedure), such as those formulated by Grice (quality, quantity, manner and relation) or Williams (accuracy and sincerity). Narrative/reporting performance is deemed unsuccessful, hence unreliable, if it fails to obey one or more of these norms. In the case of Grice's maxims, such failure will consist in the replacement of truth with falsehood, inclusion with omission, clarity and coherence with equivocation and relevance with evasion (Vincent-Marrelli 2006). Once again, both the reliability (success) and unreliability (failure) of narration are scalar in nature, and different norms can be obeyed or deviated from to different degrees.

A NARRATOR is the originator, inner-textual or actual, of the narration at hand. He is deemed (un)reliable on the basis of prior decisions regarding the (un)reliability of the telling and/or the told. The crucial dimension for assessing narrator reliability is the *mental*. A narrator is considered reliable if he is *dependable*, if he possesses the *cognitive and behavioural properties* necessary for the production of reliable claims, and non-dependable otherwise. The properties in question include information state, communicative intentions, capacities and dispositions, as well as personality traits. Properties of any of these kinds are hypothetically ascribed to the narrator by readers on the basis of cultural codes, and they (or their absence or reversal) serve in their turn as motivation or explanation for the (un)reliability of the telling and/or the told. In a further step they may also serve as the basis for constructing a personality profile of the narrator, whether actual of fictional.

It remains to be seen how much of what I have proposed is applicable to or useful for different areas (such as historiography, journalism, legal discourse), and how much needs correction, replacement or simple removal. One also needs to determine what major problem areas have been overlooked, what lacunae remain in the overall scheme, and how they should be filled in, in general or in an area-specific manner. I trust the articles in this volume go a long way towards improving what is after all just an initial and tentative integrated model.

Works Cited

Allrath, Gaby. 1998. "'But why will you say that I am mad?' Textuelle Signale für die Ermittlung von *unreliable narration*." In: Ansgar Nünning (ed.). *Unreliable Narration. Studien zur Theorie und Praxis unglaubwürdigen Erzählens in der englischsprachigen Erzählliteratur.* Trier: WVT. 59–79.

Allrath, Gaby & Ansgar Nünning. 2005. "(Un-) Zuverlässigkeitsurteile aus literaturwissenschaftlicher Sicht: Textuelle Signale, lebensweltliche Bezugsrahmen und Kriterien für die Zuschreibung von (Un-) Glaub-

würdigkeit in fiktionalen und nichtfiktionalen Erzählungen." In: Dernbach & Meyer (eds.). 2005. 174–193.
Audi, Robert. 2009. "Reliability as Virtue." *Philosophical Studies* 142.1: 43–54.
Chatman, Seymour. 1978. *Story and Discourse. Narrative Structure in Fiction and Film*. Ithaca, NY: Cornell University Press.
Currie, Gregory. 2004. *Arts and Minds*. Oxford: Clarendon Press.
Currie, Gregory. 2010. "Authors and Narrators." In: *Narratives and Narrators*. Oxford: Oxford University Press. 65–85.
Dernbach, Beatrice. 2005. "Einführung." In: Dernbach & Meyer (eds.). 2005. 11–27.
Dernbach, Beatrice & Michael Meyer (eds.). 2005. *Vertrauen und Glaubwürdigkeit: Interdisziplinäre Perspektiven*. Wiesbaden: VS Verlag für Sozialwissenschaften.
Dijk, Teun van. 2012. "Knowledge, Discourse and Domination." In: Michael Meeuwis & Jan-Ola Östman (eds.). *Pragmaticizing Understanding*. Amsterdam: John Benjamins. 151–196.
Good, David A. 2006. "Communicative Success vs. Failure." *Handbook of Pragmatics Online* (last retrieved: January 23, 2013)
Grice, Paul H. 1975. "Logic and Conversation." In: Peter Cole & Jerry Morgan (eds.). *Syntax and Semantics: Speech Acts*. Vol. 3. New York, NY: Academic Press. 41–58.
Habermas, Jürgen. 1984 [1976]. "Was heißt Universalpragmatik?" In: *Vorstudien und Ergänzungen zur Theorie des kommunikativen Handelns*. Frankfurt am Main: Suhrkamp. 353–440.
Heyd, Theresa. 2006. "Understanding and Handling Unreliable Narratives." *Semiotica* 162. 217–243.
Heyd, Theresa. 2011. "Unreliability: The Pragmatic Perspective Revisited." *Journal of Literary Theory* 5.1: 3–17.
Kindt, Tom. 2008. *Unzuverlässiges Erzählen und literarische Moderne*. Tübingen: Niemeyer.
Laucken, Uwe. 2005. "Explikation der umgangssprachlichen Bedeutung des Begriffs 'Vertrauen'." In: Dernbach & Meyer (eds.). 2005. 94–120.
Lewis, David. 1978. "Truth in Fiction." *American Philosophical Quarterly* 15: 37–46.
Margolin, Uri. 1986. "The Doer and the Deed." *Poetics Today* 7.2: 205–225.
Martínez, Matías & Michael Scheffel. 2000 [1999]. *Einführung in die Erzähltheorie*. München: C.H. Beck.
Niiniluoto, Ilkka. 1987. *Truthlikeness*. Dordrecht: Reidel.
Nünning, Ansgar. 1999. "Unreliable, compared to what? Towards a Cognitive Theory of Unreliable Narration: Prolegomena and Hypotheses."

In: Walter Grünzweig & Andreas Solbach (eds.). *Grenzüberschreitungen. Narratologie im Kontext.* Tübingen: Gunter Narr Verlag. 53–73.

Nünning, Ansgar. 2001. "Mimesis des Erzählens." In: Jörg Helbig (ed.). *Erzählen und Erzähltheorie im 20 Jahrhundert.* Heidelberg: Winter. 13–47.

Phelan, James & Peter J. Rabinowitz. 2012. "Authors, Narrators, Narration." In: David Herman, James Phelan, Peter J. Rabinowitz et al. (eds.) *Narrative Theory.* Columbus, OH: Ohio State University Press. 29–38.

Phelan, James & Mary P. Martin. 1999. "The Lessons of 'Weymouth': Homodiegesis, Unreliability, Ethics and *The Remains of the Day.*" In: David Herman (ed.). *Narratologies. New Perspectives on Narrative Analysis.* Columbus, OH: Ohio State University Press. 88–109.

Pratt, Mary L. 1977. *Toward a Speech Act Theory of Literary Discourse.* Bloomington, IN: Indiana University Press.

Rescher, Nicholas & Robert Brandom. 1979. *The Logic of Inconsistency: A Study in Non-Standard Possible-World Semantics and Ontology.* Totowa, NJ: Rowman & Littlefield.

Solbach, Andreas. 2005. "Die Unzuverlässigkeit der Unzuverlässigkeit." In: Fabienne Liptay & Yvonne Wolf (eds.). *Was stimmt denn jetzt? Unzuverlässiges Erzählen in Literatur und Film.* München: Text + Kritik. 60–71.

Steller, Max. 1989. "Recent Developments in Statement Analysis." In: John C. Yuille (ed.). *Credibility Assessment.* Dordrecht: Kluwer. 135–154.

Vincent-Marrelli, Jocelyne. 2006. "Truthfulness." *Handbook of Pragmatics Online* (last retrieved: January 23, 2013)

White, Hayden. 1980. "The Value of Narrativity in the Representation of Reality." *Critical Inquiry* 7.1: 5–27.

Williams, Bernard. 2002. *Truth and Truthfulness.* Princeton, NJ: Princeton University Press.

Yacobi, Tamar. 1981. "Fictional Reliability as a Communicative Problem." *Poetics Today* 2.2: 113–126.

LIESBETH KORTHALS ALTES
(Groningen)

What about the Default, or Interpretive Diversity? Some Reflections on Narrative (Un)reliability

> It isn't working, what you're writing at the moment. Sorry. But these sexual things you talk about, these guys, that's not you [...]. It is intellectual, artificial, what you're doing now, I'm sorry. But above all: you're not in it enough. You should be in it. You. You, Christine Angot, you. You should be in it, you. Not just a hodge-podge of what others may think of you. What you jotted down in the café, on the phone, that will never be your book. What one may think or say about you. You should be in it, you. [...]. Plus, you're writing a bad book. Because you, yourself, you're not in it. That's what we want, your style. Unique. Not just a portrait by omission. You must be in it. These things with these guys, all that, that's not you. [...] That's not interesting [...].We want your unique style. And you yourself, what you have to say, just as unique. You. Who you are. You. You who are unique. I could speak for hours about that. (Christine Angot 1998: 10–11, my translation, lka)

The preceding quotation is a fragment of a long letter written by *Claude*, addressed to his former wife, *Christine Angot*. This letter constitutes the main body of Sujet Angot, a novel by Christine Angot (the generic indication is given on the book's cover).[1] The letter is devoted to reflections on what exactly constitutes the identity, uniqueness and authenticity of person and writer *Christine Angot*, the narrator's ex-wife. With respect to the reliability of the narration, this section, like much of Angot's work, is relevant in several ways, as I shall explain. Readers are likely to be sensitive to *Claude*'s rather idiosyncratic mode of expressing himself through his writing about *Christine*, which might cast him as an unreliable narrator. My aim in this chapter is not, however, to develop a thorough analysis and interpretation of (un)reliability in Angot's autofiction. Rather, this example will allow me to ask some questions about narratological ways of theorizing and analyzing narrative unreliability, for which I will also propose a slightly shifted framing, as well as some complementary perspectives.

The main point I would like to make, which to a great extent concurs with Ansgar Nünning's (2005, 2008) position, is that narrative (un)reli-

---

1 Italics distinguish the literary characters from the homonymous real persons.

ability cannot be identified as a textual property; and that it cannot be established through a fail-safe method. While Ansgar Nünning proposes an integration of the rhetorical and cognitive approaches, I will emphasize the hermeneutic character of these—and most—narratological approaches. As I see it, cognitive theories might help explain, with recourse to frame and schemata theory, how people make meaning out of situations and communications, including literary texts. But when a scholar uses frame theory to determine the meaning and effects of a particular literary text or groups of texts, his or her approach in most cases becomes hermeneutic: one is doing interpretation; one may also explicitly reconstruct and reflect on one's own interpretive steps, a *meta*-attitude, which is also characteristic of hermeneutics; alternately, in an even stronger *meta*-hermeneutic way, one may seek to reconstruct alternative interpretive pathways, analyzing their underlying procedures and assumptions.

This meta-hermeneutic perspective will be my line of approach, especially in the last section of this chapter.[2] I will elaborate on some of the factors that, arguably, combine into an over-arching, dynamically synthetic *framing* assumed to play a steering role in readers' interpretive decisions regarding a narrator's or author's (un)reliability. This understanding of the notion of *framing* is borrowed not from frame theory, but from Erving Goffman's (1974) work, as I shall explain later on. Arguably, readers constantly accomplish acts of framing when they read a text, literary or otherwise. Such framing acts are decisive, as they determine the kind of experience readers engage in. They also activate particular interpretive attitudes and *value regimes* (the terms in italics will be explained later). Some of these over-arching framing acts work together: this seems to be the case for readers' intuitive or reasoned categorization of a narrator's and author's *ethos*, of the latter's *posture*, of the text's genre, as well as readers' normative expectations regarding literature and (literary) communication, and their interpretive strategy, which in turn probably relates to their familiarity with literary and general communicational conventions (see also Yacobi 1981 on the importance of reading strategies in establishing narrative unreliability). Whether and how these factors play the over-arching and inter-related framing role that I attribute to them deserves to be checked through empirical research. For now I will rely on argumentation and reasoned introspection, as scholars in narratology and hermeneutics often do.

Before moving on to Christine Angot's novel it might be fruitful to ask: why all this attention on unreliability in narratology? In her excellent introduction to this volume, Vera Nünning gives several convincing rea-

---

2 For an elaboration of this notion see Korthals Altes (2013, 2014).

sons for this on-going fascination. For my part, one basic answer is that the detection of unreliability belongs to intention attribution, which is of vital importance for humans, as it is for any species. For a bird preying on butterflies that may arbor fierce colors, for a banker checking a businessman's financing plan, or for a businesswoman musing about her banker's trustworthiness, an adequate assessment of the reliability of the signals emitted by these significant others is crucial. In one's own interest, and in order to predict another subject's behavior and determine one's own action range, one must correctly detect and interpret kinds and degrees of (un)reliability in another's character, words and deeds, from plain deception to playful under- or overstatement, or to irony. One also needs to master one's own verbal, facial and overall bodily expression so as to be able to project, or perhaps feign, reliability.

On a more specific level, literary scholars' interest in (un)reliability might be partly explained by the role that fiction or, more broadly, narrative art plays as the repository of individual and collective experience and as the imaginative extension of experiential learning as Aristotle already observed. Narrative art arguably works as an exercise in mind-reading (Zunshine 2006; Butte 2004) and in perspective-taking (Booth 1961; Rabatel 2009; Bruner 1990, and many others). Not only do narratives represent characters engaged in reading each others' minds, intentions, and reliability, narratives also draw their own readers into reconstructing often competing perspectives on facts, words, experiences, and evaluations belonging to the story-world, making them ponder the authority and reliability of these perspectives. Narrative fiction thus exercises our capacity for meaning and value attribution and for modalisation, i.e. our capacity to sense degrees and shades of truth and authority in information that is being presented to us. Fiction makes its audiences weigh perspectives on perspectives and the value of values, activating reflection on those processes. Doubts on the reliability of narrative transmission or of a narrator's sincerity and truthfulness are very effective for triggering such reflection.

1. Slippery Unreliabilities

Christine Angot is one of the *enfants terribles* in the contemporary French literary scene. Given her high media exposure—nasty tongues would say: given her compulsive cultivation of media attention—, French readers are likely to be sensitized to issues concerning her reliability as a writer who purports to use her own life as her material and to convey it "raw", without aesthetic mediation.

Angot exposes not only her own intimate moments, but also draws into public exposure those who shared that intimacy. Vehement dissent can be found among literary critics and readers concerning the author's underlying ethos.[3] How authentic, how reliable are the stories presented in her work and public performances? For example, did she really have an incestuous relationship with her father? To what extent is the suggestion that her work truthfully conveys real experience just a literary pose? How ethical is her exposure of others, particularly her various lovers, and to what extent does her use of that real-life material affect her reliability as an autobiographical narrator? For some critics Angot's work and public persona are without a doubt ruthlessly and painfully authentic and her account of her experiences is reliable, or at least sincere. For others her self-presentation expresses an exacerbated narcissism and a disturbing pathological (or worse, commercially clever) exhibitionism. Here, whether the narratives about her life are factually reliable may become less relevant than the moral and aesthetic functionality of their exhibition. Yet others understand her artistic enterprise as a masterful play with what Lejeune (1971) called the autobiographic pact. The point of her work then shifts again: it is less about representing one's self, and being reliable or not in that, than about exposing the norms conventionally attached to literary self-representation, such as expectations of sincerity, modesty, and reliability, and about reflecting on experiencing one's self and offering a mimesis of that experience in writing or performance.[4]

The kind of unreliability that is usually addressed in narratology is that of the text's (character-)narrator, who, at first sight, is *Claude*. His writing—his letter to *Christine*—conveys the sense that he is very much attached to his role as the guardian of her personal and authorial authenticity. Such a referential reading is paratextually encouraged, as seen in interviews when Angot mentions that her husband Claude was a decisive support for her in the early stages of her writing career. In my reading, the quoted section is a good example of the ways in which *Claude*'s reliability—especially his authority and trustworthiness—both manifests and undermines itself: he explicitly casts himself in the role of expert and judge regarding *Christine*'s personal identity and the authenticity of her writing ("I could speak for hours about that [her 'uniqueness']").[5]

---

3   Linking back to Aristotle's *Rhetoric*, this notion of ethos has been re-formulated within French/Francophone Discourse analysis by Ruth Amossy as "the image of self built by the orator in his speech in order to exert an influence on his audience" (Amossy 2001: 1). The notion can be extended to *the interpreter's* image of a speaker or writer, inferred from the latter's whole way of being, speaking or writing.

4   For more details on the reception of Angot's work, please see Korthals Altes (2005, 2014).

5   It might be useful to recall that Aristotle called attention to the various grounds for successful persuasion. He distinguished not only three main rhetorical appeals: logos (appeal

His style expresses conventional signals of goodwill ("I'm sorry...") and of good sense through argumentation markers such as: "But above all...", "because...". Yet there seems to be a disturbing excess in his zeal to defend *Christine*'s authenticity and identity, as if he were not just defining but also obsessively confining her. In my perception, authority topples over into normativity in the accumulation of apodictic formulas: "that's you", "that's not you", "it doesn't work", "you should...", "you must...". Other idiosyncratic traits in *Claude*'s style, such as colloquialisms, a halting syntax and insistent repetitions, are likely to be associated by convention with first-impulse speech and emotion, belying the stance of superior reasonable deliberation (I trust that the stylistic features to which I draw attention remain sufficiently salient in my English translation). Many sections all over the book stage *Claude* as deeply affected by their separation: he describes, for instance, how he wallows in tears, week after week, and how he is reduced to impotence in all respects. In the light of his misery, the letter often reads as apologetic, or might be interpreted as the expression of the labour of mourning over their rupture. Thus, the ex-husband's whole stance as reasonable and knowledgeable arbiter might appear unreliable, casting doubt on the views and facts this character-narrator provides on "Sujet Angot".

Claude's narration at some point appears to be embedded in that of an extra-diegetic narrator, who only intermittently becomes explicit, through dialogic glosses that interrupt *Claude*'s reflections. The theme of those interventions and the inside knowledge they presuppose suggest that they stem from *Claude*'s ex, *Christine*. Needless to say, it is Angot who signed the book; there are heavy clues, pointing to an extradiegetic (authorial?) narrative communication plane, in which other rhetorical intentions regarding *Claude*'s embedded narration may be at play, to be deciphered by the reader. The question arises whether, given the strong hints for an auto/biographic framing, one can make inferences about *Claude*'s unreliability as a narrator without imagining the author's intentions regarding the narrative's structure of telling in relation to the told.

In critics' interpretation and appraisal of Angot's work, their image of the author, of her overall aesthetic or communicative intentions, and their response to her posture in the literary and public domain indeed appear to play a significant role.[6] Critics among others broach the issue of the inten-

---

to arguments), ethos (appeal to character) and pathos (appeal to emotions); but he also singled out, within the ethos appeal, three main components: *eunoia* (good-will), *arete* (virtue, being good, with respect to the social codes), and *phronesis* (good sense, prudence, practical wisdom); Aristotle (2007 [4th C BC]); Amossy (2001) and others.

6 After Bourdieu and Viala, Meizoz defined an authorial *posture* as an author's "mode of self-presentation," his or her "personal way of investing or endorsing a role, even a social

tion the author may have had with this book, whose title foregrounds "sujet Angot", while the embedded narrative structure problematizes the access to the subject. In a circular mode, readers' ideas about what is at stake in the work inflect, I hypothesize, their sense of the author's ethos, which then feeds back into their interpretation and appraisal of the work. If a reader or interpreter has for some reason an initial image of an author's ethos (including of her (un)reliability), this image can be expected to work as a framing or classification clue. Such a framing particularly affects one's way of constructing the overall intention of the work, as well as one's perception of the tone of narration (irony? playfulness? indignation?), and of its reliability. Given the many textual and paratextual autobio prompts, this work was often framed as basically non-fictional. In such a reading strategy, Angot's/*Christine's* covert exposure of Claude's/*Claude's* unreliable narration is easily interpreted as the real author's ironical, perhaps vindictive, yet at times sympathetic exhibit of her ex-husband's distorted views of her, "behind his back:" tit for tat.

But such a reading is definitely not the only option. A quite different perspective on unreliability in this novel arises if the reader notes that *Claude*'s discursive ethos is uncannily similar, if not undistinguishable from, *Christine*'s and Angot's own style of writing. *Claude* quotes *Christine*'s reaction to a critic who dared define Angot's intentions and identity on the basis of her style (in my terms that would be: on the basis of his discursive ethos):

> The sentence is deliberately halted, there is no narrative continuity. […] she [Angot, according to the critic] pursues her autobiographic undertaking. Everyday life is omnipresent, the 'refusal of narrative' claimed by Angot, [is] extremely effective. One must recommend *Les Autres* [another book published by Angot in 1997] for the virulence of Angot's prose and subject material." (Angot 1998: 84)

To which Claude adds somewhat abruptly: "One of the things about you I find most beautiful, *Sujet Angot*, are your breasts, which make your body beautiful" (ibid.: 84). Whose discursive ethos may one read into these sentences? How reliable are the thematic and stylistic "inference invitations" (Bortolussi/Dixon 2003: 80–81) that foreground *Claude*'s take on *Sujet Angot*, inviting a referential—(auto)biographical—, psychologizing, moralizing reading? To whom could one attribute the possible humour in the

status," through which he or she "re-plays or negotiates his [or her] 'position' in the literary field" (Meizoz 2004: 51) and sets a "horizon for his/her reception," (Meizoz 2008: 2). Postures build on a repertoire engrained in the memory ideally shared by authors and their audiences. Like an ethos, a posture can be conveyed through all kinds of signals: style of writing, choice of genre, register, themes, the whole gamut of paratexts, public self-fashioning (Meizoz 2004, 2009; Heinen 2002). Postures elicit expectations regarding an author's ethos; conversely, ethos clues suggest a posture (Meizoz 2009; for elaboration, also Korthals Altes 2014).

incongruity of the shift from style to breasts? Though both may indeed be perceived as characteristic for one, as a female individual? How would a narratologist decide where the relevant communication situation and the most authoritative narrative view-point and potential issues for reliability lie? What might be the consequences of such decisions for one's "processing" of Angot's work?

These cursory comments and questions, elicited by just one literary fragment, should at least have driven home the point that to speak about unreliable narration involves complex framing and classification acts, concerning what communication level and hence whose (un)reliability might be relevant, and what (generic) interpretive and evaluative pathway readers might follow. Before expanding on this, let us examine several narratological frameworks for analyzing unreliable narration, and see what they offer to clarify these issues.

2. (Un)reliability in Narratology

The narratological research on unreliability has been summarized by Vera Nünning in this volume's introduction, and discussed, among others, in Ansgar Nünning's syntheses (2005, 2008). I do not want to duplicate all this excellent work, and only aim to highlight some salient points. There are several theoretical frameworks and corresponding methodologies for analyzing unreliable narration that became influential in narratology: structuralist narratology, which provided the initial framework for mapping narrative communication, limiting it to the text, and setting a standard for what counted as scientific work; rhetorical narratology, focusing on the communication between (implied) author and reader via the text; more recently, cognitive narratology, which concentrates on the reader's meaning-making activity; and finally, the pragmatic approach, attentive to the social conventions and norms regulating communication, including literary communication.

These approaches appear complementary, with their respective focus on the text, on the author's communicative intentions, on readers' interpretive activity, and on socially defined communication codes. They certainly get combined in practice. Not only has Ansgar Nünning proposed to integrate rhetorical and cognitive perspectives, rhetorical narratologists also tend to integrate structuralist-textual approaches, deciphering textual signals of unreliability as the expression of an (implied) author's intentions. However, such ecumenical practices risk obliterating differences in theoretical presuppositions from which different methodologies may be expected to follow. In particular, there still seems to be some confusion about the kind of scholarly enterprise one is engaging in: is one's aim to contribute a science-based, systematic, epistemologically more valid framework for the "analysis" of the narrative structures, devices, and meaning of literary (or other) texts? How then are the interpretive moves, which come up during the process of textual analysis, dealt with, especially when the reliability of narration is at stake? Why is no empirical testing envisaged? Or does one aim to reconstruct meaning-making and interpretive processes in hermeneutic ways, that is, through argumentation, reasoned speculation and induction, based on (phenomenological) introspection, and (historical) comparison? In order to clarify the debate within narratology, and also, perhaps, to offer a more solid basis to the transfer of theories of (un)reliability beyond literary narratives, it seems worthwhile to tease out some of those presuppositions.

Given that narratology was coined in relation to what came to be called French structuralism, it is with this perspective that I would like to start. Firstly, it should be noted that it was not structuralist narratology, exemplified in its heyday by Greimas, Genette and Todorov, which sparked the interest in unreliable narration. Structuralist narratologists at that stage strived, at least rhetorically, for objectivity in their reconstruction of narrative structures (Greimas 1966) and conventions (Genette 1972). In particular, they sought to stay clear of interpretation, perceived as subjective and unscientific. Hence the need to focus on the text only, omitting authors and the murky matter of their intentions, as well as readers, who *par excellence* led into the aleatory domain of interpretation and interpretive diversity. Whether this striving to eliminate interpretation and "disturbing subjective elements" (Greimas 1966: 164) was justified, and whether it had any chance to succeed, is another matter.[7] Throughout its later developments, narratology often cultivated, at least in its rhetoric, the structuralist idea, or ideal, of rigorous *methods* for textual description and analysis, and the suggestion that this rigour brings narratology closer to science than to hermeneutics.

To the extent that structuralist narratologists paid attention to issues of reliability in narration, this pertained to the distribution of truth in narration (as in Greimas and Courtés' notion of "contrat fiduciaire" [Greimas/Courtés 1979: 368]) and the effects of narrative embedding on a

---

7   In a strict sense, this striving holds true only for a limited part of initial structuralism, since Genette's focus on narrative conventions already leads to a historical poetics, which implies the idea of changing narrative writing and reading conventions. Culler, Suleiman, and many others further opened up the scope of investigation to the reader, the socio-historical contexts, and so on; see the land-mark volume on *The Reader in the text* (Suleiman/Crosman 1980).

narrator's authority (Genette 1988; Chatman 1978). Genette's or Chatman's models of narrative communication would suffice to help establish in concrete cases the relevant communicative levels, the types of narrative transmission, and the resulting hierarchy of perspectives (methodology itself was hardly discussed explicitly). Importantly, as a cornerstone of structuralist narratology, the narrator became invested with the function of marking the distinction of fiction as a mode of assertion.[8] Thus narratology could dismiss the intentions of the real author and his or her ethos, in particular his or her reliability or authority. Instead, the narrator became the last instance to which intentions and values were attributed. This was as far as the narratologist's concern was meant to go (for recent synthesizing critiques on both issues, see Schaeffer 2010 [1999]; Walsh 2007; or Patron 2009).

A structuralist orientation, i.e. text-based, classificatory, and aiming at general validity, is also found in the later systematic work on *textual* signals of unreliability (Olson 2003), and to some extent also in text-based types of unreliable narrators (Phelan/Martin 1999), and in the attempt to establish rules, reminiscent of scientific laws, such as the one according to which unreliable narration is only relevant for character-narrators. In fact, such scholarly work might also exemplify the systematic, comparative, often historically oriented research that constitutes hermeneutics' core business. But this affiliation to hermeneutics is not, usually, very openly acknowledged, and the notion of method circulating in structuralist narratology seems to express more of a 'hard-sciences' ambition than just methodical reasoning, which belongs to the very useful methods of hermeneutics.

With *Sujet Angot*, a structuralist narratologist might, for instance, point out signals of unreliability in *Claude*'s discourse, such as its emotional syntax and punctuation, which would contradict the—also discursively expressed—stance of rationality. This narratologist could also analyze the text's narrative structure, signaling the embedding of *Claude*'s narration in that of a—rarely manifest—extradiegetic narrating voice, which may cast *Claude*'s writing in another light. Yet, as has been observed by many others (among others Gibson 1996 i.a.), to theorize a narrative as a hierarchical structure in which the view-point of an extradiegetic narrator automatically trumps any embedded narrator does not do justice to the complexity of literature, nor to readers' interpretive activity, in particular, regarding

---

[8] Genette famously proposed as a "law" of literary fiction that "A *is not* N," whereas in factual narrative "A = N" (where A stands for the author, and N for the narrator). Following Genette (whose argument goes back to Searle, literary fiction as an assertion is uncoupled from factual referentiality and from its source, the author.

their emotional response to the rhetorical appeal a text may exert at various communicative levels.

While the text-centeredness, and what could be called the scientism, of the structuralist approach have been criticized on good grounds, the proposed typologies of narrators, models of narrative communication, and lists of textual signals definitely have their value. Arguably, such lists and models condense experiential and historical and comparative knowledge about social codes of behaviour and meaning-making, as well as about literary communication and representation conventions that are characteristic for certain genres, periods and (interpretive) communities. Lists of textual signals of unreliability also convey, in didactic contexts, such conventional knowledge and expectations to less experienced or reflexive readers, allowing for more complex reading experiences.[9] Such lists thus offer a precious interpretive heuristics, as well as a vocabulary, and accepted argumentative pathways through which the effects readers may perceive as textually induced can be identified, and through which texts, or readings of texts, can be compared, as in Genette's historical poetics, or in reception history.

But the association of such lists and the proposed concepts and models with analytic "tools" promises too much, as they do not allow mechanical detection or factual description of narrative unreliability, which result from a complex interpretive calculus. Moreover, there is always a hole in the bucket, as it is precisely the existence of (convention-based) semiotics of (un)reliability that allows the playful or deceptive display of such signals. The interpreter will have to decide for herself, on the basis of clues that themselves need to be assessed for authenticity and reliability, whether the narrating voice is reliable, has authority, is sincere, should be trusted, and so on. In addition, communication codes and the social appreciation of the various ethos ingredients may change over time, as Bruno Zerweck (2001) and Vera Nünning (2004 [1998]) have argued. And not only is there evident historical variation in assessing narrative (un)reliability, this assessment also varies according to people's reading strategies (Yacobi 1981, 2001; Korthals Altes 2014). *Claude*'s narration, for instance, may display a degree of subjectivity and emotionality that, according to narratologists, would signal unreliability, as they cast doubts on his rationality (Olson 2003; Nünning 1999, 2005). Yet in today's Western culture, "raw" emotion often works as a guarantee of authenticity and sincerity. Thus, *some kind of* reliability may be recuperated and estab-

---

9   A fruitful hypothesis, here, is the idea that humans need to practice their capacity for coping with cognitive dissonance; plus the connected idea that there is pleasure/benefit to be had from mastering, in the sheltered playing-ground of fiction, experiences of complexity.

lished via an alternative route, building on different ethos topoi. In sum, what is lacking in text-centered structuralist narratological approaches to unreliability is the explicit recognition of the interpretive frameworks and their underlying social-communicational and generic conventions, which prompt readers and scholars to select particular textual elements and turn them into signals.

The real interest for unreliability within narratology rather came from scholars attentive to the rhetorical, ideological, or ethical functioning of narratives, overstepping the barrier against interpretation. It has been sufficiently recalled, also in this volume, that in the rhetorical perspective on unreliable narration, coined by Booth, and developed by Phelan, Lanser, Kearns, and others, the distance between narrator and (implied) author is decisive. Booth's approach also tends to assume complicity in values and world view between interpreter and (implied) author, the latter expecting the former to dance to the tune of his or her intentions and rhetorical strategies, a complicity that the narratologist may also denounce and resist.

In the case of *Sujet Angot*, a rhetorical narratologist would seek to establish the (implied) author's stance, and distance, toward *Claude*'s narration, in particular, toward his views on *Christine* and her writing, the rapport between husband and wife, and so on. All sorts of textual elements—themes, style, composition, metaphor, evoked situations and relationships in the story world—can turn into rhetorical clues, feeding and steering one's "detection" of the narrator's reliability; more precisely, in fact, they are retrospectively invoked to justify one's interpretation. In this case, Angot-the-implied-author (I prefer Chatman's [1978] notion of inferred author, which points to the interpreter's activity) might be considered to stealthily mock poor *Claude*'s attempts to define and confine *Christine*, exposing his unreliability. Yet how can I be sure whether this is what "the text", or the real or implied Angot, want me to understand or even to focus on? In my experience, this text's rhetoric prohibits any comfortable bonding, and instead maintains what Booth called an unstable irony. Reflecting on my own interpretive process, I cannot say that narratology provides me with tools to identify the (implied) author's norms or intentions, or the distance Angot, or the text, "require" me to sense between authorial views (on *Christine*, on writing) and those exposed by *Claude*. I am not even sure whether I am meant to discern unreliability in *Claude*'s, or perhaps rather in *Christine*'s or even Angot's narration. Rather, these various ways of framing the text's design and relevant communicative level are all plausible interpretive options for me, and I rather feel I am "made to" oscillate between these.

With Phelan and Martin, quite usefully, we could at least seek to qualify what kind of an unreliable narrator *Claude* is. Narrators, Phelan observes, "perform three main roles—reporting, interpreting, and evaluating" (Phelan 2005: 50). These roles refer to three axes on which unreliability can occur: that of facts; that of values or ethics; and that of knowledge and perception. With this model in mind, I could characterize *Claude* as underreporting on the axis of knowledge (for instance, I do not get to read much about his own failures in the marriage), and as misevaluating on the axis of ethics, as when he amalgamates *Christine*'s sexual openness to other men and her proclivity to use bits of everyday exchanges as *objets trouvés* in her writing, judging both according to his jealous desire to control her, in body and style. Insightful as such distinctions might be, again, they may be a matter of argument. Moreover, as mentioned, the relevance of my focus on *Claude*'s unreliability is not even guaranteed.

Ansgar Nünning (2005, 2008) helpfully listed the methodological weaknesses displayed in Booth's discussion of unreliability: there would be no real method for establishing the unreliability of the narrator, other than to "read between the lines" or to note the "secret communication behind a narrator's back". Moreover, "the only yardstick [Booth] offers for gauging a narrator's unreliability is the implied author," a notion at least as contested theoretically and methodologically as that of unreliability itself (Nünning 2005: 91; 2008: 30–45). In addition, the rhetorical-narratological procedures for establishing unreliability would rest on the problematic assumptions that there is a *reliable* view on the world and on selves, presupposing a shared sense of psychological, moral, and linguistic normality as the default setting of narration. Instead, Nünning noted with a touch of provocation in his earlier article on the subject, "no generally accepted standards of normality exist which can serve as the basis for impartial judgment. In a pluralist, postmodernist and multicultural age like ours it has become more difficult than ever before to determine what may count as "normal moral standards" and "human decency" (Nünning 1999: 64). Nünning's later rhetorical-cognitive approach precisely aims to reconstruct such "accepted standards," reformulating them as "frames" and "scripts". In his view, this analytic reconstruction included the possibility that different readers might consider different frames and scripts to be applicable, and this is a fundamental methodological—meta-interpretive—perspective change.

Booth's lack of methodological rigour seems to be the biggest bone of contention. But isn't this rather a matter of different kinds of hermeneutics, each building on different value-laden assumptions? Booth has always been outspoken in his (moral) claims about literary communication, and also about the fact that hermeneutics form the inseparable counterpart of textual rhetoric. Hermeneutic frameworks require persuasion, as well as argumentative pathways and norms one expects to share with one's intended audience, rather than ideals of stringent methodology in any scientific sense. Activating in its own readers' minds world-views, norms and values, the rhetorical-hermeneutic analysis of fiction plays its own role in discursively relaying the negotiation of world-views that fictional works stage for their readers.

The hermeneutic character of rhetorical narratologies is indeed striking, and so is its difference, in epistemological intent, from the original structuralist approaches. Instead of shunning interpretation and subjectivity, theorizing is now considered to stand in service of good interpretation, of moral and aesthetic evaluation, and of sharing such interpretive pathways and the values they articulate. The "subjective" is, importantly, community-building, the active construction of inter-subjectivity. A good example here is Phelan's insistence on the rhetorical narratologist's careful deliberation and pondering of ethical versus aesthetic dimensions of a text; or on the need for the interpreter/narrative scholar to invest him or herself personally in his or her response to a literary text. In such a hermeneutic stance, there is nothing wrong, methodologically, with an interpreter holding normative presuppositions or attributing intentions to an author, implied or real; these are presuppositions that are widely shared within broad interpretive communities. They form part of the interpreter's "pre-understanding" (*Vorverständnis*) to refer to Gadamer's terms (Gadamer 1991 [1960]). Speaking about the intentions of an actual or implied author or text corresponds to a particular interpretive attitude and expresses a conception of art as communication ("dialogue") between reader and author via the text. Such views may be criticized for the sake of an alternative conception of literature and alternative hermeneutics, but may not be fairly criticized on the basis of a methodological stringency that the theory does not even attempt. A problem arises only if such a hermeneutic understanding of narrative fiction is put forward as a generally valid theory (in the hard sense of this notion), from which a failsafe method can be drawn.

The cognitive framework proposed more recently for narrative unreliability aims to remedy some of the identified problems for the structuralist and rhetorical approaches. In this cognitive work on unreliability, Ansgar Nünning's contribution stands out. While pinpointing the weaknesses of rhetorical and structuralist theories of unreliability, his approach integrates their most fruitful elements. In particular, Nünning draws attention to the author, textual "signals", the historical socio-cultural context, as well as, importantly, the processing rules and the cognitive frames and schemata that readers bring to their reading and interpretive activity.[10] He assumes that such schematized knowledge allows readers to fill in what counts as standard behaviour or evaluation, against which a character or narrator might then appear unreliable (Nünning 2005: 98 ff; 2008: 47–49). These frames can be drawn from everyday experience, and include social, moral or linguistic norms that are relevant for the period in which a text was written and published; they also include readers' knowledge of pertinent psychological theories of personality, and models of psychological coherence and normal human behaviour. The activated frames can also be literary, prominently comprising generic conventions, intertextual references, character prototypes, such as the picaro, or the trickster, and "last but not least the structure and norms established by the respective work itself" (Nünning 2008: 48).

Nünning very rightly, I think, concludes that the "term 'unreliable narrator' does not indicate a structural or semantic feature of texts, but a pragmatic phenomenon that cannot be fully grasped without taking into account the conceptual premises that readers and critics bring to texts." A little further he adds: "Pragmatic and frame theory present a possible way out of the methodological and theoretical problems that most theories of unreliable narration suffer from because cognitive theories can shed light on the way in which readers naturalize texts that are taken to display features of narrational unreliability" (Nünning 2008: 45, 46). One question that arises, however, regards how exactly the recourse to cognitive frame theory functions here. Nünning clearly distances himself from what he considers Booth's under-formalized and overly intuitive approach, placing himself, as I understand, on the side of methodological rigour. The aim of his own framework seems to be threefold: to offer (1) a cognitive sciences -grounded explanation of how readers detect unreliability in general; (2) a method for a more objective assessment and analysis of unreliable narration that uses cognitive theory to build on insights into readers' processing of texts, but also creates narratological lists of textual, extra- or paratextual signals that are somehow considered observable and describable; (3) a systematic hermeneutic (or meta-hermeneutic) reflection on the interpretive steps involved in assessing the reliability of a narrator. But I would argue that Nünning does not offer a method, let alone a better method, to

---

10   Various models and concepts have been proposed to account for memory's role in processing experience, such as frames (Minsky 1977), schemata, scripts (Shank/Abelson 1977), mental models (Johnson-Laird 1986), or prototypes (Rosch 1977). All of these concepts refer to the idea that memory somehow stores experience knowledge in schematized forms, reactivating and re-combining these in new situations. These concepts recall the phenomenology of the meaning-making process proposed by Iser (1976), as well as hermeneutic accounts of the human understanding process, and the so-called hermeneutic circle.

describe or detect unreliable narration. Nor are there, I argue, evidently observable textual or para- and extratextual signals, which would allow readers or scholars to establish unreliability compared to "the structure and norms established by the respective work itself." The missing piece is the reconstruction of interpreters' framing activity itself: how can the analyst access the reader's act of selecting discursive or extratextual elements and of turning these into signals (more about this in this chapter's last section)?

To the extent that the recourse to cognitive theories suggests a more scientific procedure, one might also expect empirical research on frames which readers actually activate, for example in order to establish the reliability of a narrator. Instead, Nünning's discussion of McEwan's short story, "Dead as they come" (2008: 51–56), which illustrates his cognitive-rhetorical framework, reconstructs his own negotiation of textual clues, background norms, and (textual/authorial) intentions detected in the perceived textual rhetorical steering (ibid.: 51–54). While Nünning's textual analysis appears eminently interpretive, his general account of narrative unreliability most fruitfully sets a framework for further meta-hermeneutic explorations such as my own.

A final perspective on unreliability, also distinguished by Vera Nünning, is the pragmatic approach, which foregrounds the social-communicative dimension. In particular, the idea has been retained that unreliable narration could be explained within the framework of pragmatics as a violation of the conversational maxims put forth by Grice (cf. Heyd: 2011). "This [approach] is compatible", Vera Nünning writes, "with major premises of cognitive narratology, since the theoretical framework of Grice's approach within pragmatic linguistics also stresses the role of inferences on the part of readers" (this volume, 8). Grice famously distinguished four major conversational maxims that speakers are expected to adhere to in successful communication, namely communication that is "governed by the overarching Cooperative Principle'. This principle requires speakers to adjust their utterances to the given communicative situation," and obey the maxims of Quality (truthfulness), of Quantity (informativeness), of Relation (relevance), and of Manner (clarity, mainly of style and phrasing). As Vera Nünning noted, Jürgen Habermas called attention to the rules underlying successful communication in a similar way to Grice. These rules are comprised of the following: (1) the expectation that the speaker's intention is to act in accordance with the content of the statement); (2) that the speaker is truthful and sincere; and (3) that the content of what is told is adequate (correspondence between the content and current cultural world knowledge, or with the beliefs of the listener; see Habermas 1983 i.a.).

It does not seem coincidental that literary theorists with leanings toward more (scientific) rigour showed enthusiasm for models such as Grice's or Habermas', which sought to define the default rules of communication. The problems with such approaches, however, are also quite obvious. That is: if they are taken without adding nuance. Habermas, for instance, clearly acknowledged that these norms for successful communication correspond to a democratic ideal, to be cherished as discourse ethics. He would certainly concur with Derrida, J. Hillis Miller and others that deceptive or playful untruthfulness, and lack of information, relevance and clarity also belong to standard everyday language use.

What seems lacking in theories positing such default communicational rules is the awareness of the diversity in communication genres and conventions. One glance at some seventeenth century social exchanges—for instance, letters written by literati, with their convoluted rhetoric—demonstrates how context-bound communication codes are. In fact, a rich domain lies open for investigation attentive to the codes and topoi of various rhetorics of reliability. Rich research on one such communicational ethos code, sincerity, shows that this communication rule, posited as a default by Grice or Habermas, was at times considered more of an uncivil or even risky social handicap rather than a virtue (see Martin 1997; discussed in Korthals Altes 2008; 2014: Ch. 6). Literature often dramatizes differences in codified uses of language, creating awareness of the norms and expectations that characters and readers need to internalize in order to operate in socially adequate modes, adapted to the actual communication situation and genres. Grice's or Habermas' lists of communication rules, however, usefully point to the need to reconstruct such communicational contract(s) under which any text, literary or not, may be produced and received, activating particular normative expectations.

These observations regarding the various narratological approaches to (un)reliability all point in the same direction. They call for more awareness of (various) patterns underlying the interpretive activity of readers/interpreters; and for more empirical investigation and/or for the reconstruction of such mental steps and pathways leading to readers' decisions about narrative reliability or unreliability. The last section of this chapter proposes some ideas and concepts that might be useful in a hermeneutic reconstruction, the validity of which could also be explored from another angle, that is, via systematic empirical testing.

3. Ethos and Posture Attributions, and Other Framing Acts

Adopting cognitive frame theory, as mentioned, narrative theorists have suggested that readers make sense of texts and are able to grasp the outline of situations, plot, character types or themes, by having recourse to frames, scripts, schemata, prototypes, and other mental models. But shouldn't we first ask how people select and delimit the frames, scripts, and schemata, required for understanding any artifact, communication, or situation? Frames or scripts are not directly observable in texts, nor do they lie waiting like neat piles of towels for the analyst's use. Not coincidentally, the most commonly cited example is that of the restaurant-script, which most people will meet with nods of recognition. As soon as contexts are less clear, interpreters will need to be inventive, select between potential alternatives, and argue for them. This selection, I propose, is likely to be based on the reader's classification of the kind of situation and genre he or she has at hand (for instance, some kinds of texts and some kinds of reading strategies may require that we hold in mind alternative conflicting framings and oscillate between them, as this may give pleasurable "aesthetic" mental activity).

This is where we need the concept of an overarching- or macro-frame like Erving Goffman's, which seems to work well here, except for the risk of potential terminology confusion.[11] Goffman understands frames as tools that allow us "to label 'schemata of interpretation' that allow individuals or groups 'to locate, perceive, identify, and label' events and occurrences, thus rendering meaning, organizing experiences, and guiding actions" (Goffman 1974: 21). Framing is about choosing "the correct tools", they "help us to navigate through our experiential universe, inform our cognitive activities and generally function as preconditions of interpretation," Werner Wolf explains, in an in-depth discussion of the usefulness of Goffman's notion of frame (Wolf 2006: 5).

Frames, moreover, have a recursive nature: every frame can itself be reframed. This idea applies to generic classifications of literary texts, or author's (or narrator's) ethos. Angot's novel, for instance, may seem at first to be rightly framed as autobiography, with consequences for our interpretive disposition and ethos expectations. This initial generic framing may however be superseded by another one, that of metafiction or essayistic fiction, which casts new light on both the narrator's and the author's display of authenticity or sincerity. Language allows meta-

---

11 Goffman himself borrowed the notion from Bateson (1972), who analyzed the importance of "metacommunication" in play, marking to all involved that "I am playing," "We are playing." I will mostly use the gerund form "framing," which conveys better the idea that one is performing a mental act.

communication about frames, which is crucial, as framings have decisive consequences for the kind of experience and *point* we expect the work to afford. This holds true not just in a real-life situation, as when we check whether we have properly understood a candle-lit dinner, but also in literary interpretations, when people debate over framing a book like Angot's as definitively autobiographical or not. Many conflicts or debates can, unsurprisingly, be analyzed as conflicts about framings.

Goffman paid great attention to what he called "frame borders" and "framing keys" (Goffman 1974: 43–44). In the case of literary texts, such keys are conventional paratextual and textual markers, as well as signals of fictionality, or of genre. But such framing keys are themselves signs that need to be selected, framed and interpreted, also with respect to their reliability.

Goffman's notion of "framing" seems to me indispensable for the attention it draws to acts of selection and classification that form the core of processes of interpretation. Such classifications determine what kinds of frames (in the cognitive sense) would be at all relevant to select, and, centrally, what kind of value regime would apply to the case at hand. While the risk of confusion with the cognitive use of the term is inconvenient, these two different understandings of this notion of frame—Goffman's and the cognitive one—are not deeply heterogeneous. As Werner Wolf remarks,

> all of the different approaches to 'frames' converge in one frame function, namely to guide and even to enable interpretation. [...] As 'keys' to interpretation, frames [in Goffman's sense] are 'metaconcepts,' that is, concepts that regulate the application of frames in the cognitive sense of stereotyped knowledge. (2006: 5)

(Meta-)hermeneutic research could seek to reconstruct what framing acts become over-arching and determining in readers' actual processing and interpreting of (literary) texts. It seems promising to set up cooperation with psychologists, sociologists, and cognitive scientists, in order to test how and when readers select and hierarchize framing clues, or to get better insight into readers' emotional involvement and general attention in connection to specific generic framings, to the ethos readers attribute to the author, and even to whether such ethos attributions are at all relevant. In this perspective, interpretive diversity, which constituted a problem for many narratological approaches, becomes instead a rich object of inquiry. The status of textual and extratextual or paratextual signals, in particular, also changes, as they get systematically connected to a particular kind of interpretive processing. In the case of Angot's text a psychological and immersive reading strategy is likely to focus on signals of Claude's self-expression through his mode of writing, and to apply to his writing fairly widespread moral norms and psychological frameworks ("isn't he demonstrating the enraging male superiority, which we feminists have been rightly denouncing for decennia, now?", "Doesn't his jealous bias demonstrate that he still loves her?", et cetera). Alternately, an auto/biographic reading strategy could still *psychologize* and moralize, but now about Angot's own need to take revenge on her ex, and her nasty or efficient manipulative exposure of her ex-husband's take on her. In a metafictional reading, entirely different signals achieve salience.

The Angot example points to an interesting phenomenon, which I am not the first to observe. Nünning writes that "the general effect of narrator unreliability consists of redirecting the readers' attention from the level of the story to speaker and of foregrounding peculiarities of the narrator's psychology" (Nünning 2008: 38–39; see also Wall: unreliable narration "refocuses the reader's attention on the narrator's mental processes"; Wall (1994: 23), qtd. in Nünning [2008: 39]). Such a re-direction could be described in terms of a frame-switch, in line with Goffman's understanding of framing. This frame-switch, however, is not necessarily only in the direction of a *narrator's psychology*, but can also make the reader shift—as an effect of textual rhetoric, as pointed out by Rabinowitz (1998)—toward adopting an "authorial" rather than a "narrative" (here: narratorial) perspective. It may be argued that doubts about a narrator's reliability at least activate readers to ponder what might count as the most significant communication level; this may involve a generic frame-switch, in which a narrator's psychology may even lose its salience retrospectively. If one frames and interprets *Sujet Angot* as representing the real-life experience of a couple (*Claude* and *Christine*, or even the real Claude and Angot), the psychological and moral dimensions get foregrounded, including those of the real or fictional *Claude*'s (un)reliability, or of Angot's manipulative embedding of this narration. If one interprets this work as metafiction, a less psychological and moralizing reading is likely to result, and *Claude*'s unreliability may turn into a mere device, an affective lure for the reader who gets trapped in her immersive empathic reading, which suddenly gets exposed as a sticky attempt at appropriation, similar to *Claude*'s approach to *Christine*. Different aesthetic and moral expectations then become relevant.

Factors that are likely to affect such basic framing acts include the image readers construct of characters', narrators' and the author's ethos, that is their basic characters, to the extent that it would help determine how to understand their words. These aspects will not be developed in detail in this chapter. Let me only propose that in order to establish an ethos for any discursively evoked subject, speakers and audiences refer to culturally transmitted grounds for rhetorical credit, or ethos topoi (Curtius

1979 [1948]: 70, 105; Eggs 1991: 42; Amossy 1999: 132). The signals that narratologists established for unreliability can be traced back to such topoi. Claude's, and also Angot's own, idiosyncratic way of writing (respectively, of speaking) are taken by many readers as the expression of their authentic emotion on the basis of the conventional association of such a style with the un-impeded, "hence" authentic, exteriorisation of emotion. One's interpretation of the narrative structure in *Sujet Angot*, and also of *Claude*'s unreliability, is likely to be co-determined by the ways in which one imagines the author's own ethos: do I construct Angot as a writer who exploits the register of metafiction *playfully*, or *ironically* (making her reader feel somewhat aggressed), or in a *pathologically compulsive manner*? The author's own posturing, and the ways in which her posture has been cast in the media contribute to how I would imagine her ethos, and vice-versa (these thoughts are developed in more detail in Korthals Altes, 2014).

4. Conclusion

This chapter aimed to raise some questions regarding narratology's theoretical and methodological frameworks, in particular, regarding the idea that narratology offers a method for identifying unreliable narrators. I hope to have contributed to the argument, in line with Nünning's cognitive approach, that to assess the (un)reliability of a narrative voice (or even of focalisation) is a complex interpretive calculus involving several framing operations. The relevance of the typologies that narratologists have developed lies, in my view, in the systematization of time and culture-bound codes and conventions attached to (un)reliability. But such codes require readers' semiotic "nose" to sniff them out and readers may have their noses trained or set in different ways. Narratology's lists of signals and typologies are most useful as heuristics, sharpening interpreters' procedures for close reading and offering a vocabulary and format for explaining one's interpretive acts.

Such interpretive procedures are not merely subjective: they rest on shared interpretive habits (reading in terms of real-life psychology/morals, or in terms of aesthetic stylizing, for instance). Such interpretive pathways also respond to conventional signals for an author's and narrator's posture, on ethos topoi, which relate back to 'folk' (or more sophisticated) psychology and morality. For a meta-hermeneutic narratology a combination of a semiotics with a rhetoric of reliability forms a rich domain for investigation. This perspective may avoid the psychologizing and moralizing that often characterizes research on narrative unreliability and which betrays its normative hermeneutic rather than meta-hermeneutic character. Acknowledging this (meta)hermeneutic dimension more clearly also strengthens Vera Nünning's and others' call for more attention to the cultural-historical context.

Narratology could in this respect benefit from the work that is being done in discourse-analytical and sociological research on ethos and authorial posture, which also pays minute attention to the social/institutional conditions in which these images function (in Korthals Altes 2014, I discuss several of the most relevant contributions of French/Francophone sociology and discourse analysis). The investigation should include a comparison of the codes for trustworthiness, sincerity and reliability in the many domains in which we articulate and negotiate our worldviews, such as politics, media debates, gossip, or literature.

Last but not least, cooperation with sciences that seek empirical validation of their claims is evidently relevant for such topics, especially for narratologists that claim to work in a cognitive perspective. However, this interest for interdisciplinary cooperation should not make scholars in the humanities forget the central importance of interpretation, as a scholarly tool, as an object of investigation, and as a mechanism that is constitutive for culture.

Works Cited

Amossy, Ruth. 2001. "*Ethos* at the Crossroads of Disciplines: Rhetoric, Pragmatics, Sociology." *Poetics Today* 22.1: 1–23.
Angot, Christine. 1997. *Les Autres*. Paris: Fayard.
Angot, Christine. 1998. *Sujet Angot*. Paris: Fayard.
Aristotle. 2007 [367–347 BC; 335–322 BC]. *On Rhetoric: A Theory of Civic Discourse*. Trans. George A. Kennedy. 2nd Rev. ed. New York, NY/Oxford: Oxford University Press.
Booth, Wayne. 1961. *The Rhetoric of Fiction*. Chicago, IL: Chicago University Press.
Bortolussi, Marisa & Peter Dixon. 2003. *Psychonarratology. Foundations for the Empirical Study of Literary Response*. Cambridge: Cambridge University Press.
Bruner, Jerome. 1990. *Acts of Meaning*. Cambridge, MA: Harvard University Press.
Butte, George. 2004. *I Know That You Know That I Know. Narrating Subjects from Moll Flanders to Marnie*. Columbus, OH: Ohio State University Press.

Chatman, Seymour. 1978. *Story and Discourse. Narrative Structure in Fiction and Film*. Ithaca, NY: Cornell University Press.
Curtius, Ernst R. 1979 [1948]. *European Literature and the Latin Middle Ages*. Trans. Willard R. Trask. London: Routledge & Kegan Paul.
Eggs, Ekkehard. 1999. "Ethos aristotélicien, conviction et pragmatique moderne." In: Ruth Amossy, Jean-Michel Adam, Marcelo Dascal et al. (eds.). *Images de soi dans le discours. La construction de l'ethos*. Lausanne: Delachaux & Niestlé.
Gadamer, Hans-Georg. 1991 [1960]. *Truth and Method*. Trans. Joel Weinsheimer & Donald G. Marshall. 2nd Rev. ed. New York, NY: Crossroad.
Genette, Gérard. 1972. *Figures III*. Paris: Seuil.
Genette, Gérard. 1988. *Narrative Discourse Revisited*. Trans. Jane E. Lewin. Ithaca, NY: Cornell University Press.
Gibson, Andrew. 1996. *Towards a Postmodern Theory of Narratology*. Edinburgh: Edinburgh University Press.
Goffman, Erving. 1974. *Frame Analysis. An Essay on the Organization of Experience*. New York, NY: Harper & Row.
Grice, H. Paul. 1989. *Studies in the Way of Words*. Cambridge, MA: Harvard University Press.
Greimas, Algirdas J. 1966. *Sémantique structurale. Recherche de méthode*. Paris: Larousse.
Greimas, Algirdas J. & Joseph Courtés. 1979. *Sémiotique. Dictionnaire raisonné de la théorie du langage*. Paris: Hachette.
Habermas, Jürgen. 1983. *Moralbewußtsein und kommunikatives Handeln*. Frankfurt am Main: Suhrkamp.
Heinen, Sandra. 2002. "Das Bild des Autors: Überlegungen zum Begriff des 'impliziten Autors' und seines Potentials zur kulturwissenschaftlichen Beschreibung von inszenierter Autorschaft." *Sprachkunst* 33.2: 329–345.
Heyd, Theresa. 2011. "Unreliability. The Pragmatic Perspective Revisited." *Journal of Literary Theory* 5.1: 3–17.
Korthals Altes, Liesbeth. 2005. "Ironie, ethos textuel et cadre de lecture: Le cas de *Sujet Angot*." In: Vincent Jouve (ed.). *L'Expérience de lecture*. Paris: L'Improviste. 85–100.
Korthals Altes, Liesbeth. 2008. "Sincerity, Reliability and Other Ironies— Notes on Dave Eggers' *A Heartbreaking Work of Staggering Genius*." In: Elke D'Hoker & Gunther Martens (eds.). *Narrative Unreliability in the Twentieth-Century First-Person Novel*. Narratologia 14. Berlin: De Gruyter. 107–128.
Korthals Altes, Liesbeth. 2013. "I Narratology, Ethical Turns, Circularities, and a Meta-Ethical Way Out." In : Jakob Lothe & Jeremy Hawthorn (eds.). *Narrative Ethics*. Amsterdam/New York, NY : Rodopi.

Korthals Altes, Liesbeth. 2014. *Ethos and Narrative Interpretation. The Negotiation of Meanings and Values in Fiction.* Frontiers of Narrative Series. Nebraska University Press.

Lejeune, Philippe. 1971. *L'Autobiographie en France.* Paris: Armand Colin.

Martin, John. 1997. "Inventing Sincerity, Refashioning Prudence: The Discovery of the Individual in Renaissance Europe." *The American Historical Review* 102.5: 1309–1342.

Meizoz, Jérôme. 2007. *Postures littéraires. Mises en scène modernes de l'auteur. Essai.* Genève: Slatkine.

Meizoz, Jérôme. 2009. "Ce que l'on fait dire au silence : Posture, *ethos*, image d'auteur. " *Argumentation et Analyse du Discours* (October 15, 2009): http://aad.revues.org/667 (last retrieved: August 20, 2012)

Nünning, Ansgar. 1999. "Unreliable, compared to what? Towards a Cognitive Theory of Unreliable Narration: Prolegomena and Hypotheses." In: Walter Grünzweig & Andreas Solbach (eds.). *Grenzüberschreitungen. Narratologie im Kontext/Transcending Boundaries: Narratology in Context.* Tübingen: Gunter Narr Verlag. 53–73.

Nünning, Ansgar. 2005. "Reconceptualizing Unreliable Narration: Synthesizing Cognitive and Rhetorical Approaches." In: James Phelan & Peter J. Rabinowitz (eds.). *A Companion to Narrative Theory.* Oxford: Blackwell. 89–107.

Nünning, Ansgar. 2008. "Reconceptualizing the Theory, History, and Generic Scope of Unreliable Narration: Towards a Synthesis of Cognitive and Rhetorical Approaches." In: Elke D'Hoker & Gunther Martens (eds.). *Narrative Unreliability in the Twentieth-Century First-Person Novel.* Narratologia 14. Berlin: De Gruyter. 29–76.

Nünning, Vera. 2004 [1998]. "Unreliable Narration and the Historical Variability of Values and Norms: The *Vicar of Wakefield* as a Test-Case of a Cultural-Historical Narratology." *Style* 38.2: 236–252.

Olson, Greta. 2003. "Reconsidering Unreliability: Fallible and Untrustworthy Narrators." *Narrative* 11.1: 93–109.

Patron, Sylvie. 2009. *Le Narrateur. Introduction à la théorie narrative.* Paris: Armand Colin.

Phelan, James. 2005. *Living to Tell about It. A Rhetoric and Ethics of Character Narration.* Ithaca, NY: Cornell University Press.

Phelan, James & Mary P. Martin. 1999. "The Lessons of 'Weymouth': Homodiegesis, Unreliability, Ethics, and *The Remains of the Day*." In: David Herman (ed.). *Narratologies. New Perspectives on Narrative Analysis.* Columbus, OH: Ohio State University Press. 88–109.

Rabatel, Alain. 2009. *Homo Narrans. Pour une analyse énonciative et interactionnelle du récit.* Limoges: Lambert-Lucas.

Rabinowitz, Peter J. 1998. *Before Reading. Narrative Conventions and the Politics of Interpretation*. Columbus, OH: Ohio State University Press.

Schaeffer, Jean-Marie. 2010 [1999]. *Why Fiction?* Trans. Dorrit Cohn. Lincoln, NE: University of Nebraska Press.

Suleiman, Susan R. & Inge W. Crosman (eds.). 1980. *The Reader in the Text. Essays on Audience and Interpretation*. Princeton, NJ: Princeton University Press.

Walsh, Richard. 2007. *The Rhetoric of Fictionality: Narrative Theory and the Idea of Fiction*. Columbus, OH: Ohio State University Press.

Wolf, Werner. 2006. "Introduction: Frames, Framings and Framing Borders in Literature and Other Media." In: Werner Wolf & Walter Bernhart (eds.). *Framing Borders in Literature and Other Media*. Amsterdam: Rodopi. 1–40.

Yacobi, Tamar. 1981. "Fictional Reliability as a Communicative Problem." *Poetics Today* 2.2: 113–126.

Yacobi, Tamar. 2001. "Package Deals in Fictional Narrative: The Case of the Narrator's (Un)Reliability." *Narrative* 9.2 : 223–229.

Zerweck, Bruno. 2001. "Historicizing Unreliable Narration: Unreliability and Cultural Discourse in Narrative Fiction." *Style* 35.1: 151–178.

Zunshine, Lisa. 2006. *Why we Read Fiction. Theory of Mind and the Novel*. Columbus, OH: Ohio State University Press.

VERA NÜNNING

(Heidelberg)

Reconceptualising Fictional (Un)reliability and (Un)trustworthiness from a Multidisciplinary Perspective: Categories, Typology and Functions

Though a host of studies have explored many facets of fictional unreliable narrations, the discussion has so far been confined to rather narrow lines of inquiry. As briefly argued in the introduction to this volume, literary scholars have much to gain when they attempt to broaden the path bid out by Wayne C. Booth and join the insights of literary studies with those of the multidisciplinary debate on (un)reliability and (un)trustworthiness. Since unreliable narrators abound in all kinds of social discourse, it seems fruitful to extend the field of narratological inquiry and acknowledge as well as explore several kinds of both factual and fictional narrations. Moreover, a closer look at the multidisciplinary debate on unreliability suggests that a number of aspects which have so far escaped the notice of literary scholars should be considered in the discussion of fictional unreliable narrations.

In the following, the exploration of (un)reliability and (un)trustworthiness will begin with the introduction of a number of categories and criteria from the multidisciplinary research on trust, which can arguably enrich the analysis of unreliability both in fictional and factual stories. These categories will then be partly modified and adjusted to the study of unreliable narrations, and a basic typology of three different kinds of such narrations will be developed. This framework will then be enlarged by adding a number of narratological categories which can augment the typology and render it more useful for a characterisation of different kinds of unreliable narrators, some of which have not been considered in the theoretical debate of the concept of unreliability so far. The third section of this chapter will focus on the identification of signals or clues for unreliability and highlight which presuppositions have to be given in order to characterise a fictional narrator as unreliable. In this section, the importance of narrative conventions and narrative competence will be highlighted, and Grice's conversation maxims will be employed in order to distinguish between different kinds of clues for unreliability. In the fourth section, major functions of fictional unreliability will be sketched, and the brief conclusion will point out some future areas of research.

1. (Un)reliability and (Un)trustworthiness from a Multidisciplinary Perspective

In order to gain a more thorough understanding of unreliability, it is worthwhile to start with the question of what is involved when deciding whether to call someone reliable in a given act of communication. Building on ideas put forth by Jürgen Habermas and John Searle, I want to distinguish the following three aspects that readers or listeners can rely on with regard to narrators who tell a story: first, they can rely on the engagement of the speaker; that is on his or her intention to act in accordance with the content of the statement (see Habermas 1984 [1976]: 431). This aspect focusses on the relation between the speakers' intentions and their future behaviour. Second, they can rely on the sincerity of the speakers, i.e. on their conviction that what they say is true, which implies the assumption that they express their emotions, thoughts and feelings honestly and truthfully. This second aspect refers to the relation between the content of the story and the speaker's beliefs. And third, readers and listeners can rely on the adequacy of the content of what is told. Following Habermas and others, the correctness of the narrative is not to be conceptualised as a relationship between the content of the story and the actual events, but rather as a correspondence between the story and the knowledge of the listener.[1] These are quite different meanings of the term reliable, of course, since a speaker may be sincere but still tell an incorrect story. Moreover, the first two criteria sketched above refer to the unreliability of the speaker, while the third concerns the unreliability of the "narrated product", i.e. the text. Each of these meanings of the term unreliable can be questioned from a postmodernist perspective,[2] but what we are dealing with here is not a philosophical definition of sincerity or authenticity. Instead, the focus is on what people hope or expect from others when they decide to trust them. In such situations the assumption

---

[1] See Habermas (1984 [1976]: 431–432), as well as figure 16 (ibid.: 440). The correspondence to current knowledge is also stressed by Sperber (2000: 135).
[2] Especially the assumption of sincerity would come into question; after all, it is more than just difficult to identify an authentic self; and there are no reliable stories in the sense of correspondence to the events which are related. However, these terms can be understood as ideals which (should) govern successful interaction as kinds of felicity rules in the sense of John Searle and Jürgen Habermas.

of the speaker's sincerity is an important precondition for trusting someone.[3]

In addition, another aspect which is stressed in the multidisciplinary discussion of trust should be taken into consideration: the competence of the speaker. In psychology and business studies, for instance, competence is held to be an important feature, since one has to believe not only in the sincerity of the narrators, but also in their ability to carry out their intentions.[4] This capability, which refers not only to the speakers' expertise but also to the means that they have at their disposal, seems to be quite remote from the concerns of studying literary unreliable narrators. However, some studies link the competence of speakers to their ability to tell a correct story, and the implications of this ability, which will be discussed later on, turn out to be more important than is apparent at first sight.

2. Categories and Typology for the Study of Fictional (Un)reliable Narration

In order to transfer the terms and definitions introduced above, it is necessary to acknowledge that there are major differences between the real-life situations that many conceptualisations of trust (and trustworthiness) refer to and those literary works which feature (un)reliable or (un)trustworthy narrators. These differences stem from the fact that, in the study of literary texts, scholars deal with the narrative product, while other disciplines can take the complexities of communication in given social contexts into account and analyse the performance of the narrator while considering factors that are not (or are only partially) accessible when reading fictional texts. Many studies have, for instance, shown that the reputation of narrators, their former behaviour and dispositions, play an important role in the attribution of trustworthiness.[5] In the study of fiction, however, such aspects are only important when dealing with embedded fictional narrators, since it is only with regard to those narrators that readers know

---

3 In many cases the attribution of morality or benevolence plays a role as well; trustors expect that the trustee will adhere to basic moral maxims or is benevolently inclined towards them. This is, however, not always the case, since one can 'trust' that someone will fulfill a threat. For the criterion of morality, see Schweer/Thies (2005: 47).
4 See Schweer/Thies (2005: 57) and Möllering (2001: 413). See also (Fricker 2002: 379): "the speaker is trustworthy – both sincere, and competent, that is, likely to be right about her topic".
5 See Moss (2004: 246, 248) and Rousseau/Sitkin/Burt et al. (1998: 394): "trust is at once related to dispositions, decisions, behaviors, social networks, and institutions". For a brief overview of the main topics of research on trust in the neurosciences and psychology, see Schipper/Petermann (2011).

about their former behaviour and future actions. In the case of texts told by homodiegetic narrators, readers do not have such knowledge. In these texts, criteria like the reputation of narrators do not apply: what happened before or what will happen later on is outside the scope of the analysis of this kind of fictional self-narrative.

Building on insights from multidisciplinary studies on trust, I want to distinguish three basic kinds of unreliability, which can be analysed by using different criteria. The first of these concerns the product of narration, the text, and the correspondence between the narrative discourse and the facts within the storyworld. This analysis has been at the core of most studies of unreliable narrations so far. A second major kind of unreliability concerns the (lack of) sincerity of the speaker, which distinguishes narrators who are the victim of their own delusions from those who know the facts about the events but nonetheless tell a story that is inconsistent with them. The third kind of unreliability is related to the incompetence of the narrator and to the possible lack of three areas of expertise which can—for a variety of reasons—render it impossible for him or her to tell a correct story of the events.

The first kind of unreliability concerns the relation between the narrative and the facts within the fictional storyworld, and can be analysed by having recourse to different types of criteria:

- Intratextual inconsistencies between the narrator's discourse and the feelings, words and actions that are depicted in the text; and/or
- Extratextual inconsistencies between the elements of the story and the general knowledge as well as implicit personality theories at the time of writing the story.[6]

The second kind is marked by the (in)sincerity of the narrator and defined by the relation between the narrative and the narrator's beliefs:

- With regard to homodiegetic or human-like overt narrators: (in)consistency between the actual beliefs, feelings and motives of narrators and those they profess in their tales. Whether the narrators are conscious or unconscious of the discrepancy between their tale and the facts in the fictional world is important to the analysis of their intentions as well as the identification of their motives and implicit self-characterisation.

---

[6] This neutral and rather general definition of unreliability is consistent with the terminology used in the *Clinical Assessment of Malingering and Deception*, in which unreliability is differentiated from deception, dissimulation, self-disclosure and non-disclosure (see Jarmila Mildorf's contribution in this volume). For a detailed discussion of text internal, paratextual and contextual signals of unreliable narration, see Ansgar Nünning (1997).

- With regard to covert heterodiegetic narrators: these covert narrators act as agents narrating a story, which, even as far as the description of the setting and the action is concerned, implies choices regarding wording as well as selection and perspectivisation of facts. Though it cannot be assumed that the distortion or suppression of crucial facts is a mere coincidence, in covert heterodiegetic narrations, this misrepresentation of relevant information cannot be used by readers in order to explore the narrator's implicit self-characterisation. Here, the cognitive and rhetorical functions of unreliability are foregrounded.

The third kind of unreliability is distinguished by the incompetence of the narrators and their ability to create an adequate story of the events in question:

- The narrator's inability to understand his or her own feelings and motives or the events that are depicted.
- The narrator's inability to adequately interpret his or her own feelings or the state of affairs, due to a lack of maturity and general knowledge (with regard to children or 'fools' as narrators) or due to a deficient or deviant system of norms and values.
- The narrator's inability to provide an acceptable and understandable narrative account of his or her feelings or of the affairs in question (both with regard to narrative conventions and with regard to the choice of stylistic means).[7]

This differentiation into several kinds of unreliability is based on the insights from psychology, sociology and linguistics introduced above; at the same time it is closely related to the typologies developed by Uri Margolin (this volume) and James Phelan (2005: 51–52).[8] The analysis of the first kind has been at the centre of literary studies of unreliability: consistency, completeness and the truth of correspondence between the narrator's representation and the story world can be explored by applying the narratological toolkit, and it can be determined whether there is a misrepresentation or a suppression of important facts. The second kind refers

---

7   This incompetence impairs the performance of the narrator and becomes visible in the act of narration.

8   See also Phelan/Martin (1999), who first differentiated three axes of communication and two kinds of unreliability potentially pertaining to each of them: for the axis of facts, under- and misreporting; for the axis of knowledge, perception and interpretation, under- and misreading; and for the axes of ethics and evaluation, under- and misregarding. See also Phelan (2005: 50–52). Moreover, the typology is indebted to articles by Britta Hartmann (2007) and Robert Vogt (2009; see also his contribution in this volume), who also distinguish between the kind of narrator who becomes the object of dramatic irony, and a different kind of 'ambivalent' narration.

to the disposition and intentions of the narrator as well as the possible functions of the narration, which can be deduced from the analysis of the text. The last kind also refers to narrators, but instead of concentrating on their dispositions the focus lies on their abilities and breadth of knowledge. With regard to these capabilities, one can distinguish between their understanding of the facts in the storyworld and the other character's emotions and intentions as well as their own state of mind on the one hand, and their interpretative skills as well as their abilities of applying adequate standards of evaluation and of drawing correct conclusions on the other. These two criteria specifying the field in which the narrator is (in)competent correspond to the three axes of communication proposed by James Phelan according to which a narrator can be said to misrepresent, misinterpret or misevaluate the facts on the level of the story.[9]

The final criterion concerning the (in)competence of narrators, their ability to create a story that conforms to the narrative conventions required in the context, has not yet been applied to the study of unreliable narration. This criterion refers to the process of narration and can be analysed with regard to Paul Grice's conversational maxims, which can be used in order to provide standards for assessing the unreliability of the narrative act.[10] Generally, however, literary scholars have concentrated on the first kind, on intratextual and extratextual inconsistencies as well as paratextual clues, while the other criteria have only been mentioned in passing. In fact, some literary studies have asked whether a sincere narrator—like the butler Stevens in *The Remains of the Day*—can be called unreliable at all (cf. Wall 1994).

Since all of the aspects mentioned above can play a role in determining whether a narration is unreliable, it seems pertinent to distinguish between different possible combinations of kinds of unreliability in a given text. The exploration of these can not only characterise the particular mixture leading to the conclusion that a fictional narrator is unreliable, it can also help to elaborate a more nuanced typology of unreliable narrators. Put simply, one should, for instance, be able to distinguish between a competent liar on the one hand, and a sincere narrator that is the victim of his or her own delusions on the other. Moreover, it is necessary to bear in mind that with regard to all of these criteria, specific narrations and narrators can be placed on a sliding scale between the poles

---

9   See Phelan (2005: 50–52) and Phelan/Martin (1999). While Phelan distinguishes between interpretations and evaluations, they are put in the same category here, since it is extremely difficult to disentangle them in any given text.

10 Theresa Heyd (2011) connects Grice's maxims to the study of unreliable narration. However, she proceeds from different theoretical premises than those which will be explicated later.

of 'very reliable/sincere/competent' and 'extremely unreliable/insincere/incompetent'.[11]

In order to come to a more comprehensive understanding of the types of fictional unreliable narrators, it seems necessary to consider some additional categories. First of all, one has to distinguish between the different diegetic levels of a fictional text. On the level of the story, there can be any number of narrators who are untrustworthy—including the former self of the narrator who later tells a truthful story—without giving a major twist to the story that induces readers to re-interpret the events in a significant way.[12] Such embedded untrustworthy narrators can be found in detective stories, for instance, in which many characters tell stories that consciously or unconsciously provide a completely inadequate representation and interpretation of the fictional events. Embedded unreliable narrators are often included in stories which, on the whole, present the facts of the fictional world in a reliable way. When exploring these narrators, it can be useful to look at aspects that are of great importance in multidisciplinary studies on trust, such as the former reputation and the future behaviour of the speakers. Moreover, with regard to embedded narrators, factors like the particular context, the relations between the characters or their body language—facial expressions, gestures and movements—are often rendered in detail and can serve to evaluate their reliability, sincerity and competence.[13]

In the analysis of unreliability in fictional texts, the category of multiperspectivity should also be taken into account (cf. Menhard 2009). This does not only concern the study of embedded narrators, but also the exploration of unreliability on the level of narrative mediation. From Wilkie Collins' novel *The Moonstone* onwards, there has been a tradition—which was recently revived—of featuring more than one homodiegetic narrator, i.e. of rendering and juxtaposing conflicting narratives of several characters telling their stories, without the device of an omniscient voice that organises the tales and embeds them in its own discourse. From a structural point of view, these narrators are placed on the level of narrative mediation and therefore differ only in number, but not in kind

---

11 The use of sliding scales, has, among others, been advocated by Phelan/Martin (1999).
12 These criteria are also mentioned by Hartmann (2007: 37, 40–42, 45–46).
13 In face-to-face communication, any number of factors concerning outer appearance and body language can influence judgements on the reliability of narrators. Cab drivers, for instance, not only take the outer appearance of passengers into account, but also aspects like their "sitting behavior" (cf. Henslin 1968: 149). See also Chang/Doll/Wout et al. (2010: 88). The most pertinent non-verbal as well as non-dispositional factors which influence ascriptions of trustworthiness in interactive situations are succinctly stated in James Henslin's summary of Ervin Goffman's concept of "the front: (a) the setting, (b) the appearance of the performer, and (c) the *manner* of the performer" (Henslin 1968: 142).

from those in novels with one (un)trustworthy narrator. However, novels which juxtapose the stories of several (partly untrustworthy) narrators can be compared to those featuring embedded narrators, since contrastive stories are plainly put next to each other so that the reader is in a position to compare the individual accounts and arrive at his or her own conclusion. A narrator such as Miss Clack in *The Moonstone* would be considered highly untrustworthy regarding the degree of her delusions, but the mistaken judgements, interpretations and values of her narration can be easily detected and are of minor significance as far as the interpretation of the whole story is concerned. In contrast, novels told by one homodiegetic narrator leave the other characters with only a marginal voice and position, which makes it more difficult to detect inconsistencies.

The criterion of the textinternal, diegetic positioning of the narrator is therefore related to that of the significance of unreliability for the interpretation of any given text. Following Booth, most theorists reserve the term 'unreliable' for those narrators whose story is re-interpreted by readers in a way that deviates decisively from the tale the narrator intends to tell. In such cases the attribution of untrustworthiness changes the meaning of the whole story; the interpretation hinges upon the question of untrustworthiness. It seems reasonable, however, to include embedded unreliable narrators into the typology and consider the degree as well as the scope of the narrator's distortions: These may concern key issues and influence the comprehension of the whole story, but they can just as well refer to only a few instances.[14] The discussion of the typology of unreliable narrators should be reframed with regard to the diegetic positioning of the narrators and the scope of their narrations.

Within the framework suggested here, the controversial discussion of whether unreliability depends on the presence of a human or human-like narrator whose personality becomes visible to readers can be discarded. The link between unreliable and homodiegetic narration makes sense within the tradition of Booth's definition, since the narrator has to be recognisable as a personality who unwittingly lays bare his or her faults, be it their psychological dysfunction or obsession, their lack of knowledge, interpretative faculties or morals. This anthropomorphisation of the narrator has been associated with the (homodiegetic) narrator's presence in the

---

14 For this criterion, Greta Olson (2003: 96–104) has introduced the distinction between untrustworthy or unreliable narrators whose disposition is responsible for the telling of a tale which deviates "from the general normative standards implicit in the text" (2003: 96) and those that are fallible, i.e. when only a few instances of mistaken interpretations are concerned, and their mistakes are "*situationally motivated*" (2003: 102). The differences with regard to scope and diegesis are also considered in an article by Britta Hartmann (2007), who provides a helpful table of criteria for distinguishing between several kinds of unreliability in films (cf. ibid.: 37).

fictional world by a host of scholars; but, following insights put forward by Gunther Martens, I agree with most of the contributors to this volume that both homodiegetic and omniscient, heterodiegetic narrators can potentially be untrustworthy.[15]

Since homo- as well as heterodiegetic narrators can be unreliable, it seems sensible to emphasise the difference between sincere and insincere unreliable narrators, between those who unwittingly become the dupe of their own delusions, and those who are aware of the facts but mislead the reader by withholding or distorting crucial information; this difference can be used as a major category for distinguishing between several kinds of unreliability.[16] The first kind refers to either homodiegetic or personalised overt heterodiegetic narrators who unconsciously misinform readers, and who often unintentionally provide a plethora of clues to the unreliability of the tale. The second kind consists of stories in which a homodiegetic or heterodiegetic narrator misleads the reader by telling a story which seems to be trustworthy throughout the major part of the text, but which is revealed as incorrect at the very end of the story. This kind is distinguished from the first one by the fact that readers are more or less unable—at least on first reading the story—to detect the unreliability through the recognition and interpretation of textual inconsistencies; rather, they are told at the end in plain terms that what was told before does not correspond to the facts in the fictional world.

However, with regard to this latter kind of narration, which cannot be explained by the lack of abilities of narrators, one should distinguish between homodiegetic and overt heterodiegetic narrators on the one hand, and covert heterodiegetic narrators on the other. While both kinds of narration provide stories which seem to be reliable for a major portion of the text, they invite different reader reactions: with regard to personalised narrators it is possible to search for motives and potential faults of the narrator and ask why he or she gave a wrong account of the facts in the first place. With regard to covert heterodiegetic narrators, however, searching for motives is a futile proposition; instead of looking for personal reasons, it makes much more sense to inquire into the functions that this kind of narration serves. A typical example of the personalised narrator who deliberately deceives the reader is the overt homodiegetic narrator in Agatha Christie's novel *The Murder of Roger Ackroyd*, which is told by a Dr. Watson-like speaker, a sober, respectable physician living in

---

15 For a criticism of this position, see Tamar Yacobi (2001). For the study of unreliable heterodiegetic overt narrators, see Martens (2008).
16 This distinction is also emphasised by Bo Pettersson in this volume, who establishes a scale of intentionality, ranging from unintentional fallibility to deception. Uri Margolin (in this volume) also stresses the importance of the criterion of intentionality.

a village where a murder has taken place. This narrator helps the detective in his investigations, and reveals only at the very end how he purposefully deceived the reader by leaving out all reference to his murder. A similar, but nonetheless different kind of narration can be found in Ambrose Bierce's famous short story "An Incident at Owl Creek Bridge", where a covert heterodiegetic narrator tells a tale that seems to show that a man, who is just about to be hanged at the beginning of the story, makes a miraculous escape and reaches his home, while at the end it becomes obvious that this is just the man's final fantasy, not lasting more than a second or so, before he is executed. Whereas Christie's novel, told by an overt homodiegetic narrator, raises the question of the narrator's motives and ethics, Bierce's narrative raises the question of the possible functions of unreliability in the short story.

If one characterises the two kinds of narrators in terms of the framework sketched above, the following picture emerges: the first type of narrator, the object of dramatic irony, tells a story that is unreliable, which is recognisable by internal or external inconsistencies. At the same time he or she is sincere, and in some way incompetent with regard to his or her ability of reporting, interpreting or evaluating the facts; or with regard to his or her storytelling capabilities. The second type of narrator is not the object of dramatic irony as he chooses to tell a false story, revealing the deception at the end of the text. This narrator is also unreliable with regard to the fictional facts, but in contrast to the first type he or she is insincere at the same time and usually very competent as far as his or her endeavour to mislead the reader is concerned. Since it is generally possible for readers to recognise the incorrectness of the stories of sincere but incompetent narrators at an early point in the story, their tales appear to be more untrustworthy due to their lack of guile and deception. Insincere and competent unreliable narrators, by contrast, seem to be trustworthy throughout the major part of the text. Their tales are usually cunningly told, featuring next to no inconsistencies or other markers of unreliability, which makes it extremely difficult to detect them by way of textual clues. Both types are unreliable—but in a very different way and for completely different reasons and with diverse consequences for the type of text and textual clues they produce.

Moreover, the insincere but highly competent kind of narrator who only reveals the correct version of the story in the end can be differentiated into two sub-types: The first one consists of personalised narrators who are recognisable by their comments and judgements. Since readers are able to understand their motives and intentions and evaluate them accordingly, these human or human-like narrators, who can be homo- or heterodiegetic, to some extent resemble sincere but incompetent narrators.

This kind of explanation and evaluation of unreliability is not possible when the story is told by covert heterodiegetic unreliable narrators who refrain from comments and do not provide any clues as to their personality traits, values or motives.[17] With regard to these narrations, the search for motives does not make any sense; instead, the functions of unreliability are placed in the foreground.

A refined typology of unreliability in fiction should differentiate not only between the three kinds of unreliability and the different types of narrators, but also take the other categories that have been introduced above into consideration: the diegetic positioning of the narrator, the question of multiperspectivity, and the significance of unreliability for the interpretation of the story as a whole. This allows for a more nuanced categorisation of the kind of unreliability that can be found in a given text. The literary study of unreliable narration has so far mainly been restricted to the study of sincere, but incompetent homodiegetic narrators, and a few discussions of narrations in which the facts are revealed in the end, but the unreliability of narrators extends beyond the scope of just the two major types of narrators. There has been no exploration of impostors who are unreliable only with regard to the textinternal discrepancies on the level of the story, where there are inconsistencies between their intentions, words and actions on the one hand, and purported social status on the other. Just like picaros, such narrators are often solely unreliable as far as their embedded narrations on the level of the story are concerned; they can be sincere as well as competent on the level of narrative mediation and tell a trustworthy story to the reader.[18]

The integration of the category of diegetic positioning makes it possible to include the analysis of the unreliability of focalizers into the discussion. Though focalizers differ from embedded narrators in that they do not tell a story and therefore are not motivated by their desire to deceive others in telling their tales, there are a number of similarities between unreliable focalizers and sincere but incompetent narrators. Both are characterised by their inability to perceive, interpret or evaluate the situation or their own desires and intentions. In addition, the criterion of multiperspectivity (or the number of and balance between different focalizers) as well as that of the degree of unreliability of the whole narration can also be applied to the interpretation and categorisation of

---

[17] There are, of course, cases in which a seemingly trustworthy heterodiegetic narrator is revealed to be an unreliable homodiegetic narrator in the end. A famous example of this is Ian McEwan's novel *Atonement* (2001).

[18] According to Ervin Goffman, the feeling of being duped is sometimes connected to the question of "whether or not the performer is authorized to give the performance in question" (1973 [1959]: 59).

unreliable focalizers. The combination of the categories and criteria suggested above therefore offers a typology which can accommodate quite different types (and degrees) of unreliable narrators as well as focalizers.

3. How to Identify Fictional Untrustworthy Narrators: Preconditions and Signals

The categorisation of types of untrustworthy narrators can only begin, however, after they have been identified. Only after detecting signals which show that the story told by the narrator does not correspond to the facts in the fictional world and/or that his norms and values are questionable are readers in a position to ask for possible reasons for these discrepancies; only then can they decide whether the narrator is (un)reliable, (in)sincere and/or (in)competent. With regard to the identification of a fictional untrustworthy narrator, a few overarching decisions have to be taken before a close interpretation of subtle signals of untrustworthiness begins.

The first precondition pertains to the acceptance of literary conventions: Readers have to be willing to immerse themselves in the fictional world, to take the characters and their deeds 'as if' they were real. They also have to be versed in the use of genre conventions. In text types such as fantasy or science fiction novels as well as in fables or fairy tales, the fictional world may include human-like beings with super-human powers or talking animals, but with regard to such genres, it does not make sense to question the trustworthiness of the narrator just because he or she is an animal or flies a spaceship. There can be unreliable narrators in these genres as well, of course, but they would have to sport distinct features of unreliability such as internal inconsistencies, insincerity, etc. Moreover, while it still seems reasonable to suspect narrators' reliability within such text types, this becomes meaningless with regard to postmodern works, which feature "unnatural" or impossible worlds, in which a host of internal and external contradictions abound. In such tales, which depart from "'natural' (real-world) cognitive frames, i.e., our assumptions about time, space, and other human beings in the actual world" (Alber 2013: 44), it is not possible to create a coherent mental model of the fictional world. There is neither a naturalisation strategy which can explain the contradictions by referring to an unreliable narrator nor a final reversal which provides a coherent interpretation of what has been narrated before.

Another precondition for deciding whether a narrator is trustworthy or not is the acceptance of a literary convention which allows for the possibility of omniscient and omnipresent extradiegetic narrators, who know what the characters think and feel. Such knowledge is obviously unattainable for human beings, and a homodiegetic narrator in a realistic novel who claims to be able to read all the thoughts of his friends and foes would have to be considered unreliable. Heterodiegetic, omniscient narrators, however, are held to be especially trustworthy as far as establishing the facts of the fictional worlds are concerned. As Uri Margolin (1992: 110) has pointed out, it is also important to recognise the significance of historically variable genre conventions. In Shakespeare's time, for instance, an aristocratic character could speak in blank verse; and even though this did not match the actual behaviour of the nobility, this mode of speaking is accepted as part of the fictional world. Cultural beliefs at the time of production also have to be considered; in the eighteenth century, it was not unusual if a narrator enjoyed the spectacle of a particularly gruesome execution; in the nineteenth century, such a narrator would be highly suspect.[19] Last but not least, the norms and values established by a work itself are of crucial importance. Though they do not conform to given cultural beliefs or genre conventions, the excessive speech of the characters and the narrator in Victor Hugo's *Les Misérables* does not indicate their untrustworthiness.[20] Each work establishes its own norms of what is held to be normal.

It is therefore a precondition for the possible identification of unreliable narration that the narrative has to be perceived as realistic to the extent that the actions and thoughts of the fictional characters and the causal patterns of the plot appear plausible and coherent. Often, this implies that the workings of the characters' minds correspond to the general beliefs of the time of production. These include knowledge about folk psychology, motivation, causal connections and prevalent values, and genre conventions. This does not exclude genres like fantasy, science fiction or magical realism; as long as the characters act in a plausible way in their specific (and perhaps fantastic) environment, the narrative can be perceived to be realistic. Only with regard to fictional works which fit the definition of "perceived realism" is it possible to talk about trustworthy or untrustworthy narrators.[21]

---

19 It is impossible to sketch the discussion about fictional truths, which is crucial for the understanding of fictional facts as well as deviations from them in the discourse of unreliable narrators, in a few words. See, for instance, Uri Margolin, Kendall Walton, Gregory Curry as well as Tilman Köppe.
20 Cf. Vargas Llosa (2007 [2004]: 31, 36).
21 'Perceived realism', which is different from the kind of realism that defines realist novels, is related to the persuasiveness of a story in a number of publications by Melanie C. Green; see, for instance, Green (2004: 252). The features of 'perceived realism' are explored by Busselle/Bilandzic (2008).

In narratology, there have been many studies exploring the textual signals that, within realistic fiction (which is, however, usually more narrowly defined as fiction corresponding to beliefs about the real world), indicate the untrustworthiness of a narrator. Many of these studies attempt to identify the clues that might lead readers to attribute untrustworthiness to a narrator (cf. A. Nünning 1997; see also 2005). These signals fall into three categories: intratextual, paratextual, and contextual. The intratextual clues can be subdivided into two groups. The first group comprises intratextual inconsistencies with regard to a number of factors like the consistency of the discourse and the relation between a narrator's words and his actions or the different points of view of other characters within the story. The second is made up of stylistic features that signal a high degree of emotional involvement (or derangement) of narrators as well as their desire to establish contact with the reader and convince him or her of the truth of their version of the events. Contextual signals refer to the relation between the readers' beliefs about the world and the events portrayed in the story.[22]

These criteria could be enriched by considering the adequacy of the narrator's behaviour in a given social situation. This pertains not only to embedded intradiegetic narrators who interact with others in specific situations, but also to homodiegetic unreliable narrators such as Martin Amis' narrator John Self in *Money: A Suicide Note* (1984). At over 300 pages, the mere length (as well as style) of this "suicide note" gives reason to pause. The adherence to rules which govern different kinds of social intercourse is another criterion for the attribution of trust; role-based relations often require different stories than those that are called for in personal interactions.[23]

Moreover, the intratextual signals of unreliability can be grouped by relating them to Paul Grice's conversational maxims and to Dan Sperber and Deirdre Wilson's relevance theory.[24] Grice's Maxims of Quality

---

[22] Sperber (2000: 135) suggests that the search for internal and external discrepancies is the most important way to find out whether a narrator is trustworthy or not.

[23] The significance of the given social situation with its particular requirements is stressed in fields such as psychology and business studies. Cf. Laucken (2005: 99, 103); Möllering/Sydow (2005); see especially the very helpful table by Anthony Giddens (qtd. in Möllering/Sydow 2005: 80).

[24] Sperber and Wilson's relevance theory can serve as the overarching frame in which Grice's maxims can be reconceptualised. There are major differences between both theories; these concern mainly the basic theoretical assumptions concerning the nature and significance of inferences, particularly with regard to the interpretation of implicatures as well as explicit information, and the importance of inferential comprehension and psychological metarepresentation. For a brief account of the differences, see Sperber/Wilson (2002: 6–9); Wilson/Sperber (2004: 608, 611, 613). However, for the present purpose it seems possible to combine them.

(truthfulness), Quantity (informativeness), Manner (clarity, which concerns matters of style and wording) and Relation (relevance) can also serve to specify James Phelan's categories for distinguishing between different kinds of unreliability.[25] Phelan convincingly argues that under- and misreporting as well as under- and misreading (on the axis of interpretation) and under- and misevaluation are features of unreliable narrations. It remains unclear, however, what exactly the criterion for deciding that an event may be, for instance, underreported, is. There are intuitive standards, but these can be made more explicit by relating them to violations of Grice's maxims. These maxims can then be taken as clues to untrustworthiness, with the frequency and relevance of the breaches indicating the degree of the narrator's unreliability. The Maxim of Quality and the question of truthfulness are linked to both the sincerity of the speaker and to the correspondence between the facts in the fictional world and the story delivered by the narrator, which was discussed above. Breaches of the Maxims of Quantity and Manner can signal the incompetence of the speaker as far as the mode of narration is concerned.

Violations of the Maxims of Quantity and Manner can therefore provide valuable clues to questioning the competence and trustworthiness of a narrator, implicitly characterising him or her as unreliable. Breaches of the Maxim of Quantity can consist in the withholding of crucial information or in over-explicitness, i.e. belabouring the obvious. Such unnecessary repetitions or the use of superfluous explanations violate both Sperber and Wilson's principle of relevance as well as Grice's Maxims of Quantity and Relation. Textual clues corresponding to over-explicitness primarily call into question the competence of the narrator; it is only by way of implication that such an account raises suspicion concerning the correctness of the facts. With regard to the attribution of untrustworthiness, the Maxim of Manner is double-edged: As Sperber and Wilson note, it is the narrator's task to convince the audience of the relevance of his or her story—the listeners have to be motivated to invest cognitive effort with the hope of achieving a positive effect, such as gaining new knowledge.[26] A less than competent attempt to capture the attention of listeners

---

25   Cf. Grice (1989: 368–372). These maxims are useful for a categorisation of breaches of conversational rules pointing to unreliability; however, the criticism as well as additional distinctions put forward by Dan Sperber and Deirdre Wilson should be taken into account as well. Particularly with regard to the first maxim, the question of truthfulness, it seems necessary to consider what Geoffrey Leech has termed the 'Politeness Principle', since general rules of conversation often prohibit telling true stories which might be embarrassing or otherwise inappropriate. For Phelan's and Martin's categories, see the discussion of the typology of unreliability as well as footnotes 8 and 9.
26   From the vantage point of trustworthiness, one might also add that it is in the interest of communicators to persuade listeners of their trustworthiness—otherwise, there is no

and persuade them of the importance of the particular story can be interpreted as a sign of untrustworthiness. Frequent reader addresses, attempts to establish a common ground with the audience (for instance via rhetorical questions), repeated emphases as well as explanations can either serve to persuade readers to believe in the relevance of the story or to convince them of the narrator's untrustworthiness. In addition, breaches of the Maxim of Manner can be related to the emotional involvement of the speaker. Violations of this maxim are to be expected in the works of sincere but incompetent narrators who are emotionally involved in the story. Moreover, breaches of the Maxim of Relation, which is closely related to the Maxim of Quantity and has been taken up and elaborated by Sperber and Wilson, can serve as clues for unreliability. When a narrator shies away from telling certain facts and takes up different, unrelated topics instead, this can be regarded as a sign of his or her emotional involvement, narrative incompetence or even insincerity.

Even though violations of the relevance principle and the Maxims of Quantity, Manner and Relation can offer useful clues as to the untrustworthiness of the process of narration and the incompetence of the narrator, it seems unwise to re-conceptualise the whole phenomenon of unreliable narration as a violation "of the Cooperative Principle without the intention of an implicature" (Heyd 2011: 7).[27] It seems fruitful, however, to regard violations of these Maxims as signals of the unreliability of the process of narration, and integrate them into the search for clues about untrustworthy narrations. Relating the maxims to Sperber and Wilson's relevance principle, and heeding their criticism of the limitations of Grice's theory, helps to confirm a few necessary distinctions—such as that between the unwillingness and incompetence of the narrator (cf. Wilson/Sperber 2004: 612f.)—and enhances their usefulness as tools for the identification of unreliable narration.

---

expectation of any cognitive gain, and the communication fails before it has really begun. As Sperber/Wilson note in passing, "Whether the informative intention itself is fulfilled depends on how much the audience trusts the communicator" (2004: 611).

[27] Grice is concerned with overt breaches, which he calls implicatures, such as joking or irony; these, however, are not relevant for the identification of unreliability. In addition, it is questionable whether this framework, which is concerned with communicative utterances in real-life situations and not with narratives, can be meaningfully applied to fictional narratives, in which the aesthetic design as well as aesthetic devices play an important role.

4. Functions of Fictional Unreliable Narrations

Part of the attraction of unreliable narrations within the field of literary studies may be attributed to the wide range of functions they can fulfil. The differences between unreliability in face-to-face interactions and literary works come to the fore particularly with regard to their functions. In social communication, untrustworthiness poses a substantial problem for listeners, who are, for instance, exposed to the threat of personal disappointment or financial damage if they become the dupe of unreliable narrators. By contrast, no direct personal harm will be done if readers fail to recognise unreliable narration in fiction. Instead, literary unreliability offers the pleasure of suspense and detection, of trying to prove one's initial suspicions and finally being confirmed in one's opinions; it is also related to the surprise of having to revise all the previously read facts of the fictional world and interpret them in a new light at the end of the story. In the following, I will briefly consider some major epistemological, cognitive and ethical functions that unreliability can fulfil in fiction.

The cognitive functions of unreliable narrations are manifold. Probably the most typical of these is the practice of flexibility: readers have to hold the truth of the statements of the narrators in suspension; they have to accept their utterances under the proviso that they may or may not be true (and remember them accordingly) as well as revise and reinterpret these statements in light of the knowledge they acquire later.[28] Sincere but incompetent narrators who become the butt of the irony usually provide readers ample opportunity to doubt and test their opinions throughout the story. With regard to competent, but misleading narrators, who only reveal crucial pieces of information belatedly at the end of the story, this process of reinterpreting is delayed until the ending, but at that point it is more intense and extensive in scope, since it becomes necessary to make sense of a greater number of events in a completely different light. In both cases, cognitive flexibility is required; readers have to revise their first impressions, formulate and check new hypotheses and compare different possible interpretations of the same event. They have to suppress their desire for cognitive closure at least temporarily; in some works, in which it is impossible to decide which version of the events matches the facts in the fictional world, readers have to accept that they cannot achieve a coherent interpretation of the story as a whole. Since different interpretations are both possible and irreconcilable, readers have to deal with complexity and ambivalence.

---

[28] The importance of this kind of "training" of cognitive abilities with regard to metarepresentation and the questioning of the reliability of narrators is emphasised by Zunshine (2006: 51–60; 100–118).

With regard to epistemology, unreliable narrations function as a means of presenting deviating viewpoints; they require readers to practice their judgement with regard to what is held to be normal and what is not. While the recognition of subjectivity is important in most multiperspective works (cf. Menhard 2009), the presence of unreliable narrators shifts the focus from the acknowledgement of multiple truths to the question of whether there are some viewpoints which should not be accepted as adequate descriptions of the fictional events. Though there is usually a range of co-existing different subjective representations, each of which has its own legitimacy, unreliable narrations draw attention to those perspectives that suppress or distort salient facts of the fictional world—and to the question about the reasons for this particular kind of delusion or lie. It is, of course, possible that some statements by unreliable narrators turn out to provide important information on another level of interpretation—either because they allow insight into the mind of the speaker or because they can be regarded as metaphors (see Phelan 2007: 226). However, the most telling features of unreliable narrations lie beyond the border of what is regarded as epistemologically (or factually) adequate in a given narrative.

The most visible function of homodiegetic or human-like unreliable narrators is their importance as a means of self-characterisation. Personalised unreliable narrators provide insight into their strange minds, their values, delusions, emotions, and, finally, into their (sometimes twisted) ways of thinking. While every explicit characterisation or evaluation of others always amounts to an implicit self-characterisation, and literary characters constantly characterise themselves by way of their actions, feelings and thoughts, this function is more pronounced with regard to unreliable narrators, whose perceptions, interpretations and judgements deviate from what is considered normal human behaviour.[29] Both with regard to unreliable focalizers and narrators, it becomes possible to understand just how a very different personality interprets the world. Such insights are valuable, since they provide the opportunity to gather knowledge about the way human minds may work.

In addition, unreliable narrations serve to enrich and refine readers' implicit personality theories with regard to aspects which cannot be observed in normal social interactions. Especially with respect to madmen, paedophiles or murderers, reading fiction offers a more pleasant way of acquiring such information than real-life communication. Moreover, readers get the opportunity to come to know various causes for unreliability and recognise the consequences of obsessions or other kinds of psy-

---

[29] The implicit self-characterisation of unreliable focalizers has been analysed in a pioneering article by Shen (1989).

chological dysfunction. The stories of unreliable narrators allow readers to distinguish between different reasons for misinterpretations, among them self-delusion and the negation of thoughts that might threaten dearly held beliefs and aspects of one's self-image. At the other end of the spectrum, they highlight how narrators cunningly concoct lies in order to achieve personal gain. In addition, even those homodiegetic narrators who deliberately mislead readers cannot simply be put in the same category as far as ethical evaluation is concerned. Readers have to differentiate and decide how they want to evaluate and position themselves towards, for instance, the narrator of *Roger Ackroyd*, who fails to get away with murder, and a narrator like Briony in Ian McEwan's *Atonement* (2001), who twists the truth in order to atone for a childhood mistake and cope with her guilt.

Another function of fictional unreliability lies in questioning truisms and prevailing cultural norms and values. That unreliable narrations can serve to implicitly criticise cultural concepts has been explored within the frame of a gender-oriented narratology. The deviant opinions or emotions of untrustworthy narrators can be used either to sketch alternative conceptions of identity or to criticise existing ones. The idea is at least as old as the eighteenth century, when one of the first novels by women, Mary Davys' *The Accomplished Rake* (1727), "inaugurates a tactic of women's fiction: characterizing undesirable male characters by allowing them to pontificate foolishly on their mistaken ideas about women's nature".[30] When such unattractive and untrustworthy embedded narrators voice widely held opinions about the many weaknesses of women, they render these truisms suspect. Though this function has only been studied with regard to gender identities, unreliable narrators can serve to implicitly criticise culturally entrenched beliefs about other domains, for instance about ethnicity, religion or social behaviour, equally effectively.

While all of the functions of unreliability mentioned so far depend on "perceived realism" and the use of devices like the detailed representation of consciousness, the de-automatisation and de-familiarization of perception and interpretation that unreliability can also serve to foster is closely connected to aesthetics. If, as Viktor Shklovsky claimed, it is the major function of fiction to make the well-known "'unfamiliar', to make forms difficult, to increase the difficulty and length of perception" (1965 [1917]: 12), unreliable narrators fulfil this function. The representation of their strange ways of perceiving, interpreting and evaluating can be regarded as a means of de-familiarization. Unreliable narrators can show familiar objects and events in a new light; their unusual, highly subjective ways of

---

30   See Staves (2006: 186). For functions of unreliability with regard to gender, see Allrath (2005).

thinking can bring new aspects of familiar phenomena to the foreground. This mode of presentation can provide insight into the phenomena that are depicted in such an unfamiliar way, and also stimulate reflection about what is deemed normal.

To question the borderline between what is held to be normal and abnormal is closely connected to one of the ethical functions of unreliability. Being immersed in the thoughts and world-views of unreliable narrators, following their thoughts and perhaps even sharing their feelings, readers practice empathy with others who are radically different from themselves. They experience alterity; they see the other in his or her difference. In a number of recent novels, this distance between self and other is gradually diminished; it may even give way to positive feelings towards the other, to an appreciation of his or her idiosyncrasies and to an understanding of just why he or she sees the world in that particular way. The initial experience of alterity can be replaced by the recognition of personality traits or ways of thinking that readers have in common with the narrator and by the insight that even highly unreliable narrators are perhaps not as different and alien as they might seem at first sight.[31] In trying to understand and share the narrator's thoughts and feelings, readers practice empathy with the kind of narrators for whom it is most difficult to conjure up that feeling, those who deviate from their own dispositions, norms and values. By cognitively following the thoughts and sharing the feelings of unreliable narrators, readers increase not only their knowledge about, but also their understanding of people who are different from themselves.

5. Conclusion and Suggestions for Further Research

Joining insights from the multidisciplinary discussion of trust with those of literary studies leads to a considerable expansion of the field of research. In the seminal volume on unreliable narration published by Elke D'hoker and Gunther Martens in 2008, most chapters dealt with homodiegetic narrators in twentieth century fiction. While the contributors significantly enlarged the corpus of texts and concentrated on unreliable narrators in a broad range of languages and cultures, they affirmed the focus on homodiegetic narrations in contemporary fiction. If one takes this volume as a point of comparison to the argument developed in this article, a number of new departures become visible.

---

31 See V. Nünning (2008). For the difference between distancing and bonding unreliability, see Phelan (2007).

Drawing on research in sociology, psychology and linguistics, it became possible to distinguish between the (in)correctness of the facts told in the story as well as the (in)sincerity and (in)competence of the narrator. This distinction could be correlated with insights into the importance of textinternal and -external discrepancies, with the differences between human-like and covert heterodiegetic narrators, and with three different areas of expertise which are involved in the production of narratives. While two of these three different abilities could be connected to Phelan's and Martin's distinction between the three axes of communication, the criterion of narrative competence was related to Grice's conversation maxims, which can serve as a measure for determining what is 'over'- or 'underreported'. Moreover, the integration of additional aspects such as the diegetic positioning of narrators, the importance of multiperspectivity and the significance of unreliability for an understanding of the text as a whole further served to elaborate the typology of unreliable narrations. In addition, the generic preconditions for unreliable narrations could be clarified by having recourse to the concept of "perceived realism", which makes it possible to explain why there can potentially be unreliable narrators in genres like fantasy or science fiction, while it does not make sense to look for unreliability in "unnatural" narratives.

At the same time, this reconceptualisation of the field raises a number of questions which are worthy of exploration. First, the conceptualisation of human or human-like narrators as well as their self-delusions or insincerity presupposes a conceptualisation of individuals, agency and responsibility predominant in Western stories told from the eighteenth century onwards. It is an open question, however, to what extent they can be applied to texts from earlier periods and other cultures. The device of embedded unreliable narrators can be found in a host of earlier works, for instance in medieval chronicles, where they often serve a didactic purpose,[32] and it would be interesting to look at the stories told in earlier texts—for instance by the heroes in Homer's *Ulysses*—from the point of view of unreliable narration, and determine their commonalities as well as differences with modern unreliable narrators. The close analysis of embedded narrators in many texts, such as Geoffrey Chaucer's *Canterbury Tales* and the stories told by historical characters in medieval chronicles, could provide insight into the cultural and historical variability of unreliable narration and make it possible to determine which role cultural values, general knowledge, and assumptions concerning agency and individuality play.

32　I owe this suggestion concerning the importance of embedded unreliable narrators in medieval texts to Jörg Rogge.

An even more intricate problem is posed by the consideration of unreliable extra-diegetic narrators of medieval or ancient texts. The criterion of sincerity or conscious misleading on the part of narrators does not seem applicable in these cases; it seems necessary to put forward different criteria and conceptualisations of unreliability for the analysis of such narratives.[33] In some contexts, it is not the personality and trustworthiness of the narrator that is involved in evaluating the reliability of a story. The reliability of medieval stories about the lives of saints, for instance, was not judged by comparing them to the supposed facts or by taking the personality traits of the teller into account. Instead, it was the correspondence of the virtues, deeds and values of the saint with the stories told in the Bible, which served as the pretext which legitimised the truth of the tale (cf. Koschorke 2012: 83). To determine the preconditions and criteria of unreliable narrations in texts written before the eighteenth century is thus worthy of further research; specifically interesting in this context is the importance of pre-texts, genre conventions and narrative traditions as opposed to the individual responsibility of narrators.

Moreover, more research is necessary with regard to the unreliability of semi- and non-fictional narratives. Promising fields of study are the authority and legitimisation of homodiegetic narrators, as well as the tension between the stress of their own experiences (for instance in travel literature) and the correspondence of the story with well-known pretexts and general knowledge of the contemporary audience. After all, it is sometimes those texts which we now believe to be factual that were held to be untrustworthy at the time of publication, such as Marco Polo's report, while accounts including fictitious events, such as Mandeville's, were believed to be true.

In addition to the significance of pretexts, the functions of unreliable narrations are worthy of further study. In many early modern texts, didactic functions may dominate, but it seems worthwhile to consider the propagandistic, cognitive or entertaining functions, too. As far as fictional narratives are concerned, a further differentiation of the functions of unreliable narration seems to be both possible and necessary, since the distinctions sketched above apply to nearly all types of unreliable narrators, while it stands to reason that different types can be related to different functions.

Fascinating though the topic of unreliability is, it is important to bear in mind that not every narrator who tells a story that does not conform to

---

[33] The remarks on covert heterodiegetic narrators and the concentration on the functions instead of personalised reasons might serve as a starting point for the investigation of such cases. Moreover, the generic tradition might play a similar role here as in the example of medieval legends introduced below.

the facts can be called unreliable. The boundaries of the phenomenon have to be marked as well. It is debatable, for instance, whether the criterion of sincerity can be applied to narrators in genres which developed before the eighteenth century. Is the Münchhausen-type of narrator, who tells tales which could not have happened on the level of the story (that is, who is unreliable as far as extratextual inconsistencies between story and context are concerned) insincere or sincere when he pretends that these stories are true? And is this question relevant for understanding the stories, or should it be discarded from the outset? Further research can help to clarify to which genres the concept of unreliability can and cannot be applied. Even though many valuable insights have been achieved by scholars during the last fifteen years or so, it seems that the phenomenon of unreliable narration still raises more questions than can be answered at the moment. More research is needed in order to fully comprehend a concept that turns out to be much more complex than was initially assumed.

Works Cited

Alber, Jan. 2013. "Unnatural Narratology: The Case of the Retrogressive Temporality in Martin Amis's *Time's Arrow*." In: Vera Nünning (ed.). *New Approaches to Narrative: Cognition—Culture—History*. Trier: WVT. 41–54.

Allrath, Gaby. 2005. *(En)Gendering Unreliable Narration. A Feminist-Narratological Theory and Analysis of Unreliability in Contemporary Women's Novels*. Trier: WVT 2005.

Booth, Wayne C. 1961. *The Rhetoric of Fiction*. Chicago, IL: University of Chicago Press.

Busselle, Rick & Helena Bilandzic. 2008. "Fictionality and Perceived Realism in Experiencing Stories: A Model of Narrative Comprehension and Engagement." *Communication Theory* 18.2: 255–280.

Chang, Luke J., Bradley B. Doll, Mascha van 't Wout et al. 2010. "Seeing Is Believing: Trustworthiness as a Dynamic Belief." *Cognitive Psychology* 61.2: 87–105.

Dernbach, Beatrice & Michael Meyer (eds.). 2005. *Vertrauen und Glaubwürdigkeit. Interdisziplinäre Perspektiven*. Opladen: VS Verlag für Sozialwissenschaften.

Fricker, Elizabeth. 2002. "Trusting others in the sciences: *a priori* or empirical warrant?" *Studies in History and Philosophy of Science* 33.2: 373–383.

Goffman, Ervin. 1973 [1959]. *The Presentation of Self in Everyday Life*. Woodstock, NY: The Overlook Press.

Grice, Paul H. 1989. *Studies in the Way of Words*. Cambridge, MA: Harvard University Press.

Green, Melanie C. 2004. "Transportation Into Narrative Worlds: The Role of Prior Knowledge and Perceived Realism." *Discourse Processes* 38.2: 247–266.

Habermas, Jürgen. 1984 [1976]. "Was heißt Universalpragmatik?" In: *Vorstudien und Ergänzungen zur Theorie des kommunikativen Handelns*. Frankfurt am Main: Suhrkamp. 353–440.

Hartmann, Britta. 2007. "Von roten Heringen und blinden Motiven. Spielarten Falscher Fährten im Film." In: Patric Blaser, Andrea B. Braidt, Anton Fuxjäger et al. (eds.). *Falsche Fährten in Film und Fernsehen*. Maske und Kothurn 53. 2–3. Wien/Köln: Böhlau. 33–54.

Henslin, James M. 1968. "Trust and the Cab Driver." In: Marcello Truzzi (ed.). *Sociology and Everyday Life*. Upper Saddle River, NJ: Prentice Hall. 138–158.

Heyd, Theresa. 2011. "Unreliability. The Pragmatic Perspective Revisited." *Journal of Literary Theory* 5.1: 3–17.

Korthals Altes, Liesbeth. 2008. "Sincerity, Reliability and Other Ironies—Notes on Dave Egger's *A Heartbreaking Work of Staggering Genius*." In: Elke D'hoker & Gunther Martens (eds.). *Narrative Unreliability in the Twentieth-Century First-Person Novel*. Berlin/New York, NY: De Gruyter. 107–128.

Koschorke, Albrecht. 2012. *Wahrheit und Erfindung. Grundzüge einer Allgemeinen Erzähltheorie*. Frankfurt am Main: Fischer.

Laucken, Uwe. 2005. "Explikation der umgangssprachlichen Bedeutung des Begriffs Vertrauen und ihre lebenspraktische Verwendung als semantisches Ordnungspotenzial." In: Dernbach & Meyer (eds.). 2005. 94–120.

Margolin, Uri. 1992. "The Nature and Functioning of Fiction: Some Recent Views." *Canadian Review of Comparative Literature* 19.1: 101–117.

Martens, Gunther. 2008. "Revising and Extending the Scope of the Rhetorical Approach to Unreliable Narration." In: Elke D'hoker & Gunther Martens (eds.). *Narrative Unreliability in the Twentieth-Century First-Person Novel*. Berlin/New York, NY: De Gruyter. 77–106.

Menhard, Felicitas. 2009. *Conflicting Reports: Multiperspektivisches Erzählen und unzuverlässiges Erzählen im englischsprachigen Roman seit 1800*. Trier: WVT.

Möllering, Guido. 2001. "The Nature of Trust: From Georg Simmel to a Theory of Expectation, Interpretation and Suspension." *Sociology* 35.2: 403–420.

Möllering, Guido & Jörg Sydow. 2005. "Kollektiv, kooperativ, reflexiv: Vertrauen und Glaubwürdigkeit in Unternehmungen und Unternehmungsnetzwerken." In: Dernbach & Meyer (eds.). 2005. 64–93.
Moss, Pamela A. 2004. "The Meaning and Consequences of 'Reliability'." *Journal of Educational and Behavioral Statistics* 29.2: 245–249.
Nünning, Ansgar. 1997. "'But why *will* you say that I am mad?' On the Theory, History, and Signals of Unreliable Narration in British Fiction." *Arbeiten aus Anglistik und Amerikanistik* 22.1: 83–105.
Nünning, Ansgar. 2005. "Reconceptualizing Unreliable Narration: Synthesizing Cognitive and Rhetorical Approaches." In: James Phelan & Peter J. Rabinowitz (eds.). *A Companion to Narrative Theory*. Oxford: Blackwell. 89–107.
Nünning, Vera. 2008. "Ethics and Aesthetics in British Novels at the Beginning of the Twenty-First Century." In: Astrid Erll, Herbert Grabes & Ansgar Nünning (eds.). *Ethics in Culture: The Dissemination of Value Through Literature and Other Media*. Berlin/New York, NY: De Gruyter. 369–392.
Nünning, Vera. 2013. "*Unreliable Narration* als Schlüsselkonzept und Testfall für neue Entwicklungen der Postklassischen Narratologie: Ansätze, Erklärungen und Desiderata." *Germanisch-Romanische Monatsschrift* 63.1: 135–160.
Olson, Greta. 2003. "Reconsidering Unreliability: Fallible and Untrustworthy Narrators." *Narrative* 11.1: 93–109.
Phelan, James & Mary P. Martin. 1999. "'The Lessons of 'Weymouth': Homodiegesis, Unreliability, Ethics and *The Remains of the Day*." In: David Herman (ed.). *Narratologies. New Perspectives on Narrative Analysis*. Columbus, OH: Ohio State University Press. 88–109.
Phelan, James. 2005. *Living to Tell About It. A Rhetoric and Ethics of Character Narration*. Ithaca, NY: Cornell University Press.
Phelan, James. 2007. "Estranging Unreliability, Bonding Unreliability, and the Ethics of Lolita." *Narrative* 15.2: 222–238.
Rousseau, Denise M., Sim B. Sitkin, Ronald S. Burt et al. 1998. "Not so Different after All: A Cross-Discipline View of Trust." *Academy of Management Review* 23.3: 393–404.
Schipper, Marc & Franz Petermann. 2011. "Trust—a Subject for Social Neuroscience?" *Zeitschrift für Neuropsychologie* 22.4: 245–255.
Schweer, Martin K. W. & Barbara Thies. 2005. "Vertrauen durch Glaubwürdigkeit—Möglichkeiten der (Wieder-)Gewinnung von Vertrauen aus psychologischer Perspektive." In: Dernbach & Meyer (eds.). 2005. 47–63.
Shen, Dan. 1989. "Unreliability and Characterization." *Style* 23.2: 300–311.

Shklovsky, Viktor. 1965 [1917]. "Art as Technique". In: Lee T. Lemon & Marion J. Reis (eds.). *Russian Formalist Criticism. Four Essays*. Lincoln, NE: University of Nebraska Press. 3–24.

Sperber, Dan. 2000. "Metarepresentations in an Evolutionary Perspective." In: Dan Sperber (ed.). *Metarepresentations: A Multidisciplinary Perspective*. Oxford: Oxford University Press. 117–137.

Sperber, Dan & Deirdre Wilson. 2002. "Pragmatics, Modularity and Mindreading." *Mind and Language* 17.1–2: 3–23.

Staves, Susan. 2006. *A Literary History of Women's Writing in Britain, 1660–1789*. Cambridge: Cambridge University Press.

Vargas Llosa, Mario. 2007 [2004]. *La tentación de lo imposible*. Madrid: Punto de lectura.

Vogt, Robert. 2009. "Kann ein zuverlässiger Erzähler unzuverlässig erzählen? Zum Begriff der 'Unzuverlässigkeit' in Literatur- und Filmwissenschaft." In: Susanne Kaul (ed.). *Erzählen im Film. Unzuverlässigkeit—Audiovisualität—Musik*. Bielefeld: Transcript. 35–53

Wall, Kathleen. 1994. "*The Remains of the Day* and its Challenges to Theories of Unreliable Narration." *Journal of Narrative Technique* 24.1: 18–42.

Wilson, Deirdre & Dan Sperber. 2004. "Relevance Theory." In: Laurence R. Horn & Gregory Ward (eds.). *The Handbook of Pragmatics*. Oxford: Blackwell. 607–632.

Yacobi, Tamar. 2001. "Package Deals in Fictional Narrative: The Case of the Narrator's (Un)Reliability." *Narrative* 9.2: 223–229.

Zunshine, Lisa. 2006. *Why We Read Fiction. Theory of Mind and the Novel*. Columbus, OH: Ohio State University Press.

BO PETTERSSON
(Helsinki)

Kinds of Unreliability in Fiction: Narratorial, Focal, Expositional and Combined

The reason why unreliability in fiction can be so hard to pin down is that unreliability comes in so many different guises and is based on a host of aspects. In an attempt to provide a cognitive narratological account of unreliability I have elsewhere discussed aspects such as verisimilitude, unreliable narrators and characters, veracity, existential presuppositions, referential familiarity, morality, intentionality and consistency (see Pettersson 2005). In this paper I attempt to view the by now traditional narratorial and the somewhat more recent focal types of unreliability in fiction on a scale from unintentional to intentional, with fallibility and deception at either ends and delusion—in a variety of forms—in the middle. Then I suggest that there is also a rather unrecognized kind of unreliability in fiction that I term *expositional manipulation* and go on to present some of its types and how they are combined with narratorial and focal unreliability.

My aim is to study the spread of different kinds of fictional unreliability by considering a wide variety of fiction. Before doing so, let me just tip my hat to the important recent theoretical work done on fictional unreliability, such as Tamar Yacobi's (2000) interpretive mechanisms of integration, Vera Nünning's (2004) historical contextualization, Per Krogh Hansen's (2005) new textual typology as well as James Phelan's (2005) work that continues Wayne C. Booth's (1983 [1961]) rhetorical tradition and Ansgar Nünning's (2008) broad scope of unreliability. My hope is that the kinds of unreliability I distinguish will animate this multifaceted theoretical discussion.

1. Narratorial and Focal: A Scale of Intentionality

A very basic—perhaps the most basic—form of unreliability could be viewed on a scale of intentionality which is based on whether the communicator has the knowledge and ability to communicate what he or she intends to communicate. Let me flesh out this scale by analyzing the many ways in which character narrators and characters can be unreliable.

Fallible character narrators and characters are in fact seldom entirely fallible. Huck Finn may be fallible in that he lacks all sorts of knowledge and ability but in many ways he is streetwise and can also deceive when need be. Most importantly, however, he is not fallible morally: he stands up for his friend Jim, the runaway slave, even if he were to go to hell for it—according to his skewed view of how racism and Christianity are coupled. Still, despite William Riggan's (1981) categorization of him as a naif, he is also a kind of moral pícaro who declines being "sivilized" and lights out for the Territory (see Pettersson 1999). Often the fallible clowns or pícaros, such as the character narrators in Laurence Sterne's *Tristram Shandy* or Apuleius' *The Golden Ass*, do not learn much, however intelligent or well-read they are.[1] But other fallible narrators go through a development comparable to that of the protagonist in a *Bildungsroman*. The main character in Voltaire's *Candide* may remain as naive as he was at the start but his final decision to tend his garden promises a safe and happy old age for him.

Another simple-minded gardener, Chance or Chauncey Gardiner in Jerzy Kosinski's (1996 [1970]: 103–104) *Being There*, may not develop, but through his simplistic adages he is nevertheless finally about to be asked to run for vice president of the United States. He is a kind of latter-day version of Candide, but his naivety is misinterpreted as great wisdom by leading politicians and the media, who are deluded in taking his comments about gardening as deep allegorical statements, even if they are not intended as deceptive. Winston Groom's Forrest Gump in the novel by that title may have an IQ of "near 70", yet he has read enough stories of naifs and pícaros—such as *King Lear* (with reference to its Fool), Dostoevsky's *The Idiot*, Faulkner's *The Sound and the Fury*, Lee's *To Kill a Mockingbird* and Steinbeck's *Of Mice and Men*—to know that "idiots [are] always smarter than people give them credit for" (Groom 1995 [1986]: 9, 10). In fact, Gump has a formidable career and ends up owning a five-million dollar business. These brief notes on fallible narrators and characters suggest that there is a wide variety of them: intelligent or intellectually challenged, moral or immorally acting naifs and pícaros, who may or may not develop during the course of the story.

But there are also cases in which it is hard to decide whether the character narrator is fallible or deluded. Throughout Sarah Waters' (2010 [2009]) *The Little Stranger* the Georgian house Hundreds Hall, which the

---

1 As Riggan (1981: 47) notes, the final conversion of Lucius in *The Golden Ass* seems "merely tacked on to provide a serious counterweight to the general levity of the foregoing portions of the work".

narrator Dr Faraday has known since childhood, is subject to visitations by poltergeist phenomena.[2] Either Dr Faraday—like the governess in Henry James's *The Turn of the Screw*—is a reliable narrator and there are actually supernatural visitations or he is fallible or deluded and *unbeknownst to himself* embodies something like a poltergeist. If so, it is he who is responsible for all the ghastly incidents in Hundreds Hall, as his name may suggest: he—or the poltergeist he embodies—is in a kind of paranormal Faraday's cage. The very last sentences of the novel seem to suggest as much:

> If Hundred's Hall is haunted, however, its ghost doesn't show itself to me. For I'll turn, and am disappointed—realising that what I am looking at is only a cracked window-pane, and that the face gazing distortedly from it, baffled and longing, is my own. (Waters 2010 [2009]: 499)

Thus, to the very end he appears unaware of what he may have done and is either fallible or, if indeed in some way he is aware of it but does not face up to it, deluded or self-deceptive.

Deluded narrators and characters are another motley crew. Stevens in Kazuo Ishiguro's (1996 [1989]) *The Remains of the Day* is self-deluded in the sense that the butler's work ethic he inherits from his father ruins much of his private life and that of Miss Kenton (later Mrs Benn), who once was his potential fiancée and wife. At the end of the novel he does not abandon his delusion as much as decides to make the best of the rest of his life, as the title implies. The constellation between John Marcher and May Bartram in Henry James's (2001 [1903]: 460) story "The Beast in the Jungle" is rather similar: the (main) character focalizer Marcher is deluded in thinking that a beast awaits him and gets Bartram to wait for it with him, until Marcher at her grave finally realizes that the beast has been "the chill of his egotism", including his not having understood the love they could have shared.

Riggan (cf. 1981: 109–143) discusses an assortment of "self-deluding" fictional madmen, such as those of Gogol and Dostoevsky, but two other mad diarists may show the broader spectrum of delusion. The diary of Guy de Maupassant's (1997 [1885]) judge in "The Diary of a Madman" is only found after his death: it turns out that during his seemingly impeccable life he has both killed and knowingly sent innocent people to death and never been caught. He has deceived everyone, but seems neither fallible nor deluded as such—he has simply acted on an instinct he cannot comprehend, hence giving his diary the heading "Why?" (Maupassant

---

2 The rest of this paragraph discloses the end of the novel, so if you are going to read *The Little Stranger* you may want to pass over it.

1997 [1885]: 113). In some sense his murderous cravings are instinctual (unintentional), in some sense planned (intentional), but as a confession his diary seems completely reliable, even if its contents and the frame story of how the diary was found prove that throughout his life he has deceived everybody to think he is highly moral man.

Lu Xun, one of the founders of modern Chinese literature, seems to take his cue from Gogol and Maupassant in his "Diary of a Madman". The frame story notes that the madman has "long since made a complete recovery" and claims that his diary shows that he suffered from a "persecution complex" in that it depicts his growing fear of cannibalism (Lu Xun 2009 [1918]: 21). Thus, when writing it the madman seems to be deluded to think that cannibalism was widespread in China. However, as Lu Xun was openly critical of the political mismanagement in China after the toppling of the Qing dynasty in 1911, the fear of cannibalism was understood as both real and allegorical.[3] The story mentions famine leading to cannibalism, of which there were reported cases when the story was penned, and ends with the oft-quoted words "Save the children…" (Lu Xun 2009 [1918]: 31). This may seem deluded in terms of the diarist's exaggerated fear of cannibalism, but was understood as pointing to a new generation taking over in China, especially to the unrest leading to the May Fourth demonstrations in the year after its publication.[4] What seems deluded in the diary and is corroborated as such by the frame story has both real and allegorical socio-critical meanings intended by Lu Xun. In other words, the diarist may be deluded but nevertheless acts as a soothsayer.

Deception too comes in many shapes in fiction. According to Robin Trivers (2011), deception and delusion are closely connected, as is suggested by the subtitle of his major study *Deceit and Self-Deception. Fooling Yourself the Better to Fool Others*. That is, in his view (which is still debated, at least in its strong form), you delude yourself in order to deceive others. In literary studies James Phelan (2008) has intriguingly analysed one of the central techniques by which Vladimir Nabokov makes Humbert Humbert in *Lolita* so ambiguous: he is not only an "estranging" unreliable narrator (that is, shows that he is a paedophile), but he is also a "bonding" one (he seeks sympathy through rhetorical persuasion). Phelan goes on to show how there are different kinds of bonding unreliability, just as he has earlier shown how in *Lolita* there is a process in Humbert's narration from self-

---

[3] For instance, according to Knight (2012: 104), the story "cries out against exploitation in a hallucinatory modernist mode".

[4] See Howard Goldblatt's (2000: 479) view that "Lu Xun [in the story] turns the May Fourth slogan *lijao chiren* – established rituals and moral tenets have cannibalized the Chinese people – into an extended metaphor for the Chinese".

absorption to a more defensive position with—at least on the face of it—some concern for Lolita's well-being (Phelan 2005: 98–131).

In other novels with unreliable character narrators, deception lies less in the narrative than in the strangely motivated actions they claim to have performed. John Banville's (2003 [2002]) character narrator in the novel *Shroud* is a case in point. He may start out apparently deceiving his readers: "The name, my name, is Axel Vander, on that much I insist", but his entire narrative is for the most part a reliable confession-like account of how as a young man he took on the name and identity of his deceased friend Axel Vander (Banville 2003 [2002]: 7). The novel is full of different kinds of ironic turns, as when, unwittingly, by turning into Axel Vander the protagonist takes on a Jewish personality in Belgium during the Nazi occupation. He is clearly a rather despicable character, who compares himself at times to Christ during his sojourn in Turin, the home town of the title's Turin Shroud, most likely the ultimate artefactual hoax in the history of Christianity. In *The Book of Evidence*, another Banville novel, the character narrator and murderer Frederick Montgomery may at times—perhaps even throughout—be an unreliable narrator, but he confesses that he has committed numerous nasty deeds and even decides to plead guilty to murder in the first degree, even if he could get away with a more lenient sentence if pleading otherwise. He repeatedly points out that he does not try to exonerate himself (in fact, he shows in great detail what a callous man he is), and focuses on his double identity, which makes his bourgeois self feel liberated by having set free the beast. Thus, these two Banville characters are less unreliable as narrators than as characters: they mainly portray how deceptive and despicable they are as well as the motivations to their deceptions. In this way they exemplify something that has seldom been discussed in terms of unreliability, namely—in part, at least—that characters' frankness about their misdemeanour may override their unreliability. That is, they gain some sympathy—in Phelan's (2008) terms, bond with their readers—in rather candidly confessing their horrid deeds.

In short, fallibility, delusion and deception figure in narration and characterization; they come in different shapes and degrees; and their nature and meaning can change in the course of the story. But different kinds of unreliability can also be combined in intriguing ways. To take a recent instance: in Amity Gaige's (2013) novel *Schroder* the protagonist Erik Schroder as a young man changes his identity to Eric Kennedy in Dorchester, Massachusetts, where he as an East German immigrant is taken—and intends to be taken—to be related to *the* Kennedys. Later, when having been divorced for a year, he fails to return his six-year-old daughter Meadow to his ex-wife and goes on a trip that by lengthening the weekend into almost a week becomes a case of abduction. During the trip he lies and deceives a number of people, including Meadow, and in his life story and in the action portrayed during the trip he is multiply deceptive. But he is also repeatedly deluded in thinking that he is a good father to Meadow: he neglects and endangers her repeatedly, feeds her mainly doughnuts and caffeinated lemonade, and finally his negligence causes her to have a life-threatening asthmatic attack. What is more, the novel is composed of a story of the trip written as a confession in jail by Schroder to his ex-wife in order to explain the motives, both for his false identity and his abduction of their daughter. Since his detailed story shows how narcissistic he has been not only towards his wife and child but also to his father (whom he has not seen for years, so as not to disclose his new identity), as a narrator he is mainly fallible: he thinks he is not such a bad man and does not seem to be aware that he actually discloses a wealth of evidence showing his true nature. Finally, the author points to his true identity by calling the novel by the real name he has never been able to discard, despite living for decades as Eric Kennedy: willy-nilly, he is the East German immigrant he has always been, Schroder. As narrator and character he is fallible, deluded as well as deceptive. Still, just as in the case of Banville's narrators, by Gaige's skilful narration readers understand the motivation behind his unreliable behaviour and may feel some sympathy for him (not least as a father who really does love his daughter deeply), despite his immoral actions.

Thus, a central way of viewing literary narrators and characters is on a scale of intentional agency, which is dependent on the knowledge and skills they have. For instance, as Schroder simply does not have the skills to be the good father he would very much like to be, his intention is undercut by his deficient parenting. As a matter of fact, the scale of intentionality has in many ways been what the literature on unreliable narration has focused on, but usually without overtly exploring intentionality. Perhaps a context-sensitive use of such a scale of intentionality in terms of both narration and characterization could be combined with Phelan's (2005: 49–53) six types of unreliability concerning reporting, regarding and reading in terms of *mis*- and *under*—and I would add *over-reporting* and *over-regarding* (see Pettersson 2005: 85–86n11). An instance of, say, *over-reporting*—that is, of the narrator telling more than he knows—is to be found in Banville's *The Book of Evidence* in which the narrator gives names to characters—such as Reck, Mrs Reck and Cunningham—whose names he admits he does not know.

But, as I see it, the main shortcoming of the scholarship on literary unreliability is that it has by and large centred on narrators and (later) focalizing characters, whereas unreliability in literature in fact often seems to go beyond narrators and characters and be lodged in the exposition as such or in combinations of expositional, narratorial and focal unreliability.

2. Expositional and Combined: Exposition as Manipulation

As far as I know, the most important work on exposition in fiction was written in Israel in the 1970s. In his major work *Expositional Modes and Temporal Ordering in Fiction* Meir Sternberg (1978: 1) starts out by noting that "the function of exposition [is] to introduce the reader into an unfamiliar world, the fictive world of the story, by providing him [*sic*] with the general and specific antecedents indispensable to the understanding of what happens in it". He goes on to show that exposition appears in many forms, such as preliminary and delayed, and that the latter includes "expositional gaps" employed "with a view to exciting interest" (cf. Sternberg, 1978: 35–55). Further on, Sternberg discusses the detective story in which "the author does his utmost to mystify, misdirect, and baffle" what he terms "the curious reader" through

> a retardatory structure that achieves its effects—sustained curiosity and suspense—by distributing the expositional material piecemeal throughout while postponing the concentrated, true exposition—the opening part of the fabula—to the end of the sujet. (ibid.: 180–182)

What comes across both explicitly and implicitly is that although text-centred in the best tradition of classical narratology, Sternberg is aware that there is an intentional agent who aims to familiarize his or her readers with the fictional world and who can make use of exposition to trick or manipulate them in order to maintain curiosity or suspense. His reference to the scene in which the exposition is completed in the thirty-third chapter of Charlotte Brontë's (1953 [1847]: 437) *Jane Eyre* in this connection shows his awareness of the use of such manipulation in other kinds of fiction (see Sternberg 1978: 182).[5]

At about the same time as Sternberg and well aware of his work, Menakhem Perry studied what he termed "Literary Dynamics" in his influential 1979 essay.[6] He shows how the order of a fictional text can create meanings, also so that "the reader may be said to be led into a 'trap', i.e. is not supposed to identify the organizing principle, merely to be

---

5   In fact, this is an ancient technique: even the character narrator Lucius on the first page of Apuleius' (2008: 1) *The Golden Ass* places hints of writing his story on "Egyptian paper inscribed with the sharpened point of a reed from the Nile" that are only understood in the last book when the Egyptian goddess Isis restores his human shape.
6   In fact, Perry (1979: 35) notes that he published a version of this essay in Hebrew as early as 1973.

affected by it" (Perry 1979: 40). According to Perry's convincing reading, William Faulkner's story "A Rose for Emily" includes "a series of factual deceptions with which the story misleads its readers". Since the story does not have character narrator as such (it is narrated in the first-person plural by the townsfolk as "we"), the deceptions are less due to the deluded narrators than to the organization of the exposition. In the course of his reading of the story Perry makes other theoretical and interpretive points, but let me only single out two of the most important ones. First, there are two kinds of comparisons with Emily in the story: that between the "real" Emily and the thwarted view of her by the expositionally manipulated readers, which is brought to coincide with that of the real Emily at the end when they learn that she is a murderer. The readers' view is also set in contrast to that of the townsfolk, who in narrating the story as "we" clearly also have a thwarted view of Emily, and they too learn the truth about her at the end (see Perry 1979: 354). Second, when meanings in a fictional text are "consistently constructed or rejected", "the reader maintains the rejected meanings as a system of 'hovering' meanings", which are part of the text's "intentions" (Perry 1979: 356). Thus, Perry discusses what I would term *expositional manipulation* on the levels of narration, characterization and interpretation and demonstrates that even discarded meanings are part and parcel of the meaning of a fictional narrative.

As I see it, the study of unreliability in fiction should take into account the various types of expositional manipulation of readers. By structural or rhetorical means such manipulation suggests a view of a character or the action that is later shown to be untenable. Let me note that calling such indirection *irony* would in my opinion stretch that term beyond its scope.[7] There is play with multiple, corrected and thwarted meaning of all kinds, but it is not necessarily ironic as such. Rather, as Sternberg notes, it aims to create suspense and curiosity in readers—as well as, I would add, a deepened interest in the plot and the motivations of its characters, thus displaying a broader understanding of the complexity in human behaviour and morals. Also, despite the diffident ways Sternberg and Perry mostly speak of actual intentional agents, all such manipulation is of course due to the author in the first place, even though it may be channelled by narrators (thereby adding to the complexity, as in the case of the first-person plural narrators in "A Rose for Emily"). That is, the scale of intentionality in narrators and characters discussed above is not necessarily separate from expositional manipulation, since narratorial, focal and expositional kinds of unreliability are intentional in one way or another and can

---

7   Booth (1983 [1961]: 492) famously viewed unreliable narration as a "kind of irony", which I find too narrow, also in terms of narratorial and focal kinds of unreliability.

occur simultaneously. What Sternberg and Perry also demonstrate is the complex and processual nature of what I have termed expositional manipulation, which can give us more detailed tools to deal with unreliability in fiction. More recently, Phelan (2007: 15–22) has been one of the very few who have analysed the ways exposition is used throughout narratives, but what we still lack is a broader understanding of the various ways in which exposition is used to convey unreliability in fiction.

On the basis of the groundwork provided by Sternberg and Perry I will now present a preliminary survey of some *techniques and features of fictional unreliability by expositional manipulation, often in combination with narratorial and focal features*. Some of them are more or less work-specific, but many are also informed by particular genres or subgenres.

Speculative (narratorial). One of Nathaniel Hawthorne's (1987 [1835]: 75) most famous stories, "Wakefield", starts out like this: "In some old magazine or newspaper, I recollect a story, told as truth, of a man—let us call him Wakefield—who absented himself for a long time from his wife". Even in Hawthorne's day, showing that the basis of a story is speculative was an old narrative trick, but Hawthorne puts it to multiple use: the unnamed narrator does not remember where he read about a man, whose name he apparently does not recall, and notes that the story is "told as truth", as is so much gossip and legend. The story is full of such hedging, speculation and hypothesis, as for instance when the narrator suggests: "Let us now imagine Wakefield bidding adieu to his wife" (1987 [1835]: 75). He continuously hedges in his narration (by "perhaps"), apostrophizes Wakefield, poses questions and then answers them by hypothesizing his actions (see below), such as "What sort of a man was Wakefield? We are free to shape out our own idea, and call it by his name" (Hawthorne 1987 [1835]: 76). In this speculative and hypothetical form Hawthorne's readers finally learn the entire story of Wakefield's absence including a moral drawn from it, if not his motivation or his reception when returning home. We could call this an instance of what Brian McHale has termed "*epistemological* hesitation" in fantastic and modern fiction (1982: 223, emphasis original).

The narratorial speculative technique was taken on by Hawthorne's friend Herman Melville (2002 [1851]: 18) in his famous opening line of *Moby-Dick*—"Call me Ishmael"—in the first chapter subtitled "*Loomings*", and then even more prevalently employed in the fiction of Henry James in terms of what is known about the characters, their actions and morals. The point I am making is that such speculation is not only narratorial but shows that the very exposition too is manipulated, sometimes intentionally by narrators and their use of exposition (*Daisy Miller* by James, see below), sometimes by inadequate, speculative or hypothetical information ("Wakefield"). Thus, the action as depicted is simply unreliable. Of course, modernist fiction was to put speculation to an even greater variety of uses.

Speculative (focal). In Adam Haslett's (2003 [2002]) short story "The Good Doctor" the narrative is focalized by the main character Frank from the East Coast, who having recently graduated as a psychiatrist has landed his first position at a county clinic. He goes on a house call to see the severely traumatized housewife Mrs Buckholdt, who has merely asked for her sedatives to be renewed, but this cannot be done without a doctor meeting the patient. The story is all about how Frank does his best to be the good doctor of the title and how he thinks he knows what is best for Mrs Buckholdt, since he is convinced that "[p]eople like this needed him, needed a person to listen to" (Haslett 2003 [2002]: 44). Much of the story is about how he speculates as to her condition and tries to form a diagnosis by talking to her. In the course of the story it becomes clear that—in the words of his ex-girlfriend—Frank is "a romantic clinging to an old myth about the value of talk" (Haslett 2003 [2002]: 28), that is, it is he rather than Mrs Buckholdt who has a need to talk. Apparently, Frank has led a fairly comfortable and secure life, so his speculation—or rather diagnosis—of Mrs Buckholdt seems wrong, which he does not see but Haslett's readers do. With his naivety and background, he simply has no insight into her life and condition, so to the very end of the story he is deluded about being a good doctor and understanding the needs of Mrs Buckholdt. This is a case of how a character throughout the exposition of the story is unreliable in focalizing his speculations as to his own identity, his professional identity and that of the other main protagonist.

Biased (by comparison). All unreliable narration and focalization is about bias in one way or another, but at times bias can be in focus by the juxtaposition of different narratives of the same event. Ryonosuke Akutagawa's short story (1959 [1922]) "In a Grove" is famous not least for providing the basic plot for Akira Kurosawa's film *Rashomon* (1950).[8] In the film there are four versions of the same event, but in Akutagawa's rather brief story there are seven accounts relating to the death—apparently a murder by a bandit—of a man in a grove. Most of them seem—at least after the entire story is read—unreliable, since the last version is "THE STORY OF THE MURDERED MAN, AS TOLD THROUGH A MEDIUM" and thus apparently reliable (cf. Akutagawa 1959 [1922]: 26–28). Despite the title of this final version, which suggests the man is murdered, it seems to be the definitive version (that is, if indeed a man's dead spirit could speak, it would hardly lie) that throws light on the other six. It discloses

---

[8] The title of the film and the setting of its frame story is based on another story by Akutagawa (1959 [1915]) called "Rashomon".

that the man committed suicide, since he had been disgraced by having witnessed a bandit raping his wife.

In this way it also shows that most of the other versions are unreliable: the woodcutter lies because he has stolen the sword by which the man committed suicide; the policeman is fallible, since he too easily jumps to the conclusion that the bandit Tajomaru is the murderer; Tajomaru lies that he killed the man in combat, so as to preserve his bandit's honour; and the man's wife claims Tajomaru killed her husband, since she—according her husband's final version—asked the reluctant bandit to kill him to preserve her honour (the moral code she abides by can only accept that one man alive has known her intimately). The other two versions seem largely reliable: that of Buddhist monk, who saw the man and his wife on the road before having been assaulted by the thief, and that of the man's mother-in-law, who tells how the couple started out on their journey. Unlike the film *Rashomon* in which the four stories are left juxtaposed, thus producing what later has been termed *the Rashomon effect* of biased memory, the story does not only demonstrate how biased different versions of the same event are but also that there in fact seem to be truthful accounts. Also, it thematizes the different honour codes that override death or jail for the three protagonists. More common than such balancing of bias is, however, that either bias (as in the above example of focal speculation) or ambiguity prevails.

Ambiguous. Perhaps the best-known instance of ambiguity in unreliable narration is Henry James's (1974 [1898]) novella "The Turn of the Screw", where readers are hard-pressed to know whether to trust the governess as narrator. But ambiguity in fiction can also be due to delayed exposition and such ambiguity can be even more perplexing. Joanne Harris's novel (2011 [2010]) *blueeyedboy* is completely composed of texts supposedly posted on the Internet as web journals and comments on them, which makes everything written supremely unreliable. As the main web journal author and protagonist **blueeyedboy** puts it: "On WeJay [web journal] I can vent as I please, confess without fear of censure; be myself—or indeed, someone else—in a world where no one is quite what they seem" (Harris 2011 [2010]: 25). The characters in the novel take on different personalities, both in their lives and as net characters, and may steal other people's passwords so they can impersonate them or rather their fictitious web personalities. Since the actual persons behind central nametags are unfolded late in the novel, with a central one disclosed close to the end (unless possibly impersonated by someone else, as the protagonist thinks), the novel is expositionally ambiguous. Close to the end **blueeyedboy** may still reflect: "Real life makes so little sense; only fic [net fiction] has meaning", but real life is to have its vengeance—in the fiction authored by

Harris (2011 [2010]: 496–497), of course. Since for much of the novel the identity of the persons are in question before they are finally disclosed, the exposition also makes use of *hypothetical* and *processual* forms of unreliability (see below).

Contradictory (narratorial). One of the most widely discussed instances of unreliable narration, Ford Madox Ford's *The Good Soldier*, also includes expositional unreliability. Most evidently, in telling his story the character narrator John Dowell leaves a crucial scene last. This is the one in which he walks out on his friend Edward Ashburnham, well knowing that Edward is about to commit suicide (Ford 1995 [1915]: 162). A few pages earlier he has professed that Edward is "one of the two persons [he] has ever really loved", the other being his deranged beloved Nancy Rufford— in the same paragraph that he calls Edward and Nancy the "villains" of his story (Ford 1995 [1915]: 160). Dowell does indeed seem to belong to "the slightly-deceitful" who "flourish", while "the passionate, the headstrong, and the too-truthful are condemned to suicide and madness" (Ford 1995 [1915]: 161). Many readers may agree with Eugene Goodheart (1995 [1986]: 377) that Dowell in his feelings and responses is "ambivalent and inconsistent", whereas others, Paul B. Armstrong (1995 [1987]: 388) among them, would claim that he "struggles, with mixed and increasing success, to give a trustworthy account of his history". In my view, for Goodheart the unreliability in *The Good Soldier* is *ambiguous* while for Armstrong it is at first ambiguous as to reliability but that ambiguity decreases *processually* until Dowell is trustworthy.

Contradictory in thought versus speech or action (focal). One of Virginia Woolf's most widely used techniques to show the complexity in her characters is the contradiction inherent in what the characters say or do and what they think. A veritable showcase of this is the story "Together and Apart" in which one of the two protagonists, the main focal character Miss Anning, even comments on her mixed feelings on having met Mr Serle: "Of all things, nothing is so strange as human discourse, she thought, because of its changes, its extraordinary irrationality, her dislike being now nothing short of the most intense and rapturous love" (Woolf 1989 [1944]: 193). Throughout the story both Miss Anning and Mr Serle have long trains of thought, but what they say are mere platitudes, as when the former having just met the latter and having thought about the night sky utters "What a beautiful night!" and straightaway thinks that such an utterance is "Foolish! Idiotically foolish!" (Woolf 1989 [1944]: 189).

Similarly, the actions and opinions of the characters in Ford's tetralogy *Parade's End* are much like those of Sylvia Tietjens and her husband Christopher, "the products of caprice" or "a matter of contrariety" (Ford

2013 [1924–1928]: 137). What the characters think and say is largely contradictory throughout the four novels. For instance, Valentine Wannop, Christopher's lover later on, reflects: "She wanted to say: 'I am falling at your feet. My arms are embracing your knees!'", but admits that "[a]ctually she said: 'I suppose it is proper to celebrate together today!'" (Ford 2013 [1924–1928]: 592). This technique often serves the exposition of Woolf's and Ford's fiction in that the complex disposition of the characters is revealed in delayed ways. It is much like the corrections typical of unreliable narration, yet often it does not throw suspicion on the character, but rather is in line with Ford's (1995 [1914]: 265) view that literary impressionism attempts to convey "an illusion of reality", and thus it is not primarily employed to suggest unreliability.[9]

Misleading. Most Golden Age detective novels à la Agatha Christie or Dorothy L. Sayers knowingly spread red herrings in their narratives so as to keep readers guessing who the culprit is. Still, as we have seen when discussing Sternberg's and Perry's views of exposition, much general fiction makes use of misleading by expositional manipulation in order to increase the readers' engagement in the fictional world and its characters.

Processual/partial. Michael Frayn's (2002) *Spies*, whose unreliability I have analysed elsewhere (Pettersson 2005), is for most of the novel fallibly focalised by the protagonist Stephen Wheatley as a boy, whereas as the adult narrator, he is deceptive in not letting on what he knows and is thus misleading. That is, the novel is a case of dissonant narration (with the narrating self separated from his experiencing self) until the closing pages when Wheatley finally discloses the actual meaning of the actions and pronouncements he misunderstood as a young boy, after which the narration is entirely reliable. In Raymond Carver's (1989 [1988]) story "Blackbird Pie", the narrator thinks somebody is impersonating his wife's handwriting in a farewell letter to him, until he finally gains the insight that he has been deluded in thinking that he really knows his wife and her handwriting and so turns into a reliable narrator. Such shifts from unreliability to reliability in narration often occur in *Bildungsroman*-like stories as the result of a long process (*Spies*) or a sudden insight ("Blackbird Pie"). They may occur simultaneously in the narration and the exposition, that is, the process or the shift occurs when the narrator discloses or realizes a fact that completes the exposition.

Shifts from unreliability to reliability are quite common, but there can also be shifts from reliability to unreliability. In James's novella *Daisy Miller*

---

9   In fact, modernist fiction could be viewed as extending the descriptive impetus of realist and naturalist fiction to the cognition of characters, in which case the use of impressionism is at the service of a kind of realism.

a young American man called Winterbourne focalizes much of the story and seems quite a reliable focalizer for a while. In his eyes the other protagonist Daisy Miller is quite a flirt and behaves badly, while after she has died of Roman fever readers understand that, in the words of another of her suitors, "she was the most innocent" young lady (James 1974 [1878]: 241). Since her death is in part caused by his callousness towards her, Winterbourne's focalization finally comes across as unreliable, whereas Daisy is now seen as a moral, if naive young lady victimized by Winterbourne.[10]

Local/overridden. Unreliability can occur locally in different ways. As noted above, Stevens in *The Remains of the Day* is mainly deluded, but he occasionally deceives people to believe that he is an aristocrat. However, these local instances of deception do not make him a deceptive narrator; he remains mainly deluded, which is the overriding feature of his character and narration. In Homer's (2007 [1967]) *The Odyssey* Odysseus as narrator and character is largely reliable even though he is repeatedly cunning enough to lie and cheat in order to get back to Ithaca alive.[11] In *The Kalevala* (1990 [1847]: 194) the trickster-like god Väinämöinen's lies are often fortuitous—he simply knows he will not be able to get away with them and finally gives up and confesses, as for instance in canto 16 to the girl of Tuoni: "If I did lie a little [/] was a fraud the second time [/] now I'll tell the truth". Such instances of unreliability are local enough not to tarnish the reliability of the in part trickster-like heroes. Still, one should remember that all kinds of mythological literature include trickster characters who are heroes precisely owing to their unreliability. In such cases, much like sympathetic fallible narrators such as Huck Finn or Forrest Gump, the narratorial unreliability, however encompassing, is overridden by other features, such as heroism, morality and/or sympathy.

Hypothetical. Actions and pronouncements in fiction can be merely hypothesized and in this sense be unreliable. When Hawthorne's narrator speculates about the protagonist and his actions in "Wakefield", he also hypothesizes a great many moves that Wakefield may or may not have made. Similarly, T. S. Eliot's (1989 [1915]) "The Love Song of J. Alfred Prufrock" is a narrative poem that hypothesizes a walk and uses many hypothesizing techniques in order to suggest what could or might have happened (see Pettersson, 2013). Hypothetical action may also be used in fantastic fiction, which in one way or another includes a what-if premise. But this does not mean that all fantastic fiction is but rather can be unreliable.

---

10   For a detailed reading of this inversion in *Daisy Miller* see Norrman (2000: 149–216).
11   In a web paper Skalin (n.d.) analyses five scenes in which Odysseus lies.

Fantastic. First I would like to question the oft-repeated claim that "unreliable narration is deeply rooted in the realist novel because it depends on kinds of naturalization based on real-world frames of reference" (Zerweck 2001: 170). It may be true in the sense that even fantastic fiction makes use of realist, pseudo-realist or logical aspects in portraying fictional worlds and characters, but not in the sense that only realist fiction can be unreliable. Even a brief look at literary history shows that different kinds of unreliability are prevalent, which proves that unreliability occurs much before its alleged starting-point in the eighteenth century or so. In fact, decades ago Riggan (1981: 39–48) already discussed the character narrator Lucius in Apuleius' *The Golden Ass* as an unreliable pícaro. At about the same time as that ancient novel, the second century CE or so, in what is sometimes considered the first science-fiction novel, Lucian's (2008: 621) *A True Story*, the character narrator starts out tongue-in-cheek by criticizing Homer and other authors of writing "fantastic yarns" with "literary horseplay", that is, of "lying". He goes on to claim: "I will say one thing that is true, and that is that I am a liar"—but of course he calls his narrative *A True Story* (Lucian 2008: 622). Is such play with the status of fiction unreliable? Well yes, at least in the sense that it leaves his audience spinning in the delightfully vicious circle of the liar's paradox.

What about the what-if premise in fantastic fiction? Since this premise is usually not presented explicitly and there may even be a claim that the story is "true" (which often gives it away as fiction), much fantastic fiction seems closely related to unreliable narration. In *The Arabian Nights* there are many unreliable narrators and characters, such as the black slave, who lies that he has cuckolded a man in "The Tale of the Three Apples", which makes the man kills his wife. The father-in-law feels so much pity for his son-in-law grieving for the wife he has murdered that he in turn lies by confessing to the murder. Not only the is actual murderer finally acquitted (owing to the supposedly understandable rage caused by the slave's lie) but also the slave, since his master is able to tell the story so well—the supreme virtue in *The Arabian Nights*—that the Caliph "laughed till he fell on his back and ordered that the story be recorded and be made public amongst the people" (*The Arabian Nights* 2004 [2001]: 153). Hence, the exposition is delayed, so that the lies, the actual murderer and the fates of all characters are exposed in delayed ways—in keeping with what was to become the structural device of detective fiction, except for the twist that all culprits are acquitted.

In both Boccaccio's *Decamerone* and Chaucer's *Canterbury Tales* one of the key delights for readers is to try to assess the reliability of the various narrators and characters. In fact, since Chaucer the Pilgrim—that is, the narrator—in his "Prologue" to *The Canterbury Tales* repeatedly emphasizes that his intention is not to tell a "tale untrewe" and compares himself to "Crist [...] in Holy Writ" as well as to Plato, he evidently protests too much and his readers know that his tongue is firmly in his cheek (Chaucer 1979 [1964]: 34–36; ll. 737–741). Similarly, *Don Quixote* is a kind of fictional treatise on the difference between appearance and reality, on various kinds of deceptions and delusions. It is told by a fictitious Moorish narrator, who knows the thoughts in Don Quixote's mind as well as the adventures where no-one is present except Don Quixote and Sancho Panza, a fact which the latter even comments on, thus questioning the narrator's truthfulness (see Cervantes 2005 [2003]: 23, 472). Later, when the English novel started out, unreliability was often used. For instance, Daniel Defoe (1972 [1722]: 1) announces it in the preface of *Moll Flanders* by complaining that "The world is so taken up of late with novels and romances, that it will be hard for a private history to be taken for genuine". He goes on to note that the not very reliable ex-prostitute Moll at the end "pretends to be" "penitent and humble"—just as her author pretends that "[all] possible care [...] has been taken to give no lewd ideas" (Defoe 1972 [1722]: 1). From here on—and as we have seen, much earlier—there are many different kinds of unreliability, not least in fiction, but of course in poetry and drama too, even though they have so far been given very little attention in this respect (see however Hühn, Nünning/Schwanecke, this volume).

Finally, let me note that in the history of fiction there is a wide area between realist and fantastic fiction. The premise of Markus Zusak's (2007 [2005]) *The Book Thief* may be fantastic: the novel is narrated by death personified, but the story is a rather realistic, if somewhat sentimental story of Nazi Germany. Jenny Diski's novel (1990 [1988]) *Like Mother* does not just have a fantastic premise but an utterly impossible one: most of the novel is narrated by an anhydranencephalic newborn infant, that is, by a baby girl without a brain, but her description of her and her mother's lives is very realistic. One possible way of reading the novel is that her mother needs to tell the story of her and her baby's symbiotic lives and does so as a separate narrator in dialogue with the infant (who, according to a final twist, may not have existed at all)—hence the title which seems drawn from the saying "like mother, like daughter" (see Diski 1990 [1988]: 187–189). This shows how closely related imagination (the fantastic narrative perspective), realistic depiction and unreliability can be.

Of course, these notes on unreliability in fantastic fiction only indicate that it appears in various forms throughout literary history and that there is a vast unexplored area that awaits further analysis, not least in terms of specifying the variety of fictional unreliability.

What I hope this section on expositional and combined forms of unreliable fiction has shown is that the study of unreliability must be broadened to include expositional forms that alone or together with narratorial and focal means add to the plethora of unreliable usages in fiction.

3. Conclusion

The kinds of unreliability in fiction surveyed in this paper may be of use in two ways. First, by viewing the received forms of unreliability in narrators and characters on an intentional scale, they may corroborate the fact that fictional beings, like real ones, are assessed on the basis of whether their actions are unreliable and, if so, in what sense and to what extent they are intentional. Fallibility, delusion and deception and their combinations are better pinpointed when they are viewed along this general scale of intentionality, which of course is understood in different ways depending on when and where fiction is written or read. Second, when this scale is in place it is easier to focus on expositional manipulation of which a preliminary list was presented. Thus, unreliability in fiction can be understood as appearing in narrators and characters and their actions and pronouncements as well as in the narrative form which may be unreliable in the sense that it manipulates readers to believe what later is shown not to be the case. The intentional agents crafting fiction or figuring as narrators and characters should be studied in greater detail so that the different kinds of unreliability can be better identified. Even the fiction examined here suggests that the forms and combinations of unreliability in fiction are not only extremely diverse but also elemental in enriching the experience of reading.

Works Cited

Akutagawa, Ryonosuke. 1959 [1915]. "Rashomon." In: *Rashomon and Other Stories*. Trans. Takashi Kojima. New York, NY: Bantam. 29–39.

Akutagawa, Ryonosuke. 1959 [1922]. "In a Grove." In: *Rashomon and Other Stories*. Trans. Takashi Kojima. New York, NY: Bantam. 13–28.

Apuleius. 2008 [1994]. *The Golden Ass*. Trans. Peter G. Walsh. Oxford/New York, NY: Oxford University Press.

The Arabian Nights. Tales from A Thousand and One Nights ("The Tale of Three Apples"). 2004 [2001]. Trans. Richard F. Burton. New York, NY: The Modern Library. 145–154.

Armstrong, Paul B. 1995 [1987]. "[Dowell as Trustworthy Narrator]." In: Ford 1995 [1915]. 388–391.
Banville, John. 1990 [1989]. *The Book of Evidence*. London: Minerva.
Banville, John. 2003 [2002]. *Shroud*. London: Picador.
Booth, Wayne C. 1983 [1961]. *The Rhetoric of Fiction*. 2nd ed. Chicago, IL/ London: University of Chicago Press.
Brontë, Charlotte. 1953 [1847]. *Jane Eyre*. New York, NY: Pocket Books.
Carver, Raymond. 1989 [1988]. "Blackbird Pie." In: *Elephant and Other Stories*. London: Collins Harvill. 91–109.
Cervantes, Miguel de. 2003. *Don Quixote*. Trans. Edith Grossman. London: Vintage.
Chaucer, Geoffrey. 1979 [1964]. *Canterbury Tales & Tales of Caunterbury*. A. Kent Hieatt & Constance Hieatt (eds.). New York, NY: Bantam.
Defoe, Daniel. 1972 [1722]. [*The Fortunes and Misfortunes of the Famous*] *Moll Flanders*. London/New York, NY: Dent & Dutton.
D'hoker, Elke & Gunther Martens (eds.). 2008. *Narrative Unreliability in the Twentieth-Century First-Person Novel*. Narratologia 14. Berlin/New York, NY: De Gruyter.
Diski, Jenny. 1990 [1988]. *Like Mother*. London: Vintage.
Eliot, Thomas S. 1989 [1915]. "The Love Song of J. Alfred Prufrock." In: *The Complete Poems and Plays*. London: Faber & Faber. 13–17.
Ford, Ford Madox. 1995 [1914]. "On Impressionism." In: Ford 1995 [1915]. 257–274.
Ford, Ford Madox. 1995 [1915]. *The Good Soldier*. Ed. Martin Stannard. 2nd ed. New York, NY/London: Norton.
Ford, Ford Madox. 2013 [1924–1928]. *Parade's End*. Ware, Hertfordshire: Wordsworth.
Frayn, Michael. 2002. *Spies*. London: Faber & Faber.
Gaige, Amity. 2013. *Schroder. A Novel*. London: Faber & Faber.
Goldblatt, Howard. 2000. "The 'Saturnicon'. Forbidden Food of Mo Yan." *World Literature Today* 74.3: 477–485.
Goodheart, Eugene. 1995 [1986]. "What Dowell Knew." In: Ford 1995 [1915]. 375–384.
Groom, Winston. 1995 [1986]. *Forrest Gump*. London: Black Swan.
Hansen, Per Krogh. 2005. "When Facts Become Fiction: Facts, Fiction and Unreliable Narration." In: Lars-Åke Skalin (ed.). *Fact and Fiction in Narrative: An Interdisciplinary Approach*. Örebro: Örebro University. 283–307.
Harris, Joanne. 2011 [2010]. *blueeyedboy*. London: Black Swan.
Haslett, Adam. 2003 [2002]. "The Good Doctor." In: *You Are Not a Stranger Here*. London: Vintage. 24–47.

Hawthorne, Nathaniel. 1987 [1835]. "Wakefield." In: James McIntosh (ed.). *Nathaniel Hawthorne's Tales*. New York, NY/London: Norton. 75–82.
Homer. 2007 [1967]. *The Odyssey*. Trans. Richmond Lattimore. New York, NY: Harper Perennial Modern Classics.
Frayn, Michael. 2002. *Spies*. London: Faber & Faber.
Ishiguro, Kazuo. 1996 [1989]. *The Remains of the Day*. London: Faber & Faber.
James, Henry. 1974 [1878]. "Daisy Miller: A Study." In: *Daisy Miller and The Turn of the Screw*. New York, NY: Scholastic Book Services. 157–243.
James, Henry. 1974 [1898]. "The Turn of the Screw." In: *Daisy Miller and The Turn of the Screw*. New York, NY: Scholastic Book Services. 1–155.
James, Henry. 2001 [1903]. "The Beast in the Jungle." In: John Lyon (ed.). *Selected Tales*. London: Penguin. 426–461.
The Kalevala. 1990. Ed. Elias Lönnrot. Trans. Keith Bosley. Oxford/New York, NY: Oxford University Press.
Knight, Sabina. 2012. *Chinese Literature. A Very Short Introduction*. Oxford/New York, NY: Oxford University Press.
Kosinski, Jerzy. 1996 [1970]. *Being There*. London: Black Swan.
Lu, Xun. 2009 [1918]. "Diary of a Madman." In: *The Real Story of Ah-Q and Other Tales of China. The Complete Fiction of Lu Xun*. Trans. Julia Lovell. London: Penguin. 21–31.
Lucian. 2008. *A True Story*. In: Bryan P. Reardon (ed.). *Collected Ancient Greek Novels*. Trans. Bryan P. Reardon. Berkeley, CA: University of California Press. 621–649.
Maupassant, Guy de. 1997 [1885]. "The Diary of a Madman." In: *The Dark Side. Tales of Terror and the Supernatural*. Trans. Arnold Kellett. New York, NY: Carroll & Graf. 113–119.
McHale, Brian. 1982. "Writing about Postmodernist Writing." *Poetics Today* 3.3: 211–227.
Melville, Herman. 2002 [1851]. *Moby-Dick*. Ed. Hershel Parker & Harrison Hayford. 2nd ed. New York, NY/London: Norton.
Norrman, Ralf. 2000. *Wholeness Restored. Love of Symmetry as a Shaping Force in the Writings of Henry James, Kurt Vonnegut, Samuel Butler and Raymond Chandler*. Frankfurt/Berlin: Peter Lang.
Nünning, Ansgar. 2008. "Reconceptualizing the Theory, History and Generic Scope of Unreliable Narration: Towards a Synthesis of Cognitive and Rhetorical Approaches." In: D'hoker & Martens (eds.). 2008. 29–76.

Nünning, Vera. 2004. "Unreliable Narration and the Historical Variability of Values and Norms: *The Vicar of Wakefield* as a Test-Case of a Cultural-Historical Narratology." *Style* 38.2: 236–252.

Perry, Menakhem. 1979. "Literary Dynamics. How the Order of a Text Creates its Meanings [With an Analysis of Faulkner's 'A Rose for Emily']." *Poetics Today* 1.1–2: 35–64; 311–361.

Pettersson, Bo. 1999. "Who Is 'Sivilizing' Who(m)? The Function of Naivety and the Criticism of *Huckleberry Finn*—A Multidimensional Approach." In: Irma Taavitsainen, Gunnel Melchers & Päivi Pahta (eds.). *Writing in Nonstandard English*. Amsterdam: John Benjamins. 101–122.

Pettersson, Bo. 2005. "The Many Faces of Unreliable Narration. A Cognitive Narratological Reorientation." In: Harri Veivo, Bo Pettersson & Merja Polvinen (eds.). *Cognition and Literary Interpretation in Practice*. Helsinki: Helsinki University Press. 59–88.

Pettersson, Bo. 2013. "Hypothetical Action: Poetry under Erasure in Blake, Dickinson and Eliot." In: Roger D. Sell, Adam Borch & Inna Lindgren (eds.). *The Ethics of Literary Communication: Genuineness, Directness, Indirectness*. Amsterdam/Philadelphia, PA: John Benjamins. 129–145.

Phelan, James. 2005. *Living to Tell about It. A Rhetoric of Ethics and Character Narration*. Ithaca, NY: Cornell University Press.

Phelan, James. 2007. *Experiencing Fiction. Judgments, Progressions, and the Rhetorical Theory of Narrative*. Columbus, OH: The Ohio State University Press.

Phelan, James. 2008. "Estranging Unreliability, Bonding Unreliability, and the Ethics of *Lolita*." In: D'hoker & Martens (eds.). 2008. 7–28.

Riggan, William. 1981. *Pícaros, Madmen, Naïfs, and Clowns. The Unreliable First-Person Narrator*. Norman, OK: University of Oklahoma Press.

Shakespeare, William. 1975 [1608]. *King Lear*. The Arden Shakespeare. Kenneth Muir (ed.). London: Methuen.

Skalin, Lars-Åke. "Stories in Disguise: On Odysseus' Ithacan Lies and Their Relevance to the Device of the Unreliable Narrator." http://www.oru.se/PageFiles/5354/Lars-%c3%85ke%20Skalin%20%20Stories%20in%20Disguise.pdf (last retrieved: March 26, 2013).

Sternberg, Meir. 1978. *Expositional Modes and Temporal Ordering in Fiction*. Baltimore, MD/London: The Johns Hopkins University Press.

Trivers, Robert. 2011. *Deceit and Self-Deception. Fooling Yourself the Better to Fool Others*. London: Allen Lane.

Twain, Mark. 1988 [1885]. *Adventures of Huckleberry Finn*. The Works of Mark Twain. Vol. 8. Walter Blair & Victor Fischer (eds.). Berkeley, CA: University of California Press.

Waters, Sarah. 2010 [2009]. *The Little Stranger.* London: Virago.
Woolf, Virginia. 1989 [1944]. "Together and Apart." In: Susan Dick (ed.). *The Complete Shorter Fiction.* 2nd ed. San Diego, CA: Harcourt Brace Jovanovich. 189–194.
Yacobi, Tamar. 2000. "Interart Narrative: (Un)reliability and Ekphrasis." *Poetics Today* 21.4: 711–749.
Zerweck, Bruno. 2001. "Historicizing Unreliable Narration: Unreliability and Cultural Discourse in Narrative Fiction." *Style* 35.1: 151–178.
Zusak, Markus. 2007 [2005]. *The Book Thief.* London: Black Swan.

ROBERT VOGT

(Gießen)

Combining Possible-Worlds Theory and Cognitive Theory: Towards an Explanatory Model for Ironic-Unreliable Narration, Ironic-Unreliable Focalization, Ambiguous-Unreliable and Alterated-Unreliable Narration in Literary Fiction

"The theory of unreliable narration is obviously one of the current boom-sectors of what Manfred Jahn and Ansgar Nünning have called the 'narratological industry'," writes Tom Kindt (2008: 129f.). Since "it has been 'refigured' (Currie), 'reexamined' (Phelan), 'reconceptualized' (Nünning), 'rethought' (Baah), and 'reconsidered' (Olson) […]" (ibid.: 130), it is difficult—even for literary critics—to keep track of the different concepts. The fact that heterogeneous texts such as Ian McEwan's "Dead as They Come" (Nünning 1998), Mark Twain's *The Adventures of Huckleberry Finn* (Riggan 1981), Ford Madox Ford's *The Good Soldier* (Chatman 1993), Bret Easton Ellis' *American Psycho* (Phillips 2009), or Ian McEwan's *Atonement* (Menhard 2009) are all subsumed under the label 'narrative unreliability' not only shows that the concept serves as an umbrella term covering a range of different phenomena but also raises the question of what literary critics actually mean when they speak of narrative unreliability. I suggest that it encompasses three different phenomena.

First, unreliability can be understood as a trait of a homodiegetic narrator or a focalizer which manifests as a questionable account or interpretation of the events in the narrative world.[1] In texts featuring such a type of narrator or focalizer, readers detect a discrepancy between the narrative world and the account or interpretation that the narrator or focalizer offers, and they naturalize these inconsistencies by resorting to

---

1 Cf. Yacobi (2000: 712): "Ever since Wayne Booth (1961) focused the concept, '(un)reliabi-lity' has been accepted by most scholars as a character trait that attaches to the figure of the narrator (or reflector, hence all speaking/thinking subjects)".
   See also Margolin's helpful typology in this volume.

the narrator's or focalizer's mind (cf. Shen 1989: 300; Nünning 1998).[2] For this reason, "unreliability cannot be simply attributed to an impersonal narrator: it must be motivated in terms of the psychology of a narrating character" (Walsh 2007: 79). This form of narrative unreliability is frequently regarded as a special form of ironic communication 'behind the narrator's or focalizer's back' (Booth 1983 [1961]: 304; Chatman 1990: 153f.) or as a form of dramatic irony at the narrator's or focalizer's expense (Nünning/Nünning 2007: 69).[3] For this reason, I will call this form *ironic-unreliable narration* or *ironic-unreliable focalization* (depending on whether the butt of irony is situated on the discourse-level or on the story-level). An ironic-unreliable narrator can be found, for instance, in Edgar Allan Poe's "The Tell-Tale Heart" (Nünning 1998) or Kazuo Ishiguro's *The Remains of the Day* (Phelan 2004), while James Joyce's *A Portrait of the Artist as a Young Man* (Fludernik 1999: 78) or Henry James *What Maisie Knew* (Nünning 1998: 7) serve as prime examples of texts featuring ironic-unreliable focalizers.[4] In addition to this type of narrative unreliability—which without question has received the most attention in literary studies—there are two other types which do not involve dramatic irony.

Second, unreliability can be regarded as a feature of the narrative discourse which leaves open whether or not a narrator or a focalizer depicts or evaluates the narrative world in an adequate way. In contrast to texts featuring ironic-unreliable narrators or focalizers, the reader "cannot know whether the narrator [or focalizer] is reliable or not and whether the events he records are to be taken on trust or to be treated with ironic disbelief" (Rimmon-Kenan 1977: 15). Rimmon-Kenan explains the differences between irony and ambiguity in an illuminating way:

> Irony is incompatible with ambiguity because its drift is unequivocally implied by the discourse. The very fact that we can identify a narrative as ironic implies a foregone choice of the correct reading, in the light of which we subvert every detail of the 'false' version. The moment we can assert that a narrator or a character in a given narrative is unreliable and that our reading should proceed in direct opposition to his account, we have abandoned the realm of 'ambiguity' for that of 'irony'. Ambiguity exists in the in-between land of hesitation […]. (1977: 15)

---

[2] As a result, ironic-unreliable narrators are frequently categorized according to socio-cognitive parameters. E.g. Riggan (1981) differentiates the pícaro, the madman, the naïf and the clown.

[3] For the differences and similarities between (what I call) ironic-unreliable narrators and ironic-unreliable focalizers, see Nünning/Nünning (2007) and Chatman (1990) (who speaks of fallible filters instead of unreliable focalizers).

[4] One might further subdivide ironic-unreliable narrators or focalizers according to different socio-cognitive types—as Riggan (1981) proposes—or distinguish different kinds in which narrators reveal their unreliability, as Phelan (2004: 49ff.) does with his taxonomy of misreporting/underreporting, misreading/underreading and misregarding/underregarding.

Following Rimmon-Kenan, I call this second type of narrative unreliability *ambiguous-unreliable narration* in order to highlight its difference from texts featuring ironic-unreliable narrators or focalizers.[5] In contrast to the latter, unreliability doesn't refer to a narrator's or focalizer's trait but to a feature of the narrative discourse (that cannot be assigned to a narrator or focalizer)—specifically, "the existence of a central permanent gap and of mutually exclusive systems of clues designed to fill in" (Rimmon-Kenan 1977: 126). Prime examples of this type of narrative unreliability can be found in Henry James' *The Turn of the Screw*, Bret Easton Ellis' *American Psycho*, or Thomas Pynchon's *The Crying of Lot 49*.

Third, unreliability can also designate a feature of the narrative discourse which leads the reader astray about the actual events in the fictional world.[6] In these texts, readers construct a false image of the fictional world until an unexpected plot twist pulls the rug out from under their feet, forcing them to call into question and revise their assumptions about the facts and events in the story. Contrary to other (rather genre specific) narrative strategies found for instance in *whodunits*, the plot twist in these texts springs an absolute surprise on the reader who is not aware that he might get duped about the facts and events in the fictional world (Hartmann 2005: 156). Since this effect is achieved by a manipulative distribution of narrative information, I call this type *alterated-unreliable narration* (with regard to Gérard Genette's [1980: 195] concept of narrative alteration—meaning an "infraction" of the narrative code).[7] Examples of this type of narrative unreliability range from texts such as Agatha Christie's *The Murder of Roger Ackroyd* (Fludernik 1999: 76), Chuck Palahniuk's *Fight Club*, Nabokov's *Pnin* (Bode 2011 [2005]: 271) to heterodiegetic narratives such as Ambrose Bierce's "An Occurrence at Owl Creek Bridge" (Zipfel 2011).

---

5   It has to be noted that Rimmon-Kenan's concept of ambiguous narration is much broader than the concept of ambiguous-unreliable narration that is proposed here. While her concept captures all sorts of ambiguities within a narrative, mine is solely restricted to those cases where the narrator's or focalizer's depiction, perception or evaluation of the events in the fictional world is at stake. Another concept—which I need to distance unreliable-ambiguous narration from—is Martínez and Scheffel's (2007 [1999]: 103) mimetic-undecidable narration in which the reader cannot decide what is the case in the fictional world. However, Martínez and Scheffel's examples encompass highly metafictional texts in which no cognitive center is to be found. Thus, mimetic-undecidable narration covers all sorts of narratives in which the reader is not able to construct a coherent narrative world. Contrary to that, ambiguous-unreliable narration refers to cases where this phenomenon is linked to the (un)reliability of the cognitive center (as narrator or focalizer).
6   See also Vogt (2009).
7   For the lack of better terms and to avoid confusion with other narrative strategies such as red herrings, I refer to Genette's concept of alteration (1980), being aware that the concept is used slightly differently by the French narratologist.

The function of this typology is not to establish clear-cut boundaries between the different forms of narrative unreliability,[8] but to serve as a starting point to map the field of narrative unreliability. In the following, I wish to propose a model for describing and explaining these different types of narrative unreliability. The essay is divided into four parts: After addressing some of the theoretical stumbling blocks narratologists face when theorizing narrative unreliability in fictional works (section 1), I will outline how insights from literary possible-worlds and cognitive narratology might help to develop a better understanding of how readers construct fictional universes in texts featuring ironic-unreliable narration/focalization, ambiguous-unreliable narration and alterated-unreliable narration. Section 2 will introduce main assumptions of literary possible-worlds theory and explain how the concepts can be used not only to describe a fictional universe in unreliable narratives but also how they may lay the foundation for explaining the different types of narrative unreliability. Since fictional universes are always the result of reader's interpretative processes, section 3 will address the question of how a reader constructs fictional universes in unreliable narratives. The essay will be concluded by a brief outlook of how the proposed model can be of use for a transmedial theory of narrative unreliability.

1. Challenges in Explaining Narrative Unreliability in Fictional Works

In a groundbreaking essay from 1998, Ansgar Nünning (1998: 20) raises one of the most pertinent questions surrounding the debates about narrative unreliability by asking: "Unreliable—compared to what?" Although the answer to that question is certainly very complex and beyond the scope of this essay, I believe that we can identify at least two positions. While rhetorical approaches regard the implied author's ethical norms and values as the frame of referenc[9], the majority of narratological approaches take the narrative world (or mental model of the narrative world) as the

---

8   Moreover, it needs to be pointed out that different forms of narrative unreliability are frequently found in the same work. For instance, in the first part of Ian McEwan's *Atonement* (2001) we find different ironic-unreliable focalizers. In addition to that, the novel also serves as an example of alterated-unreliable narration since the reader is misled about the ontological status of the first three parts of the novel (in the fourth part of the novel, it is revealed that the preceding parts were written by a character in the novel). Furthermore, we learn that (in contrast to the depiction in the preceding parts) the two lovers have not reunited but have died instead.
9   For instance, for Booth in his classic definition a narrator is reliable "when he speaks for or acts in accordance with the norms of the work (which is to say, the implied author's norms), unreliable when he does not" (Booth 1983 [1961]: 158f.).

central yardstick.[10] For instance, Herman writes that "[in unreliable narration] the teller of a story cannot be taken by his or her word, compelling the AUDIENCE to 'read between the lines'—in other words, to scan the text for clues about how the STORYWORLD really is, as opposed to how the NARRATOR says it is" (Herman 2009: 194).

Since the concept of the narrative world is obviously of central importance, it may come as a surprise that it leads a rather shadowy existence in most theories of unreliable narration, posing a number of challenges to traditional narratological approaches—as I will illustrate with recourse to ironic-reliable narration. A central problem for narratologists lies in the fact that on the one hand, they assume that the narrator is the "unique source" (Chatman 1990: 153) of the fictional world, while on the other hand, they regard the fictional world (as depicted by the narrator) as the frame of reference to evaluate the narrator's (un)reliability. Obviously, we are caught in circularity. Ryan (1981: 530) cuts right to the heart of the matter when she incisively reflects:

> As natural as the possibility of unreliable discourse may be in narrative fiction, it conceals a rather paradoxical situation. In natural communication, the hearer is able to detect lies, errors and other faulty declarations because he has other ways of access to the frame of reference. He can either compare the speaker's representation of facts to his own experience, or to the content of another discourse. But in fictional narration, the text constitutes the reader's sole source of information about the represented state of affairs. How then can he test the accuracy of the narrator's declarations?

In order to solve this problem, structuralist and rhetorical approaches draw on the implied author as an instance which can communicate "beyond the awareness of the narrator" (Phelan 2004: 50). According to this position, the reader concludes "by 'reading out' between the lines that the events and existents could not have been 'like that'," (Chatman 1993 [1978]: 233) and thus questions the narrator's depiction or evaluation. Not surprisingly, other critics have dismissed this explanation as being too metaphorical since it can neither explain how such a secret communication actually works nor how the actual reader detects the implied author's hidden message (Nünning 1998: 14).

Cognitive narratologists propose a model which focuses on the actual reader and his interpretation strategies to make sense of inconsistencies in a text. According to this approach, the reader naturalizes textual inconsistencies and incoherences by resorting to the narrator's psychology. Furthermore, Nünning (1998: 27f.; 2008: 44f.) provides a detailed list of potential textual signs which alert the individual readers to the narrator's unreliability. However, as he admits,

---

10   See Chatman (1990); Martínez/Scheffel (2007 [1999]); Rimmon-Kenan (2002).

> [w]hat is needed [...] is a more systematic exploration between readers' identification of elements in the narrative discourse (including decisions about the narrator's unreliability) and the 'story' or represented world that readers project. An alliance between narratology and possible worlds theory could thus be an important force in the current reconceptualization of narrative theory, opening up productive new possibilities for the relation between indeterminacies on the level of discourse and the represented worlds of the level of the story, which are projected by the reader. (Nünning 2008: 68)

Taking up Nünning's proposal seems productive for a number of reasons. First, as literary possible-worlds theory focuses on fictional worlds, it offers a differentiating terminological toolkit to describe the fictional universe (including the relation between the fictional world and the narrator's mental representation of it). Second, although possible-worlds theory is by no means a cognitive theory, literary possible-worlds theory lays a foundation for explaining how readers construct fictional universes and can be complemented with insights from cognitive narratology. Moreover, a combination of possible-worlds theory and cognitive narratology provides a theoretical framework which enables one to explain not only ironic-unreliable narration and focalization but ambiguous-unreliable and alterated-unreliable narration as well.

2. Describing Narrative Unreliability by Means of Possible-Worlds Theory

Possible-worlds theory originates in analytical philosophy "to solve problems in formal semantics" (Ryan 2001: 99). The theory's basic premise is that reality

> is a universe composed of a plurality of distinct worlds. [...] This universe is structured like a solar system: at the center lies a world commonly known as 'the actual world', and this center is surrounded by worlds that are possible but not actual. These worlds lie at a variable distance from the actual world and resemble it to various degrees [...]. (Ryan 2006: 644)

This model provides "a framework within which it is possible to determine the truth-values of propositions beyond the constraints of the actual world, and particularly to define the concepts of possibility and necessity" (Semino 1997: 58). Accordingly, a proposition is necessarily true when it is true in all worlds, it is possibly true when it is true in at least one of the worlds, and it is necessarily false when it is false in all of the worlds (ibid.). Possibility (as understood in this framework) can be equated with epistemological accessibility, meaning that "a world is possible if it satisfies the logical laws of noncontradiction and of excluded middle" (Ryan 1991: 31).

Literary possible-worlds theory has adopted these ideas to analyze the relationship between different worlds within a fictional universe and between the reader's actual world and the fictional world. Ryan (1991: 32) calls these intrauniverse and transuniverse relations. In the following, I will take both of these relations into account to develop a model of narrative unreliability. While intrauniverse relations provide a conceptual frame for describing the relations between different worlds in the fictional universe, transuniverse relations serve as a theoretical backdrop to explain the different ways in which a reader detects and makes sense of narrative unreliability.

According to Ryan, fictional works create their own modal system of reality which consists of a multitude of worlds. In the center of each fictional universe is the so-called 'textual actual world' (TAW) surrounded by the different characters' mental worlds. A character's mental world can be further subdivided according to different propositional attitudes: one may distinguish between a knowledge world, an obligation world which encompasses the moral values of a character, a wish world, an intention world, and a fantasy universe (including the character's dreams and fantasies) (Ryan 1991: 113–119). Since "[t]he possible worlds of a character's domain are built out of truth-functional propositions; they are collections of facts which can be compared to the facts of the actual world" (Ryan 1991: 111). For this reason, narrative unreliability has been conceived of as a discrepancy or a conflict between the narrative world and the narrator's mental world (see Ryan 1991: 113; Àlvarez Amorós 1991; Zipfel 2011).

However, if we reduce the description of the fictional universe to TAW and the narrator's world, little is gained. In fact, Ryan (1991: 113) herself, being one of the most prominent advocates of possible-worlds theory, falls back on the concept of the implied author as a communicative instance to explain narrative unreliability. This seems unsatisfying since it does not really exhaust the theory's full potential. Instead, it seems reasonable to take other mental worlds into account as well. If a narrator recounts or interprets the events in the narrative world in an inadequate way, one can assume that there are other mental worlds within the fictional universe in which these events are perceived, interpreted, or evaluated differently (cf. Àlvarez Amorós 1991). Consequently, we can assume that conflicts between different kinds of worlds are constitutive elements of unreliable narratives (ibid.).

If conflicting worlds are constitutive of narrative unreliability, it is necessary to distinguish between a variety of world conflicts. Since possible-worlds theorists have mostly neglected the discourse level,[11] it seems advisable to modify and expand the terminology of possible-worlds theory by means of structuralist-narratological terminology in order to differentiate between various types of mental worlds in the fictional universe. Therefore, I wish to propose a distinction between a narrator's world, a focalizer's world, a narratee's world and a character's world. A narrator's world presupposes a homodiegetic narrator to whom the reader can attribute certain mental states (such as beliefs, intentions or a value system)[12], while a narratee's world necessitates an explicit narratee (who does not need to be a clearly identifiable or individualizable character within TAW).[13] A focalizer's world is the mental world of a focalized character, while a character's world encompasses the desires, beliefs, and ethics of a character that does not serve as focalizer. The differences in the reading process and in the way the reader reconstructs these different mental worlds are manifold: In the case of a homodiegetic narrator or a focalizer, the reader has direct access to the thoughts and emotions of the characters—and thus to their mental worlds. In contrast to narrator's and focalizer's worlds, the reader cannot directly access the mental worlds of narratees and of non-focal characters. Consequently, the reader has to reconstruct the character's worlds, for instance, solely on the basis of their outward appearances, statements, and actions.

The expansion of terminology allows us to distinguish between a variety of world conflicts which challenge a narrator's or a focalizer's mental worlds. For instance, a narrator's world and a narratee's world contradict each other when the narrator assumes that his addressee has a different perspective on an event than himself. An example of this kind of world conflict is found in the famous first sentence of Edgar Allan Poe's "The Tell-Tale Heart" in which the narrator asks: "True!—nervous—very dreadfully nervous I had been and am; but why will you say that I am mad?" (Poe 2004 [1843]: 317) While the narrator believes he is perfectly sane (though nervous), he infers that the narratee might regard him as a lunatic (and thus offering an alternative view on his own mental state of mind). A conflict between a narrator's world and a character's world arises when the narrator's account or interpretation is called into question by a character within the narrative world. For instance, in Bret Easton Ellis' *American Psycho*, the narrator Patrick Bateman depicts how he kills his

---

11 The only exception is the category of the homodiegetic narrator, whose mental world is termed the "narratorial actual world" (Ryan 1991: 113).
12 Although heterodiegetic narrators can be explicit as well, it seems difficult to attribute particular intentions or desires to these instances.
13 A narratee's world is a special case as it can be regarded as the speaker's mental projection of the knowledge, norms and values, wishes and intentions of his addressee.

colleague Paul Owen, disposes of the corpse, and meets and kills prostitutes in his victim's apartment. The narrator's world, however, is contradicted by another character's world at a later point in the novel. When the narrator confesses his brutal murders to his attorney a couple of weeks later, the latter does not take Bateman's depiction seriously, claiming he had dinner with Paul Owen in London only a couple of days before.

Instead of spelling out all different kinds of conflicts, the following table provides a broad overview of potential kinds of conflicting worlds found in unreliable narratives.

Conflict between a narrator's world and TAW	a homodiegetic narrator contradicts himself about the facts and events in TAW
Conflict within a narrator's world	a homodiegetic narrator questions his own account or evaluation of the facts and events in TAW
Conflict between different narrators' worlds	two or more homodiegetic narrators depict or evaluate the same fact or event in TAW differently
Conflict between a narrator's world and a focalizer's world	a homodiegetic narrator ("narrating I") contradicts the assumptions and values of the focalizer ("experiencing I")
Conflict between a narrator's world and a character's world	a homodiegetic narrator's account or evaluation of facts and events in TAW is contradicted by another character's assumptions or evaluation
Conflict between a narrator's world and a narratee's world	a homodiegetic narrator infers that his addressee would depict or evaluate the facts and events in TAW differently
Conflict between a focalizer's world and TAW	a focalizer's world is contradicted by the facts and events in TAW (as depicted by a heterodiegetic narrator)
Conflict within a focalizer's world	a focalizer questions his own perception or evaluation of the facts and events in TAW
Conflict between different focalizers' worlds	two or more focalizers perceive or evaluate the same fact or event in TAW differently
Conflict between a focalizer's world and a character's world	a focalizer's perception or evaluation of the same facts and events in TAW is contradicted by another character's assumptions or evaluation

Typically, we find different kinds of world conflicts in unreliable narratives which draw the reader's attention to certain moral or epistemological issues. In Edgar Allan Poe's "The Tell-Tale Heart", to take up the story once more, the reader is not only confronted with conflicts between the narrator's world and the narratee's world concerning the narrator's lunacy (see above) but also with conflicts between the narrator's world and other characters' worlds. In the story, the narrator (or rather the focalizer) murders and dismembers his roommate hiding his body parts under the floorboards. He is then visited by three policemen who were alerted by neighbors who heard the roommate's shrieks. After convincing the policemen that everything is fine, he chats with them. During the conversation, however, the narrator starts to hear the beating of his victim's heart, while the police officers apparently do not notice anything—hence, we have a conflict between the narrator's world and other characters' worlds.

A systematic analysis of world conflicts in narratives offers several advantages and can shed light on different aspects of narrative unreliability. For example, one may ask: What kinds of world conflicts arise? Are these world conflicts about facts in the narrative world (as in a conflict between different knowledge worlds) or rather about the evaluation of events or other characters (as in a conflict between moral values in different obligation worlds)?[14] What kind of epistemological or moral questions are being addressed via the conflicting worlds? Furthermore, one may ask: Whose worlds are in conflict? When do world conflicts occur? Do world conflicts increase or decrease in the course of a story? The answer to the last question, for instance, can provide insights into the development of a narrator or of a focalizer. An increase in world conflicts might indicate an increase in the narrator's or focalizer's unreliability, as is the case with Charlotte Gilman Perkins' "The Yellow Wallpaper". A decrease of conflicting worlds, on the other hand, frequently points to a decrease of the cognitive center's unreliability, as in the case of Charles Dickens' *David Copperfield*, where the ironic-unreliable focalizer matures and becomes more and more reliable throughout the course of the story.

But intrauniverse relations not only serve as a means to describe the fictional universe in unreliable narratives, they also lay the foundation for an explanation model of narrative unreliability. As noted before, a central challenge for traditional approaches to unreliability lies in the fact that on the one hand the fictional world (or the mental model of it, as in cognitive approaches) is the yardstick for determining the narrator's or focalizer's unreliability, while on the other hand the reader can frequently construct

---

14   See also Zipfel (2011) on that question.

the fictional world solely on the basis of the narrator's account or the focalizer's perception. By means of intrauniverse relations this dilemma can be solved: Since world conflicts provide different perspectives on the same event, they counteract the assumption that the reader is solely dependent on the narrator's account of the fictional world. Consequently, there is no need to speak of a "secret communication behind the narrator's back". Instead, world conflicts indicate, as Àlvarez Amorós (1991: 62f.) argues, a narrator's or focalizer's potential unreliability because the reader can only regard one of the conflicting worlds as being in accordance with the narrative world. Hence, conflicting worlds are not only helpful to describe the fictional universe in unreliable narratives but also serve as signals for the reader to question the narrator's account or focalizer's perception of the narrative world.

This assumption shifts the focus unto transuniverse relations (the relation between the reader and the fictional world) and the question of how a reader reconstructs a fictional universe in ironic-unreliable narration/focalization, ambiguous-unreliable narration and alterated-unreliable narration. The main difference between these forms of narrative unreliability, as will be argued, lies in the ways a reader identifies and distinguishes different worlds, detects conflicting worlds and puts these in a hierarchical order (to decide what is the case in TAW). In the case of ironic-unreliable narration or ironic-unreliable focalization the reader detects a discrepancy between TAW and the narrator's account or evaluation of the events. Hence, one can conclude that the reader can identify and distinguish different worlds, he can detect world conflicts, and he believes another world to be more adequate in relation to the fictional world than the narrator's or focalizer's. This specific hierarchization is justified by attributing some kind of epistemological or moral defect to the narrator or focalizer, e.g. by qualifying them as naïve or insane (as in Poe's "The Tell-Tale Heart"), etc. Due to the hierarchization of worlds, the reader reconstructs an alternative course of facts and events in the fictional world.

In the case of ambiguous-unreliable narration, the reader cannot be sure whether to trust the narrator's or focalizer's account or evaluation of the facts and events in TAW. With recourse to conflicting worlds, we can find two possible explanations for the uncertainty towards the story's cognitive center. Either the reader is not able to decide whether or not a narrator's or focalizer's world is contradicted by another world, or—if he detects a world conflict—the reader is unsure how to put these worlds in a hierarchical order (and thus to decide what is the case in TAW). Even after having finished the narrative, the conflicting worlds remain unresolved for the reader. For this reason, the reader can construct separate fictional universes on the basis of the same text—one in which the narrator is ironic-unreliable and another one in which he is to be trusted (cf. Ryan 1991: 127).

In texts featuring altered-unreliable narration the reader is led up the garden path about the facts and events in TAW. In terms of conflicting worlds, one can conclude that the reader might not be able to distinguish between different worlds during a first reading (which is why he mistakes a character's mental world with TAW). Another possibility is that a reader identifies and distinguishes worlds in the fictional universe but fails to detect conflicts between them (hence, he will not doubt the narrator's or focalizer's depiction of TAW). A third explanation of why a reader constructs a false image of TAW is that he (having identified a world conflict) puts the conflicting worlds in a hierarchical order that proves wrong in the course of the narration. At some later point in the story (frequently at the end), however, a world conflict occurs that forces the reader to question and revise his mental model of the fictional world and to reconstruct a new fictional universe from scratch.

The following table summarizes the differences in the reader's reception of conflicting worlds in narrative unreliability. The (+) marks cases when the reader's interpretation is in accordance with the fictional universe, the (-) indicates that a reader's interpretation is initially false (but this mistake will be detected and revised by the reader). The (?) marks the reader's uncertainty about his own interpretive choices.

Ironic-Unreliable Narration/ Ironic-Unreliable Focalization	– Identifying and Distinguishing Worlds (+) – Detecting World Conflicts (+) – Hierarchizing the Conflicting Worlds (+)
Ambiguous-Unreliable Narration	– Identifying and Distinguishing Worlds (+) – Detecting World Conflicts (?) – Hierarchizing the Conflicting Worlds (?)
Altered-Unreliable Narration	– Identifying and Distinguishing Worlds (-) – Detecting World Conflicts (-) – Hierarchizing the Conflicting Worlds (-)

If this is so, one may ask why a reader can identify and distinguish different worlds in some texts and not in others? In which cases can he detect world conflicts, in which cases does he fail? And how does a reader put conflicting worlds in a hierarchical order? Or, to pose a more general question: how does a reader construct a fictional universe? Although the possible-worlds theory assesses the relation between reader and the fictional universe and even understands fictional texts as "instructions" (Doležel 1998: 205) for a reader of how to reconstruct the specific fictional universe, "[p]ossible worlds theory is by no means a cognitive theory" (Semino 2003: 88). Hence, in order to answer these questions, the theoretical framework needs to be expanded by referring to insights from cognitive psychology.

3. Explaining Narrative Unreliability by Means of Cognitive Science: Identifying Worlds, Detecting World Conflicts and Hierarchizing Worlds in Unreliable Narratives

A central premise of cognitive studies is that text comprehension relies on an interaction of textual data (data-driven-processes or bottom-up-processes) and on the reader's stored knowledge structures (schemata or categories) which are activated by textual cues in the reading process (top-down processes) (cf. Schneider 2001: 611). Furthermore, it is agreed upon that a reader constructs various levels of mental representations of a text. The *surface structure* "preserves the exact wording and syntax" (Claassen 2012: 29), the *textbase* "contains the explicit propositions" (ibid.), while the *situation model* depicts a mental representation of

> a microworld with characters who perform actions in pursuit of goals, events that present obstacles to goals, conflicts between characters, emotional reactions to characters, spatial setting, the style and procedure of actions, objects, properties of objects, traits of characters, and mental states of characters. (Graesser/Olde/Klettke 2002: 230f.)

As this definition indicates, a situation model is the mental representation of what literary possible-worlds theorists call a fictional universe—including individual mental models of TAW (or, "microworld") as well as characters and their mental worlds (or "mental states").[15] In addition to that, a number of researchers assume that readers not only construct a mental representation of the described states of affairs, but also of the pragmatic context in which the specific communication between teller and addressee takes place (cf. Claassen 2012: 56f.).[16] The *pragmatic model* designates the mental representation of the specific communication situation within the fictional universe, that is, of the characters (narrator and narratee), of the time and place in which the act of the narration takes place as well as of

---

15   In the following, I will refer to fictional universe instead of situation model.
16   With regard to text processing in fictional works, it is likely that a reader constructs two different pragmatic models (cf. Claassen 2012: 61)—one including a mental representation of the intratextual communication between homodiegetic narrator and narratee, while the other extratextual pragmatic model encompasses the mental representations of the implied author. Although this mental representation of the (implied) author is beyond any doubt pertinent for a cognitive approach to narrative unreliability (cf. Nünning 2008), this essay will neglect the category for reasons of brevity.

the narrator's intentions. It needs to be pointed out, however, that the construction of the pragmatic model is optional—only in texts with homodiegetic narrators does a reader construct a mental model of the pragmatic model including the narrative agent (cf. Graesser/Wiemer-Hastings 1999: 85f.).

Having sketched premises and key concepts of cognitive research on text comprehension, I will focus more closely on the cognitive processes underlying the construction of TAW and of mental worlds, the detection of conflicting worlds and the principles of putting them in a hierarchical order. It is common consensus that when reading a fictional work, the reader assumes a similarity between his reality and the fictional world. According to Marie-Laure Ryan's principle of minimal departure (Ryan 1991: 52f.), a reader will first and foremost rely on his general world knowledge (such as knowledge about physical laws, places, entities etc.) when constructing TAW until he receives information which indicates a discrepancy between TAW in the fictional universe and the reader's actual world. However, since "an essential aspect of reading comprehension consists of distinguishing a domain of autonomous facts—what I call the textual actual world—from the domains created by the mental activity of characters" (Ryan 2001: 103), the reader cannot integrate all textual data equally in the construction of TAW but has to consider and evaluate the source of the information—he needs to distinguish between TAW and a narrrator's, a focalizer's or a character's worlds.

The reader's distinction between TAW and characters' mental worlds goes hand in hand with what cognitive psychologists call "metarepresentation" and "decoupling". According to them, (most) human beings have metarepresentational capabilities meaning that they differentiate between "a primary representation (the world as it is)" and a "metarepresentation (the world as quoted)" (Iversen 2011: 133). According to this view, the mind stores information differently: some information is stored in the semantic memory as "architectural truth", while other information is "decoupled" from the semantic memory in scope syntaxes being bound to a specific source tag (a "time-specifying tag", a "place-specifying tag", or, most importantly in the context of this essay, an "agent-specifying tag") (cf. Iversen 2011: 133; Zunshine 2006: 51). The proposition within the scope syntax is regarded as true in relation to its source ("it is true that X believes that the world is a disc"). Hence, decoupling can be understood as the cognitive process with which a reader distinguishes between a narrative world and a character's world or between different mental worlds and assigns certain propositions to certain mental worlds (be it to a narrator's, focalizer's, narratee's, or a non-focalized character's world). When a statement is attributed to a heterodiegetic narrator, a reader will regard this information as architecturally true—and hence as a fact in TAW, while propositions which are assigned to homodiegetic narrators, focalizers, or characters will be provided with a source tag. Hence, identifying and distinguishing different worlds by means of decoupling is of central importance for the reconstruction of TAW.

To identify a narrator's or focalizer's world and distinguish it from TAW relies on textual signals. A homodiegetic narrator is first and foremost marked by the first-person pronoun. Furthermore, the "I" not only refers to a speaker but also to a character in the story and can be assigned "a proper name" and "a specific social identification (e.g. class, race, religion, profession, political affiliation)" (Bortolussi/Dixon 2003: 65). If these prerequisites are fulfilled, the reader constructs a mental model of the specific narrating character and a pragmatic model and assigns the narrator's statements with a specific source tag (character X narrates…). In a similar vein, textual indicators such as pronouns, infinite and definite articles, verbs of perception, cognition and emotions, tenses and verbal moods, evaluative lexical items and marked syntax (Herman 2004: 306–309) serve to identify a focalizer's perspective and thus serve to ascribe propositions to a specific focalizer's world.

While the identification and distinction of worlds is rather simple in most texts, some altered-unreliable narratives trick the readers about the ontological status of the constructed world. For instance, due to the lack of textual indicators a reader might confuse TAW with a narrator's mental world. A case in point is Nabokov's *Pnin*, a story about a Russian-born professor living in the USA and seemingly told by a heterodiegetic narrator. In the last chapter of the novel, it is revealed that Pnin's story is actually told by another character in TAW named N. In the light of this new information, the reader is forced to question everything he has read before, source tag all the statements (N. narrates that Pnin thinks…) and construct a pragmatic model in which a homodiegetic narrator tells the story. A similar example in which a reader confuses a focalizer's world with TAW is Bierce's "An Occurrence at Owl Creek Bridge" (cf. Vogt 2009; Zipfel 2011) in which the protagonist's escape turns out to be only an illusion.

Having identified different worlds, a reader needs to compare them in order to detect potential conflicts. To do so, a reader initially has to construct the individual narrator's, focalizer's and character's worlds—relying on textual data on the one hand, and specific social and literary knowledge on the other (cf. Schneider 2001: 611f.). The reader's mental representations of fictional characters (including homodiegetic narrators and focalizers) include their traits and mental states (their beliefs, assumptions or desires), while the latter corresponds to what possible-worlds theorists call a mental world.[17] When constructing a mental world of a narrator, focalizer or character, a reader engages in what cognitive psychologists call 'mind-reading'. Mind-reading designates "our ability to explain people's behavior in terms of their thoughts, feelings, beliefs, desires. Thus we engage in mind-reading when we ascribe to a person a certain mental state on the basis of her observable action [...]" (Zunshine 2006: 6).[18] Attributing mental states first and foremost depends on the observer's interpretation of whether he regards the behavior as an intentional act or not. If interpreted as unintentional, the observer explains it in terms of causes.[19] If an action is regarded as intentional, the observer infers specific reasons for the intention—primarily the "agents' mental states (primarily beliefs and desires) in light of which they formed an intention to act" (Malle 1999: 36). Hence, attribution of mental states is always dependent on the specific situational context in which a character's action takes place. With regard to fictional characters, it can be assumed that the reader's construction of narrator's, focalizer's and non-focalized character's mental states (beliefs, emotions etc.) is different. As the reader has no direct access to the minds of non-focalized characters (in contrast to those of narrators and focalizers), the reader is solely dependent on the character's behavior and outward appearance to infer his mental states.[20]

Detecting a world conflict (in ironic-unreliable narration or focalization) is a fairly easy endeavor especially when the narrator's account or focalizer's perception is explicitly called into question by other worlds. However, detecting world conflicts can be challenging in those cases in which a character's world needs to inferred on account on their behavior. The passage from Jess-Cooke's *The Boy Who Could See Demons* illustrates how readers detect conflicting worlds via mind-reading: "Miss Holland

---

17   Although it is safe to say that the construction of traits and mental states/worlds go hand in hand in the reception process and affect each other (cf. Jannidis 2004: 190), they will be discussed separately. Broadly speaking, traits are attributed by means of top-down processes such as categorization and/or bottom-up processes such as personalization in which the construction of character traits is more dependent on specific textual data (cf. Schneider 2001).
18   E.g. he stumbled (=unintentional behavior) because he was drunk.
19   E.g. he hit the man (=intentional behavior) because he thought (mental state) he was being attacked.
20   Although narratologists agree that a reader has direct insights into a narrator's or focalizer's mind, one should not jump to the conclusion that mind-reading is not necessary in these cases (see also Palmer 2002: 42). For instance, since a homodiegetic narrator rarely shares all his inner thoughts, mind-reading is necessary to infer his intentions, beliefs or feelings. As with characters, the reader has to consider the specific context (= the pragmatic model) of the behaviour (= the narration) to engage in mind-reading. Hence, the question of who the narrator's addressee is might be of importance for attributing certain intentions and other mental states to the narrator.

came over to my desk and asked what was wrong. I told her about the monsters in the corner. She took off her glasses very slowly and pushed them into her hair, then asked if I was feeling all right" (Jess-Cooke 2012: 2). Due to his mind-reading abilities, a reader concludes that Miss Holland takes off her glasses and asks the narrator if he is alright not because she believes that he has a cold but because she does not see any monsters in the classroom and worries about the boy's sanity.

However, detecting world conflicts via mind-reading can prove difficult. In ambiguous-unreliable narratives, a reader might be uncertain why a character behaves in a certain way in a specific situation. For instance, in James' *The Turn of the Screw* we find several incidences where it is impossible for the reader to decide whether Miles' and Flora's behavior can be seen as proof that they see ghosts or not. Hence, the reader is left in the dark about whether Miles' and Flora's character worlds are in accordance or in conflict with the narrator's. In the case of altered-unreliable narratives a reader might attribute false mental states to characters because he lacks crucial information about the specific context and thus fails to discern conflicting worlds. For instance, in Palahniuk's *Fight Club* the reader initially does not know that the narrator suffers from schizophrenia and that he and his friend Tyler are in fact the same person. Although most characters in the fictional universe know the narrator as Tyler, the reader does not discern this fact because—no matter how awkward their behavior might seem at times—he attributes false mental states to the other fictional characters.

When a reader detects a conflict between different worlds, he has to establish a hierarchy of these worlds in order to determine which one is in accordance with TAW. In other words, in order to decide what is true in TAW, we have to consider the source of a statement to evaluate its truth value (Zunshine 2006: 60). As noted before, metarepresentation and decoupling helps to explain how a reader hierarchizes conflicting worlds. Statements by heterodiegetic narrators are always regarded as fictional truth (as they are not source-tagged) when in conflict with statements which are assigned to other sources.[21] When solely mental worlds collide, the reader relies on real-world parameters. Assuming readers process fictional characters like people in their real life, as Bortolussi and Dixon (2003: 140) claim, it is likely that they assign different degrees of trustworthiness to characters based on real-life parameters such as age, gender, race, traits, or reputation in TAW (see Surkamp 2000: 127). For example,

---

21   A model of hierarchization based on linguistic-pragmatic assumptions is proposed by possible-worlds theorists—see for example, Doležel's concept of "authentication" (1998: 145ff.) or Ryan's concept of "textual authority" (1981).

if the narrator is a patient in a psychiatric hospital, such as the narrator in Kesey's *One Flew Over the Cuckoo's Nest*, one might consider his mental world inferior to conflicting worlds of characters who are regarded as sane in the fictional universe. In addition to the mental model of the specific source, other factors might determine how a reader solves a world conflict. When world conflicts concerning facts or properties in the TAW occur, it seems likely that a reader relies on what Surkamp (2000: 128) calls "shared actual world". When a majority of characters believes that something is fact in TAW, readers are likely to hierarchize these worlds over a singular mental world which contradicts this view. In addition to that, a reader might compare his own mental model of TAW and other character's worlds with those constructed by a narrator or focalizer and hierarchize conflicting worlds on this account. As Palmer (2009: 293) has argued, attributing traits and mental states to characters is not only an activity of readers, but also one that fictional characters are engaged in. Hence, a reader can monitor how a narrator or a focalizer makes sense of data and arrives at his conclusions and evaluations about the events in the fictional universe and compare these with his own interpretative processes.

The problems of hierarchizing conflicting worlds in ambiguous-unreliable narratives can be manifold. For instance, when an equal number of characters share the same beliefs about the facts and events in TAW, a reader might be unsure whom to trust, as is the case with James' *The Turn of the Screw*. In other cases, the reader cannot hierarchize the conflicting worlds because all characters seem (un)trustworthy to a similar degree. In Ellis' *American Psycho*, we cannot solve the conflict between the narrator's and a character's world concerning Paul Owen's death (see above). Since the narrator and the character both seem untrustworthy for different reasons, the reader cannot make out whose version is right.[22]

In some alterated-unreliable narratives, the reader hierarchizes conflicting worlds falsely and only learns retrospectively about his own false assumptions about the events in the narrative world. In McEwan's *Enduring Love*, the reader is faced with a multitude of conflicting worlds that cast doubt on the narrator's account and interpretation of the events. For this reason, the reader is likely to regard the narrator's world as somewhat untrustworthy and therefore to question his account of the events. "In the end, however, it turns out that every single far-fetched and obscure assumption, descriptive detail, or judgment of the narrator was absolutely true (within the fictional world)" (Zerweck 2001: 163f.), forcing the reader to revise his assumptions about the narrator and the events in the fictional world.

---

22 It goes without saying that there are more world conflicts in these novels.

4. Conclusion and Further Outlook: Towards a Transmedial Theory of Narrative Unreliability

In this essay I have proposed to distinguish three different types of unreliability: ironic-unreliable narration or focalization, ambiguous-unreliable narration and altered narration. Having pointed to the discrepancy between the importance of the fictional world and the surprising neglect of the concept in most theories of narrative unreliability, I have delineated some of the challenges the concept poses. To solve these problems, a theoretical framework was proposed that combines concepts from literary possible-worlds theory and cognitive science. Possible-worlds theory serves a means to describe a fictional universe in unreliable narratives. Assuming that conflicts between different worlds are constitutive of narrative unreliability, these conflicts furthermore serve as signals for the reader to question a narrator's or focalizer's account or evaluation of the facts and events in the fictional world. It was further argued that the main difference between the three forms of narrative unreliability lies in the way a reader makes sense of these conflicts: how he distinguishes different worlds, how he detects conflicting worlds and how he puts conflicting worlds in a hierarchical order to determine what is fact in the fictional universe. Building up on these assumptions, concepts from cognitive psychology were applied to explain how readers construct mental representation of the fictional universe in unreliable narratives.

Although solely applied to literary fiction, the proposed model may also open a path for a transmedial theory of narrative unreliability and can shed light on the media-specific means of narration in films, graphic novels or video games. For instance, ironic-unreliable narration or focalization are found in movies such as Robert Zemeckis' *Forrest Gump* or Terence Malick's *Badlands*, ambiguous-unreliable narration is found in Christopher Nolan's *Inception*, while Bryan Singer's *The Usual Suspects* or M. Night Shyamalan's *The Sixth Sense* employ altered-unreliable narration. While the semantic approach with conflicting worlds can generally be applied to unreliable narratives in different media, the focus of a transmedial theory of narrative unreliability would have to be on the media-specific narrative means of world-making and the similarities and differences of the reception-processes.

Works Cited

Àlvarez Amorós, José A. 1991. "Possible-World Semantics, Frame Text, Insert Text, and Unreliable Narration: The Case of 'The Turn of the Screw'." *Style* 25.1: 42–70.

Bierce, Ambrose. 1984 [1890]. "An Occurrence at Owl Creek Bridge." In: Ernest J. Hopkins (ed.). *The Complete Short Stories of Ambrose Bierce.* Lincoln, NE: University of Nebraska Press. 305–313.

Bode, Christoph. 2011 [2005]. *Der Roman. Eine Einführung.* Tübingen: Francke.

Booth, Wayne C. 1983 [1961]. *The Rhetoric of Fiction.* Chicago, IL: University of Chicago Press.

Bortolussi, Marisa & Peter Dixon. 2003. *Psychonarratology. Foundations for the Empirical Study of Literary Response.* Cambridge: Cambridge University Press.

Chatman, Seymour. 1990. *Coming to Terms. The Rhetoric of Narrative in Fiction and Film.* Ithaca, NY: Cornell University Press.

Chatman, Seymour. 1993 [1978]. *Story and Discourse. Narrative Structure in Fiction and Film.* Ithaca, NY: Cornell University Press.

Claassen, Eefje. 2012. *Author Representations in Literary Reading.* Amsterdam: John Benjamins.

Doležel, Lubomír. 1998. *Heterocosmica. Fiction and Possible Worlds.* Baltimore, MD: Johns Hopkins University Press.

Ellis, Bret Easton. 2006 [1991]. *American Psycho.* London: Picador.

Fludernik, Monika. 1999. "Defining (In)Sanity: The Narrator of *The Yellow Wallpaper* and the Question of Unreliability." In: Walter Grünzweig & Andreas Solbach (eds.). *Grenzüberschreitungen. Narratologie im Kontext.* Tübingen: Gunter Narr Verlag. 75–95.

Genette, Gérard. 1980. *Narrative Discourse.* Trans. Jane E. Lewin. Oxford: Blackwell.

Graesser, Arthur C. & Katja Wiemer-Hastings. 1999. "Situation Models and Concepts in Story Comprehension." In: Susan R. Goldman, Arthur C. Graesser & Paul van den Broek (eds.). *Narrative Comprehension, Causality, and Coherence. Essays in Honor of Tom Trabasso.* Mahwah, NJ: L. Erlbaum Associates. 77–92.

Graesser, Arthur C., Brent Olde & Bianca Klettke. 2002. "How Does the Mind Construct and Represent Stories?" In: Melanie C. Green, Jeffrey J. Strange & Timothy C. Brock (eds.). *Narrative Impact. Social and Cognitive Foundations.* Mahwah, NJ: L. Erlbaum Associates. 229–262.

Hartmann, Britta. 2005. "Von der Macht erster Eindrücke: Falsche Fährten als textpragmatisches Krisenexperiment." In: Fabienne Liptay

& Yvonne Wolf (eds.). *Was stimmt denn jetzt? Unzuverlässiges Erzählen in Literatur und Film.* München: Text + Kritik. 154–174.

Herman, David. 2004. *Story Logic. Problems and Possibilities of Narrative.* Lincoln, NE: University of Nebraska Press.

Herman, David. 2009. *What's the Story? Basic Elements of Narrative.* Oxford: Wiley-Blackwell.

Iversen, Stefan. 2011. "States of Exception: Decoupling, Metarepresentation, and Strange Voices in Narrative Fiction." In: Per Krogh Hansen, Stefan Iversen, Henrik Skov Nielsen et al. (eds.). *Strange Voices in Narrative Fiction.* Narratologia 30. Berlin/New York, NY: De Gruyter. 127–146.

James, Henry. 1999 [1898]. "*The Turn of the Screw.*" In: Deborah Esch & Jonathan Warren (eds.). *Henry James: The Turn of the Screw. Authoritative Text, Contexts, Criticism.* New York, NY: Norton. 1–85.

Jannidis, Fotis. 2004. *Figur und Person. Beitrag zu einer historischen Narratologie.* Narratologia 3. Berlin/New York, NY: De Gruyter.

Jess-Cooke, Carolyn. 2012. *The Boy Who Could See Demons.* London: Piatkus.

Kesey, Ken. 1963. *One Flew Over the Cuckoo's Nest.* London: Signet.

Kindt, Tom. 2008. "Werfel, Weiss and Co.: Unreliable Narration in Austrian Literature of the Interwar Period." In: Elke D'hoker & Gunther Martens (eds.). *Narrative Unreliability in the Twentieth-Century First-Person Novel.* Narratologia 14. Berlin/New York, NY: De Gruyter. 129–146.

Martínez, Matías & Michael Scheffel. 2007 [1999]. *Einführung in die Erzähltheorie.* München: C.H. Beck.

McEwan, Ian. 2002 [2001]. *Atonement.* London: Vintage.

Menhard, Felicitas. 2009. *Conflicting Reports. Multiperspektivität und unzuverlässiges Erzählen im englischsprachigen Roman seit 1800.* Trier: WVT.

Nabokov, Vladimir. 1989 [1957]. *Pnin.* New York, NY: Vintage Books.

Nünning, Ansgar. 1998. "Unreliable Narration zur Einführung: Grundzüge einer kognitiv-narratologischen Theorie und Analyse unglaubwürdigen Erzählens." In: Ansgar Nünning (ed.). *Unreliable Narration. Studien zur Theorie und Praxis unglaubwürdigen Erzählens in der englischsprachigen Erzählliteratur.* Trier: WVT. 3–40.

Nünning, Ansgar. 2008. "Reconceptualizing the Theory, History and Generic Scope of Unreliable Narration: Towards a Synthesis of Cognitive and Rhetorical Approaches." In: Elke D'hoker & Gunther Martens (eds.). *Narrative Unreliability in the Twentieth-Century First-Person Novel.* Narratologia 14. Berlin/New York, NY: De Gruyter. 29–76.

Nünning, Ansgar & Vera Nünning. 2007. "Dramatische Ironie als Strukturprinzip von *unreliable narration, unreliable focalization* und *dramatic monologue*: Ein kommunikations- und erzähltheoretischer Beitrag zur Rhetorik der Ironie im literarischen Erzähltext." In: Thomas Honegger, Eva-Maria Orth & Sandra Schwabe (eds.). *Irony Revisited. Spurensuche in der englischsprachigen Literatur. Festschrift für Wolfgang G. Müller*. Würzburg: Königshausen & Neumann. 51–82.

Palahniuk, Chuck. 2005 [1996]. *Fight Club*. New York, NY/London: Norton.

Palmer, Alan. 2002. "The Construction of Fictional Minds." *Narrative* 10.1: 28–46.

Palmer, Alan. 2009. "Attributions of Madness in Ian McEwan's *Enduring Love*." *Style* 43.3: 291–308.

Phelan, James. 2005. *Living to Tell about It. A Rhetoric and Ethics of Character Narration*. Ithaca, NY: Cornell University Press.

Phillips, Jennifer. 2009. "Unreliable Narration in Bret Easton Ellis' *American Psycho*: Interaction between Narrative Form and Thematic Content." *Current Narratives* 1.1: 60–68.

Poe, Edgar Allan. 2004 [1843]. "The Tell-Tale Heart." In: Gary R. Thompson (ed.). *Edgar Allan Poe: The Selected Writings of Edgar Allan Poe. Authoritative Texts, Backgrounds and Contexts, Criticism*. New York, NY: Norton. 317–321.

Riggan, William. 1981. *Pícaros, Madmen, Naïfs, and Clowns. The Unreliable First-Person Narrator*. Norman, OK: University of Oklahoma Press.

Rimmon-Kenan, Shlomith. 1977. *The Concept of Ambiguity. The Example of James*. Chicago, IL: University of Chicago Press.

Rimmon-Kenan, Shlomith. 2002 [1983]. *Narrative Fiction: Contemporary Poetics*. London/New York, NY: Methuen.

Ryan, Marie-Laure. 1981. "The Pragmatics of Personal and Impersonal Fiction." *Poetics* 10.6: 517–539.

Ryan, Marie-Laure. 1991. *Possible Worlds, Artificial Intelligence, and Narrative Theory*. Bloomington, IN: Indiana University Press.

Ryan, Marie-Laure. 2001. *Narrative as Virtual Reality. Immersion and Interactivity in Literature and Electronic Media*. Baltimore, MD: Johns Hopkins University Press.

Ryan, Marie-Laure. 2006. "From Parallel Universes to Possible Worlds: Ontological Pluralism in Physics, Narratology, and Narrative." *Poetics Today* 27.4: 633–674.

Schneider, Ralf. 2001. "Toward a Cognitive Theory of Literary Character." *Style* 35.4: 607–640.

Semino, Elena. 1997. *Language and World Creation in Poems and Other Texts*. London/New York, NY: Longman.

Semino, Elena. 2003. "Possible Worlds and Mental Spaces in Hemingway's 'A Very Short Story'." In: Joanna Gavins & Gerard

Steen (eds.). *Cognitive Poetics in Practice*. London/New York, NY: Routledge. 83–98.
Shen, Dan. 1989. "Unreliability and Characterization." *Style* 23.2: 300–311.
Surkamp, Carola. 2000: "Die Perspektivenstruktur narrativer Texte aus der Sicht der *possible-worlds theory*. Zur literarischen Inszenierung der Pluralität subjektiver Wirklichkeitsmodelle." In: Vera Nünning & Ansgar Nünning (eds.). *Multiperspektivisches Erzählen. Zur Theorie und Geschichte der Perspektivenstruktur im englischen Roman des 18. bis 20. Jahrhunderts*. Trier: WVT. 111–132.
Vogt, Robert. 2009. "Kann ein zuverlässiger Erzähler unzuverlässig erzählen? Zum Begriff der 'Unzuverlässigkeit' in Literatur- und Filmwissenschaft." In: Susanne Kaul, Jean-Pierre Palmier & Timo Skrandies (eds.). *Erzählen im Film. Unzuverlässigkeit—Audiovisualität—Musik*. Bielefeld: Transcript. 35–56.
Walsh, Richard. 2007. *The Rhetoric of Fictionality. Narrative Theory and the Idea of Fiction*. Columbus, OH: Ohio State University Press.
Yacobi, Tamar. 2000. "Interart Narrative: (Un)Reliability and Ekphrasis." *Poetics Today* 21.4: 711–749.
Zerweck, Bruno. 2001. "Historicizing Unreliable Narration: Unreliability and Cultural Discourse in Narrative Fiction." *Style* 35.1: 151–178.
Zipfel, Frank. 2011. "Unreliable Narration and Fictional Truth." *Journal of Literary Theory* 5.1: 109–130.
Zunshine, Lisa. 2006. *Why We Read Fiction. Theory of Mind and the Novel*. Columbus, OH: Ohio State University Press.

GUNTHER MARTENS
(Ghent)

Unreliability in Non-Fiction: The Case of the Unreliable Addressee

1. Introduction

In this article, I aim to explore unreliability in non-fictional narration. Departing from the widespread conviction that unreliable narration is only possible in fiction, I set out to define the contours of rhetorical approaches to narratology that have paved the way for the discussion of unreliability in non-fiction. I then explore unreliability in relation to non-fictional discourse, especially that found in hybrid genres such as literary documentary and docu-fiction. My argument begins by identifying stylistic criteria as a key element in the assessment of degrees of reliability and unreliability. I then go into questions of the cultural and ethical underpinnings of unreliability judgments by dealing with forms of experimental journalism and with Laurent Binet's documentary novel *HHhH*, which is discussed as a third-person antithesis to Jonathan Littell's *Les Bienveillantes*. I conclude by advocating a more addressee-oriented narratology.

2. Some Preliminaries: Towards a Rhetorical Narratology of Unreliability

"Only in fictional narrative do we have true cases of unreliability", Monika Fludernik (2001: 100) writes in "Fiction vs. *Non-Fiction*". Dorrit Cohn (2000: 307) argues that in non-fiction the unreliability rests with the author rather than the textual speaker. Most attempts to discuss non-fictional unreliability have been directed towards unreliable autobiography, i.e. in texts paying particular attention to the homodiegetic narrator (cf. Phelan 2005: Ch.2). If "true" unreliability is seen as a privilege of fiction, this is mainly due to the fact that fiction allows us quite easily and readily to reconstrue the profile of a narratorial voice solely on the basis of textual clues. But it needs to be pointed out that other paratextual and extratextual signs of unreliability have always been on the horizon of narratological theory. Tamar Yacobi's pioneering article is a typical example of a structuralist-functionalist approach to unreliability: She singles out five potential sources of unreliability: genetic, generic, existential, functional, and perspectival (1981: 114). Yacobi argues that narrative unreliability applies only in the case of perspectival unreliability, i.e. unreliability generated by the skewed perspective of an intratextual agent. Peritextual and extratextual circumstances may attenuate the communicative situation, but these were assumed not to belong to the study of narratology proper.

In a previous contribution, I presented a case for unreliability in third-person narration. I saw the necessity to do so in response to a number of strong statements as to its theoretical impossibility (see Martens 2008). In the meantime, it is feasible to say that the idea of heterodiegetic unreliability has begun to gain sway as evidenced both through specific examples such as McEwan's *Atonement* and new methodologies borrowing from analytical philosophy (cf. Köppe/Kindt 2011; Zipfel 2011). Zipfel (2011: 126) cites the specific case of Ambrose Bierce's "An Occurrence at Owl Creek Bridge" as an example. Zipfel states that it seems difficult to conceive of a narrational text with a completely covert narrator, i.e. a narrator without any personalising features, as unreliable. That is indeed the case. Almost all cases of unreliable heterodiegetic narration involve narrators stepping out of their roles. In fact, my own argument for heterodiegetic unreliability was part of a broader scrutiny of the conditions under which we assume unreliability to occur. I highlighted that Dorrit Cohn allowed for the detection of unreliability even in those cases where "corrective information" can be supplemented by other perspectival agents. She does so by squarely addressing the idea of narrative competence. Under the label of discordance, she posited "the possibility for the reader to experience a teller as normatively inappropriate for the story he or she tells" (Cohn 2000: 307). This opens up the possibility of considering stylistic overtness as a source of unreliability. In the present article, I wish to extend my considerations into the domain of non-fictional narration. This leads us to address related questions: Beyond the homodiegesis/heterodiegesis divide, why is it that we continue to privilege fiction and to link unreliability to narrators and not, for instance, to addressees? And how can we take into account gendered and other culturally determined markers of reliability? Before we can answer these questions, we need to take into account some of the basic methodological options underpinning the various branches of rhetorical narratology.

In the North-American context, the influence of Neo-Aristotelianism as propagated by the Chicago school has led to a branch of rhetorical narratology that explores the ways in which authors address and engage audiences (see Booth, Phelan, Rabinowitz, Kearns). Wayne C. Booth's *The*

Rhetoric of Fiction gained notoriety for opposing New Criticism's strict reservations concerning the 'affective fallacy'; his disciples have strengthened the links with narrative studies. This has led to a branch of narratology which focuses on volition and reader-author interaction. Its rhetorical focus on narrative, however, differs from that of stylistics or cognitive poetics: Booth and Phelan put emphasis on synthetic notions like plot, character, and genre rather than on the analysis of style, poetic diction, and figurativity as rhetorical strategies in literary communication. Wayne Booth capitalizes on the sense of collusion that irony accrues (which is definitely a rhetorical tool) and on the sense of social inclusion/exclusion that it evokes (cf. *The Company We Keep*). Phelan's taxonomy of unreliable narration presents a sophisticated development of the Boothian model while sticking to its basic tenets (including the implied author).

In a widely acclaimed article, Ansgar Nünning (1993) criticised the notion of the implied author on account of endowing textual features with human agency. Vera and Ansgar Nünning set out to give both a comprehensive structure and a history to the metaphorical notion of secret communication "behind the narrator's back" (see V. Nünning 2004; A. Nünning 2008); i.e. a story which transpires in spite of quite different intentions on the part of the narrator (conference description/introduction; cf. Vogt 2009: 38). In order to study unreliability within its historical and cultural context, Nünning, seconded by Zerweck (2001: 154f), argued that narrative theory needed to take into account both textual features and context.

At a 2005 conference in Leuven (documented in D'hoker/Martens 2008), James Phelan and Ansgar Nünning had the opportunity to cross swords and directly discuss their viewpoints. To the surprise of many, the expected clash did not take place. Phelan and Nünning concluded that their approaches were largely compatible. This unexpected outcome is due, I argue, to the phenomenological underpinnings of both theories. Booth's hypothesis of the implied author resonates with the core characteristics of a phenomenological approach to literature. It considers intention (both of the author and of the reader) as a yardstick, hence the centrality of the "implied author". In the case of Nünning, the confluence of his ideas with phenomenology is less forthcoming. But whenever constructivist principles are called upon, phenomenology is behind the corner. It turned out that Phelan's phenomenological approach and (the culturalist and rhetorical extension of) Ansgar Nünning's structuralist-functionalist approach shared a common ground. However, crucial differences cannot be ignored: In Phelan's account, the reader wants to join the "authorial audience" by definition (1996: 93). This echoes the assumptions of Chaïm Perelman's (humanist) view of the universal audience. The emphasis on judgments chimes in with Gadamer's hermeneutics and its rehabilitation of prejudice (i.e. of that which comes before reading, as detailed by Rabinowitz [1998]). In the Nünnings' account, the readers' norms are the outcome of a dynamic process contingent on shifting memory contests and involving worldmaking throughout various modes and media. The addressee is embedded in a community of memory, conceived of as a culturally and historically variable notion shaping the evaluation of facts and events. This emphasis visibly shifts attention away from the narrator and allows for the study of genres and media that rely less on the profiling of a narratorial instance (cf. Nünning/Schwanecke, in this volume).

This kind of unreliability does not primarily pertain to *facticity* (the question whether the narrative gets the extratextual facts right), nor to any psychological property of the narrating instance (since these may have been given short shrift). Rather, the unreliability inheres in the extent to which the unreliability of the addressee is brought into play. This can be achieved by exploiting the ambiguity of the deictics involved in second-person address or by the self-same procedures of dramatic irony (cf. Nünning/Schwanecke, in this volume) that apply in the case of docu-drama and docu-fiction. An added advantage of the rhetorical approach is that it is media-independent. Liesbeth Korthals Altes (2008) has advanced an encompassing contextual approach by drawing on the rhetorical notion of ethos. It is clear that the debate on unreliability has evolved to include an ever-wider range of genres and media, leading up to the question of whether there is still a common core to the concept. Brütsch (2011, and in this volume) argues that there is a fundamental difference between unreliability in literature and in film. In film, the status of events is thrown into relief by a surprise twist in retrospect although the previous report of these events is not attenuated by any conspicuous cues, e.g. argumentativeness of a profiled narrating instance. In literary fiction, Brütsch argues, unreliability is the object of a more gradual unravelling. The reader may resort to repair mechanisms in order to naturalize the conspicuous features of the discourse, but over the course of time these hypotheses will fail to resolve the inconsistencies. While I am convinced that these differences are legitimate, they appear not to neatly separate into options available exclusively to literature or film. In fact, the combination of reframing existing signifiers and of subjecting information to a specific stylistic profile is especially important in order to arrive at a comprehensive notion of unreliability in non-fiction.

3. Unreliability in Non-Fiction?

The previous considerations are important to arrive at a definition of unreliability in non-fiction. The strong assumption that true unreliability is particular to fiction at least implicitly suggests the reverse conclusion that reliability is the default case in non-fictional narration. This account is wrong-headed in many respects: In non-fictional (especially oral) communication, judgments about reliability are made at various levels long before the semantics of the message is even considered. In addition, the assessment of reliability is a matter of scale rather than a binary all-or-nothing option. Various branches of rhetoric and its modern successors—pragmatics, linguistics and sociology (Goffman)—have studied the interplay of phenomena including:

- sound: 'normal' and/or consistent psychological motivation for the telling of the story;
- body language: poise, precipitation, including the asymmetrical signs that point towards the speaker's dissociation from the message, as in 'tongue-in-cheek' irony;
- audience adaptation: including the '*captatio*', the strategic pose of unreliability in order to court the attention or the benevolence of the audience;
- hedging (gender-specific): the amount of diffidence and 'tact' appropriate or necessary in view of the authority of the audience[1];
- voice (pitch);
- iconicity: from physiognomy to UX, i.e. design in view of optimal user experience); even applies in the case of written scientific communication; cf. (Waugh/Barletta/Smith et al. 2004);
- reputation and prestige of communication channel (publication outlet).

Any of these factors can be exploited for strategic purposes. Given its allegiance to the system of language rather than the individual performance, classical narratology has prided itself in the ability to do away with these aspects to a large extent. This has also led to a persistent preoccupation with fictional story material, as narratology long cherished its ability to reconstruct the profile of a narratorial voice solely on the basis of textual

---

1 Cf. Goethe's maxim in *Die Wahlverwandtschaften*: "He who addresses others for very long without flattering them evokes antipathy. Every assertion provokes its contrary." [„Wer vor andern lange allein spricht, ohne den Zuhörern zu schmeicheln, erregt Widerwillen. Jedes ausgesprochene Wort erregt den Gegensinn." (Goethe 1971: 118)]

clues. While this focus has many merits, it would be wrong to deduce from the disjunction between fiction and non-fiction that unreliability would only apply in the former case. This is nevertheless the position defended by Ryan on account of the premises of speech-act theory.

> In natural communication, the hearer is able to detect lies, errors and other faulty declarations because he [or she] has other ways of access to the frame of reference. He [or she] can either compare the speaker's representation of facts to his own experience, or to the content of another discourse. But in fictional narration, the text constitutes the reader's sole source of information about the represented state of affairs. (Ryan 1981: 530)

I do not propose to call into doubt the fact that non-fiction offers other ways of fact-checking. But especially narratorial stances that ship with a lot of authority and reliability are prone to experimentation. In a recent article, Staes discusses encyclopaedic novels as "narratives that obscure the fiction/nonfiction divide" (Staes 2013, n. pag.). Given the fact that novels such as those written by Richard Powers and William T. Vollmann abound with references to realia, the conventional certitude that "an author or narrator's invocation of an external source gives her or him an air of reliability" (ibid.) is fatally overturned.

Narrativity itself is a mode that confers a specific authority to a communicative utterance. It owes its appeal to the depiction of a consistent storyworld, which used to be signalled through the dominant usage of the past tense. Present-tense narration poses a challenge to theories of unreliability. In texts like Irmgard Keun's *The Artificial Silk Girl* (1932) and Brett Easton Ellis' *American Psycho*, the present tense can still be seen as a sign pointing to a troubled mind. But the most recent historical fictions (e.g. Hilary Mantel's *Wolf Hall*) persistently use the present-tense in an unmarked way. Definitions of narrative themselves have shifted away from the rehashing of past experience (and from units of narrative typically enclosed within the confinements of book covers) in favour of a set of media-transitive criteria. This shift is of primary importance for the discussion of narrative unreliability since the detection of unreliability typically used to involve the detection of traits of oral discourse undermining the structured (typically written) ordering of experiences. Scholars have since drawn on theories of worldmaking that go beyond the domain of fiction strictly (see, e.g. A. Nünning 2010; V. Nünning 2010).

4. From Gonzo Journalism to Unreliable News Reports

The usage of unreliability in non-fictional discourse can be exemplified in a very palpable way by means of experiments in literary journalism. Literary, stylized forms of journalism trespass on the realm in which the journalistic narrator is expected to remain covert. In the standard interview situation, even questions are left out, so that one seems to have access to a person's verbatim discourse and to an innermost reality straight from the horse's mouth. Various extra-textual registers reinforce culturally specific norms of authority (gender, age, etc.): For a very long time, television newsreaders tended to be male by default. In order to challenge these conventions, Hunter S. Thompson launched Gonzo journalism, a type of factual storytelling which puts the emphasis on the opinions of the interviewer. Instead of the passive attitude, the journalist took the stage.

This mixture of journalistic and literary conventions has been the object of much debate. In the German-speaking context, the case of Tom Kummer gained notoriety. The former reporter of the unconventional journal *Tempo* caused a scandal when it was revealed that he had invented many of his interviews with famous Hollywood stars (which he had not met at all). In his defence, Kummer argued that his interviews were meant to satirically expose the norms of lifestyle and human interest journalism and that they were so obviously made up that any well-meaning reader would have noticed their unreliability. From a narratological point of view, one can indeed say that any type of rendering verbatim discourse involves representation, narrativization and "filling in". Kummer lost his job, but Doll accurately observes that in the long run the pose of the recalcitrant, disrespectful journalist itself was not deemed inadequate (cf. Doll 2012: 328). Quite to the contrary: This interviewing style has become mainstream. Meanwhile, Doll argues that former journalists of *Tempo* like Chistian Kracht, Benjamin von Stuckrad-Barre, and Peter Glaser took their writing to books rather than to magazines (cf. Doll 2012: 328). He links the move with an increased concern with ethical and moral standards, which occurred after 9/11. In the relatively 'safer' fictional context of novels, unreliable narrators could be given free reign.

Arguably, Christian Kracht's *Faserland* (1995) features an unreliable narrator quite reminiscent of Brett Easton Ellis' *American Psycho*. Revelling in a string of *juste milieu* references to expensive brands and trendy places, Kracht's narrator drifts in and out of the superficialities of party life. The narrator is very critical of people with ecological and moral concerns. The book was a major success due to its large amount of referentiality. One can read the book as a risky reportage underpinned by the scenario of a travel report and spiced up with participatory observations about drugs and music.

Prior to its domestication as a fictional genre, the endeavour to lend credibility to stories straining the categories of the ordinary or the believable feeds on age-old narrative traditions of story materials (legends, hagiography, urban legends) and storytelling tactics. The persistence and success of urban legends hinge on a balance achieved via rhetorical means and by merging the ordinary and the familiar with the unwarranted. The reliance on small forms ("kleine Formen" in the words of the pre-structuralist folk narratologist André Jolles), also indicates that unreliable non-fiction owes its success to the felicity of speech acts. An interesting (fictional) experiment that puts this strategy of rhetorical authorisation into perspective is Thomas Glavinic' bestselling novel *Wie man leben soll* (2004), translated as: *Pull Yourself Together* (Glavinic 2012). This novel recounts the story of a young couch potato who makes his way into life by taking the advice from self-help manuals. The manuals are a substitute for his lack of parental guidance. "One is utterly convinced that in some book one may find the answer to the question: who am I and what do I have to do?"[2] The persistent usage of gnomic sentences adds to the unreliability: The narrator casts his maturing insight into matters of sexuality and family life into lofty, aphoristic utterances which contrast starkly with his naivety and ignorance. Although we consider the psychology contained in such trashy manuals as sketchy or even trivial, the genre owes its appeal to the persistence of schemata of edifying literature and the felicity of directive and commissive speech acts (the promise that 'if you change this minor aspect in your life, happiness will ensue'). This explains why counselling continues to be such a widespread phenomenon in management, even in the management of our own private lives. Glavinic pokes fun at the sense of trust that ensues from such life manuals and ventures to write a kind of counter-manual (cf. Peeters/Niehaus 2012).

Notwithstanding all experiments and innovations, journalistic narration is still strongly supposed to be reliable by default. This can be deduced from the amount of scandal that experiments continue to elicit. We conclude this section by dealing with *Bye Bye Belgium*, a fake television documentary that shocked Belgium (cf. Dutilleul 2008). In 2006, the French-speaking national television interrupted its regular programme for a "breaking news" report. In the setting of the regular TV news studio, the regular, iconic news speaker announced that the Northern, Flemish-

---

[2] „Man ist fest überzeugt, in irgendeinem Buch dieser Welt sei zu finden, wer man ist und was man tun soll." (Glavinic 2008: 116, my translation, GM)

speaking part of the country had declared its independence. Footage showed how public transport had come to a halt at a new border dividing the country. Only after a few minutes, a subtitle indicated that the news was fiction. Of course, the unreliability of the news report could have been confirmed by switching channels: Flemish television channels were broadcasting their usual soaps and reality TV. But given the relative separation of the country's public spheres, few people were inclined to do so. The fictional news report led to a severe scandal, although it did not cost any journalists their jobs. The unreliable report was defended as an act of engaging journalism; the journalist wanted to elicit the debate. In terms of rhetorical narratology, it is interesting that the notice "Ceci est une fiction" was subliminally overturned. A reference to the Belgian surrealist René Magritte, it was meant to stress unreality, but in reality it corroborated the sense that the country's structure is so complex that reality indeed borders on surrealism. In addition, it was accompanied by an iconic picture by the painter Félicien Rops depicting a blinded lady escorting a pig. Within the attention economy of television, the visual is more reliable than the textual; moreover, any direct negation is likely to backfire. Experimental psychological research has amply shown that warnings about false claims are counterproductive and actually lend more credibility and familiarity to erroneous beliefs (Schwarz/Sanna/Skurnik et al. 2007). Thus, despite the ludicrous content, the documentary managed to authenticate or authorise itself by repurposing existing signifiers such as surrounding the country's endless debate on its federal structure and autonomist tendencies in the North and by using all the standardised signals of liveness (i.e. the interruption of an ongoing programme, even a somewhat outdated intervention by phone call). There were quite some contradictions: for instance, despite the urgency, there were many visibly prerecorded interviews. But the fact that the deliberate signals of unreliability went by unnoticed is of course due to the institutional setting overshadowing the actual narrative aspects of the message. The docu-fiction is no longer a vehicle for information, it creates a (somewhat cheap) sense of urgency and is naturally prone to reinforce the stereotypes which the two language communities harbour for one another. Deemed unacceptable by many professional journalists, the fake breaking news was unparalleled in the sense of urgency that it instated in the political issue. In the Anglophone context, the Yes Men have undertaken similar experiments, particularly in the domain of unreliable corporate storytelling (cf. Doll 2012: 391–416).

In times of information overload, media and advertising business themselves increasingly cater to the resisting, recalcitrant reader. Companies and cities order their marketing by 'rebellious' theatre groups because an unreliable, extraneous representation yields more credibility than an inside view. To some extent, unreliability has become the new norm to target addressees. These addressees are increasingly assumed to be equipped with more sophisticated decoding capacities, but they are also increasingly at a loss of cues expressive of stable irony that allow for a sense of collusion behind the back of an unreliable speaker. This is due to the increased hybridisation of formerly unified cultural and social discursive communities (pace Hutcheon).

5. New Sincerity: Binet's *HHhH*

Theorising unreliability in relation to non-fiction or hybrid fiction requires us to take into account not only media specifics but also new tendencies and trends in the literary system. Practitioners of unnatural narratology have raised unreliable narrators to the norm: "[O]ne goes from unreliable narrators to incompetent ones to delusional and then completely insane storytellers" (Richardson 2006: 2). Recent developments in literature even aim to counteract the sense that unreliability has increasingly become the norm. David Foster Wallace's ambiguous plea for post-irony and reliability is a good example:

> The next real literary 'rebels' [...] might well emerge as some weird bunch of anti-rebels, born oglers who dare somehow to back away from ironic watching, who have the childish gall actually to endorse and instantiate single-entendre principles. Who treat of plain old untrendy human troubles and emotions [...] with reverence and conviction. (1993: 192)

After postmodernism, writers like Wallace embraced and favoured new types of post-irony and sincerity (cf. Khortals Altes 2008). A typical representative of the "New Sincerity" is Laurent Binet, whose novel *HHhH* (2010) will now be discussed. The novel's title is an acronym standing for "Himmlers Hirn heißt Heydrich", pointing to a wry joke that allegedly circulated at the time of the Nazi occupation suggesting that Himmler was the real mastermind of the Nazi system. Binet's prizewinning, experimental novel *HHhH* recounts the plot to assassinate Heydrich, one of the highest-ranking members of the SS and the infamous architect of the Final Solution. The first part of the book is a kind of metafiction that deals with the narrator's frustrations and attempts to arrive at a reliable version of the story. This kind of speculative epistemology is not new; it is also present in W. G. Sebald's work and is typical of a modernist style applied to the traumas of the twentieth century.

The narrator highlights that he is not the most competent speaker by indicating that his command of German is sketchy. To some extent, this puts him into the disadvantaged position of the 'real' witnesses who had first-hand experience but did not survive the events. The metafiction qualifies him as a more reliable speaker for the purposes of the story at hand. In the second part, the narrator seems to shed his scruples and switches to a fast-paced account of the events in Prague. The novel does not attribute unreliability exclusively to the perspectival limitations of narrator, but ships with a radical doubt as to the validity of fiction as such.

The narrator refuses to make anything up; this leads him to extensively review various other books about the topic and also other fictionalizations and film adaptations. The narrator is more like an aggregator. This is another venture into the grey area that Dorrit Cohn mentioned in *Distinction of Fiction*: Explicit references to sources normally belong to historiographical discourse. Binet refers to his book as an "infra-novel" (Binet 2012: 241). To most critics, the narrator's concern with sincerity and his precautions have appeared excessive and even pedantic. Nevertheless, I think the petty concerns are justified, and they even elevate the suspense. The lengthy digressions as to whether Heydrich's convertible Mercedes was either green or black are of little importance, but they point to a broader sense of unreliability that hints at a fundamental sense of impropriety. Binet confronts the addressee with his or her propensity to fill in the gaps on the basis of story material sedimented in collective memory but also with an innate tendency towards voyeurism:

> [T]he proliferation of the 'docu-drama' bears testimony to the voyeuristic need to 'be there' and to enjoy fiction-like participation, not only in imaginary worlds, but also in historical events. (Ryan 1999: 120)

As the trauma theorist Dori Laub pointed out, there are no reliable witnesses to the events surrounding the Holocaust, even though these witnesses were sincere. At the same time, Binet's narrator raises awareness about the genre conventions to the extreme, so that the text runs the risk of becoming self-defeating: "And just so there's no confusion, all the dialogues I invent (there won't be many) will be written like scenes from a play. A stylistic drop in an ocean of reality" (Binet 2012: 21). Binet does engage in short dialogue scenes, which, however, he immediately rejects. This act of abrupt rejection is spectacular and breath-taking. As a reader, one grows aware of the immense emotional impact that these dialogues have in conventional approaches to retelling historical events.

Laurent Binet shares his epistemological concerns with Daniel Kehlmann, another prize-winning author. *Die Vermessung der Welt* (2005, translated as *Measuring the World*) solved the conundrum by taking recourse throughout the text to the German-speaking journalistic convention of the subjunctive mode, which signals objectivity as well as distance through the restriction to verbatim report. This somewhat quaint and jarring style (not retained in the English translation) allows Kehlmann to dodge the artifice of attributing dialogues and thoughts to historical characters and is explored to comic effect, since it is also used to render intimate bedroom scenes.

> He threw himself on her, felt her shock, paused for a moment, then she wound her legs around his body, but he apologized, got up, stumbled to the desk, dipped the pen, and without lighting a candle wrote *sum of square of diff. betw. Obs'd and calc'd >Min.* It was too important, he couldn't forget it. He heard her say she couldn't believe it, and she wasn't believing it either even though it was happening right in front of her. But he was already done. On the way back he hit his foot against the bedpost." (Kehlmann 2007: 127)[3]

The context of post-postmodernist New Sincerity and New Narratability may point in the direction of a generalised surpassing of unreliability. This becomes particularly evident in Binet's almost sentimental account of the last hours of the resistance fighters. At this point, the narration slips into the narrator's present: "Today is May 27, 2008. When the firemen arrive, about 8:00 a.m., they see the SS everywhere and a corpse on the pavement" (Binet 2012: 315).

The dates obviously point to the time of writing rather than that of the historical action. In a similar way, iconic film scenes are recalled in order to visualise the action.

> While this is going on, Gabčík keeps running. Tie flapping in the wind, hair messed up, he looks like Cary Grant in *North by Northwest* or Jean-Paul Belmondo in *That Man from Rio*. But obviously Gabčík, though very fit, does not have the supernatural endurance that the French actor would later display in his spoof role as a hero. Unlike Belmondo, Gabčík cannot keep running forever. (ibid.: 267)

These associations are anachronistic from the point of view of the story-world; hence, they might come across as unreliable to historians, since these personal associations clearly indicate the personal involvement of the narrator in the way in which he recounts the narrated events. Nevertheless, in a world more geared towards visual media and strategies of sampling, they are very apt to capture the atmosphere and possibly also more reliable than a painstaking reconstruction of the actual historical settings.

Binet's critical foil in writing the novel is Jonathan Littell, whom he accuses of indulging in the voyeurism and fake realism that Binet's

---

3   „Er wälzte sich auf sie, und weil er fühlte, dass sie erschrak, wartete er einen Moment, dann schlang sie ihre Beine um seinen Körper, doch er bat um Verzeihung, stand auf, stolperte zum Tisch, tauchte die Feder ein und schrieb, ohne Licht zu machen: *Summe d. Quadr. d. Differenz zw. beob. u. berechn.* → *Min.*, es war zu wichtig, er durfte es nicht vergessen. Er hörte sie sagen, sie könne es nicht glauben und sie glaube es auch nicht, selbst jetzt, während sie es erlebe. Aber er war schon fertig. Auf dem Weg zurück stieß er mit dem Fuß gegen den Bettpfosten."(Kehlmann 2005: 149)

narrator refrains from simulating. In view of its cynical, unreliable narrator and its cold, trenchant style, Binet (2012: 241) dubs Littell's novel unfavourably as "Houellebecq chez les nazis". Littell's novel evokes the perspective of a refined aesthete, leaving it up to the reader to decide whether this is a reliable perspective to judge the events of the Holocaust. The unity of this personality is not without fabrication (the protagonist is present at all the theatres of war and the most iconic crime scenes, including Auschwitz, Belaja Zerkow etc.), but it is clearly the monologic discourse of an unreliable narrator. The detection of a number of gaps and incoherencies allows the reader to pierce through the ideology of the amiable character. Littell's narrator is unreliable due to the fact that he does not offer a moral corrective to his cool and dispassionate *désinvolture* faced with extreme violence and killings, although he visibly suffers the somatic and psychic consequences of repressing his trauma. Unlike Littell's novel, Binet's book is written in the third-person, although the narrator's persona is more profiled than is usually the case. Binet's digressive narrator insists on plain and old-fashioned notions of truth and insincerity, although he continually points out the limits of knowability. It is important to note that both authors have moved on to write non-fiction, to wit journalist chronicles of political events. Binet (2013) wrote a book on Francois Hollande's presidential campaign, which is not a heroical portrait but rather a rebellious report in the sense outlined above. Littell (2012) wrote an embedded report on the civil war in Syria. Both approach their projects as explicitly fallible observers. Once more, the opinionated look is more effective than the laudatory, as Hunter S. Thompson found out. This indicates that there is some similarity between the two authors. In terms of docu-fiction, however, Binet clearly holds the view that a dispassionate, documentary approach would amount to a complicity with the perpetrator of the crimes, which were facilitated through an anonymous bureaucracy.

Binet's docu-fiction veers away from the ontological pluralism and especially the linguistic materialism of historiographical metafiction. The novel explores the relation between the referentiality of documentary narration and ethical responsibility, which is very much unlike the detective type of unreliability. It introduces a new type of naïve authenticity. As such, Binet's novel is a deliberate rebuff to our passion for unreliability. Ever since Edgar Hilsenrath's *Der Nazi & der Friseur (The Nazi and the Barber, 1971)*, we revel in the perpetrator's perspective, idiom, habitus and rhetoric; in Quentin Tarantino's *Inglourious Basterds*, only the addressee well-versed in film history (and in the director's oeuvre) will see that the 'nazi chic' is kept in check by the references to G. W. Pabst and others. When attempts are made to introduce some reliable corrective to this unreliable perspective, e.g. by the mature counterparts to the secretary

Traudl Jung in *Der Untergang* or the young lover in Schlink's *Der Vorleser*, this attempt is nowadays often experienced as inauthentic and superfluous.

6. Conclusion

By foregrounding the addressee in its title, this article aimed to interrupt the ritualised collocation of "unreliable" and "narrator". Non-fiction gives less weight to the rationale for telling a story, which might even be motivated by institutional and extratextual parameters. Hence, the narrator figures less prominently in the list of possible sources or signs of unreliability. It turns out, however, that this circumstance itself foregrounds the unreliability of the narratee as a witness and as a participant in the act of communication, especially in media which seek to engage addressees through interactivity.

Unlike fictional narratives, non-fictional narratives can in principle be subjected to fact-checking. However, the mere possibility of fact-checking non-fictional narrative does not imply that people actually take advantage of this possibility. Hybrid text genres like docu-fictional novels successfully disturb the ability to discern between fact and fiction. This observation helps to highlight historical and contextual determinants: Unreliable docu-fictions exploit tensions that have beset the rise of the modern novel since its own institutionally still underdetermined outset. The novel owed its rise to fame precisely because of the persistent encroachments on the border between fiction and non-fiction. This transitional and unstable (Richard Walsh would say rhetorical) aspect of the notion of fiction prevents us from saying that forms of non-fictional unreliability simply amount to local acts of fictionalisation. Fictional texts might indeed be self-consciously aware that they performatively bring into being a non-existing reality. But non-fictional texts are also increasingly aware of how they function as speech-acts, which is corroborated by the observation that seemingly reliable speech-act situations can be ironically overturned in non-fiction too.

Works Cited

Binet, Laurent. 2012. *HHhH*. New York, NY: Random House.
Binet, Laurent. 2013. *Rien ne se passe comme prévu*. Paris: Hachette.
Brütsch, Matthias. 2011. "Von der ironischen Distanz zur überraschenden Wendung. Wie sich das unzuverlässige Erzählen von der Literatur- in

die Filmwissenschaft verschob." *Künste Medien Ästhetik* (1/2011–1): http://www.kunsttexte.de/index.php?id=711&idartikel=37876&ausg abe=37742&zu=121&L=1. (last retrieved: January 26, 2012)
Cohn, Dorrit. 2000. "Discordant Narration." *Style* 34.2: 307–316.
D'hoker, Elke & Gunther Martens (eds.). 2008. *Narrative Unreliability in the Twentieth-Century First-Person Novel.* Narratologia 14. Berlin: De Gruyter.
Doll, Martin. 2012. *Fälschung und Fake: Zur diskurskritischen Dimension des Täuschens.* Berlin: Kulturverlag Kadmos.
Dutilleul, Philippe. 2008. *Chronique d'une imposture assumée: l'émission choc du 13 décembre 2006.* Tielt: Lannoo Uitgeverij.
Fludernik, Monika. 2001. "Fiction Vs. Non-fiction: Narratological Differentiations." In: Jörg Helbig (ed.). *Erzählen und Erzähltheorie im 20. Jahrhundert. Festschrift für Wilhelm Füger.* Heidelberg: Winter. 85–103.
Glavinic, Thomas. 2012. *Pull Yourself Together.* Trans. John Brownjohn. Seattle, WA: AmazonCrossing.
Glavinic, Thomas. 2004. *Wie man leben soll.* München: Deutscher Taschenbuch Verlag.
Goethe, Johann W. von. 1971. *Elective affinities.* Trans. Reginald J. Hollingdale. Harmondsworth: Penguin
Kehlmann, Daniel. 2005. *Die Vermessung der Welt.* Reinbek: Rowohlt.
Kehlmann, Daniel. 2007. *Measuring the World.* Trans. Carol Brown Janeway. New York, NY: Vintage Books.
Köppe, Tilmann & Tom Kindt. 2011. "Unreliable Narration With a Narrator and Without." *Journal of Literary Theory* 5.1: 81–93.
Korthals Altes, Liesbeth. 2008. "Sincerity, Reliability and Other Ironies— Notes on Dave Eggers' *A Heartbreaking Work of Staggering Genius.*" In: D'hoker & Martens 2008: 107–128.
Littell, Jonathan. 2012. *Carnets de Homs.* Paris: Gallimard.
Martens, Gunther. 2008. "Revising and Extending the Scope of the Rhetorical Approach to Unreliable Narration." In: D'hoker & Martens 2008: 77–106.
Nünning, Ansgar, 2008. "Reconceptualizing the Theory, History and Generic Scope of Unreliable Narration: Towards a Synthesis of Cognitive and Rhetorical Approaches." In: D'hoker & Martens 2008: 29–76.
Nünning, Ansgar. 2010. "Making Events—Making Stories—Making Worlds: Ways of Worldmaking from a Narratological Point of View." In: Vera Nünning, Ansgar Nünning & Birgit Neumann (eds.). *Cultural Ways of Worldmaking. Media and Narratives.* Berlin: De Gruyter. 191–214.
Nünning, Vera. 2004. "Unreliable Narration and the Historical Variability of Values and Norms: The *Vicar of Wakefield* as a Test-Case of a Cultural-Historical Narratology." *Style* 38.2: 236–252.

Nünning, Vera. 2010. "The Making of Fictional Worlds: Processes, Features, and Functions." In: Vera Nünning, Ansgar Nünning & Birgit Neumann (eds.). *Cultural Ways of Worldmaking. Media and Narratives*. Berlin: De Gruyter. 215–244.

Peeters, Wim & Michael Niehaus. 2012. "Zum diskursiven Ort von Anti-Ratgebern. Eine kleine Blütenlese." In: David Oels, Michael Schikowski, Ute Schneider et al. *Non Fiktion. Arsenal der anderen Gattungen*. 1.2: 71–86.

Phelan, James. 1996. *Narrative as Rhetoric. Technique, Audiences, Ethics, Ideology*. Columbus, OH: Ohio State University Press.

Phelan, James. 2005. *Living to Tell About It. A Rhetoric and Ethics of Character Narration*. Ithaca, NY: Cornell University Press.

Rabinowitz, Peter J. 1998. *Before Reading. Narrative Conventions and the Politics of Interpretation*. Columbus, OH: Ohio State University Press.

Richardson, Brian. 2006. *Unnatural Voices. Extreme Narration in Modern and Contemporary Fiction*. Columbus, OH: Ohio State University Press.

Ryan, Marie-Laure. 1981. "The pragmatics of personal and impersonal fiction." *Poetics* 10.6: 517–539.

Ryan, Marie-Laure. 1999. "Immersion vs. Interactivity: Virtual Reality and Literary Theory." *SubStance* 28.2: 110–137.

Schwarz, Norbert, Lawrence J. Sanna, Ian Skurnik et al. 2007. "Metacognitive Experiences and the Intricacies of Setting People straight: Implications for Debiasing and Public Information Campaigns." *Advances in Experimental Social Psychology* 39: 127–161.

Staes, Toon. 2013. "The Fictionality Debate and the Complex Texts of Richard Powers and William T. Vollmann." *Neophilologus*. 1–16.

Vogt, Robert. 2009. "Kann ein zuverlässiger Erzähler unzuverlässig erzählen? Zum Begriff der 'Unzuverlässigkeit' in Literatur- und Filmwissenschaft." In: Susanne Kaul, Jean-Pierre Palmier & Timo Skrandies (eds.). *Erzählen im Film. Unzuverlässigkeit—Audiovisualität—Musik*. Bielefeld: Transcript. 35–56.

Wallace, David Foster. 1993. "E Unibus Pluram: Television and US Fiction." *Review of Contemporary Fiction* 13.2: 151–194.

Waugh, Linda R., Norma Barletta, Susan Smith et al. 2004. "Peircean Theory, Diagrammatic Iconicity and Academic Texts: Global Structure, Abstracts, and The Role of Narrative." *Logos and Language V* 1: 39–62.

Yacobi, Tamar. 1981. "Fictional Reliability as a Communicative Problem." *Poetics Today* 2.2: 113–126.

Zerweck, Bruno. 2001. "Historicizing Unreliable Narration: Unreliability and Cultural Discourse in Narrative Fiction." *Style* 35.1: 151–178.

Zipfel, Frank. 2011. "Unreliable Narration and Fictional Truth." *Journal of Literary Theory* 5.1: 109–130.

TRANSGENERIC AND INTERMEDIAL APPROACHES

PETER HÜHN
(Hamburg)

Unreliability in Lyric Poetry

1. Problem and Approach

The term *unreliability*, originally introduced by Wayne Booth (1961) for the critical evaluation of first-person narration in fiction, is hardly ever used in the discussion and analysis of poems. If the term is applied to poetry at all, then to the sub-genre of the dramatic monologue, where the untrustworthiness of the speaker is obvious and, in fact, a constitutive feature.[1] However, the dramatic monologue is not typical of the genre of poetry as a whole but rather presents a special case on account of its hybrid combination of poetic and dramatic elements: the performance of an utterance by a persona (who is clearly dissociated from the author) addressed to a listener within an interpersonal communicative situation. Instead of exploring such obvious cases, I will approach the question of reliability specifically in lyric poems and on a more systematic basis. Furthermore, while most studies of unreliability in narrative fiction concentrate on the *reception* side, namely on the problem of how to decide whether a narrator in his utterance is reliable or not, my argumentation will start at the other end, the causes and sources of unreliability.[2]

The point of departure for the following argument is the basic condition of the communicative constellation underlying lyric poetry. Lyric poems prototypically present the monological utterance of a situated speaker in the first person.[3] Such utterances routinely employ narrative structures, predominantly of a mental kind, e.g. in the form of expe-

---

[1] For an explicit early reference to this phenomenon, see Hühn (1998: 220). The most comprehensive study of unreliability in dramatic monologues is Rohwer-Happe (2011).
[2] The present article is an elaboration and specification of the argumentation in Hühn (1998).
[3] A look at standard anthologies of English poetry shows that more than three quarters of all poems included conform to this prototype. Poems with a first-person perspective or a self-reflexive speaker comprise 88% of those selected in Hayward, ed. (1956), 76% of those in Ricks, ed. (1999), and 74% of those in Keegan, ed. (2000). Cf. also Petzold (2012: 148–151).

riences, recollections, perceptions, changes of attitude etc.[4] However, the pervasive narrative organization of lyric poems is less relevant to the present argument than the *monological stance* employed in the mediation of those narrative elements. This stance allows for variation in two respects: The speaker either addresses some other person (as is typical, for instance, in love poetry) or he soliloquizes, i.e. speaks to himself alone. As to the question of reliability, if the speaker addresses someone else, he may be either truthful or deliberately distort or conceal the truth for personal reasons. If he speaks to himself alone, the problem of reliability occurs in a different guise, as the result of *self-deception*[5] or, more generally speaking, of what I will call *self-intransparency*. To be sure, self-intransparency on principle may also function as an additional factor of unreliability in constellations where the speaker addresses someone else.

In order to explore possible causes of unreliability in lyric poetry it is therefore helpful to focus systematically and at a high level of abstraction on the stance of a person addressing himself alone and investigate his or her perspectival conditions. Lyric poems offer rich opportunities for the observation of such a single speaker in his situatedness and his perspective by directly presenting, i.e. quoting, his utterance and at the same time foregrounding the verbal medium. Thus, s/he renders the mediating text conspicuous in its (acoustic and visual) materiality and its artistry by superimposing additional regularities on the natural language material, such as prosodic patterns, lexical repetitions, parallelisms, syntactical manipulations etc. This set-up is basically equivalent to the distinction between *histoire* and *récit*, story and discourse in narrative prose fiction, but poetry differs from prose in that here the medium is given an additional, conspicuous structure clearly beyond the consciousness and responsibility of the speaker[6], which establishes an external focus on his internal perspective. To highlight this *difference in perspective* between these two levels of the poetic text, I will refer to them by the terms *enounced* and *enunciation* introduced by Antony Easthope (1983). And for the other end of the communication process, the side of reception and analysis, I will employ the analogical distinction between two reading operations, as proposed by Jonathan Culler (1981: 78–79), the contrast between *referential* and *rhetorical* interpretations, which focus on the enounced and enunciation, respectively.

---

4   See the detailed arguments for a narratological approach to poetry and the various model analyses in Hühn (2004) and Hühn/Kiefer (2005).
5   For an insightful study of the problem of self-deception in philosophy and literature, cf. Marcus (2007).
6   With the exception of poet-speakers who self-reflexively thematize the fact that they are writing poetry, i.e. their utterance is intended as a poem, as in several of Shakespeare's sonnets (e.g. 18, 65, 74, 107). Cf. Petzold (2012: 153).

2. Functions of the Double Perspective in Lyric Poetry

The single point-of-view utterance as the prototypical set-up of lyrical texts can be used and frequently has been used—by poets in their production and by readers in their reception—as the allegedly authentic self-expression of the author, suggesting emotional intimacy and private experience and variously functioning as a forum for the self-presentation of individual identity and the self-exploration of mind and consciousness, for the constitution and expression of subjective attitudes, perceptions, and emotional states. Historically, this function occurred, for instance, in classical Latin poetry in Augustan Rome, in the chivalric and Petrarchan love lyric of the late Middle Ages, in seventeenth century "metaphysical" poetry in England and again in Romanticism. Such function of seemingly unmediated self-expression is facilitated by the inherent ambivalence of the lyric genre between fictionality and factuality, between focusing on the enounced or on the level of enunciation.[7] Whether poems are treated as fictional or factual depends on historical and cultural conventions as well as on the attitude of authors and readers.

But on the other hand, the conspicuous doubleness of lyric poetry may also be utilized to *expose* the limitations and biases of perspective and consciousness. For communicating the speaker's perspective inevitably entails the logical and perspectival problems inherent in any form of self-reflexivity (as in visual perception, psychology, or mental cognition), namely the partial intransparency of the reflecting self to itself. The mind can merely see parts of itself and the self can never observe itself while observing itself—this operation will always remain a blind spot. Nor can the self, because of the fundamental perspectivism of human consciousness, ever be aware of all its qualities, motivations and conditions. In particular, the self will not see those aspects of itself which do not fit its self-image and therefore threaten its self-esteem. It will overlook, ignore, or re-interpret those features which it is unwilling or unable to face. Although limitedness of consciousness and partial self-intransparency is a universal human condition, it need not be thematized in a poem, i.e. it is not of necessity foregrounded as a problem. In fact, poems predominantly tend to neglect this aspect altogether or deliberately play it down, in their speakers' attempts, for instance, to constitute themselves as stable identities—and readers routinely and intuitively tend to trust the speaker's view and judgment.

In this respect, there is a clear structural similarity between poetry and the narrative genre in that in both cases a voice (the speaker and the

---

7   See Zipfel (2011); Zymner (2009: 10–12); Hühn (2014).

narrator, respectively) presents a specific internal or external state of affairs, a view of a supposedly real, imagined, or fictive world from a restricted position and perspective. It is within this context that one may address the question of the causes of unreliability in first-person utterances in poems and of its possible functions. So far, this phenomenon has rarely been discussed with respect to poetry, in spite of its analogy to narrative texts.[8]

3. Two Models for Analyzing First-Person Utterances

For the analysis of such utterances, I will employ an approach that focuses on the processes and perspectives of *observation* as they occur at various levels of the text, combining models developed in poetics (Easthope) and systems theory (Luhmann). Both models conceive of the self as constituted of human consciousness and as the result of a dynamic interaction between two dimensions of the mind.[9] The combination of these models provides a close conceptual link between the operations of consciousness and the organization of poetic form, between self and poetry.

Drawing on linguistic and psychoanalytic theories (Benveniste; Jakobson; Lacan), Easthope (1983: 40–47) distinguishes two subjects in poetry, i.e. dimensions in the written text of the poem—the subject of the *enounced* and the subject of *enunciation*. The subject of the enounced is the grammatical subject of the reported happenings, and in the case of first-person utterances, the explicit speaker or persona who produces what is actually and consciously communicated. The subject of enunciation refers to the agent who—by the very act of composing the poetic text— produces the subject of the enounced, creating and shaping the enounced utterance as a material process of signifiers, with particular intentions and, possibly, hidden implications. The speaker of the text merely seems to be the subject of the reported events and perceptions, and poems usually tend to play down or even hide the existence of the higher level, that of the subject of enunciation. In the last analysis this is, of course, the actual author of the poem. However, since the writer may not have been fully aware of all implications of his text and of all his own motives, it seems

---

[8] An exception is Petzold (2012: 154), who briefly illustrates the application of this term to poetry by Blake's "The Chimney Sweeper" and—unspecifically—by Browning's dramatic monologue "My Last Duchess".

[9] These two models—Easthope's concept of verbal communication (*enounced/enunciation*) and Luhmann's notion of perspective (*observation of the first order/the second order*)—might be supplemented by Mead's (1964 [1934]) symbolic interactionism, his social psychological model of identity (*I/Me*).

preferable to call this agent neutrally *subject of enunciation* to avoid biographical speculation.[10] It is this level which—through the material structure of the text, such as connotations of words, implications of images and syntactical patterns, stylistic biases etc.—contains what is repressed, distorted or hidden and therefore absent from the level of the enounced. These two dimensions of the language of the poem correspond to Culler's distinction between the *referential*, referring to the enounced, and the *rhetorical*, referring to enunciation (1981: 78).

The complication of levels can be specified further by applying Niklas Luhmann's notion of *observation*, a concept which comprises all forms of sensory perception, mental imagination, artistic creation, interpretation and judgment, not only of empirical but also of fictive phenomena, objects and states of affairs (Luhmann 1990: 23–25; 1997: 1117–1124; 1998: 46–50). Observation always operates through selecting and structuring that which is being observed by distinguishing it from what it is not and thereby creating what Luhmann calls a "form". However, there is always something which unavoidably escapes observation—the blind spot, especially the observer himself and his own standpoint. The individual consciousness observes the world and it observes others observing the world. But it can also—through self-reflection—observe itself, though only partially and, ultimately, only retrospectively. Thus, a hierarchical succession of levels is established: first-order observation observes objects; second-order observation observes another observer; if someone observes another observer observing an observer, this is an instance of third-order observation. In the last analysis, third-order observation is also a form of second-order observation, albeit on a higher level. Poetry, like art in general, provides a particularly apt medium—and model—for the conscious mind (of the persona) to observe itself and, furthermore, to allow for the possibility of observing the mind observing itself.

Since every observation of necessity excludes parts or areas of the observer himself, his standpoint and motivation as blind spots, the observation of oneself *after the event*, on the next higher level makes these blind spots visible. But the second-order observation, in its turn, necessarily creates new blind spots for itself: its own position, motivation, attitude etc. The identity—as rendered on the level of the enounced, the first-order

---

10 The term "subject of enunciation" is meant to replace the controversial terms "implied author" or "abstract author" frequently used in discussions of unreliability in narrative fiction. One concomitant question connected with all these terms, namely whether unreliability is ultimately to be attributed to the speaker/narrator, the structure of the text (against the presumed conscious intentions of the author) or the author's disposition, has to be answered individually and specifically in each case, with respect to context and author's oeuvre and biography. In many cases this question will ultimately be undecidable.

observation of the mind—can never comprise the whole of the individual. That this is so can be perceived from the next higher level, the second-order observation, i.e. the perspective of the subject of enunciation. But, with respect to the poetic utterances, the entire set-up is made observable for the reader, who then is able to take the position of a third-order observer identifying the blind spots and biases of the subject of the enounced and, moreover, also those of the subject of enunciation, though the latter requires more of a conscious effort.[11]

Observing observers opens additional scopes of meaning and enables new strategies of understanding. While to the first-order observer the world or the state of affairs—that which is being observed—seems to be unquestionably what it is, for an observer of the second order everything becomes *contingent* ("it could be otherwise"): he can see that "*what* is observed depends on *who* is being observed" (Luhmann 1998: 48). Thus, second-order observation offers a choice with regard to *attribution*, which likewise applies to the reader of poetry:

> [the] choice [...] whether certain designations are to be attributed to the observed observer [i.e. the persona of the poem], thereby characterizing him, or seen as characteristics of what he observes. Both attributions, observer attribution and object attribution, are possible. (ibid.)

To combine Luhmann's categories with Culler's and Easthope's terms: Any utterance may be read either referentially or rhetorically, depending on whether the particular rendering of a state of affairs is attributed to the subject of the enounced or to the subject of enunciation. Attribution one way or the other may be supported by referring to stylistic and formal signals in the text, for instance, to internal discrepancies or contradictions which would have to be ascribed to the level of enunciation.

By way of exemplification, I will apply these analytical categories to two poems with different degrees of complexity, representing two types and functions of unreliability in lyric poetry.

4. William Wordsworth's "The World Is Too Much with Us"

The first—relatively simple—example is William Wordsworth's sonnet "The World Is Too Much with Us" (1802), which presents a typical Romantic form and function of self-intransparency.

> 1   The world is too much with us; late and soon,
>   Getting and spending, we lay waste our powers:

---

[11] In order to detect unreliability, the reader has to identify textual clues and interpret them with respect to relevant schemata and conceptual frameworks. Cf. Nünning (2005).

           Little we see in Nature that is ours;
           We have given our hearts away, a sordid boon!
     5   This Sea that bares her bosom to the moon;
           The winds that will be howling at all hours,
           And are up-gathered now like sleeping flowers;
           For this, for everything, we are out of tune;
           It moves us not.—Great God! I'd rather be
     10   A Pagan suckled in a creed outworn;
           So might I, standing on this pleasant lea,
           Have glimpses that would make me less forlorn;
           Have sight of Proteus rising from the sea;
           Or hear old Triton blow his wreathèd horn.[12]

The speaker (the subject of the enounced, the first-order observer) states and laments the meaninglessness and disenchantment of the world: "we lay waste our powers: / Little we see in Nature that is ours" (2–3), "for everything, we are out of tune" (8). He sees this fundamental loss as caused especially by commercialism and, implicitly, concomitant rationalism, indicated by the phrases "the world" and most specifically "getting and spending", which can be taken to refer to the contemporary process of economic modernization in Britain, the growing dominance of the market principle regulating people's behavior and motivation. But in the course of his lament, the speaker comes to describe the actual natural scenery first in metaphorical (5–7) and finally in mythological terms (13–14), which effectively constitutes an experience of animated nature after all and thus inadvertently belies the statement of loss: "This Sea that bares her bosom to the moon; / The winds [...] are up-gathered now like sleeping flowers" (5–7) and "Have sight of Proteus rising from the sea; / Or hear old Triton blow his wreathèd horn" (13–14). The unwitting transformation of the speaker's perception of, and attitude towards, nature as expressed in these descriptions is accompanied by a surreptitious shift in the pronouns, paralleled at the formal level by the sonnet's traditional volta, namely the shift from the plural "we"/"us" in the octave (1–9) to the singular "I"/"me" in the sestet (9–14), from the collective and social realm to the individual's subjective position. That is, by distancing himself from general modern developments, the individual proves capable of preserving in his mind the archaic capacity of spontaneous creative imagination. This internal self-contradiction within the expression of his lament reveals the speaker's utterance as unreliable.

The unreliability in Wordsworth's sonnet is not caused by the speaker's intention to deceive or to hide discreditable aspects of his

---

12 In: Selincourt/Darbishire, eds. (1946: 18–19).

personality or deficits in his character, but rather by self-intransparency, his ignorance about his still-existing capacity of vitalizing response to nature. From its higher vantage point, the subject of enunciation (the second-order observer) demonstrates how the speaker's desperate complaint about this loss in conjunction with the passionate desire for such a meaningful experience inadvertently leads to the imaginative re-enchantment of the world—re-animating nature and re-creating the ancient gods in their living presence. The clarity of this self-contradiction suggests that the process and the result have been arranged deliberately by the (real or implied) author, whose operations the readers—as superior (third-order) observers—can then perceive and analyze. The poetic text purposefully stages the complaint about the loss of meaning in order to evince the still extant, merely latent creative vitality of the mind. Self-intransparency in this poem has the function of preventing excessive self-consciousness and self-observation, which would block spontaneous imagination, which for Romantic poets is the prime vital source of artistic creativity. In this respect the poem enacts the process by which the speaker's mind, if the attention is momentarily directed elsewhere, proves still capable of spontaneously creative imagination. In other words, the utterance of the sonnet can be attributed both as an experience to the subject of the enounced, powerlessly lamenting the loss, but also as a strategic action to the subject of enunciation, manipulating the lament for the demonstration of imaginative poetic writing. Assuming that the author deliberately conveyed this purpose, the reader can read the rhetorical meaning referentially, as pointing to, and evincing, the actual author's own poetic creativity under modern disillusioning conditions.[13]

5. Sir Thomas Wyatt's "They Flee from Me That Sometime Did Me Seek"

The second—much more complex—example is Wyatt's poem "They Flee from Me That Sometime Did Me Seek" (probably written in the 1530s). Pragmatically, the text presents a soliloquy because the speaker addresses himself alone and not his lady, although one can, of course, imagine the utterance indirectly intended for an audience.

---

[13] Interestingly, there is almost no discussion of this sonnet in Wordsworth criticism, presumably because critics have failed to see the fundamental problem and the strategy of its solution underlying this poem. One rare exception is a brief unspecific comment in Davies (1986: 143). Davies identifies the "delicate balance between imaginative and self-critical impulses" but then merely states the impulsive progress in the course of the poem from the acknowledged lack to the mythic glimpses. He does not recognize the underlying problem and denies that there has been any kind of self-deception.

1	They flee from me that sometime did me seek,
	With naked foot stalking in my chamber.
	I have seen them gentle, tame, and meek
	That now are wild and do not remember
5	That sometime they put themself in danger
	To take bread at my hand; and now they range
	Busily seeking with a continual change.
	Thanked be fortune it hath been otherwise
	Twenty times better, but once in special,
10	In thin array after a pleasant guise,
	When her loose gown from her shoulders did fall
	And she me caught in her arms long and small,
	And therewithal all sweetly did me kiss
	And softly said, 'Dear heart, how like you this?'
15	It was no dream: I lay broad waking.
	But all is turned thorough my gentleness
	Into a strange fashion of forsaking.
	And I have leave to go of her goodness
	And she also to use newfangleness.
20	But since that I so kindly am served,
	I would fain know what she hath deserved.[14]

The persona, the subject of the enounced, situates himself within the discourse of Petrarchism (in the role of the unrequited lover, though not of the poet) only to announce the repudiation of the entire convention. The referential intention of the utterance on the level of first-order observation is the relinquishment of the role of the Petrarchist male lover and the rejection of the lady because of her betrayal of him. In another respect, the Petrarchan convention is already undermined retrospectively when the speaker recalls the consummation of their love in the past (14) and when he hints at a plurality of former loves (1 ff.). In his present observation of their past relationship, the speaker distributes right and wrong quite one-sidedly between himself and his former lady. The technique the speaker employs is meant to disparage her morally in two ways: On the one hand, he accuses her directly of promiscuity ("they range / Busily seeking with a continual change," 6–7; "use newfangleness", 19). On the other, he ironically takes the blame for her behavior: "But all is turned thorough my gentleness / Into a strange fashion of forsaking" (16–17). Not only did his behavior, he insinuates, not justify her turning away from him but, on the contrary, its very exemplariness ought rather to have strengthened her attachment to him. That she should have taken unfair advantage of his civilized attitude is condemned ("observed") as particularly discrediting. When the speaker sarcastically describes his treatment by her as "I so

---

14 In: Rebholz, ed. (1978: 116–117).

kindly am served" (20), he both reverses the conventional roles (the male lover should be the one that serves) and denigrates her very nature—and possibly that of the female sex in general—as immoral ("kindly" also meaning "naturally", "according to her nature"[15]). These attacks, ironies (in "goodness" and "kindly"), and his demand for a just punishment all project the self-image of the gentle self-restrained male lover who feels wronged and vents his sufferings in manly indignation.

The enunciation of the poem, i.e. the rhetorical presentation of the utterance, the choice of words and especially their connotations, constitutes the level of second-order observation, a perspective that lies outside the speaker's consciousness and allows the reader to observe his blind spots, that which he is unable or unwilling to see. The blind spot in this case concerns the underlying *motives* of his vented indignation, which are chiefly conveyed through the connotations of the metaphors used and defined in terms of *power relations*, as a tension between control and freedom. While the speaker styles himself as passive, the lady—or woman in general (as the plural seems to suggest)—is associated by him with activity and natural freedom, underlined by the animal metaphors in the first stanza. The woman is said to be wild by nature and untamed. She temporarily and voluntarily suspended her independence to become "gentle, tame and meek" (3) while she was in love with the speaker, only to revert to her unrestricted natural freedom later: "now are wild" (4), "now they range" (6), "a strange fashion of forsaking" (17). But the context and the wording betray that the speaker's passivity is merely a form of suspended and hidden power, an indirect but effective manner of acting, as revealed by the expression "they put themself *in danger* to take bread at my hand" (5–6): The phrase "in danger" in early modern English means "in (my) power"[16] as well as "in peril". He suspended his power and used a kind of bait ("bread") to induce, in fact to seduce, her to give up her freedom (her wildness) and become "tame". The same phenomenon is then described in non-metaphorical terms: "my gentleness" (16) implies voluntary civilized relinquishment of force, aggressiveness and rudeness. Furthermore, that this passivity is only a disguised form of power is betrayed by his self-righteous indignation about her leaving him despite his gentleness. He resents this freedom which by his whole attitude ("gentleness") he had seemed to generously grant her. His resentment is also revealed by the fact that he maliciously discredits her independence by equating it with morally reprehensible promiscuity. The bad faith inherent in his indignation becomes apparent against the background that he had welcomed her love

---

15   See *Oxford English Dictionary* s.v. "kindly" (I.1.a.).
16   See *Oxford English Dictionary* s.v. "danger" (A.1.a).

and that he himself has had numerous affairs, too, as acknowledged by the plural in the first stanza ("they"; "them").

The speaker's implied motives for accusing his lady—resentment and desire for power as the result of the loss of power—are clearly not part of his conscious utterance since they are discreditable emotions and would undercut his communicative strategies. The mind has to remain partially intransparent to itself in order to be able to make this accusation and stabilize itself morally in a crisis of loss.[17]

It is debatable whether Wyatt deliberately arranged the text to present the disappointed Petrarchist lover's perspective as well as a superior perspective which allows for the observation of the hidden motives. One can assume that he was at least semi-conscious of this discrepancy[18], but that his gender-specific involvement in these discourses prevented a detached view of the contradictory motives (Friedman 1967). However, regardless of the question of authorial intention, "They Flee from Me That Sometime Did Me Seek" is an early example of unreliability in English poetry, of self-intransparency and the implicit thematization of unacknowledged motives. The reader as a third-order observer is able to compare the first- and second-order observations with one another and assess how they develop their respective strategies of presenting particular concepts of the self.[19] The male individual is caught in the interplay of various discourses: the gender-specific discourse of courtly love and that of male self-assertion on the one hand, the general discourse of power on the other. Whereas the subject of the enounced uses a specific strategy to stabilize himself and gain his objectives partly by hiding his own motives from himself, the subject of enunciation betrays these very motives. One might add that this second-order observer in turn hides the motives for unmasking the motivation of the subject of the enounced. The reader can then speculate on these motives: disillusionment, debunking, sympathetic understanding?

From a social perspective this complex set-up fits into the precarious and highly pressurized situation at the absolutist court of Henry VIII, which forced the courtiers to develop elaborate techniques of role-acting, self-fashioning, and dissimulation. Wyatt, because of his own practical

---

17 Some critics have noticed the disparity in this poem without, however, clearly identifying the phenomenon of self-deception, bad faith and unreliability. Cf., for example, Panja (1988) and Graham (1989). This also goes for the more specific description of the differences and distinctions in the presentation of speaker and lady as well as their confusing and dissolution in Heale (1998: 52–53).

18 Cf. the discussion of the moral dilemma entailed in the use of rhetorical eloquence in Wyatt's work by Hannen (1974).

19 That it is also possible for a reader to read this poem merely referentially and accept the speaker's utterance as reliable is exemplified by Brigden (2012: 23–28).

experiences in this environment, was intimately familiar with the contradictory conditions of the courtier's existence. Moreover, he was particularly sensitive to the potentials of language and its ambiguity in role-acting as well as to the function poetry could have in fashioning and presenting a self. But personally he was so caught up in the contradictory codes of love, power, and self-fashioning that his attitude towards them remained fundamentally ambivalent.[20]

6. Conclusion

These two examples of unreliability in lyric poetry document two different functions. In Wordsworth's sonnet, self-intransparency is utilized (by the subject of enunciation) to enable—inadvertently and spontaneously—the production of meaning, structure and order in a situation of loss, instability and decay. This recovery and re-stabilization is achieved by screening off the vital, creative areas of the mind against debilitating self-observation and paralyzing self-consciousness, thus allowing a new insight, a new meaning, a new confidence to emerge spontaneously. The reader can then vicariously participate in this experience. Adopting James Phelan's terminology (Phelan 2007), one can tentatively designate this type of unreliability or self-intransparency as a *bonding* strategy. To sketch a few further comparable examples, significantly by Romantic and Post-Romantic poets: In Coleridge's "Kubla Khan" (1798)[21], the speaker's lament about his failure to complete a work of art is surprisingly granted fulfillment, behind his back, in the innovative—fragmentary—artistic form of the very lament itself. Somewhat similarly, in Shelley's "Ode to the West Wind" (1820)[22], the poem as such belies the speaker's complaint about his lack of artistic creativity, whereas Keats's "Ode on a Grecian Urn" (1819)[23] shows how after two failing attempts to find consolation and relief from human misery in the imaginary world of art, the work of art itself inadvertently seems to utter a consoling statement. In Yeats's "The Second Coming" (1920)[24], the speaker, shattered by a fundamental cultural crisis, inadvertently can orient and stabilize himself through a visionary insight, which (like in Keats's ode) is not warranted by any independent

---

20 Cf. Greenblatt's (1980: 150–156) detailed interpretation of this poem. Greenblatt highlights a dialectical tension between manipulative manly self-representation and critical independence but does not precisely locate and relate these two forces.
21 In: Coleridge, ed. (1967: 295–298). The narrative introduction about the "vision in a dream", normally not printed, has to be considered an integral part of the text.
22 In: Keegan, ed. (2000: 642–643).
23 In: Keegan, ed. (2000: 637–638).
24 In: Ricks, ed. (1999: 525–526).

clues but has to be classified as a spontaneous subjective projection not seen through by the speaker himself; and although the aging speaker in Yeats's "Sailing to Byzantium" (1928)[25] insists on seeking a new artistic existence only outside nature and all natural forms, he inadvertently envisages himself finally in the shape of a singing bird, thereby betraying his inescapable attachment to the natural world.

In Wyatt's poem, in contradistinction to Wordsworth, unreliability refers to hidden, potentially discreditable motives, which the speaker has to repress or overlook to stabilize himself and protect his self-love in a situation of crisis; in this case unjustified resentment and accusation. Should the speaker become fully aware of his motives, these would undermine his positive unified self-image and force him to act differently. Using Phelan's terms, one can call this an *estranging* strategy on the part of the subject of enunciation. Other examples are Wyatt's "My Lute, Awake" (1530s)[26], in which the speaker's elaborate renunciation of his lady and his desire to take revenge betray his unrecognized lasting attachment. In Blake's "London" (1794)[27], the speaker—by rigorously uncovering and criticizing repressive and authoritarian structures everywhere—inadvertently reveals a similar absolutist rigorism in himself, and in several of Shakespeare's sonnets to his young friend (1609)[28], unreliability is deliberately staged and employed to put moral pressure on the friend: in sonnet 71, e.g. the speaker urges his friend to forget him but the very request is in fact meant to countermand this order and ensure continued remembrance; in sonnet 87, the speaker pretends to give up any claim on the friend in view of his own unworthiness, thereby surreptitiously contradicting himself by implying the very opposite, namely arrogance and inflated self-esteem on the part of the friend.[29]

Both strategies may be called enabling functions, the one (as in Wordsworth's sonnet) motivated by a *desire* for compensation in a situation of lack or loss, the other (as in Wyatt's poem) driven by *anxiety* to ward off a threatening violation of self-esteem in a situation of crisis.[30] It remains to be seen whether these two functions can be confirmed by a more comprehensive look at the history of poetry.

25　In: Keegan, ed. (2000: 892–893).
26　In: Rebholz, ed. (1978: 144–145).
27　In: Keegan, ed. (2000: 541).
28　In: Kerrigan, ed. (1986: 112, 120).
29　The deliberate staging of unreliability in Shakespeare's sonnets has to do with the communicative set-up. Most of the sonnets in the first part of the sequence are directly or imaginatively addressed to the young friend.
30　These two alternative motives for unreliability in lyric poetry can be compared to the two basic types of motivation identified by Marcus (2007: 23 ff.) for self-deception.

Works Cited

Booth, Wayne C. 1961. *The Rhetoric of Fiction*. Chicago, IL: University of Chicago Press.

Brigden, Susan. 2012. *Thomas Wyatt. The Heart's Forest*. London: Faber & Faber.

Coleridge, Ernest H. (ed.). 1967. *Coleridge: Poetical Works*. Oxford: Oxford University Press.

Culler, Jonathan. 1981. *The Pursuit of Signs: Semiotics, Literature, Deconstruction*. London: Routledge & Kegan.

Davies, Hugh S. 1986. *Wordsworth and the Worth of Words*. Ed. John Kerrigan & Jonathan Wordsworth. Cambridge: Cambridge University Press.

Easthope, Antony. 1983. *Poetry as Discourse*. London: Methuen.

Friedman, Donald M. 1967. "The Mind in the Poem: Wyatt's 'They Flee from Me'." In: *Studies in English Literature 1500–1700*. 7.1: 1–13.

Graham, Kenneth J. E. 1989. "The Performance of Conviction: Wyatt's Antirhetorical Plainness." *Style* 33: 374–394.

Greenblatt, Stephen. 1980. *Renaissance Self-Fashioning. From More to Shakespeare*. Chicago, IL: University of Chicago Press.

Hannen, Thomas A. 1974. "The Humanism of Sir Thomas Wyatt." In: Thomas O. Sloan & Raymond B. Waddington (eds.). *The Rhetoric of Renaissance Poetry from Wyatt to Milton*. Berkeley, CA: University of California Press. 37–57.

Hayward, John (ed.). 1956. *The Penguin Book of English Verse*. Harmondsworth: Penguin.

Heale, Elizabeth. 1998. *Wyatt, Surrey and Early Tudor Poetry*. London/New York, NY: Longman.

Hühn, Peter. 1998. "Watching the Speaker Speak: Self-Observation and Self-Intransparency in Lyric Poetry." In: Mark Jeffreys (ed.). *New Definitions of Lyric: Theory, Technology, and Culture*. New York, NY/London: Garland. 215–244.

Hühn, Peter. 2004. "Transgeneric Narratology: Applications to Lyric Poetry." In: John Pier (ed.). *The Dynamics of Narrative Form: Studies in Anglo-American Narratology*. Narratologia 4. Berlin/New York, NY: De Gruyter. 139–158.

Hühn, Peter & Jens Kiefer. 2005. *The Narratological Analysis of Lyric Poetry: Studies in English Poetry from the 16th to the 20th Century*. Narratologia 7. Berlin/New York, NY: De Gruyter.

Hühn, Peter. "Problems of Fictionality and Factuality in Poetry." *Narrative* 22.2: 155–168.

Keegan, Paul (ed.). 2000. *The New Penguin Book of English Verse*. London: Alan Lane & Penguin.
Kerrigan, John (ed.). 1986. *William Shakespeare: The Sonnets and A Lover's Complaint*. Harmondsworth: Penguin.
Luhmann, Niklas. 1990. "Weltkunst." In: Niklas Luhmann, Frederick D. Bunsen & Dirk Baecker (eds.). *Unbeobachtbare Welt. Über Kunst und Architektur*. Bielefeld: Cordula Haux. 7–45.
Luhmann, Niklas. 1997. *Die Gesellschaft der Gesellschaft*. 2 vols. Vol. 2. Frankfurt am Main: Suhrkamp.
Luhmann, Niklas. 1998. *Observations of Modernity*. Trans. William Whobrey. Stanford, CA: Stanford University Press.
Marcus, Amit. 2007. *Self-Deception in Literature and Philosophy*. Trier: WVT.
Mead, George H. 1964 [1934]. *Mind, Self and Society from the Standpoint of a Social Behaviorist*. Charles W. Morris (ed.). Chicago, IL: University of Chicago Press.
Nünning, Ansgar. 2005. "Reconceptualizing Unreliable Narration: Synthesizing Cognitive and Rhetorical Approaches." In: James Phelan & Peter J. Rabinowitz (eds.). *A Companion to Narrative Theory*. Oxford: Blackwell. 89–107.
Panja, Shormishta. 1988. "Ranging and Returning: The Mood-Voice Dichotomy in Wyatt." *English Literary Renaissance* 18.3: 347–368.
Petzold, Jochen. 2012. *Sprechsituationen lyrischer Dichtung. Ein Beitrag zur Gattungstypologie*. Würzburg: Königshausen & Neumann.
Phelan, James. 2007. "Estranging Unreliability, Bonding Unreliability, and the Ethics of *Lolita*." *Narrative* 15.2: 222–238.
Rebholz, Ronald A. (ed.). 1978. *Sir Thomas Wyatt. The Complete Poems*. Harmondsworth: Penguin.
Ricks, Christopher (ed.). 1999. *The Oxford Book of English Verse*. Oxford: Oxford University Press.
Rohwer-Happe, Gislind. 2011. *Unreliable Narration im dramatischen Monolog des Viktorianismus. Konzepte und Funktionen*. Göttingen/Bonn: V&R unipress & Bonn University Press.
Selincourt, Ernest de & Helen Darbishire (eds.). 1946. *The Poetical Works of William Wordsworth*. Vol. 3. Oxford: Clarendon.
Zipfel, Frank. 2011. "Lyrik und Fiktion." In: Dieter Lamping (ed.). *Handbuch Lyrik. Theorie, Analyse, Geschichte*. Stuttgart/Weimar: Metzler. 162–166.
Zymner, Rüdiger. 2009. *Lyrik. Umriss und Begriff*. Paderborn: Mentis.

Ansgar Nünning & Christine Schwanecke
(Gießen)

The Performative Power of Unreliable Narration and Focalisation in Drama and Theatre: Conceptualising the Specificity of Dramatic Unreliability

1. Prologue: Unreliable Narration and Focalisation in Drama and Theatre as Lacunae in Narratology[1]

Although the unreliable narrator has been an important concept in narratology ever since Wayne C. Booth first proposed it as a category of textual analysis in 1961, the forms and functions of unreliable narration have mainly been studied in conjunction with narrative fiction. The recent boom in transgeneric and intermedial narratology (cf. Nünning/Nünning 2002; Meister 2005; Ryan 2005) has led to an extension of scholarly interest in the uses of unreliable narration in other genres and media, though narratologists have, so far, largely focused on film (cf. Ferenz 2008; Laass 2008) and poetry (cf. Anastasopoulos 2011; Rohwer-Happe 2011).

In view of this state of research, it is rather astounding that one major genre which also often features unreliable narrators, namely, drama, has not yet received as much narratological attention as it arguably deserves. As Brian Richardson stated,

> [p]erhaps the most flagrant omission in point-of-view theory is the absence of any discussion of the dramatization of an individual consciousness in the theater. [...] [I]t is presumed that dramatic representation is invariably objective, unmediated, devoid of subjectivity, and in Bakhtinian terms, entirely monological. (1988: 204)

Unfortunately, this statement still holds true one quarter of a century later. Although there are some laudable exceptions to this rule (e.g., Richardson 1988; Hesse 2009) narratologists have not yet displayed much interest in the dramatisation and staging of individual consciousness and in the uses and functions of unreliable narration in drama and theatre. This comes as

---

[1] We would like to cordially thank our colleague Elizabeth Kovach for her careful proofreading of our article at various stages of its development and for making valuable suggestions for stylistic improvements.

a bit of a surprise because both the extra-diegetic narrators and focalisers that we find in a host of plays of the twentieth and twenty-first centuries, as well as characters who tell stories within the storyworlds of many plays, can be, and often are, unreliable narrators. Unreliable narration is arguably a transgeneric, transmedial, and interdisciplinary phenomenon, though the forms and functions in which it becomes manifest may vary considerably from one genre, medium, or discourse to another.

Drawing upon state-of-the-art research on unreliable narration in narratology, we would like to begin by pointing out that the conceptualisation of the phenomenon which has been found to occur in literary texts has always been at least implicitly linked to drama and drama theory—a crucial fact which often goes unnoticed or unmentioned by narratologists. This is why we emphasise that, from the very beginnings of research on the subject, unreliability has been conceptualised in terms of irony,[2] especially of '*dramatic* irony'.[3] Against this backdrop, some blind spots in narratology can be revealed. Firstly, since instances of unreliable narration that occur in literary narratives are structurally similar to cases of 'dramatic irony,' which has been a traditional and common stylistic feature in drama, it is certainly worth asking to what extent narratology and drama theory can mutually illuminate each other in their attempts at coming to terms with the phenomenon of unreliability. Secondly, given that unreliability in literary texts has often been explained with recourse to concepts and terms originating within drama theory, new light could be shed on both fields by taking into consideration the trajectory of the 'travelling concepts' (*sensu* Bal) of dramatic irony and unreliable narration as they have travelled from drama theory to narratology and potentially back again. This could also help to uncover the hitherto unexplored uses of unreliability in drama and theatre. These issues become all the more pertinent in the context of the recent interest in transgeneric phenomena in narrative theory.

What has come to be known as 'transgeneric narratology' (cf. Nünning/Nünning 2002) has successfully managed to redirect narratological attention to genres that were traditionally considered to be non-narrative and, thus, beyond the scope of narratological inquiry. It is quite

---

[2] Wayne C. Booth understands 'irony' as a device triggering unreliable narration (cf. Booth 1961: 304). Note also Greta Olson's reading of Booth's (1975 [1974]) explanation of how we process irony in a literary work (cf. Olson 2003: 94–95).

[3] Ansgar and Vera Nünning have gone one step further than Olson, pointing out that the text-internal and text-external processes involved in understanding unreliability can be explained in terms of 'dramatic irony': "Um die Mechanismen zu erklären, auf denen der Eindruck mangelnder Glaubwürdigkeit eines Erzählers oder einer Fokalisierungsinstanz beruht, bedarf es daher eines Rückgriffs auf das Konzept der dramatischen Ironie." (Nünning/Nünning 2007: 66)

striking, though, that drama still seems to have remained the stepchild of transgeneric narratology. While theorists have been primarily concerned with developing narratological models that apply to lyric poetry (cf. Hühn/Schönert 2002; Hühn 2004; Hühn/Kiefer 2005), only relatively few narratologists have also extended their scope of research to include drama (cf., however, e.g., Nünning/Sommer 2002; Hühn/Sommer 2009). Even the few narratologists who actually have focused on the relations between narrative and drama (cf. Sommer 2005; Fludernik 2007) and who have taken steps towards a narratology of drama (cf., e.g., Richardson 2007; Muny 2008; Nünning/Sommer 2008) have hardly addressed the question of 'unreliable narration in drama' or attempted to develop theoretical frameworks for getting to grips with this particular transgeneric phenomenon. The same holds true for those seminal articles in transgeneric narratology which explore "narrative voice and agency in drama" (Jahn 2001), "voice and narration in postmodern drama" (Richardson 2001), and the "performative power of narrative in drama" (Nünning/Sommer 2011) yet only mention unreliable narration in passing, if at all.

Without intending to gloss over or devaluate the fact that the abovementioned developments in transgeneric narratology are still extremely relevant and fruitful, one can safely state that narratological research on drama and especially on unreliable narration in drama and theatre still belong to the lacunae of narratology, and, unjustly so, as we will try to show. This article will, therefore, make a modest attempt at redressing the balance by applying recent reconceptualisations of unreliable narration that synthesise cognitive and rhetorical approaches (cf. Nünning 2005, 2008) to drama and by exploring the specificity of dramatic unreliability and the performative power that unreliable narration can have in dramatic scripts and, even more so, on the stage. Drawing on recent attempts to establish a narratology of drama and on unreliability research in transmedial narratologies, we will develop a theoretical and analytical framework that takes into consideration both the specificity of dramatic storytelling and the distinctive features and possible uses of unreliable narration in drama and plays.

We will start by laying out the narratological 'state of the art,' looking at the spectrum of current research in the blossoming field of transgeneric narratology and reconceptualising both the generic scope of unreliable narration and the specificity of its dramatic uses. We will also introduce narratological research on drama and show the need for general, transmedial conceptualisations of storytelling in drama (Section 2). In the next section, we will make first steps towards establishing a theory of unreliability in drama by remodelling traditional conceptualisations of unreliability and suggesting a possible typology of dramatic and theatrical unreliability (Section 3). We will then test this analytical framework and typology, examining five different plays, to explore and exemplify some concrete forms and functions of unreliability in contemporary drama (Section 4). In a short epilogue, we will summarise the most important findings and make some suggestions for further research (Section 5).

2. The Narratological 'State of the Art' and Points of Departure, or: Reconceptualising the Generic Scope of Unreliable Narration and the Specificity of Dramatic Unreliability

To reconceptualise unreliable narration in drama as a narratological research object, we will begin by taking stock of what is already there and make some modest suggestions as to how and in which directions existing approaches can be extended even further. Secondly, we will provide a short account of how 'narration in drama' has been generally addressed within the field of transgeneric narratology and consider possible points of departure for analysing unreliable narration in drama.

Studies on the subgenres known as the 'dramatic monologue' (cf. Bennett 1987) and the 'memory play' (cf. Brunkhorst 1980) exemplify that the use of unreliable narrators is not confined to narrative fiction. These hybrid genres cut across established generic categories of poetry, drama, and narrative: with its limitation to a single, often unreliable speaker usually revealing key episodes of his or her life, the dramatic monologue combines poetic diction with dramatic presentation and story-telling elements. Similarly, the memory play is a type of drama with distinct narrative characteristics, typically featuring an unreliable first-person narrator. Many post-war English plays prove critics and theorists wrong who, like Elam (1980: 111), maintain that drama is "without narratorial mediation". Nonetheless, the study of both unreliable narration and point of view or focalisation in drama has hardly received any attention to date. In the only available article on the subject, Brian Richardson convincingly shows that the deployment of narratorial mediation and the appearance of unreliability in plays call "for the kind of analysis of point of view usually reserved for modern fiction" (1988: 194). But narratologists have not yet taken heed of his clarion call.

Memory plays such as Tom Stoppard's *Travesties* (1975 [1974]) and Peter Shaffer's *Amadeus* (2002 [1979]), which feature Henry Carr and Antonio Salieri as narrators, respectively, demonstrate that post-war English playwrights have made refined use of unreliable narration. In the stage directions of his play, Stoppard explicitly draws attention to Carr's unreliability, which results from the old man's poor memory and his reactionary prejudices: "the scene (and most of the play) is under the erratic control of Old Carr's memory, which is not notably reliable, and also of his various prejudices and delusions" (Stoppard 1975: 11). The main reasons for Salieri's unreliability, on the other hand, are his limited knowledge, high degree of emotional involvement, and problematic value-system. In *Amadeus*, dramatic irony results primarily from the tension between what the audience sees and what Salieri describes, while *Travesties* contains a wide range of textual clues about Carr's unreliability.[4]

Hybrid literary subgenres like the dramatic monologue (cf., however, Rohwer-Happe 2011) and memory play demonstrate that unreliable narration appears cross-generically, but, like other neglected (sub)genres, they have not yet received the narratological attention they arguably deserve: not only particular subgenres like 'memory plays' or other kinds of drama that feature first-person narrators, but also dramatic unreliability in general have yet to be properly conceptualised. As we will show, unreliable narration in drama and theatre is so widespread and multifaceted that it surely deserves to receive the same amount of attention that filmic unreliability has been accorded in recent years (cf., e.g., Liptay/Wolf 2005; Laass 2008).

Recent transgeneric contributions to a narratology of drama (cf. Richardson 2001; Nünning/Sommer 2006, 2011) provide useful bases for a systematisation of the spectrum of unreliable narration and narrative forms in plays. They foster the application of narratological categories, models, and methods to drama theory and analysis, facilitating a transgeneric exploration of the different forms and functions of diegetic narrativity and narrators across media and genres. They also open up the possibility of a transgeneric examination of single and multi-perspective forms of representation on a more theoretically advanced level. In addition, transferring narratological models to the analysis of drama and testing narrative categories of analysis by means of a dramatic text corpus can expose blind spots within narratology. To do justice to the characteristics of dramatic storytelling and unreliable narration in drama, the performative quality of dramatic narration must be kept in mind. After all, we are not dealing with texts meant for reading but for theatrical performance.

Brian Richardson's and Manfred Jahn's studies constitute a first frame of reference and demonstrate that diegetic narrativity in dramatic texts is a profitable object for narratological examination. Richardson, for instance,

---

4 Other examples of plays which violate naturalistic stage conventions by relying on unreliable narration would be Samuel Beckett's *Krapp's Last Tape* (1958) and Harold Pinter's *Landscape* (1968), the latter being composed of alternating and independent acts of narration spoken by two characters (cf. also Morrison 1983).

points out that a model for the narratological analysis of drama could both give classic narratology new impulses and make the rich tradition of narrative forms accessible to the study of drama.[5]

Richardson's approach is particularly productive because it does not conceive of dramatic narration as an exception to the rule of mimetic imitation of actions and speech acts. Rather, Richardson considers narrative elements to be part of the repertoire of dramatic representational techniques which playwrights have used on a regular basis with varying intentions throughout the course of drama's history. According to him, the use of narrators ranks first on a long list of narrative techniques. In contrast to the meaning of the word 'narrator' in classic drama analysis, his definition moves beyond narrators such as messengers who summarise events happening off-stage. Rather, he refers to characters who function as narrators in a narratological sense (cf. Richardson 1988: 194). Ranging from modes of presenting consciousness to narrative situation and the implied author, Richardson's examples show that narrative mediation, or what Nünning and Sommer (2008) have called "diegetic narrativity", can be found in drama as well. There are various kinds of narration on different dramatic levels. However, most researchers have applied 'narration' in a rather restricted, hardly transgeneric sense, because they have failed to consider forms of dramatic storytelling that are unmediated and detached from narrator figures, such as focalisation processes (a laudable exception is Muny 2008). Moreover, hardly any attempts have been made to apply some of the other concepts and theories of narratology to drama and theatre, such as the staging and semantisation of time and space, processes of hybridisation and intermedialisation, and, most notably, the concept of 'unreliability'.

Zooming in on the main differences between 'unreliability' in narrative fiction and drama, we have to state that, to the best of our knowledge, transgeneric narratology has not even begun to address these differences, let alone to develop theoretical or typological frameworks for the topic at hand. Whether we are foolish to rush in where sober narratologists have so far feared to tread will remain to be seen, but we should like to venture four hypotheses about the specific quality and uses

---

5   Cf. Richardson (1988: 194): "[S]everal important works on cinematic narration have appeared. Comparable investigations of the theater, however, are still extremely rare. This is an unfortunate state of critical affairs for two reasons: it is important to acknowledge the rich tradition of narration in drama, and by doing so it will allow us to identify certain blind spots in theories of point of view based too narrowly on post-Jamesean novels. Analysis of narration on stage can also lead to interesting questions about other aspects of traditional narrative theory such as the relations between mimesis and diegesis, consciousness and representation, and even the author and the text."

of dramatic unreliability, which can be summarised under the heading of the 'performative power of storytelling in drama'.

Our first hypothesis is that unreliable narration and focalisation in drama and theatre often do much more than just influence the progress of the action. Unreliable storytelling in drama has a world-making capacity in that it constitutes the storyworlds in which the characters live and act (cf. Nünning/Sommer 2006; Nünning/Sommer 2011: 201ff.), and the storyworlds the audience sees: the performative quality or even power of theatrical uses of unreliable narration determines what is supposed to be 'really' the case in the dramatic storyworld. In some cases, characters' narratives establish what they and the audience believe to be the actual storyworld. At the same time, however, dramatic unreliability undermines the credibility of these narrative accounts in highly theatrical ways—by mimetic means, such as actions, gestures, and stage effects that call the veracity of a narrator's version into doubt, or in diegetic ways, e.g., through counter-narratives that question and even contradict the stories told. Thus, complex possible worlds can be staged and juxtaposed in drama and theatre that oscillate between truth and lies, fact and fiction.

Secondly, the performative power of dramatic unreliability lies in its theatrical embodiment. In contrast to the disembodied voices of unreliable narrators and focalisers which are encountered in narrative fiction, unreliable narrators in staged plays are (usually) physically present on stage. In dramatic unreliable focalisation, even mental constructs can be materialised and seen on stage. The actual physical presences of both unreliable narrators and the contents of the minds of dramatic focalisers tend to underscore the authenticity and the realness of the phenomena and narrative versions which are told and performed on stage.[6]

A third characteristic is the heightened degree of indeterminacy in plays characterised by unreliability, oscillating as they do between the actual textual world and various subjective worlds projected by the stories and minds of unreliable narrators and focalisers. It is thus usually much more difficult for the audience of plays than for the readers of novels to determine whether there is reliable or unreliable narration or focalisation at work. If something that the audience sees enacted on stage turns out to be nothing but a projection of an unreliable narrator's or focaliser's distorted mind or imagination, it might be even more shocking or difficult to accept for the audience than for readers dealing with unreliable depictions

---

6　This not only makes it difficult for the audience to spot unreliability; it also makes it difficult for the production complex (author, director, actor, etc.) to disclose unreliable narration or focalisation. If the producers want to disclose unreliability, they have to give additional clues (with, e.g., inconsistencies in the plausibility structure, the lighting, or revealing facial expression).

in literary texts. It is the performative power of narrative in drama that lends unreliable narration additional force and verisimilitude, while also enhancing its ambivalence.

Fourthly and finally, similar to the poems Peter Hühn analyses in this volume, plays often establish highly complex arrangements of contrasting points of view and equally complex hierarchies of levels of observation. Spectators observe narrators on various extra-diegetic and intra-diegetic levels, and they see characters on extra- and intra-diegetic levels. While extra-diegetic narrators can watch what intra-diegetic characters do and say, the latter are typically not aware of the existence of narrators situated on a superior level of communication, e.g., the type that Richardson has called 'generative narrators': "[H]e [the generative narrator] generates a fictional world (hence my name for this practice) in a manner similar to that of an omniscient narrator" (2001: 685). What is more, characters on the intra-diegetic level observe each other and often question each other's points of view. Needless to say, with so many different points of view on various levels of communication, it becomes the rule rather than the exception that perspectives and levels of observation often contradict each other. This is especially the case if the production complex (author, dramatic advisor, director, actors, etc.) does not emphasise which point of view and hierarchical level of observation is dominant and trustworthy. The performative power of dramatic unreliability, therefore, also lies in the dramatic complexity of observational levels: conflicting and competing points of view are often played off against each other, and it is the reader's and audience's task to gauge the respective degrees of (un)reliability that can be attributed to the different perspectives presented in a play read or staged.

Against the backdrop of these hypotheses about the specificity of dramatic unreliability, it becomes evident that the distinctive features of dramatic storytelling have far-reaching consequences with regard to how acts of unreliable narration and focalisation can be staged as well as how unreliable narration and focalisation can be gauged from the point of view of the reader or the spectator. In addition to the signals and frames of reference that recent contributions to a cognitive reconceptualisation of unreliable narration have tried to systematise for narrative fiction (cf. Nünning 1999b, 2005), other aspects and frameworks have to be taken into consideration if we want to get to grips with the complex processes involved in unreliable narration and focalisation in drama.

3. Towards a Theory and Typology of Dramatic and Theatrical Unreliability

To begin to fill in the lacunae in narratology regarding 'unreliability in drama,' it is necessary to adapt and revise some of the basic notions of fictional unreliability that have been developed for narrative fiction. We would like to remodel some of literary theory's basic assumptions on unreliable narration to make it applicable to drama.[7] However, one should be aware of the dangers which may lie in transferring a theory developed for one genre or medium to another. Since the concept of unreliability is transgeneric and even transdisciplinary, it makes sense to first focus on the general features which might cause an artefact to appear unreliable.

In order to make unreliability theory compatible with the forms of unreliability that occur in dramatic texts and their stagings, at least three issues have to be considered and reconceptualised: (1) the role of the narrator as a trigger of unreliability, (2) the question of how unreliability is generated, and (3) narrative unreliability's relation to dramatic irony.

As far as the role of the narrator as the focus and source of unreliability is concerned, most recent research has attributed unreliable narration to the existence of a first-person narrator.[8] Lately, however, this attribution has been challenged and it has been acknowledged that a work of art can feature (un)reliable narration without presenting a narrator. Emily Anderson even goes so far as to suggest that we should "revisit our definition of 'narrator' and perhaps of 'narration' itself" (2010: 81).

This suggestion becomes all the more pertinent when one takes the medial and generic specificities of film and drama into account. In plays and films, the plots are typically not recounted by a narrator, but expressed by way of many verbal as well non-verbal means, which in their entirety constitute dramatic (and filmic) narration (cf. Chatman 1990: 153–154; Pfister 1991 [1988]: 6–9), including its potential (un)reliability. It is thus not necessary to assume the existence of a (first-person) narrator as *the* source of narrative unreliability. On the contrary, it may not even be productive to regard filmic, dramatic, or other literary narrative instances as anthropomorphic beings (cf., e.g., Vogt 2009: 36, 51).

---

[7] In an article like this, we cannot discuss all of the many problems currently discussed in unreliability research, e.g., the tensions and boundaries between normative and factual unreliability, or the ongoing debate revolving around the 'implied author' as a point of reference for detecting unreliability in a narrator and determining the degree of unreliability.

[8] Monika Fludernik, for example, once claimed that "[o]nly first-person narrators can be properly unreliable" (cf. Fludernik 2003 [1996]: 213) and recent edited volumes which are exclusively concerned with 'first-person novels' (cf. D'hoker/Martens 2008) attest to the unbroken popularity of this thesis in literary theory. Cf. also Nünning (1998: 6); Zerweck (2001: 155–156); Olson (2003); Allrath (2005: 76 *et passim*).

Trying to find out which instances, then, constitute dramatic, filmic, and other kinds of narrative unreliability, it is helpful to look at another prevalent (and much travelled) concept: the communication model of narrative texts. In order to come to terms with the difference between unreliable narration in narrative fiction and in drama, the model of 'cinematic communication' that Eva Laass (2008: 44) has adapted from the communication model of dramatic texts (cf. Pfister 1991 [1988]) provides a useful foil.

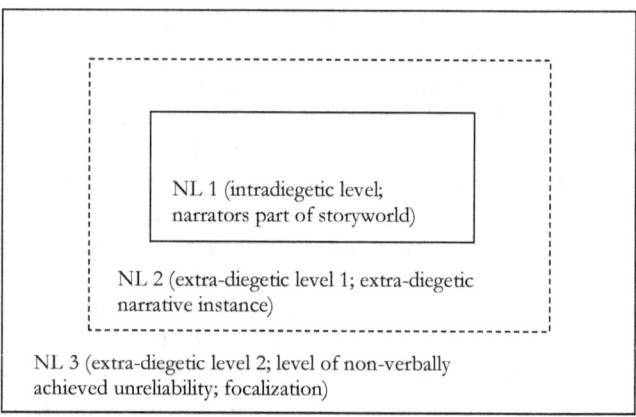

Figure 1. 'Intratextual Communication in Drama/Onstage Communication in Theatre;' a model adapted from Laass (2008: 44)

In her model, Laass (cf. 2008: 43–79) draws attention to unreliability on a first narrative level (NL 1), the level of action. At this level, acting characters, narrating characters, and/or generative narrators (cf. Richardson 2001: 685) may be sources of *dramatic* unreliability. On NL 2, the level of explicit narrative communication which is not constitutive of traditional realist drama, Laass identifies voice-over narration as the cause of unreliability. In plays, this kind of 'unreliable explicit narration' may be produced by voices off-stage or by extra-diegetic narrative instances like generative narrators or other narrating instances who may also appear on the intra-diegetic level, i.e., NL 1 (e.g., choruses or prologues). The level of 'implicit narrative communication' (NL 3) describes a level on which non-verbal information is communicated; it refers, e.g., to focalisation or perspectivisation strategies, which may be assessed along a scale of subjectivity and objectivity. Both dramatic focalisation and perspectivisation may be characterised by selectivity and/or the restricted presentation of characters' histories, stories, and actions. In contrast to 'dramatic focalisation,' which can be defined as "a means of selecting and restricting narrative information, of seeing events and states of affairs from somebody's point of view, of foregrounding the focalizing agent, and of creating an empathetical or ironical view on the focalizer" (Jahn 2005: online), 'dramatic perspectivisation' is not bound to any character or narrator figure appearing on the first or second level of dramatic communication.

Before adapting Laass' narrative level 4 (the level of text-external communication; NL 4) to outline a theoretical framework for the forms of unreliability in drama, one can venture the following hypotheses: 'unreliability' or 'dramatic unreliability' is an abstract and transgeneric term. It is 'abstract' because it is not necessarily bound to an anthropomorphic instance, that is, it can occur in conjunction with an unreliable (usually first-person) narrator, but it can also be separable from an overt narrator. It is 'transgeneric' because it can appear across a wide range of different genres. To find out which narrative instances may cause 'unreliable discourses in drama,' one can fruitfully adapt Laass' cinematic communication model for the theatre. We would like to argue that in drama and theatre, unreliability can be constituted in a number of different ways, viz. by:

(1) unreliable narration in a more restricted sense, relating to the question of 'who speaks?' In Drama and theatre, such narrators can appear
   (a) in the form of anthropomorphic instances on the intra-diegetic level NL 1,
   (b) in the form of anthropomorphic or non-anthropomorphic instances on the extra-diegetic level NL 2, e.g., as 'generative narrators' whose perspectives and versions can be more or less subjective or objective, and who often turn out to be the focalising instances of the action on NL 1),
   (c) as a combination of both 1.a and 1.b, or
(2) (un)reliable focalisation (relating to the questions of 'who perceives?') or (un)reliable perspectivisation (concerning any selection and presentation of events not attributable to any anthropomorphic being) on the level NL 3, which may oscillate between various instances of
   (a) subjective perspective(s) of one or more character(s),
   (b) a more or less objective perspective, resonant with omniscience,
   (c) unmarked "theatrical staging[s] of mental events" (Richardson 1988: 204),
   (d) a combination of 2.a and 2.b, 2.b and 2.c, or 2.a-c,
(3) various combinations of the variants listed under 1 and 2.

As the typology delineated in the schematic overview above shows, reconceptualising unreliability and adapting the concept for drama and theatre lead us to the following insights: firstly, dramatic unreliability can be generated by acts of actual narration, that is, by narration or storytelling in a literal sense. Secondly, it can be caused by forms of focalisation and perspectivisation, that is, dramatic narration or presentation in a broader sense. Thirdly, strategies of unreliable narration, focalisation, and perspectivisation may be combined in plays in any number of ways, resulting in mixed forms.

The communication model delineated above (see Fig. 1) allows us to pinpoint the levels on which unreliability can occur in plays and how various kinds of dramatic unreliability can be combined: on the intra-diegetic level, characters often assume the role of storytellers, and their versions of the events can contrast with their actions and/or the actions and perspectives of other characters, i.e., these storytellers' narratives may be contradicted by those of other characters who tell their own stories. In addition, unreliable narration can and quite often does occur on an extra-diegetic level. When considering drama's entire history, one has to state, though, that instances of extra-diegetic unreliable narration are relatively rare, at least until the second half of the twentieth century. As we pointed out in Section 2 above, an exception of this rule is the 'memory play.' In this genre, the storyworld is typically presented by an extra-diegetic narrator who, more often than not, turns out to be unreliable. Memory plays conjure up a sophisticated dramatic scenario in which an unreliable extra-diegetic narrator, who often turns out to be the older or younger self of one of the characters, recounts or even 'generates' what happens on the embedded level of action. Whereas an unreliable extra-diegetic narrator is a common and even constitutive feature of the dramatic subgenre of the memory play, in other genres extra-diegetic unreliable narration is the exception rather than the rule. Narrative instances on extra-diegetic levels, however, must neither be actors present on stage nor anthropomorphic beings: narratives can be presented in written form, e.g., on banners, as was the case in Brecht's time, or on digital panels. They can even be mediated through other media, as in stagings which, by way of introducing the story, present film clips.

Although all these examples of both intra-diegetic and extra-diegetic narration can and should be distinguished for the sake of theoretical clarity, they may, of course, also occur in various combinations. In addition to the instances of explicit or overt narration in drama, unreliability may also be evoked by implicit means, namely, by focalisation or perspectivisation. The complex semiotic ways in which characters and events can be extra-diegetically selected and presented in drama and theatre may result in an unreliable perspective on what happens on stage. This perspective structure may depend on anthropomorphic figures (focalisation) or not (perspectivisation); it may be quite subjective (cf. point-of-view shots in film) or rather objective; and it may include the unmarked staging of mental events or merge some (or all) of these points. Finally, dramatic narration, focalisation, and perspectivisation can be combined to achieve complex effects of unreliability.

As far as the second issue involving reconceptualising unreliability is concerned, i.e., the questions of how unreliability is generated and how it can be accounted for, disagreement prevails among narratologists, with rhetorical, structuralist, and cognitive narratologists championing different models. Researchers working in the tradition of rhetorical narrative theory (e.g., Phelan 2004) still go back to, and rely on, Booth's original definition, in which unreliability is attributed to the tension between the norms of a narrator and those of an implied author. Others maintain that Booth's definition has been undermined, arguing that the 'unreliable narrator' is commonly understood in an every-day-like manner as someone who "distorts the fictional facts" (Köppe/Kindt 2011: 81). Within the current debate, an alternative to Booth's rhetorical approach has been developed by a cognitive-pragmatic approach. Cognitive reconceptualisations of unreliable narration emphasise that text-external elements, most notably the reader and his/her cultural frames of reference, have to be taken into consideration in order to come to terms with the complex phenomenon of unreliable narration. A synthesis between cognitive and rhetorical approaches not only provides a fruitful basis for reconceptualising the theory and generic scope of unreliable narration (cf. Nünning 2005, 2008); it can also account for a transgeneric reframing of 'unreliability,' in general, and 'dramatic unreliability,' in particular.

To explain how unreliable discourse and its sub-phenomena of unreliable narration (on the levels of action [NL 1] and of explicit unreliable narration [NL 2]) and unreliable focalisation or perspectivisation (NL 3) work, we would like to draw on 'dramatic irony' (cf. also Nünning/Nünning 2007: 66), which refers to "the ironic contradictions that are created when the internal [NL 1–3] and the external [what Laass has termed 'NL 4'] communication systems conflict with each other" (Pfister 1991 [1988]: 56). Inferring an incongruity between the fictional, intra-textual level and non-fictional, extra-textual level of reception involves pragmatic processes. More specifically, it results from a cognitive process on behalf of the recipients (and perhaps also of the plays' production complex). The experience of dramatic unreliability (in the various typological manifestations delineated above) thus results from a discrepancy between the norms, values, and information presented by either narrating, focalising, or perspectivising instances on the various intra-textual levels (NL 1–3) and the cognitive frames (the norms, values, and information) of the production complex and the audience on the extra-textual level (NL 4). An unreliable dramatic discourse, thus, features at least two stories or meanings, an explicit and one (or more) implicit one(s) which has/have to be unravelled by the audience (cf. Nünning/Nünning 2007: 69, 74).[9]

In order to account for discrepancies and inferences between the various perspectives and levels, it is helpful to reconceptualise dramatic unreliability in terms of dramatic irony. When narratologists resort to the notion of dramatic irony in unreliability studies, they typically assume that the narrator is the butt or target of irony. According to this view, the narrator is unaware of his/her fallibility, while readers notice contradictions or other signals of unreliability because they are in a position of superior audience awareness. When we apply this explanation to dramatic unreliability, however, we have to acknowledge that there is a large number of plays in which the information is disseminated in such a way that the audience in fact has less knowledge than the characters. Thus, defining unreliability just in terms of superior audience awareness is not sufficient. Cases in point of 'inferior audience awareness' are, for instance, the so-called '*rückwirkende Überraschungsgeschichten,*' that is, (literary, dramatic, filmic) stories which at the very end feature either final plot twists or final discursive twists which trigger *anagnorisis* in the audience (and sometimes also in the focalising character) and cause recipients to (re)interpret everything they have heard, read, or seen beforehand (cf. Robert Vogt's article in this volume).[10] One example is Terry Johnson's *Hysteria* (2001 [1993]): not until the very end does it become clear that the main character Sigmund Freud has been dreaming the story presented on stage. Dramatic stories like this can be called 'unreliable,' since they only reveal their 'true' meanings in retrospect. Until these revelations occur, the joke/irony is at the expense of the recipient.

The cognitive-pragmatic definition of an unreliable story as an 'ironic discourse,' therefore, presupposes a 'discrepancy' between the norms, values, and information presented on the text-internal level (NL 1–3) and those prevalent on the extra-textual level (NL 4). This discrepancy can occur in at least two forms: it becomes manifest not only in a recipient's

---

[9] Cf. also Olson (2003: 104): "The reader judges the narrator's unreliability based on textual signals, and then moves beyond a literal reading of the text and attributes fallibility or untrustworthiness to the narrator".

[10] Along with Virginia Hastings Floyd, we would like to emphasise that this often neglected form of unreliability within the context of drama and theatre research is more common as a dramatic convention than one might have thought (cf. Hastings Floyd 1972: 14).

'superior awareness' but also in his/her 'inferior awareness', and sometimes even a 'congruent awareness,' namely, when conflicting textual and performative clues are out in the open while the recipients, just like the characters on the diegetic level [NL 1], do not know what to make of them. This opening up of the concept of 'dramatic irony' and narrative unreliability can serve to shed new light on film and drama and potentially on literary studies as well. In this rather new light, retrospectively surprising stories like, e.g., Guy de Maupassant's short story "La Parure"/"The Necklace" (1884) or Cyril Hare's detective story "It Takes Two…" (ca. 1959) can arguably be analysed in new and interesting ways.

4. Forms and Functions of Dramatic Unreliability: A Selective Overview and Some Exemplary Case-Studies

Since the focus has so far mainly been on narratological and theoretical issues, we would now like to turn our attention to the question of how we can come to terms with the actual forms and uses that unreliable narration in drama has taken, and with the functions that it can fulfil in performed plays. Instead of merely applying narratological models to dramatic instances of unreliable narration, it is not only important to develop a systematic typology of the most important forms and functions of unreliable narration in drama and plays, but also to explore the specificity and distinctive features and functions of dramatic storytelling in concrete plays. To test the analytical potential and heuristic value of our hypotheses, we are now going to briefly analyse five dramas which all feature different forms of unreliable discourse. Their differences largely depend on divergent qualities of unreliability, the various ways in which these qualities are generated (i.e., theatrical techniques), and the diverse levels of dramatic communication that are involved.

Testing the usefulness of the typology of theatrical unreliability sketched out in Section 3, we will look at a variety of works: two plays in which unreliability is caused by narration (either on the level of action [NL 1] or on the extradiegetic level of narrative communication [NL 2]); two works in which unreliability is generated by unreliable focalisation or perspectivisation (NL 3); and one dramatic text in which dramatic narration and focalisation are combined to evoke unreliability. To counter Beatrix Hesse's criticism that scholars always appear to cite the same "handful of plays" (Hesse 2009: 27) when trying to account for unreliability in drama,[11] which, in her opinion, creates the impression that unreliability is uncommon in dramatic literature, we will reference plays which, to our knowledge, have not yet been considered in the context of unreliability studies. After all, there actually *are* a great number and variety of plays over and above the by now quite well-known examples of the memory-play which feature various forms of unreliability—innovative plays and instances of dramatic unreliability which are just waiting to be explored.

Neil LaBute's *autobahn, A Short-Play Cycle* (2005 [2003]), for example, provides a paradigm example of a play that turns out to be unreliable in an interesting way. It consists of seven one-act plays, each of which is set inside cars. The private spaces of these cars' interiors motivate the play's protagonists to betray the masks they bear in everyday life. Restricting the possibilities of what can be done besides driving and talking, the cars' confinement induces talk—the telling of life stories as either monologues or dialogues in which characters unconsciously reveal things they have hitherto tried to hide or of which they have been unaware. The young girl in "Bench Seat", the second play in the cycle, for instance, implicitly characterises herself as an unreliable narrator, misjudging situations, relationships, and herself. The nice teaching assistant she is dating has driven her up a long, winding road and stopped at a secluded spot with a view—the cliché of a romantic site for a young couple in love. After they have kissed, the girl reveals her suspicion that he has brought her to that spot to dump her, even though he has not indicated this intention in any way. After initially delaying an explanation as to why she would suspect such an outcome ('underreporting;' cf. Phelan/Martin 1999), the girl eventually tells her story. Only at this point, in the middle of the act, do the boy and the audience finally understand why she expects to be dumped: two years earlier, she "got dumped here once" (LaBute 2005: 25)—that is, at the same spot and in an unexpected manner (cf. ibid.: 25–26).

As the play moves on, a discrepancy is established between what the girl has told the boy and how she begins to act which serves to signal her unreliability and to shed further light on its background. Returning repeatedly to her suspicion and to the matter with her ex-boyfriend, the girl contradicts herself: she has not really made peace with her past and, after a while, admits that she is still "jumpy" (ibid.: 31). Additionally, the young woman seems to confuse past and present by completely misjudging and mishandling the positive circumstances she actually finds herself in, even becoming reproachful with her date. When the young

---

11 Hesse refers to Arthur Miller's *Death of a Salesman*, Eugene O'Neill's *The Emperor Jones*, Thornton Wilder's *Our Town*, and Tennessee Williams's *The Glass Menagerie*.

man, in turn, feels alienated by her conduct, physically and emotionally withdrawing from her, the girl gets more and more agitated and even threatening, mentioning that, after her ex-boyfriend separated from her, she took revenge (for instance, by sending him dead field mice and a picture of a horse dropping excrement into the mouth of a girl; cf. ibid.: 31), implying that the same could happen to her current boyfriend. What starts out as a seemingly cosy date in the back seat of a car turns out to be a nightmare for the college student, who eventually does seem to want to break off the relationship. Through her bizarre behaviour, the girl supplies the audience with markers indicating that she is not just a naïve and erratic woman, but also an unreliable narrator. It is likely that she has also misrepresented her role in her past breakup (which Phelan and Martin 1999 call 'misregarding'). She seems to completely misjudge the situation as well as herself, her beliefs, and values (unable to see that sending dead mice to people with whom she is angry might be a little over the top). She also appears unable to interpret situations correctly, accusing her date of wanting to dump her when he actually wants to kiss her. Finally, the discrepancy between her initial story and her implicit self-characterisation suggests that her ex-boyfriend might have had the same experience as that of the shocked young boy sitting next to her. In sum, various theatrical techniques including the discrepancy between explicit and implicit self-characterisation, or discrepancies between the stories told, the setting, and the action on the story-level serve to undermine the girl's story, revealing the degree of her normative untrustworthiness.

While LaBute's short-play cycle *autobahn*, and particularly "Bench Seat", exemplifies unreliable narration on the story-level (NL 1) of a play, Brian Friel's *Dancing at Lughnasa* (1990) exemplifies another way in which dramatic unreliability can emerge through a narrator figure. Friel's play features a frame narrative and an overt narrator on the extra-diegetic level of narrative communication (NL 2), in which Michael, a young man, introduces his childhood memories of the summer in which he was a boy of seven. This memory, which is framed and repeatedly interrupted by Michael's diegetic renderings, is enacted (or mimetically narrated) on the story-level (NL 1). The set of the memory play on NL 1 is the interior of a cottage situated in a small, rural town in Ireland, in which the narrator lives with his aunts and mother, five sisters, and his uncle Jack, a missionary. The play takes place in 1936—during two days in August and September, around the Celtic festival of Lughnasa. These days turn out to be the last in which the family lived (not well off, but quite happily) together; as we learn from the narrator, the family is disrupted and financially and emotionally impoverished shortly thereafter.

What is striking about this unreliable narrator's story is, paradoxically, his honesty, especially concerning his limited trustworthiness. Unlike other examples of overt unreliable narrators, who are embedded in dramatic discourse structurally similar to Friel's, such as Salieri in Shaffer's *Amadeus* or Carr in Stoppard's *Travesties* (cf. Section 2), the narrator on the extra-diegetic level NL 2 freely admits his fallibility regarding the action presented on the level of action (NL 1). What is more, he embraces the fallibility of his account, openly acknowledging the unsurmountable gap between his subjectively tinged retrospective version of the events and factual truth: "But there is one memory of that Lughnasa time that visits me most often; and what fascinates me about that memory is that it owes nothing to fact" (Friel 1990: 56).

The complex dramatic structure of narrative transmission does not make it particularly easy for the reader or audience to work out that there are manifold deviations from factual truth and that the narrator's version is highly unreliable. While the performative power of the act of narration exerts a strong theatrical presence, Michael's childhood self is invisible on the discourse level. Although the adults refer and talk to him (to which Michael, the young man, replies from his extra-diegetic position, which the other characters are not aware of), it is never quite clear where the witness of these days, the seven-year-old, is actually standing/sitting or if he is present at all. It follows that Michael, the adult, does have a clear recollection of himself as a child, which gives rise to the suspicion that there are also errors and gaps in his memory concerning the adults' world and concerns. What nurtures this distrust even more is the fact that the boy seems to have lived innocently in his own world by building kites and only sporadically interacting with the adults. Consequently, he is unlikely to have paid very close attention to the things going on in the adult world, the very same world he now presents to the audience. This fact is established at the beginning of the play—albeit less explicitly than in the narrator's final monologue.

When the extra-diegetic narrative turns to the action on the intra-diegetic level, the audience is implicitly warned that it will have to be careful in putting its trust all too willingly in the hands of the adult narrator, whose unreliability is gradually revealed. Michael introduces us to a scene (cf. Friel 1990: 2) in which his aunts and mother talk and interact—a scene he never witnessed. When, a couple of minutes into this 'memory,' Michael's aunt Agnes asks her sister, "What's that son of yours at out there?" (ibid.: 4), the audience becomes aware of the fact that the boy could not possibly have witnessed the scene, because he is actually playing outside. This opening informs the audience that Michael is not only a storyteller but also a story-inventor, and an unreliable narrator at that.

Despite not bearing witness to all of the incidents of 1936 (and maybe having even forgotten some, too), Michael presents the audience with a remarkably coherent story by imagining (parts of) it. Factual unreliability, therefore, is rendered less directly than the way it is employed in "Bench Seat", and it is less unsettling than a rendering of subjective memories full of fissures, repetitions, and variations like those staged in other memory plays like *Travesties*. Factual unreliability in *Dancing at Lughnasa* is a means of evoking a dreamlike, nostalgic atmosphere, which nevertheless is able to capture what an adult feels in relation to his past. This is ultimately acknowledged by Michael's adult self in a direct way, which somewhat diminishes the grade of Michael's unreliability: "In that memory atmosphere is more real than incident and everything is simultaneously actual and illusory" (ibid.: 56). After all, the discrepancy between the information provided within the play and the external (until then supposedly superior) audience's awareness is exposed as deliberate and purposeful and, to a certain extent, levelled and excused.

While superior audience awareness is often a prerequisite for triggering an experience of dramatic unreliability, inferior audience awareness first causes ambiguity and is then resolved with an *anagnorisis* in the audience, exposing the focalising perspective on the level of non-verbal, 'implicit narrative communication' (NL 3) as erroneous. This also means that, in contrast to the forms of unreliability exemplified so far, which are generated by narration on different dramatic levels, yet another form of dramatic unreliability exists, one which is caused by particular kinds of focalisation (cf. Jahn 2005). Even when this is not verbally explicated in the primary text as in our previous examples, narrative information can be imparted from the selective and restricted point of view of one protagonist. For example, in *Mindgame* (2000), a play by English playwright Anthony Horowitz, a character's restricted perspective is presented throughout almost the entire play, generating dramatic unreliability (cf. type 2.a). A similar case in point is Alan Ayckbourn's play, tellingly entitled *Woman in Mind* (1986), in which the action of the play largely consists of a dramatic representation of the very active and equally unreliable fantasy life of the central character Susan, who supplies the play with an idealised family that remains invisible to the other characters. And in *Gorgeous Avatar* (2006), Scottish dramatist Jules Horne combines various forms of unreliable dramatic focalisation (cf. type 2.d of dramatic unreliability).

Just like many other unreliable narrators that represent or evoke one of the standard types that William Riggan discusses in his monograph *Pícaros, Madmen, Naïfs, and Clowns* (Riggan 1981), the focaliser in *Mindgame* turns out to be just as prototypically unreliable as the narrators in many novels and short stories which narratological research has been concerned with: he is a madman. This is, however, only revealed after a final twist in the play's discourse structure occurs. Until then, and in contrast to *Dancing at Lughnasa*, the theatre audience of *Mindgame* has no reason to question the reliability of what is shown, at least if they have not paid much attention to the play's title.[12] In the beginning, the audience is led to believe that they are observing Mark Styler, an author of books on serial killers, who is trying to convince Dr Farquhar, the head of Fairfields "experimental hospital for the criminally insane", to grant him an interview with one of the institution's most unpredictable, dangerous, and especially violent inhabitants, a man called Easterman. What we really witness, though, is a therapy method called 'psychodrama,' which has been developed by the founding psychotherapist of the clinic, Karel Ennis. This technique delivers treatment in the form of role-playing, in which serial killers impersonate other people and therapists imitate serial killers so that the inmates can see themselves from an outside perspective. At the end of this therapy session or 'mindgame,' Styler turns out to be Easterman, Dr Farquhar is Karel Ennis, the real head of the hospital, and a nurse also involved in the therapy session actually turns out to be the therapist, Dr Farquhar (cf. Horowitz 2000: 104). This knowledge is revealed after a change in the focalising perspective transpires: most of the action on NL 1 is seen through Styler's/Easterman's eyes and interpreted through his deluded mind, but the focalisation shifts towards the end of the play, when the therapist closes the psychodrama session (cf. ibid.: 102–104), allowing the audience to see things through the eyes of the therapist. The audience discovers their inferior awareness only at the very end.

Throughout the play, three different interpretations are possible,[13] although the recipients are, by way of focalisation, led to believe that the version they see is the correct one. Only in retrospect can the audience

---

12 Whereas readers are informed in the secondary text that, in the staging, a "shifting, faulty perception" (Horowitz 2000: 7) should be evoked, the theatre audience is not in command of this crucial piece of information.

13 Interpretation 1: Styler is Styler, an interviewer who has to realise that the hospital has been taken over by Easterman and the other mad inhabitants, who have killed all the staff. Interpretation 2: A therapy session, a 'psychodrama,' is going on; Styler is Easterman, imagining what happens in interpretation 1. Interpretation 3: It is impossible to decide which version is the correct one, as there are constant reminders of unreliability, e.g., the subtly changing stage set and explicit remarks made by Farquhar to Styler: "The man who put it on you [that you were mad] might believe that you were, in his opinion, mad. But it might occur to you, it might cross your mind that it was in fact the reverse that was true. You might believe that it was he who was mad and you who were perfectly sane." (Horowitz 2000: 57) In this case, the recipient cannot choose between alternative interpretations (cf. also Liptay 2006: 202).

infer possible alternative interpretations of the events presented. There are, however, triggers which may signal dramatic unreliability by initially indicating a twisted and false perception of Styler/Easterman. First of all, the stage design slowly changes. The stage direction reads: "the scenery will play a game with the audience […] parts of it changing while their attention is elsewhere. The aim is to suggest a shifting, faulty perception, a feeling that you cannot trust your eyes" (ibid.: 7). Additionally, there are inconsistencies in the play, for instance, Styler, the writer, calling Dr Farquhar a "rude bastard" (ibid.: 10) without even knowing him. Following Helbig (cf. 2005: 143–144), we would like to suggest that such strategies may be the first signs of the development of an emerging hybrid form of unreliability, viz. a new kind which is characterised by filmic and dramatic unreliability caused by restricted focalisation and followed by a final twist in discourse.

There are, of course, other plays which present a combination of unreliable dramatic focalisation and perspectivisation (cf. type 2.d), with Jules Horne's *Gorgeous Avatar* being an innovative case in point. Horne's play stages dreams and other mental events, oscillating between a strong subjectivity and objectivity and even including references to the notoriously unreliable realm of the fantasy worlds acted out or projected on the Internet. The combination of unreliable focalisation and perspectivisation in *Gorgeous Avatar* triggers empathy towards Horne's main focaliser and character Amy, a lonely woman in her thirties. She has not left her flat for quite some time and never meets people, except her neighbours Rose, a woman in her fifties, and Dan, a man her age, both of whom frequently drop in to wrench the young woman from her isolation. Amy does, however, meet plenty of people on the Internet, including the American man she has fallen in love with and married—online! The two act play is set in her flat in Scotland the day she is going to see her husband, Rafi, for the first time. He is about to visit her when we witness her slight uneasiness about what Rafi might be like in real life. Her worries are not addressed directly: they only become evident in what turn out to be Amy's delusions. Before Rafi actually appears in the second act, she imagines three different arrivals. Her thoughts are acted out on the stage, with the actor embodying Rafi standing before the audience and interacting with the actress playing Amy, without, however, providing any indications of their imaginary nature. Theatrical unreliability occurs because the audience has been entangled by the performative power of unreliability in drama: the subjective wish-worlds of the character's untrustworthy imagination are scenically represented, and the audience does not know that it cannot even trust what it sees. It is only when the action becomes outrageous and fantastical (e.g., Rafi rips off his moustache; Rafi tries to kill Amy; Rafi, Rose, and Dan sing and dance) that it becomes clear that the perspectivisation, not bound to any character, must have slowly changed from an external, seemingly objective point of view, presenting 'real life' events, to an instance of focalisation characterised by Amy's internal, subjective point of view, staging mental, dream-like incidents (cf., e.g., Horne 2006: 20, 38, 50).

Horne's play differs from classic representations of mental events in theatre, in which it is usually highlighted when characters' dreams are being staged. In *Gorgeous Avatar*, the transmutation from reality to dream and back again is unmarked, which is the precise cause of the play's theatrical unreliability. What is more, there is a consistent oscillation between ontological levels that establishes a pattern: reality (with Rose and Dan), dream- or wish-world (with Rafi), reality (with Rose and Dan), dream- or fear-/wish-world (with Rafi), etc. The first theatrical visualisation of Amy's fears are probably not interpreted as such; however, upon the second and third instances in which Rafi appears at Amy's door, the audience is no longer surprised by, and might even anticipate, the fact that it is witnessing a dream. The combination of different focalisation and perspectivisation strategies and the recurrent staging of mental events (and their subversion in Act II) cause a constant insecurity on behalf of the recipients regarding the correct interpretation of the onstage events, being similar to the insecurity Amy feels about Rafi. Thus, the continuous game with knowledge distribution and the audience's inferior awareness causes the audience to remain on constant guard and is probably best understood as a special configuration of unreliability, namely, ambiguity.

Our last example of theatrical unreliability combines instances of unreliable narration on the diegetic level (NL 1) and unreliable focalisation (producing inferior audience awareness) on the level of focalisation (NL 3): Edward Albee's *Who's Afraid of Virginia Woolf* (1965 [1962]). This landmark of modern American drama displays very salient and virtuoso instances of dramatic and theatrical unreliability (cf. type 3) and it is remarkable that, in spite of its wide reception, Albee's play has, to our knowledge, not even been considered in this context before. The play is set in the on-campus living room of a dysfunctional couple, namely, George, a professor of history, and Martha, his older wife and the daughter of the college's president. Martha has invited George's young, new colleague Nick and his wife Honey over to prolong a college staff party. Subsequently, the older couple plays a game of cat and mouse with the younger couple, telling reliable and unreliable stories. Among these are the story George tells of an acquaintance who accidentally killed his own parents; the story Nick tells about Honey's nervous pregnancy; the story George and Martha tell about their son, who will soon return home to celebrate his 21st birthday. Some instances of narration on the intra-diegetic level are revealed as lies during the play, e.g., when Martha states that George's story about an acquaintance having accidentally killed his parents is not a story about an acquaintance but rather about George himself. These rather direct revelations of unreliability are counterpointed with extra-diegetically triggered, indirect disclosures. In the beginning, what the audience knows about the incidents happening on stage roughly equates to what little knowledge Honey and Nick have about the couple they—like the audience—have just met. This is why neither the young couple nor the audience is able to deduce what is truly going on between George and Martha, who seem to have more than one skeleton in the closet. In other words, the recipients are confronted with a focalisation that is close to Nick's and Honey's restricted viewpoints, who ask more than once: "What are you two [George and Martha] talking about?" (Albee 1965: 137). The restrictedness of the focalisation is opened up, however, in a final twist, when Nick suddenly realises along with the audience, that George and Martha's son never even existed.

In sum, we hope to have indicated that dramatic texts and plays are subjects worthy and in need of being taken into consideration in research on unreliability, providing genre-specific instances of various kinds of dramatic unreliability and thus shedding new light on this complex phenomenon. Moreover, plays feature a rich variety of dramatic, narrative and theatrical strategies that can evoke unreliable storyworlds, establish misapprehensions and trigger recognition. The stories that the characters and narrators tell in the plays examined as case-studies above may not provide objective renderings of events. But they depict, in very realistic ways, the illusions and self-deceptions of the narrators and focalisers themselves, while at the same time exerting the performative power of dramatic storytelling.

5. Epilogue: Conclusions and Suggestions for Further Research

Since unreliability is a transgeneric, transmedial and interdisciplinary phenomenon, narratology would certainly benefit from opening its generic scope to dramatic and theatrical matters. As we have tried to show, however, it does not suffice to simply apply narratological conceptualisations developed for novels if one tries to get to grips with the forms, functions, and uses of dramatic unreliability. Adapting Laass' cinematic communication model for our purposes, we have delineated three main kinds of theatrical unreliability—unreliable narration on an intra-diegetic and an extra-diegetic level, unreliable focalisation on a non-verbal, extra-diegetic level, and a mixture of unreliable narration and focalisation that can appear on several intratextual levels. Dramatic unreliability, thus, can be recognised if there is a discrepancy between narration and focalisation on intratextual levels and the reader's—superior or inferior—awareness on the extratextual level.

However, since dramatic texts can either be read or performed and watched on stage, the realisation of unreliability in drama depends on whether we are dealing with the written text or an actual play put on stage. In the latter case, the actualisation of unreliability can be very much influenced by the play's staging. In contrast to watching a play in the theatre, reading dramatic texts includes paying attention to the stage directions, which can include signals of unreliable narration that clearly reveal that what is to be presented is not to be trusted. The stage directions in Alan Ayckbourn's play *Woman in Mind* (1986) are a case in point, as the following example at the beginning of the play illustrates: "Throughout the play, we will hear what she [the main character Susan] hears; see what she sees. A *subjective viewpoint* therefore and one that *may at times be somewhat less accurate*" (Ayckbourn 1986: 9, our emphasis). The authorial stage directions thus foreground the fact that what the reader and audience will see and hear will not provide reliable information about the characters and events of the actual textual world. What they will be confronted with instead are episodes and projections emanating from a highly subjective, distorted and fallible viewpoint. The reader of the dramatic text will thus be less surprised to encounter unreliability in Ayckbourn's *Woman in Mind* as well as in similar plays than the theatre audience, which in cases like these will experience the performative power of unreliability in drama directly, having to work it out for itself that what you see on stage is much more ambivalent than what meets the eye and ear.

Further studies must address the questions of how we can distinguish between dramatic and theatrical unreliability, and how the differences in production and reception between dramatic texts and performed plays can be explored. What in a printed drama is unmistakeably and deliberately unreliable or ambiguous can, in a staged play, become disambiguated, or be made even more ambiguous, for that matter, depending on the choices the directors or actors make. Even plays which are ambiguous throughout, like John Patrick Shanley' *Doubt* (2005), could be disambiguated. When analysing a play in terms of the forms and functions of unreliability, these differences in reception (and probably even the performative power of drama) should be taken into account.

As these concluding observations already indicate, there are still several important issues and new territories to be explored in the as yet largely unmapped field of the kinds, degrees and effects of dramatic and theatrical unreliability. Bolstered by performative and transgeneric frameworks, the analysis of unreliable narration and focalisation in drama can, first, bridge the gap which has separated narratology and drama theory for much too long—to the detriment of both narratological inquiry and the analysis of drama. Secondly, the cognitive, performative, and transgeneric reconceptualisations of both dramatic storytelling, in general, and unreliable narration, in particular, can fruitfully be applied to unreliable storytelling in plays. Thirdly, the combination of a transgeneric theory of unreliable narration and concepts developed by possible-worlds theory can be useful for understanding how readers and spectators make sense of dramatic storytelling and conjure up different kinds of possible worlds evoked by the stories that characters and narrator figures tell (in addition to the actual textual world, e.g., the dream-, fantasy- and wish-worlds projected by the subjective viewpoints of the dramatic storytellers).

As far as the kinds, uses and functions of unreliable narration in drama and plays are concerned, there are several other important issues which have yet to be adequately explored. One of them is the development of a far more exhaustive and fully-fledged theory of dramatic forms of unreliable narration than the one sketched above, which would require a separate study. Another is an adequate typology of unreliable narration and focalisation in drama that would allow the critic to distinguish different kinds of unreliable dramatic narration (e.g., unreliable generative narrators, intra-diegetic characters that serve as narrators) and focalisation. Thirdly, a more subtle and systematic account of the clues that indicate unreliable narration and focalisation in drama and theatre is needed; these clues are arguably at least partly different from those found in narrative fiction. Fourthly, the different uses of unreliable narration in the works of both contemporary playwrights and dramatists from earlier periods are just waiting to be explored. Fifthly, both the history of storytelling in drama and the development of unreliable narration in American and British drama have yet to be written (cf. Sommer 2012). Sixthly, the generic scope of dramatic unreliability has thus far neither been properly defined nor even gauged, and the same holds true for the two-way traffic between the rise of the novel and the development of storytelling in drama. Although a small number of articles exist on the subject, the forms and uses of dramatic unreliability in dramatic subgenres other than memory plays and innovative hybrid genres deserve more attention than they have hitherto been given. Lastly, considering both the cognitive strategies and the culturally accepted models and frames that readers and critics (often unconsciously) deploy when they naturalise dramatic and narrative texts in terms of unreliable storytelling, narratologists have to assess the possible links between the historically variable notions of subjectivity and the equally changing uses of what has come to be known as unreliable narration.

Many recent plays do indeed suggest that there is something to Wall's (1994: 22) hypothesis "that changes in how subjectivity is viewed will inevitably be reflected in the way reliable or unreliable narration is presented". Like contemporary fiction, many recent plays such as *Doubt* or *Mindgame* tend to challenge the processes of naturalisation involved in the projection of unreliability and call conventional notions of the phenomenon into question. Wall (1994: 18) has demonstrated that Kazuo Ishiguro's *The Remains of the Day* not only "challenges our usual definition of an unreliable narrator" but also "deconstructs the notion of truth, and consequently questions both 'reliable' and 'unreliable' narration and the distinctions we make between them" (ibid.: 23). The same point could be made with respect to many post-war and contemporary plays that feature unreliability, including some of the plays that feature dramatic unreliability discussed above. But much more work needs to be done if we want to come to terms with the complex set of narrative strategies and cognitive processes that, ever since the good old days of Wayne C. Booth, have been subsumed under the wide umbrella of the term 'unreliable narration,' especially as far as drama and theatre as well as 'unreliable focalisation' and 'perspectivisation' are concerned.

On the basis of a cognitive, performative, and transgeneric theory of unreliability, the answer to the question "Unreliable, compared to what?" (cf. Nünning 1999a) can be summed up in one brief sentence: unreliable, not compared to the implied author's norms and values, but to the reader's, spectator's, or critic's conceptual knowledge of the world and his or her (usually unacknowledged) frames of reference, norms, and values. This answer, just like the theoretical framework and hypotheses delineated above, is not, however, meant to be the last word on the unchartered territory of unreliable narration in drama but rather a modest contribution to a transgeneric reconceptualisation of the subject that tries to take the specificity of dramatic storytelling and its performative quality into consideration. If we are to make sense of the complex uses of unreliable narration and focalisation in drama and theatre, we would arguably be wise to take the performative power of narrative in plays into account and recognise the worldmaking quality of dramatic storytelling on the page as well as on the stage.

Works Cited

Albee, Edward. 1965 [1962]. *Who's Afraid of Virginia Woolf.* Harmondsworth: Penguin.

Allrath, Gaby. 2005. *(En)Gendering Unreliable Narration: A Feminist-Narratological Theory and Analysis of Unreliability in Contemporary Women's Novels.* Trier: WVT.

Anastasopoulos, Dimitri. 2011. "Present without Memory: Self-Forgetfulness, Omniscience, and Non-Narration in the 2003 State of the Union Speech and in Lautréamont's 'Maldoror'." *Journal of Narrative Theory* 41.1: 12–33.

Anderson, Emily R. 2010. "Telling Stories: Unreliable Discourse, Fight Club, and the Cinematic Narrator." *Journal of Narrative Theory* 40.1: 80–107.

Ayckbourn, Alan. 1986. *Woman in Mind: December Bee.* London: Faber & Faber.

Bennett, James R. 1987. "Inconscience: Henry James and the Unreliable Speaker of the Dramatic Monologue." *Forum* 28: 74–84.

Booth, Wayne C. 1961. *The Rhetoric of Fiction.* Chicago, IL: University of Chicago Press.

Booth, Wayne C. 1975 [1974]. *A Rhetoric of Irony.* Chicago, IL: University of Chicago Press.

Brunkhorst, Martin. 1980. "Der Erzähler im Drama: Versionen des *memory play* bei Fry, Shaffer, Stoppard und Beckett." *AAA* 5.2: 225–240.

Chatman, Seymour. 1990. *Coming to Terms: The Rhetoric of Narrative in Fiction and Film.* Ithaca, NY/London: Cornell University Press.

D'hoker, Elke & Gunther Martens (eds.). 2008. *Narrative Unreliability in the Twentieth-Century First-Person Novel.* Narratologia 14. Berlin/New York, NY: De Gruyter.

Elam, Keir. 1980. *The Semiotics of Theatre and Drama.* London/New York, NY: Methuen.

Ferenz, Volker. 2008. *Don't Believe His Lies: The Unreliable Narrator in Contemporary American Cinema.* Focal Point: Studies in English and American Media 9. Trier: WVT.

Fludernik, Monika. 2003 [1996]. *Towards a 'Natural' Narratology.* London: Routledge.

Fludernik, Monika. 2007. "Narrative and Drama." In: John Pier & José Á. García Landa (eds.). *Theorizing Narrativity.* Narratologia 12. Berlin/New York, NY: De Gruyter. 355–383.

Friel, Brian. 1990. *Dancing at Lughnasa.* London/New York, NY: Samuel French.

Hastings Floyd, Virginia. 1972. "Point of View in Modern Drama." In: Esther M. Doyle & Virginia Hastings Floyd (eds.). *Studies in Interpretation*. Vol. 2. Amsterdam: Rodopi. 13–27.

Helbig, Jörg. 2005. "'Follow the White Rabbit!': Signale erzählerischer Unzuverlässigkeit im zeitgenössischen Spielfilm." In: Fabienne Liptay & Yvonne Wolf (eds.). *Was stimmt denn jetzt? Unzuverlässiges Erzählen in Literatur und Film*. München: Text + Kritik. 131–146.

Hesse, Beatrix. 2009. "Amadeus and Narrative Unreliability." In: Sabine Coelsch-Foisner, Dorothea Flothow & Wolfgang Görtschacher (eds.). *Mozart in Anglophone Cultures*. Frankfurt am Main/New York, NY: Lang. 25–36.

Horne, Jules. 2006. *Gorgeous Avatar*. London: Nick Hern Books.

Horowitz, Anthony. 2000. *Mindgame*. London: Oberon Books.

Hühn, Peter. 2004. "Transgeneric Narratology: Applications to Lyric Poetry." In: John Pier (ed.). *The Dynamics of Narrative Form. Studies in Anglo-American Narratology*. Narratologia 4. Berlin/New York, NY: De Gruyter. 139–158.

Hühn, Peter & Jörg Schönert. 2002. "Zur narratologischen Analyse von Lyrik." *Poetica* 34.3–4: 287–305.

Hühn, Peter & Jens Kiefer. 2005. *The Narratological Analysis of Lyric Poetry. Studies in English Poetry from the 16th to the 20th Century*. Trans. Alastair Matthews. Narratologia 7. Berlin/New York, NY: De Gruyter.

Hühn, Peter & Roy Sommer. 2009. "Narration in Poetry and Drama." In: Peter Hühn, John Pier, Wolf Schmid et al. (eds.). *Handbook to Narratology*. Narratologia 19. New York, NY: De Gruyter. 228–241.

Jahn, Manfred. 2001. "Narrative Voice and Agency in Drama: Aspects of a Narratology of Drama." *New Literary History* 32.3: 659–679.

Jahn, Manfred. 2005. "Narratology: A Guide to the Theory of Narrative." http://www.uni-koeln.de/~ame02/pppn.htm#N3.2 (last retrieved: December 6, 2012)

Johnson, Terry. 2001 [1993]. *Hysteria*. In: *The Methuen Book of Modern Drama: Plays of the '80s and '90s*. London: Methuen. 101–205.

Köppe, Tilmann & Tom Kindt. 2011. "Unreliable Narration With a Narrator and Without." *Journal of Literary Theory* 5.1: 81–93.

Laass, Eva. 2008. *Broken Taboos, Subjective Truths: Forms and Functions of Unreliable Narration in Contemporary American Cinema. A Contribution to Film Narratology*. Trier: WVT.

LaBute, Neil. 2005 [2003]. *autobahn: A Short-Play Cycle*. London: Faber & Faber.

Liptay, Fabienne. 2006. "Spinn' es noch einmal, Spider! Ambiguität als Voraussetzung für die doppelte Filmlektüre am Beispiel von David Cronenbergs *Spider*." In: Jörg Helbig (ed.). *Camera doesn't lie: Spielarten*

erzählerischer Unzuverlässigkeit im Film. Focal point: Studies in English and American Media 4. Trier: WVT. 189–223.
Liptay, Fabienne & Yvonne Wolf (eds.). 2005. *Was stimmt denn jetzt? Unzuverlässiges Erzählen in Lit. und Film*. München: Text + Kritik.
Meister, Jan C. (ed.). 2005. *Narratology beyond Literary Criticism. Mediality, Disciplinarity*. Narratologia 6. Berlin/New York, NY: De Gruyter.
Morrison, Kristin. 1983. *Canters and Chronicles. The Use of Narrative in the Plays of Samuel Beckett and Harold Pinter*. Chicago, IL/London: University of Chicago Press.
Muny, Eike. 2008. *Erzählperspektive im Drama: Ein Beitrag zur transgenerischen Narratologie*. München: Iudicium.
Nünning, Ansgar. 1998. "*Unreliable Narration* zur Einführung. Grundzüge einer kognitiv-narratologischen Theorie und Analyse unglaubwürdigen Erzählens." In: Ansgar Nünning (ed.). *Unreliable Narration: Studien zur Theorie und Praxis unglaubwürdigen Erzählens in der englischsprachigen Erzählliteratur*. Trier: WVT. 3–40.
Nünning, Ansgar. 1999a. "Unreliable, compared to what? Towards a Cognitive Theory of Unreliable Narration: Prolegomena and Hypotheses." In: Walter Grünzweig & Andreas Solbach (eds.). *Grenzüberschreitungen: Narratologie im Kontext/Transcending Boundaries: Narratology in Context*. Tübingen: Gunter Narr Verlag. 53–73.
Nünning, Ansgar. 1999b. "Reconceptualizing the Theory and Generic Scope of Unreliable Narration." In: John Pier (ed.). *Recent Trends in Narratological Research. GRAAT: Publications des Groupes de Recherches Anglo-Américaines de Tours* 21: 63–84.
Nünning, Ansgar. 2005. "Reconceptualizing Unreliable Narration: Synthesizing Cognitive and Rhetorical Approaches." In: James Phelan & Peter J. Rabinowitz (eds.). *A Companion to Narrative Theory*. Oxford: Blackwell. 89–107.
Nünning, Ansgar. 2008. "Reconceptualizing the Theory, History and Generic Scope of Unreliable Narration: Towards a Synthesis of Cognitive and Rhetorical Approaches." In: Elke D'hoker & Gunther Martens (eds.). *Narrative Unreliability in the Twentieth-Century First-Person Novel*. Narratologia 14. Berlin/New York, NY: De Gruyter. 29–76.
Nünning, Ansgar & Roy Sommer. 2002. "Drama und Narratologie: Die Entwicklung erzähltheoretischer Modelle und Kategorien für die Dramenanalyse." In: Vera Nünning & Ansgar Nünning (eds.). *Erzähltheorie transgenerisch, intermedial, interdisziplinär*. Trier: WVT. 105–128.
Nünning, Ansgar & Roy Sommer. 2006. "Die performative Kraft des Erzählens: Formen und Funktionen des Erzählens in Shakespeares Dramen." In: Ina Schabert & Sabine Schülting (eds.). *Shakespeare Jahrbuch* 142. Bochum: Verlag & Druckkontor Kamp. 124–141.

Nünning, Ansgar & Roy Sommer. 2008. "Diegetic and Mimetic Narrativity: Some further Steps towards a Transgeneric Narratology of Drama." In: John Pier & José Á. García Landa (eds.). *Theorizing Narrativity*. Narratologia 12. Berlin/New York, NY: De Gruyter. 331–354.

Nünning, Ansgar & Roy Sommer. 2011. "The Performative Power of Narrative in Drama: On the Forms and Functions of Dramatic Storytelling in Shakespeare's Plays." In: Greta Olson (ed.). *Current Trends in Narratology*. Narratologia 27. Berlin/New York, NY: De Gruyter. 200–231.

Nünning, Vera & Ansgar Nünning. 2002. "Produktive Grenzüberschreitungen: Transgenerische, intermediale und interdisziplinäre Ansätze in der Erzähltheorie." In: Vera Nünning & Ansgar Nünning (eds.). *Erzähltheorie transgenerisch, intermedial, interdisziplinär*. Trier: WVT. 1–22.

Nünning, Vera & Ansgar Nünning. 2007. "Dramatische Ironie als Strukturprinzip von unreliable narration, unreliable focalization und dramatic monologue: Ein kommunikations- und erzähltheoretischer Beitrag zur Rhetorik der Ironie im literarischen Erzähltext." In: Thomas Honegger, Eva-Maria Orth & Sandra Schwabe (eds.). *Irony Revisited: Spurensuche in der englischsprachigen Literatur*. Würzburg: Königshausen & Neumann. 51–82.

Olson, Greta. 2003. "Reconsidering Unreliability: Fallible and Untrustworthy Narrators." *Narrative* 11.1: 93–109.

Pfister, Manfred. 1991 [1988]. *The Theory and Analysis of Drama*. Trans. John Halliday. Cambridge: Cambridge University Press.

Phelan, James. 2004. "The Implied Author and the Location of Unreliability." In: *Living to Tell about It: A Rhetoric and Ethics of Character Narration*. Ithaca, NY/London: Cornell University Press. 31–65.

Phelan, James & Mary P. Martin. 1999. "'The Lessons of 'Weymouth': Homodiegesis, Unreliability, Ethics and *The Remains of the Day*." In: David Herman (ed.). *Narratologies: New Perspectives on Narrative Analysis*. Columbus, OH: Ohio State University Press. 88–109.

Richardson, Brian. 1988. "Point of View in Drama: Diegetic Monologue, Unreliable Narrators, and the Author's Voice on Stage." *Comparative Drama* 22.3: 193–214.

Richardson, Brian. 2001. "Voice and Narration in Postmodern Drama." *New Literary History* 32.3: 681–94.

Richardson, Brian. 2007. "Drama and Narrative." In: David Herman (ed.). *The Cambridge Companion to Narrative*. Cambridge: Cambridge University Press. 142–155

Riggan, William. 1981. *Pícaros, Madmen, Naifs, and Clowns: The Unreliable First-Person Narrator*. Norman, OK: University of Oklahoma Press.

Rohwer-Happe, Gislind. 2011. *Unreliable Narration im dramatischen Monolog des Viktorianismus: Konzepte und Funktionen.* Göttingen: V&R unipress GmbH.

Ryan, Marie-Laure. 2005. "On the Theoretical Foundations of Transmedial Narratology." In: Jan C. Meister (ed.). *Narratology beyond Literary Criticism: Mediality, Disciplinarity.* Narratologia 6. Berlin/New York, NY: De Gruyter. 1–23.

Shaffer, Peter. 2002 [1979]. *Amadeus.* Stuttgart: Reclam.

Shanley, John P. 2005. *Doubt: A Parable.* New York, NY: Dramatists Play Service, Inc.

Sommer, Roy. 2005. "Narrative and Drama." In: David Herman, Manfred Jahn & Marie-Laure Ryan (eds.). *Routledge Encyclopedia of Narrative Theory.* London/New York, NY: Routledge. 119–124.

Sommer, Roy. 2012. *Von Shakespeare bis Monty Python: Eine transmediale Geschichte der englischen Komödie zwischen pragmatischer Poetik und generischem Gedächtnis.* Trier: WVT.

Stoppard, Tom. 1975 [1974]. *Travesties: A Play.* New York, NY: Grove Press.

Vogt, Robert. 2009. "Kann ein zuverlässiger Erzähler unzuverlässig erzählen? Zum Begriff der 'Unzuverlässigkeit' in Literatur- und Filmwissenschaft." In: Susanne Kaul (ed.). *Erzählen im Film. Unzuverlässigkeit—Audiovisualität—Musik.* Bielefeld: transcript. 35–55.

Wall, Kathleen. 1994. "*The Remains of the Day* And Its Challenges to Theories of Unreliable Narration." *Journal of Narrative Technique* 24.1: 18–42.

Zerweck, Bruno. 2001. "Historicizing Unreliable Narration: Unreliability and Cultural Discourse in Narrative Fiction." *Style* 35.1: 151–178.

MATTHIAS BRÜTSCH

(Zurich)

Irony, Retroactivity, and Ambiguity: Three Kinds of "Unreliable Narration" in Literature and Film

It has become commonplace to label the narratological concept of unreliable narration a "mixed bag" or an "umbrella term", containing or denoting a variety of different types which should be set apart. While I agree with this statement from a transdisciplinary perspective, I would argue that within literary and film theory one can identify a particular narrative form predominantly invoked when unreliability is the topic in each of these fields. Interestingly, the two narrative constellations usually referred to—one with ironic distance and the other with retroactivity as its central feature—appear considerably different and in some respects even contrary to each other. As I have argued for this claim in more detail elsewhere (Brütsch 2011b, 2014), I will content myself here with an introductory note presenting the major results of this transdisciplinary comparison.

In addition, I will discuss a third narrative form, marked by ambiguity, sometimes referred to as unreliable narration in both literary and film studies. Here I will examine the conditions under which it makes sense to call narrators generating Todorov's (1975 [1970]: 24–40) "fantastic hesitation" unreliable and the relations and differences between the "destabilization" and the "unreliability" of narrators and their accounts. While maintaining my claim throughout that none of the three constellations are media-specific or bound exclusively to either homo- or heterodiegetic forms of narration, I will nevertheless point to differences in the way literary and filmic works establish ironic distance and ambiguity or destabilize their own narrative authority.

1. The Standard Examples in Literary and Film Studies

In literary studies, unreliable narration is generally associated with a homodiegetic narration shaped in such a way as to allow readers to adopt an understanding of diegetic reality which differs from the narrator's account. The discrepancy between these two assessments establishes a distance that accords a privileged position to the reader from which he or she can obtain an understanding unavailable to the narrator. The "uninformed" version of the narrator is the only one explicitly conveyed. An implicit meaning at odds with the narrator's account must be actively constructed by the reader, drawing on knowledge of the world in general and of fictional narratives in particular.[1] The narrator is usually not aware that his account or judgments would seem problematic to the addressee. For this reason, he cannot be considered guilty of deliberate deception.[2] Conflicts between the narrator's statements and the reader's understanding usually arise early on, and the discrepancy between the two often persists until the end. This narrative constellation can be considered ironic. The narrator's statements themselves, however, are not ironic. He really means what he says. But the narrative text as a whole is shaped in such a way so as to suggest an alternative or even opposite interpretation.[3] Examples of this "prototype" are Mark Twain's novel *Huckleberry Finn* (1884), in which the narrator blames himself for helping an African-American slave to escape from his master—a judgment which can be expected to be inverted by readers condemning slavery—and Ian McEwan's short story "Dead as They Come" (1978), in which the narrator tells the story of his passionate love to a woman who we soon find out is not a living human being but a mannequin in a shop window.[4]

When film scholars use the term unreliable narration, they often refer to the following constellation:[5] filmic narration presents the events of the story in such a way so as to prompt the audience to make erroneous inferences about the reality of characters, events, or entire worlds. The real state of affairs is only revealed in the ending. The narrative's dynamic is thus geared towards a final plot twist. The narration usually deceives the spectator by restricting perspective and knowledge to the central character, who turns out to be the victim of an illusion of some kind.[6] The

---

[1] For a detailed analysis of the reader's cognitive activity involved in projecting unreliability, see A. Nünning (1998b: 23–32; 2005: 99–104).

[2] The concept of unreliability has sometimes been expanded to include consciously deceptive narrators, even though this implies a major shift in the narrative constellation and, consequently, in the effect on the reader.

[3] Whether readers actually adopt a diverging view by projecting unreliability onto the narrator depends to a large degree on their own world-view and predispositions, which may change over time, as Vera Nünning (1998) has shown from a cognitivist stance.

[4] Further examples are "The Yellow Wallpaper" (1892) by Charlotte Perkins Gilman, "Oil of Dog" (1911) by Ambrose Bierce, "Haircut" (1925) by Ring Lardner, and *The Remains of the Day* (1989) by Kazuo Ishiguro.

[5] E.g. Liptay/Wolf (2005b: 15), Helbig (2005, 2006b), Hartmann (2005), Lahde (2005, 2006), Thoene (2006), Laass (2006: 257–258), Orth (2006) and Poppe (2009).

[6] Typically the narration gives various clues as to the illusory nature of the protagonist's perceptions before the ending but makes sure the hints are subtle enough not to give away the surprise. See Helbig (2005) and Brütsch (2011a: 182–211).

aligning of spectator and character continues until the end, since the final revelation usually enlightens them both. On the other hand, the surprise ending establishes a distance between the spectator and the narration in which crucial information turns out to have been withheld. Examples of this "prototype" are *La Rivière du Hibou* (Robert Enrico, France 1962), in which we learn at the end that the protagonist's adventurous escape from captivity and execution was only a last-minute fantasy before dying,[7] or *The Sixth Sense* (M. Night Shyamalan, USA 1999), in which the main character, a psychologist watching over a boy who sees ghosts, is himself revealed to be a ghost.[8]

2. Dissimilarities between the Two Standard Examples

In order to highlight the differences between these two notions of unreliable narration (subsequently referred to as the literary and filmic prototypes), I have compiled a list of important dissimilarities:

- *Deception*: In the literary prototype, the reader is not deceived (or is so only at the very beginning) but, on the contrary, recognizes illusions or misunderstandings on the part of the narrator. In the filmic prototype, the spectator just as the main character is deceived until the surprise ending.
- *Distance between narrational instances*: In the literary prototype, there is a distance between reader and narrator but none between the reader and the narrative text as a whole. In the filmic prototype, there is no distance between spectator and character but rather, implicitly, between the spectator and the narrative text as a whole, which becomes explicit in the final revelation.
- *Discrepancy*: In the literary prototype, there is a discrepancy between the narrator's version of the story and the reader's understanding and reconstruction of that same story. In the filmic prototype, there is a discrepancy between the story version first conveyed by the narration and the one it reveals in the ending.
- *Irony*: The narrative constellation in the literary prototype is ironic since an implicit meaning can be construed which differs from the explicit one. In the filmic prototype, there is no such ironic

---

[7] For a close analysis of the narrative structure in Enrico's short film, see Brütsch (2011a: 204–207; 292–295).

[8] Further examples are: *Dans la Nuit* (FR 1929), *The Woman in the Window* (USA 1944), *Angel Heart* (USA 1987), *Abre los ojos* (Spain/FR/IT 1997), *The Matrix* (USA 1999), *A Beautiful Mind* (USA 2001), *The Others* (Spain/FR/USA 2001), *Identity* (USA 2003) and *El Maquinista* (Spain 2004).

duplicity (in any case, not on first viewing) since the reconstruction of the alternative version is explicitly carried out by the filmic narration.
- *Dramaturgy*: In the literary prototype, the discrepancy is established early on and remains until the end. In the filmic prototype, the discrepancy becomes apparent only at the moment when it is finally revealed.
- *Surprise*: In the literary prototype, there is no surprise effect (or only a minor one at the beginning). In the filmic prototype, the entire dramatic structure is oriented towards the final plot twist.
- *Focalization/Subjectivity*: In the literary prototype, even though the point of view is restricted, the reader is able to acquire a broader perspective by projecting unreliability and drawing on his own knowledge. The dynamic thus elicits objectivity from subjectivity. In the filmic prototype, it turns out that the spectator was restricted to the experience of the central character in a much more fundamental way than at first seemed the case. The dynamic thus elicits (revealed) subjectivity from (apparent) objectivity.[9]

In view of this long list of differences, one may raise the question whether there are any similarities at all between the two constellations, especially given that many film scholars have transferred the concept of unreliable narration from one to the other. There are, of course, parallels between the two on a general level. The fact that there is some kind of deception and discrepancy connected to the process of narration and reception, that something must be interpreted differently than the narration suggests, seems to be the common ground that justifies the transfer. Nonetheless, the list I have presented shows that these rather unspecific similarities are outweighed by a number of important differences that become obvious as soon as one examines the exact location of the discrepancies and deceptions.

One may object that my prototypes exaggerate differences and disregard distinctions already made by several authors. The distinctions between *misevaluating* and *misreporting* (Phelan/Martin 1999) or *normative* and *factual unreliability* (A. Nünning 1998b: 12–13), which have gained general acceptance, are not identical, however, with the distinction between my literary and filmic prototypes; for the literary narrator often misreports on the basis of his erroneous judgments (as is the case in "Dead as They Come"), and false evaluations also play a significant role in the filmic prototype, albeit not at the level of narration but of reception. There is a

---

9   The only publications, to my knowledge, that address several of these differences systematically are Vogt (2009) and Koch (2011).

partial match, though, since the literary prototype has an affinity to the normative and the filmic prototype to the factual type of unreliability. But this link is not exclusive because mis- or underreporting does not necessarily mislead readers/spectators (as would have to be the case in the filmic prototype) but can just as well be detected from the start (as in the literary prototype).

3. The Literary Prototype in Film (and Vice-Versa)

How did the term "unreliable narration" come to be used in neighbouring fields for two narrative constellations more different than similar? One of the reasons seems to have been that literary and film scholars alike were eager to stress differences between the two media, especially the fact that in literature narration can be personalized, whereas in film, at least at the highest level, it necessarily remains impersonal and abstract without psychological attributes.[10] This view is based on the assumption that, contrary to verbal narration, to narrate by means of sound and image about past events is not a common form of human expression. Therefore it appears much more natural to presuppose a personal narrator when reading a novel than when watching a film. Moreover, film production is a collaborative enterprise that normally resists the projection of a single entity responsible for the overall design of the work.

However reasonable this view seems, it ignores the exceptional case in which a filmmaker is established as being responsible for the film's narration not on a secondary level as the author of a film within the film but on a primary level as the individual accountable for all images and sounds. Just as novelists can create narrators who appear to be in charge of the narration, filmmakers may invent directors appearing to be in charge of narration. As a result of this operation we get fake documentaries in which fictional filmmakers report on their lives or the lives of others. Examples of this kind are *David Holzman's Diary* (Jim McBride, USA 1967) or *Zusje* (*Little Sister*, Robert J. Westdijk, Netherlands 1995). The narrative constellation in these films corresponds to first-person narratives in literature, where the narrator claims to report on real events and persons he has known and observed.

The question is whether filmic narration which can thus become personalized may be as unreliable as the first-person narrator in literature. An example of this kind would confirm the hypothesis that the narrative

---

10 E.g. Liptay/Wolf (2005b: 13–14), Helbig (2005: 131–134), Lahde (2005: 294), Laass (2006: 254–256), Orth (2006: 286–288) and Poppe (2009: 70).

constellation of the literary prototype, often labelled "genuinely literary" (e.g. Martínez/Scheffel 2002 [1999]: 101), may also be found in film. *C'est arrivé près de chez vous* (*Man Bites Dog*, Rémy Belvaux/André Bonzel/Benoît Poelvoorde, Belgium 1992) is just such an example. It pretends to be a documentary about Ben's daily life as shot by three filmmakers. Ben's occupation, however—murdering and robbing people—is rather uncommon. What is striking about this mockumentary is that the filmmakers, who repeatedly appear onscreen or are heard on the soundtrack, not only let Ben go on with his killings without interfering, but they eventually even participate in them. Moreover, they ask Ben all kinds of questions, but never why he is killing people or how he feels about what he is doing. This omission is foregrounded in a scene in which Ben loses his bracelet while chasing a victim. The film director immediately asks him whether the lost bracelet has any sentimental value to which he gives a prolonged, affirmative answer. The film crew's attitude can thus be qualified as unreliable in the sense of Phelan and Martin's *underregarding*. In addition, analysis of the film's aesthetic qualities provides examples of *misregarding* such as when the filmmakers show Ben's killings in a swift montage-sequence, attempting to present his activities in a stylish manner worthy of their admiration, or when they help Ben dispose of the victim while laughing at his racist and sexist jokes.

The explicit message of the fictional documentary is that Ben's behaviour is funny, admirable, and a good example to be followed. Analytical detachment or critical questions are not necessary. The implicit meaning of *Man Bites Dog*, however, can be understood as the exact opposite: a sharp critique of reality-TV shows and their lack of critical stance towards their protagonists. The fictional filmmakers are not aware of this implicit meaning, even though their roles are played by the real filmmakers themselves. The controversial reactions provoked by the mockumentary reveal that not all spectators were willing to make this distinction. An ironic reading, however, is possible and demonstrates that filmic narration is capable of unreliability corresponding to the literary prototype.

Conversely, that the narrative constellation typical for the filmic prototype—false leads ending in a major plot twist—can be found in literary fiction is even more easily demonstrated since short stories and novels such as Ambrose Bierce's "An Occurrence at Owl Creek Bridge" (1890)[11] or Leo Perutz' *Zwischen neun und neun* (1918)[12] are more common than the exceptional case of *Man Bites Dog*. These examples are not usually con-

---

11 The short film *La Rivière du Hibou*, mentioned above, is based on Bierce's short story.
12 Just as in "An Occurrence at Owl Creek Bridge," most of the events narrated in Perutz' novel turn out to be a mere fantasy of the dying protagonist who jumped from the roof of a building to escape from two policemen.

sidered unreliable narratives despite corresponding exactly to works so labelled in the other media.[13]

4. Ambiguity and Its Relation to Unreliable Narration

A prominent work of fiction belonging neither to the literary nor to the filmic prototype but sometimes discussed as an example of unreliable narration is *The Turn of the Screw* (1898) by Henry James. Booth himself called the governess (author of the intradiegetic manuscript, which constitutes the major part of James' novella) "only one of a great number of indeterminately unreliable narrators who have led readers into public controversy" (1983 [1961]: 315). In her account as it is conveyed to us by an unnamed narrator who has heard the manuscript read, the governess tells about her stay at the country estate Bly where she had been employed to look after Miles and Flora, the nephew and niece of a wealthy young bachelor. Given full charge of the children, the young and inexperienced woman at first feels insecure about the big assignment but is quickly reassured and even delighted by the charm of the two children. The only matter disturbing the harmonious atmosphere at this point is a letter from the headmaster stating that young Miles has been expelled from school. There are no reasons given and the governess, hesitating to directly confront the boy, explains the matter away by telling herself that there might be a mistake or that the headmaster overreacted. Soon thereafter, the governess starts noticing a man and a woman on the premises who are not residents of the estate. When she describes them to the housekeeper, she discovers that their appearance corresponds exactly to that of Peter Quint, a former Valet at Bly, and Miss Jessel, the governess' predecessor, who both died under mysterious circumstances. Although no one else acknowledges their presence, the Governess is soon convinced not only that the apparitions are ghosts of the former employees but also that the children are aware of them and under their bad influence. The governess urges Flora to confess that she has been secretly communicating with Miss Jessel, but the girl strongly denies this and demands to be taken away from the governess, a wish she is granted due to her feverish condition. Left

---

[13] Martínez and Scheffel are among the few who classify novels such as Perutz' *Zwischen neun und neun* as a form of factual unreliability ("mimetisch teilweise unzuverlässiges Erzählen", 2002 [1999]: 102–103), but by doing so they contradict their own definition of unreliable narration as a form of ironic communication (ibid.: 100–101). In recent contributions— probably due to the influence of film scholars' publications—it has become more common to mention retroactive constellations in discussions of literary unreliability (cf. articles in this volume by, for example, Vogt, Pettersson, Nünning/Schwanecke, Nünning).

alone with the boy, the governess is about to confront Miles about his expulsion from school when the figure of Peter Quint appears again. The governess tries to shield the boy from the evil apparition and to squeeze a confession out of him only to realise after the figure has vanished that he has died in her arms.

The Turn of the Screw has been discussed in relation not only to the concept of unreliable narration but also to the concept of the fantastic. For Todorov (1975 [1970]), the fantastic arises when, in a fictional world that seems to obey the laws of our world, strange happenings occur that defy these laws and can be accounted for by two mutually exclusive explanations, one natural and the other supernatural. The hesitation on the reader's part between the two is what constitutes for Todorov the genre of the fantastic. Besides *La Vénus de l'Ille* (Prosper Mérimée, 1837), *The Turn of the Screw* is the only example Todorov gives of the "pure fantastic", i.e. of narratives which sustain the reader's uncertainty until and beyond the end. James' novella, Todorov writes, "does not permit us to determine finally whether ghosts haunt the old estate, or whether we are confronted by the hallucinations of a hysterical governess victimized by the disturbing atmosphere which surrounds her" (1975 [1970]: 43).

Todorov does not explicitly invoke the concept of the unreliable narrator introduced by Booth less than a decade earlier. And among the scholars taking up Todorov's theory and developing it further, only some have seen a connection (e.g. Simonis 2005; Horstkotte 2007) while others have explicitly cautioned against confusing the two concepts (e.g. Wörtche 1987; Durst 2007).

5. Unreliability vs. Destabilization

I would like to now turn our focus to the question of whether narrators of fantastic tales can be called unreliable in the sense of the literary prototype. Wörtche and Durst both argue that a special kind of narrator is called for in order to achieve the effect of the fantastic, but they call him or her "destabilized", "shattered" ("zerrüttet") or "disintegrated" ("demontiert") rather than unreliable (Wörtche 1987: 159). Discussing a particular strategy by which his or her authority may be undermined (modalisations such as the use of "as if"-clauses), they make the distinction between the two explicit:

> Wörtche is right to note that the disintegration of the narrator is not to be confused with the concept of the unreliable narrator [Wörtche 1987: 102]. Booth calls a narrator unreliable when he does not "speak for or act in accordance with the norms of the work (which is to say, the implied author's norms)" as for in-

stance "in Huckleberry Finn [wherein] the narrator claims to be naturally wicked while the author silently praises his virtues behind his back" (Durst 2007: 190, my translation).

While I see good reasons for distinguishing between the instability or disintegration and the unreliability of the narrator, I argue that there is nevertheless a match between the two, albeit only a partial one: unreliable narrators are often destabilized, but destabilized narrators need not be unreliable.

What is meant by the "instability" or "destabilization" of the narrator and his or her account? Authors using these terms alongside or instead of "unreliability"[14] usually refer to the following aspects:

- the character traits, behaviour, psychological disposition and mental health of the narrator;
- his or her situation;
- the narrative perspective adopted;
- the way he or she relates what happened.

The more dubious the character, odd the behaviour, fragile the disposition, and stressful the situation, the more probable that the narrator may appear destabilized to the reader. As for the narrative perspective, most authors agree that a more or less strong restriction to the narrator's subjective experience is an important prerequisite for his or her destabilization.[15] And concerning the manner in which the narrator tells his or her story, the following features are said to destabilize his or her account:

- the use of modalizing formulas such as "it was as if", "it seemed", "you could almost say that", etc., which immediately cast doubt on what is asserted.
- explicitly expressed doubts by the narrator about his own ability to accurately remember or relate what happened.
- the "grammatical disintegration" ("grammatische Zerrüttung"; Durst 2007: 191) of the language used.

---

14 Spiegel uses "destabilized" and "unreliable" synonymously (2010: 60), Simonis makes some distinctions but also sees close relations (2005: 199–229) while Wörtche and Durst draw a line between the two (see above).

15 For Todorov, only first person narrators can fully guarantee the fantastic effect, since assertions by third-person narrators are too authoritative to allow for the necessary doubt on the reader's part (1975 [1970]: 83). This (pre-genettien) position overlooks the fact that restriction to the subjective experience of a single character is the pertinent factor here, and that this kind of perspective, while not necessarily implied by homodiegetic narration, can just as well be established by heterodiegetic narration (cf. Durst 2007: 188).

6. *The Turn of the Screw* vs. *The Green Man*

The Green Man by Kingsley Amis (1969), reputed as an instance of a fantastic tale with an unreliable narrator by Horstkotte (2007), may exemplify the above mentioned strategies of destabilization and at the same time establish a difference to *The Turn of the Screw* despite similarities in the alleged supernatural occurrences (i.e. the appearance of ghosts). The novel's homodiegetic narrator, Maurice Allington, freely admits he is "on a bottle of Scotch a day" habit which "had been [his] standard for twenty years" (Amis 1969: 12). In his mid fifties, he begins to suffer from various symptoms of old age and is repeatedly troubled by a combination of hypnagogic jactitation and hallucinations, which, as he explains in detail, are involuntary spasms of the muscles before falling asleep accompanied by visual illusions. He is in charge of a large inn and must cope with undependable employees, his daughter and second wife, who both feel neglected, and the death of his father, who suffers a lethal stroke early in the story. Alongside these troubles, he engages in a secret sexual adventure with the wife of his doctor; all of this amounts to a lot of stress (subdued with alcohol and pills) and little sleep.

When a character in such circumstances starts seeing ghosts, it is only natural for us readers to be somewhat sceptical about their real existence. This attitude is reinforced when the narrator uses phrases like "I vaguely saw [...]" (ibid.: 13), "I heard, or thought I heard [...]" (ibid.: 87, 118) or when he makes assertions only to disqualify them right away as in the following passage: "However, I felt certain that this was the first time tonight I had seen what I now saw. Feeling certain of that kind of thing is very far, in cases like mine, from being certain" (ibid.: 121). The unbelieving reactions of the characters around him, of which the following statement by his doctor is a typical instance, are another factor weighing on our judgement:

> Right. Now, whatever you see in this way can't harm you. I can understand your being frightened by these things, but try to remember that that's as much as they can do. Delirium tremens is a warning, not a disaster in itself, and we can deal with it. It's usually brought on by emotional strain, plus drink, of course, and I'd put all this down to your father's death. I think these ghosts of yours were a sort of prelude to the business in the bathroom, and your general idea that there are sinister and hostile characters around is very common in these cases. Are you with me? (ibid.: 159)

Unlike in many horror stories where reassurances like this one are only meant to highlight the isolation of the hero whom nobody believes except us as readers, here it is an objection to be taken seriously, especially since the narrator himself, at least till the last part of his narrative, regularly takes up arguments against the real existence of his ghosts as the following passage shows:

> I could not tell Lucy or anyone else, including myself, that I had not read the affidavit before. It was possible—I disbelievingly supposed it to be just possible—that my earlier couple of readings had impressed the facts on some buried part of my mind, from which something had dredged them up to create an illusion. (ibid.: 106)

The effect of the fantastic, as described by Todorov, would not be established, of course, if there were not also factors in support of the ghost theory. First of all, the fact that a character is in poor shape and that his account appears "destabilized" does not mean that he could not be right about his supernatural perceptions. Second, as the apparitions grow in number and concreteness, they seem to affect the real world in a way that is not so easily explained away, as when objects (apparently) put into play by the alleged ghosts are found by Allington outside of his paranormal encounters and are tangible for other characters as well or when his daughter is attacked by one of the creatures (or did she only dream it and get hurt while sleepwalking?).

Is the narrator of *The Green Man* not only destabilized but also unreliable as Horstkotte claims in his analysis? Reconsidering the central feature of our definition of literary unreliability—ironic distance between reader and narrator resulting from a discrepancy in knowledge and understanding—we have to acknowledge that, rather than being distanced and feeling better informed, we are led to share Allington's insecurity throughout a large part of the narrative. And when in the last part of the story evidence of the ghosts' real existence grows stronger and he starts to be convinced that they are not just hallucinations, so are we. Since Amis' novel does not establish the kind of evaluative or cognitive discrepancy typical of unreliable narration, I claim that its narrator cannot be called unreliable in the sense of the literary prototype.

Is that to say that narrators of fantastic tales are always reliable even if they are severely destabilized? Let us refer back to *The Turn of the Screw* to answer this question. The governess in James' novella is healthy and does not drink alcohol or swallow pills, but she is young and inexperienced, emotionally instable, easily excitable, rather fanciful, and under heavy pressure to live up to her responsibilities in an unfamiliar environment. Preoccupied first by her big assignment, then by Miles' expulsion from school and finally by the sinister apparitions, and unable to turn to her employer for help—he made it clear not to be bothered under any circumstances—she stays awake for nights on end and shows more and more signs of agitation and isolation. Thus, in her own way, she appears just as destabilized as Allington.

What about her account? In this respect, *The Turn of the Screw* differs radically from *The Green Man*. While Allington continually cautions the reader against the trustworthiness of his own perceptions and recollections, the governess is firmly convinced not only that what she sees is really there but also that the ghosts secretly communicate with the children and try to harm them. Instead of explicitly addressing the problems of her own disposition and cognitive abilities, she emphatically affirms her perceptions and inferences. The following are a few examples of this mindset.

Of her first encounter with Quint she writes:

> The gold was still in the sky, the clearness in the air, and the man who looked at me over the battlements was as definite as a picture in a frame. [...] So I saw him as I see the letters I form on this page [...]. (James 2008 [1898]: 26–27)

The account of her first sight of Miss Jessel reads:

> I began to take in with certitude and yet without direct vision the presence, a good way off, of a third person. [...] There was no ambiguity in anything; none whatever at least in the conviction I from one moment to another found myself forming as to what I should see straight before me [...]. (ibid.: 45)

On the question of Quint's intentions, she conveys her thoughts and dialogue with Mrs. Grose:

> On the spot there came to me the added shock of a certitude that it was not for me he had come. He had come for someone else. [...] "He was looking for little Miles." A portentous clearness now possessed me. "*That's* whom he was looking for."—[Mrs. Grose:] "But How do you know?"—"I know, I know, I know!" My exaltation grew. "And *you* know, my dear!" She did n't deny this, but I required, I felt, not even so much telling as that. [...] I had an absolute certainty that I should see again what I had already seen [...]. (ibid.: 32, 39–40)

And concerning the ghost's menace to the children, she writes:

> I was a screen—I was to stand before them. The more I saw the less they would. I began to watch them in a stifled suspense, a disguised tension, that might well, had it continued too long, have turned to something like madness. What saved me, as I now see, was that it turned to another matter altogether. It didn't last as suspense—it was superseded by horrible proofs. Proofs, I say, yes—from the moment I really took hold. (ibid.: 43–44)

"Definite", "certitude", "no ambiguity", "conviction", "clearness", "certainty", "proofs", etc.: expressions like these leave no doubt as to the governess' firm belief in the ghosts' actual presence and threat—an attitude in sharp contrast to Allington's hesitation in deciding whether the ghosts he sees are real or not. So the narrator's stance is clear,[16] but what about the reader's? The question of the ghosts' reality in *The Turn of the*

---

[16] The Governess has her moments of doubt, although not concerning the existence of the ghosts, but the children's complicity.

Screw has triggered a heated debate with critics arguing for and against it or maintaining that undecidability is the central effect. James' novella is a telling instance of the historical variability of readers' responses to works of fiction since, according to Peter G. Beidler's survey, "virtually all of James' contemporaries read it as a spine-chilling ghost story" (2004: 192) whereas positions making a case for the governess' insanity gained prominence from the 1930s to the 1960s. Later, a dualistic view focusing on the text's ambiguity started to dominate critical discourse, with Todorov's *The Fantastic*, mentioned above, paving the way for this position.[17]

For our purpose, which is more theoretical than historical, suffice it to say that soon after *The Turn of the Screw* was published the first reviews appeared arguing against the governess' version of the story and that the dominant critical stance from the 1970s has been a bipolar reading highlighting the effects of hesitation and insecurity. If the governess' version is not taken at face value, either because it is rejected outright or because the possibility of an alternate version is taken into account, then the reader distances himself from the narrator. And since the only version explicitly conveyed is the one given (or, rather, emphatically asserted) by the governess, an alternative reading has to be grounded on implicit clues. In *The Turn of the Screw*—contrary to *The Green Man*—the conditions for unreliability in the sense of the literary prototype are thus met. On the relation between the concepts of the fantastic and unreliability, we can conclude that in cases where the narrator does not hesitate between a natural and a supernatural explanation but firmly believes in the latter while implicit clues invite the reader to waver between the two, unreliability plays a crucial role insomuch as the reader's hesitation is not just between two kinds of fictional worlds but also between two kinds of narrators, one reliable and one unreliable. In cases where the narrator hesitates in accord with the reader, on the other hand, I would argue that unreliability in the above sense is not a central feature.[18]

---

17 This is of course a simplified account of Beidler's critical history, which is only meant to show the range and changeability of points of view.

18 Todorov already pointed to the fact that the character-narrator's uncertainty is only an optional ingredient to the fantastic effect, for which the readers' hesitation is essential (1975 [1970]: 31–33). On this point, Simonis is inaccurate when she writes that "Todorov however still locates the attitude of hesitation primarily (even if not exclusively) on the level of the characters in action who are surprised by strange occurrences [...]" (2005: 208, my translation).

7. Signs of Unreliability Reconsidered

What then are Horstkotte's arguments for calling the narrator of *The Green Man* unreliable? He refers to textual clues established as signs of unreliability by some of the most prominent scholars in the field:

(1) strong personalization of the narrative situation (Zerweck);
(2) the narrator's untrustworthy personality and character (Allrath);
(3) his or her unintentional self-incrimination (Zerweck);
(4) contrasts between descriptions of events and their explanations and interpretations (Booth; A. Nünning);
(5) the narrator's self-conscious raising of issues of (un)reliability (A. Nünning).

Horstkotte sees strong evidence for all of these signs in *The Green Man*: (1) Allington is a strongly personalized first-person narrator; (2) his behaviour towards most of the other characters is questionable; (3) he obviously has a drinking problem which might directly be connected to his visions but is casual about it; (4) when confronted with justified accusations by his wife or son, his thoughts are somewhere else; and (5) he repeatedly and self-consciously muses about his memory lapses.

Against these points, I submit the following rebuttal:

(1) The personalization of the narrative situation is, as Zerweck and Horstkotte themselves admit, only a prerequisite for unreliability, not a sign of it.

(2) To directly infer anything from the character and personality the narrator was at the time the events in the story took place (i.e. from his or her behaviour towards other characters) about his or her reliability as a narrator (i.e. to his or her present relation to the narratee) is highly problematic. For readers of *Huckleberry Finn* who condemn slavery, its narrator is at the same time behaving exemplary *and* narrating unreliably (in the normative sense). And the narrator of "Dead as They Come" does not appear unreliable because of "abusing" a dummy, but because he talks about it as if it had been a living human being.[19]

---

19 This is why I believe that, even if "a male chauvinist fetishist who gets his kicks out of making love to dummies is unlikely to detect any distance between his norms and those of the mad monologist," as A. Nünning (1997: 101) puts it, this kind of reader would probably still be struck by the inadequateness of taking a dead object for a living being and thus detect a discrepancy in cognitive abilities sufficient to project unreliability. The distance between narrator and reader depends on the similarity of their assessment and evaluation of what happened in the story, which is only partly determined by factors such as their sexual orientation and behaviour. A pederast, to take A. Nünning's second example (ibid.), if more conscious of the wrongness of seducing children than Humbert Humbert, could very well notice inconsistencies in the account of his relation to Lolita even if he shares the same perverse sexual orientation.

(3) & (4) I do not see much of either in *The Green Man* and do not think Horstkotte's examples are valid instances of these clues. There are many passages of self-incrimination, to be sure, but, as mentioned above, most of them are *intentional and self-conscious* rather than unintentional. Which brings me to (5), a point worthy of a more detailed discussion.

There is no doubt that Allington raises the issue of the potential unreliability of his perceptions and memories again and again, thus openly destabilizing his own account in the sense discussed above. But is that a sign of narrative unreliability? Examining A. Nünning's catalogue of 13 textual clues for unreliability (1998b: 27–28) to which Horstkotte refers[20] (and which is one of the most advanced of its kind), we observe that all but two of the entries are either forms of contradictions, discrepancies or contrasts directly inviting readers to take their distances towards the narrator (clues 1–7) or signs of his or her strong subjectivity, emotional involvement and efforts to gain the understanding of the narratee (8–11), which are not, strictly speaking, direct clues to unreliability but nevertheless may caution readers to be on their guard and thus prepare the ground for their detachment. The last two signs (*acknowledged* untrustworthiness and *acknowledged* partiality), on the other hand, tend to *approximate* rather than to distance the reader's and the narrator's views—provided, of course, the readers agree with this judgement (which is, I would say, the case in *The Green Man*). They are no doubt indications that what the narrator reports may be inaccurate and how he comments may be biased, but unreliability as conceived above is not primarily a matter of knowing what really happened and how best to evaluate it but of what stance the reader takes vis-à-vis the narrator and his account. If reader and narrator *both* suspect that things might have happened differently than how the latter remembers and describes them, then they are united in their doubt rather than separated by differing standpoints. In this constellation, acknowledged untrustworthiness and acknowledged partiality are signs of narrative *reliability* rather than of narrative unreliability!

Unreliability is a relational phenomenon. That a narrator's account cannot be trusted is not enough to make him unreliable. What are needed additionally are signs of his belief in his version of the story without which there is no (ironic) distance and thus no unreliability (in the sense of the literary prototype). Because of the relationality of the concept, a narrator's "emphatic assertion" and his "acknowledged untrustworthiness" may *both* serve to form an unreliable narrative constellation, although they are diametrically opposed attitudes—on condition that readers are led to take a contrary stance, entertaining doubts in the former case (as in *The Turn of*

---

20 Horstkotte refers to Nünning (1997) which by and large discusses the same textual clues.

the Screw) and trusting in the narrator's good faith despite his open self incrimination in the latter case (as in *Huckleberry Finn*).[21]

Narratives with fantastic ambiguity as their central feature are interesting test cases in yet another respect. Among the signs of unreliability to be found in the violation of narrative conventions, Gaby Allrath calls attention to focalizations of other character's consciousness not accounted for in any way (1998: 68–69). The governess' report clearly contains transgressions of this kind since she repeatedly tells us about thoughts and emotions of the children to which as a restricted homodiegetic narrator she cannot have direct access and which can hardly be gained by mere outside observation. How can the ambiguous structure which pivotally relies on the hesitation between projecting and not projecting unreliability be maintained despite these apparent signs of unreliability? The solution lies in the subordination of norms of focalization to the conventions of genre. In a *realist setting*, it is implausible for a character to intuitively sense without much external evidence what other characters feel and think. In a *marvellous world* (as defined by Todorov) with supernatural laws, on the other hand, the powers of insight may well be stronger and render the governess' code of focalization much less transgressive and therefore also less unreliable. And because most readers of James' novella hesitate between assuming exactly these two kinds of fictional worlds, its dualistic design is not only undisturbed but even perfectly enhanced by the clue to unreliability mentioned by Allrath, which in this context is only potential.

We are now in a position to better differentiate between narrative destabilization and unreliability. The former method aims at (depending on its force) casting doubts on or clearly discrediting what is asserted, the latter at establishing a discrepancy between the narrator's and the reader's assessment and evaluation. The two only coincide if destabilization goes as far as completely discrediting or, in the case of only casting doubt, if the narrator is not himself conscious of the epistemic precariousness of his account.

Concerning the concept of the fantastic, we can observe that a frequent strategy to achieve ambiguity is to confront a narrator (as experiencing character) who already appears destabilized by his disposition and situation with frightening and apparently supernatural occurrences throwing him completely off track but leave it to the reader to decide whether his behaviour is justified—after all, it is quite natural to be highly troubled

---

21 Complemented accordingly, A. Nünning's twelfth and thirteenth entries may well remain in the catalogue.

when encountering evil-minded ghosts—or a sign of mental illness (which would account for the hallucination of paranormal activities).²²

8. Ambiguity, Destabilization, and Unreliability in *The Blair Witch Project*

So far I have only mentioned literary examples. What about ambiguity and its relation to destabilization and unreliability in film? In her book-length study of the fantastic genre in literature, Simonis briefly turns to film but only to deplore the gapless hyper reality of Hollywood's fantasy-blockbusters,

> obviously going directly against the fundamental principles of the narrative tradition [...] and the specific appeal of the genre of the fantastic [...] which are substantially based on techniques of suggestion and allusion actively involving the reader and his power of imagination in the process of constructing the story (2005: 60–61, my translation).

If we were to adhere to Simonis' view, we could close the subject without further consideration. But she not only unquestioningly takes fantasy films to correspond to the genre of the fantastic (while in Todorov's system most films so labelled would rather belong to the marvellous), she also obviously did not look beyond Hollywood mainstream to find any more convincing examples.

Discussing the literary prototype of unreliability in film, it appeared above that the filmic equivalent to personalised homodiegetic narration are fake documentaries in which filmmakers report audiovisually on what they experience. A fantastic film involving unreliability in the literary sense would thus have to be looked for in this genre which is the domain of independent low budget productions rather than Hollywood. *The Blair Witch Project* (Daniel Myrick/Eduardo Sanchez, USA 1999), one of the first movies that comes to mind because of its huge success at the turn of the millennium, seems to be a promising candidate.²³

The film opens with the following caption: "In October of 1994, three student filmmakers disappeared in the woods near Burkittsville, Maryland while shooting a documentary. A year later their footage was found." Next, blurry images taken from a Hi-8 camcorder appear and a voice can be heard saying: "It's already recording!" Then a girl, Heather, comes into

---

22 *La Vénus de l'Ille* is a special case insofar as a fantastic effect is achieved despite the fact that its (homodiegetic) narrator—who is observing from a distance—does not appear destabilized and also does not believe in the supernatural explanation given by the characters directly involved with the ominous statue.
23 For a general discussion of the applicability of Todorov's (literary) concept to film, see Carroll (1990: 144–157).

focus showing her home and explaining that these are the comforts she will be leaving for the weekend to explore the Blair Witch. In the next scene, still conveyed to us through the handheld camcorder, a guy, Josh, with a 16mm camera and other shooting equipment joins the girl and sets his own camera into motion in response to her recording. Through parallel editing, this response results in a switching back and forth between footage from the two cameras, each showing the other person and camera in action. The next bit of footage shows them picking up a third member of the crew, Mike, and setting out to shoot their documentary.

In more than one respect, this beginning recalls the frame set up in *The Turn of the Screw*. Both narrations establish early on that the bulk of what will be conveyed to us is a record left behind by someone (or a group of people) who has (have) died or disappeared, that no other points of view will be offered than the one given in this chronicle, and that we are to expect a sinister turn of events. In addition, *The Blair Witch Project* establishes a series of parameters important for the (relative) plausibility of what follows. The crew members are introduced as persons who are obsessively filming every step of their investigation and who let the camera roll even during their own personal interactions. The dialogue is supposed to make us believe that there is enough battery power to shoot for a long time without recharging and we grow accustomed to the (unexplained) fact of seeing the footage (from both cameras) in edited form.

To briefly sum up the itinerary of the crew: First, they travel to Burkittsville to ask local people about the Blair Witch. Then they start to explore the woods nearby to look for signs of her and to visit sites where, as legend has it, people disappeared or were found dead. As they move deeper into the woods, they lose track of their location on the map and are finally unable to find where they parked the car. Forced to camp in the woods much longer than planned and unable to find a way out of it, they start to tire out and at the same time to notice more and more strange objects and eerie sounds that point to the real existence and close proximity of the witch. During the fifth night, Josh disappears, and the following night screams of horror are heard, but Heather and Mike are not sure they are Josh's. Finally, the two arrive at an abandoned house, from the inside of which the same kinds of screams resonate. Convinced they have found Josh, they search the house, but, as Mike reaches the basement, his camera drops to the floor. As Heather hurries to catch up with him, her camera briefly shows Mike standing motionless in the corner, facing the wall, before it is forced to the ground and stops rolling.

Like *The Turn of the Screw*, *The Blair Witch Project* introduces a number of uncanny elements but never actually establishes the existence of the supernatural as an irrefutable fact. In many respects, it creates a fantastic effect as defined by Todorov. How is this possible, given the photographic nature of the medium and the fact that what we are seeing is presented (within the fictional framework set up in the beginning) as audiovisual recordings? The most important strategy the film adopts to enable fantastic hesitation despite technological factuality is to never show the putative witch onscreen and to only present possible signs of her evil doings. In addition, the signs are such that they can not only be explained supernaturally but also naturally. To be more concrete: Since the beginning of their investigation, the crew (and we as spectators) have been suspicious that some of the local people (who know they are in the woods looking for the legendary witch) could play a nasty trick on them. All of the sounds they hear and traces they find (e.g. piles of stones, wooden figures, slime, a blood-soaked tooth and tongue) could just as easily be explained by animal or man-made causes.

The limited scope of the cameras, especially at night in the dense wood, is another factor enhancing the fantastic effect. The fact that the crew members, who started out enthusiastic, are more and more frightened and hide with their cameras in the tent or run away from apparent signs of the witch explains why the footage left to us is not only fragmentary but often also jittery or blurry and never really catches a clear view of anything that could prove the existence of the witch beyond reasonable doubt.

Are the crew members, the sole "producers" of the record left to us[24] (and in this respect resemble homodiegetic verbal narrators), destabilized and/or unreliable in the above defined (literary) sense? Concerning destabilization, we can affirm that the circumstances of their derailed investigation together with the effects of hunger, exhaustion, coldness and fear clearly meet the conditions "stressful situation" and "fragile (physical/psychological) disposition" mentioned above. More interesting, however, is the question whether the second and third criteria ("restriction to the narrator's subjective experience" and "destabilization of his or her account"), which are more media-specific than the former two, can also be fulfilled if the "language" used is audiovisual rather than verbal.

Despite the fact that there is a mechanical basis to audiovisual recordings and that cameras and microphones can be used to register images and sounds independently of human presence and interference,[25] the equipment of the crew and the circumstances of shooting in *The Blair*

---

24 As mentioned above, editing is the only element not accounted for in this context.
25 As is partly the case in *Paranormal Activity* (Oren Peli, USA 2009). Cf. Spiegel (2010: 133–139) who analyses some of the differences between this film and *The Blair Witch Project*.

Witch Project[26] are such that there is a strong relation between the crew members and how and what they film. The cameras are always hand-held, only built-in microphones are employed, and the camera lights are used as torches at night, thus establishing an obvious parallel between human perception and mechanical recording. The "live" recording also automatically eliminates any distance between experiencing and "narrating".[27] Furthermore, through dialogue, self-talk and exclamations, the crew members convey much information about what they think and how they feel. The quality and "style" of the footage, wherein whole stretches are out of focus, jittery or off the mark, also allow the viewer to draw inferences about the physical and psychological disposition of the persons holding the cameras, especially in a context where the declared aim was to shoot a documentary shedding light on a mystery rather than to create a piece of experimental cinema. In a way, these moments are the filmic equivalent to Durst's "grammatical disintegration", with the final dropping of the cameras as the ultimate loss of control over one's means of expression.

To sum up, destabilization, both of a general and a media specific kind, plays an important part in establishing the fantastic effect of *The Blair Witch Project*. But what about unreliability? In this regard, I see a closer resemblance to *The Green Man* than to *The Turn of the Screw*. Although in the course of the film there may be some differences between characters and spectators in evaluating the probability of supernatural occurrences, I would claim that the overall movement for both is one from more to less doubt and that the potential discrepancy (and, thus, possibility to project unreliability), though present, is weaker than in *The Turn of the Screw*. However, here, as in all the other examples discussed, spectators (and readers) may not agree and therefore may project unreliability to a variable extent.

9. Homo- vs. Heterodiegetic Narration

To conclude, I would like to look at a last question concerning all three narrative constellations invoked in this paper: Can ironic distance and ambiguity only be established with homodiegetic character narrators and retroactivity only in heterodiegetic narrative situations or is the inverse nexus possible as well? My answer is: yes, it is possible in all three cases,

---

26 I am referring to the crew and circumstances of (documentary) shooting *as fictionally established*, of course, and not to the real circumstances of shooting the fake documentary.
27 The literary genre closest to this kind of shortcut between experience and report is diary fiction.

even if there is a clear affinity between ironic distance and the former[28] and a certain affinity between retroactivity and the latter (while ambiguity seems to work equally well with both). Examples in support of my point are "The Disappearance" (a short story by Chitra Banerjee Divakaruni, 1995)[29] and *Einspruch III* (a short film by Rolando Colla, Switzerland 2002)[30] for ironic distance with heterodiegetic/impersonal narration, *Fight Club* (novel and film, USA 1996/1999) for retroactivity with homodiegetic character narrator and *Rosemary's Baby* (novel and film, USA 1967/1968)[31] or *El Labyrinto del Fauno* (Mexico/Spain/USA 2006)[32] for ambiguity with heterodiegetic/impersonal narration. However, two of these constellations do not involve unreliable narration (neither in the sense of the literary nor of the filmic prototype): namely, ambiguity without ironic distance and ironic distance without homodiegetic narrator.

Works Cited

Allrath, Gaby. 1998. "'But why will you say that I am mad?' Textuelle Signale für die Ermittlung von *unreliable narration*." In: Nünning (ed.). 1998a. 59–79.

Amis, Kingsley. 1969. *The Green Man*. London: Jonathan Cape.

Beidler, Peter G. 2004. "A Critical History of *The Turn of the Screw*." In: Peter G. Beidler (ed.). *Henry James, The Turn of the Screw. Complete, Authoritative Text with Biographical, Historical, and Cultural Contexts, Critical History, and Essays from Contemporary Critical Perspectives*. 2nd ed. Boston, MA/New York, NY: Bedford/St. Martin's. 189–222.

Booth, Wayne C. 1983 [1961]. *The Rhetoric of Fiction*. 2nd ed. Chicago, IL: University of Chicago Press.

Brütsch, Matthias. 2011a. *Traumbühne Kino. Der Traum als filmtheoretische Metapher und narratives Motiv*. Marburg: Schüren.

Brütsch, Matthias. 2011b. "Von der ironischen Distanz zur überraschenden Wendung. Wie sich das unzuverlässige Erzählen von der Literatur- in die Filmwissenschaft verschob." *Künste Medien Ästhetik* (1/2011–1): http://www.kunsttexte.de/index.php?id=711&idartikel=37876&ausgabe=37742&zu=121&L=1 (last retrieved: January 26, 2012).

---

28 This is why ironic distance is less common in film than in literary narration which is much more easily personalized.
29 Cf. Fludernik (2005: 53–56).
30 Cf. Brütsch (2011b: 7).
31 Cf. Brütsch (2011a: 335–343).
32 Cf. Spiegel (2010: 161–171).

Brütsch, Matthias. 2014. "From Ironic Distance to Unexpected Plot Twists. Unreliable Narration in Literature and Film." In: Jan Alber & Per Krogh Hansen (eds.). *Beyond Classical Narration. Unnatural and Transmedial Narrative and Narratology*. Berlin/New York, NY: De Gruyter. 57–79.

Carroll, Noël. 1990. *The Philosophy of Horror or Paradoxes of the Heart*. New York, NY/London: Routledge.

Durst, Uwe. 2007. *Theorie der phantastischen Literatur*. Berlin: LIT.

Fludernik, Monika. 2005. "Unreliability vs. Discordance. Kritische Betrachtungen zum literaturwissenschaftlichen Konzept der erzählerischen 'Unzuverlässigkeit'." In: Liptay & Wolf (eds.). 2005a. 39–59.

Hartmann, Britta. 2005. "Von der Macht erster Eindrücke. Falsche Fährten als textpragmatisches Krisenexperiment." In: Liptay & Wolf (eds.). 2005a. 154–174.

Helbig, Jörg. 2005. "'Follow the White Rabbit!' Signale erzählerischer Unzuverlässigkeit im zeitgenössischen Spielfilm." In: Liptay & Wolf (eds.). 2005a. 131–146.

Helbig, Jörg. (ed.). 2006a. *Camera Doesn't Lie. Spielarten erzählerischer Unzuverlässigkeit im Film*. Trier: WVT.

Helbig, Jörg. 2006b. "'Open Your Eyes!' Zur (Un-)Unterscheidbarkeit filmischer Repräsentationen von Realität und Traum am Beispiel von David Finchers *The Game* und Cameron Crowes *Vanilly Sky*." In: Helbig (ed.). 2006a. 169–188.

Horstkotte, Martin. 2007. "Unreliable Narration and the Fantastic in Kingsley Amis's *The Green Man* and Nigel Williams's *Witchcraft*." *Extrapolation* 48.1: 137–151.

James, Henry. 2008 [1898]. *The Turn of the Screw and Other Short Fiction*. 2nd ed. New York, NY: Bantam.

Koch, Jonas. 2011. "Unreliable and Discordant Film Narration." *Journal of Literary Theory* 5.1: 57–80.

Laass, Eva. 2006. "Krieg der Welten in Lynchville. *Mulholland Drive* und die Anwendungsmöglichkeiten und -grenzen des Konzepts narrativer UnZuverlässigkeit." In: Helbig (ed.). 2006a. 251–284.

Lahde, Maurice. 2005. "Der unzuverlässige Erzähler in *The Usual Suspects*." In: Liptay & Wolf (eds.). 2005a. 293–306.

Lahde, Maurice. 2006. "Den Wahn erlebbar machen. Zur Inszenierung von Halluzinationen in Ron Howards *A Beautiful Mind* und David Cronenbergs *Spider*." In: Helbig (ed.). 2006a. 43–72.

Liptay, Fabienne & Yvonne Wolf (eds.). 2005a. "*Was stimmt denn jetzt?" Unzuverlässiges Erzählen in Literatur und Film*. München: Text + Kritik.

Liptay, Fabienne & Yvonne Wolf. 2005b. "Einleitung. Film und Literatur im Dialog." In: Liptay & Wolf (eds.). 2005a. 12–18.

Martínez, Mathías & Michael Scheffel. 2002 [1999]. *Einführung in die Erzähltheorie*. 3rd ed. München: C. H. Beck.
Nünning, Ansgar. 1997. "'But why will you say that I am mad?' On the Theory, History, and Signals of Unreliable Narration in British Fiction." *Arbeiten aus Anglistik und Amerikanistik* 22.1: 83–105.
Nünning, Ansgar. 1998a (ed.). *Unreliable Narration. Studien zur Theorie und Praxis unglaubwürdigen Erzählens in der englischsprachigen Erzählliteratur.* [*Unreliable Narration: Studies in the Theory and Practice of Unreliable Narration in English Narrative Fiction*]. Trier: WVT.
Nünning, Ansgar. 1998b. "*Unreliable Narration* zur Einführung. Grundzüge einer kognitiv-narratologischen Theorie und Analyse unglaubwürdigen Erzählens." In: Nünning (ed.). 1998a. 3–40.
Nünning, Ansgar. 2005. "Reconceptualizing Unreliable Narration: Synthesizing Cognitive and Rhetorical Approaches." In: James Phelan & Peter J. Rabinowitz (eds.). *A Companion to Narrative Theory*. Oxford: Blackwell. 89–107.
Nünning, Vera. 1998. "Unreliable narration und die historische Variabilität von Werten und Normen. *The Vicar of Wakefield* als Testfall für eine kulturgeschichtliche Erzählforschung." In: Nünning (ed.). 1998a. 257–285.
Orth, Dominik. 2006. "Der unbewusste Tod. Unzuverlässiges Erzählen in M. Night Shyamalans *The Sixth Sense* und Alejandro Amenábars *The Others*." In: Helbig (ed.). 2006a. 285–307.
Phelan, James & Mary P. Martin. 1999. "The Lessons of 'Weymouth'. Homodiegesis, Unreliability, Ethics, and *The Remains of the Day*." In: David Herman (ed.). *Narratologies. New Perspectives on Narrative Analysis.* Columbus, OH: Ohio State University Press. 88–109.
Poppe, Sandra. 2009. "Wahrnehmungskrisen. Das Spiel mit Subjektivität, Identität und Realität im unzuverlässig erzählten Film." In: Susanne Kaul, Jean-Pierre Palmier & Timo Skrandies (eds.). *Erzählen im Film. Unzuverlässigkeit—Audiovisualität—Musik*. Bielefeld: Transcript. 69–83.
Simonis, Annette. 2005. *Grenzüberschreitungen in der phantastischen Literatur. Einführung in die Theorie und Geschichte eines narrativen Genres*. Heidelberg: Winter.
Spiegel, Simon. 2010. *Theoretisch Phantastisch. Eine Einführung in Tzvetan Todorovs Theorie der phantastischen Literatur*. Murnau am Staffelsee: *p.machinery* Haitel.
Thoene, Tina. 2006. "Er liebt mich—er liebt mich nicht: Abweichende Wahrnehmung und erzählerische Irreführungen in Laetitia Colombianis *A La Folie … Pas Du Tout*." In: Helbig (ed.). 2006a. 73–93.

Todorov, Tzvetan. 1975 [1970]. *The Fantastic. A Structural Approach to a Literary Genre*. Trans. Richard Howard. Ithaca, NY: Cornell University Press.

Vogt, Robert. 2009. "Kann ein zuverlässiger Erzähler unzuverlässig erzählen? Zum Begriff der 'Unzuverlässigkeit' in Literatur- und Filmwissenschaft." In: Susanne Kaul, Jean-Pierre Palmier & Timo Skrandies (eds.). *Erzählen im Film. Unzuverlässigkeit—Audiovisualität—Musik*. Bielefeld: Transcript. 35–56.

Wörtche, Thomas. 1987. *Phantastik und Unschlüssigkeit. Zum strukturellen Kriterium eines Genres. Untersuchungen an Texten von Hanns Heinz Ewers und Gustav Meyrink*. Meitingen: Corian.

Zerweck, Bruno. 2001. "Historicizing Unreliable Narration. Unreliability and Cultural Discourse in Narrative Fiction." *Style* 35.1: 151–178.

MARKUS KUHN
(Hamburg)

(Un)reliability in Fictional and Factual Audiovisual Narratives on YouTube

1. Introduction: In Search of Unreliable Narratives on YouTube

To illustrate what will be discussed in this article, I start in *medias res*, with a telling example: a user-generated clip posted on YouTube by the user "Robobos" in 2006. The clip is simply titled "Shining"[1] and looks like a movie trailer. After a silent still—showing the green band that is typical for movie trailers—the clip's first scenes visually introduce the two main characters, Jack and Danny, and a couple of other characters, including Danny's mother. The characters are shown in a few characteristic situations, while an extradiegetic male voice-over narrator explains the context: "Meet Jack Torrance … He's a writer, looking for inspiration … Meet Danny … He's a kid, looking for a dad … Jack just can't finish his book…" The utterances of the voice-over narrator and the intermissions he makes between them guide the rhythm of editing. The short scenes (that sometimes contain short dialogues) illustrate what the voice-over tells and add some necessary information about Danny and his mother that the voice-over narrator does not give.

The next part of the clip is a short sequence of shots, bridging the two main parts of the clip. This bridging sequence shows Danny opening a door and entering a room very carefully, while the voice-over explains: "But now … sometimes … what we need the most … is just around the corner." A few distorted piano cords create a tension that is resolved with the beginning of the song "Solsbury Hill" by Peter Gabriel, which—together with a fast dissolve to a white screen—marks the beginning of the third part of the clip, where we see Jack, Danny and his mother in a few scenes that show them as a happy patchwork family (see fig. 1). The clip ends with a black screen with the word "Shining" in white letters. The voice-over narrator articulates the same word with a mixture of promise and yearning in his voice.

---

1   "Shining." YouTube clip (http://www.youtube.com/watch?v=sfout_rgPSA (last retrieved: August 1, 2013)). The clip was uploaded on February 27, 2006 and reposted several times.

Let us imagine that someone watches this clip without knowing the background. The clip "Shining" promotes a movie about Jack Torrance, "a writer looking for inspiration," and Danny, a boy of about six years of age who lives with his mother and is "looking for a dad." It is a narrative clip: It represents the story of how Jack Torrance and the boy learn that the solution to their problems is to become closer to each other and to build some kind of family with the boy's mother. The dominant voice-over narrator is widely complemented by the moving pictures. The music on the soundtrack emphasizes the clip's dramaturgical structure: In the first part we see the main characters governed by their problems, in the second part we see a happy family and a relieved Jack Torrance, continuing his writing project. The introduction of the gentle song "Solsbury Hill" by Peter Gabriel marks the turning point. Taking all these aspects into account, it is quite obvious that the clip is a movie trailer for a family comedy with a happy ending.

My basic understanding of unreliable narration in this paper relies mainly on the positions of cognitive narratology, developed by Tamar Yacobi (1981), Monika Fludernik (1996, 2005), Ansgar Nünning (1998, 1999, 2005), and others. Therefore one of the presuppositions for unreliability is that there must be a contradiction, tension, or incongruity that cues the recipient to search for an interpretation strategy to *naturalize* this contradiction. One of these naturalization strategies—which Tamar Yacobi explains in her famous article "Fictional Reliability as a Communicative Problem" (1981)—is to consider the narrator, or to argue more abstractly, the narration itself, as unreliable.

Thus, to search for signposts that guide the reader to take the narration of the clip "Shining" as unreliable, I start searching for contradictory elements. As any audiovisual narrative, a YouTube clip bares the capability for contradictions in its multimodal mediality, or in other words, its multi-channel-structure. In this clip there is, actually, a contradiction between the verbal and the visual narration. On the one hand the verbal narrator explains—in a complementary interplay with parts of the visual narration and supported by the soundtrack—that this is the story of a writer who finds a family and regains his inspiration and mental balance. On the other hand, some of the pictures signal something different: Jack Torrance does not look like a writer merely in search of inspiration (see fig. 2) and does not appear to be as happy as the voice-over tells us he is (and as we would assume when following the storyline and the character's ostensible development). Having a closer look we recognize the gaze of Jack Torrance, which indicates some kind of madness.² Thus, we can register a contradiction between the *explicit* characterization of the male main character by the voice-over narrator and the *implicit* characterization by the *visual narrative instance*.³ This contradiction is, I must admit, not so obvious that every viewer would notice it. A crucial question is whether one interprets Jack Torrance's gaze as mad only because one is aware of the role biography of the actor Jack Nicholson.

I will stop my text-based analysis at this point, because almost everybody who has seen this clip knows that one does not have to search for intra-textual signposts to find a striking contradiction. We should rather start discussing the extra-textual dimension of this clip. The clip is supposed to be a movie trailer, signaled by conventional elements of movie trailers, especially the green band at the beginning (see fig. 3). Like any movie trailer, this clip has an obvious intermedial dimension (signaled by the title, the actors, specific key scenes etc.). It refers to a movie that ought to be forthcoming soon, or has, as in this case, already been released as the feature film *The Shining* by Stanley Kubrick with Jack Nicholson as Jack Torrance (USA 1980). Many media-conscious viewers know—even though they have not seen the movie—that *The Shining* has nothing to do with a family or comedy movie at all, but is in fact a horror movie about a father and writer who goes insane and tries to kill his family (see fig. 4).⁴ The clue of this fake-trailer is that it purports to be a trailer for a completely different film, while still using audiovisual material from the original. By editing the material in a different order, using different music as a soundtrack and adding the specific voice-over, this clip presents itself as a heart-warming comedy for the whole family. In this sense, compared to the movie that it ought to refer to, we can say that the clip is *unreliable*.

This example demonstrates that if we want to analyze such forms of unreliability on YouTube the question of the point of reference is crucial. To expound on this, I start with some remarks on my theoretical framework (Section 2). I will then point out a couple of narrative YouTube genres which may have notable potential for unreliable narration (Section 3), before I select a prominent YouTube genre, the video blog, and analyze the specific form of unreliability we can find within that genre

---

2   That holds true for his gaze on figure 2 (which is taken from the first part of the trailer), and—to a certain degree—even for his gaze on figure 1 that ought to show a 'happy patchwork family'.
3   For the concept of the *(audio)visual instance* in film see Kuhn (2011a: 83 ff.).
4   Cf. *The Shining* film poster (*IMDb* "Pictures & Photos from Shining", http://www.imdb.com/media/rm4034713856/tt0081 505 (last retrieved: August 28, 2013). For a summary, see Vossen (2009) and Koebner (1995).

(Section 4/5). To do so, I have to introduce the concept of authenticity and describe how it is related to the field of (un)reliability on YouTube. Eventually, I discuss whether the question of 'unreliable authenticity' is not only of crucial importance for many YouTube users but whether it is also highly dependent on the perceived authenticity of the YouTube users (Section 6), and how researchers could deal with this methodologically (Section 7).

2. Working Hypotheses: The Importance of Frames of Reference

If we want to regard those kinds of user-generated fake trailers like "Shining" as forms of unreliable narration—which is, as we have just seen, an obvious perspective—we have to focus not only on the intra-textual markers and signposts but also on the *frame of reference*, which is, in this case, an *intermedial* frame of reference. A YouTube clip refers to a movie and guides viewers to activate their media knowledge. The contradiction lies between the vision of a movie created by the fake trailer and the famous horror film *The Shining*. That brings me to my first working hypothesis. I assume that *intermedial* and other kinds of *media-based frames of reference* are essential for discussing forms of unreliable narration on YouTube in almost every case. It is not only the relation between the text and the reader's *world knowledge* that is important when discussing frames of reference, but also the intertextual and intermedial dimension or, in other words, *intermedial* and other *media- and genre-specific* contextual frames of reference. The knowledge the viewer activates to understand the clip is mostly related to knowledge about other media products and guided by the intermedial, interactive and interconnected dimension of the YouTube clip itself. My understanding of these frames of reference, which I call intermedial, media- and genre-specific, is based on the concept of Ansgar Nünning's *literary frames of references* (see 1998, 1999), modified and transferred for another medium and other media environments.

In his article "Unreliable, compared to what?" Nünning suggests a reconceptualization of the notion of unreliable narration in terms of frames of reference:

> The question of whether a narrator is described as unreliable or not needs to be gauged in relation to various frames of reference. More particularly, one might distinguish between schemata derived from everyday experience and those that result from knowledge of literary conventions. (1999: 67)

Nünning proposes two referential frameworks, the first one referring to "the readers' empirical experience and criteria of verisimilitude" (ibid.), and a second one that "involves a number of specifically literary frames of reference" (ibid.: 68). This second referential framework, or group of frames of reference, is what I take as basis for my concept of intermedial and media- and genre-specific frames of references (I return to Nünning's first referential framework when I discuss my second hypothesis). Nünning explains, referring to Harker (1989: 473), that the "experienced reader of literature brings to the text a set of schemata learned from previous literary reading experience" (ibid.), and registers the following:

- general literary conventions […]
- conventions and models of literary genres,
- other parameters of the respective generic and stylistic framework,
- intertextual frames of reference, that is reference to specific pre-texts,
- […],
- and last but not least the structure and norms established by the respective work itself. (Nünning 1999: 68)

Taking these categories and modifying them in terms of other media, I come to my concept of media-based, genre-based, and intermedial frames of references. Accordingly, I modify the list as follows:

- general media conventions,
- conventions and models of media genres (in this case: film and YouTube genres),
- other parameters of the respective generic and stylistic framework,
- intermedial frames of reference, that is reference to specific media pre-texts (in the case of a movie trailer: the movie it refers to)
- the structures and norms established by the respective work itself.

Nünning explains "the reader can always resort to one of these frames of reference in order to naturalize the text" (ibid.). I would like to emphasize that—with regard to YouTube clips—these frames of reference are important for both discovering tensions and contradictory elements and naturalizing these disparate items. When talking about unconscious cognitive processes one cannot separate the processes of detecting a contradiction and of naturalizing it. In the case of fake trailers like "Shining" the viewer resorts to an intermedial frame of reference to discover, to understand, and to naturalize the contradiction.

My article takes this hypothesis and the idea of intermedial, media- and genre related frames of reference as a first point of departure. A second attempt will focus on the relation between the representation within the clip and the sense of reality and authenticity of the user, or, more precisely, the model of realistic and authentic media-specific representation a group of users of a medium has in a certain period of time. I claim that in some narrative YouTube clips and genres, for instance video blogs, curiosity clips, semi-professional fashion blogs, or user-generated documentary clips, the question of reliability is closely related to questions of authenticity, and the discussion about the fictional or factual state of a clip by the users. I take this as my second hypothesis. In these cases it is another frame of reference that is important. The crucial question is what do viewers take as authentic or factual in a specific medial context and what do they not? This concept can be compared to Nünning's first referential framework mentioned above.

> A first referential framework should be based on the readers' empirical experience and criteria of verisimilitude [...] rather than on literary models. These frames depend on the referentiality of the text, the assumption that the text refers to or is at least compatible with the so called real world. (1999: 67)

I will narrow the points Nünning mentions for the purpose of this article to the question of authenticity and factuality. And I would like to stress what users take for authentic and/or real is highly dependent on both the medial context and the media experience of the users. Certain artifacts in certain historical media contexts use strategies of authenticity that influence the media knowledge of the users. In turn, users' media usage influences the strategies used. I will explain this in detail with regard to the example of YouTube in section 4, 5 and 6.

What both hypotheses I propose have in common is that they take the question "unreliable, compared to what?"—which Ansgar Nünning raised in the headline of the quoted article (1999)—as the major question for discussing YouTube clips in terms of unreliability, untrustworthiness and verisimilitude. In asking this question we gain important insights in how these examples are structured, how they are comprehended and interpreted in the reception process, and how we could find a point of departure for a theory of unreliability on YouTube.

3. Narrative Forms and Genres on YouTube and Their Capabilities for Unreliable Narration

Narrative on the Internet is a broad field of research as there exists a diversity of forms and modes of narration: From novels to everyday storytelling via weblog, from movies to private video clips, from public communication platforms to the micro accounts on twitter, narrative is almost everywhere on the Internet. Some of these forms are mainly based on language, pictures, sounds, or moving images, others on a combination thereof. Some are mono-modal, others multimodal, some are based on one-channel media, others on multichannel media (Kuhn 2014). Hence, in general, one can find on the Internet every form of narrative that appears in literature, film, TV, graphic novels, audio drama, and other analogue and digital media. Ultimately, the Internet has the potential to represent almost any kind and type of unreliable narration that we find in these media. Thus, a broad theory of unreliability on the Internet should be aware of all approaches in literary, film, media and art studies. This field is certainly too broad to be elaborated within the discipline of media studies alone. What should definitely be the goal of media and Internet studies, however, is to identify media-specific forms of reliable and unreliable narration. Collecting and modifying some suggestions by Mary-Laure Ryan (2004), Nick Montfort (2007), Terry Harpold (2008) and others[5], and adding quite a few narrative forms of my own, I suggest a list of crucial narratives on the Internet that may be complex enough to bare the capability for unreliable narration (see table 1). All those different narrative forms are, I presume, candidates that should be discussed with regard to the question of unreliability. Focusing on media-specific forms one must not overlook examples of other media that are transformed or adapted for the Internet. It is important for both forms—media-specific and transmedial forms—to consider the influence of the medial environments into which these products and artifacts are embedded.

– hypertexts	– multi-modal self narration on Facebook
– interactive fiction; interactive drama	– podcasts
– online games (e.g.: MMORPG—massively multiplayer online role-playing games)	– flash cartoons/flash cartoon series
	– interactive animation
– everyday storytelling via blog and weblogs (also: commercial storytelling; fictional storytelling on blogs and weblogs)	– web comics
	– email chain letters
	– commercials; pseudo-commercials; viral marketing via storytelling
– interactive video-clips/audiovisual narratives	– collaborative authorship projects (novels, comics, pop songs, …)
– non-serial and serial micro-narratives on twitter (e.g. "tiny tales" by Florian Meimberg)	– alternate reality games
	– transmedia storytelling projects; storytelling across media
– interconnected and cross-linked video-clips on different platforms	– fan fiction (that uses written or spoken language, pictures, moving pictures, sounds, comic strips, etc.)
– multi-modal narratives on home pages of professional, semi-professional, or amateur users	
– audiovisual web series	
– multi-modal, interconnected, and cross-linked narration and self-representation on the social web (by amateur users, pop stars, politicians, …)	

Table 1. Forms and modes of narration on the Internet

---

5   See Kuhn (2012, 2014).

Talking about YouTube clips as forms of narration is like cutting a small piece out of a big cake: 'Narrative across new or digital media' is a small part of the field of 'narrative across media;' 'narrative on the Internet' is an even smaller one. Within that framework, research on 'audiovisual forms on the Internet' exclusively focuses on all kinds of filmic and audiovisual narration, which is generally based on a combination of moving images, sounds and language (Kuhn 2014). Last but not least, this article concentrates particularly on audiovisual narratives on YouTube. Not every YouTube clip is a narrative, but there are many clips and genres that are narratives to a certain degree if we operate with a broad and gradual definition of *narrativity* and define a representation of a change of state as the core condition of narrative, regardless in which medium this representation happens (see Kuhn 2011a: 55–61). Table 2 shows a choice of YouTube genres and forms that have narrative potential and therefore also potential for unreliable narration. As the range of YouTube genres is much bigger, there are certainly more forms that hold the capability for reliable and unreliable narration. Moreover, it is possible to see complete movies or TV series on YouTube, usually separated into a series of interconnected short clips. Thus, nearly every form of unreliable narration we can find in Cinema or on TV can eventually be found on YouTube. But this is, again, not the core business of Internet studies.

– web series (professional/ semiprofessional/amateur; fictional/ pseudoauthentic/documentary; series/serial …) – mash ups – fake trailers – video blogs/YouTube channels that are used as video blogs – commercials; viral marketing via video clips (e.g. "Ron Hammer") – fake commercials – (fake)skills videos – interactive video-clips – digital attraction videos (videoclips that use and promote visual effects) – mockumentary clips – event and experience clips (clips that represent outstanding events and experiences; narratives that bear a high potential of eventfulness and experientiality)	– fail videos – animated clips (e.g. cartoons and digital or stop motion animation) – audiovisual fan fiction – machinima – tech demos (e.g. for video game engines) – re-enactments – audio-visual narrative Internet memes – narrative music videos – narrative documentary clips (investigative and citizen journalism) – political and socio-critical propaganda campaigns (from professional propaganda campaigns over viral and semi-professional clips to the field of counter-public and grassroots culture) – comedy clips – parody video

Table 2. YouTube genres and forms with narrative potential

The structure of unreliability in many fake trailers can be compared to the example of the "Shining" clip I discussed above. Differences are down to the grade of contradictory elements within the clip, and the prominence of the movie they refer to. A lot of *mash ups* have a similar structure, except that they refer to not one, but to two or more different media texts. This extends more or less to *audiovisual fan fiction* that expands or re-creates the storyworlds of popular films, TV series, comics, or transmedia story worlds. I will now, however, turn to serial clips on YouTube that have a more complex structure and single out the field of *serial video blogs*. As I highlighted above, we cannot discuss their reliability without touching the question of authenticity.

4. (Un)reliability in Serial Video Blogs: Creating and Faking Authenticity in Factual Clips and Fictional Web Series

To discuss the question of (un)reliability on serial video blogs on YouTube, there is no better place to start than with *lonelygirl15*:

> Hi, guys. Um, so, this is my first video blog. I've been watching for a while and I really like a lot of you guys on here. [...] Well, I guess the video blog is about me. My name is Bree. I'm sixteen. Um, I don't really wanna tell you where I live because ... you could stalk me. [...]

In 2006, under the username *lonelygirl15*, a cute girl with big brown eyes recounts events from her everyday teenage life. In most of the first 33 clips, she is sitting in her room, talking directly into the webcam about her best friend, about being homeschooled in summer, about her parents' strange 'religion' (see fig. 5).[6] Her clips very quickly became "most discussed" on YouTube and broke visitor records of 2006.[7] Her clips are highly narrative because Bree narrates as an intradiegetic verbal narrator, mediated through the camera. Later in the series of clips, the clips themselves become more complex and represent audiovisual narratives, mediated through an extradiegetic audiovisual narrative instance (constituted by parameters of the hand-held camera and editing).

Is this clip reliable or unreliable? To answer this question, I will have to take a diversion to the concept of authenticity. As many of the comments on the clips indicate, the question whether one can trust Bree

---

6   For a more detailed description and an analysis of the *lonelygirl15* clip series, see Näser (2008); Simanowski (2008: 84–88); Burgess/Green (2009a: 27ff.; 2009b: 95f.); Kuhn (2011b; 2012: 51 ff.; 60 ff.; 71. ff).
7   See Davis (2006); Näser (2008: 2) and Burgess/Green (2009a: 27f.).

and regard her accounts as reliable was, for most viewers, inseparably linked to the question of whether Bree was authentic and real or not.[8]

To develop an idea of the core concept of *authenticity* in audiovisual media, I start with Manfred Hattendorf's remarks on authenticity and documentary film (1999 [1994]). Hattendorf distinguishes between *authentic*—in German *authentisch*—and *authenticity*—in German *Authentizität*:

(1) 'Authentic' refers to the objective 'validity' of an event that is at the basis of cinematic depiction. If an event is labeled authentic, the cinematic depiction renders the event appropriately and the process of shooting the film has had no impact on the course of events. The authenticity derives from the source.

(2) Authenticity is the product of editing. Therefore the 'trustworthiness' of an event is dependent on the effect of its cinematic depiction at the moment of reception. Authenticity derives from both formal features and the act of reception.[9]

Hattendorf's first definition refers to the 'pre-filmic event', which is the basis for the process of filming, or, simply put, the event that is recorded with the camera. If a filmic representation is called *authentic* in the first sense it means that the event happened without being influenced by the process of filming. The event is not staged in any sense and would have happened the same way if there had not been a camera or a film team recording it. The second definition of Hattendorf refers to the processing of the filmic representation, i. e. the act of mediation through the recorded, edited and post-produced filmic material—or, in other words, the act of narrative mediation in audiovisual media. Authenticity in the second sense is linked to the idea of believability or trustworthiness and depends directly on the effect that certain filmic strategies have in the moment of reception. Authenticity—in this sense—is thus a result of both formal aspects and the act of reception.

Hattendorf's first definition of *authentic* should go with my concept of *factuality*. A *factual* audiovisual narrative is a narrative that represents an

---

8   See Näser (2008) who analyses the case of *lonelygirl15* and especially focuses on the comments to several clips from the perspective of cultural anthropology.

9   See: „(1) ‚Authentisch' bezeichnet die objektive ‚Echtheit' eines der filmischen Abbildung zugrundeliegenden Ereignisses. Mit dem Verbürgen eines Vorfalls als authentisch wird impliziert, dass eine Sache sich so ereignet hat, ohne dass die filmische Aufnahme den Prozess beeinflusst hätte. Die Authentizität liegt in der Quelle begründet.
(2) Authentizität ist ein Ergebnis der filmischen Bearbeitung. Die ‚Glaubwürdigkeit' eines dargestellten Ereignisses ist damit abhängig von der Wirkung filmischer Strategien im Augenblick der Rezeption. Die Authentizität liegt gleichermaßen in der formalen Gestaltung wie der Rezeption begründet." (Hattendorf 1999 [1994]: 67; translated by Sebastian Beckmann).

event which happened in the extra-medial reality[10] and which is as such not influenced by the process of filming. Correspondingly, an audiovisual narrative that is *fictional* represents events that did *not* happen in the extra-medial reality or that would, at least, not have happened in exactly this way, without the process of arranging them for the purpose of filming—in short, they only happened because they were staged.

To develop a concept of *authenticity*, which is not bound to factuality or fictionality in a fundamental sense, I would like to take Hattendorf's *second* definition as a starting point. According to that, authenticity refers to a quality of the narrative text or artifact. That means that there must be evident structures or properties within the narrative that function as strategies for authenticity. Thus, I assume that inherent structures and stylistic devices exist that can indicate authenticity in a certain context. I will call these stylistic patterns and devices *signposts of authenticity*. They can be used consciously or unconsciously by producers of films and videos. They can be detected within the artifact through detailed analysis. Likewise, they may be noticed by the audience, consciously or not, or go unnoticed. Signposts of authenticity are not stable or constant, but rather dynamic, context-sensitive, and subject to historical change.

Hence, we can discuss the question of authenticity at least relating to (a) the circumstances of production, (b) the audiovisual narrative itself, and (c) the reception of the narrative. Producers sometimes pretend that an audiovisual product is factual. The product itself can be based on structures and patterns that function as signposts of authenticity within a certain historical period and a certain medial, generic, and social context. And the spectators can perceive a narrative as factual, because they react to the signposts of authenticity within the narrative or because there are other paratexts or contextual signals that underlie the factuality of the narrative. There is the possibility of failure at any of these levels. There is the possibility that viewers classify a narrative as factual which is in fact fictional, or that producers present a narrative as fictional which is actually factual.

Let me suggest a few crucial terms to clarify some aspects of this knotty problem. Once producers or authors have the intention that a narrative should be perceived as factual, we can speak of an *intention of authenticity*. This intention makes producers and authors use *strategies for authenticity* when they produce a narrative. Those strategies could result in (a) *intra-textual signposts of authenticity* and/or (b) *paratextual* and/or *contextual*

---

10 The definition of factuality and documentary relating to events which happened in the extra-medial reality is quite common in German film and media studies (see, for example, Hickethier 2012: 183).

markers of authenticity. If a spectator regards a factual narrative as factual, one can speak of an *assumption of authenticity*. As a consequence, one can furthermore speak—freely adapted from Hattendorf's "Wahrnehmungs-vertrag" (1999 [1994]: 75 ff.; 311)—of a successful *contract of authenticity*, or, in other words, a successful *documentary pact* between author and/or producer on one side and user and/or spectator on the other. Strategies for authenticity can be used independently of the actual factual or fictional state of a narrative.

5. Signposts of Authenticity in User-Generated Content

To search for signposts of authenticity that may be of relevance for YouTube in its early years, I have selected one of the first YouTube videos ever, "Me at the Zoo," recorded in the San Diego Zoo, uploaded in April 2005.[11] The clip shows a man standing in front of an elephant enclosure saying (see fig. 6):

> All right, so here we are in front of the elephants. Um, the cool thing about these guys is that they have really, really, really long, um, trunks, and that's, that's cool. And that's pretty much all there is to say.

I think I do not have to explain the self-evident irony of this clip. A few signposts of authenticity are obvious at first glance: (a) the noticeable unsteady camera, (b) the man's address directly into the camera, (c) the seemingly unscripted speech, (d) the filler words, (e) the reiteration of words, (f) the use of colloquial language, (g) the gestures he uses to emphasize what he is saying, and (h) that he looks over his shoulder in the direction of the elephant enclosure. But why are those signs so obvious?

This private clip is not in a documentary format. If anything, it looks a bit like persiflage, or a poor imitation of a newscast report. The reporter stands in front of the object, place or event which is the topic of the report and talks directly into the camera to address the presumed audience. Compared to a professional TV-report, there are quite a few tokens of non-professionalism in this clip. These tokens are, at the same time, signposts of the self-made and private nature of this clip. In other words, all those signposts signal that this clip should belong to authentic user-generated content.

In its first year, YouTube, as a participatory platform for uploading and watching short video clips, was one of the major examples of web 2.0.

---

11 "Me at the Zoo." YouTube clip (http://www.youtube.com/user/jawed? feature=watch (last retrieved: August 20, 2013)). The clip, uploaded April 23, 2005 at 8.27 pm, shows Jawed Karim, one of the founders of YouTube (along with Chad Hurley and Steve Chen).

The 'big promise' of web 2.0 was the boundless participation of all users, a concept that was enthusiastically received. The old borders between producers and users were blurred in the concept of the new 'producer-user', or, in short, 'prod-user.' All prod-users work together to create something new in a fundamentally democratic, open-minded, grassroots culture that requires no professsional training or status whatsoever. However, we all know by now that the enthusiasm has cooled down quite a bit.

The clip "Me at the Zoo" is a typical example of such user-generated content,[12] and the signposts we have just collected are typical elements of this user-generated content. In this context *authentic* just means private, self-made, and unprofessional. That is why these indicators of un-professionalism alone can serve as signposts of authenticity in the context of YouTube in the first two or three years. Furthermore, in "Me at the Zoo" we can see some basic patterns that developed rapidly in conventional YouTube genres, for example the direct address into the camera. This formal situation creates an open communicative situation that blurs the borders between the audiovisual text and the extratextual context: The speaker transcends the so-called 'fourth wall' and talks directly to the YouTube community. This pattern became the aesthetic paradigm for a very typical YouTube genre called the *video blog*. The difference between the clip "Me at the Zoo" and a common video blog is that the latter is ordinarily recorded with an unmoved camera, a web cam, or a consumer camera that is put on a static object.

Lonelygirl15, like a lot of other amateur video bloggers, also looks and speaks directly into the camera. Some of the strategies for authenticity used in the clips of *lonelygirl15* are those typical patterns of user-generated content present in the clip "Me at the Zoo," for example, the use of colloquial language, filler words, and the hesitations while searching for the right phrasing. In other *lonelygirl15* clips we find another typical signpost of authenticity: the use of hand-held consumer cameras, evident in the clips "My Parents … Let Us Go Hiking!!!"[13] and "Swimming!".[14] In these clips the characters take a consumer camera with them, film each

---

12 I have chosen this clip although it was uploaded by one of the founders of YouTube. Despite its clearly amateur nature, it would be naïve to assume that there have been no economical interests by the uploader. Among many other aspects, this early YouTube video already proves that no clear borderlines between amateur and professional users can be drawn. As Burgess/Green (2009b) point out there are other user types "beyond the professional-amateur divide."
13 "My Parents … Let Us Go Hiking!!!" YouTube clip (http://www.youtube.com/watch?v= iRO4J P81 Hpo (last retrieved: August 1, 2013)).
14 "Swimming!" YouTube clip (http://www.youtube.com/watch?v=5Q_y0HdJ4x8 (last retrieved: August 1, 2013)).

other and other events in a playful manner. Effects of 'hand-camera filming' connote authenticity in almost all audiovisual media, at least since the hand-held camera was used excessively in the documentary *direct cinema* movement in the 1960s (see Kuhn 2013).

Another *contextual* strategy for authenticity is that *lonelygirl15* tries to refer to famous factual video clips on YouTube. Even in her very first clip she directly mentions the well-known video bloggers *TheWineKone* and *Paytotheorderofofof2* and uses the 'answering function' to link her clip to successful amateur YouTube users. The formal and thematic parallels of *lonelygirl15*'s first clip and the first clip of *Paytotheorderofofof2*[15] is striking. A girl of seventeen years is sitting in front of a webcam, talking directly to the audience (see fig. 7):

> Hi. Um, this is my first video blog. I don't know if I'll keep up with it. But I've been watching people's video blogs for a while on YouTube [...]. My Name is Emily, I'm seventeen. I just finished my second semester in college. I'm from North Carolina, United States [...].

One can compare this clip with *lonelygirl15*'s first blog (see above). Especially the very beginning of Bree's introduction—"Hi, guys. So, this is my first video blog. I've been watching for a while and I really like a lot of you guys on here. [...]"—is a variation of the opening by *Paytotheorderofofof2*. Another paratextual marker of authenticity is that *lonelygirl15* joins in the discussions in the comments section of her clips, common practice for private video bloggers (see fig. 8).

These signs of authenticity, along with other aspects, led users to feel that Bree was a bona fide teenager and many followers discussed her problems online. Eventually, Bree became a very successful YouTube user. The development of her success and how other users interacted with her can be reconstructed and analyzed with the help of the commentaries (see Näser 2008). Looking closer, one notices that in the beginning the majority of users considered the clips to be authentic and entered a kind of 'contract of authenticity.' Throughout the first 33 clips the users became more skeptical and began to doubt the authenticity, reliability, and, at last, factuality of *lonelygirl15*, because they noticed successively more and clearer attributes within the clips that broke with the assumed authenticity. They discovered an increasing quality, professional postproduction and post-dubbing, some contradictions amongst Bree's different statements, as well as some details that seemed too private to be shared online. So some of the followers canceled the 'contract of authenticity.' And around September 10—when Bree posted her 33rd clip—the hoax was dis-

---

15 "Blog 1." YouTube clip (http://www.youtube.com/watch?v=4PDpnxHcEJ8 (last retrieved: August 1, 2013)).

covered: The followers who had trusted Bree found themselves cheated. Journalists had found out that the narration was not factual but fictional, that the series was not authentic but staged. Bree was a fictional character, performed by the 19-year-old actress Jessica Rose.[16]

The strategies for authenticity have, nevertheless, been very effective: A fictional product was taken for a factual one and the users trusted Bree and believed her accounts—at least for quite a while. The *lonelygirl15* example proves that the signposts of authenticity can be 'misused' to deceive.

The case of *lonelygirl15* found its way to all kinds of traditional media (see Kuhn 2011b). This made it possible for the producers to continue the series with nearly the same success after the hoax had been discovered. They carried on—with more action and more suspenseful events, with more violence and more mystery—through over 500 episodes, and a lot of spin offs (see ibid.). Nevertheless, it is important to stress that *lonelygirl15* has become a professional fictional web series without abandoning the forms of videoblog aesthetics that had been established in the first clips. Two basic patterns of the first episodes have stayed distinctive for the rest of the series: First, the direct address into the camera that suggests an open communication with the community; second, that the characters take consumer cameras with them and try to spontaneously cover every interesting event that happens. In this way, these 'unreliable signposts of authenticity' became typical patterns of a subgenre of a web series, which I call the *pseudo-authentic web series* (see Kuhn 2012: 60; 2014). All the other characters of the growing storytelling cosmos of the *lonelygirl15* series were established as if they were private bloggers too (see Kuhn 2011b: 128 ff.; 2012: 72 ff.).

6. (In)authenticity and (Un)reliability as a Result of Negotiation between Users?

The case of *lonelygirl15* has shown how effective some strategies for authenticity can be in the context of YouTube. Regarding the successful hoax, the establishment of a new serial audiovisual narrative on the Internet and its interactive structures, the web series *lonelygirl15* is a unique phenomenon that could only have happened in a certain period of the development of YouTube. Such a link between strategies for authenticity on one side and technical and medial developments on the other is not

---

16 See Patalong (2006); Munker (2006); Davis (2006); Burgess/Green (2009a: 27ff) and Kuhn (2012: 52 f.)

new if we compare it with developments in other media. A famous example is the use of documentary techniques in the fictional feature film *David Holzman's Diary* (Jim McBride, USA) in 1967, which was announced as a self-documentary: The film shows the protagonist David Holzman producing a filmic diary about his everyday life. The film is actually a fiction presenting itself as a documentary. During the film there are quite often scenes in which David sits in front of his camera, reflecting on the concepts and details of his project, showing his recording equipment in a self-reflexive manner by using mirror effects (see fig. 9). The production of the filmic diary rules his everyday life. Consequently, the film ends after someone has stolen David's camera equipment (see Kuhn 2011a: 174–177).

David Holzman's Diary plays—like another well known example, *The Blair Witch Project* (Daniel Myrick/Eduardo Sánchesz, USA 1999)—with the borders between factual and fictional narration. In both cases we have fictional movies that were produced by real directors who are not represented within the film. And, at the same time, both films are marked as pseudo-factual documentary films purportedly directed and produced by fictional directors that are visually and acoustically represented within the film. In both cases there were spectators who felt cheated as they recognized that these were in fact feature films and not documentaries. Both are highly media- and self-reflexive. *David Holzman's Diary* transferred features of the documentary film—especially the use of 16-millimeter hand-held cameras in the *direct cinema*[17]—into the fictional movie, where they created the illusion of authenticity. *Lonelygirl15* did a similar thing, just in another medial context. It also used user-generated aesthetics that had already been established as signposts of authenticity in the context of YouTube. Since the fictional nature of the *lonelygirl15* project has been revealed, the YouTube user community has become highly skeptical about such strategies of authenticity (see Näser 2008: 14). Nowadays, one finds a lot of discussions in YouTube comments questioning the authenticity of clips. I would like to add one more example that is highly noted on YouTube regarding its reliability and its factual status. The clip "Adler greift Kind im Park an" was hotly discussed at the end of 2012 and the beginning of 2013, not only in the clip's comments but also on other platforms and online magazines.[18]

The clue of this clip is quite simple: It uses a hand held camera and a couple of the signposts of authenticity discussed above to signal that it

---

[17] For an overview of the development of *direct cinema* (in relation to *cinéma vérité*), see Ellis/McLane (2005: 219ff.).

[18] "Adler greift Kind im Park an." YouTube clip (http://www.youtube.com/watch?v=kWFoX1xeRlg (last retrieved: August 1, 2013)).

represents a true story. It surprises the viewer at first, because what happens—an eagle hitting a child (see fig. 10)—seems unreal. To solve this contradiction the viewer must rely on his media knowledge, watching and analyzing the clip again and again. A lot of users did so and posted their results on different platforms, and even as new clips on YouTube, like "Adler greift Kind. Adler schnappt sich ein Kind xxmanpower,"[19] "Eagle snatches baby is a fake,"[20] or on *Spiegel Online*.[21]

7. Conclusion

I suppose that these processes of negotiation about what is authentic and what not—that kind of permanent uncertainty about authenticity and factuality—will accompany YouTube for the next decade. I take this as a point of departure for my concluding hypotheses: The process of using new technical devices and media developments for establishing patterns of authenticity in a medium, straight to the point where these patterns are being functionalized for false authenticity, took years in a medium like the movie, but happens much faster in the context of YouTube. If one compares the function of hand-held camera filming in film history with the functions of signposts of authenticity in the short history of YouTube one clearly sees the difference: Within less than two years the typical constellations of webcam communication and user-generated aesthetics were responsible for the near simultaneous developments of YouTube genres that were supposed to be amateur documentary clips or video blogs, and, nearly at the same time, they could be used for non-authentic and fictional clips that simulated such documentary forms or video blogs. The development of structural and thematic patterns as an ongoing process on YouTube is comparable with processes of genre development in cinema and TV. In the context of YouTube there is, however—besides the higher pace—simultaneity of processes of establishing conventions, and subverting them with the function of delusion, persiflage, or media-reflexivity. Thus, the process of establishing conventional patterns happens at the same time as the deconstruction of these patterns, and the

---

19   "Adler greift Kind. Adler schnappt sich ein Kind xxmanpower." YouTube clip (http://www.youtube.com/ watch?v=dnHPGJJXiTI (last retrieved: April 1, 2013)).
20   "Eagle snatches baby is a fake." YouTube clip (http://www.youtube.com/watch?v= CMIZCAbMvVQ (last retrieved: August 1, 2013)).
21   See "Adlerangriff auf Kleinkind: Spektakuläres Video ist spektakuläre Fälschung." *Spiegel Online* (http://www.spiegel.de/wissenschaft/natur/angebliche-adler-attacke-in-kanada-youtube-video-ist-eine-faelschung-a-873960.html (last retrieved: August 1, 2013)).

use of conventions with distinct functions within one genre occurs at the same time as the 'misuse' of other functions in another genre.

This does not make the research for distinct signposts of authenticity impossible, but makes the attempt to link them to the question of fictional or factual narratives rather difficult. What can be taken as factual and/or authentic in the context of YouTube, is more and more a result of processes of negotiation between the users. These negotiation processes can be analyzed, maybe quantified, with the help of the commentaries on the video clips. As a final question, we can ask whether authenticity on YouTube happens to be the result of measurable negotiation processes between YouTube users. From a methodological point of view, I suppose, we would have to go on analyzing single cases, because the question of authenticity will be justified case-by-case. And the answer to this question will depend notably on the practices of all kinds of different YouTube actors and agencies, ranging from amateur users, activists, cultural institutions, and semi-professional uploaders to big media companies that seek to make high profits with viral strategies.

To put it in a nutshell: Discussing unreliability in the context of YouTube is highly fruitful if we do it in a context-sensitive way. As the structure of YouTube is highly cross-linked, interactive and intermedial as well as influenced by usage practices, we have to link the concept of unreliability with either the concept of intermediality or the concept of authenticity. For one thing, contextual, intermedial, media-, and genre-based frames of references are of crucial importance for mash-ups, fake trailers, audiovisual fan fiction, and all other YouTube genres in which 'uploaders' make use of intermedial relations, or play with forms and stereotypes of other media like cinema and TV. Furthermore, to discuss user-generated content, curiosity clips, video blogs, pseudo-authentic web series and private as well as semi-professional documentaries and their reliability, the concept of un(reliability) has to be linked with the concept of authenticity. In this article, I could only give some initial insights, highlight a few problematic issues, and present some building blocks for a theory of unreliable narration on YouTube. There is a lot of research and theoretical work to be done, all the more if we want to spread the focus to the Internet in general, which seems to be a promising project. And it certainly is, as I stressed before, a broad interdisciplinary mission even if we concentrate just on YouTube as a start.

Works Cited

Burgess, Jean & Joshua Green. 2009a. *YouTube: Online Video and Participatory Culture*. Cambridge/Malden, MA: Polity.

Burgess, Jean & Joshua Green. 2009b. "The Entrepreneurial Vlogger: Participatory Culture Beyond the Professional-Amateur Divide." In: Pelle Snickars & Patrick Vonderau (eds.). *The YouTube Reader*. Stockholm: National Library of Sweden. 89–107.

Davis, Joshua. 2006. "The Secret World of Lonelygirl: How a 19-year-old actress and a few struggling Web filmmakers took on TV. A *Wired* exclusive." *Wired* 14.12 (December 2006): http://www.wired.com/wired/archive/14.12/lonelygirl.html (last retrieved: August 10, 2013)

Ellis, Jack C. & Betsy A. McLane. 2005. *A New History of Documentary Film*. New York, NY: Continuum.

Fludernik, Monika. 1996. *Towards a 'Natural' Narratology*. London/New York, NY: Routledge.

Fludernik, Monika. 2005. "Unreliability vs. Discordance: Kritische Betrachtungen zum literaturwissenschaftlichen Konzept der erzählerischen 'Unzuverlässigkeit'." In: Fabienne Liptay & Yvonne Wolf (eds.). *'Was stimmt denn jetzt?' Unzuverlässiges Erzählen in Literatur und Film*. München: Text + Kritik. 39–59.

Harker, W. John. 1989. "Information Processing and the Reading of Literary Texts." *New Literary History* 20.2: 465–481.

Harpold, Terry. 2008. "Digital Narrative." In: David Herman & Manfred Jahn & Marie-Laure Ryan (eds.). *Routledge Encyclopedia of Narrative Theory*. London/New York, NY: Routledge. 108–112.

Hattendorf, Manfred. 1999 [1994]. *Dokumentarfilm und Authentizität. Ästhetik und Pragmatik einer Gattung*. Konstanz: UVK.

Hickethier, Knut. 2012. *Film- und Fernsehanalyse*. 5th Rev. ed. Stuttgart/Weimar: Metzler.

Koebner, Thomas (ed.). 1995. *Filmklassiker. Beschreibungen und Kommentare*. Stuttgart: Reclam.

Kuhn, Markus. 2011a. *Filmnarratologie. Ein erzähltheoretisches Analysemodell*. Berlin/New York, NY: De Gruyter.

Kuhn, Markus. 2011b. "YouTube als Loopingbahn. *lonelygirl15* als Phänomen und Symptom der Erfolgsinitiation von YouTube." In: Julia Schumacher & Andreas Stuhlmann (eds.): *Videoportale: Broadcast yourself? Versprechen und Enttäuschung*. Hamburger Hefte zur Medienkultur 12. Hamburg: IMK. 119–136.

Kuhn, Markus. 2012. "Zwischen Kunst, Kommerz und Lokalkolorit: Der Einfluss der Medienumgebung auf die narrative Struktur von Webserien und Ansätze zu einer Klassifizierung." In: Ansgar Nünning, Jan

Rupp, Rebecca Meyer et al. (eds.). *Narrative Genres im Internet. Theoretische Bezugsrahmen, Mediengattungstypologie und Funktionen*. Trier: WVT. 51–92.

Kuhn, Markus. 2013. "Das narrative Potenzial der Handkamera. Zur Funktionalisierung von Handkameraeffekten in Spielfilmen und fiktionalen Filmclips im Internet." *DIEGESIS. Interdisziplinäres E-Journal für Erzählforschung* 2.1: 92–114. https://www.diegesis.uni-wuppertal.de/index.php/diegesis/article/download/127/149 (last retrieved: August 1, 2013)

Kuhn, Markus. 2014. "Between User Generated Aesthetics and Self-Reflexive Narration: The Web Series Pietshow and Other Examples for the Diversification of Audiovisual Serial Narration on the Internet." In: Jan Alber & Per Krogh Hansen (eds.). *Beyond Classical Narration. Unnatural and Transmedial Narrative and Narratology*. Berlin/New York, NY: De Gruyter. 137–160.

Montfort, Nick. 2007. "Narrative and Digital Media." In: David Herman (ed.). *The Cambridge Companion to Narrative*. Cambridge: Cambridge University Press. 172–188.

Munker, Barbara. 2006. "Die Enttarnung von Lonelygirl15." *Stern.de* (September 14, 2006): http://www.stern.de/computertechnik/internet/570087.html?nv=cb (last retrieved: August 28, 2013).

Näser, Torsten. 2008. "Authentizität 2.0—Kulturanthropologische Überlegungen zur Suche nach 'Echtheit' im Videoportal YouTube." *Kommunikation@gesellschaft* 9.2: http://www.soz.uni-frankfurt.de/K.G/B2_2008_Naeser.pdf (last retrieved: August 1, 2013).

Nünning, Ansgar. 1998. "*Unreliable Narration* zur Einführung: Grundzüge einer kognitiv-narratologischen Theorie und Analyse unglaubwürdigen Erzählens." In: Ansgar Nünning (ed.). *Unreliable Narration: Studien zur Theorie und Praxis unglaubwürdigen Erzählens in der engischsprachigen Erzählliteratur*. Trier: WVT. 3–40.

Nünning, Ansgar. 1999: "Unreliable, compared to what? Towards a Cognitive Theory of Unreliable Narration: Prolegomena and Hypotheses." In: Walter Grünzweig & Andreas Solbach (eds.). *Grenzüberschreitungen: Narratologie im Kontext/Transcending Boundaries: Narratology in*. Tübingen: Narr. 53–73.

Nünning, Ansgar. 2005. "Reconceptualizing Unreliable Narration: Synthesizing Cognitive and Rhetorical Approaches." In: James Phelan & Peter J. Rabinowitz (eds.). *A Companion to Narrative Theory*. Oxford: Blackwell. 89–107.

Patalong, Frank. 2006. "Nur falsch ist wirklich echt." *SPIEGEL ONLINE* (September 11, 2006): http://www.spiegel.de/netzwelt/web/0,1518,436070,00.html (last retrieved: August 10, 2013).

Ryan, Marie-Laure. 2004. "Will New Media Produce New Narratives?" In: Marie-Laure Ryan (ed.). *Narrative across Media. The Languages of Storytelling*. Lincoln, NE/London: University of Nebraska Press. 337–360.

Simanowski, Roberto. 2008. *Digitale Medien in der Erlebnisgesellschaft. Kultur—Kunst—Utopien*. Reinbek bei Hamburg: Rowohlt.

Tophinke, Doris. 2009. "Wirklichkeitserzählungen im Internet." In: Christian Klein & Matías Martínez (eds.). *Wirklichkeitserzählungen. Felder, Formen und Funktionen nicht-literarischen Erzählens*. Stuttgart/Weimar: Metzler. 245–274.

Vossen, Ursula (ed.). 2009. *Filmgenres. Horrorfilm*. Stuttgart: Reclam

Yacobi, Tamar. 1981. "Fictional Reliability as a Communicative Problem." *Poetics Today* 2.2: 113–126.

Appendix

Figure 1. 'Happy patchwork family' in "Shining" (Screenshot from "Shining")

Figure 2. Jack writing his 'book' (Screenshot from "Shining")

(Un)reliability and Narratives on YouTube   267

Figure 3. The green band indicating a movie trailer (Screenshot from "Shining")

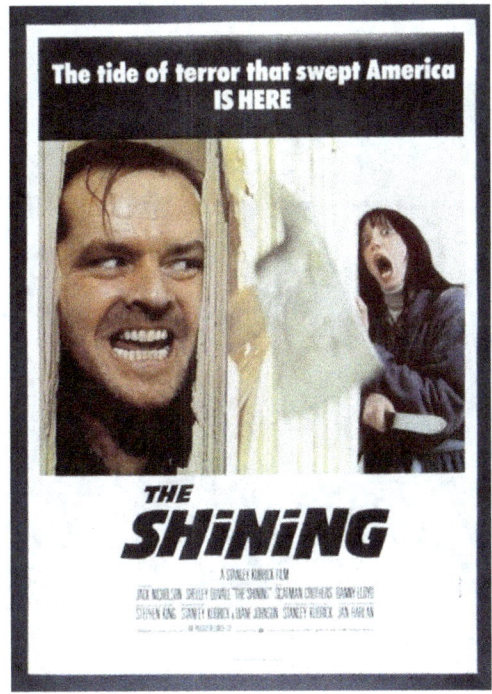

Figure 4. *The Shining* (film poster)

Figure 5. Bree talking to the youtube audience (Screenshot from *lonelygirl15*)

Figure 6. Jawed Karim in "Me at the zoo" (Screenshot)

Figure 7. Emily's "Blog 1" (Screenshot)

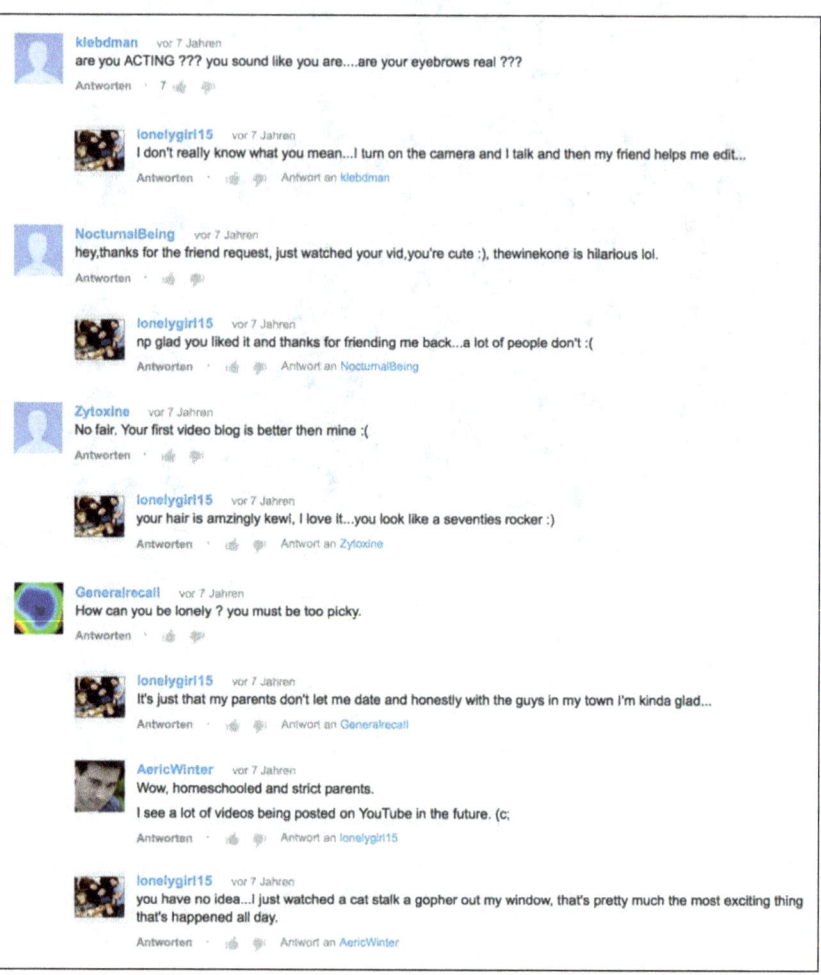

Figure 8. Commentaries on *lonelygirl15*'s "First Blog / Dorkiness Prevails" on YouTube

Figure 9. David and his equipment in *David Holzman's Diary* (Screenshot)

Figure 10. Eagle attacking a child in "Adler greift Kind im Park an […]" (Screenshot)

CHRISTOPH BIETZ
(Köln)

Tracing Televised 'Truth':
Reality Effect and Unreliable Narration in TV News

1. Introduction: News Theory and Narratology

How is one to start a text on the narrativity and truth of TV news if this cannot be done without admitting from the first that one's own words might create a kind of story themselves whilst claiming to promote somewhat true insights about how the subject it deals with can best be understood—namely as stories?

What this observation carries along is not only the non-negligible imperative of self-reference striking any text that deals with narrativity or narratological issues; it is also the fact that the idea of narrating and the idea of truth are always and inevitably intertwined with one another within narrative worlds: Where there is narration, there is a speaker who (usually) claims truth for the spoken; where there is said to be truth, there has to be some utterance formulating that very truth.[1]

As we cannot avoid a certain degree of scientific vulnerability concerning the first phenomenon,[2] we are forced to disregard further discussions on this admittedly interesting philosophic matter and concentrate on the second point (which is the main interest of this essay anyway since we do not want to trail off the paths of narratology too much). So again: How is one to start an essayistic 'story' on narrativity and truth within TV news?

Besides the already mentioned interconnection between *narrative* and *truth*, there is another pair of words that necessarily comes to one's mind when dealing with journalistic texts known as 'news'. Those are said to

---

[1] However, a 'true' utterance does not, of course, necessarily have to be labelled narrative; 'truth' can also be expressed within an argumentative or descriptive utterance, as in: 'The earth is not a disc'. Still, if we consider a certain world to be a narrative one (like the narrative world of a newsstory that reports on events within the world we live in), any 'truth' within this world is inevitably narrative as it contributes to creating this very narrative universe.

[2] Like one of the most well-known liars in 'history' and literature, Baron Münchhausen, who tried to make his addressees believe that he drew himself out of the morass only with his own hands, we follow the arguments of a discipline that could very well apply its instruments on itself.

report 'the truth' about political, social or economic events. News is therefore based on the notion of 'truth' insofar as it claims veracity for the things recounted. Telling the truth about certain events is the basic journalistic premise of any news text or film.

At this point, we can already see how and why the matter of unreliability in TV news falls within the scope of an academic publication that has an interdisciplinary approach towards unreliable narration as its main purpose. As we will hopefully be able to show, TV news can not only serve as a prime example of narrative unreliability in journalism, but also support the (narratological) thesis that 'truth' within any narrative text, no matter if it is fictitious or factual, is always to be understood as a medially constructed truth. This necessarily affects the general notion of truth as well, since it suggests that, from an epistemological point of view, there is no such thing as 'literal' truth at all—but rather only relative truth.

Let us start with the first point: Especially journalistic narration has a lot to do with the phenomenon of (un)reliability, as journalistic texts are paradigmatic instances of how narrators put all their effort into being trustworthy.[3] Discovering 'the truth' is the essence of every news item in every newspaper or news-show, and, in that, it resembles the classic detective story. That alone may already raise one's awareness in matters of reliability: As Jonathan Culler has shown by analyzing the narration of Diderot's *Jacques le fataliste et son maître*, narrators often emphasize their own trustworthiness which automatically includes the possibility of lying and being untrustworthy *ex negativo*.[4]

But how are we to describe the trustworthiness (or untrustworthiness) of a journalistic story? By claiming that narratology and its concept of unreliable narration provide a suitable approach for analyzing journalistic reliability, we first have to deliver reasonable arguments why news does indeed tell stories just like novels do. Until today, an interdisciplinary ap-

---

[3] For distinctive features of the terms (un)reliability, (un)trustworthiness and further narratological terms describing different forms of narrative inconsistencies, see Vera Nünning's introducing contribution to this volume. Also Greta Olson (2003) and, recently, Jonas Koch (2011) have contributed to further differentiation. Olson distinguishes between untrustworthy and fallible narrators, Koch between discordant and unreliable narration. In my paper, I am following Nünning's suggestion to use 'trustworthiness' for all different kinds of narrative inconsistencies—whether we are talking about the narrator's intentions, competence or sincerity. Reliability, on the other hand, has, historically seen, been the first term on the narratological schedule to deal with the phenomenon in question. And it is probably also the most well known term in the whole discussion. I will therefore firstly use the two terms as synonyms before making little adjustments in the last chapter.

[4] Cf. Culler (1975: 149f).

proach towards the science of narrative is still in the fledging stages, and most narratological works deal solely with novels.⁵

Anyway, the term 'narrative' has gained much interest during the past years, especially after the so-called narrative turn, which led to a burst of the term's usage.⁶ "We no longer need [...] to be told that the narrative mode of discourse is omnipresent in human affairs", writes Christopher Nash (1990: xi) in the introduction to his volume *Narrative in Culture—The Uses of Storytelling in the Sciences, Philosophy, and Literature*. The narrative turn did in fact help spread the 'narrative word', but it did not concern itself with formulating the basics of an interdisciplinary narratology. Rather, narratology is still more often neglected than used when it comes to different adoptions of the term 'narrative'. This is also true (and the writer of these lines can assure you he is reliable in this matter) for the prevailing scientific discourse concerning 'news': the so-called *news value theory*.

Classic approaches of this theory go back to the American journalist and sociologist Walter Lippmann and his work *Public opinion*, in which Lippmann is primarily concerned with the question in what way newspapers, or newsstories in general, modify the events they report—or, to be more concrete, in what way they distort reality.⁷ Some news theorists have lately argued that one reason for the distortion of reality through news lies in a certain kind of narrativity which is generated in the news-making process.⁸ The label 'narrativity' clearly has a negative connotation here as it corresponds to journalistic failure. More on this later.

Most interesting in this discussion is the notion of 'faithfulness to the truth'. It plays a crucial role within the scientific discourse about news, just like it does within narratology. The only actual difference to its narratological usage is a difference of terminology: Classical news theory calls this matter a matter of 'objectivity', whereas narratology subsumes such questions of consistency under the term reliability. When Jonathan Culler describes narrative reliability by writing that an account of events is reliable as long as it "can be trusted not to distort things while taking its own course" (1975: 150), it becomes pretty clear that the narratological concept of (un)reliability may well be applicable to news and news theory. Both news theory *and* narratology use the term 'distortion' to explain a certain

---

5 Famous narratologists like Shlomith Rimmon-Kenan, Gérard Genette or Wolf Schmid have strictly confined their analyses to fictional verbal narratives like the novel (cf. Rimmon-Kenan 1983; Genette 2010 [1998]; Schmid 2005). Others like Roland Barthes, Seymour Chatman or Gerald Prince have emphasized that narrativity can also be a feature of other medial texts like films, comics or theatre (cf. Barthes 1975; Chatman 1978; Prince 1982). Still, most narratological research deals with verbal fiction.
6 Cf. Kreiswirth (1992); Lamarque (1990).
7 Cf. Lippmann (1922); Galtung/Ruge (1966).
8 Cf. Haußecker (2007); Hörmann (2004).

unfaithfulness of textual manifestations towards 'truth'—whatever the latter may be exactly.

The idea of 'distortion' is only *one* of many parameters within news theory that could be cited as evidence for the thesis that the classical news theory covertly seems to borrow its central arguments from structuralist narratology.[9] Thereby the latter has a central advantage: Unlike news theory, it does not run into aporias when trying to label a text as 'unreliable'.

A narratological approach towards news and towards TV-News therefore lies at hand. But we can go even further than that by arguing that a narratological approach can overcome theoretical difficulties and aporias that the news value theory inevitably brings about. While news theory claims that the news making process leads to untruthfulness but at the same time cannot deliver evidence for this claim, the narratological category of unreliable narration provides an interpretive method for analyzing the credibility or the truthfulness of news.

Before we are going to do exactly this in the final chapter of this little study, we first have to outline a reasonable argument saying why news can be classified as narrative texts telling stories, and why narratology is therefore an appropriate instrument of analyzing them. This would be another main purpose of this study: to tear down disciplinary borders around a promising theory like narratology in order to make it applicable to different text forms in different media.

2. The Untrustworthy Newsstory: A Not Very Trustworthy Stereotype

But before we get to the core of this paper, we should shortly have a look at the common stereotype that has already been mentioned. In Germany, especially commercial TV-channels are always being accused of not giving objective and trustworthy accounts of reality in their newsshows.

Critics include news theorists who have supposedly found a way of proving their accusations: By ascribing so-called news-factors to certain political or social events that have been covered by the news, these theories gather empirical data that is supposed to give reasons why some events become news while others do not.

The idea that the news making process is a process of selection is central to any news theory. Regarding Johan Galtung and Mari Holmboe

---

9   Interestingly, Ansgar Nünning (1998: 26) uses the idea of distortion when he explains unreliability as he speaks of a „verzerrten Wirklichkeitssicht des Erzählers" ('the narrator's distorted view of reality'). For an elaborate survey on the shortcomings of the news value theory and its dissolution by narratological categories, cf. Bietz (2013).

Ruges significant essay "The Structure of Foreign News" as an important basis for news value theory, we can name the following terms as typical so-called 'news-factors' that drive the selective process: conflict, reference to persons, meaningfulness, and unexpectedness.[10] The logic of the common theory works as follows: The more conflict an event bears, the more it refers to well-known or socially or politically important people, the more meaningful for a huge number of people it is and the more unexpected it is—the more probable a possible newsstory about this event becomes. Assuming that the theory is right, this would lead to a preference of events that fulfil the list of factors, while other events would remain ignored by the media. One result of this selective mechanism is, according to news value theorists, an over-representation of top dog nations and an under-representation of underdog nations.[11]

On this basis, the main argument of news theories lies at hand: News distorts reality. Or put in another way: News does not represent reality objectively and it therefore does not fulfil its own standards.[12] And, raising even more awareness from a narratological point of view, especially a phenomenon called narrativization is not seldom suspected of contributing to the assumed growing untrustworthiness of television news.[13] Stefanie Hörmann describes "the use of narrative structures" within TV news as an "entertaining device" that forwards a trend towards dramatization and therefore distorts reality. Also Tamar Liebes is sure that "journalism is increasingly concerned with entertaining—that is, with telling a good story" (1994: 1).

But as constructivism has shown, there is no access to an objective reality whatsoever. Ernst von Glaserfeld wrote:

> At the very beginning of occidental epistemology, in presocratic times, it was already clear to certain thinkers that the concept of knowledge as a more or less truthful mirror of an in itself independent ontological reality leads to an inextricable paradox.[14]

---

10 Cf. Galtung/Ruge (1970 [1965]).
11 Cf. Galtung/Ruge (1970 [1965]: 259). The news value theories rising in the 1960s were closely linked to peace studies. A central assumption back then was that the uneven representation of reality in newspapers would mirror the unjust distribution of power and economic strength in the world. This is another debate, however.
12 The journalistic demand for objective reporting is not as old as many might think. It was not until the nineteenth century (when new technologies like photography were introduced) that it became common sense among journalists: "News was to be a strictly photographic reflection of the objectively visible world" (Schiller, 1979: 52).
13 Cf. Liebes (1994).
14 Original quote: „Schon in den ersten Anfängen der abendländischen Erkenntnislehre zur Zeit der Vorsokratiker war es einigen Denkern klar, daß die Vorstellung von Wissen als einer mehr oder weniger wahrheitsgetreuen Spiegelung einer an für sich unabhängigen

Engrossing in a philosophical-epistemological discussion about objectivity would certainly lead us too far here, yet a central finding of scepticism should be kept in mind: Knowledge, and truth along with it, are always a matter of perspective; there is no mind-independent objective view on the world. Empirical news studies are therefore inevitably doomed to fail when it comes to checking their basic premise: namely the alleged disparities between the event reported and the report on the event. "No one will ever be able to compare the perception of an object with the postulated object itself, which is supposed to have caused the perception".[15]

Plus, if one allows the possibility of truthfulness on the basis of an objective reality and at the same time claims the theoretical possibility of compliance between the real event and the reported event, then one automatically neglects a central fact: Namely the fact that a news report is always a matter of mediation. A news-narrator narrates a newsstory to an audience. And this is exactly the point where unreliability might come into play. So *if* someone has the suspicion that a news report might 'distort the truth', then that someone will have to treat it as a *story*, as narratology is based on the distinction between story and discourse, the distinction between telling and told, between teller and audience.

Especially when investigating TV news, it becomes quite obvious that giving an account on reality always has to do with giving this account from a certain *point of view*—because the camera always shoots from a certain angle. News theories are admittedly right when they assure us that the news making process is a process of selection. But in doing so, they again remind us that this process is a narratological process, because selection is a central feature of story-telling, as we will show in the next chapter. Moreover, the mediation of any event inevitably means selection and perspectivization.

After all, the common stereotype of non-objective newsstories is not provable and thus not a very trustworthy one as it remains an accusation without evidence. Selection and mediation are not the manifestations of an ill-driven process, but inevitable components of any news-generating process. So the question is not how we can prove the disparities between event and report, but rather how we can find a better way of describing a phenomenon that news theorists claim to have already detected long ago: The untrustworthiness of TV news. This essay proposes the following

---

ontologischen Wirklichkeit zu einem unauflösbaren Paradoxon führt" (Glasersfeld 1997: 38, my translation).

15 "[N]iemand wird je imstande sein, die Wahrnehmung eines Gegenstandes mit dem postulierten Gegenstand selbst, der die Wahrnehmung verursacht haben soll, zu vergleichen" (Glasersfeld, 1997: 12; translated by Bernard Woodley).

answer: Scientists can best trace the truth in newsshows by understanding the inherent narrativity of news and then analyzing newsstories with the instruments provided by narratology, which would be, among many others, the concepts of unreliable narration and possible worlds.

3. Towards a Narratology of TV News

3.1 Breaking Borders between Fact and Fiction

Before an analysis of unreliability in TV news can start, it is necessary to take one step back and establish TV news as an inherently narrative textform which can best be apprehended by making use of narratological concepts such as unreliable narration. For televised news to be introduced into the studies of narratology, the latter has to overcome two disciplinary boundaries which traditionally separate it from being applied to a broader field of different textforms.

The first boundary is the one between mimetic and diegetic modes of expression.[16] Far too often in contemporary narratological approaches, film and other media are obviously not part of the object of interest. Even important narratologists like Genette, whose theory is indispensable when it comes to establishing an intermedial narratology (although this is far from what Genette wants to do), explicitly state literariness, e.g. the written word, as a distinctive feature of narrativity.[17] But if we acknowledge that the cinema, for instance, can predominantly be seen as a huge *Erzählmaschine*, then we as narratologists have to find ways of including forms of media undeniably narrative into our studies.

The second border we will have to overcome is the one between fictional and factual narratives. Almost all narratological studies concentrate on (literary) fiction. Film studies are the only discipline besides literary theory that has come up with a kind of narratology of its own. So until now, narratology almost solely deals with fiction, which also has historic reasons, of course.[18] But even today, narratology, and with it the concept of unreliable narration, is still closely linked to analyzing literary fiction. As a result, the following observation made by Vera and Ansgar Nünning is still valid: "Aside from film narratology, which is in part relatively far developed already, the narratological investigation of other

---

16 Cf. Nünning/Sommer (2008).
17 Cf. Genette (2010 [1998]).
18 Today's classical structural narratology has derived from Russian formalism, French structuralism and the German *Erzähltheorie*. It nowadays also has a strong Anglo-American branch.

media is only just in its beginning stage" (2002: 18, my translation). Especially when it comes to television, there has not yet been *any* serious narratological approach at all.

This might serve as a reason (but not as an excuse) as to why news theorists are terribly mistaken when using the terms 'narrative' and 'narrativization' to explain how news items distort reality. By doing this, these theories do not only disregard the fact that narrativity is not a news factor at all but rather a characteristic feature inherent to all kinds of newsstories, they also tend to confuse narrativity and fictivity by claiming that the news-generating process adds narrativity to an 'objective' event in order to *sell it* as news and that by doing this, news distorts truth.

But narrativity and fictivity are two distinct phenomena in the spectrum of text-types. Both *factual* and *fictional* texts can be *narrative* texts. Gerald Prince writes: "Narrative, indeed universal and infinitely varied, may be defined as the representation of *real or fictive* events and situations in a time sequence" (1982: 1, emphasis added). This argument has already been brought forward in French structuralism when Roland Barthes spoke of "countless forms of narrative in the world" (1975: 237). As Marie-Laure Ryan and Paul Ricœur argue, every single personal life in itself can be seen as one huge narrative.[19] And Mark Turner writes in *A Literary Mind*:

> Everything we do, from making the bed to making breakfast to taking a shower (and notice how these combined—in any order—make a multi-episode narrative) can be seen, cast and recounted as a narrative—a narrative with a middle and end, characters, setting, drama (difficulties resolved), suspense, enigma, 'human interest', and a moral. (1996: viii)

Therefore, experiencing and understanding life and single life events always bares narrativity. By accepting that factual texts can indeed be narrative just as well as fictional texts, and on the basis of the constructivist insight that there is no objective account of reality anyway, we can conclude that the fictional and the factual story are just subcategories of the text-type 'narrative'.[20]

And as Paul Ricœur puts it, narrativity is what these two text types have in common—and narrativity always has to do with mimesis, that means with configuring or re-figuring time and space and the dimensions of real life.[21] Whereas fictional stories construct an *illusion of time and space*, factual stories try to *reconstruct* or refigure *actual time and space*. By doing so,

---

19 Cf. Ryan (2005: 345ff); Ricœur (1988 [1983]: 98).
20 It was not until the 1990s that 'narrativity' finally broke free from its hostile embracement by 'fictivity': Cf. Ryan (1991), where she finally strictly distinguishes between literariness, fictivity, and narrativity.
21 Cf. Paul Ricœur's comprehensive study, *Time and Narrative*.

both rely on each other, which means that factuality and fictivity are always characterized by the intersection of history and fiction, i.e. by a reciprocal relationship to one another. Ricœur understands the crossing of history and fiction as an ontological and epistemological fundamental structure; a structure due to which both narrative modes, i.e. history and fiction, inevitably borrow parts of their own intentionality from the intentionality of the other narrative mode respectively.[22] A *fictional* text, sensu Ricœur, always refers to a totality which borrows its propositions and preconditions from the *real* world, and a *factual* text always has to *fictionalize* its story substratum by generating points of view from where to report about the action—an action not directly and objectively perceivable once it lies in the past. For Ricœur, this non-perceivableness of the past goes along with a certain need for fictionalization when it comes to factual narratives such as history.[23]

Consequently, *any* text has to select and arrange information—it has to *construct its own story*. News production can therefore never result in a one-to-one-depiction of real events; it is rather to be understood as a transformation of narrative propositions from story to discourse, from abstract ideas of what has happened into medial manifestations like words, pictures and sounds.

3.2 Central Categories: Narrative Instances and Possible Worlds

This leads us to the central categories of narrativity that can be stated as the two main obligatory requirements of narrativity: *eventfulness* and *mediacy*. Both are reflected in Seymour Chatman's famous and narratologically unquestionable distinction between *story* and *discourse*: "In simple terms, the story is the *what* in a narrative that is depicted, discourse the *how*" (1978: 19). According to this basic narratological distinction, any narrative can be divided into its content and its mediation: Narrative content by definition is made of events in which persons participate, and it thereby generates a whole narrative universe, a *possible world* as Marie-Laure Ryan calls it. Narrative mediation, on the other hand, always means that there has to be someone or something that *tells* the story by selecting certain events out of the indefinite universe of the narrated *possible world*. And this is exactly where unreliable narration manifests itself as it describes a narrative situation in which the narrator seems to deceive the narratee

---

22 Cf. Ricœur (1991 [1985]: 295).
23 Cf. Ricœur (1991 [1985]: 296).

with respect to the facts of the *possible world* recounted. More on this in the next section.

So despite tendencies within the discipline which try to postulate the possibility of a narration without the existence of a narrator,[24] we have to insist that there generally has to be a narrator where there is a story— simply because there is narration, and simply because narration means mediation, and mediation means that we are dealing with some sort of communication which could not take place if there was no communicator. "Narratives have to have a teller, and that teller, no matter how backgrounded or 'invisible', is always important" (Toolan 2001: 5).

Taken the existence of a narrative instance for granted, it is necessary to find a general terminology with respect to an intermedially and transgenerically applicable narratology. 'Narrator', for example, simply does not fit to films very well, and neither does it work with television. There might be a voice-over-narrator, but this alone does not cover the whole narratorial process of audiovisual narration. For cinematic narration, Manfred Jahn has thus introduced the term *filmic composition device* (in short: FCD).[25] This term can well be used for any audiovisual narration: All information in any audiovisual rendering of any story (including factual stories in TV news) is to be ascribed to this theoretical narrative instance called FCD. "Because the FCD is the highest authority in the hierarchy, all filmic information ultimately flows from its mediation, choice, organization, and arrangement" (Jahn, 2002: 8). In addition to that, Markus Kuhn has further differentiated between two special types of filmic narration. Due to the different narratorial channels in a film, Kuhn (2009: 261f) speaks of an *audiovisual narrative instance* on the one side and a *verbal narrative instance* on the other, both of which the FCD makes use of in order to forward the filmic story. This can be helpful, especially for analyzing TV news, where the main information about the story is given by a voice-over-narrator.

So at first glance, one tends to name two possible narrative instances when looking at TV news from a narratological perspective: Logically, the first one would be the anchorman or anchorwoman who obviously starts a newsstory at its beginning (see Figure 1).[26] Then, if a newsfilm should follow, a voice-over-narrator seems to take over the narratorial function from the anchorman.

Both suggestions are not totally wrong, but neither are they totally right. Neither the anchorman nor the voice-over-narrator can be seen as

---

24 Cf. Bach (1997); Bordwell (1985); Stanzel (2001 [1979]).
25 Cf. Jahn (2002).
26 For reasons of readability, I will from now on refer to 'anchorman/anchorwoman' by just using the masculine form.

the main narrative instance although they in fact do fulfill a narratorial function. It is to be acknowledged that although the anchorman does indeed have a narrative voice, he is part of the staging and of the mise-en-scene at the same time, so there has to be a higher function that orchestrates the whole narrative situation. In addition to that, the newsstory is not told exclusively by the anchorman, but also by virtual pictures or pictographs in the background generating information about the newsstory as well. Moreover, when a newsfilm takes over later on, it is not only the voice-over that tells the story, but also moving pictures, sounds and verbal quotes. Thus there must also be an *audiovisual narrative instance* that provides information about the story world in a news film—for example, information about spatial components or protagonists who are part of the action.

After all, we can subsume that during the newsfilm, the FCD combines different narrative channels like moving pictures and a voice-over in order to convey the newsstory at hand. This is different in case of the anchorman, which has hierarchic reasons having to do with the distinction between story and discourse: The film (i.e. the FCD) *shows* the audience pieces of the narrated world while the anchorman *tells* the audience about pieces of the narrated world.[27] Therefore, anchorman and FCD are being settled on the same level of the narrative process, namely on the level of discourse. Thus, the anchorman can never be a product of the FCD that narrates the film—he is rather the product of an even higher medial instance that also equips the FCD with its narratorial function.

We therefore have to complement our terminology. On Jahn's basis, we want to assign the overall narratorial process to an instance we call *televisionary composition device* (in short: TCD).[28] All selective and perspective operations within TV news have to be traced back to this overall narrative instance. Usually, the TCD installs a TV studio and an anchorman as a narrative situation first in which the recounting of a certain newsstory begins. Later on, the TCD 'hands over' the narratorial function to the FCD with its different narrative instances (i.e. Kuhn's audiovisual and verbal narrative instances).

Having set the vocabulary for the level of medial discourse, we now shortly have to take a look at the other narrative side: The narrative world, i.e. the *What* of narrative. Marie-Laure Ryan's possible-worlds theory has already been indicated above and it fits into the idea of an intermedial narratology perfectly because it is closely linked to the discussion about

---

27 The distinction between showing and telling is a very common one when dealing with different types of narration. It goes back to Percy Lubbock (1929 [1921]).
28 Cf. Bietz (2013: 209).

the dichotomy between fact and fiction. A short look at the status of fictive narrative worlds is helpful here as it might explain the ontological status of factual narration on the basis of the reciprocal trace of fictivity, as already mentioned, within factual narrative worlds.

From the viewpoint of radical constructivism or modal realism, every fictional text creates a narrative universe that can be seen as an ontologically equal *alternative possible world* next to the *real world* or *actual world*. David Lewis observes:

> It is uncontroversially true that things might be otherwise than they are. I believe, and so do you, that things could have been different in countless ways. [...] I therefore believe in the existence of entities that might be called 'ways things could have been'. I prefer to call them 'possible worlds'. (1979: 182)

This observation has a lot to do with a phenomenon Roland Barthes (1994 [1968]: 482) calls 'reality effect' (or *effet de réel*). Although a work of fiction is not able to convey every single detail of the narrative it produces, the reader thinks the story to be part of a larger narrative universe that is automatically being created by the process of narrating. If a book tells a story about a certain person, the reader will assume that this person has been born at some point in the world his or her story is being set in. The reader will also assume that this person has usual human traits like we know them from our 'real' world. As long as the narration does not convince us of the opposite, we assume everything not explicitly mentioned to be similar to the world we know as ours.

Nevertheless, the equality of possible worlds and actual worlds claimed by modal realism is not maintainable. Nicolas Rescher stresses a central constraint: "Only *actual* things and states of affairs can unqualifiedly be said to exist, not those that are possible but unrealized. By definition, only the *actual* will ever exist in the world, never the unactualized possible" (1979: 168). It becomes pretty clear here that in case of fictional narratives, the story is based on an *alternative possible world* that owes its existence to an act of imagination. It tells us what *could* be but what *is* not. There is no access towards the givens of a fictional story except through the act of narration.

But, and this is essential for an intermedial narrative theory, the same is true for factual stories like news items: Due to their inherent mediacy, a transformation of narrative levels takes place. If a story reports on the election campaign of German chancellor Angela Merkel, we must not confuse the depiction of her in the newsstory with the actual person. We do not witness Merkel in a real situation (and even if we would, her being there could, in a strict constructivist sense, not objectively be verified as there is no such thing as objectivity), but rather see an image of her on screen. This moving image in fact tells us: Merkel was there in this certain surrounding being part of the real world! But how do we know for sure? After all, the chancellor on screen is just a two-dimensional effigy, only a sign that signifies a signified Angela Merkel. So when analyzing the according newsstory, we cannot talk about Merkel herself, but rather a 'Merkel-prime' (Merkel'), i.e. a protagonist in a factual narrative telling a story about someone called Angela Merkel who is the German chancellor campaigning for her re-election. Through the eye of the camera, we see Merkel' (i.e. Merkel-prime) on a stage from a certain angle. Had we been there, we would have seen her from a different angle realizing different things due to a varied perspective. This would lead to another version of the story 'Angela Merkel in a certain village during her campaign'. The effect becomes pretty clear when we think of different newsstories on the same topic. None of them tells exactly the same story.

Therefore, according to Marie-Laure Ryan, even every *factual* story constructs an *alternative possible world*—no matter where this world is said to be situated. By the inevitable fact of mediation which includes perspectivization and selection, *any* narrative, no matter if it tells a story supposedly taking place in the actual world or in an imagined world, is a closed system generating its own world—and with it, its own truth as well. And when we deal with factual narratives, we indeed deal with something that is said to 'have really happened' in our actual world—the same world we live in. But we cannot control the value of truth this story conveys with respect to reality. The corresponding events are in the past, and the only way to experience these past events is by recounting them. Therefore, there is no direct access to 'the real event' per se, to a perspective where we could retrospectively see a 'what has *really* happened'. "If we travel to an APW, and from there to one of its alternatives, we will never return to the actual world" (Ryan 1991: 18f).

Despite all that, it would not make any sense to equate fiction and fact. An essential ontological difference remains. Factual and fictional story-worlds correspond to different worlds: A fictional movie or a novel, on the one hand, generates a *textual actual world*, i.e. a narrative universe, that relates to a so-called *textual reference world* which is fictive—at least from the viewpoint of our actual world, because it does not exist. A newsstory, on the other hand, constructs a *textual actual world* that refers to the *actual world*, to reality itself. It claims to tell a story that has really occurred. But still this story is constructed and therefore the textual actual world must not be confused with reality.

Picking up the typical criticism that news tends to distort *the truth*—which truth are we then talking about? And how is it possible to detect evidence for this allegation?

After all, the ideas of the *possible-worlds theory* provide narratological instruments for solving the problems of unreliability in TV news as they pay respect to the ontological refinements of factual narratives. But there are even more advantages of this approach: on the outlined basis, PWT is the surely the best narratological concept to explain the ontological status of newsstories in general and in TV specifically. At this point, it makes sense to finally move on to an analysis of TV news.

4. Approaching TV News

4.1 Narrative Verisimilitude and Unreliable Narration

The narratological fact that every story creates a universe, an *alternative possible world*, is certainly 'true' for all kinds of stories, no matter what their point of reference may be. As we have learnt, this world is usually characterized by a striking similarity to the *actual world*. Jonathan Culler confirms what Barthes calls *reality effect* by defining a narrative as a

> discourse which requires no justification because it seems to derive directly from the structure of the world. We speak of people as having minds and bodies, as thinking, imagining, remembering, feeling pain, loving and hating, etc. (1975: 140)

This underlying narrative verisimilitude makes a story's addressee believe what s/he is being told—it makes the story trustworthy.

A good example for the inherent verisimilitude of any narrative is the filmic or televisual image, which is in fact always a result of a selective process showing no reality but rather framed excerpts of something that is said to be real: it owes its existence to the process of filmic construction. Nevertheless we assume that beyond the frame, the world shown on our screens goes on. And whenever the camera pans towards any direction, we are assured that this assumption is right.

According to Culler, this natural verisimilitude effect is a guiding principle of telling stories. And it can also help us understand the journalistic credo of objectivity and faithfulness to the truth—but from a narratological point of view.

Narrators "are typically trusted by their addressees", writes Toolan (2001: 3), and his observation fits perfectly to journalism, which people tend to regard as reliable with respect to its faithfulness to what 'really happened'.[29] For a start, this means that any event or proposition of the story told deserves the label 'true' within the corresponding narrative universe—but, of course, only as long as there is no indication that suggests

---

29 The same is true for journalists themselves who regard their reports as objective.

that this certain event or proposition could be false within the boundaries of that very story. This goes along with the core definition of (un)reliable narration that Shlomith Rimmon-Kenan has formulated on Wayne Booth's basis:

> A reliable narrator is one whose rendering of the story and commentary on it the reader is supposed to take as an authoritative account of the fictional truth. An unreliable narrator, on the other hand, is one whose rendering of the story the reader has reasons to suspect. (1983: 100)[30]

But as long as there are no reasons for suspicion, the 'presumption of innocence', so to say, is also valid for the process of televisionary news narration, i.e. for the so-called televisionary composition device and all its secondary narrative devices like the anchorman or the audiovisual narrative instance. Journalistic narration can even be seen as a perfect example for analyzing the narratological phenomenon of narrative reliability as journalistic texts are paradigmatic instances of how narrators put all their efforts into being trustworthy or at least into being *seemingly* trustworthy. Discovering 'the truth' is the essence of any news item in any news-show. This might encourage us to analyse newsstories as certain kinds of detective stories.

Ryan's possible world semantics can be helpful to do so: If we assume a news-narrative to be reliable, then we can conclude that the textual actual world it produces features a great similarity to the 'actual world' we know to be real—and its textual *reference* world, i.e. the world it refers to, can even be equated with the actual world, i.e. with reality itself. In this case, the corresponding journalistic rendering of the events in question could—in Ryan's words—be categorized as 'nonfictional accurate discourse'.[31] This accurate rendering of story-events would lead to the greatest possible degree of narrative reliability in a newsstory.

However, a central problem remains: How can we tell if a TV-news-story is *really* reliable and accurate, how can we tell if it is 'telling the truth' or 'distorting reality' or not? Due to epistemological restrictions, *objectivity cannot be verified*. There is no way of comparing reality with the depiction of events in a newsfilm. Thus even narratology cannot solve the aporias that lead to the 'scientific untrustworthiness' of empirical news value theories.

But it brings about an essential advantage: A narratological approach towards TV news does not run into the mentioned aporias as it is not aiming at a comparison between the *real* and the *told* at all. The only thing narratological analyses can look at is the graspable level of the textual

---

30 For an intermedial narratology, 'fictional truth' is to be substituted with 'narrative truth', of course.
31 Cf. Ryan (1991: 109).

actual world, which, in case of TV news, would be the audivisual manifestations of the newsstory—like a newsfilm, for example, and its propositions. "The only observable level is the text of the narrative. All other levels are abstractions."[32] Through these manifestations it is possible, in a second step, to make (abstract!) assertions about the characteristics of the underlying textual reference world, which, in case of factual narratives, is equal to reality. Nevertheless, the textual reference world is, just as the actual world it refers to, not directly perceivable or accessible. Like all components of the newsstory, it owes its existence merely to the process of narration. This is the reason why Marie-Laure Ryan proposes recursivity as a rule for generating *alternative possible worlds* (and news items are exactly this)—but not reversibility.[33] Once a story takes place in a mediated *alternative possible world*, there is no way back to reality from within its storyworld.

So if one wants to detect untrustworthiness in a news-narrative (which corresponds with the wish of news-theories to detect non-objectivity), the only way to do so is by analyzing the medial text on the concrete level of discourse. After all, like all narratives, newsstories do not depict reality itself but rather something that is said to *relate* to reality. Niklas Luhmann has called this phenomenon second-order observation: It is not reality that we witness when we watch TV, it is just an *observation* of reality that we ourselves observe when we watch the News. And any observation means selection and construction and therefore cannot convey a direct reality whatsoever.[34] According to Luhmann's Systems Theory, any medial text, as a closed system, has to generate its indicators of reality on the level of its own operations.[35] Transferred to narratology, this means that we cannot test the trustworthiness of a narrative account by comparing it with the extradiegetic world, but only within its own boundaries. Although many narratologists have rightly indicated that narrative inconsistencies can also be a result of extradiegetic factors, we have to disregard these approaches as they usually refer to the interplay between a work of fiction

---

32 "Die einzige der Beobachtung zugängliche Ebene ist der *Text des Erzählwerks*. Alle anderen Ebenen sind Abstraktionen" (Schmid 2005: 269; translated by Bernard Woodley).
33 This leads to a logical mistake within Ryan's theory: If we acknowledge the fact that if "we travel to an APW, and from there to one of its alternatives, we will never return to the actual world" (Ryan 1991:19), then we cannot go along with Ryan's equation of the *textual reference world* and the *actual world* when it comes to factual narratives. These two epistemic dimensions can never be equalized in an absolute way. Theoretically, an equation of the two could nevertheless be understood as an ideal projection of the axioms of the possible-worlds theory.
34 Cf. Luhmann (2004 [1996]: 153).
35 Cf. Luhmann (2004 [1996]: 159).

and the 'real' world surrounding it.[36] For news-narratology, the following general argument can be taken as a basic rule for analyzing matters of reliability: "In unreliable narration, the authority of the narrator is undermined by internal contradictions, and the reconstruction of the facts of TRW necessitates the rejection or the correction of some narratorial declarations" (Ryan 1991: 27). Dealing with news, especially the following is our major subject of interest: Are there any discrepancies between the narratorial account of what has happened and other textual elements? How can we detect a particular insincerity in matters of faithfulness to the 'truth' regarding the textual reference world? In the subsequent section, we will shortly outline some examples explaining how to identify traces of untruthfulness on behalf of the narrative instance, i.e. the instances of the televisionary composition device.

4.2 Forms of Unreliable Narration in TV News

The first example is taken from the most famous and most viewed German news-show *tagesschau*—aired by the public broadcaster ARD.

> In the military action in Mali, French and governmental troops are moving towards Timbuktu. The city is famous for its Islamic shrines many of which were destroyed in the fundamentalists' advancement. Meanwhile, the fundamentalists have supposedly withdrawn to the North. This makes Kidal their last major stronghold. Yesterday, governmental troops had recaptured Gao, a strategically important city.[37]

The anchorman, Jan Hofer, starts a story on a military action executed by the French army which took place in Mali at the beginning of 2013, when Islamic extremists occupied large parts of Northern Mali. The narration is mainly descriptive, it sketches main movements of the antagonistic forces. Everything does make sense—while the French move on, the rebels move back. There is no reason to mistrust any of the narratorial assertions, we

---

36   For example, Vera Nünning lists different types of narrative untrustworthiness such as an untrustworthiness with respect to the historical context of a text's genesis (see Nünning's paper in this volume). Also, Ansgar Nünning (1998: 22) states that unreliable narration is not to be seen as a "purely textimmanent phenomenon" („rein textimmanentes Phänomen") and lists "normal moral standards" and "basic common sense" as quality factors for reliability (ibid.).

37   „Beim Militäreinsatz in Mali rücken die Truppen Frankreichs und der Regierung auf Timbuktu zu. Die Stadt ist berühmt für islamische Heiligtümer, von denen aber viele beim Vormarsch der Fundamentalisten zerstört wurden. Inzwischen sollen sich die Islamisten nach Norden zurückgezogen haben. Damit ist Kidal ihre letzte größere Hochburg. Gestern hatten die Regierungstruppen die strategisch wichtige Stadt Gao zurückerobert." (Transcript of Jan Hofer's moderation, *tagesschau* (January 27, 2013); translated by Bernard Woodley).

may thus call Hofers account on what has happened reliable: The propositions given lead to a consistent textual actual world.

This textual actual world of the *tagesschau*, however, could be seen as a part of larger series called 'German TV news'—a series to which other channels contribute their story versions as well. They add different narrative perspectives and further details.[38] Thus the next example originates from the news-show *heute journal* aired by Germany's second big public broadcaster ZDF. Anchorman Claus Kleber starts the Mali-story with the following text:

> The French military action in Mali is, at least that's how it is presented in Paris, going as planned. French units alongside those of the Mailian government, are already in control of the cities Diabali, Konna, Douenza and Gao. Timbuktu is said to be surrounded, but this picture may be misleading. The difficult phase might begin once the French troops have settled in the area. Usually, the loosely organized Islamist aren't keen on occupying cities or land anyway. Independent coverage about incidents at the front is being hindered. Our reporter, Timm Kröger, is trying to get as close as possible to the events.[39]

As we can read (or hear), Kleber talks about the French action just like Hofer does—but his tone of narration is a bit more reluctant and reserved. From the beginning, Kleber's verbal narration binds its claims to particular perspectives: "[A]t least that's how it is presented in Paris" („[S]o wird es in Paris jedenfalls dargestellt"). This leads to a certain distance between the telling and the told: It is no longer the verbal narrative instance (i.e. Kleber) that claims that everything goes according the plan—this assertion is ascribed to the French government. Furthermore, the little phrase 'at least' implies that things could be different to what is reported. Here, the TCD already leaves room for mistrust. Later on, this room is filled when the audiovisual narrative instance (= FCD or filmic composition device) constructs an exact narrative story space by establishing a map of the country, showing which parts of Mali are under the rebels' control (see Figure 2). At the same time, Kleber admits that the conveyed story-image "could be deceptive". This is a clear indication for unreliabi-

---

38 For a more complex account to the serial structure of TV-news, see Bietz (2013: 224–231, 367ff).

39 „Die französische Militäroperation in Mail läuft, so wird es in Paris jedenfalls dargestellt, genau nach Plan. Die Einheiten aus Frankreich kontrollieren gemeinsam mit den Truppen der malischen Regierung schon die Städte Diabali, Konna, Douenza und Gao. Timbuktu soll zumindest eingeschlossen sein, aber dieses Bild könnte trügen. Die schwierige Phase könnte beginnen, wenn sich die französischen Truppen in der Region einmal festgesetzt haben. Auf Städte- und Geländegewinn sind die irregulären Verbände der Islamisten in der Regel überhaupt nicht scharf. Unabhängige Berichterstattung vom Frontgeschehen wird behindert. Unser Reporter Timm Kröger versucht, der Sache so nahe wie möglich zu kommen." (Transcript of Claus Kleber's moderation, *heute journal* (January 27, 2013); all quotes from Kleber were translated by Bernard Woodley).

lity because the overall TCD constructs two channels of information that slightly contradict one another: While we get a pretty clear image of story space by the audiovisual narrative instance, Kleber's verbal narrative instance confronts us with a trace of insincerity. But are we really dealing with an unreliable narrator here? On a plain textual level: Yes—due to the analysis above. But going deeper into the narrative structure, one can realize that the narration in total might still be trustworthy: The verbal instance makes use of the grammatical form of the German *Konjunktiv* 'könnte', which means that it does not claim absolute truth for its assertion. *Things seem to be like we see them here on this map, but at the same time, they might differ from that picture.* This narrative strategy of allowing a pinch of contradiction helps the TCD to gain trustworthiness on the highest narrative level. It therefore only adds to the TCD's trustworthiness that Kleber, towards the end of his introduction, forwards an important reason for the already overtly admitted narratorial unreliability: The whole journalistic narration, he suggests, is involuntarily subject to a restriction of perspective: "Independent coverage about incidents at the front is being hindered." And then he goes on: "Our reporter, Timm Kröger, is trying to get as close as possible to the events"—*in spite of the hindrances, Kröger will succeed*, we could add, as we are now being assured: This guy (and with him the whole TCD) is doing his best to get as close to the truth as possible. So why not trust him?

What we get here is a typical narrative technique of TV news: the admission of unreliability turns into narrative credibility as the teller is not only aware of but also lets the recipient know about his limited point of view. At this point, we can make a first step towards a more differentiated terminology and draw a distinction between two kinds of narratorial unreliability in TV news: Paying tribute to our just detected first form of unreliability on the surface level of narrative content, we want to establish the notion of an *insincerity of narration* (corresponding to Vera Nünning's term): Here, facts are (or might be) not exactly as they are being constructed by the TCD's narration. The second form of televisionary unreliability affects the deeper narrative structure; or, to be more concrete, the sensitive point of transition from *story* to *discourse*. Logically, narrative events (which are 'real' events in case of TV news) have already happened before they can be transformed into stories by the act of narrating. But due to the rule of non-reversibility, these events will never again unfold in the exact way they happened. Therefore, no one can ever know *what really happened*. So if in a factual discourse the narrative instance overtly shows its own dilemma between trying to find out the truth and not being able to find out the truth at all, this leads to a *structural unreliability* that, in a second step of interpretation, can be valued as to contribute to an overall trustworthiness we could narratologically describe as *credibility*.

If this self-reflexivity is omitted, it could be argued, this could even affect the trustworthiness of news-narration in a negative way. This phenomenon becomes clear when we look at the level of serial news narration: In the interplay of the two cited moderations, Kleber's confession of potential inaccuracy makes Jan Hofer's account seemingly unreliable—as it has stated its facts of the liberation of the North without any hesitation and without questioning the value of the information on which the report is grounded.

Moreover, *credibility* and *reliability* in TV news are closely linked to audiovisual capabilities of the TCD, namely the audiovisual narrative instance. Interestingly, the maxim of journalistic objectivity is historically connected to the invention of photography. Dan Schiller writes the following about the rise of the premise of objectivity in American news reporting in the nineteenth century: "News was to be a strictly photographic reflection of the objectively visible world" (1979: 52). Almost the same time, around 1895, the cinema, characterized by a close medial relationship to photography, experienced its 'big bang', and from its very beginning, the moving image was said to be capable of providing a direct access to reality. Early film scientists like Siegfried Kracauer emphasized the ability of film to generate an 'illusion of reality',[40] and especially television was seen as a medium,

> which does not mediate or construct reality, but seemingly makes reality immediately accessible and observable. The technical mediation is not visible on TV and respectively the impression of a direct participation is created.[41]

We cannot discuss the mediacy of film and television here in detail. But we do not have to do so anyway, because the mediacy of any media is to be regarded as a non-negotiable narratological fact. As we have found out with Luhmann and others, each medium constructs its own reality, and mediacy always remains a central feature of any narrative. But, nevertheless, it has to be acknowledged that, in film and TV, the mode of audiovisual narration tends to 'cover' the act of narration (Chatman speaks of 'covert narration' here)[42] and therefore bares a fake-immediacy that results in a certain mode of 'directness'. To cut a long story short: Moving pictures have a natural tendency to suggest reliability, since the human eye

---

40   Cf. Kracauer 1985 [1960].
41   „das Realität eben nicht vermittelt oder konstruiert, sondern diese scheinbar unmittelbar zugänglich und damit direkt wahrnehmbar mache. Die technische Vermittlung wird im Fernsehen ausgeblendet, so dass sich der Eindruck unmittelbarer Teilhabe einstellt." (Bartz, 2007: 249; translated by Bernard Woodley).
42   Cf. Chatman (1978: 181ff).

tends to believe what it sees. Television, therefore, has been seen, from its very beginning, as the *Fenster zur Welt*—the 'window to the world'.⁴³

Seeing on the recipient's side of the narrative situation means *showing* on the narrator's side. And showing, just like seeing, always has to do with perspective and 'point of view'. Like 'narrator', 'discourse', or 'story', 'point of view' (or 'focalization') is an obligatory category for any narrative theory. Also classic news theories stress the need for selection during the process of news production, and this notion of selection describes the central process of narration. Theoretically, a narrator *selects* events and protagonists out of the infinity of a narrative universe (the story's 'textual reference world') in order to *follow* these characters and events by telling their *story*. Rick Altman writes:

> With the introduction of following, concentrating attention on a particular character, we paradoxically also sense the existence of a narrational instance—someone, some thing, some system deciding who should be followed. (2008: 16)⁴⁴

Narration and point of view are always intertwined with each other: "[T]here is no such thing as a story without perspective".⁴⁵

This is also true for TV news. Point of view and the concept of focalization (introduced by Genette for literary analysis and later adopted for film analysis in order to account for the peculiarities of audiovisual point of view) have to be borne in mind when it comes to uncovering unreliable TV news narration.⁴⁶ Let us stay with the Mali story: After Claus Kleber's introduction, the report begins, and as we can see, the recipient indeed gets close to the Malian army (just like Kleber promised) as the reporter's camera (its point of view has already been announced) accompanies the soldiers from one city to another. The result is a kind of internal focalization—we witness the events told from the perspective of the protagonist, which is the Malian army fighting the rebels. Over-shoulder shots (see Figure 3) are connected with point of view shots (see Figure 4) generating a subjective perspective by showing the viewer exactly what the soldiers (and with them the reporter) see. Later on, we hear people paying their respect to France and more people being liberated from the rebels' terror. Although there is an audiovisual limitation of perspective, a limitation to the prevailing point of view, this narrative process leads to a high verisimilitude, to a high degree of credibility, and reliability as well. The narrative

---

43 Cf. Elsner/Müller/Spangenberg (1992).
44 Altman (2008: 16). The idea of 'following' a story goes back to French structuralist Claude Brémond. Cf. Chatman (1978: 20).
45 „eine Geschichte ohne Perspektive kann es nicht geben" (Schmid, 2005: 246; translated by Bernard Woodley).
46 Cf. Genette (2010 [1998:121 ff, 217 ff]; Deleyto (1996).

information of the verbal narrative instance fits together with that of the audiovisual narrative instance. We hear about people being liberated, and we see them happy and cheering. In the end, the report affirms what was previously depicted as potentially inaccurate by Kleber when he said that the picture "may be misleading". If the anchorman, as a verbal narrative device, admits from the beginning that the TCD's information might be unreliable, and if then, the filmic composition device uses an internal focalisation to show how the army has in fact freed the people, the viewer retrospectively appreciates the anchorman's honesty and assigns him a high degree of credibility.

This is not always the case. As another story-example shows, striking contradictions between *telling* and *showing* can lead to a strong unreliability of narration. Figure 5 and 6 show the Japanese power plant 'Fukushima Daiichi' before and after the tsunami, as well as several explosions in the reactors in March 2011. The fact of total devastation is hardly arguable. Nevertheless, many newsshows kept reporting how firemen and other helpers were trying to fight a *possible* worst-case-scenario, a nuclear meltdown—even days after the disaster started: "The nuclear power plant Fukushima is laying in ashes. [...] Still, nuclear radiation is escaping the remains, and still the army is trying to prevent a meltdown".[47] While the audiovisual narrative instance tells a story of total devastation that suggests that the fight had already been lost before it even began, the verbal narrative instance insinuates that damage control is still under way. Even two weeks after the explosions, RTL-anchor Peter Kloeppel stays pretty conservative with respect to the meltdown: "There are hints according to which a meltdown might be taking place in the nuclear power plant Fukushima".[48] The following report then only speaks of a 'looming nuclear meltdown',[49] which implies that the meltdown has not happened yet. At the same time, other narrative voices within the reports tell different stories: "There has definitely been a total melt-down",[50] says Susanne Holst hosting the ARD-newsshow *tagesthemen*, and Claus Kleber observes: "Radiation may invisible, but it is pretty obvious that these remains can

---

[47] „Das Atomkraftwerk Fukushima in Schutt und Asche. [...] Noch immer entweicht radioaktive Strahlung aus den Trümmern, noch immer versucht die Armee eine Kernschmelze einzudämmen." Transcript from *tagesschau* (March 17, 2011; translated by Bernard Woodley).
[48] „Es gibt Hinweise, dass im Atomkraftwerk Fukushima eine Kernschmelze ablaufen könnte." Transcript from *RTL aktuell* (March 25, 2011; translated by Bernard Woodley).
[49] „[H]ier droht eine Kernschmelze." Transcript from *RTL aktuell* (March 25, 2011).
[50] „Zu einem GAU ist es jetzt definitiv gekommen." Transcript from *tagesthemen* (March 12, 2011).

hardly be impermeable".[51] Furthermore, nuclear scientists that are given a voice within the reports stress a strong likelihood that a nuclear meltdown has been proceeding constantly since the beginning of the catastrophe.[52] These contradictions in the 'detective newsstory' about 'what is really happening in the power plant' lead to a considerable unreliability of narration. Facts of the *narratorial actual world* of certain *verbal narrative instances* differ from the facts of the *textual actual world* that is being *shown* by the *audiovisual narrative instance* with its narrative directness and high degree of natural verisimilitude: Fukushima is looking as bad as it can get—it seems simply unimaginable that a meltdown might be prevented. Due to these inconsistencies, the overall narration is subject to a remarkable insincerity on the level of narrative content.

But the inaccurate rendering of narrative facts also leads to a structural unreliability here. Thanks to their serial character, TV news can be regarded as an ongoing story about different world events. The series of all different newsshows share one common *textual reference world*: The actual world. The dilemma of not being able to give direct accounts on reality leads to a kind of natural and constantly underlying structural unreliability which is boosted to a general untrustworthiness every time it is explicitly unfolded. During the first days of the Fukushima disaster, the narrative insincerity is implicitly present, but not explicitly proven. This changes during the continuation of the serial story: Later on in the course of this news-narrative, the Japanese government and the operator of the affected power plant find out that the worst case scenario, a nuclear meltdown, had already started on the very first day, shortly after the tsunami. All newsshows now include the new state of affairs into their reconsiderations of the story at hand—and by doing so, they construct a new textual actual world that differs from the one they forwarded only weeks before. This is a typical case in which the facts of the textual reference world, i.e. the facts of the narrative universe, have undermined the telling of the narrative instance. Nevertheless, this evidence still does not come from the outside world, from reality itself, but rather from the intradiegetic level within the borders of the story (*sensu* Luhmann). And here, the structure of the story told during the first weeks does not reflect the structure of the underlying narrative world it refers to. Especially retrospectively, the narration about the fight against a possible meltdown is structurally and factually highly untrustworthy.

---

51 „Strahlung kann man nicht sehen, aber dass diese Ruine nicht zuverlässig dicht sein kann, ist ziemlich offensichtlich". Transcript from *heute journal* (March 27, 2011).
52 Cf. *RTL aktuell* (March 13, 2011); *heute journal* (March 13, 2011).

5. Conclusion

In the preceding, different variations of unreliability within TV news have been described, and the important observation that *admitting* the possibility of unreliability can, in some cases, ironically strengthen the overall credibility of factual news narration has been made. TV news draws its credibility from its narrative character—and therefore also from its subjectivity due to the selective operations of point of view and focalization. The ill-driven empirical notion of journalistic objectivity, no matter if it is formulated as a scientific utopia or a professional self-description, is a result of TV's natural verisimilitude which is a mixture of audiovisual 'directness' and the narrative reality effect. The term 'journalistic objectivity', thus, has to be reformulated narratologically as 'narrative credibility', and news theorists should no longer speak of the idea of objective journalism but rather of credible, reliable, trustworthy journalism. Journalistic objectivity, after all, is not an achievable textual characteristic, but rather a narrative strategy, because reliability or unreliability can always be found only within the frame of a certain narrative form. Therefore, journalistic untrustworthiness can only be detected by an interpretive "reconstruction of the facts of TRW" (Ryan 1991: 27). 'What really happened' is already a construct within that very frame—a construct that may vary.

> First, while we can perhaps detect unreliability, [...] we cannot use such means to construct a definitive version of events. Second, even this method does not with certainty separate what the narrator is somehow aware of from what we have cleverly concluded. (Wall, 1994: 30)

This final statement shall now frame the narratological story of (un)reliability in TV news at hand. And within this very frame it wants to be regarded as true. Though this might just be another story.

Works Cited

Altman, Rick. 2008. *A Theory of Narrative*. New York, NY: Columbia University Press.

Bach, Michaela. 1997. *Erzählperspektive im Film. Eine erzähltheoretische Untersuchung mithilfe exemplarischer Filmanalysen*. Essen: Item-Verlag.

Barthes, Roland. 1975. "An Introduction to the Structural Analysis of Narrative." *New Literary History* 6.2: 237–272.

Barthes, Roland. 1994 [1968]. "L'Effet de Réel." In: *Œuvres complètes. Livres, Textes, Entretiens 1962–1967*. Vol. 2. Paris: Seuil. 479–484.

Bartz, Christina. 2007. *MassenMedium Fernsehen. Die Semantik der Masse in der Medienbeschreibung*. Bielefeld: transcript.

Bietz, Christoph. 2013. *Die Geschichten der Nachrichten. Eine narratologische Analyse telemedialer Wirklichkeitskonstruktion.* Trier: WVT.
Bordwell, David. 1985. *Narration in the Fiction Film.* London: Routledge.
Chatman, Seymour. 1978. *Story and Discourse. Narrative Structure in Fiction and Film.* Ithaca, NY: Cornell University Press.
Culler, Jonathan. 1975. *Structuralist Poetics. Structuralism, Linguistics and the Study of Literature.* London: Routledge & Kegan Paul.
Deleyto, Celestino. 1996. "Focalisation in Film Narrative." In: Susana Onega Jaén & José A. García Landa (eds.). *Narratology. An Introduction.* London/New York, NY: Longman. 217–233.
Elsner, Monika, Thomas Müller & Peter M. Spangenberg. 1992. "Zwischen utopischer Phantasie und Medienkonkurrenz. Zur Frühgeschichte des Deutschen Fernsehens (1926–1935)." In: Knut Hickethier (ed.). *Fernsehen. Wahrnehmungswelt, Programminstitution und Marktkonkurrenz.* Frankfurt am Main: Peter Lang. 131–144.
Galtung, Johan & Mari Holmboe Ruge. 1970 [1965]. "The Structure of Foreign News." In: Jeremy Tunstall (ed.). *Media Sociology.* London: Constable: 259–298.
Genette, Gérard. 2010 [1998]. *Die Erzählung.* Paderborn: Wilhelm Fink.
Glasersfeld, Ernst von. 1997. "Konstruktion der Wirklichkeit und des Begriffs der Objektivität." In: Heinz Gumin & Armin Mohler (eds.). *Einführung in den Konstruktivismus.* München: Piper. 9–40.
Haußecker, Nicole. 2007. "Nachrichtenberichterstattung über Terrorismus. Eine Analyse der TV-Nachrichten über die Terroranschläge in Kenia 2002." *conflict and communication online* 6.1: 1–18.
Hörmann, Stefanie. 2004. *Die Angleichung öffentlich-rechtlicher und privater Nachrichten unter den Mechanismen des journalistischen Feldes am Beispiel ausgewählter Hauptnachrichtensendungen im deutschen Fernsehen.* Aachen: Shaker.
Jahn, Manfred. 2002. "A Guide to Narratological Film Analysis." http://www.uni-koeln.de/~ame02/pppf.htm (last retrieved: November 11, 2013)
Koch, Jonas. 2011. "Unreliable and Discordant Film Narration." *Journal of Literary Theory* 5.1: 57–80.
Kracauer, Siegfried. 1985 [1960]. *Theorie des Films. Die Errettung der äußeren Wirklichkeit.* Frankfurt am Main: Suhrkamp.
Kreiswirth, Martin. 1992. "Trusting the Tale: The Narrativist Turn in the Human Sciences." *New Literary History* 23.3: 629–657.
Kuhn, Markus. 2009. "Film Narratology: Who Tells? Who Shows? Who Focalizes? Narrative Mediation in Self-Reflexive Fiction Films." In: Peter Hühn, Wolf Schmid & Jörg Schönert (eds.). *Point of View,*

Perspective, and Focalization. Modeling Mediation in Narrative. Berlin/New York, NY: De Gruyter. 259–278.

Lamarque, Peter. 1990. "Narrative and Invention: The Limits of Fictionality." In: Christopher Nash (ed.). *Narrative in Culture. The Uses of Storytelling in the Sciences, Philosophy, and Literature.* London: Routledge. 133–146.

Lewis, David. 1979. "Possible Worlds." In: Michael J. Loux (ed.). *The Possible and the Actual. Readings in the Metaphysics of Modality.* Ithaca, NY: Cornell University Press. 182–189.

Liebes, Tamar. 1994. "Narrativization of the News. An Introduction." In: Tamar Liebes (ed.). *Narrativization of the News. A Special Issue of the Journal of Narrative and Life History.* London: Routledge. 1–8.

Lippmann, Walter. 1922. *Public Opinion.* New York, NY: Harcourt, Brace & Co.

Lubbock, Percy. 1929 [1921]. *The Craft of Fiction.* London: Jonathan Cape.

Luhmann, Niklas. 2004 [1996]. *Die Realität der Massenmedien.* Wiesbaden: Verlag für Sozialwissenschaften.

Nash, Christopher. 1990. "Foreword." In: Christopher Nash (ed.). *Narrative in Culture. The Uses of Storytelling in the Sciences, Philosophy, and Literature.* London: Routledge. xi-xiv.

Nünning, Ansgar. 1998. "*Unreliable Narration* zur Einführung. Grundzüge einer kognitiv-narratologischen Theorie und Analyse unglaubwürdigen Erzählens." In: Ansgar Nünning (ed.). *Unreliable Narration. Studien zur Theorie und Praxis unglaubwürdigen Erzählens in der englischsprachigen Erzählliteratur.* Trier: WVT. 3–40.

Nünning, Ansgar & Roy Sommer. 2008. "Diegetic and Mimetic Narrativity: Some further Steps towards a Transgeneric Narratology of Drama." In: John Pier & José Á. García Landa (eds.). *Theorizing Narrativity.* Narratologia 12. Berlin/New York, NY: De Gruyter. 331–354.

Nünning, Vera & Ansgar Nünning. 2002. "Produktive Grenzüberschreitungen: Trans- generische, intermediale und interdisziplinäre Ansätze in der Erzähltheorie." In: Vera Nünning & Ansgar Nünning. (eds.). *Erzähltheorie transgenerisch, intermedial, interdisziplinär.* Trier: WVT. 1–22.

Olson, Greta. 2003. "Reconsidering Unreliability: Fallible and Untrustworthy Narrators." *Narrative* 11.1: 93–109.

Prince, Gerald. 1982. *Narratology. The Form and Functioning of Narrative.* Berlin: Mouton.

Rescher, Nicholas. 1979. "The Ontology of the Possible." In: Michael J. Loux (ed.). *The Possible and the Actual. Readings in the Metaphysics of Modality.* Ithaca, NY: Cornell University Press. 166–181.

Ricœur, Paul. 1988 [1983]. *Zeit und Erzählung. Zeit und historische Erzählung.* Vol. 1. Trans. Rainer Rochlitz. München: Wilhelm Fink.
Ricœur, Paul. 1989 [1984]. *Zeit und Erzählung. Zeit und literarische Erzählung.* Vol. 2. Trans. Rainer Rochlitz. München: Wilhelm Fink.
Ricœur, Paul. 1991 [1985]. *Zeit und Erzählung. Die erzählte Zeit.* Vol. 3. Trans. Rainer Rochlitz. München: Wilhelm Fink.
Rimmon-Kenan, Shlomith. 1983. *Narrative Fiction: Contemporary Poetics.* London: Methuen.
Ryan, Marie-Laure. 2005. "Narrative." In: David Herman, Manfred Jahn & Marie-Laure Ryan. *Routledge Encyclopedia of Narrative Theory.* London/New York, NY: Routledge. 344–348.
Ryan, Marie-Laure. 1991. *Possible Worlds, Artificial Intelligence, and Narrative Theory.* Bloomington, IN: Indiana University Press.
Schiller, Dan. 1979. "An Historical Approach to Objectivity and Professionalism in American News Reporting." *Journal of Communication* 29.4: 46–57.
Schmid, Wolf. 2005. *Elemente der Narratologie.* Berlin/New York, NY: De Gruyter.
Stanzel, Franz K. 2001 [1979]. *Theorie des Erzählens.* Göttingen: Vandenhoeck & Ruprecht.
Toolan, Michael J. 2001 [1988]. *Narrative. A Critical Linguistic Introduction.* London/New York, NY: Routledge.
Turner, Mark. 1996. *The Literary Mind. The Origins of Thought and Language.* Oxford: Oxford University Press.
Wall, Kathleen. 1994. "*The Remains of the Day* and Its Challenges to Theories of Unreliable Narration." *Journal of Narrative Technique* 24.1: 18–42.

Appendix

Figure 1. Claus Kleber. *heute journal* (January 27, 2013)

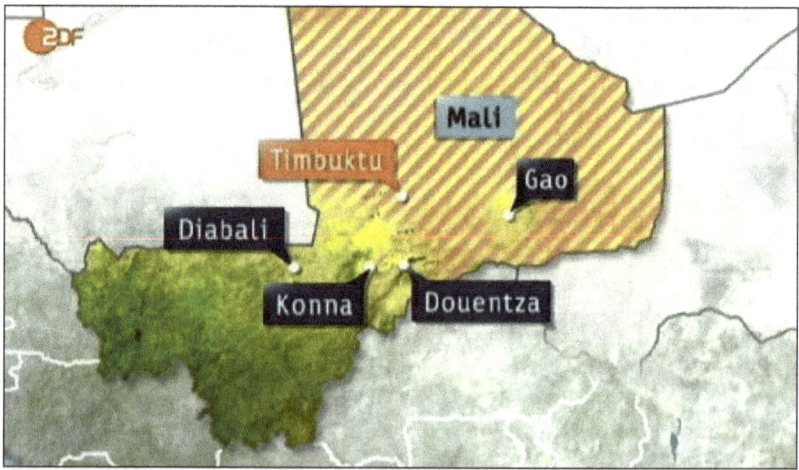

Figure 2. Map. *heute journal* (January 27, 2013)

Reality Effect and Unreliable Narration in TV News 301

Figure 3. Over-shoulder-shot. *heute journal* (January 27, 2013)

Figure 4. Point-of-view-shot. *heute journal* (January 27, 2013)

Figure 5. Fukushima Daiichi before explosions. *tagesschau* (March 11, 2011)

Figure 6. Fukushima Daiichi after explosions. *heute journal* (March 28, 2011)

Interdisciplinary Perspectives on (Un)reliability

BEATRICE DERNBACH
(Nürnberg)

(Un)reliable Narration in Journalism:
The Fine Line between Fact and Fiction

1. Introduction

Due to its social function of information and orientation, journalism is supposed to be reliable. The German sociologist Niklas Luhmann (2000: 1) wrote: "Whatever we know about our society, or indeed about the world in which we live, we know through the mass media." Journalism is expected to be reliable because it reports on events all over the world and it is for the most part our main source of information. In a normative sense we have to believe and we have to trust. But can we be sure that journalists tell us the truth? That they select the truly important news from thousands of events every day? Journalists are conventionally classified as reliable storytellers. They seem to be authentic because we believe that they are witnesses, that they saw with their own eyes what they are telling us. Nevertheless, there are some circumstances that could make journalistic storytelling appear less reliable. The three examples given in this article, not the only but the most prominent ones, lend themselves the questions of reliability and unreliability, trustworthiness, truthfulness, credibility, mistrust, and trust in and of journalism, of a reliable combination of facts and fiction and of the future of storytelling in times of media crisis and the booming Internet.

This article will refer to findings of media and communication research (Kohring 2004; Dernbach 2005) and theories of literature and cognitive narratology (Nünning 1998; Nünning/Allrath 2005). One crucial distinction this article will make is that, for instance between the media system and the journalism system. Among laymen and in everyday practice, this distinction is not made, and as a result there has been much debate as to whether journalism can both inform and entertain or if the latter is only reserved for the media. This debate motivates a closer investigation of the relationship between journalism and literature. There are certainly many connections between these two fields. However, there are well-defined limits which have been trespassed by certain groups of journalists. Elements of literature and fiction influence non-fictional reports in journalism. The question is: How far can the fine art of storytelling in journalism go without casting doubts on reporters' reliability? So called storytelling has established itself as a technique in journalism. Covering events in a way that attracts awareness and interest, appeals to a wide audience, and embeds itself deeply in recipients' memories, promises not only public but also economic success. It is obvious that this means walking the thin line between reliable and unreliable storytelling.

2. Media and Journalism: Two Systems of Narration

The development of professional journalism as we know it today is related to the development of (a) modern society in the nineteenth century (Blöbaum 1994). A central characteristic of this development has been the separation of social systems like politics, economics, law, and the media. The increasing complexity of society demanded the differentiation of the media system into more subsystems: journalism, public relations and advertisement emerged. As part of the development of the popular press, editorial offices were established as professional organization units and departments were formed as internal structures (Meier 2002) with corresponding operational programs (selection, research, presentation etc.) and different professional role models (editors, publishers etc.) (Blöbaum 1994).

The normative functions of journalism have been to inform, to criticize and control actors in other subsystems, mainly politicians and economists and to take the role of advocate for those who do not have access to use the mass media as transmitters of their messages. Journalism observes the social subsystems, selects information, processes it on the basis of news value (topicality, geographical and emotional closeness, celebrity etc.), and publishes reports in professsional and idiosyncratic formats (Rühl 1980; Weischenberg 1996; Görke 2002; Meier 2011). Thus, journalism has developed genres which are more focused either on facts (news and reports) or on opinion (comments).

The main question discussed to this day is whether journalism just reduces the complexity of the world while remaining purely descriptive or if it creates its own reality (Merten/Schmidt/Weischenberg 1994; Baum/Schmidt 2002; Pörksen 2006). There is a broad consensus in academic research that journalism does not produce an undistorted picture of reality because of the way it selects and presents topics and information. Indeed, some approaches of communication and media research, especially research on the impact and effects of media, have shown a correlation between public perception and agenda setting in journalism. However, recipients do not believe the media blindly and they do not automatically trust information simply because it is printed in black and white (Dernbach 2005).

Having made this point, a brief digression is necessary: In laymen's everyday perception, the media and journalism are often the same. But in times of economical and journalistic crisis, it has become clear that the media and journalism are different organizational systems. "They can be distinguished with respect to their services, their programs, their structures and the way in which they are managed" (Altmeppen 2006: 17).[1] However, journalism is dependent upon the financial contributions, the production possibilities, and the means of distribution of the media system. This coupling creates some opportunities, but also certain risks: journalism transported via newspapers and magazines was drawn into the economic crisis affecting print media and publishing companies. Even though publishers assert that they plan to pay for quality journalism in the future, it appears as if they are taking counterproductive measures: The closing of the economic press section of the Gruner & Jahr Publishing Company, as well as the insolvencies of the *Frankfurter Rundschau* and the press agency *dapd* are good examples, just looking at the year 2012.

The media recipients, who are mostly laymen and not experts in media research or media policy, do not, and do not have to, distinguish between media and journalism. They use media primarily to satisfy two important needs: information and entertainment. Generally, the media—and not journalism—are praised for good offers, programmes, and news and criticized for bad ones. For example, the former President of Germany, Christian Wulff, was chased out of office by "media campaigns". For recipients, credibility, reliability, truthfulness in the media are identical to confidence in journalism. Excellent media journalism reflects on itself or—as Maja Malik (2004) calls it—"journalism-journalism" always draws the attention to this disparity. However, there is no research about the effects of criticizing the media on readers, listeners, TV-audiences and Internet-users.

The only long-term study of media use, conducted since 1964 in a five-year cycle, shows that recipients obviously trust those media most that not only provide words and texts but also pictures: TV has been perceived as the most reliable medium for decades (63% of 4500 interviewees), closely followed by the newspaper (60%). The reliability of the radio has stagnated for years at 49 % and, parallel to the increasing

---

1   All quotes from German sources—books, articles—were translated by the author Beatrice Dernbach.

number of access possibilities and longer usage, the acceptance of the Internet has increased slowly but steadily to 29%. These results are surprising taking into consideration the changes of the media system in the last 46 years, but, they clearly show that there is a stable demand for the elementary needs of media use: information and entertainment (Reitze/Ridder 2011). Especially with regard to TV, these main needs separate the market between public broadcasting stations and private companies. Unfortunately, these differences cannot be discussed further in this paper.

One could question this media research when comparing the data with that from the Bundesverband der Deutschen Zeitungsverleger (BDZV): In the year 2004, the Zeitungsmarketing Gesellschaft ZMG found the newspaper to be in first place, far ahead of TV, when focusing on the criterion of credibility; 43 % of young people 14 years or older believe print media are reliable, while only 27 % regard the programs of ARD, ZDF and similar stations to be trustworthy. There must be an important reason why the Zeitungsverlegerverband has not updated these charts.

Since 1959, the US-American opinion research institute Roper has asked the American public one question which was and still is repeated analogous in most of the surveys, also in Germany: "If TV, radio, the newspapers and magazines offered different reports about one event, which version would you believe most?" (cf. Bentele 1998: 308). The term reliability has never been clearly defined and critically scrutinised before but it is assumed to be understandable for everyone. In the above-mentioned long-term-study "Massenkommunikation", reliability is one of 14 factors concerning media images that were investigated. TV, radio, newspapers, and the Internet are compared in the form of a semantic analysis independent from real use. The descriptors range from "ambitious", "reliable" and "modern" to "factual" and "independent" (Reitze/Ridder 2011: 300). In comparison to the functions and images of public and the commercial broadcasters, additional factors play an important role: balancing political reporting, pointing out injustices and failures, giving those people a voice who deal with social issues communicating values in our society, contributing to the formation of political opinions, supplying reliable and credible information, etc. (cf. ibid.: 309). Only the positive value of credibility is being measured, but not the negatively connoted factor of unreliability.

3. Trust in Journalism

What is credibility? Günter Bentele (1998: 305) defines it as "a quality allocated to human beings, institutions or their communicative products (oral or written texts, audiovisual products) by someone (recipients) with respect to something (events, facts etc.)". In addition, communication scientists have formulated a basic "theory of public trust" (e.g. Bentele 1994). It is based upon the idea that in the present information and communication society, trust in institutions, organizations, enterprises, and persons is essentially formed by the media. Thus, political, economical and other social actors try to lastingly influence this trust building process using public and strategic communication. Matthias Kohring is one of the German communication and media scientists who intensively worked on the topic of trust in journalism. In his monograph on the subject, Kohring (2004) explains his intention and motivation to work on this subject: He regards trust as fundamental for today's modern, highly differentiated and complex media society. But there is no reliable instrument to measure trust and credibility. Kohring (2004: 18–19) provides the state of the art of the research in this field, differentiating behavior, content, sources, and context. In Kohring's view, the most promising instrument to evaluate credibility is an orientation towards behavior and content. However, early studies by Hovland and others have focused very much on sources and contexts. They focused, and still focus, on the criteria of expertise and trustworthiness (Hovland/Janis/Kelley 1959). Indicators for competence are age and (life) experience, position and leadership roles; for trustworthiness these indicators are the intention to manipulate and indications of professional communication behavior.

To put it briefly: For American scientists like Hovland—and also German researchers in their tradition—allegedly fixed characteristics of the communicators themselves are much more important than those attributed externally by the recipients. However, Matthias Kohring considers the allocation process of credibility and trust to be directed from the recipient to the communicator. He (2004: 171ff.) distinguishes systematically between four different dimensions of credibility in journalism: the selection of issues, the selection of facts, the correctness of description and the trust in validation. Looking at the selection of topics one can ask if journalism has chosen the most current and relevant ones. The public expects journalism to always extract those events which are highly important for the target groups. Also, placing events in political, economical and social contexts is important for journalism. It gives background information, allowing readers, listeners, viewers, and users to assess the information with regard to their expectations and to classify them based on their experiences. Kohring's third dimension is the accuracy of descriptions: "This means the trust in the verifiable and generally acceptable accuracy of the description or the designation of the selected facts and issues" (cf. ibid.: 172). Is the number of dead and injured people correct? Is the term disaster accurate if nine people died in a flood? In what case is a disease an epidemic in the medical sense?

If the selection of information is some sort of validation, the explicit validation is another dimension to describe trust in journalism. Explicit validation can be found in journalistic genres like commentary, editorials, and glosses. In these formats, one can find concrete information about the journalist's view.

These four dimensions are being tested every day. Again a good example is the case of the former president of Germany, Christian Wulff. Did the media select the alleged mistakes of this politician as relevant and newsworthy among a lot of other possible issues? Did they research the facts correctly? Did they evaluate the incidents reasonably? Media analyses and opinion polls show that people first trusted the CDU politician more than the media. Many people, and also many conservative politicians, described and perceived the media coverage as a character assassination attempt. This perception changed after the interview between Christian Wulff and two correspondents of the public broadcasters ARD and ZDF, Ulrich Deppendorf and Bettina Schausten, on January 4, 2012 in Berlin. While the courts are still investigating the facts, the media, the political world, and the (German) population have already passed their verdicts.

4. Information and/or Entertainment

"Facts, facts, facts!" In a TV spot, the former editor of *Focus*, Helmut Markwort, drummed these words on the table in the editing office. This slogan was supposed to show all the stakeholders—the actual and potential readers, the political and economical actors, and even the competitors in the media—that for *Focus*, objective and verifiable information is the most important value. Also other media, like the national newspapers *Süddeutsche Zeitung, Frankfurter Allgemeine Zeitung, Die Zeit* and the news magazine *Spiegel* cultivate their image as serious, quality newspapers. They claim to research their stories carefully, to investigate facts that others tend to keep secret, and to classify and validate events correctly. These media organizations are regarded as opinion leaders— they often provide what is published in other media days and weeks later. But, obviously, for years the scope of how to interpret information journalism has been broadening. While the Anglo-American rule "facts are sacred, comment is free"[2] was true for German journalists after World War II and despite the existence of ethical guidelines regarding personal rights and issues related to religion and medicine formulated in the Press Code of the German Press council, tendencies towards tabloidization can be noted even in quality media. Is it possible to distinguish clearly between information and tabloid journalism, represented by *BILD* or TV programs like *RTL Explosiv*, for example? Generally, there is no, or only a small, difference between the respective journalism techniques regarding selection, research, writing, speech, photography and film. But: "News factors in tabloid journalism are always factors of narration. Important narration strategies are emotionalization, simplification and moralization" (Burkhardt 2005: 34).

Journalists working for so called serious media emphasize that they are different from others. This is illustrated by what happened during the Henri-Nannen-Award 2012 on May 15: The award for the best investigative research was given to Martin Heidemanns und Nikolaus Harbusch for their report "Controversy over private loans—did Wulff lie to Parliament?" The two authors are editors at the tabloid *BILD*, which, on the one hand, meant that for the first time a tabloid won the prestigious award and, on the other hand, that the reporters of the *Süddeutsche Zeitung*, Hans Leyendecker, Klaus Ott and Nicolas Richter, who had also won the prize, chose to give back their award in protest. The jury's decision was heavily criticized by the Netzwerk Recherche among many others: "Obviously, the jury has again shown a lack of understanding for journalistic criteria. Giving the award to *BILD*, the Jury confused a successful 'scoop' with the best investigative performance" (Die Recherche-Plattform von news aktuell: http://www.presseportal.de).

The question whether tabloid journalists also investigate true stories, research carefully, and publish adequately is clearly answered by the journalist association:

> To investigate does not mean—as the jury appears to believe—to produce a scandalous headline or to be frequently cited by other media. These effects are at best just concomitant. To investigate means to pursue a relevant issue for society with persistence, to research despite resistance, to generate new findings and to present them understandably. Thus, to perform investigative journalism in the best sense. (ibid.)

The debate in journalism science is not only emotional but also fundamental. It is taking place on at least two levels: on the level of the normative function the question is if journalism should only provide

---

[2] The long-term editor of The Manchester Guardian C. P. Scott (at the centenary of *Manchester Guardian*, that is, the precursor of *The Guardian*) wrote in 1921 the essay "A Hundred Years", in which he stated: "comment is free, but facts are sacred".

information and news or if it is also allowed to entertain. On the other hand, on the micro level of journalism skills and thus with a focus on storytelling, the question is if a journalist is allowed to tell stories in which facts and fiction are not clearly discernible by the recipients?

First, some comments on the debate on the macro level of the function of journalism and entertainment. Media scientists arguing strongly normatively and from the point of system theory distinguish between the public systems of information and of entertainment. This is based on historical developments, as information journalism is seen in the tradition of Enlightenment. In a society based on leisure and fun, the media assumes the function of entertainment. Görke (2007: 93), for example, attributes the functions of synchronization of the social subsystems and the construction of topicality to journalism. To implement this function, journalism provides programs for arrangement, for representation, for selection and for inspection (Blöbaum 1994). Görke (2007) considers entertainment a construction of possibilities. It is not necessarily current and it has developed special and different programs than journalism: Narration and presentation are the main focus here. While journalism informs, entertainment tells a story. But Görke also accepts that this distinction based on system theory is not comparable with the current development in journalism. He argues that journalism and entertainment are different forms of public communication, but that forms of hybridization are possible and real (infotainment) (cf. ibid.: 88).

Journalism researchers like Margreth Lünenborg (2007) analyze the relationship between information and entertainment in journalism not from the producers' but from the recipients' perspective. People use the media to satisfy certain needs. As can be seen in the study "Massenkommunikation", the recipients searching for gratification based on their expectations, distinguish between media types, formats and concrete programs. While the newspaper is clearly used for information, the offers of fiction in private programs are supposed to meet the audience's needs for recreation and entertainment. From the perspective of Cultural Studies, entertainment, as well as journalism, is seen as a part of the modern culture industry, but it is not disqualified. Recipients decide and act independently on their own and not on the basis of external normative qualifications that define entertainment as negative and information as most useful for a democracy. Why shouldn't journalism entertain and why shouldn't recipients be entertained by journalism and also get satisfaction for their emotional needs?[1]

This debate about information and entertainment, facts and fiction, is as old as journalism in mass media itself. It can be observed on several levels: on the level of functions, the level of the journalists themselves, and on the level of genres. In his study "The Emergence of German journalism" Dieter Paul Baumert (1928) called the phase between the middle of the eighteenth and the end of nineteenth century the *period of literary journalism*. A fair number of writers, like Josef von Görres, Heinrich Heine, and Theodor Fontane, were more or less part time journalists for newspapers, for example for *Rheinischer Merkur*, *Augsburger Allgemeine Zeitung* and *Vossische Zeitung*.

5. The Relationship between Journalism and Literature

Thus, the relationship between literature and journalism, between fictional and non-fictional narration, comes into focus. Professor for journalism, Bernd Blöbaum, and literary scientist Stefan Neuhaus, published a book in 2003 which deals with this relationship and is still unique in the field. Blöbaum (2003: 30) writes: "Both systems share the intermediation of reality—be it socially necessary and/or imaginary. In the case of journalists this happens through information about current events that is bundled into issues. In the case of writers, this happens through fiction."

Blöbaum sees the largest difference between the two communication systems in the broad creative space:

> The up-to-date objectivity of journalism limits the creative space and the utilization of creative potentials of journalists who work with restricted forms of presentation in routinized processes. In contrast, the personal attitude of the literary writer, his creativity and the less time-related opportunity for the processing of reality remain a space with comparably little structure. The creative space for text production is much larger in literature than in journalism. (2003: 32)

Egon Erwin Kisch (1885–1948) is one of the publicists who most obviously represent this state of tension. Kisch was "The racing reporter" (Kisch 1924), the "everyday author" (Augstein 2004). Kisch (1924: 7) said: "[t]he reporter does not have any tendencies, he must not legitimize anything and he has no position. He must be an impartial witness and he has to give impartial testimony, as reliable as a statement can be made".

Jakob Augstein, who in 2004 published a short biography of Kisch in the book "The conscience of their time", edited by Wolfgang Langenbucher and Hans-Jürgen Jakobs, described Kisch's life experiences, especially during wars all over the world, and his way of working. He concluded:

> Impartial? No position? No way. And what about the truth? Sometimes it has to suffer. Kisch himself described how he resorted to his imagination in his first task […] as a volunteer, because the results of his research were too thin. His colleagues complained that his fiction was much better than the reality and that he should have told them beforehand. (Augstein 2004: 145)

This description leads to "simply" another negative example, Tom Kummer, born on January 14, 1963, in Bern, caused a long lasting media scandal with his fictional interviews. In the mid-eighties he worked as a reporter for the newly founded magazine *Tempo*. As a Hollywood correspondent from 1993 onwards, he delivered his articles also to the *SZ-Magazin*, the *Tagesanzeiger-Magazin*, to the *Zeit*, the *Spiegel*, the *Neue Zürcher Zeitung* and other publications. His interviews with Pamela Anderson, Sharon Stone and others were completely faked. These stories deeply shook the media landscape, and their repercussions are felt to this day. Authors like Tom Kummer and the Zeitgeist-Magazin *Tempo*, implemented a new basic idea of journalism: "Smart people can write about gummy bears as well as about Helmut Kohl, Hollywood, AK-47s, polluted oceans, the sex life of pigeons, Gucci, pop and politics" (Kummer 2012).

Kummer, who many colleagues called a "bad boy" and "borderline journalist" after the scandal, has his own views on journalism and its practice:

> Objectivity, like truth and reality, is a pure myth in the media. I think that journalism only can regain credibility when journalists openly admit that their task of information presenting involves not just simply providing information, but constructing completely different conceptualizations of reality. [...] Much more important for me is another insight: if there is too much pressure or no money for field-work, one can simply find pictures of huts and coca farmers in Bolivia to describe the landscape and the villages. [...] I don't see that as a swindle. You can read the work of local authors and you can do excellent research about the issue via the internet and if you have some writing talent, it is no problem not only to create a sense of authenticity but to deliver a plausible message. And with such an article you are closer to a deep truth than somebody else who did a large amount of field-work and who is under pressure to subordinate his feelings and visions to his research, the reality he found and the untruth. (Kummer 2012)

The two editors-in-chief of the *SZ-Magazin*, Ulf Poschardt and Christian Kämmerling, lost their jobs after Kummer's practices were revealed. The Swiss journalist continued in the business: he writes under a pseudonym und as a ghostwriter, but he does not draw public attention to himself. Meanwhile, his art form is also in demand in public relations. The energy supplier RWE published a fictional interview between Andy Warhol and Joseph Beuys in its magazine entitled "Art meets intelligent energy" (www.vorweggehen.de). In 2010 a documentary about "Bad Boy Kummer" was released in cinemas, though it never became a blockbuster. Today, to be on the safe side journalists convey authenticity in their interviews by integrating personal observations about the interviewee, the room, the atmosphere etc.

6. (Un)reliable Narration in Fiction and Non-Fiction

There are elements common to non-fictional journalism and fictional narrative: Both have a narrator who communicates the story in a special way to an audience. The reliability and credibility of the narrator and the narrative not only depend on text-immanent, e.g. structural and semantic characteristics, but also and mainly on external and contextual characteristics and thereby mainly on the recipient, his experience, his knowledge, his system of norms and values and his knowledge of literary conventions (Nünning 1998). Ansgar Nünning modifies and transfers the findings of cognitive narratology related to the phenomenon of unreliable narration in fictional texts where the main focus of his research is to non-fictional genres (Nünning/Allrath 2005). Based on that the most important differences are:

- Fictional unreliable narration often is a rhetorical and/or aesthetic strategy. "In non-fictional narratives the lack of believability or credibility of a narrator is not an assessment the author intends the reader to make" (ibid.: 184).
- In contrast to recipients of fictional narration, readers of non-fictional stories have the opportunity to add, to modify or to question the credibility of a narrator using additional information (ibid.).
- While the author of a fictional narration always establishes a narrator, in authentic communication "a narrator usually is identical with the creator of the narrative, meaning that a non-fictional narrator only uses strategies to undermine the credibility of what he has said consciously under exceptional circumstances" (ibid.: 185). In contrast, the narrator of real stories will always try to strengthen his credibility.
- The "social identity" of an actor is important in fictional as well as in non-fictional narration. For the former, it is important that there are no contradictions between the narrator's description and his value judgements, but a non-fictional narrator can be identified by other characteristics. Physical characteristics like appearance, clothes, body language, mimicry and gestures are key factors in audiovisual media for the evaluation of the credibility and trust of a communicator (ibid.: 186–187).

But non-fictional narration also offers a number of strategies. So,

> the clever selection and presentation of the facts could cause an illusion of consistency. By leaving out information that could modify or call into question what was said, potential inconsistencies and inaccuracies which could undermine the credibility of the narration are suppressed. (Nünning/Allrath 2005: 187–188).

Cultural patterns are relevant for the recipient-oriented evaluation of the communicator's credibility in fiction and non-fiction. The set of standards and values, morality and ethics of the recipients determine whether the narrative is perceived as possible, plausible and believable ("the narrative coherence"; ibid.: 189). While fictional literature tries to break taboos and to push boundaries, journalism cannot afford to break social and professional rules. Tom Kummer shocked German journalism and perhaps his recipients with his style of Zeitgeist-journalism. Today journalists try to avoid untrustworthiness and unreliability by conveying authenticity, e.g. by printing not only their questions and the interviewee's answers but also describing the atmosphere, the circumstances, the clothes and the interviewee's behavior.

The following two examples are similar but not quite the same. On July 10, 2012, Heribert Prantl published this portrait of Andreas Voßkuhle, President of the Federal Constitutional Court, on page three of the *Süddeutsche Zeitung*. It has had a great after-effect.

> One has to experience him at the kitchen table. One has to see how he prepares a large meal. At Voßkuhles', no one sits at the dining table waiting to see what is being dished up. An invitation [...] starts in the kitchen: One guest cleans the mushrooms, another the beans, a third washes the salad. And there is some wine to accompany the preparation of the meal. Naturally, the host prepared everything very carefully, naturally, the menu is clear; but everything is created by everybody together. Everyone plays his part, everyone has to cut, boil and cook something, everybody has something to talk about: the pasta, the kitchen roll, and the world. Voßkuhle stirs the dressing himself. One can imagine how he acts as a chief justice. (Simon 2012)

For an appropriate assessment some background information is necessary.

Heribert Prantl is a lawyer with a PhD who worked as a judge and prosecutor. He started his journalistic carrier as an editor in the political department of the *Süddeutsche Zeitung* at the end of the eighties. He is regarded as a

> big player in German journalism. Whenever the country is engaged in an important legal issue or a court established an important principle, the reader of the *Süddeutsche Zeitung* wants to know what Prantl has to say. His pointed editorials have weight. The readers trust his expertise [...]. (Simon 2012)

This expert published a harmless and friendly portrait of the President of the Constitutional Court Andreas Voßkuhle under the headline "The protector of the constitution", which began with the paragraph cited above. The delicate issue about this apparently authentic scene is that Heribert Prantl never witnessed it with his own eyes. This was revealed when the President's spokesman stated "that Mr Prantl had never been invited for a private dinner, not for this article or at another time, so he could not be familiar with the cooking practices" (ibid.). Searching this case with Google you can find a lot of hits, but neither the abovementioned article nor the apology from the *Süddeutsche Zeitung* the day after are among them (cf. Mediaa.de). Other media, especially newspapers, reported about this case in a more or less gloating tone and quickly named it "Voßkuhle-Gate".

This case has created a significant stir because many people remember an article from the year 2010. In the *Spiegel* No. 33, René Pfister wrote a portrait of the CSU chairman and Bavarian State Premier Horst Seehofer:

> A few times a year, Horst Seehofer climbs down into the basement of his cottage in Schamhaupten, at Christmas and Easter, and also now in the summer, whenever he takes a few days off. His model train is there, a scale 1:87 Märklin HO model, he has been working on it for years. The train is a model of Seehofer's life. There is a replica of the train station in Bonn, the town where Seehofer's career started. After 2004, when he lost his highest post over the conflict about health policy, he built his "shadow train station" as he calls it, a track going down into the darkness. Just recently, Angela Merkel received a place at Seehofer's cellar, too. He had thought long and hard about where to put her. A few months ago he cut out her picture, made a smaller copy, stuck it on a plastic figure, and put her in a diesel locomotive. Since then, the chancellor has been riding around on Seehofer's train as well. Seehofer has created a world according to his own will, he stands at the control table and the figures in the trains move whenever he gives the order. It is a place where Seehofer's play instinct pairs with his passion to rule. In his case, this does not appear like a favorable combination. (2010: 41)

This story also created quite a stir. The rather sweet irony in this case is that the author René Pfister was supposed to be awarded the well-known Henri-Nannen-Award for his article in 2011. Holding the trophy in his hands he incidentally mentioned that he had never witnessed this scene but assembled it from other sources. As a consequence, he did not get the award. However, both Prantl and Pfister retained their jobs.

The question is whether recipients, especially newspaper readers, would have been aware of these cases without the reactions in other media. Obviously, self-awareness and self-control through media journalism worked in this case. Is that true for journalism in general? Does journalism watch itself so intently that it discovers every regulatory breach, every violation? Are recipients so media-literate that they are able to distinguish facts from fiction?

In general, Prantl and Pfister played by the rules of non-fictional narration: Both are well-known editors of serious national newspapers; they both found protagonists with a similarly high social status. The scenes they described sounded authentic, plausible, and possible. The information could have been proven by other sources and they were shown as being factually correct. Furthermore, the stories correspond to the standards and values of the readers of *Süddeutsche* and *Spiegel*.

If one cannot find unreliability in the narrator, the narrative or in the evaluations—then where else? It can be found in the disappointment of the deeply rooted belief (held especially by the journalists themselves) that reporters only authentically report what they really saw, heard, felt, and tasted. The cases described above have stirred up, and perhaps divided, the business because an unwritten rule was violated: tabloid journalism lies and crosses the line—that's what we have known since the descriptions by Günter Wallraff. Serious journalists do not play with truth and credibility. But it has happened, more than once. What does that mean for journalism?

7. The Fine Art of Storytelling

It can be observed that well told stories sell well, especially if they are entertaining, emotional, and partly also satisfy the need for relaxation or even voyeurism. This can be nicely illustrated by the history of travel journalism. The factual description of travel experiences started in antiquity. The best example is the Greek Herodot (born 490 BC). "When he collected and brought back his impressions people at home received his cultural and geographical reports enthusiastically. In the Latin word 'reportare' the meaning of bring-back-home is embedded" (Kleinsteuber/ Thimm 2008: 31). The travel report can be seen as an archetype of journalistic reporting. For "easy chair travellers" the stories experienced far away served as information about distant countries, and foreign people and cultures. Whether those who stayed at home would ever visit those countries was not the primary motivation for travel journalism—they were "instructions for dreams" (ibid.: 41). The issue of travelling is excellently suited to show the close link between the "literary description of a journey", the practical travel guide and enlightening travel journalism (ibid.: 49). These forms cannot be entirely separated.

The topic of travel itself is not yet the story. The journalist only discovers whether there is a story worth telling if he makes experiences for himself, sorts, selects, and weights his impressions, experiences, information, and notes. Furthermore, "he who investigates as a storyteller searches for emotions, looks for amusement, the human factor, the extraordinary, which at the same time enables him to convey the relevant information" (Lampert/Wespe 2011). The focus, the main message, the hero/protagonist, the action, and the place must be determined. The storyteller also has to decide on the beginning, the development, and the end of the story.

This kind of storytelling is not really an innovation in New Journalism but for years it has found its way into German journalism.

> This journalistic literary genre called New Journalism was developed in the early sixties of the 20th century in New York and is considered the original form of modern lifestyle- and Zeitgeist-journalism because of different innovative elements with regard to how issues were presented, language, and narrative perspective. (Wallisch 2005: 320)

Tom Wolfe was and still is one of the pioneers and protagonists of New Journalism. Together with Edward Johnson, the American edited an anthology with relevant texts in 1973. In his preface and the introduction he describes his motivation and approach to his style of journalism which he sees as a mixture of a literary novel, a report, and a feature article. Also Wolfe does not claim to have invented something new—on the contrary he appeals to authors like Balzac, Dickens, Mark Twain, and others. The most important thing for Wolfe/Johnson is the journalist's approach:

> When one moves from newspaper reporting to this new form of journalism, as I and many others did, one discovers that the basic reporting unit is no longer the datum, the piece of information, but the scene, since most of the sophisticated strategies of prose depend upon scenes. Therefore, your main problem as a reporter is, simply, managing to stay with whomever you are writing about long enough for the scenes to take place before your own eyes. (1973: 50)

The special characteristic of these new reports was their subjectivity aimed at triggering emotions instead of a kind of abstract objectivity, dialogues which could have taken place in reality, and an extraordinary and sometimes bizarre sounding writing style adapted from everyday life (cf. Wallisch 2005). One cannot find out from the text who the narrator and the protagonist are. Free associations, references to the everyday world and to hippie culture in the sixties bring back that "Zeitgeist".

New Journalism challenges both journalists and communication scientists. Some people presumed that authors like Wolfe did not do enough research—but the critized authors showed the opposite with the help of detailed notes. The New Journalists did not want to separate themselves from traditional journalistic investigation but wanted to prepare and to present their very well researched material in another form and style. This separation between form and content was not the consensus among all authors, but most of them crossed the border between fact and fiction (cf. Pörksen 2004: 20). Wolfe and his colleagues called the principle of objectivity and truth in journalism into question. No one can separate observations and observed people from the observer. Subjectivity cannot be prevented and therefore it is important to make one's own position explicit (cf. ibid.: 20–21).

From a scientific and also a practical perspective one can see a lot of possibilities for narrative journalism (cf. Müller 2008) and for storytelling. For years these forms can be observed for example in the USA in the field of science. In the last few years new products, formats, and programs were developed in print media but also especially in television that have been well received and in which people have placed high hopes in the face of the newspaper crisis (cf. Müller 2008; Dehm 2008). The great challenge for all kinds of journalism, but especially for science coverage, is the reduction of complexity of things and events so that laymen can understand them while remaining accurate enough for experts with regard to content and facts. Science journalist and professor for journalism Deborah Blum appreciates narrative writing in journalism for two reasons:

> First, it's seductive. It speaks to readers who are not naturally drawn to science topics but can be caught by narrative itself. And second, it's subversive. It seeks to educate readers by weaving information into a story, so that they learn about science without feeling—or even realizing—that they are receiving instruction at all. (Blum 2008: 550)

This approach to journalism has nothing to do with the invention of facts or lies. But indeed, it refers to the question discussed above: How strong and in what ways is journalism allowed to select, reduce, to put into another context, and to formulate the facts so that the content on the factual level is correct but the information function takes a back seat? To what extent can it take literary elements and forms without violating the standards of topicality, relevance, understandability, correctness, and clarity?

Furthermore, this discussion not only exists in science journalism but also in the sciences themselves. While one group of scientists sees storytelling as a main part of their science and the communication of science, others equate storytelling with "bad science" (Gardner/Marsack/Trueman et al. 2007: 510).

Where are the limits of narration in journalism? Christopher Bartone made the following point in a study about the coverage of the Iraq war from 2001 to 2003:

> Mainstream news media organizations have adopted classical Hollywood narrative storytelling conventions in order to convey vital news information. In doing so, these organizations tell news stories in a way, that paints political realities as causal agents, delicate international crises as sensational conflicts, and factual profiles of public figures as colorful characterizations. (2006: 3)

Bartone concludes that the media have reduced themselves to "henchmen of the political system". Script writing and journalism are two forms of storytelling and their meanings are absolutely different. While journalism provides information collected on one side and forwarded to the other, the traditional Hollywood story guides its audience through a fictional story to a logical conclusion. Because of the tendency towards sensationalism in the news the distinctions between the storytelling of journalists and Hollywood script writers have disappeared.

Especially topics in the field of justice and crime are mostly presented in a narrative form, in particular if they contain tragic, sensational, and very unusual aspects. This is a result of Jane Johnston's and Caroline Graham's study (2012) of two Australian newspapers. Articles about fashion, art, and theatre also show narrative elements, especially if they describe the individual success or the lives of the actors. In contrast, economical and political issues are composed in the classical news style of the inverted pyramid.

8. Conclusion: The Fine Line

The phenomenon of unreliable narration in journalism can be studied on three levels: on the macro level of media and journalism, on the meso level of organizations in journalism, and on the micro level of journalistic actors and their actions. On the macro level of journalism, which media transports into society, the focus lies on the allocation of reliability based on the motivation for media use, expectations, and trust. While we know much more about the world through media than through primary experience and the information cannot be checked because of its complexity, it would be naïve to believe that the observer system journalism describes the world as it is. Journalism cannot fulfill the normative requirement of completeness for the simple fact that it selects just a small number out of many potential topics. Nevertheless, journalism is and will continue to be one of the most important narrators in our modern information and communication society. The media as a kind of technical channel does not matter and a journalistic narrator is considered much more trustworthy and reliable in comparison to narrators appearing in the domain of advertisement and public relations. While TV provides authenticity via audio and pictures, the printed word in serious quality newspapers and magazines is considered, per se, reliable. Media and journalism produce a common cultural understanding through narration (Klaus/Lünenborg 2002: 155).

In any case, the journalism system has lost its value for society in the past few years. This is demonstrated by the declining circulation number of newspapers since 2001. Media studies show that mainly elderly people read newspapers as their primary source of information. For young people obviously the Internet fills this information gap. The great challenge for media organizations is that news and information are free in the Internet. Nevertheless, publishers and editors continue to think about how to motivate people to pay for informative quality journalism. This problem for the media also is a problem for journalism. An additional problem is that: sometimes it looks like journalism constructs a "life world" which has nothing to do with the audience's world. It creates hype for events which are not important. It spreads rumors, something which always has been part of oral narration culture (Raether 2012), but which is not expected in fact-orientated journalism. It provides real and pseudo scandals (cf. Bergmann/Pörksen 2009) within a matter of seconds via the digital network. Therefore, media experts and sociologists have demanded a new (media) ethics (cf. Pörksen 2012).

This acceleration has contributed to another negative development: the error rates have increased at the same time as no one is investing money into quality assurance in editing offices. Furthermore, in German speaking countries, a "correction culture" comparable to that in the USA has never been developed. Many American newspapers correct newsstories at fixed places, so called "correction corners". Colin Porlezza, Stephan Ruß-Mohl and Marta Zanichelli (2010) and Stephan Ruß-Mohl (2009) cite a study by Scott R. Maier from the University of Oregon who analyzed 4800 articles from 14 different US newspapers. He found that there is indeed a correction culture in editing offices and 58 percent of the journalists "believed a few years ago, that every suspected reporting error is always followed by correction" (Ruß-Mohl 2009). But Maier found that in contrast to the self-evaluation of journalists more than 98 % of all errors are not corrected.

Stephan Ruß-Mohl (2009) did a similar study for newspapers in Switzerland and Italy with similar results. The research team identified fundamental fact based errors: lurid headlines, distorted quotes, incorrect numbers/wrong data, wrong information about places and names, and orthographic errors. The Swiss team concludes: "Obviously, the error incidents in journalism is a problem in general and the error typology is similar across cultures" (Ruß-Mohl 2009).

In any case, the Swiss researchers conclude: "Not all the faults are obviously so serious that they have direct and negative effects on the reliability of newspapers. Nevertheless, the editing offices should intensively cope with the accuracy of reporting especially in times of increasing digitalization". Not only the columns of correction help but also the establishment of so called complaints offices like they exist at the *Westdeutsche Allgemeine Zeitung* or *Mainpost*. The reader should have a contact for questions, praise, criticism, and feedback. Possibly, this can strengthen reliability and trust in editing offices and the media.

But other aspects also threaten reliability: Many issues from social reality are not covered by journalism. Every year the "Initiative Nachrichtenaufklärung" presents the top topics which did not make it but which have a lot to do with the reality of people's lives. Probably, the unreliability of journalism partly stems from results speaking to the fact that journalists represent only a small portion of society because of their academic education and their income. They do not know the environment of others and it is not high on their agenda (cf. Weischenberg/Malik/Scholl 2006).

Let us go back to the new digital media: With the Internet, a new channel has come along which also publishes journalism, among many other things. Different media are coming closer together because traditional publishers and broadcasting stations are developing into integrated multimedia companies. Moreover, the border between producers and consumers is disappearing (cf. Deuze 2008; Berning 2011). On the one hand, these developments present opportunities for journalism while on the other hand they also present risks. The border between information and entertainment, between fiction and non-fiction has become blurred even more today, for example because of tabloid tendencies in the traditional printed and audiovisual media. The new media offer the option for everyone to check the information they get from the traditional journalistic media. The most important features of these new media are their enormous memory capacity, encyclopedia, data bases, chats, forums, and multimedia tools. Furthermore, it is much easier for the recipients to become part of the journalistic process by providing topics and information or producing their own tracks, videos, articles, and blogs. Mark Deuze (2008) calls this development "convergence culture". Not all welcome the collaboration of professsional journalists and amateurs, called for example "citizen journalism", but, on the contrary, complain about the de-professionalization of journalism. It is clear that journalism is changing under this pressure. It has to demonstrate its necessity and legitimize its work. It has to show how it can tell authentic, objective, exciting, and reliable stories about society, which create follow-up communication using innovative multimedia and narrative techniques by both producers and recipients (cf. Berning 2011). This story is starting right now. In any case, in most of the editing offices of German media the idea of reliable crossmedia storytelling has neither arrived nor been implemented (cf. Heijnk 2013).

Works Cited

Altmeppen, Klaus D. 2006. *Journalismus und Medien als Organisationen. Leistungen, Strukturen und Management.* Wiesbaden: VS Verlag für Sozialwissenschaften.

Augstein, Jakob. 2004. "Der Tagesschriftsteller. Egon Erwin Kisch 1885–1948." In: Hans-Jürgen Jakobs & Wolfgang R. Langenbucher (eds.). *Das Gewissen ihrer Zeit. Fünfzig Vorbilder des Journalismus.* Wien: Picus Verlag. 143–148.

Bartone, Christopher A. 2006. *News Media Narrative and the Iraq War, 2001–2003. How the Classical Hollywood Narrative Style Dictates Storytelling Techniques in Mainstream Digital News Media and Challenges Traditional Ethics in Journalism.* Thesis (MA), College of Fine Arts of Ohio University.

Baum, Achim & Siegfried J. Schmidt (eds.). 2002. *Fakten und Fiktionen. Über den Umgang mit Medienwirklichkeiten.* Konstanz: UVK.

Baumert, Dieter P. 1928. Die Entstehung des deutschen Journalismus. Eine sozialgeschichtliche Studie. München/Leipzig: Duncker & Humblot.

Bentele, Günter. 1994. "Öffentliches Vertrauen—normative und soziale Grundlage für Public Relations." In: Wolfgang Armbrecht & Ulf Zabel (eds.). *Normative Aspekte der Public Relations.* Opladen: Westdeutscher Verlag. 131–158.

Bentele, Günter. 1998. "Vertrauen/Glaubwürdigkeit." In: Jarren Otfried, Ulrich Sarcinelli & Ulrich Saxer (eds). *Politische Kommunikation in der demokratischen Gesellschaft. Ein Handbuch mit Lexikon.* Opladen: Westdeutscher Verlag. 305–311.

Bergmann, Jens & Bernhard Pörksen (eds.). 2009. *Skandal! Die Macht öffentlicher Empörung.* Köln: Herbert von Halem Verlag.

Berning, Nora. "Narrative Journalism in the Age of the Internet: New Ways to Create Authenticity in Online Literary Reportages." *Text praxis. Digitales Journal für Philologie* 3 (February 2011): http://www.uni-muenster.de/Textpraxis/nora-berning-narrative-journalism-in-the-age-of-the-internet (last retrieved: February 13, 2013)

Blöbaum, Bernd. 1994. *Journalismus als soziales System.* Opladen: Westdeutscher Verlag

Blöbaum, Bernd & Stefan Neuhaus (eds.). 2003. *Literatur und Journalismus. Theorie, Kontexte, Fallstudien.* Wiesbaden: Westdeutscher Verlag.

Blöbaum, Bernd. 2003. "Literatur und Journalismus. Zur Struktur und zum Verhältnis von zwei Systemen." In: Bernd Blöbaum & Stefan Neuhaus (eds.). *Literatur und Journalismus. Theorie, Kontexte, Fallstudien.* Wiesbaden: Westdeutscher Verlag. 23–51.

Blum, Deborah. 2008. "Narrative Style in Science Journalism." In: Holger Hettwer, Markus Lehmkuhl, Holger Wormer et al. (eds.). *Wissens-Welten. Wissenschaftsjournalismus in Theorie und Praxis*. Gütersloh: Verlag Bertelsmann Stiftung. 550–554.

Burkhardt, Steffen. 2005. "Boulevard-Journalismus." In: Siegfried Weischenberg, Hans J. Kleinsteuber & Bernhard Pörksen (eds.). *Handbuch Journalismus und Medien*. Konstanz: UVK. 31–35.

Dehm, Ursula. 2008. "Zwischen Lust und Lernen—Wissens- und Wissenschaftssendungen: Ergebnisse, Möglichkeiten und Grenzen von Medienforschung." In: Holger Hettwer, Markus Lehmkuhl, Holger Wormer et al. (eds.). *WissensWelten. Wissenschaftsjournalismus in Theorie und Praxis*. Gütersloh: Verlag Bertelsmann Stiftung. 483–500.

Dernbach, Beatrice. 2005. "Was schwarz auf weiß gedruckt ist… Vertrauen in Journalismus, Medien und Journalisten." In: Beatrice Dernbach & Michael Meyer (eds.). *Vertrauen und Glaubwürdigkeit. Interdisziplinäre Perspektiven*. Wiesbaden: VS Verlag für Sozialwissenschaften. 135–154.

Deuze, Mark. "Towards professional participatory storytelling in journalism and advertising." *First Monday* (July 4, 2005): http://firstmonday.org/ojs/index.php/fm/article/view/1257/1177 (last retrieved: February 13, 2013)

Gardner, Janet, Peter Marsack, John Trueman et al. 2006. "Story-telling: an essential part of science." http://www.researchgate.net/publication/6075767_Story-telling_an_essential_part_of_ science (last retrieved: February 13, 2013)

Görke Alexander. 2002. "Journalismus und Öffentlichkeit als Funktionssystem." In: Armin Scholl (ed.). *Systemtheorie und Konstruktivismus in der Kommunikations-wissenschaft*. Konstanz: UVK. 69–90.

Görke, Alexander. 2007. "Argwöhnisch beäugt: Interrelationen zwischen Journalismus und Unterhaltung." In: Armin Scholl, Rudi Renner & Bernd Blöbaum (eds.). *Journalismus und Unterhaltung. Theoretische Ansätze und empirische Befunde*. Wiesbaden: VS Verlag für Sozialwissenschaften. 87–116.

Heijnk, Stefan. 2013. "Zu viel Hü und zu viel Hott." *Message* 1: 69–71.

Hovland, Carl D., Irving L. Janis & Harold H. Kelley. 1959. *Communication and Persuasion. Psychological Studies of Opinion Change*. 3rd ed. New Haven, CT: Yale University Press.

Jakobs, Hans-Jürgen & Wolfgang R. Langenbucher (eds.). 2004. *Das Gewissen ihrer Zeit. Fünfzig Vorbilder des Journalismus*. Wien: Picus Verlag.

Johnston, Jane & Caroline Graham. 2012. "The New, Old Journalism." *Journalism Studies* 13.4: 517–533.

Kirsch, Egon E. 1924. *Der rasende Reporter*. Köln: Kiepenheuer & Witsch.

Klaus, Elisabeth & Margreth Lünenborg. 2002. "Journalismus: Fakten, die unterhalten—Fiktionen, die Wirklichkeiten schaffen." In: Achim Baum & Siegfried J. Schmidt (eds.). *Fakten und Fiktionen. Über den Umgang mit Medienwirklichkeiten.* Konstanz: UVK. 152–164.

Kleinsteuber, Hans J. & Tanja Thimm. 2008. *Reisejournalismus. Eine Einführung.* Wiesbaden: VS Verlag für Sozialwissenschaften.

Kohring, Matthias. 2004. *Vertrauen in Journalismus.* Konstanz: UVK.

Kummer, Tom. "Vom Mythos des Realen." (February 6, 2012): http://www.vocer.org/de/artikel/do/detail/id/105/vom-mythos-des-realen.html?onePage=1 (last retrieved: February 13, 2013)

Lampert, Marie & Rolf Wespe. 2011. *Storytelling für Journalisten.* Konstanz: UVK.

Luhmann, Niklas. 2000. *Reality of Mass Media.* Cambridge: Polity Press & Blackwell Publishers.

Lünenborg, Margreth. 2007. "Unterhaltung als Journalismus—Journalismus als Unterhaltung: theoretische Überlegungen zur Überwindung einer unangemessenen Dichotomie." In: Armin Scholl, Rudi Renner & Bernd Blöbaum (eds.). *Journalismus und Unterhaltung. Theoretische Ansätze und empirische Befunde.* Wiesbaden: VS Verlag für Sozialwissenschaften. 67–85.

Malik, Maja. 2004. *Journalismusjournalismus. Funktion, Strukturen und Strategien der journalistischen Selbstthematisierung.* Wiesbaden: VS Verlag für Sozialwissenschaften.

Meedia. "SZ 'bedauert' Prantls Voßkuhle-Gate." (July 31, 2012): http://meedia.de/print/sz-bedauert-prantls-vosskuhle-gate/2012/07/31.html (last retrieved: February 13, 2013)

Meier, Klaus. 2002. *Ressort, Sparte, Team. Wahrnehmungsstrukturen und Redaktionsorganisation im Zeitungsjournalismus.* Konstanz: UVK.

Meier, Klaus. 2011. *Journalistik.* Konstanz: UVK.

Merten, Klaus, Siegfried J. Schmidt & Siegfried Weischenberg (eds.). 1994. *Die Wirklichkeit der Medien. Eine Einführung in die Kommunikationswissenschaft.* Opladen: Westdeutscher Verlag.

Müller, Julia. 2008. *Narrativer Journalismus in US-amerikanischen Tageszeitungen.* Thesis (MA), Leipzig University.

Netzwerk Recherche. "Nach Nannen-Eklat: Zeit zum Umdenken." (May 12, 2012): http://www.netzwerkrecherche.de/Presse/120512-Nach-Nannen-Eklat-Zeit-zum-Umdenken/ (last retrieved: February 13, 2013).

Nünning, Ansgar. 1998. "*Unreliable Narration* zur Einführung: Grundzüge einer kognitiv-narratologischen Theorie und Analyse unglaubwürdigen Erzählens." In: Ansgar Nünning (ed.). *Unreliable Narration. Studien zur*

Theorie und Praxis unglaubwürdigen Erzählens in der englischsprachigen Erzählliteratur. Trier: WVT.

Nünning, Ansgar & Gaby Allrath. 2005. "(Un-) Zuverlässigkeitsurteile aus literaturwissenschaftlicher Sicht: Textuelle Signale, lebensweltliche Bezugsrahmen und Kriterien für die Zuschreibung von (Un-)Glaubwürdigkeit in fiktionalen und nichtfiktionalen Erzählungen." In: Beatrice Dernbach & Michael Meyer (eds.). *Vertrauen und Glaubwürdigkeit.* Wiesbaden: VS Verlag für Sozialwissenschaften. 173–193.

Pfister, René. 2010. "Am Stellpult." *Der Spiegel* No. 33: 40–43.

Pörksen, Bernhard."Die Wutmaschine." *Süddeutsche Zeitung* (December 22/23, 2012): 2.

Pörksen, Bernhard. 2004. "Das Problem der Grenze. Die hintergründige Aktualität des New Journalism—eine Einführung." In: Joan K. Bleicher & Bernhard Pörksen (eds.). *Grenzgänger. Formen des New Journalism.* Wiesbaden: VS Verlag für Sozialwissenschaften. 15–28.

Pörksen, Bernhard. 2006. *Die Beobachtung des Beobachters. Eine Erkenntnistheorie der Journalistik.* Konstanz: UVK.

Porlezza, Colin, Stephan Ruß-Mohl & Marta Zanichelli. "Fehler über Fehler." *Journalistik Journal* (October 6, 2010): http://journalistik-journal.lookingintomedia.com/?p=540 (last retrieved: February 13, 2013)

Raether, Elisabeth. "Haben Sie schon gehört?" *ZEIT-Magazin.* (December 13, 2012): 16–24.

Reitze, Helmut & Christa-Maria Ridder (eds.). 2011. *Massenkommunikation. Eine Langzeitstudie zur Mediennutzung und Medienbewertung 1964–2010.* Vol. 8. Baden-Baden: Nomos Verlagsgesellschaft.

Rühl, Manfred. 1980. *Journalismus und Gesellschaft.* Mainz: von Haase & Köhler.

Ruß-Mohl, Stephan. "Wir entschuldigen uns für diesen Fehler." *European Journalism Observatory* (April 17, 2009): http://de.ejo-online.eu/369/ethik-qualitatssicherung/wir-entschuldigen-uns-fur-diesen-fehler (last retrieved: February 13, 2013)

RWE. "Kunst trifft intelligente Energie." http://www.vorweggehen.de/energieeffizienz/kunst-trifft-intelligente-energie/ (last retrieved: February 13, 2013)

Scott, Charles P. 1921. "A Hundred Years." (May 5) http://www.theguardian.com/commentisfree/2002/nov/29/1 (last retrieved: August 15, 2013)

Simon, Ulrike. "SZ-Autor trickst bei Voßkuhle-Porträt." *Frankfurter Rundschau* (July 30, 2012): http://www.fr-online.de/medien/klage-gegen-sueddeutsche-sz-autor-faelscht-vosskuhle-portraet,1473342,16754242.html (last retrieved: February 13, 2013).

Wallisch, Gianluca. 2005. "New Journalism." In: Siegfried Wieschenberg, Hans J. Kleinsteuber & Bernhard Pörksen (eds.). *Handbuch Journalismus und Medien*. Konstanz: UVK. 320–322.

Weischenberg, Siegfried, Maja Malik & Armin Scholl (eds.). 2006. *Die Souffleure der Mediengesellschaft*. Konstanz: UVK.

Weischenberg, Siegfried. 1996. *Journalistik. Medientechnik, Medienfunktionen, Medienakteure*. Vol. 2. Opladen: Westdeutscher Verlag.

Wolfe, Tom & Edward W. Johnson (eds.). 1973. *The New Journalism*. New York, NY: Harper & Row.

ANDREAS ELTER

(Köln)

Unreliable Narratives in the US Elections: How Much Reliability Can a Campaign Take?

Narrative has only featured rarely in research on political communication to date, even though this field contains all the ingredients necessary for storytelling: narrators, a wide audience, a suitable space in interviews, reports, talk shows, biographical pieces, as well as—possibly the most fascinating aspect of narrative in the political context—meaning. It is all about mobilisation, trust, power, influence, interpretational prerogatives. The basic prerequisite for all of this is reliability. This term appears regularly, particularly during election campaigns.

1. Problem: Unreliable Narratives in Elections

Election campaigns lie at the heart of democracy; Sarcinelli (2009: 217) describes them as "the key phase of democratic legitimation in a representative system". Elections and election campaigns are constituent parts of political competition (cf. Kaase 1998: 44f.). However, academia to date has paid only little attention to narrative as a campaign strategy, even though narratives doubtlessly play a central role in the representation of identity, in individual memory, in the collective state of groups, regions and nations, and in ethnic and sexual identity (Currie 1998: 2). Because of the importance of narrative journalists are often concerned with the controversial issue of the truth of the statements made. Habermas regards truth as the essence of democracy—for him, a "post-truth-democracy" is no longer a democracy (2005: 150f.). And Brunkhorst (2009: 500) states that a democratic political culture is damaged or at least obstructed by the absence of a claim to truth.

However, a claim to truth does not necessarily go hand in hand with truth itself. Citizens are unable to easily test the statements and promises made and the stories told during election campaigns. Often, they simply have to trust that politicians are trying to live up to democracy's claim to truth. They have to place their faith in the reliability of the narrative. In election campaigns, it is this reliability that decides over victory and defeat, power and the lack of it. But when are narratives reliable, and when are they not?

The term "myth" is used here as the foundation of our analysis. Myth can help us classify both reliable and unreliable political narratives. Subsequently, classic election campaigns will be used to reveal the importance of these myths. Using historic US election campaigns, an analytical framework will be developed and applied to the US election of 2012 as a case study. Finally, the conclusion will develop a four-sphere model of reliability in election campaign narratives, and our case study will be classified according to this model.

2. Myths and Plausibility

Reliability is intrinsically connected to trust. McGregor (1938) already describes trust as a central social attitude, linked to the content-level assumption that an interacting partner will behave in a benevolent manner. The object of trust is thus evaluated positively, resulting in a tendency to act accordingly in an act of trust. Furthermore, according to Luhmann (1968) one of trust's main functions is to reduce complexity. It is only through trust that actions such as an actor's election to a government office become possible.

Trust is the result of plausibility, on which its implementation depends. Plausibility is a central topic of communications research. According to Götsch (1994), it is made up of the communicator's assumed intentions and the competency ascribed to him or her. Plausibility is created by the communication of trustworthy actions, that is, actions that show benevolence towards their recipient, an alignment with ethical and moral principles, and distributive justice (cf. Schweer/Thies 2005: 48, 56ff.).

Narratives can serve to increase plausibility. This is the case with both literary and everyday narratives. Plausibility is a topic that transcends the boundaries of individual academic disciplines. Within literary studies, narratology is concerned with the plausibility of narrators and narratives. In 1961, Wayne C. Booth introduced the term of "unreliable narration" to scholarly debate in the field of literature. Other academic disciplines have also laid increased importance on the question of "reliable" and "unreliable" narration and what distinguishes reliability from unreliability. The decision of whether a narrator can be trusted applies not only to literary narrative texts, but also to everyday and real-life narratives. In literary studies, judging the reliability of narrators is based primarily on the audience's general knowledge, values, morals and ideas of what constitutes normality. Allrath and Nünning (2005: 179f.) list a number of prerequisites for unreliable narration: firstly, a figural narrative situation; secondly, the presence of a fictional textual world; and thirdly, the conflation of narrator and main character (key term: first person narrator). Contradictions, inconsistencies and other signals are necessary for the audience to recognise that the narrative is unreliable.

Actions that measure up to or exceed the audience's standards of reliability and thus create a positive image of the actor are often communicated using narrative elements and a mode of storytelling that approaches the mythical. In the Platonic dialogue "The State", Socrates already defined "myth" as a sequence of episodes in the past, present or future, as a simple narrative or as an imitation or combination of both. Narratives, particularly mythic ones, want stories to enable statements about the main character that can be generalised in a wider context. Like Plato, Aristotle's starting point was a highly technical definition of myth, with no theoretical, religious or philosophical connotations. He defined myth as an ordering of events, literally the "composition of events", which is at the same time the representation of the action.

The special feature of myth is its cyclicality, but in many narratives this is interrupted: this is particularly the case in fairy stories, which usually end in the marriage between prince and princess. Similarly, many of the transformed stories represent mere episodes that can be seen as abbreviations of genuine myths and as layering these with a concrete original event (Marcou/Balzer 1988: 204).

In myths, heroes are larger than life and exceed the audience's expectations. The creation of meaning and identity are two important aspects of modern mythology, and the utopian impulse is a third (cf. Müller-Funk 2008: 103f.). For the people, myth stands for

> [...] the utopian longing for narrative order, which allocates humans, homeless and alienated from themselves and others, a shared space. The New Myth is a place of absolute *sensus communis*, created by poetry, able to reconcile the abstract and the particular, the absolute and the concrete through the synthetic power of a chemically conceived literature. (Müller-Funk 2008: 103)

Summarising and applying the insights generated from the interweaving of these terms to election campaigns, politicians are trying to gain citizens' trust through plausible stories. In doing so, they can enter the realm of reliable mythic narrative. At the same time, there is a danger of slipping into the area of unreliable mythic narrative. Thus they have to walk a fine line.

It is only stories about positive actions showing goodwill towards the citizen that will produce a tendency in the audience (the potential voter) to act in favour of the politician. However, if a story appears guided by pure utopia and not reality, it becomes unreliable myth. If it is a personal story, that is, one in which the narrating politician is the main character, he or she runs the risk of being perceived as an unreliable narrator. The story becomes implausible and trust is lost. Thus it always depends on how reliable a narrative is perceived to be. In general, myths as such are deemed unreliable and thus implausible. On the other hand, the mythic narrator—as long as he or she remains within the closely defined boundaries of reliable mythic narrative—can compensate for these deficits through personal charisma and emotional capital. Indeed, it may be precisely through myth that tendencies towards positive action are evoked in the audience. This phenomenon can be described using the popular proverb "faith can move mountains". That election campaigns in particular have a tendency towards mythic narrative is due to their implicit demands, as will be shown in the following section. Before moving on, however, a further line of thought merits closer consideration: while a reliable, non-mythic narrative is regarded as reliable by its recipients, it only offers little motivation to take action in the sense of voting. While a politician who announces that taxes will have to be raised and budgets cut may be regarded as a realist and as plausible, he or she will probably also not be elected. From a politician's point of view, an unreliable mythic narrative (pure utopia) is also hardly suited to prompting action. Potential voters may take pleasure in the utopian vision (e.g. all men will become brothers), but at the same time they will see that it is a utopia, and thus will not act. By contrast, only a reliable mythic narrative will cause voters to take action. A politician who is able to construct a narrative so that it both contains mythic traits (e.g. Obama in the 2008 campaign with the simplified slogan "Yes, we can") and the utopia developed in this myth is simultaneously seen as "feasible" (in Obama's case: change is possible) will be able to bring his or her audience to act. The obvious action in this case is to vote for the respective politician, which is the goal aimed for in the democratic system. Thus election campaigns need myths.

3. Election Campaigns Need Myths

A political campaign is understood as the strategic creation of public opinion (cf. Greven 1995: 41f.). Röttger (1998: 667) defines campaigns as dramaturgically conceived, thematically defined temporary communicative strategies designed to generate publicity, create trust in one's own plausibility and produce approval, subsequently leading to a corresponding action. This definition applies equally to election campaigns. The desired subsequent action is the vote.

The campaign has become firmly established as a means of gaining supporters and mobilising followers in the run-up to an election. However, it has been subject to strong criticism. For example, Baringhorst (1995: 35) calls campaign politics a "transformation of the political from *realpolitik* into political marketing". Campaigns are "the expression of a staging of politics conducted by politics and the media that bears only little similarity to reality", as Röttger (2006: 19) summarises. Schröder (2005: 13ff.) also sees a rise in a staged politics determined by media populism. He criticises citizens (apart from an information elite) for letting themselves be fobbed off with this superficial showmanship. Election campaigns offer this kind of staging in a ritualised form.

In Germany, this criticism is based on the many observed tendencies towards an "Americanisation" of politics, the media and also of election and political campaigns. American election campaigns are seen as the ideal form of personalised campaigning with a reduction of elections to a competition between candidates, an aggressive form of campaigning, a high degree of professionalisation, a marketing approach and event and theme management (cf. Schulz 1997: 186f.).

In advanced media democracies such as the United States, politicians are dependent on the media and thus align themselves with and indeed take over the media system's logic. This is a key characteristic of modern election campaigns, and expresses a steadily progressing modernisation (cf. Donges 2006: 134). Two traits are particularly striking: the use of marketing strategies and personalisation. Because of recipients' limited attention resulting from the immense offer available, the media system demands simple messages modelled on advertising and a concentration on individuals, as they are easily identified with. These traits can be observed increasingly in all media election campaigns, and of course they also influence the stories told as part of campaigns.

In contrast to real descriptions, such as those ideally found in journalism, advertising makes no claim to reality; indeed, it often openly admits the lack of it (cf. Merten 2008: 52). If campaigns are modelled on advertising, then this ideal is transferred to the narratives told as part of election campaigns. One of the simplest models is the so-called AIDA model. According to this, advertising tries to gain a customer's attention, raise interest in a product, create a desire to own the product and finally lead to action, that is, buying the product. Its goal is thus to promote sales, or in the case of politicians, to achieve a maximum number of votes, by creating attention and a need. In order to do this, the stories told do not have to be true; they only have to follow this short-term goal. If marketing manages to appeal to consumers' desires, it is successful. If the stories told by politicians about utopias and ideal behaviour appeal to the population's desires, then they are myths.

The increasing personalisation of elections and election campaigns is the result of insights gained from electoral analysis, particularly the analysis of the election decision. This decision is preceded by cognitive deliberation processes that require psychological explanation. The voter's individual decision forms the centre of interest. In modern electoral analysis, this decision is described in the extremely popular Michigan approach based on Campbell, Gurin and Miller (1954). According to this approach, the individual election decision is not motivated by socio-structural factors, but is the result of a range of long- and short-term influences. Besides long-term party identification and the topics of the respective election campaign, the candidate's orientation is also an influencing factor (Roth 2008: 42f.). In order to cater to voters' need for personal alternatives, election campaigns are increasingly focused on candidates. Topics are personalised, and in order for this to be successful the campaigns need the candidates' personal stories.

In comparison with Germany, elections and election campaigns in the USA are highly centred on the candidates, financed by the candidates, focused on the individual and dominated by television. Not only the presidential election is a candidate-focused election; congress elections are, too. Candidates' images play a significant role, and the campaign needs to render them accessible to the voters (cf. Müller 2002: 190f.).

If a voter perceives their party identification and a candidate's orientation as aligned, then one can assume he or she will vote for that candidate. According to Roth (2008: 46), candidates' stories need to match up with the topics and goals of the party. This aspect is particularly pronounced for myths. These narratives want to create meaning and identity—belonging to a party is such an identity, and voters' party identification is one of an election campaign's most important goals.

4. Myths in the US Elections

To this day, electoral campaigns and indeed the entire political culture of the USA are rooted in the structures of the nineteenth century. Many well-known canvassing strategies of that period are still used today. One central element is the public speech. More than in any other country in the world, the speech is a medium used to appeal to voters and gain their attention (cf. Müller 2002: 189). The content of these speeches may include elements of myth-creation, as they refer back to extant myths, propagate them and above all attempt to find a connection between existing myths and the respective candidate/speaker. Looking at various US presidents from a historical perspective, similar key themes appear again and again, even if they have had to be decoded afresh for the respective period. One might almost call these recurrent key topics the archetypal *topoi* of US history or its underlying myths. In my opinion, it is possible to identify four main myths and traditions:

(1) Firstly, the horror vision of a too-powerful state with unbridled federal power—which *de facto* is a myth, as it never existed. Nevertheless, it is reflected in countless statements, such as the criticism of Washington and what is decided "there" usually voiced during election campaigns. This is closely related to a fear of elites, voiced for instance by Nixon among others in a speech given on November 3, 1969 as part of the presidential election campaign. Nixon contrasted the East Coast intellectual elite that had hijacked the country with his myth of the "silent majority" (cf. Galinsky 1980), whose representative he wished to appear. Translated to the German context, this would be the position of the "advocate of the little man", which—in reference to politics—can also usually be classed as belonging to the realm of myth. In the US, the success of this myth can be explained by the widespread fear of excessive central government power and of controlling, separatist elites.

(2) Another commonly cited myth is that of unity. Thus US President Johnson, for example, spoke of the "Great Society" (cf. Zarefsky 1979). This refers to the geographical and social cohesion of the Union, even given all its differences (diversity paradigm). For example, Abraham Lincoln made a plea for the cohesion of the United States in his oft-cited "House Divided" speech, which attributes a mystical element to the unity of the population:

> A house divided against itself cannot stand. I believe this government cannot endure, permanently, half slave and half free. [...] Either the opponents of slavery will arrest the further spread of it, and place it where the public mind shall rest in the belief that it is in the course of ultimate extinction; or its advocates will push it forward, till it shall become lawful in all the States, old as well as new—North as well as South. (A. Lincoln on June 17, 1858, cited in Foner 2010: 99f.)

(3) The central American myth is, of course, the "American dream". It says that any citizen is capable of achieving social advancement, regardless of class, race or religion. This belief is firmly established. The term itself goes back to the historian James T. Adams, who first used it in 1931. The basic principle of the "American Dream" forms part of the USA's Declaration of Independence, which is in turn based upon the French Revolution's promise of equality. The Declaration states among other things that the population is allowed

to depose an unjust ruler—referring to the King of England—and choose their own political system. While the absolutist European rulers of the eighteenth century continued to oppress people using force, the American Constitution guaranteed inalienable rights, particularly the right to resist government. This in turn made individual, free development possible. Equality before the law and the same rights also make it possible for Everyman to advance socially—this was and remains the central message of the American Dream. This led many settlers to emigrate from Europe to America (cf. Musick/Wilson 1998; Monteyne 2004).

(4) The fourth myth that should be mentioned here is the myth of the "West". This refers to both the possibility and the success of permanent change. The borders of the USA once lay in the East, but during the course of history westward migration and constant shifts in the border constantly changed the "gap" between the two oceans—until the Pacific was finally reached. "New frontiers" were often mentioned in connection with social development, frontiers that could be overcome just as in history geographical and natural boundaries (the Appalachians, the Rockies) had been conquered. Thus the frontier myth of the West was translated to the realms of medicine, technology, science or space exploration. In a popular sense, it forms the basis for statements such as "Everybody can make it", or indeed "Yes, we can".

In the following, we will show that these subliminal myths also appear in the US presidential election campaign of 2012.

5. Method and Analytical Framework: When Does Myth Become Unreliable Narrative?

The definitions of plausibility, trust, unreliability and myths on the one hand and a campaign's success factors on the other result in an inherent problem: election campaigns demand reliable myths. However, if myths are narrated by their own main character, then the candidate risks being perceived as an unreliable narrator.

The better a story about a candidate's actions fits in with party goals, thus creating identity and meaning, the clearer a utopian vision is described, and the more consistently a range of events are woven to create a story, the more likely the result will be a reliable mythic narrative, which in campaign logic will contribute to success by maximising votes.

However, this conflicts with the characteristics of the unreliable narrator listed above. Unreliable narrators narrate their own actions only from a first person point of view. So if the story about positive actions is told by a third party, it will be more plausible than if told by the actor him- or herself. The story's degree of personalisation is a further factor. So if the story is only about the candidate him- or herself and they are thus perceived as egocentric, in the context of the election campaign this renders the story implausible. Then again, the candidate needs to be recognisable as a person and cannot become faceless. This is a fine line, just like the line between unreliable and reliable mythic narrative. The third factor cited by Allrath and Nünning, the textual world, can be disregarded here. Differences between candidates are hardly to be expected here. Basically we can assume that stories corresponding with the characteristics of unreliable narrative reduce a candidate's plausibility. In the following, speeches from the US presidential election 2012 will be analysed on the basis of these preliminary considerations. We hope to identify whether a candidate's speech can be classified as unreliable mythic narrative and he then accordingly as an unreliable narrator.

The speeches of Barack Obama and Mitt Romney at their parties' presidential nominating conventions have been selected, as these had a huge resonance in the media across the entire USA via television and the Internet and thus probably were the speeches that reached the most citizens. In the various stages of the election, the national party conventions kick off the main phase of the election campaign. They are the only events besides the TV debates to reach a national audience and are thus ritualised as key events, with extensive coverage both prior to and following the occasion (Müller 2002: 203f.).

Family members and partners of both candidates also speak at both party conventions. Their role can be seen as that of eye witnesses to the myth-creating process. However, the main focus of the present study lies on the candidates themselves. For this reason, only their speeches will be analysed—and within these, only the narrative passages. Given the study's leading question of to what extent narratives in the US election campaign serve to create myths and can be classed as unreliable, this seems an appropriate method of procedure.

6. Case Study Romney vs. Obama 2012

The 57th presidential election of the United States took place on November 6, 2012. On November 6, the electors of the Electoral College were formally appointed. They cast their votes for the offices of the president and vice-president on December 17. In the presidential election of 2008, the Democrat candidate Barack Obama had won against the

Republican John McCain. The dominant theme of that presidential election was the desire of the US electorate for change, for which Obama's slogan "Change" provided a simple and effective match.

The Democrats and Republicans have dominated the US party landscape for about 150 years. The Democrats are more employee-friendly and are stronger supporters of civil liberties and state welfare. The Republicans stand for lower taxes and restricted state spending, a strong army and a strict justice system. This also includes adhering to capital punishment (Radler 2008).

According to the constitution, candidates for the office of president have to have been born in the United States, be at least 35 years of age and to have lived in the country for at least 14 years. All the parties held party conventions in order to determine their candidates. Romney was officially elected the Republican presidential candidate at the Republican National Convention held in Tampa, Florida, between August 27 and 30, 2012. 2061 of 2286 delegates voted for him. Besides Romney, Paul Ryan was nominated as vice-presidential candidate. In early September 2012, Barack Obama was officially nominated for a second presidential candidacy at the Democrat party convention. Even without prior campaigning, he was able to command the majority of delegate votes. Vice-president Joe Biden was once again elected vice-presidential candidate.

In their speeches,[1] held only a few days apart, both candidates explained why they were the better choice compared to their opponent. They both employed narrative strategies and told stories from their past and about people they had met who symbolically represented their arguments. However, there are significant differences in their stories' content, narrative perspective, the main characters and length.

Mitt Romney gave his speech on August 30, 2012 at the Republican Party's nominating convention. A substantial portion of his speech (50%) was given over to introducing himself, with the main emphasis on his family history, the founding of his business, his family and his upbringing. His five-point plan for the future of the US was only explained in a brief passage.

Using excerpts from his family history, he attempted to integrate voters—migrants make up a considerable part of the US electorate:

> My dad had been born in Mexico and his family had to leave during the Mexican revolution. I grew up with stories of his family being fed by the US Government as war refugees. My dad never made it through college and apprenticed as a lath and plaster carpenter. (NPR 2012a)

---

[1] Transcripts of the speeches are analysed (sources: NPR 2012a and NPR 2012b).

Here Romney already alludes to one of the four central myths: the American Dream. This forms the underlayer of his story, which can be seen as a classic immigrant narrative. Here, Romney tries to underline the integrative aspects of his character:

> It is what brought us to America. We are a nation of immigrants. We are the children and grandchildren and great-grandchildren of the ones who wanted a better life, the driven ones, the ones who woke up at night hearing that voice telling them that life in that place called America could be better. (NPR 2012a)

He also attempts to give a positive explanation of the image he has of women using examples taken from his family history, most explicitly his mother and his wife Ann:

> When my mom ran for the Senate, my dad was there for her every step of the way. I can still hear her saying in her beautiful voice, 'Why should women have any less say than men, about the great decisions facing our nation?' (ibid.)
> I knew that her job as a mom was harder than mine. And I knew without question, that her job as a mom was a lot more important than mine. And as America saw Tuesday night, Ann would have succeeded at anything she wanted to. (ibid.)

Furthermore, it is striking that Romney tries to play down his religious confession. He is a Mormon, and Mormons make up only a small portion of the US population. He attempts to calm the fears of his audience related to this fact:

> We were Mormons and growing up in Michigan; that might have seemed unusual or out of place but I really don't remember it that way. My friends cared more about what sports teams we followed than what church we went to. (ibid.)

This is one of the few passages where he actually mentions religion. Of further note is the narrative strand devoted to Romney's biography. He represents himself as successful and willing to take risks:

> So we started a new business called Bain Capital. [...] We were young and had never done this before and we almost didn't get off the ground. In those days, sometimes [...] That business we started with 10 people has now grown into a great American success story. Some of the companies we helped start are names you know. [...] At a time when nobody thought we'd ever see a new steel mill built in America, we took a chance and built one in a corn field in Indiana. Today Steel Dynamics is one of the largest steel producers in the United States. These are American success stories. (ibid.)

Although he uses the personal pronoun "we", a strong degree of personalisation and self-heroisation can be detected. Listeners cannot fail to understand that the speaker is also the centre of the action. Unlike other examples dealing with Romney's family and origin, he appears here as the main character.

The astronaut Neil Armstrong forms a further narrative element in Romney's speech. Using the example of the moon landing, Romney explains what America is capable of; the USA are the most successful nation in the world and must remain so. This is a clear reference to the underlying myth of the "West" (new frontier). Romney creates a direct link between himself and Armstrong by connecting Armstrong's story with his own biography:

> The soles of Neil Armstrong's boots on the moon made permanent impressions on OUR souls and in our national psyche. Ann and I watched those steps together on her parent's sofa. Like all Americans we went to bed that night knowing we lived in the greatest country in the history of the world. God bless Neil Armstrong. Tonight that American flag is still there on the moon. And I don't doubt for a second that Neil Armstrong's spirit is still with us: that unique blend of optimism, humility and the utter confidence that when the world needs someone to do the really big stuff, you need an American. That's how I was brought up. (ibid.)

Here, historic events are interwoven with his own story; the mythic hero Armstrong is juxtaposed with his own narrative in an attempt to link to one of the four underlying myths.

In his speech, Mitt Romney thus employs many narratives, often from his own life or about events he wants associated with himself. His family history is consistent, is interwoven with stories to create historic events, is integrated and deals with his own positive actions. In individual important passages of his speech he also switches from "we" to "I". The word "I" occurs 51 times altogether in Romney's speech.

On September 6, 2012 Barack Obama spoke at the Democratic Party nominating convention. He introduced himself only briefly. Most time was spent giving an abstract explanation of his political views. Narrative elements only make up about a quarter of his speech. He only speaks of his origins briefly at the beginning. However, much space is given to people he has met. He uses their example to explain why his presidency should be extended. This way, he is able to create a link to himself without explicit personalisation. While Romney speaks of what "we" and "I" have done, Obama turns the tables and tells of what has happened to him, what he has experienced. This is why, somewhat curiously, the word "I" occurs more frequently than in Romney's speech, even though Obama is talking about other people. I would refer to this as indirect personalisation, which Obama uses more frequently than Romney. But the incumbent president is unable to do without direct personalisation completely. Connecting his own life story with the stories and fates of others is his main focus, however.

Obama uses the example of his grandparents to explain the role of social advancement and social equity:

> My grandparents were given the chance to go to college and buy their home—their own home and fulfill the basic bargain at the heart of America's story, the promise that hard work will pay off [...]. (NPR 2012b)

In one sentence, he describes one of his positive deeds explicitly—working for the socially disadvantaged—but this first-person narrative moves straight into another example, which he can recount as an eye witness:

> I began my career helping people in the shadow of a shuttered steel mill at a time when too many good jobs were starting to move overseas. And by 2008 we had seen nearly a decade in which families struggled with costs [...]. (ibid.)

The topic of social equity is a central theme of his speech. References to the most famous underlying myth, the American Dream, are unmistakeable. Implicit here is the notion that state intervention is necessary for this dream to continue to come true—thus Obama's creed. The narrative level of this strand connects Obama's everyday experiences with his party's goals, and presents him as the alternative to Mitt Romney:

> Now, I've cut taxes for those who need it—middle-class families, small businesses. But I don't believe that another round of tax breaks for millionaires will bring good jobs to our shores, or pay down our deficit. I don't believe that firing teachers or kicking students off financial aid will grow the economy. (ibid.)

In the following, Obama continues to speak of people he has met during the course of his life. He only mentions them and their needs briefly, and does not go into their fates in depth. Rather, he "collects" their names and jobs, creating a comprehensive view of society in this *pars pro toto*, as can be seen in this selection:

> 'I've shared the pain of families who've lost their homes, and the frustration of workers who've lost their jobs [...].'
> 'The young woman I met at a science fair [...].'
> 'I've met workers in Detroit and Toledo who feared—they'd never build another American car. And today they can't build them fast enough because we reinvented a dying auto industry that's back on the top of the world.'
> 'The family business in Warroad, Minnesota, that didn't lay off a single one of their 4,000 employees when the recession hit [...].'
> 'I think about the young sailor I met at Walter Reed Hospital still recovering from a grenade attack [...].' (ibid.)

Using these examples, Obama goes step by step through his agenda for his second term of office. All of these goals are linked to his program, integrating the different characters: "I don't know if they'll vote for me. But I know that their spirit defines us" (NPR 2012b).

By integrating completely different types of people and examples, Obama shows that he wants to be a president for all the people. On the one hand, this *habitus* is typical of incumbents, as they are able to profit from their office's aura; but on the other, Obama is also taking recourse to an underlying myth—that of unity. Thus it comes as no surprise that Obama quotes the originator of this myth, Abraham Lincoln himself. He indirectly links the quote from Lincoln to himself and the responsibility connected with his presidency:

> And while I'm proud of what we've achieved together—I'm far more mindful of my own failings, knowing exactly what Lincoln meant when he said, 'I have been driven to my knees many times by the overwhelming conviction that I had no place else to go', for I have held in my arms the mothers and fathers of those who didn't return. (NPR 2012b)

Considering the attributes selected, we can see that Obama also makes use of mythic elements. He weaves separate stories together, integrates these into his individual utopia, talks of distributive justice but dwells less on his own actions. His narrative is less consistent. He himself only appears occasionally as the narrative's main character. Thus Obama hardly speaks of himself and his own story. Although the word "I" appears 74 times in total, which at first glance would seem to suggest a first person narrator, Obama personalises himself far less than Romney does. This is due to the observer's perspective he takes. It is not ABOUT him, but rather VIA him—in the sense of an eye witness: "I have observed", "I know that", "I notice"—these and similar phrases explain the frequent use of the first person singular. But at the same time they also explain that the intention is not to create content-related personalisation, but rather that this is merely a grammatical phenomenon.

7. Conclusion:
Classifying the Case Studies According to the Four-Sphere Model

The insights gained through the analysis of the speeches require further systematisation, which will be provided in these concluding remarks. We noted that both Obama and Romney employed underlying myths. Furthermore, both used traits of mythic narrative—because it corresponds to the logic of election campaigns. Both presented themselves as first person narrators, although Obama did so less than Romney.

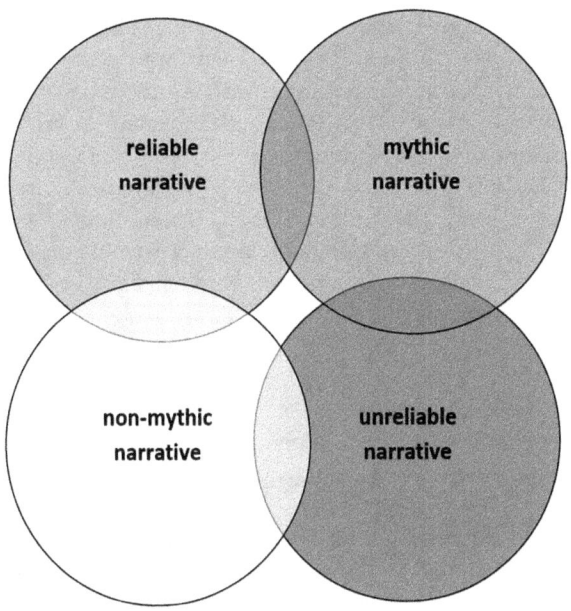

Figure 1. Four-sphere model of reliability of narratives in election campaigns (own model).

In order to represent the question of the plausibility and reliability of political narrative in election speeches (it might be possible to transfer the model to other kinds of political communication also, although we do not attempt this here), a four-sphere model was developed. It contrasts reliable narrative (above left) with non-mythic narrative (below left) and mythic narrative (above right) with unreliable narrative (below right). These pairs are those encountered most often in narratives. Usually, a mythic narrative is thus an unreliable narrative. The truth of its content cannot be verified. The opposite is the case with the reliable narrative. It is normally based on numbers, facts and dates—and thus is verifiable or falsifiable and corresponds to non-mythic narrative. To use a simple example here, the statement "We lowered the number of unemployed by […] percent" can be verified by the voter if the number of unemployed before the speaker took office is compared with current numbers. Even if the reasons for this lowering cannot be ascertained, this would remain a non-mythic, verifiable narrative. This differs in the case of statements such as "We are the only party standing for social justice". Here we are already dealing with mythic narrative, the factuality of which cannot be verified. By definition, this narrative must be classed as unreliable. But as has been noted above, it can still be more plausible—if we are dealing with a plausible myth. In other words: for our object of study and presumably political narrative in general, it is not the level of the circles themselves that are of prime interest, but only the overlaps between them.

If the characteristics of narrative reliability and the mythical are matched up, we get four areas of overlap (cf. Figure 1): reliable mythic narrative (above), reliable non-mythic narrative (left), unreliable non-mythic narrative (below) and unreliable mythic narrative (right). This four-sphere model can be used to systematically classify and compare narratives in election campaigns.

Working with this model, the differences between Obama and Romney are clear: both work with myths. However, Obama is more successful at avoiding unreliable narrative, even if not completely so. He often speaks from a first person perspective. In doing so, he hardly ever speaks about himself, but instead about what he has seen and witnessed and what people have told him. He thus remains within the overlapping area of the reliable mythic narrative. By contrast, Romney attempts to elevate his own rise and his time and a businessman. But here he lapses into the role of an unreliable narrator, whose story is less easy to verify. In the above model, Barack Obama fits in with the upper area as a reliable narrator of mythic stories, while Mitt Romney is to be classed more as an unreliable narrator of mythic stories, and thus fits in with the right-hand area of the four-sphere model.

In principle, this four-sphere model is valid for and can be applied to other case studies. It provides a suitable analytical model for narrative processes in political communication. It is based primarily on a hermeneutic, normative theoretical approach and should be evaluated as such. Whether there is a connection between reliable narrative and electoral success or the reliability of a narrative plays no role in the election outcome is a question that the model cannot answer. This is where empirical examination must follow.

Works Cited

Allrath, Gaby & Ansgar Nünning. 2005. "(Un-)Zuverlässigkeitsurteile aus literaturwissenschaftlicher Sicht: Textuelle Signale, lebensweltliche Bezugsrahmen und Kriterien für die Zuschreibung von (Un-)Glaubwürdigkeit in fiktionalen und nicht fiktionalen Erzählungen." In: Beatrice Dernbach & Michael Meyer (eds.). *Vertrauen und Glaubwürdig-*

keit. Interdisziplinäre Perspektiven. Wiesbaden: VS Verlag für Sozialwissenschaften. 173–193.

Aristoteles. 1982. *Poetik.* Manfred Fuhrmann (ed.). Stuttgart: Reclam.

Baringhorst, Sigrid. 1995. "Humanitarismus und Live Aid—Zur Moralisierung des Politischen in massenmedialen Solidaritätskampagnen." In: Helga Braun & Dörthe Jung (eds.). *Auf dem Weg in die 'Kabeldemokratie'? Frauen in der Medien- und Informationsgesellschaft.* Hamburg: Frauenanstiftung. 35–44.

Booth, Wayne C. 1961. *The Rhetoric of Fiction.* Chicago, IL: University of Chicago Press.

Brunkhorst, Hauke. 2009. "Demokratie und Wahrheit. Jürgen Habermas zum 80. Geburtstag." *Leviathan* 37.4: 491–500.

Campbell, Angus, Gerald Gurin & Warren E. Miller. 1954. *The Voter Decides.* Evanston, IL: Row Peterson.

Currie, Mark. 1998. *Postmodern Narrative Theory.* Basingstoke: Macmillan.

Donges, Patrick. 2006. "Politische Kampagne." In: Ulrike Röttger (ed.). *PR-Kampagnen. Über die Inszenierung der Öffentlichkeit.* 3rd ed. Wiesbaden: VS Verlag für Sozialwissenschaften. 123–138.

Galinsky, Hans. 1980. "Neologism in German." *American Speech* 55.4: 243–263.

Götsch, Katja. 1994. *Riskantes Vertrauen: Theoretische und emprische Untersuchungen zum Konstrukt Glaubwürdigkeit.* Münster: Lit.

Greven, Michael. 1995. "Kampagnenpolitik." *Vorgänge* 34.4: 40–54.

Foner, Eric. 2010. *The Fiery Trial. Abraham Lincoln and American Slavery.* New York, NY: Norton.

Habermas, Jürgen. 2005. *Zwischen Naturalismus und Religion.* Frankfurt am Main: Suhrkamp.

Kaase, Max, 1998. "Demokratisches System und die Mediatisierung von Politik." In: Ulrich Sarcinelli (ed.). *Politikvermittlung und Demokratie in der Mediengesellschaft.* Bonn: Bundeszentrale für politische Bildung. 24–51.

Luhmann, Niklas. 1968. *Vertrauen. Ein Mechanismus der Reduktion sozialer Komplexität.* Stuttgart: Enke.

McGregor, Douglas. 1938. "The Major Determinants of the Prediction of Social Events." *Journal of Abnormal and Social Psychology* 33.2: 179–204.

Marcou, Phillio & Wolfgang Balzer. 1988. "Dichtung, Mythos, Wissenschaft." *Erkenntnis* 29: 201–225.

Merten, Klaus. 2008. "Zur Definition von Public Relations." *Medien und Kommunikationswissenschaft* 56.1: 42–59.

Monteyne, David. 2004. "Framing the American Dream." *Journal of Architectural Education* 58.1: 24–33.

Müller, Marion. 2002. "Wahlkampf à l'americain." In: Andreas Dörner & Ludgera Vogt (eds.). *Wahl-Kämpfe. Betrachtungen über ein demokratisches Ritual.* Frankfurt am Main: Suhrkamp. 187–210.

Müller-Funk, Wolfgang. 2008. *Die Kultur und ihre Narrative. Eine Einführung.* 2nd ed. Vienna: Springer.

Musick, Marc A. & John Wilson. 1998. "*Work, Race and the American Dream.*" *Sociological Focus* 31.1: 17–30.

NPR. 2012a. *Mitt Romney's Acceptance Speech.* [Speech Transcript]. http://www.npr.org/2012/08/30/160357612/transcript-mitt-romneys-acceptance-speech (last retrieved: January 15, 2013)

NPR. 2012b. *President Obama's Convention Speech.* [Speech Transcript]. http://www.npr.org/2012/09/06/160713941/transcript-president-obamas-convention-speech (last retrieved: January 15, 2013)

Plato. 1994. "Politeia." In: Ursula Wolf (ed.). *Sämtliche Werke.* Trans. Friedrich Schleiermacher. Vol. 2. Reinbek bei Hamburg: Rowohlt.

Radler, Christian. "Land der Zwei-Parteien-Herrschaft." (March 10, 2008): http://www.tagesschau.de/ausland/meldung245842.html (last retrieved: December 14, 2012)

Röttger, Ulrike. 1998. "Kampagnen." In: Jarren Otfried, Ulrich Sarcinelli & Ulrich Saxer (eds.). *Politische Kommunikation in der demokratischen Gesellschaft.* Opladen/Wiesbaden: Westdeutscher Verlag. 667.

Röttger, Ulrike. 2006. "Campaigns (f)or a Better World?" In: Ulrike Röttger (ed.). *PR-Kampagnen. Über die Inszenierung der Öffentlichkeit.* 3rd ed. Wiesbaden: VS Verlag für Sozialwissenschaften. 9–24.

Roth, Dieter. 2008. *Empirische Wahlforschung. Ursprung, Theorien, Instrumente und Methoden.* 2nd ed. Wiesbaden: VS Verlag für Sozialwissenschaften.

Sarcinelli, Ulrich. 2009. *Politische Kommunikation in Deutschland. Zur Politikvermittlung im demokratischen System.* 2nd ed. Wiesbaden: VS Verlag für Sozialwissenschaften.

Schröder, Arne. 2005. "Politik als Inszenierung. Eine kritische Betrachtung." In: Lars Rademacher (ed.). *Politik nach Drehbuch. Von der politischen Kommunikation zum politischen Marketing.* Münster: Lit-Verlag. 13–49.

Schulz, Winfried. 1997. *Politische Kommunikation. Theoretische Ansätze und empirische Forschung.* Opladen: Westdeutscher Verlag.

Schweer, Martin K.W. & Barbara Thies. 2005. "Vertrauen durch Glaubwürdigkeit—Möglichkeiten der (Wieder-)Gewinnung von Vertrauen aus psychologischer Perspektive." In: Beatrice Dernbach & Michael Meyer (eds.). *Vertrauen und Glaubwürdigkeit. Interdisziplinäre Perspektiven.* Wiesbaden: VS Verlag für Sozialwissenschaften. 47–63.

Zarefsky, David. 1979. "The Great Society as a Rhetorical Proposition." *Quarterly Journal of Speech* 65.4: 364–378.

ANDREAS VON ARNAULD & STEFAN MARTINI
(Kiel)

Unreliable Narration in Law Courts

1. Courts and the Law

Law courts form the scene where the law of the land is interpreted, developed, put into action, applied to practical cases. When other attempts to resolve a dispute fail, parties appeal to a court; when someone is accused of a crime, the state is bound to prosecute. One should not rush to associate these legal practices with the drama of a criminal trial, though. Rather, modern society's law establishes diverse institutional settings where specialised legal bodies regulate social behaviour. While criminal proceedings shape the popular imagination of the legal system, judicial proceedings in administrative, family, or labour law may sometimes appear more technical, yet influence people's lives to no lesser extent.

Furthermore, there is more to law than court proceedings. The law lies at the centre of a variety of discursive practices, legal norms being (by a rule of thumb) conceptualised as rules originating from or being recognised by state authority and backed by an institutional apparatus (legislation, administration, courts) that shares a certain form of procedure and argumentation, monopolising the authoritative power to interpret and implement these rules. In this vein, legal norms are distinct from other social norms like ethical standards or mores—although they all demand compliance, i.e. they posit an *ought* against an empirical *is*.[1]

Court proceedings thus only partially represent legal discourse; however, they in a way epitomise this very conception of law: e.g., a person can be charged and tried for a crime *only* in state court and *only* for a crime that is established by law.[2] In criminal proceedings, state representatives have to prove, according to legally prescribed rules, that a certain crime

---

[1] This conceptualisation requires the notion of a modern legal system already departed from other social fields like the moral, religious or political universe—which cannot be upheld fundamentally through history; for a universal and historical communication and differentiation theory, see Niklas Luhmann (2004 [1993]). The *degree* of separation between law and morals depends on one's philosophical stance and may furthermore vary from one legal system to another.

[2] Art. 93 et seq., Art. 103 sec. 2 Basic Law.

has been committed, regardless of whether the crime is morally wrong or not. It is then the court's duty to compare the facts of the case (as established in the proceedings) to the relevant legal norms, a process called subsumption and traditionally conceived of as a chain of deductive reasoning.[3] Only if the judge contents herself that all the necessary elements of the legal norm are present in the "facts", only if e.g. she is satisfied that the defendant took the car purposefully and with the intent to appropriate it unlawfully, she will affirm that a crime ("theft") was committed and hand out a legally binding sentence.

Our paper will examine this complex societal set-up, where norms, institutions and individuals interact, from the perspective of narratological analysis. An emphasis on court proceedings as law's epitome notwithstanding, we try to convey at least an impression of legal discourse's diversity[4]—and to pose the question whether and how legal stories are narrated unreliably. Looking at the grave social impact law has, one should be entitled to expect that someone involved in legal activities acts—and narrates—in a reliable manner. This expectation holds both for the addressee of the law—like plaintiffs, prosecutors, defendants, witnesses, experts—and for as the producer of the law—like courts, parliaments, government agencies. We want to show how (un)reliability in various kinds of legal discourse, especially in law courts, is determined (Sections 2, 3). A case study is devoted to a recent ruling by the German Federal Constitutional Court (Section 4). Looking at law's claim to normativity, however, one can also expect some differences between (un)reliability in law and in literature—the domain from which the concept of the unreliable narrator originates.[5]

2. Looking for Narration in Legal Discourse

2.1 Legal Discourse is Diverse

As already pointed out, there is more to legal discourse than what is going on in a court of law. Looking for potential objects of a narratological analysis, one may vaguely distinguish binding and non-binding legal texts and utterances. *Binding* statements are legal norms themselves, written and non-written, and also contracts, as either legal acts between private actors recognised by the law of the state or as covenants between state entities,

---

3   A notion highly criticised, rightly so, cf. Alexy (2010 [1978]: 1); Ladeur (1990: 178).
4   Due to the authors' academic heritage, a certain emphasis will be put on the German legal system and its discourse.
5   See the introduction to this volume.

e.g. international treaties. Norms are the most abstract form of law as they ideally lay out rules for an unspecified number of future situations. Applicative acts, like court opinions and administrative acts (e.g. police arrests), share the legal validity of the norms applied, but are directed towards individual cases. Typical for a 'complete' legal norm is an 'if'-'then'-structure: If the preconditions laid down in the norm (be it a law or a contract) are met (*protasis*), if, e.g., all the elements of a certain crime are present in a given case, the legal effects laid down in the norm (*apodosis*) will follow, e.g. a fine or a prison sentence. Not all norms, however, follow this model. Rules have other contents as well: institutions may be erected, competences between state organs and federal levels delimited, legal principles set up, formalities defined by law. These sets of rules either provide the prerequisites for concretising ('complete') behavioural norms, or construct the institutional infrastructure that keeps the legal system running.

In principle *non-binding* and thus empirical statements, on the other hand, are utterances necessary to ascertain the concretisation and application of norms, like pleadings, testimonies, expert opinions, and other evidence: they present factual as well as legal knowledge to official representatives, who determine whether the elements of the relevant norms are met after having assessed the facts of the case.[6] Equally non-binding are abundant texts that teach, inform about, order[7] and criticise the law and its procedures. Despite the fact that they sometimes may be cited in court opinions and used as arguments in real cases, they can be characterised as meta-texts (or pre-texts). Textbooks and casebooks collect the legal information (norms, leading cases of higher courts) and 'wisdom' about a legal system or a specific field of law. They are mainly used in law schools to convey the major principles of the legal fields covered. Similarly, for teaching purposes, hypothetical cases are presented to law students who have to solve them according to the current (or, for example, Roman) law. These cases appear in tests, textbooks, casebooks or even student law journals. Other jurisprudential, mainly academic publications—like theses, monographs, journal articles, discussion and conference papers—devote themselves to certain legal problems or recent court decisions in order to put forward legal interpretations and solutions,

---

[6] A major difference between Civil and Common Law jurisdiction is the role of judges and what is expected from the parties to deliver the legal foundation of the court decision. In Continental jurisdiction, the role of the judge is stronger (cf. Damaška 1991).

[7] Cf. Kirchhof/Magen/Schneider (2012).

identify lines of precedent, systematise and criticise the law or its application, or propose changes in the law.[8]

2.2 How Legal Discourse Narrates

a) Non-Binding Texts and Utterances

It is rather obvious that stories are told in non-binding texts and utterances that flesh out legal cases, like testimonies and pleadings—mostly put forward in an oral, personal form. An asylum seeker has to prove her need to seek asylum by telling a convincing story of persecution. The witness of a crime is obliged to retell what happened according to his own experience before the police or the court. The prosecutor, after having studied the investigative material, will give her account of the course of events that led to a crime and will connect it to the elements of the specific crime as laid down by the law.[9] Here, one can easily identify a storyteller (being author and narrator in one person) that recounts past events—in many instances a personal story—in a certain way to state agencies. The Genettian categories of *récit*, *discours*, and *histoire* (who tells a story to whom, how, and about what?) can be clearly identified (see Genette 1983). The events as re-collected through storytelling lay the factual foundation for evidence and shape a case which then is assessed by the court according to the law in the books. This function of 'legal stories' or, in this case, legally evaluated stories, is a major difference to literary fiction. Literary fiction might follow certain aesthetic patterns, or perform social functions (e.g. reflection, entertainment), or be used to reach goals like fame, distribution and recognition. Yet, they are not integrated with the same radicalism into an institutionalised practice that is not concerned with the narratological aspects of storytelling, but determines whether legal requirements are met. The intended readers (or addressees) for these stories are primarily legal experts as well as state agencies and their representatives (although the public is regularly admitted to court proceedings and is thus also an important—additional—recipient).

Narrative structures can be detected in non-binding texts *about* the law, too.[10] This is most prominent in the already mentioned didactic, hypothetical cases where more or less fictitious characters act out a more

---

8 Cf. von Arnauld (2009: 19–23).
9 The role of the prosecutor in Germany is that of a neutral body of the administration of justice. Hence, the prosecutor is obliged to investigate objectively into the case and also has to take into account aspects in favour of the suspect (defendant), cf. § 160 sec. 2 German Code of Criminal Procedure.
10 For further details cf. von Arnauld (2009: 19–23).

or less fictitious story, in a narrative universe that needs to resemble our social reality in order to be able to connect it to the rules valid therein. In this case, as it is an example of (factual) fiction, the author-narrator divide—established for fiction—may be applied. The text can be either presented by a first- or third-person narrator, although the latter is more common.[11]

b) Binding Texts

That binding legal texts may also contain narrative elements is more subversive to traditional juridical wisdom. The storytelling element is clearly discernible in that part of a ruling (or an administrative decision) which presents the facts of the case, but it is not limited to that part alone, as we will show in greater detail in part three of this paper. The court handing out the decision is evidently the author, whereas it is impossible to discern a narrator distinct from the court or the individual judge (if one does not want to instantiate 'the law' itself as a narrator). Concerning the *discours*, one can detect a wide variety of narrative styles when comparing legal systems and cultures (cf. Lasser 2004). French style of reasoning, on the one hand, is extremely short, efficient, rational, impersonal, while in Anglo-American legal systems rulings are delivered through opinions of individual judges, which tends to inspire a narrative, personal style. German reasoning strikes a middle ground: Here, like in France, courts hand out rulings, not individual judges (with the major exception of the possibility of dissenting opinions at the Federal Constitutional Court), which leads to impersonality and rationality. Comparably, though, the German style is more learned and philosophical compared to the French discourse, as a lot of literature and precedent is cited and discussed.

It is probably least obvious to identify narrative structures in the generalised rules of law, contracts and covenants. Who is talking or telling a story when the penal act prohibits incest,[12] when tax law specifies the duty to pay taxes,[13] when the constitution grants civil rights?[14] Is the statement of the validity of a trade contract a story? Who is telling a story to whom about what here?[15] At first sight there is no story being told, rather a legal status determined.

---

11 See, e.g., von Arnauld (2012).
12 §173 German Criminal Code.
13 § 22 German Tax Code.
14 Art. 1–19 Basic Law, and a few other provisions spread in the Basic Law.
15 Cf. von Arnauld (2009: 14 et seq.).

2.3 Norms Tell Stories, Too

In ancient and medieval times, and also not uncommon in the common law tradition, legal duties were recorded by typical incidents. The description of these incidents, in words or in pictures (as e.g. in the *Sachsenspiegel* of the thirteenth century), clearly show a narrative structure. So, a legal book possessing the force of a code could describe the incident of an incestuous love affair between a brother and his sister after their parents left the house. The legal context (inferred, *inter alia*, from what Genette (1997) would call 'paratexts') makes it clear that this narration serves the function of pointing to legal consequences: 'whoever does this (or something similar or not too dissimilar), will be punished.' Thus, a quasi-third-person narration with legal force is visualised.

Similar narrative structures reappear in today's imaginations of norms. Surely, our modern laws have undergone a process of rationalisation, leaving a morally entrenched and visual language more and more behind. For example, the crime (in German categorisation: the offence[16]) of incest was abominated as "Blutschande" ('disgrace of blood') in German Law in the nineteenth century,[17] and still is in Austria until today.[18] Nowadays, even "incest" is only the title of section 173 of the German Criminal Code, while the elements of the crime follow a more clinical and scientific language: incest is defined as "an act of sexual intercourse with a consanguine descendant".[19]

Despite this rationality, interpretation is not separated from our enculturalised narrative imaginations. Reading the term "incest" in the penal code, we imagine a certain pattern, mostly the story of a daughter molested by her father, a story of violence and dependence.[20] Other constellations, on the contrary, would be viewed as atypical, of course depending on dominant cultural attitudes. The way older codes explicated laws is thus the way we tend to imagine norms until today. The subsumption and the sentencing process are governed by discovering typical stories while atypical stories require more argumentative effort (see von Arnauld 2009: 37–38). Until now, e.g., the prohibition of incest in Germany does not include homosexual acts,[21] although the official reason

---

16 A crime is called a 'crime' in Germany if its committal entails a minimum sentence of one year imprisonment—the penalisation of incest does not include this prerequisite.
17 Kanwischer (2013: 38 et seq.). It was renamed "cohabitation of relatives" in 1977, cf. Schäuble (2008: 98).
18 Sect. 211 Austrian Criminal Code.
19 Persons performing incest are not liable to prosecution if they are younger than 18, cf. § 173 sec. 3 German Criminal Code.
20 See, e.g., Kanwischer (2013: 132–133).
21 Cf. Lenckner/Bosch (2010).

given for penalising this form of sexuality, asymmetrical power relations, may arise in same sex sibling relationships as well. This exclusion is due to the imagination of the incest taboo as a protector of stable and typical reproduction structures: the story of mom and dad having children.

The process of legal construction is not only influenced by intra-legal imaginations, but also by background narratives that support and legitimise norms.[22] These narratives go back to the origin of norms and give them meaning and sense, located in the social universe.[23] Founding narratives form less obvious narrative structures in norms and can especially be found in modern-day constitutions. They prominently appear in preambles: introductions to legal texts that do not have the same force of law as the actual rules and provisions, but may have an effect on their interpretation. Preambles often tell the story of a turning-point in history, a shaking-off of the dark past, a departure into a brighter future. They mark the beginning of a new constitutional age for a society: the French constitutions of the late eighteenth century and the U.S. Constitution exemplify this type of 'positive constitutionalism'.[24]

A famous example of establishing such a founding narrative is the 1776 U.S. Declaration of Independence[25]—an important constitutional pre- and by-text with an auxiliary function for constitutional interpretation.[26] Here, an "enough is enough" story is told; it is a story of ongoing and unbearable repression: "The history of the present King of Great Britain is a history of repeated injuries and usurpations, all having in direct object the establishment of an absolute Tyranny over these States". The protagonists are the "good People of these Colonies" and the "Prince whose character is [...] marked by every act which may define a Tyrant", who is thus "unfit to be the ruler of a free people". The conclusion, the *denouement* of that story must be to end tyranny: "these United Colonies are, and of Right ought to be Free and Independent States". A kind of cogent poetic justice needs to be done: the independence of the colonies, a "necessity which constrains them [the colonies] to alter their former Systems of Government". The founding narrative of U.S. American political discourse—equality, individual liberty, independent government—is thus based on and legitimised by a story.

---

22 Public discussion with competing narratives may also try to delegitimise and change existing interpretations of norms: Seyla Benhabib calls this "jurisgenerative processes" (2006: 49).
23 See Cover (1983).
24 Cf. for this and for the opposing concept of an evolutionary constitutionalism Möllers (2011: 169 et seq.). See also Cullen (2003: 46); Anderson (1991: 193).
25 Founding even for everyday life, cf. Cullen (2003: 37).
26 Cf. Orgad (2010: 719–721).

Nevertheless, without denying normative effects of literature, there is a difference between literature and legal (or social) norms. The end of the story of a norm (and by the way, also the end of the story of a court ruling) is always a definite legal result, a demand on behalf of the law that requires factual situations to be reviewed in a certain way, and, ultimately, when at odds with the law, to be altered. That demand is symbolised by the term "ought" as opposed to the term "is". In the phrasing of the Declaration of Independence: "We, therefore, […] solemnly publish and declare, That these United Colonies *are*, and of Right *ought* to be Free and Independent States".

2.4 How Legal Discourse Can Be Unreliable

In literary criticism the notion of unreliability is primarily used to resolve intratextual incoherence. The contradiction is identified in the narrator deviating from the (implied) author's world view and norms.[27] Ansgar Nünning proposed to conceptualise it as a reading tool to account for the ambiguities and inconsistencies of a text (1999: 54).[28] Yet, unreliability can also be used to depict deviance of a text's reality from 'reality's reality', e.g. differing laws of probability.[29] This deviance has to be detected by the reader and thus is dependent on the reader's knowledge, norms, attitudes and capabilities (cf. Nünning 2004: 237).

Concerning unreliability in legal texts and utterances, there are obvious and less obvious cases. A witness may have trouble remembering or simply lie when giving testimony. Subjective recollections of past events—intentionally or unwittingly—compete with past reality. The gap between different versions of reality—which also exist in pleadings or in the court's facts of the case—creates space for unreliability. We will deal with these "distortions" with respect to courts and rulings in detail in the next section of this paper, in which we attempt a closer narratological analysis. But how about unreliability in what legal norms narrate? In modern law, there is usually no divide between author and narrator. The legislator is author and narrator at the same time: the prescriptions of norms do not contain narratological layers, they simply put forward the demands of the norm. Thus, a deviation of the author from the narrator's norms does not seem plausible in legal norms. Of course, different normative layers are possible: There is a hierarchy of norms; norms may

---

[27] Booth (1961: 158 et seq.).
[28] See also Yacobi (2001: 224).
[29] Yacobi (1981: 114 et seq.).

differ regarding their binding force (hard versus soft law).[30] A structural similarity, then, may be found in a line of jurisprudence by the German Federal Constitutional Court where the Court formulates demands on consistent legislation:[31] Here, the legislator is measured against his own concept—a deviation from this original conception might render the law unconstitutional. The author's/narrator's actual story is posed against his ideal one. Such a deviation is one of the effects of the "is"-and-"ought" divide.

There exists a significant exception from the general absence of the author/narrator-divide in modern law that has already been pointed to. Preambles to constitutions with their founding narratives are a vivid source of this kind of unreliability. First of all, preambles and constitutions present a fictitious subject issuing that law: the *pouvoir constituant*. Especially in founding constitutional moments, constitutions through their preambles—in want of real parliamentary assent[32]—can be legitimised through imagined communities (cf. Anderson 1991: 192). There are two basic choices in presenting the *pouvoir constituant*: (1) it is united or compound, (2) it is first person or third person. Especially the first choice can be an intentional effort to embrace competing political factions and entities in a crucial moment of founding a new state (cf. Rakove 2009: 106). Although forming a compound federal political body, the preamble of the U.S. constitution's subject is a united "We the People of the United States" (as it is a "We" speaking in the Declaration of Independence). Similarly, the German Basic Law, establishing a federalist state, is adopted by a single unit, "[t]he German people, in the exercise of their constituent power"—the difference to the U.S. constitution is the focality: one has to install a third-person narrator in order to make sense of the German constitution as a story about the people's proclamation of the following constitutional norms. The French constitution of 1958 follows the German example ('The French people solemnly proclaim [...]'[33]). The United Nations Charter of 1946 chooses a middle path and commences with "We the Peoples of the United Nations [...] have resolved to combine our efforts to accomplish these aims"[34].

---

30 See Arndt (2011).
31 A prominent case: BVerfGE 121, 317 (2008)—prohibition of smoking in restaurants (BVerfGE: official case selection of the German Federal Constitutional Court).
32 Moreover, parliaments need a constitutional foundation, so there is always the problem of a constitutional, democratic beginning.
33 The Declaration of Human and Civic Rights of 1789 still speaks of the "representatives of the French people".
34 The German Federal Constitutional Court—in respect of the European Union—insists that the founding subject of the transnational entity is compound: the sovereign European peoples; cf. BVerfGE 123, 267 (2009)—Lisbon Treaty.

These preambles and constitutional pre-texts present a one-sided, though 'official' version of history, with the purpose of legitimising action, action that is argued to be inevitable (as in the case of the U.S. Declaration of Independence) and consecrated by the force of (a new) law. Apart from that historical subjectivity, constitutions present a fictitious story that has nothing to do with actual historical events—not only is the *pouvoir constituant* non-existent (thereby instituting the difference between author and narrator in constitutional texts), the events that led to the foundational act almost always differ from the story told in the text: a German People never really "adopted this Basic Law", it was the product of a constitutional convention (the Parliamentary Council),[35] erected by will of the occupying powers and its representatives elected in pre-federal entities.[36] But narration is not lying in a moral sense, it has a political purpose; the narrative can fill the gap between actual historical circumstances and the need for legitimacy at the starting-point of a legal system. The constitutive act is legitimised in retrospect by weaving that narrative into the web of collective identity and by signs of explicit and implicit affirmation under a 'living Constitution'.

3. Narrative Structures in Law Courts

3.1 Courts Filter Stories

An actual scene, an actual incident, a chain of past events is always the starting point for a trial. Yet, 'the facts' and 'the law' do not come together easily; nor is it a simple logical operation to get the 'then' from the 'if' in a given case. Rather, the application of law is a complex process interweaving norms and facts (cf. Nerhot 1990: 58). Facts are collected and reconstructed already with a view to the necessity of relating them to the terms and notions of the law. The laws, on the other hand, must be given meaning with a view to social reality; they are constructed in view of actual or potential events. The application of legal norms therefore resembles a reflexive approximation of facts and norms.[37] In this process actors argue about the establishment of evidence, the scope of norms, and the resolution of possible conflicts between norms.

The asylum seeker mentioned above would be well advised to tell her story as a story of political persecution. Since e.g., discrimination against

---

35 Cf. Heun (2011: 9 et seq.).
36 The Universal Declaration of Human Rights of 1948 is more historical and less poetical in this respect, as in this document it is the General Assembly that proclaims human rights.
37 Seminal: Engisch (1963: 15); cf. further Pavčnik (2008).

women *prima facie* does not qualify as political persecution in Germany, she will have to recount grave circumstances that turn a case of discrimination into a case of persecution.[38] On the other hand, the government agent or the judge will have to reconsider the interpretation of 'political persecution' with a view to the social realities and a grown sensitivity concerning the situation of women in society, in Germany and worldwide. Or, in his presentation, the prosecutor will only refer to those facts of the case (as established by his investigation, that is) which are necessary for the legal assessment and will in turn interpret the pertinent laws with the question in mind whether they fit or should (not) fit the case at bar. Likewise, the judge (or the police officer) will direct the witness towards those points in the chain of events that are necessary for applying the relevant laws.

In a more complex, though still simplified way, decision-making in court can be reconstructed as a narrative triangle. Before court, competing narratives of what happened and how what happened should be evaluated clash.[39] The judge (or the jury) picks up those narrative strings and integrates them into her own version of legal and factual reality—eventually, she creates a legally valid and enforceable master narrative laid down in the opinion of the court.[40] Of course, this is a theoretical model. In reality, competing narratives react to each other and they are, above all, influenced by the judge, who can ask questions and direct the argumentation of the parties of the case.

3.2 What Makes a Story Before Court Reliable

"The credibility of a narrative is the extent to which listeners believe that the events described actually occurred in the form described by the narrator" (Labov 1997: 406). What William Labov writes about narration in general also holds true for what is said in law courts. It is evident that in situations of uncertainty (the normal situation before a court), may they be factual or normative, how a story is being told can exert influence on the master narrative. The question then becomes what makes the listener believe that the story told is true—and reliable? Looking at German procedural practice, one can distinguish two aspects of this question: the personal credibility of the narrator (*Glaubwürdigkeit*), and the credibility of what is being said (*Glaubhaftigkeit*). Concerning the second aspect, from the stance of the master narrative, utterances by the parties are measured

---

38 See Bumke (2002).
39 Cf. Burns (1999: 164).
40 Cf. Hannken-Illjes (2006: 213); von Arnauld (2009: 32, 35, 41).

by intra- and extra-textual standards. As a party in court, you should strive to meet these standards in order to avoid being charged with unreliability.

(1) Intra-textually, stories told before a court should be *consistent*: First of all, they should not be contradictory in themselves (cf. Alexy 2010 [1978]: 188); Wintgens 2000: 539). If you claim as an eye-witness to have seen an old woman passing the scene of a crime, while some minutes later the old woman wondrously turns into a young man, you will hardly be considered a reliable narrator. The same is true when you repeatedly have to narrate your story: what you tell the judges should be basically the same as you already told the police. However, your story should also be consistent, at least to some degree, with what others have told. If several witnesses insist on a car being blue while you describe it as red, there have to be other good reasons to believe your story. In most law cases, there will be a point at which a motif becomes dominant, because it has been repeated several times and by different people (cf. Hannken-Illjes 2006: 213, 220–221); von Arnauld 2009: 37–39). Challenging that hegemonic narrative can prove a daunting task, even if what you say is true.

(2) Occupying a field between intra- and extra-textual standards, the manner in which a story is told can also influence the credibility of what is being told. Colourful details that do not harm the overall frame of the story—such as remembering actual dialogues or specific characteristics of persons and things—enhance the credibility of the story, especially when the judge can connect these details to elements of the pertinent provision of law.[41] Furthermore, a successful testimony should not be totally unemotional, since it is presumed that *uncontrolled speech* renders lying improbable. Too much emotionality, on the other hand, will hamper the credibility of the story: one needs to find the normality range of testimonial reliability. This already points to tacit presumptions about how things should be told in a 'true' manner—and thus to extra-textual standards of legal story-telling.

(3) Extra-textually, dominant cultural standards can determine the outcome of a trial. Often, the *coherence* test, referring to assumptions about what is 'normal', will rely on standards of logic.[42] Taking the example of the ongoing proceedings against a neo-Nazi terrorist trio in Munich that murdered nine people, a man accused of assisting the trio testified he was instructed to order a firearm of German brand, not a firearm plus a muffler; a muffler was only asked for *after* he delivered the gun. If the court believes him, this detail may become crucial for assessing whether he acquiesced in the murderous activities of the trio. The normality

---

41 Cf. von Arnauld (2009: 36).
42 Cf. Wintgens (2000: 545): "making sense as a whole".

assumption associates the intent of killing and not mere defence purposes (against, e.g., the police) with a muffler.[43] Even if the coherence test relies on seemingly universal standards of logic and causality, one must bear in mind their conventional character. Our normality assumptions are modelled on our everyday experiences. This is why judges have to be sensitive to experiences different from their own. Traumatised victims e.g. will often leave out the traumatising event when telling their story; if the crucial event is not part of the story told before the court, this does not mean that the account given is unreliable. An asylum-seeker from a country culturally different from ours will refer to a sometimes radically different life-world. One needs intercultural sensitivity here, in order to avoid plausibility fallacies stemming from erroneous normality assumptions.

On the one hand, intra-textual signals of (in)consistency and veracity are looked for, on the other hand what is said in the text is compared to extra-textual social standards of *normality* and plausibility, standards so dominant that they are usually shared by the judges. Those parts of the narratives selected as reliable are in the end interwoven by the judge(s) and juries in the master-narrative of the ruling. The scattered, unordered *discours* is reconstructed as a *histoire*, a plot, following familiar behavioural patterns and trusted, 'well-known' chains of reaction.

3.3 The Ruling Also Tells a Story

Narration does not only take place in or before a court; it is also the court itself that narrates. Actually, in the court opinion taking up the plot once established and legally framing it one can detect those elements of everyday storytelling categorised by Labov and Waletzky in their seminal narratological work:[44] abstract, orientation, complicating action, evaluation, conclusion, and coda.

(1) In Germany, a ruling starts with an *abstract* conveying the gist of the decision. The caption (called *Rubrum*) informs about the parties to the case and their submissions, the composition of the court, the date of hearings and the date the ruling was delivered. It is followed by the *tenor*, the actual verdict of the court (in other legal systems, however, the verdict is placed at the end of the ruling). The highest courts in Germany often summarise the guiding principles of their decisions in clauses put ahead of the ruling (*Leitsätze*).

---

43   See Friederichsen (2013).
44   See Labov/Waletzky (1967).

(2) The *orientation* part of the ruling gives information on the factual and legal background. Especially differentiated in this respect are the rulings of the European Court of Human Rights in Strasbourg. These are divided into the sections 'Procedure', and 'The Facts', the latter being subdivided into 'The Circumstances of the Case', 'Relevant Domestic Law', and, where necessary, 'Comparative Law'.

(3) The *complicating action* can be integrated into the orientation part. Here, the ruling describes the conflict, how it came about, which arguments were raised before the court by the parties or other participants in the proceedings, etc. The issue may be a conflict between private parties, over the sale of a car for example, or the publication of private information on a public figure. But also unilateral action by state authorities, like a detention, a search, a conviction or a tax order, may be the source of an alleged violation of rights.

(4) The *evaluation* then forms the core part of a decision in which the court authoritatively interprets the pertinent norms and compares them to the facts of the case (definition and subsumption phase). Usually, the legal assessment is subdivided into two sections: In the admissibility section, the legal requirements for a case to be heard at all are discussed (jurisdiction of the court, proper representation, time-limits for an application, need for redress, etc.); the merits section then pertains to the actual legal questions of the case. A lot of effort is put into finding the relevant law, resolving legal contradictions, and into determining the meaning of the law. Depending on the legal system's style of argumentation, precedent and academic publications may be cited and discussed. The subsumption may contain complex argumentations as well, since facts or prognoses of facts may be highly uncertain (here, the question of who bears the burden of proof becomes relevant), since competing legal principles have to be balanced, etc.

(5) Every decision comes to a *conclusion*, the final result reached by the court—which in Germany, as has been said, is handed out already at the beginning of the ruling.[45] Possible results can be the affirmation or denial of a claim, conviction or acquittal, the nullification of a legal act, etc. The conclusion is finally marked by the judges' signatures.

(6) Even a *coda* may be found in decisions, e.g. when the case is referred back to a lower court to rehear it on the basis of the higher court's opinion. An 'invisible coda' might also be read into the ruling: Other state authorities have to implement it, the ruling is handed over to

---

45 Especially the German Federal Constitutional Court explicates the effects of their decision in more detail at the end of the grounds.

the public for critical discussion and to other courts to influence their decisions.[46]

3.4 Court Decisions Lie, Too

How can a court decision narrate unreliably? The ruling establishes the facts of the case; it determines the law because it is legally entitled to do so. The trope of 'legal force' (*Rechtskraft*) is a forceful social fiction. When remedies are exhausted or time limits expire, the ruling becomes final, its content true and valid,[47] no longer contestable by means of law. Differing expectations of "reader" and "author" can no longer be compared from inside the law. A veracious lawyer can only criticise the *res judicata* with regard to its potential influence on future decisions: *Roma locuta, causa finita*.

Viewed from the outside, though, the statement of facts and the legal assessments of those facts can be flawed no matter if the ruling is final and binding. Applying the Labovian terminology, the statements of facts and law in the orientation phase as well as the assessment of both in the evaluation phase can become traps for misinterpretations, misunderstandings, misperceptions, mis-findings. The recounting of events may be inaccurate compared to more convincing evidence and testimony;[48] argumentations can appear inconsistent if you juxtapose them with persuasive counter-argumentations. This is recognised by the legal order itself, as it usually provides mechanisms to alter court decisions. An appellate court has the power to reverse a ruling of a lower court—either on factual or on legal grounds. Under certain conditions, a case can be re-opened: when either new facts are presented[49] or, rarely, the law changes.[50] All legal remedies having been exhausted, however, even a false judgment remains in force. It is legal, though it may be illegitimate. Its illegitimacy can only be determined by stepping out of the perspective of the law, taking the stance of an external observer criticising the court for an unreliable account of what happened in reality or what the law has to say about the case.

---

46 See Lang (2013).
47 Of course, this is simplified. Normativity is assigned by ongoing legal events of recognition, e.g. Müller-Mall (2012); yet, in the language of legal discourse it is legitimate to talk about legal validity as "happening" and "existing" in concrete acts and cases.
48 From a radical relativist stance, there can no privileged story at all, cf. Küppers (2014).
49 § 359 German Criminal Procedure Act.
50 As happened in the recent proceedings on preventive detention: A new line of reasoning of the European Court of Human Rights persuaded the German Federal Constitutional Court to revise its past reasoning and re-hear old cases, BVerfGE 128, 326 (2011).

Moreover, the problem of correction cannot be solved that 'easily' with courts of last resort or Constitutional Courts—their rulings can only be overturned by changes in the law or the Constitution, which at least in the latter case is often unlikely because of high procedural thresholds. Rarely, legal mechanisms exist to overturn individual decisions of Constitutional Courts.[51] Otherwise, the Court has to correct itself by adjusting its jurisprudence to a new line of reasoning. Thus, a high amount of social and institutional trust must be invested in the reliability of Constitutional Courts' decisions. Unreliability may then only be ascertained by the public and professional critique of those rulings.

4. A Case Study:
The German Federal Constitutional Court on Sibling Incest

In order to illustrate how rulings can be unreliable in their argumentation, i.e. the selection, quality and presentation of arguments, let us turn to a practical example: the decision of the German Federal Constitutional Court on the penalisation of sibling incest from 2008 (BVerfGE 2008: 120, 224).[52] This decision sparked some controversy, and was finally upheld by the European Court of Human Rights in 2012,[53] more or less ending public debate on the issue in Germany.

4.1 Labov and Waletzky Visit Karlsruhe

Again, the Labovian categories prove helpful in getting a grasp of the details of the decision. In its first paragraph, the abstract of the decision is unfolded: The reader receives the basic information that the second of the Court's two Senates had to rule on the conviction of the applicant ("complainant") for committing incest. Incidental to his claim to nullify the conviction, the Court also was called to determine whether the penalisation of sibling incest is in general constitutional or not, since it forms the legal basis for the proceedings against the applicant in the individual case.

In the orientation part of the ruling, the history of the ban on incest and the history of its penalisation are outlined. The senate certifies that:

> (t)he roots of the prohibition of incest go back to ancient times. Varieties of the prohibition can be found in the codex of Hammurabi, in Mosaic […] and Islamic

---

51 For example, Art. 33 Canadian Charter of Basic Rights.
52 BVerfGE 120, 224 (2008).
53 ECtHR, 12.4.2012, Stübing v. Germany, Application no. 43547/08.

> [...] Law, in the law of ancient Greece [...], in Roman [...], in extensive forms in Canonic [...] and in Germanic Law [...] as well as in the early German penal provisions [...]. The incest motif also found its way into myths and sagas—displaying significance for the constitution of early legal cultures—, and it has always been of great importance to literature [...]. (BVerfGE 120, 224, 224–225)[54]

After having referred to the legislative history of sect. 173 of the German Penal Code, the senate also has a look at other states' current regulations:

> An expert opinion of the Max-Planck-Institute for Foreign and International Penal Law in Freiburg commissioned by the Senate, analysing prevailing legal norms in twenty states from Anglo-American, Continental-European and other, non-European legal traditions, comes to the conclusion that the law pertaining to the penalisation of sibling incest is predominantly uniform as the foundation of penalisation is concerned, yet, differences become visible when looking at the specific draftings. Accordingly, sibling incest as such—i.e. the consensual sexual intercourse between adult siblings—is a crime in thirteen of the states surveyed, not, however, in China, the Russian Federation, Turkey, Spain, France, and the legal orders (also influenced by the Napoleonic Code Pénal) of the Netherlands and Côte d'Ivoire. It has to be taken into consideration that incestuous behaviour—also between siblings—can indeed gain significance as a reason for qualified punishment; in all legal orders surveyed incest is legally disapproved of—if not through penal law then in other ways, mainly through marriage bans, in France also by denying legal recognition of children born from incestuous relationships. [...] Qualified forms of sibling incest—thus those against children or dependent persons or those committed with resort to violence—are punished in all legal orders under survey. (BVerfGE 120, 224, 230–231)

The depiction of the facts of the case including the chain of lower courts' decisions indeed lays out complicating action. We get to know a young man who is truly in love with his biological sister. He was brought up in a foster family from the age of seven; that is why he only learned of the existence of his sister after his biological mother died. When they finally met he was 23 and his sister 16 years old. They built up an intimate relationship resulting in the birth of four children. The applicant was sent to prison for ten months; his sister was acquitted for low culpability because she was found to suffer from a personality disorder and a minor mental disability.

In the evaluation part of the court opinion, a majority of seven judges to one defer to the legislator's decision to penalise sibling incest. The preservation of stable and typical family structures, the protection of sexual autonomy, and, as an additional source, public health were found to be suitable grounds to justify, in their combination, the penalisation of

---

54 All translations were made by the authors.

sibling incest. Regarding the applicant's case, the Court held his conviction to be a proportionate encroachment on his basic rights.

In his dissenting opinion, Judge Hassemer—in a somehow additional, "complicating" part of the evaluation phase—declared the ruling to be fundamentally ill-founded, since eugenic reasons are to be excluded from public decision-making, since the aim of preserving family structures could be better furthered by other, less restrictive means, and since sexual autonomy was already protected by other provisions of law. His underlying criticism was that the Court majority in fact based their ruling on a vague moral conviction[55] rather than on legal arguments, however flawed these might have been.

4.2 Karlsruhe Is a(n) (Unre)liar, Too

The majority of the Senate's judges also seem to have had some doubts about their own line of reasoning. For in the evaluation part they mention two other strings of argument, two side paths along the overall argumentative storyline that the reader already was presented with at an earlier stage of the ruling:

> The challenged criminal provision is justified by the sum of reasonable objectives to penalise, as set against the background of a societal conviction based upon cultural history and still effective to date that incest ought to be penalised, a conviction that can also be observed in international comparison […]. (BVerfGE 120, 224, 248–249)

This argumentation is remarkable because it re-connects the normative element in the evaluation part with the (allegedly) descriptive orientation phase: The continuous social conviction can only be said to be continuous because the court established it so; comparative law can only support this reasoning because the result of the analysis found in the earlier part was formulated as to point in that direction. In retrospect, the seemingly objective reproduction of facts in the orientation part attains a normative 'twist' taken up in the evaluation part of the court's opinion.

What is now unreliable in these linkages? The line of argument appears to be strictly logical in its own rhetorical universe. The historical universality of the incest ban once asserted allows for the conclusion that there is a constant social conviction to penalise incest, including sibling incest. The unreliability can only be detected if one compares the storyline of the majority opinion with other, more accurate accounts of the history

---

55 Expressly accepted as penal ground by the Hungarian Constitutional Court, AB hat. 20/1999 (VI.25).

of the penalisation of incest. Since Judge Hassemer, in his dissenting opinion, does not deal with these 'unreliabilities' but with other questions of Constitutional law, answers must be sought extratextually.

There, one can learn that the incest taboo is not as universal as the Court opines. On the contrary, the taboo has been culture-dependent and its shapes, especially the outer fringes of that shape, have varied across times and cultures.[56] Those accounts do *not* appear in the wording of the ruling and—because they argue *against* the finding of the court—appear to be suppressed by the Senate. The opinion of the court speaks of the "the prohibition" of incest and the "incest motif" reaching back to antiquity. Taken at face value, the concepts do not necessarily include either the notion of penalisation (there existed and exist other forms of legal disapproval) or the inclusion of sibling incest (which belongs to the fringes of the concept). Yet, the linkage between the evaluation and the orientation parts of the ruling relates the findings on incest in general with the legal discussion of sibling incest and thus provides the findings with another (though patched) foundation.

The necessary inclusion of sibling incest in the notion of incest is at least an incomplete account of the history of the taboo. Over time, varieties of incest have been practised, tolerated and depicted in literature. The only sanction that has been constant is the marriage ban (cf. Archibald 2001: 9)—but also here, the scope of relations covered is far from being universal. Furthermore, the central objectives of the taboo have been totally replaced. In medieval times, religious motifs to restrain individual passion and sexual appetite especially in close relationships were dominant (cf. ibid. 5–6, 237); however, in modern times more objective and societal purposes appeared on the foreground, like preserving genetic stability, family structures and roles. In particular, sibling incest has been qualified as less sinful and dangerous, which holds for elitist thinking and popular convictions alike (cf. Archibald 2001: 229). Having accepted this, an undisputed account of a universal and uniform penalisation of incest becomes untenable. At the very least, the Court would have had to acknowledge some historical differentiations or should have presented arguments for *its* interpretation of the history of incest. Therefore, the story of incest told and normatively used by the Constitutional Court is unreliable and unable to convincingly support the penalisation of sibling incest.

---

56   Cf. Rank (1974 [1926]: 387–406); Twitchell (1987: 11–12); Bramberger (1998: 36); Archibald (2001: 7, 9 et seq.); negatively, but not convincing Sidler (1971). Also in modern times, especially in the nineteenth century the penalisation of incest was widely debated, Kanwischer (2013: 170 et seq.).

5. A Two by Two Matrix of Legal Unreliability

Analytically speaking, unreliability in legal discourse, especially in respect to law courts, can be detected with the help of either intra- or extra-textual signals, occurring with regard to the assessment of either facts or norms.

Concerning facts, the concept of unreliability helps to resolve whether a story told can be accepted before a court as a representation of past reality. Intra-textually, only elements of speech and story are the clues for reliability—if there is no other direct way of proving it. Thus, the judge will look for consistency in the narration and also take into account the manner in which the story is told. Extra-textually, what is being told has to be compared ('normalised') to our normality assumptions. This coherence test should always be conducted with the awareness of the social construction and embeddedness of normality. And, of course, a story that convinced a court might turn out to be based on a lie later on. Quite a number of literary works and movie plots have taken up this motif of double jeopardy, probably most famously so Agatha Christie's and Billy Wilder's 'Witness for the Prosecution'.

Concerning the assessment of norms, we came across an example of intra-textual unreliability in the case of inconsistent legislation, regulations by law that do not abide by their own principles and standards. Extra-textual unreliability connects to the fact that legal texts claim to relate to the social world. The preamble to a constitution might narrate historical events leading up to the foundational 'constitutional moment'; this narration, however, might depart significantly from the true course of history (as far as this can be objectively reconstructed). A ruling might present a consistent line of argument which sounds compelling in itself and nevertheless disregards important socio-legal facts. The rhetorical structure of law can be misused to justify incomplete or inconsistent argumentations—omitting and ignoring pressing counter-arguments—and thus conflicts with the purpose of persuasion, i.e. to find the best solution by weighing the arguments.[57] As a result, the findings from these incomplete argumentations are unreliable—i.e. less persuasive, to the degree of making a ruling unacceptable, illegitimate, or even illegal. This understanding of unreliability (as encountered in the German Federal Constitutional Court's majority opinion on the penalisation of sibling incest) is clearly based on an 'ought': A court ought to take into account all factual and normative (argumentative) material available and discuss the relevant problems so

---

[57] Cf. Alexy (2010 [1978]: 293–294), for a concept of a correct proposition that adheres to rules of argumentation.

that the (professional) auditorium may fulfil its role by either accepting or criticising the ruling.

One problem remains: the allegation of unreliability is weak if one merely juxtaposes one version of the (argumentative) story with another. How can one determine which version is more reliable? A (persuasive) critique with a chance of approval is footed on an overarching universe of values that provides yardsticks of evaluation. Standards of argumentation and shared methods of investigating into past events that observers as well as the observed ought to adhere to are a necessary foundation. Identifying (un)reliability in law (courts) is thus a highly relative enterprise, dependent on stances and worldviews, and in this respect again comparable to the phenomenon of (un)reliability in literature.

Works Cited

Alexy, Robert. 2010 [1978]. *A Theory of Legal Argumentation: The Theory of Rational Discourse as Theory of Legal Justification.* Trans. Ruth Adler & Neil MacCormick. Oxford: Oxford University Press.

Anderson, Benedict. 1991. *Imagined Communities: Reflections on the Origin and Spread of Nationalism.* London: Verso.

Archibald, Elizabeth. 2001. *Incest and the Medieval Imagination.* Oxford: Clarendon Press.

Arnauld, Andreas von. 2009. "Was war, was ist—und was sein soll. Erzählen im juristischen Diskurs." In: Christian Klein & Matías Martínez (eds.). *Wirklichkeitserzählungen. Felder, Formen und Funktionen nicht literarischen Erzählens.* Stuttgart/Weimar: J.B. Metzler. 14–50.

Arnauld, Andreas von. 2012. *Klausurenkurs im Völkerrecht.* 2nd ed. Heidelberg/München: C.F. Müller.

Arndt, Dominik E. 2011. *Sinn und Unsinn von Soft Law: Prolegomena zur Zukunft eines indeterminierten Paradigmas.* Baden-Baden: Nomos.

Benhabib, Seyla. 2006. *Another Cosmopolitanism.* Oxford: Oxford University Press.

Booth, Wayne C. 1961. *The Rhetoric of Fiction.* Chicago, IL: Chicago University Press.

Bramberger, Andrea. 1998. *Verboten Lieben. Bruder-Schwester-Inzest.* Pfaffenweiler: Centaurus-Verlagsgesellschaft.

Bumke, Ulrike. 2002. "Zur Problematik frauenspezifischer Fluchtgründe—dargestellt am Beispiel der Genitalverstümmelung." *Neue Zeitschrift für Verwaltungsrecht* 4: 423–428.

Burns, Robert P. 1999. *A Theory of the Trial.* Princeton, NJ: Princeton University Press.

Cover, Robert M. 1983. "Nomos and Narrative." *Harvard Law Review* 97: 4–68.

Cullen, Jim. 2003. *The American Dream: A Short History of an Idea That Shaped a Nation.* Oxford/New York, NY: Oxford University Press.

Damaška, Mirjan R. 1991. *The Faces of Justice and State Authority. A Comparative Approach to the Legal Process.* New Haven, CT: Yale University Press.

Engisch, Karl. 1963. *Logische Studien zur Gesetzesanwendung.* 3rd ed. Heidelberg: Winter.

Friedrichsen, Gisela. "NSU-Prozess in München: Wie war das also mit der Waffe?" *SPIEGEL ONLINE* (June 4, 2013): http://www.spiegel.de/panorama/justiz/nsu-prozess-mitangeklagter-carsten-s-beginnt-aussage-a-903766.html (last retrieved: July 14, 2013)

Genette, Gérard. 1983. *Narrative Discourse. An Essay in Method.* Trans. Jane E. Lewin. Ithaca, NY: Cornell University Press.

Genette, Gérard. 1997. *Paratexts. Thresholds of Interpretation.* Trans. Jane E. Lewin. Cambridge: Cambridge University Press.

Hannken-Illjes, Kati. 2006. "Mit Geschichten argumentieren—Argumentation und Narration im Strafverfahren." *Zeitschrift für Rechtssoziologie* 27.2: 211–223.

Heun, Werner. 2011. *The Constitution of Germany. A Contextual Analysis.* Oxford/Portland, OR: Hart.

Kanwischer, Simon. 2013. *Der Grenzbereich zwischen öffentlichem Strafanspruch und intimer Lebensgestaltung.* Göttingen: V&R unipress.

Kirchhof, Gregor, Stefan Magen & Karsten Schneider (eds.). 2012. *Was weiß Dogmatik?* Tübingen: Mohr Siebeck.

Küppers, Julia. 2014. *Die wahre Wahrheit über die Bodenreform. Theoretische Betrachtungen rechtsgeschichtswissenschaftlicher Praxis.* Weilerswist: Velbrück Wissenschaft.

Labov, William. 1997. "Some Further Steps in Narrative Analysis." *The Journal of Narrative and Life History* 7.1–4: 395–415.

Labov, William & Joshua Waletzky. 1967. "Narrative Analysis: Oral Versions of Personal Experience." In: June Helm (ed.). *Essays on the Verbal and Visual Arts.* Seattle, WA: University of Washington Press. 12–44.

Ladeur, Karl-Heinz. 1990. "From the Deductive to the Argumentative Rationality of Law." In: Patrick Nerhot (ed.). *Law, Interpretation and Reality. Essays in Epistemology, Hermeneutics and Jurisprudence.* Dordrecht: Kluwer Academic Publishers. 169–192.

Lang, Andrej. 2013. "Wider die Metapher vom 'letzten Wort'." In: Dominik Elser et al. (eds.). *Das letzte Wort. Rechtsetzung und Rechtskontrolle in der Demokratie.* Baden-Baden: Nomos. 15–37.

Lasser, Mitchel de S.-O.-l'E. 2004. *Judicial Deliberations. A Comparative Analysis of Judicial Transparency and Legitimacy.* Oxford/New York, NY: Oxford University Press.

Lenckner, Theodor & Nikolaus Bosch. 2010. "§ 173 StGB." In: Adolf Schönke & Horst Schröder. *Strafgesetzbuch. Kommentar.* 28th ed. München: C.H. Beck.

Luhmann, Niklas. 2004 [1993]. *Law as a Social System.* Ed. Fatima Kastner, Richard Nobles, David Schiff et al. Trans. Klaus A. Ziegert. Oxford/New York, NY: Oxford University Press.

Möllers, Christoph. 2011. "Pouvoir Constituant—Constitution—Constitutionalisation." In: Armin von Bogdandy & Jürgen Bast (eds.). *Principles of European Constitutional Law.* 2nd ed. Oxford/München: Hart & C.H. Beck. 169–205.

Müller-Mall, Sabine. 2012. *Performative Rechtserzeugung. Eine theoretische Annäherung.* Weilerswist: Velbrück.

Nerhot, Patrick. 1990: "The Law and Its Reality." In: Patrick Nerhot (ed.). *Law, Interpretation and Reality. Essays in Epistemology, Hermeneutics and Jurisprudence.* Dordrecht: Kluwer Academic Publishers. 50–69.

Nünning, Ansgar. 1999. "Unreliable, compared to what? Towards a Cognitive Theory of Unreliable Narration: Prolegomena and Hypotheses." In: Walter Grünzweig & Andreas Solbach (eds.). *Grenzüberschreitungen. Narratologie im Kontext.* Tübingen: Gunter Narr Verlag. 53–73.

Nünning, Vera. 2004. "Unreliable Narration and the Historical Variability of Values and Norms: *The Vicar of Wakefield* as a Test-Case of Cultural-Historical Narratology." *Style* 38.2: 236–252.

Orgad, Liav. 2010. "The Preamble in Constitutional Interpretation." *International Journal of Constitutional Law* 8.4: 714–738.

Pavčnik, Marijan. 2008. "Das 'Hin- und Herwandern des Blickes'." *Rechtstheorie* 39.4: 557–572.

Rakove, Jack N. (ed.). 2009. *The Annotated U.S. Constitution and Declaration of Independence.* Cambridge, MA: Belknap Press of Harvard University Press.

Rank, Otto. 1974 [1926]. *Das Inzest-Motiv in Dichtung und Sage. Grundzüge einer Psychologie des dichterischen Schaffens.* Darmstadt: Wissenschaftliche Buchgesellschaft.

Schäuble, Johannes. 2008. "Auf der Suche nach einem Rechtsgut. Wie das Bundesverfassungsgericht sich (vergeblich) mühte, die Strafbarkeit des Inzests zu legitimieren." *Forum Recht* 03/08: 98–100.

Sidler, Nikolaus. 1971. *Zur Universalität des Inzesttabu. Eine kritische Untersuchung der These und der Einwände.* Stuttgart: Enke.

Twitchell, James B. 1987. *Forbidden Partners. The Incest Taboo in Modern Culture*. New York, NY: Columbia University Press.

Wintgens, Luc J. 2000. "On Coherence and Consistency." In: Werner Krawietz, Robert S. Summers, Ota Weinberger et al. (eds.). *The Reasonable as Rational? On Legal Argumentation and Justification. (Festschrift for Aulis Aarnio)*. Berlin: Duncker & Humblot. 539–550.

Yacobi, Tamar. 1981. "Fictional Reliability as a Communicative Problem." *Poetics Today* 2.2: 113–126.

Yacobi, Tamar. 2001. "Package Deals in Fictional Narrative: The Case of the Narrator's (Un)Reliability." *Narrative* 9.2: 223–229.

STEPHAN JAEGER

(Manitoba)

Unreliable Narration in Historical Studies

1. Prologue

> The city itself was not worth bombing. But on the outskirts, toward which hundreds of thousands had fled, it was more worthwhile. And for the fighters and fighter bombers there was plenty to do: namely to hunt the Germans in packs along the country roads [...]. While they [the Flying Fortresses] destroyed the houses in the suburbs, fighters and fighter-bombers chased at low-level along the country roads, attacked the farmsteads of the surrounding villages with cannon-fire and bombs. (Rodenberger 1953: 140, trans. in Taylor 2005: 430)

> The commander-in-chief of R.A.F. Fighter Command was convinced that the Luftwaffe could not be defeated over the Continent; the enemy bomber and fighter formations should, he felt, somehow be enticed or provoked into daylight battle over the British Isles, within reach of Britain's superior short-range fighter defences. With this requirement in mind, the R.A.F. launched its first attacks on targets east of the Rhine on the evening that the Rotterdam raid was announced to the world; less than twenty-five of the ninety-six bombers dispatched even claimed to have found their targets. Hermann Göring did not divert one fighter from operations supporting the Battle for France. Only after France had fallen, and after the R.A.F. had repeatedly attacked the German mainland, did the Führer direct the Luftwaffe's attention to industrial targets in and around London. (Irving 2005 [1963]: 9)

> The voices of many Jewish chroniclers will be heard in this volume, and yet all of them, as different as they may be, offer but a faint glimpse of the extraordinary diversity that was the world of European Jewry on the edge of destruction. After a steady decline of religious observance and an increase in the uncertainties of cultural-ethnic Jewishness, no obvious common denominator fitted the maze of parties, associations, groups, and some nine million individuals, spread all over the Continent who nonetheless considered themselves Jews (or were considered as such). (Friedländer 2007: 4–5)

The first quotation is a hybrid between a factual eyewitness report and a historical narrative. The historian Frederick Taylor notes that every alleged fact about the details of the American air-raid on Dresden on February 14, 1945 and the strafing of Dresden's civilians through low-fighter planes as described in the report was wrong (Taylor 2005: 430). How, then, would a reader with less expertise detect such a narrative unreliability while reading this source as an introduction to the topic? The historian would contextualize the utterance (or the whole text by Rodenberger) to find out about the context of the utterance and about the historical background of the author. He would conduct a comparison to other sources about the same or similar events (cf. Howell/Prevenier 2001: 66–68). The reader who is presented with Rodenberger's account as a factual report might have some of the historian's contextual knowledge allowing him to question the validity of the report, but he may be thrown back onto the text itself. Here, an indicator of unreliability of narration is the frequent use of evaluative attributes such as "worthwhile" or sarcasm (e.g. "plenty to do") which add a moral judgment to the report instead of focusing on concrete individual experience. This distancing casts a doubt on the validity of the narrative, while the text does not indicate the critical ability of a historian to analyze the past. The quotation seems stuck between unreliable eye-witness report and biased factual historical narration.

The second quotation is clearly a historiographical report of events in the air-war, when the Third Reich attacked Britain. Even without knowing anything about the biography of David Irving,[1] a reader can detect some warning signs of unreliability or bias in the narrative. The paragraph strongly emphasizes causality; it does not apply any notion of reflexivity (i.e. it does not ask whether there could be different causalities or on what ground the narrator draws conclusions). The narrator uses the word 'Führer' without any marked distance; and for a reader who knows about the moral debates of the air-war, the underlying message of the passage that the Germans only reacted and that they at least were not the first to bomb cities in the war displays a tendency towards a specific message marking the ideological involvement of the narrator. Thus, the text conveys markers of unreliable narration, but simultaneously aims to conceal them from the reader, who could be lured into the unbroken impression of one reality through a convincing chain of arguments.

The final quotation from Saul Friedländer's *Nazi Germany and the Jews* is different. Friedländer's historian-narrator poses a challenge for the reader: if the European Jewry is so diverse, how can the generalization of Jews in Nazi Germany and Europe actually work? There is no doubt that Friedländer, just as any historian, has a specific agenda. To represent the mechanisms of the Holocaust as the diverse voices of the victims, however, Friedländer must work against generalization. He problematizes; general description and survey narrative are interwoven with individual voices. Those are not fully utilized by the historian-narrator, but kept in their individuality and in their concrete historical situation. This allows for a constant self-reflexive narrator-voice that accompanies the historical

---

[1] Specifically his later evolution into an explicit Holocaust denier (cf. Evans 2001).

narrative. Unlike Irving, Friedländer's narrative remains open in so far as his historical interpretation never endeavors to equal reality.

Returning to the question of unreliable narration and trustworthiness in historical studies, the question arises of whether it is simply the goal of all modern academic historians to reduce unreliability to a minimum, so that the reader can trust the historian to provide the most accurate and most objective and impartial account possible. Were that the case, unreliability would be relevant only in historical method, as a precedent to the act of historiographical narration, through the analysis of the reliability of historical sources and reducing gaps and indeterminacies as much as possible. A historian who employs unreliable narration would simply be a bad historian who has not mastered the methods of the discipline or who intentionally violates the pact of historical truthfulness with the reader. Yet, the examples above show a more complex picture of unreliable narration in historical studies. Determining whether a historian is hiding bias, and therefore pretending to represent an objective reality, or is actually narrating a trustworthy story is difficult. Every narration of historical events shows the ideological, moral, and aesthetic preference of the author. At the same time, historians possess critical methods to assess the reliability of eyewitnesses and the factuality of data. Therefore, the first step in understanding unreliable narration in historical studies is to locate the historiographical dimensions that thematize unreliability (Section 2 of this chapter) before differentiating the narrative dimensions in which unreliable narration can be located (Section 3).

2. Unreliability in Historical Studies

At first glance, unreliability or untrustworthiness appears to be a useful concept for historical studies. It is the crucial task of the historian's work to determine the degree of reliability of sources or witness statements. The whole reputation of the discipline seems to depend on the fact that historians produce a critical and reliable account from source material whose reliability or trustworthiness they critique. Yet a search through encyclopedias, dictionaries, handbooks, introductory textbooks, and the Internet does not reveal the existence of a theoretical concept of reliability or unreliability.[2] Even 'trustworthiness' is mentioned merely in passing in articles about historical method and source criticism. Thus the initial

---

2   The *English Wikipedia* article entitled 'reliability' is not connected to the discipline of history, but merely to engineering, statistics, psychometrics, philosophy/epistemology, biological aging, and computer networking (http://en.wikipedia.org/wiki/Reliability (last retrieved: July 6, 2013)).

suspicion that emerged in the prologue above that unreliability is mainly a methodological problem to be overcome by a competent historian seems to be confirmed. At least for the mainstream of the discipline, historical studies or historiography are also not related to any science of prognostics, so at the surface a concept of reliability is not needed.[3] Historical studies mostly discusses methodological dimensions of unreliability and trustworthiness under four different, but closely related concepts: source criticism, hermeneutics and interpretation, objectivity and bias, and the pragmatic idea of a pact of truth or trustworthiness between historian and reader.

Source criticism in general aims to discuss the authorship and genealogy of historical sources, with a specific emphasis on its historical contextualization (its time frame) and it genuineness. The analysis about the circumstances and intentions of the author or narrator of the sources is mandatory. The sources themselves—following the concept of *ad fontes*—seem to be the guarantors of historical truth and authenticity for the antiquarians between the Renaissance and the late eighteenth century (cf. Dann 1995: 110–111). The analysis of narrative structure could support whether the stories told were inaccurate, inauthentic or faked (Howell/Prevenier 2001: 58–59). Part of the traditional practice of source criticism is the analysis of the genealogy of the historical document, of the institutional circumstances in which a document was produced, and of its originality. The reliability of the source or of the source's narrator leads to the question about his background and authorial authority (is the narrator capable of first-hand knowledge?) as well as about the narrator's competence. The latter includes questions about the psychological state of the narrator, possible prejudices, and how much the account is shaped by the discourses of the time, such as the unconscious need to conform to a dominant narrative (ibid.: 66). Finally, source criticism can analyze the trustworthiness of the source's narrator in regard to the political pressures, the genre of the source, and general bias of the narrator (cf. ibid.: 68).

Yet the verification of sources in traditional source-criticism of classical scholarship and antiquarianism has become increasingly a hermeneutic problem of the interpretation of sources (see Müller 2009: 21). To execute source criticism successfully, the historian must use a method of interpretation that balances subjective, objective, and reflexive orientations of meaning (see Reinfandt 2009: 39). Such practices of textual criticism were developed in particular in the discourse of German historical studies in the late eighteenth century. Historical scholars began to combine the

---

[3] An exception would be counterfactual or alternate history that needs to be reliable in its projections of what could have happened, if different event causalities had taken place.

antiquarian tradition concerned with collecting remnants from the past with the philosophical tradition focusing on the idea of historical development, "the quest for the meaning of history with a need for reliable documents which could back up their claims" (Müller 2009: 32). The relevance of textual criticism to verify reliability led to the inclusion of the hermeneutic circle of part and whole, past and present, as well as subject and object, as Philipp Müller discusses in its evolution through the nineteenth century from Leopold von Ranke and Johann G. Droysen to Wilhelm Dilthey: "The historian's question is the result of the entire mental content that we have unconsciously collected within ourselves and transformed into our own subjective world" (Droysen quoted in Müller 2009: 28). This means there is a "hidden relationship [for Droysen as a spiritual tendency, SJ] between the subject (the scholar) and the object of historical knowledge (the topic being studied)" (Müller 2009: 29).

The hermeneutic challenge in establishing reliability, historical knowledge, and truth indicates a constant need for historiography to consider the narrativity of its source narratives as well as the narrativity of its own discourse. Therefore, unreliability in historical studies is not merely a methodological problem, but impacts different levels of narrative. The tendency for the "hidden relationship" already indicates the inherent structural tendency of historical narrative to conceal unreliability, challenged in structural history such as the French *Annales* as well as postmodern history by emphasizing the role or actions of the historian (Carrard 1992: especially 90–92).

In regard to unreliability and trustworthiness in historical studies, the hermeneutic challenge has mainly been discussed as a dichotomy between objectivity and subjectivity or bias (in German 'Parteilichkeit'), relating to historiographic discourse and the historian in his role as author and narrator (Junker/Reisinger 1977; Koselleck/Mommsen/Rüsen 1977; Novick 1988; Rüsen 2005), starting with the advent of hermeneutics and the reflection of the point of view of the historian in the eighteenth century (Koselleck 1977). One form of bias indicates some kind of involvement of the historian in the subject-matter; it can be usually detected by finding explicit normative or moral value judgments, such as in the Irving quotation discussed above. Secondly, the historian could intentionally distort, shorten, or forge historical facts and arguments (Junker/Reisinger 1977: 228). The second form means the historian intentionally violates the standards of the profession, which makes him unreliable. In general, one stream of historians concerned with methods acknowledges that objectivity and bias are inseparable. Though they accept that historical arguments are always selective and to a certain extent political, and that they are based on the historical experience of the historian and the groups he belongs to, they work towards establishing criteria that allow historical knowledge (see Kocka 1977: 470–471). The methodological answer about the exact criteria for objectivity remains vague: The selective argumentation must be balanced and adhere to formal logic, it must follow the codes and rules of the discipline for deducing historical knowledge, and it must reduce explicit engagement for the benefit of advancing scholarly knowledge (ibid.: 472–473). In this rational paradigm, the mutual relationship of objectivity and subjectivity or bias has also been described as an opportunity, so that every generation of historians is able to advance the discipline according to their present (Mommsen 1977: 444).[4] Jörn Rüsen sees a theoretical and a practical consistency at work, allowing rational criteria in the process of inter-subjectivity, to form a meaningful historical narrative that can be plausible or maintain historical truth-claims (2005: 69).

Whereas methodologists in history try to use the historian's bias to improve the rational method of history, it has also been used in the context of the linguistic turn and postmodern history as a challenge to any kind of objectivity, following historical theorists and philosophers such as Michel Foucault, Hayden White, F. R. Ankersmit, among many others.[5] Objectivity then implies the possibility of an ideal situation in which the historian can shed all forms of bias which most historians today would clearly admit is impossible. The question of objectivity defines the very essence of the discipline of historical studies, as Peter Novick states it in a slightly polemic way:

> The objective historian's role is that of a neutral, or disinterested judge; it must never degenerate into that of advocate or, even worse, propagandist. The historian's conclusions are expected to display the standard judicial qualities of balance and even-handedness. As with the judiciary, these qualities are guarded by the insulation of the historical profession from social pressure or political influence, and by the individual historian avoiding partisanship or bias [...]. (1988: 2)

Novick sketches out an extreme, somewhat naive belief in objectivity to provoke his profession to go beyond complacency in its pragmatic objectivity "to greater self-consciousness about the nature of our activity, to stimulate alternative ways of thinking about works of history and the claims made on their behalf" (ibid.: 628–629). Thus, his goal is openness

---

4 In other words, the progress goes beyond simply accumulating further data and knowledge, each time's (or culture's) unique 'subjective' perspective adds to the advancement of knowledge.
5 See Ankersmit/Domańska/Kellner (2009), for a good synopsis of reflection upon Hayden White's impact as well as the effects of postmodernism in an age after postmodernism.

and increased self-reflexivity, not the dismantling of objectivity as a whole.⁶

The danger for the discipline of historical studies lies in the assumption that the impossibility of an ideal truth or objectivity makes all historical truth-claims equal and relative, a debate particularly hard fought in discussions about postmodern history and the role of language, the meaning of truth, reality, and time (see Macfie 2013: 10, for a synopsis of differences in historical dimensions). Unreliability would therefore be a necessary result of the interdependence of subject and object; the historian could not escape the fact that his narrative would never be reliable. However, in historiographical practice most historians agree on the possibility of a reliable narrative, rather than subscribing to the impossible ideal of objectivity or to a complete relativism.⁷

To understand different approaches to history better, a distinction between three epistemological 'genres' of history by the British historical theorist Alun Munslow proves useful. He differentiates between the reconstructionist, the constructionist, and the deconstructionist genres (Munslow 2007: 10–15).⁸ Reconstructionists view narrative with a strong empirical focus "like a wire that transmits the current of meaning from the past to the history page" (ibid.: 12). In other words, they try to represent the past as realistic, objective, and trustworthy as possible. Pure reconstructionist history is hard to find in today's academic historical profession, but it dominates the discourse of popular historiography in history magazines and TV documentaries (cf. Jaeger 2014). Generally historians tend more towards reconstructionist patterns as they narrate a past story and want their readers to re-experience a constructed past. Thus they pursue an approach of presentism (cf. Jaeger 2014). Constructionist historians emphasize an analytical approach to establish historical knowledge as a "highly complex conceptual and theory-laden social science approach" (Munslow 2007: 13). This approach dominates the German academic discourse on history. It situates historical narrative within a logical system of historical argumentation and demands a high self-reflexivity

---

6   Thomas L. Haskell argues from a more rationalistic point of view that Novick confuses objectivity and neutrality. Whereas total neutrality is impossible, Haskell identifies detachment as mechanism to ensure the possibility of objectivity. They help to channel the historian's "intellectual passions in such a way as to insure collision with rival perspectives," so that the idiosyncratic and conventional can be transcended (Haskell 1990: 134).
7   Cf. for example Haskell's soft discussion of Novick's historical practice (1990: 131–132), though he rejects the rhetorical gesture of Novick's claims; or see Mommsen (1977: 448) for a cautiously relativist position. Macfie (2013) is similarly cautious.
8   It is important to note that these are ideal genres that heavily overlap in historiographical practice.

of academic historiography (cf. Rüth 2012). It bases its narratives on hypotheses about causal explanations of the past, and identifies deeper structures in history. Munslow—clearly partial towards the postmodern-deconstructionist genre—sees the deconstructionist genre as the ultimate historiographical method, since reconstructionist and constructionist histories are based on a correspondence theory (of truth) between historical narrative and the past (Munslow 2007: 13–14): "Essentially, the deconstructionist historians hold that past events are explained and acquire their meaning as much by their representation as by their 'knowable actuality' derived by conventional (empirical-analytical) epistemological means" (ibid.: 14). Both constructionist and deconstructionist approaches demand a high level of self-reflexivity of the historian-narrator and his methodology in creating narrative expression of the past.

Even if one can question whether Munslow's three genres really describe the core of academic historiography, his distinction is useful for the discussion of unreliable narration, since depending on genre, the crucial question "Unreliable, compared to what?" (A. Nünning 1998: 20) must be answered differently. In reconstructionist history—see the Irving example above—the historiographical narrative presents the clear illusion that there is a historical reality in the past that can be made present. The constructionist historian establishes a standard of objectivity in structures of the past and reflects upon possible deviation. Friedländer's narrative as discussed in the prologue of this chapter follows this pattern. For the deconstructionist historian, the measure of reliability is at least to some degree relative, which means that historical narrative establishes the measure for truth and reliability (cf. Munslow 2007: 14).

One of the biggest differences between the discourse of historical studies and fiction emerges from the assumption that historical studies deals with infinite traces in a past world that can never be complete or fully mirrored in any kind of narrative. The historian's narration is an analysis or simulation of the past. Fiction on the contrary allows for control of its world (which only comes into being through the fiction itself). The reader can use world knowledge to evaluate whether the fictional world is probable or realistic, but in the end the reader uses his reading competency to evaluate the reliability of a fictional world, not the reliability of the fictional world referencing a world outside the text (see Doležel 2010: 29–44; Jaeger 2011a: 31–33). Because of this difference, every historian would admit that the narration of history is necessarily incomplete. In a written response by Beverley Southgate to a request by Alexander Lyon Macfie, Southgate describes histories as "stories that we tell (and are told) about the past" and pinpoints several aspects of (un)reliability in historical studies (Southgate in Macfie 2013: 4): First, there is reliable evidence, whereby through source criticism the historian establishes the reliability or unreliability of the witness narrator or the source. Second, on the level of primary sources as on the level of the production of history, facts are always mediated through somewhat biased narrators and narrative situations. Third, one can either assume that the unavoidable circumstance that history constructs or even produces the past makes all historian-narrators "equally unreliable" or that—though there is no absolute history or truth—historiographical narration can establish a measure that facilitates a pragmatic reliability or credibility of the historian-narrator. The later concept leads to the more pragmatic view of history wherein, despite its challenges to reach objectivity and suspend subjectivity as much as possible, a pact of trustworthiness exists between the historian-author and the reader (cf. Jaeger 2009: 110–111; Rüth 2005: 48–51; Ricœur 1988: 205). The reader believes that the historian attempts to represent historical reality in the best possible way. Trustworthiness is defined through a relation of equivalence between the historiographical text and the reality outside of the text. The pragmatic truth- or trustworthiness-claim makes historiographic narration a narration of reality as opposed to fiction. Up to a certain extent that is epistemologically, ideologically, and linguistically possible—depending on different theoretical approaches such as a reconstructive, constructionist, or deconstructionist approach; the reader accepts that he can test the truth-claim of the historiographical text (whereas representational styles of historiographical prose can differ). Thus, the pact of trustworthiness guarantees the academic or scientific validity of the historiographical narration and is situated outside of the actual historiographical text. Historical arguments always occur within a framework of tension between pure mimesis—the bringing to life of the past in a vivid way—and the development of criteria for historical theory and truth-claims (Rüth 2005: 49).

3. Narrative Unreliability in History and Fiction

After having identified the theoretical and methodological dimensions that relate unreliability to historical studies, it is important to distinguish three distinct narrative levels of unreliability and untrustworthiness that occur in historical studies. First, the witnesses' narratives or the sources in general could be unreliable. This locates unreliable narration on the axis of primary narration which the historian needs to verify and make reliable through source criticism and interpretation in order to balance the subjective, objective, and reflexive orientations of meaning (cf. Reinfandt 2009: 39). The second and third level both relate to the historiographic discourse and the historian, thus unreliability can be seen on the axis of secondary narration that comprise the discourse of historical studies. Second, the historian can be unreliable either because of mistakes and bad methodology or by explicitly misleading the reader by presenting apparent historical facts or making truth-claims without adequately reflecting on his own ideological or epistemological point of view. In other words, the historian—according to the rules of the discourse of historical studies—pretends an objectivity and reliability that he is not pursuing. He then fails the pact of trustworthiness with the reader. The third level of unreliable historiographic narration is a textual effect that can be, but is not necessarily bound to the entity of the historian-narrator. Here, unreliable narration consciously undermines the supposedly reliable narrative and provides for meta-reflection of historical methods, narrative, and interpretation. This can be done through an overt narrator who integrates methodological reflections, among others upon his own limitations, into the narrative, or it can be achieved through staging textual effects, e.g. multiple viewpoints or simulating specific individual and collective perspectives (Jaeger 2000; Munslow 2007: 103–109). Often this occurs in experimental historiography, but technically any historical narrative can create an experiential space and gaps for its reader (Jaeger 2011a), indicating that the historian-narrator is not in full control of narrative. Of course, one could argue that an overt narrator is far more reliable than unreliable, depending on whether a reflected methodology is regarded as reliable or whether reliability is measured against the idea of one historical reality the historian aims towards. This leads to the question of whether unreliable narration is really a useful concept for understanding narrative dimensions in historical studies. Whereas the discussion of dimensions of unreliability in historical studies has shown the presence of the term and related concepts in source criticism, theories of interpretation and objectivity, as well as in pragmatic claims of trustworthiness, to see whether the concept of 'unreliable narration' really is a tool that can add something new to the analysis of historical eye-witness accounts and historiographic narrative, can only be discussed in comparison to unreliable narration in fiction, where the concept has been developed.

The discussion of unreliable narration in fiction is always connected to a narrator whose norms the reader resists to detect and reinterpret the unreliable utterance. This discussion even incorporates the argument that only homodiegetic narrators could be regarded as unreliable.[9] Narra-

---

9 Cf. Martens (2008) for the critical discussion of this limitation and suggestions for its rhetorical extension. He points out that any overt (authorial) narrator could be unreliable, which transferred to historical studies indicates the need of discussing unreliability not

tologists have attempted to develop numerous structural typologies of unreliable narrators, whose unreliability can depend on limited knowledge, on personal involvement, or on a problematic value-scheme. Greta Olson (2003) follows Wayne C. Booth (1961) in the characterization of fallible and untrustworthy narrators. James Phelan (2005: 33–34) differentiates this into the axes of events (facts), ethics (values), and of knowledge/perception. Olson—in constant discussion with the works of Booth and with Ansgar Nünning (1998)—argues that unreliable narration always takes place between a personified narrator, the implied author or the fictional world created by the totality of textual signals, and the reader, who responds to and makes sense of divergences between the former two (Olson 2003: 99). Nünning emphasizes in his reader-centred and cognitive approach that the recognition of unreliability depends on the reader's cultural and individual frames of reference (A. Nünning 1998, 2008), which also allows for the historicization of unreliable narration, since readers from different times and contexts read unreliability differently (cf. V. Nünning 2004; Zerweck 2001). So the questions remain about whether the norms on whose basis unreliability is identified depend on a singular textual whole or on a multiplicity of possible textual wholes. To what exact standard is unreliability compared? How does this standard depend on the world knowledge and cognitive frames of the reader and on the knowledge and value system of the fictional world?

The discipline of history seems to deal with unreliability in exactly the opposite way of fiction. Historical narrative, at least in modern historiography since the nineteenth century, when it follows the pact of trustworthiness, aims for reliability. The more the subjective voice of the narrator and the reflexive voice of the academic historian disappear, the more historiographic narration conceals any possible mistrust and creates the illusion of a reliable representation of historical reality. The reader needs to apply his world knowledge to reveal this act of concealment. The historical reader changes according to time, cultural memory, ideological background, and methodological discourse: for example, a mid-twentieth-century reader would neither expect a history reflecting upon gender dimensions nor a war history that focuses strongly on the war experience of civilians, whereas a twenty-first century reader most likely would. In fiction, the reader (cf. A. Nünning 1998: 24–26) uses his or her knowledge of the world to reconcile the inconsistencies that the subjective unreliable narrator—whether due to explicit deception or lack of knowledge—has narrated. Here, unreliable narration has opened gaps to be closed by the

---

merely for first-person eyewitness accounts, but for the authorial voice of the historian and the textual-rhetorical effect of the historiographic text as well.

reader; in historical narrative, the historian aims for closing the gaps that arise in an endless number of stories from witnesses and sources. In other words, the historical discourse shows a clear tendency towards synthesizing subjectivities and closing gaps. Consequently, the reader must open the gaps again, the exact opposite of fiction.

However, the actual categories of unreliability seem, at least at first glance, very similar: There is unreliability (or fallibility) in regard to narrated events or facts (the witness or historian makes factual mistakes); there is ethical unreliability (the witness or historian either manipulates historical facts, simply conceals factual gaps, or the narrative is consciously influenced by moral values and judgments); and finally, there is unreliability based on knowledge and perception. For the historical witness, this includes the suppression of memory and the impact of other memories and stories that the witness deems to be actual remembrance of events. For the historian-narrator, this means the actual lack of possible historical knowledge at the time.

Here, the specific challenge lies in the discussion of unreliable narration in historical studies. Unreliable narration is either a bad practice by the witnesses in the source material or by the historian writing historiography, or it is a specifically reflexive historiographical tool to highlight gaps and challenges that can be epistemological, moral/ideological, or aesthetic. The second half of this chapter will consequently examine whether unreliable narration could work as a category for historical studies that exceeds the existing terminology of source criticism, objectivity and bias, and the standard hermeneutic challenges of interpreting and narrating the past.

4. Criteria and Methods for Assessing a Narrator's Unreliability

For assessing the reliability, credibility or trustworthiness of eyewitnesses, historical studies has developed numerous criteria that must be differentiated according to medium and genre. First, one can distinguish two broad categories, intentional and unintentional evidence (Bloch 1954: 60–61). Intentional documents include oral history, memoirs, diaries, first-hand journalism, and testimony. Unintentional documents do not possess an explicit first-person narrator and inform the reader directly, such as government documents, private letters, statistical data, and archeological findings (Pendas 2009: 227). Traditionally, historians seem to have preferred the unintentional, seemingly more objective sources, but theories of discourse, power, and language in the twentieth century have clearly documented that those documents could be as unreliable because of the discourse they were constructed in (cf. Pendas 2009: 227–228), so that the historian must prove the reliability of both intentional and unintentional sources through thorough source criticism. On the other hand, especially in the wake of cultural history the spectrum of sources for historical studies has been broadened to include all kinds of media and even fictional sources. One source that can be seen as either non-narrative or at least lacking an explicit narrator is images. Peter Burke points out the double-headed nature of images' testifying function: they work as evidence of the material culture of the past, but are also historical themselves (2001: 23–24). The latter makes them possibly suspicious as reliable historical evidence to materialistic historians.

When history regards unreliability as a method, historians must discuss all intentional and unintentional sources. In regard to unreliable narration, however, it mostly considers intentional sources. This first level of unreliable narration in historical studies reflects the notion from fictional narratology discussed above that unreliable narration is mainly or even exclusively located in homodiegetic narration. The narratives differ in historical distance to the events narrated, as well as in the artistic means used to refine the first-person narrators' accounts. To discuss criteria and methods, this chapter will focus on oral history and testimony. The historical sub-discipline of oral history is consistently challenged to define criteria of reliability and refine its methods to prove reliability or detect unreliability. As in fictional narration, eyewitnesses can be unreliable in facts, because of their value system, and because of interpretative challenges.

The bombings of Dresden on February 13 and 14, 1945 serve as a very good example of narratives in regard to these three unreliabilities. There are a number of debates concerning the bombings, in particular about the number of the dead through the bombings, the number of refugees in Dresden in February 1945, and whether low-flying fighter planes targeted, chased and shot civilians with machine gun fire (Müller/Schönherr/Widera 2010). Oral historians point out that subjective memories by eyewitnesses almost never prove valuable as a significant source for factual history, but rather only for processed ("verarbeitete") history (Plato/Schönherr 2010: 205). In other words, the number of dead in the Dresden bombings becomes subjectively a matter of secondary narratives that constitute a master narrative, which in turn confirms a perceived victimhood. This could be seen as interpretative unreliability, but the witnesses themselves see their narratives as factual. The legend of the low-flying fighter planes is more interesting. A historian can deduct through logical conclusions and material evidence (a sonar search of potential areas for remaining ammunition; evidence from the United States Army Air Force about the order) that these attacks did not happen, or were at least unlikely or very rare (Fleischer/Hänchen 2010). While historians today mostly agree that there were no low-level fighter planes, many eyewitnesses who were in Dresden on February 14 vividly remember these attacks.[10] Researchers argue that this is part of a collective memory process that uses the symbolic message of the uniqueness of Dresden's destruction and builds narrative elements around it, which are eventually believed by eyewitnesses, independent of historical events at that time (see Widera 2005: 110–113; 126–130). Consequently the unreliability of the narrative is involuntary, as it is one based on perception. An analysis of the witnesses' circumstances can prove whether the witness has any reason to intentionally exaggerate his accounts which could indicate an ideological or ethical unreliability. The criterion for the reliability of the witness narrative is whether the narrative tends towards exaggeration and strong emotional involvement. Good source criticism then contextualizes individual narratives in comparison to other witness accounts and known historical facts. The historian moves from the concrete witness narrative to an abstract generalization about low-flying fighter planes. Other criteria include clear contradictions: for instance, the witnesses assert that there were a high number of refugees in the city, but a much lower one is seen in their own neighborhood (see Plato/Schönherr 2010: 207). General conclusion and personal experience clash.

Testimony, unlike oral history, does not allow the historian to interact directly with the narrator. "The questions are asked by others and may or (more frequently) may not be precisely those which the historian wishes to address" (Pendas 2009: 230). This difference can be further illuminated through Aleida Assmann's distinction between four types of witnesses: historical witnesses who authenticate the past through their closeness to the historical events and persons, the witness in court, the religious witness, and the moral witness (2006: 85–92). The last category is closely linked to genocide survivors in Assmann's typology; this gives witnesses a particular performative power: they give public testimony in the arena of a moral community (ibid.: 91). This category can undermine the idea of the historical witness, so that history and memory merge.

> When presented with the witness testimony of experience of the concentration camp or other places of horror, we are dealing not with a direct representation of a naked experience but with the cultural resources that constitute the politics of identity of the whole society. (Tozzi 2012: 17)

Often, the witness in court can also be a historical witness, especially in genocide trials. Devin O. Pendas has shown that there is an important

---

[10] About 21% of the 1314 witness accounts analyzed by Dresden Historians' Commission for the Detection of the Number of Victims (Plato/Schönherr 2010: 202).

distinction between subjective trustworthiness and objective plausibility that leads to the need of both hearing and listening to testimony. Therefore, the historian's method must allow hearing, i.e. "both broad and deep historical knowledge to situate what one hears meaningfully, to cross-check one witness against others and against other kinds of sources, to notice minor and major errors," whereas listening requires "an intuitive sympathy, as well as an analytical awareness of the limits of such sympathy" (Pendas 2009: 239). Whereas a court searching for objective evidence might see a traumatized witness as too emotional, the witness might be fully trustworthy in a subjective sense that explains gaps or emotions in the testimony (Pendas 2009: 239). At the same time the trustworthiness of a witness depends on the kind of reliability that is pursued. Whereas one could argue that for "establishing the factual record concerning Nazi policies and measures of persecution […] contemporary German documents [prove] far more reliable than postwar survivor memories" (Browning 2003: 40), this proves to be very different if a moral, experiental or perceptive reliability is aimed for.[11] Consequently, the historian is forced to carefully consider what kind of reliability is needed to establish a constructionist correspondence with the past. Most constructionist historians would agree that it is possible to reconstruct events on a variety of different, often conflicting memories and testimonies (cf. Pendas 2009: 234).

The second form of unreliable narration takes place on the discursive level of historiography. This transfers the narration—in most cases, except for some utterances where the historian explicitly relates to his own work methodology in the first person (cf. Carrard 1992: 84–104)—to heterodiegetic narration. The historian-narrator is not part of the historical events. As already discussed in the prologue, the historian's voice synthesizes the witness narratives and mostly provides a historiographical reality that presents itself to the reader as a trustworthy and reliable reading. This chapter focuses on popular historiography, since it usually claims to present an objective past reality to the reader; it is the ideal of reconstructionist history (cf. Munslow 2007: especially 68–74). On the one hand, this means that it uses a covert narrator who synthesizes historical sources and facts, so that one interpretation of history can be expressed. At the same time, popular historiography uses a variety of narrative means—especially variation of focalization and historical distance—to create the impression of a history present and close to the reader (Jaeger

---

11 Cf. Browning (2003: 41–42). The Holocaust and genocide in general provide a constant challenge whether reliable insights can be gained from perpetrators as well as of traumatized victims. Browning (ibid.: especially 37–59) clearly assumes this is possible with the right historical methods.

2014). All witness accounts lose their autonomy and individuality and are synthesized in the reality of the narrator.[12] In other words, multiple voices are streamlined in a closed perspectival structure, so that they all work towards the historical reality controlled by the narrator.[13] Unlike constructionist and usually academic historiography, the illusion of the reality of the past does not allow, for analytic reflection as seen in the case of Friedländer above. Structural history is usually reduced to experiental history, stressing the collective experience of the past that the reader can re-experience in the reconstructed form in a simulated present. This kind of historiography does not allow for unreliability on the source-witness level; it only uses material appropriate to the overall argument. The reader must find and deconstruct traces of unreliability in the historian's method and voice, as shown for Rodenberger and Irving above. If the historical reality of past events seems hard to represent in the present, the reader can become suspicious of the narrative and its manipulative presentism. To detect unreliability the reader must discover traits of manipulation or at least of simplification. This can either be done by noticing the tone of the narrative and a certain bias towards one side or one interpretation (such as seeing the air-war just as a crime or just as a completely justified means of warfare), or the reader needs contextualization and world knowledge beyond the actual historiographical narrative that allows him to distance himself from the manipulative narrative and reopen historical gaps or possibilities for multiple perspectives. In academic historiography, the techniques of manipulation are more subtle, but for any covert narrator, the reader must understand the construction of the narrative to reveal the text's techniques of concealment. With an overt narrator this is considerably easier, since according to the pact of truthfulness, this historian-narrator already reflects his own method.

At first glance, references and footnotes are clear indicators of reliability. They constitute "an indispensable if messy part" of modern history (Grafton 1997: 235). Whereas for example antiquarian history in the seventeenth and eighteenth century struggled to express a coherent narra-

---

[12] There is an endless variation possible here, how much authorial power a historian-narrator leaves to witness narrators on different levels. The less the witness narrator is squeezed in a functional argument proving a specific argument of the historian-narration, the more the witness narrative—possibly on different embedded levels—remains a narrative force on its own, or in other words a reflector, possibly displaying similar narrative effects as the textual effects discussed as third level of unreliability in historical studies below. Again Friedländer's text (2008) is a good example for achieving a balance between individual voices and the historian's voice.

[13] Cf. Jaeger (2000) for the standard procedure of historiography to synthesize multiple voices in a closed perspectival structure. For a historical studies' discussion of multiple voices and perspectives, see Bergmann (1992).

tive of history, lost in endless facts, the footnote in modern historiography can imply a thorough and accountable use of historical sources and other voices from the academic discourse of historical studies. Especially for constructionist history footnotes create further space for reflection and alternate voices and interpretation. Their absence might be an indicator of unreliability or simply of easy abstraction and simplification, as is often the case in popular history. The reader must, however, be as alert to the manipulative effects of footnotes as of arguments in the text.

In summary, unreliability on the historiographical level occurs if the historian closes the infinite gaps of history by evoking the past in the present and by synthesizing a multiplicity of voices in the historical narrative. To detect possible unreliability, the reader must reveal the mechanisms of concealment that present only one historical reality or a closed historical world as a reflection of reality. If the historian is very self-reflexive as seen with Saul Friedländer such a closed world of history is not unreliable, because the historian openly displays the construction and closure mechanisms of the narrative.

The third level of unreliability is a textual effect of historiography that turns unreliability into something that should be seen in the open so that it meta-reflects that historical knowledge is infinite and never complete. The unreliability of specific narrators or persons is not important, but the performative process of making history (cf. Jaeger 2011b: especially 33–65). It displays unreliability as a historical necessity, so that it enriches the historical narrative and the reader's knowledge about and experience of the past. It is most often found in experiental historiography that can be either constructionist or deconstructionist in nature.

Two brief examples can demonstrate the richness of this third level of unreliability in historical studies. First there is the effect of an open multiperspectivity. For example, Richard Price tells in *Alabi's World* (1990) the history of Surinam from four different perspectives of which the historian is only one perspective which is not particularly privileged. There is no synthesizing authorial power. This allows the reader to experience and interpret the space that emerges in the narrative between the different value systems and different dichotomies such as past and present, black and white, or church and state (see Jaeger 2000: 332–335). In general, unreliability is emphasized because different life styles and value systems, and possibly different interpretations of the same events are presented, without or with reduced authorial power. Then—as in the cognitive approach to unreliable narration in fiction—the reader's world knowledge, interests, and emotional reaction will shape his exact reading and interpretation of reliabilities in the text.

Another form that displays unreliability at the third level is the simulation of historical atmosphere. For example, in Karl Schlögel's *Terror und Traum. Moskau 1937* (2008, *Terror and Dream. Moscow 1937*), the narrative does not focalize individual minds or collectives, but history unfolds as an event of abstract forces, loosely connected, before the eyes of the reader. The text creates a presentism of the past, so that the reader feels the forces, feelings, mood, and atmosphere of the time (Jaeger 2011a: 39–40), while the text as an almost impressionist montage explicitly displays its own constructedness. History is represented as undetermined and dependent on the arrangement of historical traces and structures. Since the reader is so explicitly integrated in the past-making process, he experiences the effects of unreliability in the past. The only way to solve this is to understand the poietic constructedness of the space (Jaeger 2011a: 31–36). Any montage technique runs the danger of reducing the history to a chronicle that lacks narrativity (White 1987: 43). Therefore, at least in the discipline of historical studies, all representations still convey a structural order that guarantees narrativity.

It is important to note that the third level of unreliability explains the difference between unreliability and trustworthiness in historical studies. In all examples, the historiographical pact according to which the reader trusts the historian to represent history accurately to his best knowledge is completely valid, as long as the historian does not disguise thought experiments and inventions as referential facts. When the narratives are trustworthy, they pinpoint the unreliability of the narrative. As in fiction, a combination of cognitive and rhetorical analysis of the narrative is required to understand the communication between text and reader. At the same time, it becomes clear that there is no true measure of reliability; unreliability relies on the infiniteness of historical worlds, on history's double existence as referential and as performative, and on its multiple voices and readers.

5. Synopsis: Functions of Unreliability

Though there is a tendency in historical studies for unreliability to be reduced for a trustworthy historical narrative, unreliability has a positive function on all three of its levels. To give room to the unreliability of witnesses allows for the understanding of memory processes and the emergence of narratives that appear to be factual though they are strongly based on often involuntary perception. Unreliability in a historical-factual sense also becomes an important tool in regard to the moral witness: for genocide survivors, the performative power of the witness can merge with historical representation; thus, unreliability demonstrates the complex conflation of the moral and the factual, as well as of representative and performative narrative.

If the historian allows unreliability and indeterminacies on the level of primary narratives to show through in the secondary narrative, a higher awareness of source criticism, hermeneutic interpretation of the past and the interdependency of objectivity and subjectivity is created. Accepting and embracing this interdependency and unreliability helps every generation, culture, or group to reflect upon the uniqueness of its own access from the present to the past. The standard idea of concealing unreliability, particularly in reconstructionist history, can be counterbalanced through more open and reflexive forms. They do not necessarily lead to relativism and the loss of the concepts of objectivity and of historical truth-claims. Reducing one's authority to the reflection upon its limitations—in constructionist and deconstructionist histories—makes unreliability a necessary component of history and includes the reader in the reflexive process of understanding history. Here, unreliability serves as a tool of the poietic process of historiographical narration. As in fiction, the narrator extends some of his authorial power to the reader who is challenged to react to the openness of the historiographical text. This allows the reader to understand the indeterminacy of the past and its reliance on different interpretative patterns. In terms of understanding the performative power of witness narratives, historiography's unreliability effect provides for any discipline that produces reality narratives—i.e. the narrative references the outside world in some way, meta-reflectional tools to understand the dependence of representations on cultural and historical dimensions. Since historical studies does not suspend its referential claim, unreliability as a concept in its own right, related to but different from fiction, proves to be a helpful concept for understanding the complex processes of narrative and methodological construction in dealing with the past in particular and human stories in general.

Works Cited

Ankersmit, Frank, Ewa Domańska & Hans Kellner (eds.). 2009. *Re-Figuring Hayden White*. Stanford, CA: Stanford University Press.

Assmann, Aleida. 2006. *Der lange Schatten der Vergangenheit. Erinnerungskultur und Geschichtspolitik*. Munich: Beck.

Bergmann, Klaus. 1992. "Multiperspektivität." In: Klaus Bergmann, Klaus Fröhlich, Annette Kuhn et al. (eds.). *Handbuch der Geschichtsdidaktik*. 4th ed. Seelze-Velber: Kallmeyer. 271–273.

Bloch, Marc. 1954. *The Historian's Craft*. Trans. Peter Putnam. Manchester: Manchester University Press.

Booth, Wayne C. 1961. *The Rhetoric of Fiction*. Chicago, IL: Chicago University Press.

Browning, Christopher R. 2003. *Collected Memories. Holocaust History and Postwar Testimony*. Madison, WI: University of Wisconsin Press.

Burke, Peter. 2001. *Eyewitnessing. The Uses of Images as Historical Evidence*. Ithaca, NY: Cornell University Press.

Carrard, Philippe. 1992. *Poetics of the New History. French Historical Discourse from Braudel to Chartier*. Baltimore, MD/London: Johns Hopkins University Press.

Dann, Otto. 1995. "Schiller, der Historiker und die Quellen." In: Otto Dann, Norbert Oellers & Ernst Osterkamp (eds.). *Schiller als Historiker*. Stuttgart: Metzler. 109–126.

Dobson, Miriam & Benjamin Ziemann (eds.). 2009. *Reading Primary Sources: The Interpretation of Texts from 19th—and 20th Century History*. London/New York, NY: Routledge.

Doležel, Lubomír. 2010. *Possible Worlds of Fiction and History. The Postmodern Stage*. Baltimore, MD: Johns Hopkins University Press.

Evans, Richard J. 2001. *Lying About Hitler. History, Holocaust, and the Irving Trial*. New York, NY: Basic Books.

Fleischer, Wolfgang & Udo Hänchen. 2010. "Tieffliegerangriffe auf Dresden am 13. und 14. Februar 1945." In: Rolf-Dieter Müller, Nicole Schönherr & Thomas Widera (eds.). *Die Zerstörung Dresdens 13. bis 15. Februar 1945. Gutachten und Ergebnisse der Dresdner Historikerkommission zur Ermittlung der Opferzahlen*. Göttingen: V&R unipress. 177–188.

Friedländer, Saul. 2007. *Nazi Germany and the Jews. 1939–1945. The Years of Extermination*. New York, NY/London: HarperCollins.

Grafton, Anthony. 1997. *The Footnote. A Curious History*. Cambridge, MS: Harvard University Press.

Haskell, Thomas L. 1990. "Objectivity is not Neutrality: Rhetoric vs. Practice in Peter Novick's *That Noble Dream*." *History and Theory* 29.2: 129–157.

Howell, Martha & Walter Prevenier. 2001. *From Reliable Sources. An Introduction to Historical Methods*. Ithaca, NY: Cornell University Press.

Irving, David. 2005 [1963]. *Apocalypse 1945. The Destruction of Dresden*. London: Parforce UK.

Jaeger, Stephan. 2000. "Multiperspektivisches Erzählen in der Geschichtsschreibung des ausgehenden 20. Jahrhunderts. Wissenschaftliche Inszenierungen von Geschichte zwischen Roman und Wirklichkeit." In: Vera Nünning & Ansgar Nünning (eds.). *Multiperspektivisches*

Erzählen. Zur Theorie und Geschichte der Perspektivenstruktur im englischen Roman des 18. bis 20. Jahrhunderts. Trier: WVT. 323–346.

Jaeger, Stephan. 2009. "Erzählen im historiographischen Diskurs." In: Christian Klein & Matías Martínez (eds.). *Wirklichkeitserzählungen. Felder, Formen und Funktionen nicht-literarischen Erzählens*. Stuttgart: Metzler. 110–135.

Jaeger, Stephan. 2011a. "Poietic Worlds and Experientiality in Historiographic Narrative." In: Julia Nitz & Sandra Harbert Petrulionis (eds.). *SPIEL* 30.1: 29–50.

Jaeger, Stephan. 2011b. *Performative Geschichtsschreibung. Forster, Herder, Schiller, Archenholz und die Brüder Schlegel*. Berlin/New York, NY: De Gruyter.

Jaeger, Stephan. 2014. "Populäre Geschichtsschreibung. Aus narratologischer Perspektive." In: Susanne Popp, Jutta Schumann & Fabio Crivellari (eds.). *Illustrierte Geschichten. Populäre Geschichtsmagazine in Europa*. Göttingen: Vandenhoeck & Ruprecht (in press).

Junker, Detlef & Peter Reisinger. 1977. "Was kann Objektivität in der Geschichtswissenschaft heißen, und wie ist sie möglich?" In: Theodor Schieder & Kurt Gräubig (eds.). *Theorieprobleme der Geschichtswissenschaft*. Darmstadt: WBG. 420–471.

Kocka, Jürgen. 1977. "Angemessenheitskriterien historischer Argumente." In: Koselleck, Mommsen & Rüsen (eds.). 1977. 469–475.

Koselleck, Reinhart. 1977. "Standortbildung und Zeitlichkeit. Ein Beitrag zur historiographischen Erschließung der geschichtlichen Welt." In: Koselleck, Mommsen & Rüsen (eds.). 1977. 17–46.

Koselleck, Reinhart, Wolfgang J. Mommsen & Jörn Rüsen (eds.). 1977. *Objektivität und Parteilichkeit*. Theorie der Geschichte. Beiträge zur Historik 1. München: dtv.

Macfie, Alexander Lyon. 2013. "Towards a new definition of history." *Rethinking History*. (April 2013): http://dx.doi.org/10.1080/13642529. 2013.774730 (last retrieved: May 13, 2013): 1–12.

Martens, Gunther. 2008. "Revising and Extending the Scope of the Rhetorical Approach to Unreliable Narration." In: Elke D'hoker & Gunther Martens (eds.). *Narrative Unreliability in the Twentieth-Century First-Person Novel*. Narratologia 14. Berlin/New York, NY: De Gruyter. 77–111.

Mommsen, Wolfgang J. 1977. "Der perspektivische Charakter historischer Aussagen und das Problem von Parteilichkeit und Objektivität historischer Erkenntnis." In: Koselleck, Mommsen & Rüsen (eds.). 1977. 441–468.

Müller, Philipp. 2009. "Understanding History. Hermeneutics and Source Criticism in Historical Scholarship." In: Dobson & Ziemann (eds.). 2009. 21–36.

Müller, Rolf-Dieter, Nicole Schönherr & Thomas Widera (eds.). 2010. *Die Zerstörung Dresdens 13. bis 15. Februar 1945. Gutachten und Ergebnisse der Dresdner Historikerkommission zur Ermittlung der Opferzahlen*. Göttingen: V&R unipress.

Munslow, Alun. 2007. *Narrative and History*. Basingstoke: Palgrave Macmillan.

Novick, Peter. 1988. *That Noble Dream. The 'Objectivity Question' and the American Historical Profession*. Cambridge: Cambridge University Press.

Nünning, Ansgar. 1998. "Unreliable Narration zur Einführung. Grundzüge einer kognitiv-narratologischen Theorie und Analyse unglaubwürdigen Erzählens." In: Ansgar Nünning (ed.). *Unreliable Narration: Studien zur Theorie und Praxis unglaubwürdigen Erzählens in der englischsprachigen Erzählliteratur*. Trier: WVT. 3–39.

Nünning, Ansgar. 2008. "Reconceptualizing the Theory, History and Generic Scope of Unreliable Narration. Towards a Synthesis of Cognitive and Rhetorical Approaches." In: Elke D'hoker & Gunther Martens (eds.). *Narrative Unreliability in the Twentieth-Century First-Person Novel*. Narratologia 14. Berlin/New York, NY: De Gruyter. 29–76.

Nünning, Vera. 2004. "Unreliable Narration and the Historical Variability of Values and Norms: *The Vicar of Wakefield* as a Test-Case of a Cultural-Historical Narratology." *Style* 38.2: 236–252.

Olson, Greta. 2003. "Reconsidering Unreliability: Fallible and Untrustworthy Narrators." *Narrative* 11.1: 93–109.

Pendas, Devin O. 2009. "Testimony." In: Dobson & Ziemann (eds.). 2009. 226–242.

Phelan, James. 2005. *Living to Tell about It. A Rhetoric and Ethics of Character Narration*. Ithaca, NY: Cornell University Press.

Plato, Alexander von & Nicole Schönherr. 2010. "Die Erfahrung Dresdens." In: Rolf-Dieter Müller, Nicole Schönherr & Thomas Widera (eds.). 2010. *Die Zerstörung Dresdens 13. bis 15. Februar 1945. Gutachten und Ergebnisse der Dresdner Historikerkommission zur Ermittlung der Opferzahlen*. Göttingen: V&R unipress.189–209.

Price, Richard. 1990. *Alabi's World*. Baltimore, MD: Johns Hopkins University Press.

Reinfandt, Christoph. 2009. "Reading texts after the linguistic turn. Approaches from literary studies and their implications." In: Dobson & Ziemann (eds.). 2009. 37–54.

Ricoeur, Paul. 1988. *Time and Narrative*. Trans. Kathleen Blamey & David Pellauer. Vol. 3. Chicago, IL: Chicago University Press.

Rodenberger, Axel. 1953. *Der Tod von Dresden. Ein Bericht über das Sterben einer Stadt.* 4th ed. Dortmund: Franz Müller-Rodenberger.
Rüsen Jörn. 2005. *History. Narration, Interpretation, Orientation.* Making Sense in History. Vol. 2. New York, NY: Berghahn.
Rüth, Axel. 2005. *Erzählte Geschichte. Narrative Strukturen in der französischen Annales-Geschichtsschreibung.* Narratologia 5. Berlin/New York, NY: De Gruyter.
Rüth, Axel. 2012 "Narrativität in der wissenschaftlichen Geschichtsschreibung." In: Matthias Aumüller (ed.). *Narrativität als Begriff. Analysen und Anwendungsbeispiele zwischen philologischer und anthropologischer Orientierung.* Narratologia 31. Berlin/New York, NY: De Gruyter. 21–46.
Schlögel, Karl. 2008. *Terror und Traum. Moskau 1937.* Munich: Hanser. [2012. *Moscow 1937.* Trans. Rodney Livingstone. Cambridge: Polity Press].
Taylor, Frederick. 2004. *Dresden. Tuesday 13 February 1945.* New York, NY: HarperCollins.
Tozzi, Verónica. 2012. "The Epistemic and Moral Role of Testimony." *History and Theory* 51.1: 1–17.
Widera, Thomas. 2005. "Gefangene Erinnerung. Die politische Instrumentalisierung der Bombardierung Dresdens." In: Lothar Fritze & Thomas Widera (eds.). *Alliierter Bombenkrieg. Das Beispiel Dresden.* Göttingen: V&R unipress. 109–134.
White, Hayden. 1987. *The Content of the Form. Narrative Discourse and Historical Representation.* Baltimore, MD: Johns Hopkins University Press.
Zerweck, Bruno. 2001. "Historicizing Unreliable Narration: Unreliability and Cultural Discourse in Narrative Fiction." *Style* 35.1: 151–178.

JARMILA MILDORF
(Paderborn)

Unreliability in Patient Narratives: From Clinical Assessment to Narrative Practice

> When you go to, when I was going to the specialist before my surgery, everything is questioned. You know, 'First of all you said your pain was like this, and now you're saying it's like this' and 'What do you mean?' and you almost feel that they're trying to tell you, 'You don't really have pain and you don't know what you're talking about'.
> But as I say, you go to a pain management clinic and it's like 'Okay you are telling the truth and we believe you' and it makes a huge difference actually, having somebody who will believe you, without questioning it. Because you go through, you go through virtually everybody questioning you and wondering if you're telling the truth or not. (Female patient suffering from chronic back pain since she was 26; aged 32 at time of interview; *Healthtalkonline*)

I begin this paper with a story told as part of an interview for an illness narrative database by a patient suffering from chronic pain. The patient talks about her encounters with medical professionals, who questioned whether she was really ill and accordingly behaved towards her in a manner that expressed their suspicion. What is at stake here is the question of reliability or, conversely, unreliability in patient narratives. Doctors may well ask themselves: Are the symptoms this patient is presenting with real or feigned? Is the story he or she is telling me truthful or not? And if it is not truthful, why is that? What are the patient's reasons for pretending to be sick?

At first glance, unreliability is not something one would expect in doctor-patient encounters. After all, patients rely on their doctors to make correct diagnoses, and then to inform them of and to implement the best treatment.[1] Likewise, when patients present with symptoms in consultations, doctors must assume that the patients rightfully seek to adopt what sociologists call the "sick role", that is, a social role that legitimates a person to withdraw from his or her regular activities and to seek the help

---

[1] As Kathryn Montgomery (2006: 191) has it: "We need medicine to be reliable and to be predictable and physicians to be agents of accumulated scientific knowhow".

of medical professionals. Sociologist Talcott Parsons (1991 [1951]: 294) writes:

> This exemption [i.e. from normal social role responsibilities] requires legitimation by and to the various alters involved and the physician often serves as a court of appeal as well as a direct legitimizing agent. [...] It goes almost without saying that this legitimation has the social function of protection against 'malingering'.

In other words, by judging whether a patient's account is truthful/reliable or not, doctors assume an important role as gatekeepers to the sick role with its rights and obligations and they are expected to prevent patients from misusing this role. This is relevant to the extent that sickness incurs huge costs to the health care system but also to the economy more generally. It is, for example, estimated that employees across Europe take over 120 million days of sick leave per year for personal reasons rather than because they are really sick (AON Consulting 2010).[2]

This example also indicates, however, that reliability is not limited to verbal interaction. People not only rely on the truth-value of what someone says but also on the sincerity and integrity on which the other person acts. In other words, reliability is also related to certain codes of conduct and practices that are adequate in a given social interaction. This also applies to doctor-patient interactions. However, things are not always as straightforward as that. For example: Do I want my doctor to tell me under any circumstances that I carry a virus which may or may not result in severe illness even if such knowledge does not at present warrant the possibility of early treatment or prevention? Does complete information lead patients to have a stronger sense of trust in their doctors? And conversely, can doctors always rely on their patients to provide truthful information and if not, when does a patient's unreliability start to have implications for the doctor's behavior towards him or her? For example, it may not be easy for a doctor to decide what measures to take, if any, when a patient tells him that he takes only the occasional drink, while his physical condition seems to tell another story. Or take the case of a drug addict who deliberately conceals his unceasing drug abuse because he fears repercussions.[3] After all, unreliability is closely connected to the ways in which people wish to present themselves in conversations, and therefore "many unreliable narratives are in a flux between conscious and unconscious behavior, often helped on by psychological suppression, manifested in euphemisms, half-truths, and diffuse hedging constructions" (Heyd

---

[2] What this study does not make sufficiently clear, however, is whether the personal reasons mentioned do not also include feelings of anxiety or stress—which may well be precursors for genuine sickness.

[3] For a more detailed discussion of denial and misreporting in cases of substance abuse, see Stein/Rogers (2008).

2011: 12). As the examples above show, patients also may or may not be conscious of the fact that they are unreliable. Furthermore, if they are deliberately unreliable they may pursue a host of different goals in being so. And finally, unreliability may depend strongly on what the doctor perceives as 'unreliable' in a given situation[4]. Can one already talk about unreliability when patients and medical professionals have different ways of explaining or expressing what certain symptoms are like (the question of qualia [cf. Cytowic 2003]) or does the term only apply to cases of downright attempts at deception, simulation and dissimulation? And how can such attempts be gauged and evaluated by doctors?

In this paper, I concentrate on those and other questions concerning unreliability in patient narratives. Of course, patient narratives as such can come in different shapes and guises. The above-mentioned examples have so far focused on direct doctor-patient interaction, where patients tell their doctors face to face, in the form of conversational storytelling, what is presumably wrong with them or what their problems are. Patient narratives can also be part of life-storytelling situations, for example, in interviews conducted for oral history databases. A good example is the *Healthtalkonline* database (healthtalkonline.org)—from which my initial example of a patient narrative is taken—which hosts a large collection of patient narratives surrounding personal experiences with a wide range of illnesses. In a situation in which an illness narrative is more or less rehearsed or perhaps structured along a catalogue of set questions, (un)reliability assumes another quality (see also Hardwig 1997). This is even more true of written or even published illness narratives. Here, issues concerning the writing process and the aims of writing down one's experiences play an important role. Moreover, editorial intervention and marketing strategies geared towards making the story 'sellable' can easily call the whole business of reliability into question (see Garden 2010). Obviously, one cannot cover all possible manifestations of patient narratives in one paper. I will therefore leave aside published patient stories and primarily pay attention to patient narratives in doctor-patient interactions. The illness narrative at the beginning of this paper will serve to illustrate some general points I will make in the end about unreliability and communication. First, however, I will outline two approaches to unreliability within medicine: clinical approaches on the one hand and discussions of the concept within narrative medicine and the medical humanities on the other.

---

4   This also corresponds with what Bode (2011: 266), building on Nünning (1998), claims for the concept of unreliability in literary narratives: whether a story is perceived as reliable or unreliable, Bode argues, depends on how readers read the text and on whether they begin to feel suspicious about what they are told.

1. The Clinical Assessment of Malingering and Deception

The title of this section is also the title of a collection of essays that deal with manifestations of unreliable patient narratives in various medical settings and with the means and methods of identifying such unreliability (Rogers 2008). In clinical psychology, there is an area of research which investigates different "response styles" in patients. Responses may range from truthful and cooperative to various shades of untruthful. The difficulty for practitioners is to detect unreliability, for researchers to define and classify different types of response styles and to develop tools for detection. Rogers notes that the medical domain is more difficult in this regard because patients can be untruthful in diverse ways:

> With medical malingering, patients can specialize in one debilitating symptom (e.g. pain), portray a constellation of common but distressing ailments (e.g. headaches, fatigue, and gastrointestinal difficulties), or specialize in complex syndromes (e.g. fibromyalgia). In light of this complexity, detection strategies for the medical domain face formidable challenges in their development and validation. (2008b: 17)

Nevertheless, researchers in this field have developed a number of statistical methods involving questionnaires in order to elicit potential forms of unreliability in patients, e.g. the MMPI (Minnesota Multiphasic Personality Inventory), the so-called Waddell signs (signs for nonorganic pain) or the Life Assessment Questionnaire (LAQ) (Rogers 2008b).[5] Ironically, these statistical methods themselves aim at reliability, validity and generalizability and may prove inadequate in certain contexts because they may not distinguish clearly enough between feigned symptoms and genuine maladaptive responses in patients with chronic conditions (cf. Rogers ibid.: 29)[6] or because they are not designed to account for variability within single patients across various situational contexts (Chassan 1957).[7]

---

5 These psychometric scales usually measure non-responding and inconsistent responding as well as over- and underreporting. It would be interesting to look at such questionnaires in detail in order to see how questions are worded, for example. For reasons of confidentiality and secrecy, however, test items are distributed to clinicians only, and consequently none of the papers in the volume edited by Rogers presents actual questions. It would be too easy for potential malingerers to learn the appropriate responses.

6 Patients can, for example, *accommodate*, which means they incorporate an illness into their identity and thereby complicate treatment, or they can *resign*, feeling overwhelmed by their predicaments and thus becoming passive sufferers (Radley/Green 1987). Granacher and Berry (2008: 145–146) also point out that physical malingering can be very difficult to distinguish from conversion disorder, for example, because the latter also involves a host of physical symptoms as a result of overwhelming anxiety.

7 Chassan (1957: 164) contends that: "The existence of variability as a basic phenomenon in the study of individual psychopathology implies that a single observation of a patient-state, in general, can offer a minimum of information about the patient-state. While such

In trying to detect signs of malingering and deception in patients, researchers of dissimulative response styles are like literary scholars investigating textual unreliability: They search for textual cues (or "read the patient as text", as Kathryn Hunter [1993] has it) and check whether these cues clash or correspond with the overall expected picture of the presented condition.[8] They also try to arrive at a typology of (textual) features of unreliability in order to make the results generalizable and applicable to a wide range of patients (literary texts). An example from dissimulation studies is Hall and Poirier's (2001) list of response styles that malingerers typically present to doctors (cf. Granacher/Berry 2008: 145): They present realistic symptoms; they deliberately make mistakes; they protest the difficult tasks and feign confusion and frustration; they perform at a fraction of their actual ability; they change their affective style. One can raise the same objection to this kind of classification that Bode (2011: 267–269) holds against similar formal typologies offered by literary narratologists. While these features may well be typical of unreliable patient response styles they can undoubtedly also be found in patients who do not merely pretend to suffer from a certain condition. The question that arises then is: What exactly in a particular patient's response style causes the doctor to suspect malingering? Is it a discrepancy between what the patient says or does and what his or her physical examination reveals? Or a discrepancy between what the patient says and what, say, another family member reports? Or are there contradictions in the patient's own account?[9] At any rate, a doctor's suspicion will ultimately depend on his or her *interpretation* of these conflicting signs and perhaps on whether he or she suspects some reason or motivation for malingering on the part of the patient.

---

information is literally better than no information, it provides no more data than does any other statistical sample of size one". In analogy, if one patient is found to be unreliable in one consultation with regard to one symptom, can one automatically take him or her to be unreliable in general or with regard to other symptoms as well?

8   In literary texts, the clash may be between what the narrator tells and what the story presents to readers or between what the narrator tells and the author's implicit discourse (Shen: sections [11]; [12]). In patient narratives, as in real-life conversational narratives in general, one may assume a personal union of author and narrator in the person telling the story, which considerably lessens the number of possible (textual) clashes. For a divergent view on speakers' "production formats" where speaker roles are divided into "author", "animator" and "principal", see Goffman (1981: 144–146). Below, I will also say more about the potential complexity of conversational narratives.

9   These examples correspond neatly with Rimmon-Kenan's (1983: 101) list of indicators of unreliability in literary narration: "[…] when the facts contradict the narrator's views […]; when the outcome of the action proves the narrator wrong […]; when the views of other characters consistently clash with the narrator's […]; and when the narrator's language contains internal contradictions". For a more extensive list that also includes rhetorical and stylistic features, see Nünning (1998: 27–28).

The first thing to note when looking at the typologies and terms used in dissimulation studies is that 'unreliability' is not a technical term *per se* in this context. As Rogers (2008a) points out in his introduction to the above-mentioned volume, there are a number of nonspecific terms used by clinicians, which only become useful if they are linked to specific response styles and are thus given more precision.[10] These terms include "unreliability", "nondisclosure", "self-disclosure", "deception" and "dissimulation" (see Table 1). Rogers (ibid.: 5) defines unreliability as "a very general term that raises questions about the accuracy of reported information. It makes no assumption about the individual's intent or the reasons for inaccurate data. This term is especially useful in cases of conflicting clinical data". In other words, there is a discrepancy between what the patient reports and what his or her physical examination suggests, but why this is so need not be evident, nor need it interest the researcher/clinician. To my mind it seems counterintuitive that medical professionals, like other human beings, should not be interested in the reasons why patients are unreliable. However, medical practice, especially in evidence-based medicine, requires of doctors that they be clinical and detached and that they must not be deterred by questions seemingly irrelevant to a case at hand. It may be sufficient for doctors to find out *that* a patient malingers or tries to deceive them rather than exploring *why* this is the case.[11]

---

[10] Precise definitions are absolutely vital for statistical research since results would otherwise be flawed and not comparable. Precision and validity in this area are also of importance because clinical psychologists often function as expert witnesses in court trials where claimants seek litigation after accidents, for example.

[11] In my research on doctors' experiences with patients suffering from domestic abuse (Mildorf 2007), one of the main reasons the GPs I interviewed gave for not following up their suspicion was lack of time in the temporally limited consultation but also their sense that, if they probed the issue further, they would open a can of worms of more complex issues, which they may then not feel equipped to deal with. Possibly, similar reasons are at stake when it comes to treating patients who are potential malingerers.

Nonspecific terms	Description/definition
unreliability	"a very general term that raises questions about the accuracy of reported information. It makes no assumption about the individual's intent or the reasons for inaccurate data. This term is especially useful in cases of conflicting clinical data."
nondisclosure	"a withholding of information (i.e. omission). Similar to unreliability, it makes no assumption about intentionality. An individual may freely choose not to disclose or may feel compelled by internal demands (e.g. command hallucinations) to withhold information."
self-disclosure	"how much individuals reveal about themselves [...]. A person is considered to have high self-disclosure when he or she evidences a high degree of openness. A lack of self-disclosure does not imply dishonesty but simply an unwillingness to share personal information."
deception	"an all-encompassing term used to describe any consequential attempts by individuals to distort or misrepresent their self-reporting. As operationalized, deception includes acts of deceit, often accompanied by nondisclosure. Deception may be totally separate from the patient's described psychological functioning..."
dissimulation	"a general term to describe an individual who is deliberately distorting or misrepresenting psychological symptoms. Practitioners find this term useful because some clinical presentations are difficult to classify and clearly do not represent malingering, defensiveness, or any specific response style."

Table 1. Nonspecific terms used to describe response styles (Rogers 2008a: 5)

Malingering falls into the category of overstated pathology in Rogers' scheme, i.e., patients report illnesses that are non-existent or are not as bad as described. For such cases Rogers recommends three different terms: the aforementioned "malingering", which involves "gross exaggeration of multiple symptoms" for specific external, but also internal reasons; "factitious presentations", which means that patients intentionally produce symptoms in order to assume the "sick role" (2008a: 5); and "feigning", which is "the deliberate fabrication or gross exaggeration of psychological or physical symptoms without any assumptions about its goals" (ibid.: 6). Rogers then delineates another group of response styles, which he terms "simulated adjustment". Here, patients under- or misreport symptoms in order to present themselves favorably. Rogers distinguishes between "defensiveness", which is the "deliberate denial or gross minimization of physical and/or psychological symptoms" (2008a: 6); "social desirability", which "involves both the denial of negative characteristics and the attribution of positive qualities" (ibid.: 6); and "impression management", which includes "deliberate efforts to control others' perceptions of an individual", with those efforts being "more situationally driven than social desirability" (ibid.: 6).[12] Finally, there are other response styles that can be applied when the ones mentioned above do not hold. For example, patients can respond in an irrelevant manner where their responses do not correspond to the clinical questions asked; they may respond in a random way, for example, when they answer an assessment questionnaire without paying attention to the actual questions asked; or they use "hybrid responding", a mixture of some of the response styles listed above (Rogers 2008a: 7).

This typology applied in medicine seems to me to include three main components, not all of which are clearly differentiated, though: (1) the manner or kind of unreliability (e.g. does a patient present false symptoms or does he or she withhold information about symptoms?); (2) the level of consciousness and, consequently, agency on the part of the patient (is the patient's unreliability deliberate or a form of behavior the patient cannot help); (3) the motivation or reason(s) behind the patient's unreliability (what benefits or advantages does the patient (consciously or unselfconsciously) seek in being unreliable?). Perhaps this typology can be a useful frame of reference for narratology, too. After all, it does remind one of similar typologies of unreliable narration in literary studies (see Hansen 2007; Phelan 2005). Researchers in dissimulation studies and literary narratologists alike are interested in questions concerning the occurrence, the extent, the quality and reasons for or causes of unreliability. The main difference seems to be that literary narratologists pay more attention to narrative mediation and to the rhetorical design of unreliable texts whereas such questions do not feature in the literature on the clinical assessment of malingering and deception. One reason might be connected to the assumed union of author and narrator in conversational narratives, which, if taken for granted, does away with the necessity to analyze various levels of a piece of narration, e.g. what the narrative says on a

---

12 It is interesting to note that these response styles are similar to speakers' verbal styles as outlined in pragma-linguistic politeness research. Thus, Geoffrey Leech (1983) added to Grice's "cooperative principle" what he termed the "politeness principle", which includes six maxims that state how speakers ought to behave in order not to be offensive or in order to portray themselves in as favorably a light as possible: the tact maxim, the generosity maxim, the approbation maxim, the modesty maxim, the agreement maxim and the sympathy maxim.

surface level and which more or less hidden message is also conveyed (cf. Phelan's [2005] "narrator" and "disclosure" functions). However, it is precisely these more finely-grained distinctions that in my view ought to be considered in real-life narratives as well. By contrast, clinical researchers and practitioners do not seem to be overly interested in *how* patients tell their stories since the discrepancies—if any are to be found—are considered to reside in *what* patients tell in contrast to clinical evidence or counter-reports by others. As I will further argue below, this could be viewed as a rather limited perspective, which may not prove to be helpful in actual doctor-patient encounters. The typology of various response styles presented above already begs the question to what extent it is applicable in everyday medical practice.

First of all, the different categories partially strike one as potentially less distinct when it comes to actual practice than they appear to be in theory. Second, these lists do not seem to distinguish clearly enough between deliberate and unselfconscious forms of unreliable narration, nor between levels of consciousness and motivation or reasons: Some terms try to capture possible motivations behind patients' behavior (e.g. malingering and defensiveness) while others do not (e.g. nondisclosure or feigning). Could one say that there are different degrees of unreliability? This is not a trivial question if one considers that unreliability in patient self-reports may be unintentional and may be attributable to factors the patient is not in control of. Research has shown, for example, that the selective functioning of our memories contributes to incomplete or distorted patient narratives surrounding their illnesses, which can in turn lead to difficulties in medical history-taking and subsequent treatment (Barsky 2002; Offer/Kaiz/Howard et al. 2000).

Phelan's discussion of degrees of unreliability along the three communicational functions of "reporting", "interpreting" and "evaluating" might be illuminating in this context. Phelan identifies six kinds of unreliability, "combining the activities of narrators and audiences" (2005: 51): "misreporting" involves the false reporting of events and facts; "misreading" is the wrong interpretation of events or facts because of lack of knowledge or wrong perception; "misregarding" includes a breach of ethical or moral codes through lying, denial, etc.; "underreporting" can be found when a narrator tells us less than he or she knows; "underreading" is an insufficient (rather than an incorrect) interpretation of events or facts due to lack of knowledge or misperception; and "underregarding" involves an evaluation that is essentially correct but does not go far enough (ibid.: 51–52). The terms "misreporting" and "underreporting" map onto what I called the manner or kind of unreliability in patient narratives, while the terms "misreading" or "underreading" and "misregarding" or "underregarding" span a continuum of unreliable behavior that takes into account the narrator's awareness/agency and his or her possible motivations or reasons. Thus, as I mentioned above, patients may be deliberately untruthful (misregarding) or they may misinterpret or insufficiently understand their own symptoms (misreading or underreading) or they may engage in half-truths out of instinctual self-protection (underregarding). Let us now turn to another area in medicine that appears to be diametrically opposed to the clinical or evidence-based approach, namely: narrative medicine.

2. Narrative Medicine:
Unreliable Stories and Patient Empowerment

Narrative medicine can be seen as an alternative paradigm to evidence-based medicine. It is closely related to the so-called medical humanities, which forges links between medicine and arts and humanities subjects (cf. Greenhalgh/Hurwitz 1998; Charon 2006). As the subtitle of Rita Charon's book *Narrative Medicine: Honoring the Stories of Illness* suggests, one of the main aims of narrative medicine is to reinstate narrative at the core of medical practice, to treat patients more holistically and to place them at the center of doctor-patient encounters. The more surprising it is that unreliability does not seem to play a major role in this research area or, if it is mentioned, the focus tends to lie on the doctor's role in this context. Perhaps this is not so surprising after all if one considers that the tacit political agenda behind narrative medicine is to give the patient a voice and thus to empower him or her. For example, Shapiro (2011: 71) argues that: "Ultimately, the patient's story belongs to the patient, not to the physician and not to the literary scholar, and needs to be approached with humility, respect and honouring, as well as mastery and critique". Potential trouble with patient narratives is rhetorically brushed aside for the cause of patient empowerment: "Stories can act as sites of oppression, self-delusion and dissimulation to be sure, but they can also serve as acts of self-empowerment" (Shapiro 2011: 70). Similarly, DasGupta contends that the problem lies with medical professionals, who in her view are unwilling to accept unreliable patient narratives as they are:

> Modern medicine struggles to gauge its relationship with patients who are clearly ignorant of or mistaken in certain clinical facts, self-deceptive, or dishonest in presenting their stories. The standard practice in medicine has been to deem certain people "bad historians"—the drug-seeking, manipulative patient; the adolescent who cannot remember her last sexual intercourse or menses; the senior citizen with no record of his numerous potentially interacting medications; the heavy alcohol drinker who obviously underreports her intake. In the increasingly

technical world of medicine, this logic is in danger of becoming extended to almost all patient stories, none of which can duplicate the unyielding veracity of an MRI, a blood hemoglobin level, a muscle biopsy. In the context of evidence-based science, where all truth has become knowable through rigorous experimentation and interpretation, the ambiguity and complexity of patient stories renders them too often at the margins of medical practice. Stories that are not corroborated by "scientific evidence" are "false," and their tellers are at best considered deluded and at worst condemned as liars. (2006: 442)

It is interesting to see that DasGupta seems to have certain kinds of unreliable patients in mind here: patients with whom we might be more inclined to feel sympathetic towards because they apparently cannot help being unreliable. Are these the kinds of unreliable patients that are taken into focus in dissimulation studies? Again, agency and patients' levels of awareness play a crucial role for those divergent views. It seems to me that narrative medicine and the medical humanities start out from a much more benevolent image of patients when it comes to questions of unreliability, yet perhaps so much so that they ignore (or at least do not discuss) the fact that unreliability in the sense of malingering and deception can also pose a problem to doctors and to society.[13]

Kathryn Montgomery, in her book *How Doctors Think*, considers this point from the doctors' perspective and identifies a general skeptical stance in medical practice, which she, however, also does not view uncritically:

Physicians are especially dependent on the personal report of events by the individual most affected, and, like political and social historians, they are well aware that the information they gather, even from a well-intentioned, honest informant, is always narrow, incomplete, and potentially flawed. [...] This skepticism does not erase the value of the patient's story. The physician's article of faith, that the patient "knows" the diagnosis or its pathognomonic clues and is by far the most important source of diagnostic information, is not inconsistent with an all-purpose skepticism: the belief that truth is less "out there" to be discovered than constructed by the clinical observer. Yet over time, in the community of discourse that is clinical medicine, that larger epistemological skepticism gives way to a persistent, commonsensical suspicion of the patient's reliability and an unwillingness to waste time, look foolish, be misled, or, worst of all, be duped. (2006: 107)

---

13 Perhaps another distinction proposed by Phelan (2007), namely that between "estranging" and "bonding" unreliability, can be informative in this context. Phelan considers the effects that certain types of unreliability in fictional stories can have on readers and claims that in cases of "estranging unreliability" the distance between narrator and audience is increased while in "bonding unreliability" it is decreased. Scholars in the fields of narrative medicine and the medical humanities seem to embrace a notion of "bonding unreliability" when conceiving of patients.

Medical professionals, Montgomery suggests, seem to extend the charge of unreliability to all patients and thus attempt to safeguard themselves against betrayal and uncomfortable situations. This point is also raised by Good and DelVecchio Good (2000: 67), who argue that: "Physicians learn to distrust patients' stories as inaccurate by purpose or by accident. They learn to "edit" patients' accounts. And at times, medical history is juxtaposed to patients' fictions as the real to the unreal". The term "fictions" here is telling. It suggests that what is at stake is also a difference in expectational frames and textual genres doctors and patients operate in. Medical charts are incongruent with patient narratives and the medical shorthand doctors use does not adequately capture the "messiness" of patients' stories.[14] Charon (2006) even refers to unreliability in fictional texts and how reading such texts may train doctors for their job because "such confuse and contradictory sets of tellings obtain regularly in the hospital" (Charon 2006: 111). Again, instead of seeing the problem in patients, Charon suggests that doctors ought to pay more attention to how patients tell their stories in order to be better able to figure out what may be going on or what may be wrong with the patient:

> How wasteful that doctors can revoke from patients the *form* of their telling, restricting them to bare content. […] If the professional listens stereophonically for what the person says and also what the body says, he or she has the rare opportunity not only to hear the body out but also to translate the body's news to the person who lives in it. (2006: 98–99)

Now, what Charon addresses here in metaphors of sound are problems in doctor-patient communication more generally rather than the specific issue of unreliability. And yet, what she has to say about doctors' listening skills could be relevant for that particular issue, too.

When it comes to unreliability in the sense of doctors and patients having difficulties in sharing the same narrative, an interesting aspect to consider is the role doctors' biases play in this context. This is a point raised by neurologist and neuropsychologist Richard E. Cytowic (2003) in his reflection on his synesthesia research. Cytowic claims that, while it is common to attribute unreliability in patient narratives to the way patients "embroider" their stories, less attention has been paid to the experimenter's or clinician's assumptions "when translating introspective reports into scientifically useful characterizations" (2003: 161). Cytowic presents synesthesia cases as examples, where patients often use metaphors to express what their sensations feel like. Since scientists in the field for a long time held on to established concepts about modularity and

---

14   As Cytowic (2003: 158) has it: "Part of the problem is that patients frequently *interpret* events instead of *reporting* them straightforwardly as one would wish ideally" (italics in original).

functionalism in the neural system, Cytowic argues, they discarded synesthesia as a non-medical condition or even denied its existence. It was only when researchers began to listen more carefully to the metaphors patients used and tried to translate those metaphors into sensory qualities that they realized they had to rethink the way they conceptualized brain organization and functioning. Cytowic contends that what is required is "interplay between first person and third person accounts. A dialogue or structured questioning between clinician and subject constitutes a second person relation between shared knowledge about experiences" (Cytowic 2003: 162).

3. Narrative Practice, Dialogue and Unreliability

The last few examples have focused on a kind of unreliability that seems to be prevalent in doctor-patient communication in general: the assumed unreliability of patient narratives that hinges around their "different" interpretations and different ways of talking about illness experiences. Whether one says one has a tingling sensation or a pricking sensation in one's arm, for example, may be important for a doctor's ultimate diagnosis. In the worst case, using the wrong words may lead to a misdiagnosis and to inadequate subsequent treatment. This is of course a far cry from the kinds of unreliability investigated in the clinical assessment of malingering and deception. Patients engaging in the latter willfully and actively present information that is untrue or distorted in order to achieve certain goals. This discrepancy shows that one first needs to define the term "unreliability" more precisely before one can continue using it to describe certain phenomena. Yet, where does one draw a line? As I discussed in this paper, unreliability may be due to the failings of one's memory rather than because one has deliberately left out vital information; or a patient's psychological disposition may include self-delusional tendencies. Clinical psychology with its research on patient response styles and forms of dissimulation offers a framework that attempts to differentiate between degrees and types of unreliable responses. However, researchers in this field also admit that their statistical methods may not be one hundred percent reliable and that it very much depends on the specific clinical context and the case at hand which measuring scale is most suitable and yields the best results. Furthermore, those measuring scales might not be of much help to non-specialists and to doctors who see a great many number of patients for very limited time spans, e.g. general practitioners. They usually have to decide within a few minutes whether what the patient presents with is plausible and, if they suspect malingering or deception, to then take or not take appropriate action. However, what that appropriate action is may be equally difficult to decide.

As far as doctors' general skepticism of patient narratives is concerned, it is difficult to gauge whether this skepticism is really all-pervasive or whether doctors are not much more lenient and sympathetic towards patients in their everyday practice. Even if they are not, this skepticism can be viewed as a means of survival and self-protection on the one hand, or as an expression of medicine's restrictive professionalism on the other. This is a point of interpretation and probably also depends on whether one considers such questions from the perspective of a patient or from that of a doctor. Finally, unreliability can be regarded as something that not only resides in patients but that medical practitioners also contribute towards because their own biases may preclude a deeper understanding of what patients have to tell them. Ultimately, I would concur with Cytowic (2003) and Charon (2006) and argue that what is needed is genuine dialogue between doctors and patients and more sensitivity on the part of doctors towards the intricacies of face-to-face communication. Such communication, one could argue, always has features of unreliability.

Let us return to the patient narrative with which I began this paper. Of course I do not suggest that this narrative is unreliable in the sense that the patient does not tell the truth about her illness experience. However, one must not forget that any kind of talk is situated, i.e. it is anchored in certain interactional and cultural frames of expectations to which interlocutors accommodate. This also means that speakers will always have their specific agenda and conversational goals they want to achieve. In this sense unreliability (in its "softer" version) is not a rare phenomenon or a curious side effect of talk but can in fact be regarded as its default condition. If one has a closer look at this patient's narrative one can find all the features that are typical of a style which aims at engaging the listener, creating involvement and establishing rapport—and which may also be used in the service of making one's story more trustworthy. Thus, the patient, for example, uses the discourse marker "you know" to ensure the listener's attention, and her story is replete with what Deborah Tannen (1989) termed "constructed dialogue", i.e. dialogue which pretends to give a verbatim rendition of an original speech situation but more likely (re)constructs it in the given verbal interaction. Thus, she recounts what the doctors said to her: "'First of all you said your pain was like this, and now you're saying it's like this' and 'What do you mean?' and you almost feel that they're trying to tell you, 'You don't really have pain and you don't know what you're talking about'" (Interview CP 21). Rather than merely enlivening the depicted scene, constructed dialogue here quite clearly assumes the additional function of transporting the attitude or implicit thoughts of some of the characters in the story (see also Mildorf 2008), in this case the medical specialist the patient went to see. The patient suggests that her doctor did not fully trust the report of her physical pain and probably thought she was only making it up or imagining it. Now, whether this assessment of the situation is correct or whether it merely reflects the patient's own projection of how she felt misunderstood and neglected cannot be firmly established by someone listening to this story. This once again shows that whether what someone says is deemed reliable information or not also depends on the interlocutor's interpretation.

Interestingly, the patient furthermore almost consistently uses the second-person pronoun "you" in her narrative while talking about her own personal experience. I would classify this "you" as "doubly-deictic *you*" (Herman 1994) because it seems to fulfill several discursive functions at once: it generalizes the experience as generic "you" would do (everyone can experience this); at the same time it addresses the interlocutor and implies him/her in the experience as though he or she could potentially experience the same (this can happen to you, too); this address function is doubled because the interview is made available to an even larger Internet audience; finally, "you" is also related to the speaker herself since she talks about her own personal experience. In this last context, "you" seems to have a distancing effect because the patient chooses precisely not to use the first-person pronoun. Together with the generalizing function, this pronoun can also be said to create a more authoritative and "reliable" account because the experience of feeling misunderstood is not merely presented as the patient's personal experience but as an experience that is presumably shared by others, too. Now, again, whether other people have the same experiences with doctors or not is for the interlocutor and for us to decide, and our assessment will depend on what we believe to be true about doctors' practices and attitudes towards patients (in other words, what our frame of expectation is). In this regard, unreliability in patient narratives also needs to be considered from a cognitive perspective in analogy to unreliability in fictional texts, where the reader's online evaluation of what he/she reads will influence the overall interpretation of the text (see also Nünning 1998).[15]

---

15 For a theoretical account of unreliability that seeks to integrate cognitive and rhetorical approaches, see Nünning (2008).

4. Conclusion

In this contribution, I have investigated the notion of "unreliability" in the context of patient narratives. I think my survey of uses of this term in different areas of medicine has shown that "unreliability" is at least as complex an issue here as it is in literary narratology. The main difference is that unreliability in patient narratives has real and often detrimental ramifications for all parties involved. The possibility of unreliability in patients creates a burden for doctors, who have the mandate to identify and to deal with it. Unreliability in the sense of Phelan's "misreading" or "underreading" may impede successful communication between doctors and patients and may, in the worst case, lead to wrong diagnoses. Deliberate malingering and deception, finally, incurs unnecessary costs for the health care system and may contribute towards a more negative image of patients. It is not least for these possible consequences that unreliability stands in great need of clarification and definition, which ultimately requires a rapprochement between clinical or scientific branches of medicine, alternative paradigms such as narrative medicine and everyday medical practice—especially that at the baseline, as it were, where doctors truly function as gatekeepers.

Furthermore, I hope to have demonstrated that there is considerable overlap between questions concerning unreliability asked in medicine on the one hand and in literary narratology on the other. This suggests that these two areas of inquiry should perhaps also enter a dialogue. What can medicine learn from narratology and narratology from medicine as regards the issue of unreliability? Narratology—and literary studies more generally—can offer medicine tools and approaches for reading and interpreting unreliability that may help sensitize medical students during their studies. What are textual features to look out for or be attentive to? Which ethical dilemmas does unreliability create for the presented characters, for narrators and for readers engaging with those characters and narrators? Practicing close reading can alert students to the intricacies of language use more generally and can help them become better listeners.[16] One should add the caveat, though, that the narratological toolkit offered for such purposes would need to be simplified and cut to measure, as it were. In turn, medicine can offer narratology fresh ways of looking at unreliability. After all, many unreliable narrators in literary texts can be classified as pathological. By comparing the terminologies applied in dissimulation

---

[16] A recent study from the area of pain management in medicine corroborates the assumption that a narrative approach is needed for doctors to be able to listen better to patients' metaphors and similes and to afford them the space to tell their stories (Clarke/Anthony/Grey et al. 2012).

studies with those used in narratology, one may be in a better position to arrive at demarcation lines and to develop an integrative core typology along the lines suggested in this paper. Clearly, more work can be done in this direction.

Acknowledgment

I thank the research team at the DIPEx charity, notably Prof. Sue Ziebland, for kindly allowing me to use the material from their Healthtalkonline website.

Works Cited

AON Consulting. "One Billion Man Hours Lost to Sickies across Europe Each Year." *AON Global Media Relations*. (July 14, 2010): http://aon.mediaroom.com/index.php?s=43&item=1957&printable
(last retrieved: December 29, 2012)

Barsky, Arthur J. 2002. "Forgetting, Fabricating, and Telescoping: The Instability of the Medical History." *Archives of Internal Medicine* 162.9: 981–984.

Bode, Christoph. 2011. *Der Roman*. 2nd ed. Tübingen: Francke.

Chassan, Jack B. 1957. "On the Unreliability of Reliability and Some Other Consequences of the Assumption of Probabilistic Patient States." *Psychiatry: Interpersonal and Biological Processes* 20.2: 163–171.

Charon, Rita. 2006. *Narrative Medicine: Honoring the Stories of Illness*. Oxford: Oxford University Press.

Clarke, Amanda, Geraldine Anthony, Denise Grey et al. 2012. "'I feel so stupid because I can't give a proper answer...' How Older Adults Describe Chronic Pain: A Qualitative Study." *BMC Geriatrics* 12.78. http://www.biomedcentral.com/1471–2318/12/78 (last retrieved: March 1, 2013)

Interview CP21. 2008. [Interview transcript].
http://www.healthtalkonline.org/InterviewTranscript.aspx?Interview=419&Clip=0 (last retrieved: March 1, 2013)

Cytowic, Richard E. 2003. "The Clinician's Paradox: Believing Those You Must Not Trust." *Journal of Consciousness Studies* 10.9–10: 157–166.

DasGupta, Sayantani. 2006. "Being John Doe Malkovich: Truth, Imagination, and Story in Medicine." *Literature and Medicine* 25.2: 439–462.

Garden, Rebecca. 2010. "Telling Stories about Illness and Disability: The Limits and Lessons of Narrative." *Perspectives in Biology and Medicine* 53.1: 121–135.

Goffman, Erving. 1981. *Forms of Talk*. Philadelphia, PA: University of Pennsylvania Press.

Good, Byron J. & Mary-Jo DelVecchio Good. 2000. "'Fiction' and 'Historicity' in Doctors' Stories: Social and Narrative Dimensions of Learning Medicine." In: Cheryl Mattingly & Linda C. Garro (eds.). *Narrative and the Cultural Construction of Illness and Healing*. Berkeley, CA: University of California Press. 50–69.

Granacher, Robert P. & David T. R. Berry. 2008. "Feigned Medical Presentations." In: Rogers (ed.). 2008. 145–156.

Hall, Harold V. & Joseph G. Poirier. 2001. *Detecting Malingering and Deception: Forensic Distortion Analysis*. 2nd ed. Boca Raton, FL: CRC Press.

Hansen, Per Krogh. 2007. "Reconsidering the Unreliable Narrator." *Semiotica* 165: 227–246.

Hardwig, John. 1997. "Autobiography, Biography and Narrative Ethics." In: Hilde L. Nelson (ed.). *Stories and Their Limits: Narrative Approaches to Bioethics*. New York, NY: Routledge. 50–64.

Herman, David. 1994. "Textual *You* and Double Deixis in Edna O'Brien's *A Pagan Place*." *Style* 28.3: 378–410.

Heyd, Theresa. 2011. "Unreliability: The Pragmatic Perspective Revisited." *Journal of Literary Theory* 5.1: 3–17.

Hunter, Kathryn M. 1993. *Doctors' Stories: The Narrative Structure of Medical Knowledge*. Princeton, NJ: Princeton University Press.

Leech, Geoffrey. 1983. *Principles of Pragmatics*. London: Longman.

Mildorf, Jarmila. 2007. *Storying Domestic Violence: Constructions and Stereotypes of Abuse in the Discourse of General Practitioners*. Lincoln, NE: University of Nebraska Press.

Mildorf, Jarmila. 2008. "Thought Presentation and Constructed Dialogue in Oral Storytelling: Limits and Possibilities of a Cross-Disciplinary Narratology." *Partial Answers* 6.2: 279–300.

Montgomery, Kathryn. 2006. *How Doctors Think: Clinical Judgment and the Practice of Medicine*. Oxford: Oxford University Press.

Nünning, Ansgar. 1998. "*Unreliable Narration* zur Einführung: Grundzüge einer kognitiv-narratologischen Theorie und Analyse unglaubwürdigen Erzählens." In: Ansgar Nünning (ed.). *Unreliable Narration: Studien zur Theorie und Praxis unglaubwürdigen Erzählens in der englischsprachigen Erzählliteratur*. Trier: WVT. 3–39.

Nünning, Ansgar. 2008. "Reconceptualizing the Theory, History and Generic Scope of Unreliable Narration: Towards a Synthesis of Cognitive and Rhetorical Approaches." In: Elke D'hoker & Gunther Martens (eds.). *Narrative Unreliability in the Twentieth-Century First-Person Novel*. Narratologia 14. Berlin/New York, NY: De Gruyter. 29–76.

Offer, Daniel, Marjorie Kaiz, Kenneth I. Howard et al. 2000. "The Altering of Reported Experiences." *Journal of the American Academy of Child and Adolescent Psychiatry* 39.6: 735–742.
Parsons, Talcott. 1991 [1951]. *The Social System*. London: Routledge.
Phelan, James. 2005. *Living to Tell about It: A Rhetoric and Ethics of Character Narration*. Ithaca, NY: Cornell University Press.
Phelan, James. 2007. "Estranging Unreliability, Bonding Unreliability, and the Ethics of *Lolita*." *Narrative* 15.2: 222–238.
Radley, Alan & Ruth Green. 1987. "Illness as Adjustment: A Methodology and Conceptual Framework." *Sociology of Health and Illness* 9.2: 179–207.
Rimmon-Kenan, Shlomith. 1983. *Narrative Fiction: Contemporary Poetics*. London: Routledge.
Rogers, Richard (ed.). 2008. *Clinical Assessment of Malingering and Deception*. 3rd ed. New York, NY: The Guilford Press.
Rogers, Richard. 2008a. "An Introduction to Response Styles." In: Rogers (ed.). 2008. 3–13.
Rogers, Richard. 2008b. "Detection Strategies for Malingering and Defensiveness." In: Rogers (ed.). 2008. 14–35.
Shapiro, Johanna. 2011. "Illness Narratives: Reliability, Authenticity and the Empathic Witness." *Medical Humanities* 37.2: 68–72.
Shen, Dan. "Unreliability." In: Peter Hühn, Jan C. Meister, John Pier et al. (eds.). *The Living Handbook of Narratology*. Hamburg: Hamburg University Press. URL = hup.sub.uni-hamburg.de/lhn/index.php?title=Unreliability&oldid=1529 (last retrieved: December 24, 2012)
Stein, Lynda A. R. & Richard Rogers. 2008. "Denial and Misreporting of Substance Abuse." In: Rogers (ed.). 2008. 87–108.
Tannen, Deborah. 1989. *Talking Voices: Repetition, Dialogue and Imagery in Conversational Discourse*. Cambridge: Cambridge University Press.

BRIGITTE BOOTHE & DRAGICA STOJKOVIĆ
(Zürich)

Communicating Dreams: On the Struggle for Reliable Dream Reporting and the Unreliability of Dream Reports

1. Unreliable Narration in Dream Reporting

I dreamt such magnificent crap last night.
(Amalie)

Looking at the narratives which are studied by psychologists and psychoanalysts, the topic of unreliability seems to be most pertinent and crucial to the analyses of dreams. Even if one takes the sincerity of speakers for granted, the fact that dreams remain obscure to the people trying to report them poses interesting problems; in narratological terms, the difference between the functions of the 'experiencing I' (the dreamer) and the 'narrating I' (the teller) shapes the dream reports which are then studied by psychologists. The ways in which tellers create narrative (dream) worlds are part of the process of understanding and interpreting dreams, and, more often than not, the listener forms an important part of the process. The study of dreams thus offers a fertile field for the exploration of (un)reliable narratives.

Dreams are mental activities which are aimed at regression; they serve as a psychophysiological regulative. The subjects of dream reports are hallucinatory events, which occur in a state of mental and physical regression and under the suspension of orientation functions. Nightly dreaming fulfills regulative functions in the regressive state of sleep. Still, there is open discussion on how these regulative functions are to be understood (see Mosch 2012; Solms/Turnbull 2002; Wiegand/Spreti/Förstl 2006). The controversial discussion ranges from a wish-fulfilling regulative of well-being, across prospective (Revonsuo 2000), problem-solving and exercise functions on up to mental reorganization. These are all more or less plausible assumptions about dreams as a regulation phenomenon (Domhoff 2005). Following Koukkou and Lehmann (1983), dreaming can be conceptualized as a manifestation of mental activities both regressive and targeted at regression. Solms (2000b) provides the neuroscientific basis for the Freudian claim (1900) that this regression-targeted mental activity benefits sleep continuity.

According to Freud, the hallucinatory impressions during sleep are a product of psychodynamic compromise and defense mechanisms. En route to being remembered this product is subject to additional psychodynamically motivated modifications; furthermore, the oral or written representation of a dream is irreducibly interwoven with articulation processes which Freud calls "secondary revision" (1953 [1900]).

As far as the study of unreliable narration is concerned, dream reports are interesting because they can be regarded as a form of biographical self-portrayal. An influential side-effect of *The Interpretation of Dreams* by Freud was the innovation of this kind of self-representation: The dream report is a form of testimony which mediates between the demands of mental life and those of external reality, combining them into a single enigmatic form. In this light, the dream protocol is a form of expressing the notoriously fragmentary and puzzling character of individual existence. Autobiographical self-reassurance manifests itself—and this became central to twentieth-century literature, arts and conceptions of identity—as a search in the face of irreducible insecurity. Beginning with the twentieth century, the *Here I am and here I avow myself* subtly transforms into the twisted stumbling of Godotesque characters, the "old man's ramblings" of the autobiographical sketches of Gregor von Rezzori. Although this was not Freud's explicit intention, *The Interpretation of Dreams* is an exemplary testimony of the "crisis of subjectivity", representing a personal history of mistaking oneself and of punctual self-reassurance. This created a model for twentieth-century articulation of subjectivity: The process of autobiographical self-reassurance manifests itself as an act of articulating, determining and searching in the face of the unknown. Let us not forget however: Freud was a physician and a scientist. He did not take an interest in the tragic or comic gesture of self-loss for its own sake. Rather, it presented an opportunity to gain insight into the realm of object relations, dependency and the psychodynamics of the various forms of internalization.

One of the most interesting features of dream reports is their oscillation between distance and appropriation. The dream report as a specific and non-interchangeable form of communication possesses a rhetorical repertoire which allows for the articulation of the moments of irreducible uncertainty, the fragmentary character and the enigmaticity of its subject. Reporting a dream means using unsaturated speech: The dream report is not self-sufficient; rather, it is part of a competitive commenting process. Dream discourse is a dialogical journey from self-alienation to punctual self-appropriation. This oscillation between distance and appropriation, the back and forth between points of reference outside the individual psyche and strategies of mental processing (primary and secondary revision) is central to dream communication.

Extensive text analytical, clinical and process-oriented documentation of dream data was made possible by the cooperation between Horst Kächele and Erhard Mergenthaler of the University of Ulm, which now provides voluminous multimethodological and interdisciplinary research on a prominent psychoanalytic case consisting of more than 500 sessions well documented through both writing and audio recording and supplemented by a comprehensive dream database, which allowed for the systematic investigation of the dream manuscripts (see Kächele/Albani/Buchheim et al. 2006; Thomä/Kächele 2006; Mathys 2007, 2008).

What occurs during a dream is experienced as real by the dreamer, but when later recounted, this sense of reality is discarded as an illusion. The occurrences in the dream become peculiar, because they cannot be understood, classified or categorized—for now—and become worthy of attention because their enigmatic character arouses interest (see Boothe 2008). How persons report their dreams demonstrates how they understand the phenomenon of the dream and how they conceive the dream event; it also influences the kind of narratives they create:

- *Claim of privacy*: In reporting a dream the person makes clear that the dream is a private experience, that it represents an event from a person's *mental life*, and not an experience that could be intersubjectively shared.
- *Privacy in a passive-receptive mode:* In reporting a dream speakers make clear that they are recipients, not stage directors of this emerging event.
- *Passive-receptive mode and naive ignorance:* In reporting a dream speakers make clear that this concerns events that, for now, defy understanding and categorization. The dreamer imparts this innocently enough, from the distance of being amazed—an important distinction from reports of psychotic experiences.
- *Privacy and shortcomings of remembering:* In reporting a dream the person makes clear that the event in the dream emanates from inner life, is past tense, and can only be grasped retrospectively and with limited certainty.
- *Claim of privacy due to reporting difficulties:* In reporting a dream speakers make clear that these are events from their mental life that are difficult to report (see Gülich 2005). Reporting is difficult because (a) the speakers are articulating experiences that are not intersubjectively shared, for which there is no common basis for understanding (privacy problem); (b) the dream evaporates quickly

from memory (elusiveness); (c) remembering cannot be validated (validation problem); and (d) the event itself is enigmatic, i.e. is not immediately grasped and categorized in its relevance and meaning (need for interpretation). Psychotic experiences are known to not be articulated in the mode of reporting difficulties but in an assured state of delusion.
- *Invitation for interpretation:* In reporting a dream the person emphasizes the non-transparent, puzzling nature of the experience and indicates that the message of the dream is not, in and of itself, sufficient, but requires supplementing. This involves an invitation for interpretation that motivates and contextualizes the dream occurrences, making them beneficial for everyday life practice.

Especially the first three aspects highlight the sincerity as well as passivity of the experiencing I. In addition, the intention of narrators to truthfully tell their experiences and understand the dream through the creation of their narratives becomes visible. A special challenge, however, results from the limited ability of the narrator. In the reflective distance of a protocol, dream reports articulate hallucinated impressions which do not bear any meaning outside the privacy of the dreamer's mind, but which, at the same time, are perceived by the dreamer as in need of interpretation.

The subject of the dream report is elusive, fragile, enigmatic, and inaccessible to others. It is only developed into a narrative world, following a narrative logic, during the process of telling what one has vividly experienced while sleeping. Dream reporters may say: "I had such a bizarre dream" or "that was a frightening dream" or—as Amalie once announced: "I dreamt such magnificent crap last night" (Boothe 2006; Mathys 2006). They emphasize the note-worthiness of the dream and—from an observing, reflective distance—report hallucinated impressions. Dream and dream commentary have a complementary relationship (see Boothe 2000). The dream teller retrospectively remodels the collection of pieces; dreamer and commentator (this can be one and the same person in two different roles) can explore the report in the narrative perspective of expectation and fulfillment (see Kilroe 2000; Knudson/Adame/Finocan 2006). The development of narrative episodes is geared, both in literature and in everyday life, towards a happy ending or a catastrophe. This means it is geared towards a wish-guided development of events, which is in line with personal, self-centered concerns (see Boothe 2004). It is important to emphasize: the narrative presentation of events transforms a person's world: the world becomes the world-for-me. The narrative cosmos organizes itself according to a dynamic that veers between fulfillment and disaster.

In the context of dream reports, unreliability should be assessed with regard to several criteria. If we apply the concept of the unreliability of reporting to dream protocols, the following picture emerges:
- The points of reference are exclusively private, withdrawn from intersubjective accessibility and difficult to remember. *We are dealing with referential unreliability.*
- Dreams are phenomena which are difficult to recapitulate. Dream-reporters engage in a sequential structure of dream articulation, in which the processuality of formulating, gaps, ruptures and fragmentation at the expense of transparency und conciseness play a central role. *We are dealing with unreliability as precarious to the conciseness of the report.*
- The dream report lacks self-sufficiency: it is akin to a question or a riddle. Every possible contextualization and narrativization ex post is bound to remain in a state of uncertainty. *We are dealing with unreliability as the irreducible tentativeness of interpretation.*
- On the one hand, the author of a dream report is unreliable: His articulative and mnemonic capabilities are—according to psychoanalytical doctrine—inevitably influenced by unconscious wish-defense-dynamics. On the other hand, he is reliable: His report has the sole purpose of recounting the remembered impressions of nightly dreaming to the best of his memory and the best of his ability to communicate with potential listeners. *We are dealing with the reliability of the honest reporter.*

Communicating a personal dream implies dealing with unreliable impressions, which are articulated by a reliable reporter employing unreliable means.

Narratives about dreams demand contextualization; moreover, the addressee assumes an important role, since dreams are often re-created on the basis of dialogical reflection. Recounting dreams is linked to the expectation that a subsequent (inter- or intrapersonal) conversation provides a retrospective contextualization, which helps to establish the relevance of the mental life in dream-state for waking life concerns. Dream reports are directed towards a recipient who enters a dialogical reflection on the mental processes during dreams. Recounting a dream means to retroactively give a narrative account of one's memory of a hallucinated event, to lexically stage and dialogically communicate the moments of being seized and struck, the bewilderment, loss of control and opacity in the state of dreaming. In contrast to other animals, human beings are capable of (fragmentary) recapitulation of nightly sensory input. Human beings are able to set themselves in relation to these findings through language: The nightly hallucinations form the basis for memory traces, which the dreamer in the awake state documents by means of everyday language. This document serves as the starting point for the analysis of and commenting on a dream.

Communicating a dream is making a claim for the relevance of a private matter, representing mental life and impressions which one has been exposed to, and marking one's reliance on a communicative response. To report one's dream is to give narrative form to the obscure (see Boothe 2001: 101–113). The speaker is prone to carry out extensive work when it comes to formulating the dream. His struggle for articulation apostrophizes the challenge to put into words the problems of formulation. Dreams are not the only private sensations, though, which pose a considerable articulative challenge, as Gülich and Schöndienst (1999: 199–227) point out in reference to oral recapitulation of epileptic auras by individuals concerned. In dreams and in certain extraordinary states of mind like epileptic auras, the ego is confronted with impressions which are not suited for adaption and connection in everyday conversation, but which, nevertheless, force the subject to communicate. There is a tension between the desire for a response in the face of being seized by peculiar sensations and the possibility of articulating them in a manner suitable for discourse within a cultural space. Dream articulation is inventive and aims at establishing the willingness to respond as well as emotional participation by the listener and dialogue partner. This is achieved by the readiness of the recipient to engage in the formulation process, to participate in a common search for possibilities of communication. The listener becomes a companion in travelling through unstable terrain. To encounter a dialogue partner is to put an end to being on one's own when facing the intrusion of that which is difficult to utter; it means replacing an individual struggle with a shared quest for rendering possible and shaping articulation.

2. A Person Reporting a Dream Offers an Unreliable Collage of Recollections

What are the distinctive features of the articulation of dreams? First, it has to be stressed that a person reporting a dream offers an unreliable collage of recollections. In addition, psychoanalytic, depth psychological, *daseins*-analytical literature as well as data collected by empirical dream research provide a vast array of references (cf. Strauch/Meier 1996). The following reflections will focus on the dream reports presented by Freud in *The Interpretation of Dreams* (1900). We will be able to observe the linguistic practices by virtue of which a person marks the fact that he is communicating a dream. We want to retrace how he linguistically exhibits the unavailability of his personal mental life and we will be granted insight into how he connects his dreams to reality. When talking about dreams we are involved in a joint effort to envision what has been experienced—the dreamer by engaging in mental work aimed at remembering and formulation, the listener by mentally recreating images and scenes under the guidelines of the descriptions uttered by the dream reporter. We receive dream reports and we recount dreams by discursively accentuating the fact that we are alluding to an event retrospectively classified as hallucinatory. We articulate a reference. The reference to an event, which, without action on our part and unintentionally, has taken place in our imagination during sleep, an incident beyond the sphere of influence of our self-disposal. A fleeting and enigmatic mental occurrence consigned to the interpretative attentiveness of the other. The reporter of a dream presents himself in a state of *naive ignorance*. He retells a dream as an event which has happened both within and to him. To be recapitulated only by one person, i.e. the dreamer himself, the constituent parts of the event are regathered from memory in order to be put into place and strung together by means of linguistic fixation. The reporter establishes a distance of astonishment. This does not suggest however, that he necessarily lacks education or psychological knowledge. Sometimes a person presents a dream and goes on to interpret it himself. In this case he goes back and forth between the position of the naive reporter and that of the oneirological expert—as it is the case in Freud.

Even under this condition, these two points of view, the position of the reporter on the one hand, who articulates his dream in a naive self-detached manner, and the position of the listener on the other, who integrates what has been uttered into a motivated context, remain systematically discernible. Although the reporter can point out connections to the events of the previous day, can suggest links to everyday reality and can subsequently take on the role of the dream expert, he typically abstains from personal statements. Rather, he releases his dream into an open space of questioning in order to "leave commenting to" the listener. Usually listeners take on this task voluntarily. Only in the case of transparent dreams, however, is commenting on their pictoriality obvious—though merely at first glance. In this case the communicative motion of "leaving to" is tantamount to initializing a closing process, which manifests itself as a staging of the absence of adoption and of naive disclosure. This gives rise to the characteristic impression that a dreamer unknowingly and in a state of naive self-detachment presents himself to a person capable of judgment. The listener receives the uncommented rapport and determines a way of reading the dream, which he either keeps to himself or shares with the dreamer.

What renders the dream rapport into a form of articulation dependent on dialogical supplementation? Is it the complementing commentary recontextualizing and shedding new light on the report? Let us take the first sentence of the following example:

> On account of certain events which had occurred in the city of Rome, it had become necessary to remove the children to safety, and this was done. The scene was then in front of a gateway, double doors in the ancient style […]. (Freud 1953 [1900]: 441)

Two different dream reports start as follows: "I received a communication from the town council of my birthplace …" (ibid.: 435) and: "I said to my wife that I had a piece of news for her, something quite special …" (ibid.: 558).

Prima facie, these examples do not feature what one might think of as distinctive oneiric features. We nevertheless ought to pay attention to how the speaker depicts the situation. It is important to point out the lack of a *motivating framework*.

For clarification, let us consider two further examples:

> A hill, on which there was something like an open-air closet: a very long seat with a large hole at the end of it. Its back edge was thickly covered with small heaps of faeces of all sizes and degrees of freshness. There were bushes behind the seat. I micturated on the seat; a long stream of urine washed everything clean; the lumps of faeces came away easily and fell into the opening. It was as though at the end there was still some left. (ibid.: 468–469)

The unquestioned acceptance of an immediately occurring event beyond reason and purpose, beyond a motivating framework, discloses a space of intransparency within the seemingly transparent. The impression of intransparency does not arise because of the obscurity of the reported actions, but rather because the event, even if it was inconspicuous und ordinary, remains uncontextualized. Something happens and this is perceived as, in the literal sense of the expression, *note-worthy*, because nobody tells us why it happens. It is 'left to' us, the listeners, to establish a motivating framework. The use of the rhetorical stratagem of 'leaving to/grant permission to' (epitrope) directly engages us, assigning us the role of commenting dialogue partners in the articulation process. The lack of a motivating framework is closely linked to the principle of the articulation of *collage-like sequencing*. The speaker combines pieces into pictures; take for example the *open-air closet* (see above). One part joins another. The speaker additively connects elements, thus creating the impression of a montage. Performing this kind of collage-like combination emphasizes the tentativeness of the composition, underlining the fragility of the inner cohesion of the image and its proneness to evaporate.

The dream reporter edits shots into sequences and takes inventory. Another good example is the short dream about a friend named Otto: *"My friend Otto was looking ill. His face was brown and he had protruding eyes"* (ibid.: 269). What is noteworthy about the recapitulative speech here, is that the speaker sequences shots, which allude to dramaturgy. Take the "coltsfoot" example:

> A crowd of people, a meeting of students.—A count (Thun or Taajfe) was speaking. He was challenged to say something about the Germans, and declared with a contemptuous gesture that their favourite flower was colt's foot, and put some sort of dilapidated leaf—or rather the crumpled skeleton of a leaf—into his buttonhole. I fired up—so I fired up, though I was surprised at my taking such an attitude. (Then, less distinctly:) It was as though I was in the Aula; the entrances were cordoned off and we had to escape [...]. (Freud 1953 [1900]: 209–210)

The speaker recapitulates *scenic figurations* or, as in the dream about the uncle, mere images or impressions. He is employing exactly the kind of ordinary, unornamented language which roman rhetorician Quintilian assigns to treating topics of everyday private life (Ueding 1976: 231 ff.). On the other hand, communicating one's dream is neither mundane nor random, but rather—in a naive way—laconic and solemn. This is probably due to the fact that the reporter finds himself being forced to express the visual and linguistic impressions which he received from mysterious sources, in the mode of *clarifying and specifying*, so he starts employing rhetorical devices such as *accumulatio, comparatio, climax* and verbose *amplificatio*. Thus, the listener is confronted with an articulation process which puts on display the struggle for the representation of hallucinated images. The closet dream is a graphic effort of accurate reproduction. The long "coltsfoot" dream highlights this struggle at various points:

> A count (Thun or Taajfe) was speaking ...; ... (Then, less distinctly:) It was as though I was in the Aula ...; ... (Becoming indistinct again) ... It was as though the second problem was to get out of the town, just as the first one had been to get out of the house .... I was now sitting in the compartment, which was like a carriage on the Stadtbahn [the suburban railway]; and in my buttonhole I had a peculiar plaited, long-shaped object, and beside it some violet-brown violets made of a stiff material. This greatly struck people. (At this point the scene broke off.). (Freud 1953 [1900]: 209–210)

Additionally, memories can be shaped by *emphasis, insistence and emotional charging*, as in the dream about the uncle:

> I. ... My friend R. was my uncle.—I had a great feeling of affection for him. II. I saw before me his face, somewhat changed. It was as though it had been drawn out lengthways. A yellow beard that surrounded it stood out especially clearly. (ibid.: 137)

The example illustrates the process of remembering from the point of view of a recipient, who remains unable to make sense of the message presented to him. Reassurement by virtue of revisualization is articulated in the following manner: *What happened? Is this what actually happened? What exactly happened?* A moment of intentionality—the emphatically accentuated affectionateness—is *added* to the impression and remains distant and enigmatic for this very reason. The search process is especially noticeable when dreams are being commented on with regard to their clarity, strangeness, or continuity. Grammatical particles like 'somehow' are very common. The often used term 'suddenly' marks the abruptness of a transition. The comparative 'as though' ("*It was as though it had been drawn out lengthways*"; "*as though it had been taken from a herbarium*") creates the impression of an event being hard to grasp (ibid.: 169). The before mentioned *articulation of the search process* further emphasizes the enigmatic distance. In this case, the speaker comments on the representation of dream events with respect to their level of clarity/opacity, familiarity/strangeness and continuity/discontinuity. Let us return to Freud's "coltsfoot" dream:

> [...] (Then, less distinctly:) It was as though I was in the Aula [...] (Becoming indistinct again)... It was as though the second problem was to get out of the town, just as the first one had been to get out of the house ..." "I was now sitting in the compartment, which was like a carriage on the Stadtbahn [the suburban railway]; and in my buttonhole I had a peculiar plaited, long-shaped object, and beside it some violet-brown violets made of a stiff material. This greatly struck people. (At this point the scene broke off.). (Freud 1953 [1900]: 209–210)

The dream report as a specific and non-interchangeable form of communication utilizes a rhetorical repertoire capable of articulating the fragmentary character, the enigmaticity and irreducible uncertainty of its subject. To communicate a dream is to employ a form of unsaturated speech: The dream rapport is not self-sufficient; rather, it raises the question of the origin and meaning of dream events. Offers to contextualize dreams range from an array of competing scientific methodologies to various prescientific practices of interpretation and communication. Not only tackling dreams but also discarding them reaches far back: Their proverbial rejection as null ("dreams are ten a penny") is far older than its neuroscientific plausibilization (see Hobson/McCarley 1977) and can be traced back to ancient literature. We are dealing with both an affinity and aversion to dreams on a historical, cultural and individual level. These attitudes may shift and take turns with regard to their dominance. It is the merit of psychoanalysis to have given a greater scientific importance to attitudes willing to take dreams seriously.

There is a unique relation between the impressive unreliability of dream reports and the privacy of the source of a dream, i.e. the privacy of dream genesis. Starting from the distanced dream rapport, professional dream analysis attempts to arrive at individual appropriation. This means:
- Paying attention to the dreamer's day residues and exploring them together,
- determining the system of relevances and preferences of the reporter,
- establishing a motivational context,
- contextualizing the dream with regard to the dreamer's situation in life and the therapeutic relationship,
- retroactively integrating the dream report into a coherent dynamic organization.

Dream memories are static or processual and they manifest themselves as individual impressions or whole sequences. After waking up, the remembered impressions are often perceived as findings or fragments of more extensive dreams. As a consequence, the dreamer engages in retroactive sequencing and narrativization. He creates a narrative construction site. He is communicating findings and fragments, which can be combined into bigger compositions by the joint exploration of the dreamer's situation in life and the expertise of the professional commentator.

How do you turn a narrative building site into a narrative structure? On the basis of an *assumption* and with the aid of a *construction*. The *assumption* is that a dream—as a regressive mental phenomenon—creates relief, the *construction* is that the dream dialogue retroactively turns the narrative building site into a fully developed narrative.

The hallucinated dream impressions were experienced as real in the dreamer's sleep. The dream impressions transform reality. The strategy of dream analysis, as suggested in Freud's pioneering discoveries (Freud 1953 [1900]), is based on precisely this tension between world transformation as motivated appropriation and reporting observations and impressions. The material of nightly dreams is comprised of impressions from waking life. These impressions are—if one goes along with the idea that dream work is mental appropriation work—subjected in the dream to the regime of a self-centered wish regulation and made suitable for presenting a wish-fear-defense scenario. The way from a distanced dream rapport to the individual appropriation follows a narrative logic (Boothe 2004), navigating between expectation and fulfillment within a personal system of preferences. The orientation towards important concerns of the dreamer can then be made useful for the practice of dream analysis in a therapeutic context.

In conclusion, there are several points to be emphasized. On the one hand, the release of Freud's *The Interpretation of Dreams* in 1900 initiated psychophysiological dream research; on the other hand, psychoanalysis laid the foundations for a theory of memory work as a set of dramaturgical rules employed by the dreamer to transform everyday life into dream reality under the horizon of wish-oriented mentality. Dreaming puts on display sensations which present themselves as characters, stage props, sceneries and actions without exhibiting any organizing principle. They lie in front of us as objects to be gazed at. They do not reveal their origin and they do not indicate their native environment. Communicating a dream is a search for words in order to grab hold of fleeting images which would otherwise disappear quickly and deny us any chance of gaining further access to them. The dream narrative is the prototypical form of unreliable communication in everyday life: First of all, its referentiality is unreliable; secondly, the report is rarely transparent and hardly comprehensible; third, the dream articulation is not self-sufficient, rather, it is a form of unsaturated speech: dream reports demand commenting. Dialogical dream communication enacts an everyday crisis of self-reference: To communicate one's dream is to underline the fact that one is not master in one's own house, stressing one's reliance on the responsive and commenting other when it comes to obtaining self-knowledge. Reporting a dream is a process of articulation on the unstable terrain of fleeting memory, communicating the limits of understanding within the narrative process.

Translated by Philippe Haensler

Works Cited

Boothe, Brigitte. 2000. *Der Traum—100 Jahre nach Freuds Traumdeutung*. Zürich: vdf.

Boothe, Brigitte. 2001. "The Rhetorical Organisation of Dream-Telling." *Counselling and Psychotherapy Research* 1.2: 101–113.

Boothe, Brigitte. 2004. *Der Patient als Erzähler in der Psychotherapie*. Gießen: Psychosozial.

Boothe, Brigitte. 2006. "Wie erzählt man einen Traum, diesen herrlichen Mist, wie porträtiert man seinen Analytiker?" In: Michael Wiegand, Flora von Spreti & Hans Förstl (eds.). *Schlaf und Traum. Neurobiologie, Psychologie, Therapie*. Stuttgart: Schattauer. 159–170.

Boothe, Brigitte. 2008. "Die Ordnung der Sprache im Traum." In: Brigitte Boothe (ed.). *Ordnung und Außer-Ordnung. Zwischen Erhalt und tödlicher Bürde.* Bern: Huber. 288–306.

Domhoff, G. William. 2005. "Refocusing the Neurocognitive Approach to Dreams: A Critique of the Hobson versus Solms Debate." *Dreaming* 15.1: 3–20.

Freud, Sigmund. 1953 [1900]. "The Interpretation of Dreams." In: *The Standard Edition of the Complete Psychological Works of Sigmund Freud.* Vols. 4/5. London: Hogarth.

Gülich, Elisabeth. 2005. "Unbeschreibbarkeit: Rhetorischer Topos—Gattungsmerkmal—Formulierungsressource." *Gesprächsforschung—Online-Zeitschrift zur verbalen Interaktion* 6: 222–244.

Gülich, Elisabeth & Martin Schöndienst. 1999. "'Das ist unheimlich schwer zu beschreiben.' Formulierungsmuster in Krankheitsbeschreibungen anfallskranker Patienten: differentialdiagnostische und therapeutische Aspekte." *Psychotherapie und Sozialwissenschaft* 1.3: 199–227.

Hanke, Michael. 2001. *Kommunikation und Erzählung. Zur narrativen Vergemeinschaftungspraxis am Beispiel konversationellen Traumerzählens.* Würzburg: Königshausen & Neumann.

Hobson, J. Allan. & Robert W. McCarley. 1977. "The Brain as a Dream State Generator: An Activation-Synthesis Hypothesis of the Dream Process." *The American Journal of Psychiatry* 134.12: 1335–1348.

Kächele, Horst, Cornelia Albani, Anna Buchheim et al. 2006. "Psychoanalytische Verlaufsforschung: Ein deutscher Musterfall Amalia X." *Psyche* 60.5: 387–425.

Kilroe, Patricia A. 2000. "The Dream as Text, The Dream as Narrative." *Dreaming* 10.3: 125–137.

Knudson, Roger M., Alexandra L. Adame & Gillian M. Finocan. 2006. "Significant dreams: repositioning the Self Narrative." *Dreaming* 16.3: 215–222.

Koukkou, Martha & Dietrich Lehmann. 1983. "Dreaming: The functional state-Shift hypothesis. A neuropsychophysio-logical model." *British Journal of Psychiatry* 142.3: 221–231.

Mathys, Hanspeter. 2006. "'Ich hab heut Nacht so einen herrlichen Mist geträumt.' Eine erzählanalytische Untersuchung von Traumberichten." In: Michael Wiegand, Flora von Spreti & Hans Förstl (eds.). *Schlaf und Traum. Neurobiologie, Psychologie, Therapie.* Stuttgart: Schattauer. 141–158.

Mathys, Hanspeter. 2008. "'Ein ganz böser Traum'—Nächtliches Widerfahrnis bei Tageslicht betrachtet." In: Brigitte Boothe (ed.). *Ordnung und Außer-Ordnung. Zwischen Erhalt und tödlicher Bürde.* Bern: Huber. 269–287.

Mosch, Simone. 2012. "Regulative Funktion des Traumes unter neuropsychoanalytischer Perspektive." In: Brigitte Boothe, Andreas Cremonini & Georg Kohler (eds.). *Psychische Struktur und kollektive Praxis*. Würzburg: Königshausen & Neumann. 55–62.

Revonsuo, Antti. 2000. "The reinterpretation of dreams: An evolutionary hypothesis of the function of dreaming." *Behavioral and Brain Sciences* 23: 793–1121.

Solms, Mark. 2000a. "Dreaming and REM sleep are controlled by different brain mechanisms." *Behavioral and Brain Sciences* 23.6: 793–1121.

Solms, Mark. 2000b. "Freudian Dream Theory Today." *Psychologist* 3.12: 618–619.

Solms, Mark & Oliver Turnbull. 2002. *The Brain and the Inner World. An Introduction to the Neuroscience of Subjective Experience*. New York, NY: Other Press.

Strauch, Inge & Barbara Meier. 1996. *In Search of Dreams: Results of Experimental Dream Research*. New York, NY: State University of New York Press.

Thomä, Helmut & Horst Kächele. 2006. *Psychoanalytische Therapie*. Heidelberg: Springer.

Ueding, Gert. 1976. *Einführung in die Rhetorik. Geschichte, Technik, Methode*. Stuttgart: Metzler.

Wiegand, Michael, Flora von Spreti & Hans Förstl (eds.). 2006. *Schlaf und Traum. Neurobiologie, Psychologie, Therapie*. Stuttgart: Schattauer.

Notes on Contributors

ANDREAS VON ARNAULD is director at the Walther Schücking Institute and professor for Public Law, International and European Law at Kiel University. His publications centre around human rights law, international, national and European constitutional law, law and literature, as well as legal theory. He has authored a casebook on International law in 2012, the second edition of which is about to be published. He is the co-editor of the journal *Die Friedens-Warte/Journal for International Peace and Organization*.

CHRISTOPH BIETZ is a TV-journalist and media scientist currently working for the political talk show "Günther Jauch" (ARD) in Berlin. He has recently published his dissertation on the narrativity of TV news (*Die Geschichten der Nachrichten*, WVT 2013), discussing the reality of news as a medial construct deriving from its onto-epistemic status as a narrative text. His studies so far have focused on film analysis, intermedial and structuralist narratology, media theory and psychoanalytical film theory. He has also been working as a news-journalist and reporter for n-tv and RTL Television in Cologne.

BRIGITTE BOOTHE was professor for Clinical Psychology at Zürich University (until 2013), where she also acted as director of the Master of Advanced Studies in Psychoanalytic Psychotherapy (MASP). She has published books on female development in a psychoanalytic view, on psychotherapy, psychoanalysis, narrative and interaction, and (co-)edited many volumes on empirical and conceptual matters in the book series *Psychoanalyse im Dialog* and *Interpretation Interdisziplinär*. Among her most recent works are *Frauen in Psychotherapie* (co-edited with Anita Riecher-Rössler, 2013) and *Wenn doch nur—ach hätt ich bloss: Die Anatomie des Wunsches* (2013).

MATTHIAS BRÜTSCH is senior lecturer in Film Studies at the University of Zurich. He is the author of *Traumbühne Kino: Der Traum als filmtheoretische Metapher und narratives Motiv (Screening the Dream: Cinematic Metaphors, Oneiric Narration and the Function of Dreams in Film*, Schüren 2011; PhD thesis) and a number of articles on film narratology and aesthetics. He has co-directed the International Short Film Festival Winterthur from 1999–2003, worked as a script analyst for the Zurich Film Foundation from 2003–2007 and has been a member of both the board of trustees of the Swiss Arts Council and the promotion agency Swiss Films from 2007–2011.

BEATRICE DERNBACH has been professor for Journalism at the Technische Hochschule Nürnberg since March 2014. From October 1999 to February 2014 she taught and pursued research in the field of journalism, media and communication at the University of Applied Sciences Bremen. She has published books on specialised journalism, the relation between journalism and public relations, and science communication. Her main interest is in the question how journalists and other communication experts can explain complex information in a way people understand—one possibility being storytelling. Before starting her academic career, she worked as an editorial journalist at a newspaper.

ANDREAS ELTER has been professor of Journalism at Macromedia University for Media and Communication in Cologne and in Berlin since 2007; currently, he is head of the televisual department at the ARD-ZDF-Medienakademie. He taught at the universities of Leipzig, Cologne and Munich and carried out research at the German Historical Institute in Washington, the national archives in Maryland and Duke University in North Carolina. He is a journalist, editor, and director and has worked for various television channels including ZDF, WDR and RTL. He has published books on politics as well as the history of US-media policy in wartime, and media strategies of terror groups. His book publications include *Die Kriegsverkäufer: Geschichte der US-Propaganda 1917–2005* (Suhrkamp 2005) and *Propaganda der Tat: Die RAF und die Medien* (Suhrkamp 2008).

PETER HÜHN is professor of English Literature at Hamburg University (retired since 2005). He has published books and articles on the theory of poetry and the history of British poetry, narratology, the application of narratology to poetry analysis, detective and crime fiction. He is author of *Geschichte der englischen Lyrik* (Francke, 1995), *Eventfulness in British Fiction* (De Gruyter, 2010), co-author of *Der Entwicklungsroman in Europa und Übersee* (with Heinz Hillmann, 2001), *Die europäische Lyrik seit der Antike* (with Heinz Hillmann, 2005), *The Narratological Analysis of Lyric Poetry: Studies in English Poetry* (with Jens Kiefer, 2005), *Lyrik und Narratologie: Textanalysen zu deutschsprachigen Gedichten* (with Jörg Schönert and Malte Stein, 2007), co-editor of the *Handbook of Narratology* (with John Pier, Wolf Schmid and Jörg Schönert, 2009), and editor-in-chief of the online edition of the *Living Handbook of Narratology* (since 2010) and of the second print edition of the *Handbook of Narratology* (2014).

STEPHAN JAEGER is Full Professor of German Studies and Head of the Department of German and Slavic Studies at the University of Manitoba.

He has published extensively on historiographical narratology, history and literature, documentary history in historiography, film, and the museum, representations of war, and romantic and modern poetry. He has published two monographs, including *Performative Geschichtsschreibung* (De Gruyter 2011), and co-edited five books, most recently *Fighting Words and Images: Representing War Across the Disciplines* (with Elena V. Baraban and Adam Muller, 2012) and a special issue of *Seminar* (Feb. 2014): *Representations of German War Experiences*. He is co-coordinator of the Interdisciplinary Network *War and Violence* of the German Studies Association.

LIESBETH KORTHALS ALTES is professor of general literature and literary theory at the University of Groningen. She is Chair of the Department of Arts, Culture and Media, Director of the Groningen Research Institute for the Study of Culture, and Director of studies of the research masters Literary and Cultural Studies at the University of Groningen, Faculty of Arts. She has published widely on narrative theory, the relation between literature and values, ethics, as well as on modern French literature. Her recent publications include *Authorship Revisited: Conceptions of Authorship around 1900 and 2000* (co-edited with Gillis Jan Dorleijn and Ralf Grüttemeier, 2010), "The End of Literature as a Basis for a Renewed Disciplinarity", in: *Grenzen der Literatur* (2009), and *Ethos and Narrative Interpretation: The Negotiation of Values in Fiction* (University of Nebraska Press 2014).

MARKUS KUHN is professor of media studies at the University of Hamburg. His research interests are film and transmedial narratology, web series, genre theory, biographical pictures, transmedia storytelling, narration on the Internet, comic and animation studies. From 2008 to 2009, he was a postdoctoral research scholar at the University of Bremen, where he supervised the doctoral research group "Textuality of Film". His dissertation *Filmnarratologie: Ein erzähltheoretisches Analysemodell* was awarded the graduate prize by the "Studienstiftung Hamburg" in 2009 and was published in 2011 at De Gruyter (available as paperback since 2013). Recent publications include *Filmwissenschaftliche Genreanalyse: Eine Einführung* (ed., with Irina Scheidgen and Nicola V. Weber, 2013).

URI MARGOLIN is professor emeritus of Comparative Literature at the University of Alberta, Edmonton, Canada. His areas of research and publication include literary meta-theory and methodology, classical and post-classical narratology, possible-worlds semantics, theory of character and Soviet semiotics (the Moscow-Tartu school). He has published over

70 articles in international professional journals and in collective volumes, including several volumes of the *Narratologia* series.

GUNTHER MARTENS is a Research Professor of German Literature at the Department of Literary Studies at Ghent University. He is co-director of the Ghent Centre for Digital Humanities and executive board member of the European Narratology Network and the Internationale Robert Musil Gesellschaft. His research interests include German literature, rhetorical narratology and the encyclopedic novel. Relevant publications include: *Narrative Unreliability in the Twentieth-Century First-Person Novel* (as co-editor, with Elke D'hoker, 2008); "Channelling Figurativity through Narrative: the Paranarrative in Fiction and Non-fiction", in: *Language and Literature* 2013 (with Benjamin Biebuyck); "Narratorial Strategies in Drama and Theatre: a Contribution to Transmedial Narratology", in: *Beyond Classical Narration* (with Helena Elshout, 2014).

STEFAN MARTINI is a legal clerk in Berlin and research assistant for Public Law at Kiel University with Prof. Dr. Andreas von Arnauld. His doctoral thesis discusses comparative reasoning by constitutional courts. His research interests are constitutional law thinking, comparative law, sociology of law, as well as law and literature. Upcoming is a report on constitutional reasoning by the German Federal Constitutional Court (with Michaela Hailbronner, in: *Constitutional Reasoning in a Comparative Perspective*). Martini is also a founding editor of a young scholars' blog in public law called juwiss.de.

JARMILA MILDORF did her PhD in sociolinguistics at the University of Aberdeen and is now a Senior Lecturer for English language and literature at the University of Paderborn. Her research interests are in narratology, sociolinguistics, dialogue studies, stylistics, gender studies, as well as literature and medicine. She is the author of *Storying Domestic Violence: Constructions and Stereotypes of Abuse in the Discourse of General Practitioners* (University of Nebraska Press 2007) and has co-edited five books, among them *Narrative: Knowing, Living, Telling* (with Matti Hyvärinen and Kai Mikkonen, special issue of *Partial Answers* 2008) and *Imaginary Dialogues in American Literature and Philosophy: Beyond the Mainstream* (with Till Kinzel, 2014).

ANSGAR NÜNNING is professor of English and American Literature and Cultural Studies at the University of Giessen. He is the founding director of the Giessener Graduiertenzentrum Kulturwissenschaften (GGK), of the International Graduate Centre for the Study of Culture (GCSC), and of the European PhD Network "Literary and Cultural Studies". He has published widely on narrative theory, English and American literature, cultures of memory, and literary and cultural theory, including 15 monographs and text books as well as more than 200 scholarly articles in refereed journals and collections of essays. His narratological publications include articles on narratological approaches and concepts, e.g. unreliable narration, the implied author, multiperspectivity, description, and meta-narration. Recent publications include a special issue on "Recent Trends in Narratology" of the journal *GRM: Germanisch-Romanische-Monatsschrift* (2013).

VERA NÜNNING is professor of English philology at Heidelberg University, where she has also acted as pro-rector for international affairs. She has published books on eighteenth, nineteenth and twentieth century British literature, and (co-)edited 21 volumes on contemporary literature and narrative theory. Her articles deal with narrative theory, gender studies, cultural history from the sixteenth to the nineteenth century, and British literature from the eighteenth to the twenty-first century. Among her most recent works are *New Approaches to Narrative. Cognition—Culture—History* (ed., 2013) and *Ritual and Narrative* (co-edited with Jan Rupp and Gregor Ahn, 2013). She was a fellow in two Institutes of Advanced Studies and is associate editor of two book series and the international journal *English Studies*.

BO PETTERSSON is Professor of American Literature and former Head of English at the Department of Modern Languages, University of Helsinki. He has published widely on Anglo-American literature in relation to literary, narrative and metaphor theory, and serves or has served on a range of national and international boards related to literary studies, publishing and academic exchange. He is now the director of the interdisciplinary research community "Interfaces between Language, Literature and Culture" at the University of Helsinki. In 2011, he was elected member of The Finnish Society of Sciences and Letters.

CHRISTINE SCHWANECKE is coordinator of the International PhD Programme 'Literary and Cultural Studies' (IPP) at Justus Liebig University, Giessen (Germany). She has published articles on inter-mediality, metareference and generic hybridity as well as a monograph, *Intermedial Storytelling: Thematisation, Imitation and Incorporation of Photography in English and American Fiction at the Turn of the 21st Century* (WVT 2013). Since 2012, she has been writing her second thesis (Habilitation), concept-tualizing a narratology of drama. She co-edited a volume on *The Cultural*

Dynamics of Generic Change in Contemporary Fiction (with Michael Basseler and Ansgar Nünning, 2013).

DRAGICA STOJKOVIĆ has studied psychology and comparative literature at the University of Zürich and is about to finish her PhD on suicide notes. She is a practicing psychoanalyst and is doing her training at the Freud-Institute Zürich. She contributed to the editorial board of the student's magazine *aware*, the literature magazine *delirium*, as well as the *Journal für Psychoanalyse*; current editorial contributions for *Psychoscope* and *che vuoi?*. Her research interests are: Suicide notes; structure, process, and function of wish(ing) and dream(ing); theory of language, rhetoric and poetology.

ROBERT VOGT is a member of the European PhDnet-Network "Literary and Cultural Studies" and the International Graduate Centre for the Study of Culture (GCSC) at the Justus-Liebig-University Giessen. His dissertation project focuses on unreliable narration. His publications include essays on narrative unreliability in literature and film, transmediality, turning points, and on the American short story writer Ambrose Bierce.

Index

Adame, Alexandra L. 418
Akutagawa, Ryonosuke
   "In a Grove" 118
Albani, Cornelia 417
Albee, Edward
   Who's afraid of Virginia Woolf 210 f.
Alber, Jan 94
Alexy, Robert 348, 358, 366
Allrath, Gaby 39, 49, 101, 197, 234, 236, 305, 315, 331, 337
Altman, Rick 293
Altmeppen, Klaus D. 307
Àlvarez Amorós, José A. 137, 141
Amis, Kingsley
   The Green Man 230 f.
Amis, Martin
   Money: A Suicide Note 96
Amossy, Ruth 62 f., 78
Anastasopoulos, Dimitri 189
Anderson, Benedict 353, 355
Anderson, Emily R. 197
Angot, Christine 59–62
   Sujet Angot 17, 59 f., 62–65, 67–70, 75–78
   Les Autres 64
Ankersmit, Frank 376
Anthony, Geraldine 410
Apuleius
   The Golden Ass 110, 115, 123
The Arabian Nights. Tales from A Thousand and One Nights 123
Archibald, Elizabeth 365
Aristotle, 61–63, 331
Armstrong, Paul B. 120
Arnauld, Andreas von 23, 24, 350–352, 357 f.
Arndt, Dominik 355
Assmann, Aleida 384
Audi, Robert 33
Augstein, Jakob 313
Ayckbourn, Alan
   Woman in Mind 207, 212

Bach, Michaela 282
Balzer, Wolfgang 331
Banville, John
   Shroud 113
   The Book of Evidence 113 f.
Baringhorst, Sigrid 333
Barletta, Norma 159
Barsky, Arthur J. 403
Barthes, Roland 275, 280, 284, 286
Bartone, Christopher A. 320
Bartz, Christina 292
Baum, Achim 306
Baumert, Dieter P. 313
Beckett, Samuel
   Krapp's Last Tape 193
Beidler, Peter G. 233
Benhabib, Seyla 353
Bennett, James R. 192
Bentele, Günter 308 f.
Bergmann, Jens 322
Bergmann, Klaus 386
Berning, Nora 323
Berry, David T. R. 398 f.
Bierce, Ambrose
   "An Occurrence at Owl Creek Bridge" 12, 92, 133, 145, 156, 226
   "Oil of Dog" 222
Bietz, Christoph 22, 276, 283, 290
Bilandzic, Helena 95
Binet, Laurent
   HHhH 155, 164–167
The Blair Witch Project 237–240, 260
Blöbaum, Bernd 306, 312 f.
Bloch, Marc 382
Blum, Deborah 320
Boccaccio, Giovanni
   Decamerone 123
Bode, Christoph 133, 397, 399

436 Index

Booth, Wayne C. 2 f., 5 f., 9, 12, 18, 61, 69, 70, 72, 83, 90, 109, 116, 131 f., 134, 156 f., 173, 189 f., 201, 214, 227 f., 234, 287, 330, 354, 381
Boothe, Brigitte 25, 417 f., 420, 425
Bordwell, David 282
Bortolussi, Marisa 64, 145, 147
Bosch, Nikolaus 352
Bramberger, Andrea 365
Brigden, Susan 183
Brontë, Charlotte
   Jane Eyre 115
Browning, Christopher R. 385
Bruner, Jerome 61
Brunkhorst, Hauke 329
Brunkhorst, Martin 192
Brütsch, Matthias 20 f., 158, 221–223, 241
Buchheim, Anna 417
Bumke, Ulrike 357
Burgess, Jean 253, 257, 259
Burke, Peter 383
Burkhardt, Steffen 311
Burns, Robert P. 357
Burt, Ronald S. 1, 3, 7, 85
Busselle, Rick 95
Butte, George 61
C'est arrive près de chez vous / Man Bites Dog 226

Call, Josep 2
Campbell, Angus 334
Carpenter, Malinda 2
Carrard, Philippe 375, 385
Carroll, Noël 237
Carver, Raymond
   "Blackbird Pie" 121
Cervantes, Miguel de
   Don Quixote 47, 124
Chang, Luke J. 89
Charon, Rita 404, 406, 408
Chassan, Jack B. 398
Chatman, Seymour 39, 67, 69, 131 f., 135, 197, 275, 281, 292 f.
Chaucer, Geoffrey
   Canterbury Tales 103, 123 f.

Christie, Agatha 121
   The Murder of Roger Ackroyd 12, 91 f., 101, 133
   Witness for the Prosecution 366
Claassen, Eefje 143
Clarke, Amanda 410
Cohn, Dorrit 155 f., 165,
Collins, Wilkie
   The Moonstone 89 f.
Cosmides, Leda 2
Courtés, Joseph 66
Cover, Robert M. 353
Crosman, Inge W. 66
Cullen, Jim 353
Culler, Jonathan 66, 174, 177 f., 274 f., 286
Currie, Gregory 40, 51, 131
Currie, Mark 329
Curtius, Ernst R. 77
Cytowic, Richard E. 397, 406–408

D'hoker, Elke 15, 102, 157, 197, 432
Damaška, Mirjan R. 349
Dann, Otto 374
Darbishire, Helen 179
DasGupta, Sayantani 404 f.
David Holzman's Diary 225, 260
Davies, Hugh S. 180
Davis, Joshua 253, 259
Defoe, Daniel
   Moll Flanders 124
Dehm, Ursula 320
Deleyto, Celestino 293
DelVecchio Good, Mary-Jo 406
Dernbach, Beatrice 6, 19, 22 f., 32, 305, 307
Deuze, Mark 323
Dickens, Charles 319
   David Copperfield 140
Dijk, Teun van 42
Diski, Jenny
   Like Mother 124
Dixon, Peter 64, 145, 147
Doležel, Lubomir 142, 147, 378,
Doll, Bradley B. 89
Doll, Martin 161, 163

Domańska, Ewa 376
Domhoff, G. William 415
Donges, Patrick 333
Durst, Uwe 228 f., 240
Dutilleul, Philippe 162

Easthope, Antony 174, 176, 178
Eggs, Ekkehard 78
Eliot, Thomas S.
    "The Love Song of J. Alfred Prufrock" 122
Ellis, Bret Easton
    American Psycho 131, 133, 138f., 148, 160 f.
Ellis, Jack C. 260
Elsner, Monika 293
Engisch, Karl 356
Evans, Richard J. 372

Faulkner, William
    The Sound and the Fury 110
    "A Rose for Emily" 116
Ferenz, Volker 189
Finocan, Gillian M. 418
Fleischer, Wolfgang 384
Fludernik, Monika 132 f., 155, 191, 197, 241, 246
Foner, Eric 335
Ford, Ford Madox
    The Good Soldier 120 f., 131
    Parade's End 120 f.
Förstl, Hans 415
Frayn, Michael
    Spies 121
Freud, Sigmund 202
    The Interpretation of Dreams 416, 420–425
Fricker, Elizabeth 85
Friedländer, Saul 371–373, 378, 386 f.
Friedman, Donald M. 183
Friel, Brian
    Dancing at Lughnasa 205 f.

Gadamer, Hans-Georg 71, 158
Gaige, Amity
    Schroder 113 f.

Galinsky, Hans 335
Galtung, Johan 275–277
Garden, Rebecca 397
Gardner, Janet 320
Genette, Gérard 66–68, 133, 275, 279, 293, 350, 352
Gerrig, Richard J. 4
Gibson, Andrew 67
Gilbert, Daniel S. 6
Glasersfeld, Ernst von 278
Glavinic, Thomas 162
Goethe, Johann Wolfgang
    Die Wahlverwandtschaften 159
Goffman, Erving 16, 60, 75–77, 89, 93, 159, 399
Goldblatt, Howard 112
Good, Byron J. 406
Good, David A. 46
Goodheart, Eugene 120
Görke, Alexander 306, 312
Götsch, Katja 330
Graesser, Arthur C. 143 f.
Grafton, Anthony 386
Graham, Caroline 321
Graham, Kenneth J. E. 183
Granacher, Robert P. 398 f.
Green, Joshua 253, 257, 259
Green, Melanie C. 95
Green, Ruth 398
Greenblatt, Stephen 184
Greimas, Algirdas J. 66
Greven, Michael 332
Grey, Denise 410
Grice, H. Paul H. 8–11, 17, 47–49, 53, 55, 73 f., 83, 88, 96–98, 103, 402
Groom, Winston
    Forrest Gump 110, 122, 149
Gülich, Elisabeth 417, 420
Gurin, Gerald 334

Habermas, Jürgen 7, 46, 73 f., 84, 329
Hall, Harold V. 399
Hänchen, Udo 384
Hannen, Thomas A. 183
Hannken-Illjes, Kati 357 f.
Hansen, Per Krogh 109, 402

Hardwig, John   397
Hare, Cyril
   "It Takes Two…"   203
Harker, W. John   249
Harpold, Terry   251
Harris, Joanne
   blueeyedboy   119 f.
Hartmann, Britta   12, 87, 89 f., 133, 222
Haskell, Thomas L.   377
Haslett, Adam
   "The Good Doctor"   118
Hastings Floyd, Virginia   202
Hattendorf, Manfred   21, 254–256
Haußecker, Nicole   275
Hawthorne, Nathaniel
   "Wakefield"   117 f., 122
Hayward, John   173
Heale, Elizabeth   183
Heijnk, Stefan   323
Heinen, Sandra   64
Helbig, Jörg   209, 222, 225
Henslin, James M.   89
Herman, David   135, 145, 409
Hesse, Beatrix   189, 203 f.
Heun, Werner   356
Heyd, Theresa   8 f., 15, 46 f., 73, 88, 98, 396
Hickethier, Knut   255
Hobson, J. Allan   424
Homer
   Ulysses   103
   The Odyssey   122 f.
Hörmann, Stefanie   275, 277
Horne, Jules
   Gorgeous Avatar   207, 209 f.
Horowitz, Anthony
   Mindgame   207 f., 214
Horstkotte, Martin   228, 230 f., 234 f.
Hovland, Carl D.   309
Howard, Kenneth I.   403
Howell, Martha   372, 374
Hugo, Victor
   Les Misérables   95
Hühn, Peter   19, 124, 173–175, 191, 196
Hunter, Kathryn M.   161, 167, 399

Ishiguro, Kazuo
   The Remains of the Day   88, 111, 122, 132, 214, 222
Iversen, Stefan   144

Jaeger, Stephan   21 f., 24 f., 377 f., 385 f.
Jahn, Manfred   132, 191, 193, 199, 207, 282 f.
Jakobs, Hans-Jürgen   313
James, Henry   117, 194
   The Turn of the Screw   111, 119, 133, 147 f., 227 f., 230–240
   "The Beast in the Jungle"   111
   Daisy Miller   121 f.
   What Maisie Knew   132
Janis, Irving L.   309
Jannidis, Fotis   146
Jess-Cooke, Carolyn
   The Boy Who Could See Demons   146 f.
Johnson, Edward W.   319
Johnson, Terry
   Hysteria   202
Johnston, Jane   321
Joyce, James
   A Portrait of the Artist as a Young Man   132
Junker, Detlef   375

Kaase, Max   329
Kächele, Horst   417
Kaiz, Marjorie   403
The Kalevala   122
Kanwischer, Simon   352, 365
Keegan, Paul   173, 184, 185
Kehlmann, Daniel
   Die Vermessung der Welt/Measuring the World   165 f.
Kelley, Harold H.   309
Kellner, Hans   376
Kerrigan, John   185
Kesey, Ken
   One Flew Over the Cuckoo's Nest   148
Kiefer, Jens   174
Kilroe, Patricia A.   418
Kindt, Tom   15, 46–48, 131, 156, 201
Klaus, Elisabeth   321

Kleinsteuber, Hans J.   318
Klettke, Bianca   143
Knight, Sabina   112
Knudson, Roger M.   418
Koch, Jonas   224, 274
Kocka, Jürgen   376
Koebner, Thomas   247
Kohring, Matthias   306, 309 f.
Köppe, Tilmann   15, 95, 156, 201
Korthals Altes, Liesbeth   6, 16 f., 21, 60, 62, 64, 68, 74, 78 f., 158
Koschorke, Albrecht   104
Koselleck, Reinhart   375
Kosinski, Jerzy
    Being There   110
Koukkou, Martha   416
Kracauer, Siegfried   292
Kreiswirth, Martin   275
Kuhn, Markus   19, 21, 247, 250 f., 253, 258–260, 282 f.
Kummer, Tom   161, 314, 316
Küppers, Julia   361

Laass, Eva   189, 193, 198 f., 201, 211, 222, 225
Labov, William   357, 359, 361 f.
LaBute, Neil
    autobahn, A Short-Play Cycle   204 f.
Ladeur, Karl-Heinz   348
Lahde, Maurice   222, 225
Lamarque, Peter   275
Lampert, Marie   318
Lang, Andrej   361
Langenbucher, Wolfgang R.   313
Lasser, Mitchel de S.-O.-l'E   351
Laucken, Uwe   7, 33, 96
Leech, Geoffrey   9, 97, 402
Lehmann, Dietrich   415
Lejeune, Philippe   62
Lenckner, Theodor   352
Lewis, David K.   43, 46, 284
Liebes, Tamar   277
Liptay, Fabienne   12, 193, 208, 222, 225
Littell, Jonathan
    Les Bienveillantes   155, 166 f.
    Carnets de Homs   167

lonelygirl15   253 f., 257–260
Lu, Xun
    „Diary of a Madman"   112
Lubbock, Percy   283
Lucian of Samosata
    A True Story   123
Luhmann, Niklas   1, 176–178, 288, 292, 295, 305, 330, 347
Lünenborg, Margreth   312, 321

Macfie, Alexander Lyon   377 f.
Malik, Maja   307, 323
Marcou, Phillio   331
Marcus, Amit   174, 185
Margolin, Uri   15 f., 52, 87, 91, 95, 131
Marsack, Peter   320
Martens, Gunther   12, 15, 19, 91, 102, 156 f., 197, 380
Martin, John   74
Martin, Mary P.   16, 67, 70, 87–89, 96 f., 103, 204 f., 224, 226
Martínez, Matías   40, 133, 135, 226 f.
Mathys, Hanspeter   417 f.
Maupassant, Guy de
    „'The Diary of a Madman"   111 f.
    "La Parure"/"The Necklace"   203
McCarley, Robert W.   424
McEwan, Ian
    "Dead as They Come"   73, 131, 222, 224, 234
    Atonement   93, 101, 131, 134, 156
    Enduring Love   148
McGregor, Douglas   330
McHale, Brian   117
McLane, Betsy A.   260
Mead, George H.   176
Meier, Barbara   420
Meier, Klaus   306
Meister, Jan C.   189
Meizoz, Jérôme   63 f.
Melville, Herman
    Moby-Dick   117
Menhard, Felicitas   89, 100, 131
Merten, Klaus   306, 333
Meyer, Michael   6
Mildorf, Jarmila   7, 14, 25, 86, 400, 409

Miller, Warren E.   334
Möllering, Guido   6 f., 85, 96
Möllers, Christoph   353
Mommsen, Wolfgang   375 f., 377
Monteyne, David   336
Montfort, Nick   251
Montgomery, Kathryn   395, 405 f.
Morrison, Kristin   193
Mosch, Simone   415
Moss, Pamela A.   85
Müller, Julia   320
Müller, Marion   334, 337
Müller, Philipp   374 f.
Müller, Rolf-Dieter   383
Müller, Thomas   293
Müller-Funk, Wolfgang   331
Müller-Mall, Sabine   361
Munker, Barbara   259
Munslow, Alun   377, 385, 377 f., 380
Muny, Eike   191, 194
Musick, Marc A. Plato   336

Nabokov, Vladimir
    Pnin   133, 145
    Lolita 112 f., 234
Nash, Christopher   275
Nerhot, Patrick   356
Neuhaus, Stefan   313
Niehaus, Michael   162
Niiniluoto, Ilkka   43
Norrman, Ralf   122
Novick, Peter   375–377
Nünning, Ansgar   10, 20 f., 39, 49 f., 59 f., 65, 68, 70–73, 77 f., 86, 96, 109, 124, 131 f., 134–136, 143, 157 f., 160, 178, 189–191, 193–197, 201 f., 214, 222, 224, 227, 234–236, 246, 248–250, 276, 279, 289, 305, 315, 331, 337, 354, 378, 381, 397, 399, 409
Nünning, Vera   65, 68, 73, 79, 102, 109, 132, 157 f., 160, 189 f., 201 f., 227, 274, 279, 289, 291, 381

Offer, Daniel   403
Olde, Brent   143

Olson, Greta   67 f., 81, 90, 131, 190, 197, 202, 274, 381
Orgad, Liav   353
Orth, Dominik   222, 225

Palahniuk, Chuck
    Fight Club   133, 147
Palmer, Alan   146, 148
Panja, Shormishta   183
Parsons, Talcott   396
Patalong, Frank   259
Patron, Sylvie   67
Pavčnik, Marijan   356
Peeters, Wim   162
Pendas, Devin   382–385
Perkins Gilman, Charlotte
    "The Yellow Wallpaper"   140, 222
Perry, Menakhem   18, 115–117, 121
Petermann, Franz   7, 85
Pettersson, Bo   18, 91, 109 f., 114, 121 f., 227
Petzold, Jochen   173 f., 176
Pfister, Manfred   197 f., 201
Pfister, Réné   317
Pinter, Harold
    Landscape   193
Phelan, James   4, 10, 16, 39, 48, 67, 69–71, 87–89, 97, 100, 102 f., 109, 112–114, 117, 131 f., 135, 156 f., 184 f., 201, 204 f., 224, 226, 381, 402 f., 405, 410
Phillips, Jennifer   131
Plato   124, 331
Plato, Alexander von   383 f.
Poe, Edgar Allan
    "The Tell-Tale Heart"   132, 138, 140 f.
Poirier, Joseph G.   399
Poppe, Sandra   222, 225
Pörksen, Bernhard   306, 319, 322
Porlezza, Colin   322
Pornpitakpan, Chanthika   7
Pratt, Mary L.   38, 47
Prevenier, Walter   372, 374
Price, Richard
    Alabi's World   387

Prince, Gerald 275, 280
Pynchon, Thomas
    The Crying of Lot 49 133

Rabatel, Alain 61
Rabinowitz, Peter J. 77, 156, 158, 170
Radler, Christian 338
Radley, Alan 398
Raether, Elisabeth 322
Rakove, Jack N. 355
Rank, Otto 365
Rashomon 118
Rebholz, Ronald A. 181, 185
Reinfandt, Christoph 374, 379
Reisinger, Peter 375
Reitze, Helmut 308
Rescher, Nicholas 43, 284
Revonsuo, Antti 415
Richardson, Brian 164, 189, 191–194, 196, 198, 199
Ricks, Christopher 173, 184
Ricoeur, Paul 280 f., 379
Ridder, Christa-Maria 308
Riggan, William 110 f., 123, 131 f., 207
Rimmon-Kenan, Shlomith 132 f., 135, 275, 287, 399
Rodenberger, Axel 371 f., 386
Rogers, Richard 396, 398, 400–402
Rohwer-Happe, Gislind 3, 173, 189, 193
Roth, Dieter 334
Röttger, Ulrike 332 f.
Rousseau, Denise M. 1, 3, 7, 85
Rühl, Manfred 306
Rüsen Jörn 375 f.
Ruß-Mohl, Stephan 322
Rüth, Axel 378 f.
Ryan, Marie-Laure 135–138, 142, 144, 147, 160, 165, 189, 251, 280 f., 283, 285, 287–289, 296

Sanna, Lawrence J. 163
Sarcinelli, Ulrich 329
Sayers, Dorothy L. 121
Schaeffer, Jean-Marie 67
Schäuble, Johannes 352
Scheffel, Michael 40, 133, 135, 226 f.

Schiller, Dan 277, 292
Schipper, Marc 7, 85
Schlögel, Karl 388
Schmid, Wolf 275, 288, 293
Schmidt, Siegfried J. 306
Schneider, Karsten 349
Schneider, Ralf 143, 145 f.
Scholl, Armin 323
Schöndienst, Martin 420
Schönert, Jörg 191
Schönherr, Nicole 383 f.
Schröder, Arne 333
Schulz, Winfried 333
Schwarz, Norbert 163
Schweer, Martin K.W. 7, 85, 330
Scott, Charles P. 311
Selincourt, Ernest de 179
Semino, Elena 136, 143
Shaffer, Peter
    Amadeus 192 f., 206
Shakespeare, William 95, 174, 185
    King Lear 110
Shanley, John Patrick
    Doubt 212, 214
Shapiro, Johanna 404
Shen, Dan 100, 132, 399
Shklovsky, Viktor 101
Sidler, Nikolaus 365
Simanowski, Roberto 253
Simon, Ulrike 316
Simonis, Annette 228 f., 233, 237
Sitkin, Sim B. 1, 3, 7, 85
Skalin, Lars-Åke 122
Skurnik, Ian 163
Smith, Susan 159
Socha, Monika 3
Solbach, Andreas 34
Solms, Mark 415
Sommer, Roy 191, 193–195, 213, 279
Spangenberg, Peter M. 293
Sperber, Dan 1 f., 9, 84, 96–98
Spiegel, Simon 229, 239, 241
Spreti, Flora von 416
Staes, Toon 160
Stanzel, Franz K. 282
Staves, Susan 101

Stein, Lynda A. R. 396
Steller, Max 49
Sternberg, Meir 115–117, 121
Sterne, Laurence
    Tristram Shandy 110
Stoppard, Tom
    Travesties 192 f., 206 f.
Strauch, Inge 420
Suleiman, Susan R. 66
Sulzbacher, Laura 3
Surkamp, Carola 147 f.
Sydow, Jörg 6 f., 96

Tannen, Deborah 408, 413
Taylor, Frederick 371
Thies, Barbara 7, 85, 330
Thimm, Tanja 318
Thoene, Tina 222
Thomä, Helmut 417
Todorov, Tzvetan 20, 66, 221, 228 f.,
    231, 233, 236 f., 239, 243
Tomasello, Michael 2
Tooby, John 2
Toolan, Michael J. 282, 286
Tozzi, Verónica 384
Trivers, Robert 112
Trueman, John 320
Turnbull, Oliver 415
Turner, Mark 280
Twain, Mark 319
    The Adventures of Huckleberry Finn 110,
    122, 131, 222, 229, 234, 236
Twitchell, James B. 365

Ueding, Gert 423

Van 't Wout, Mascha 89
Vargas Llosa, Mario 95
Vincent-Marrelli, Jocelyne 46, 48, 55
Vogt, Robert 12, 18, 20, 22, 87, 133, 145,
    157, 197, 202, 224, 227
Voltaire
    Candide 110
Vossen, Ursula 247

Waletzky, Joshua 359, 362
Wall, Kathleen 77, 88, 214, 296
Wallace, David Foster 164
Wallisch, Gianluca 319
Walsh, Richard 67, 132, 168
Waters, Sarah
    The Little Stranger 110–111
Waugh, Linda R. 159
Weischenberg, Siegfried 306, 323
Wespe, Rolf 318
White, Hayden 41, 376, 388
Widera, Thomas 383 f.
Wiegand, Michael 415
Wiemer-Hastings, Katja 144
Williams, Bernard 33, 46 f., 55
Wilson, Deirdre 9, 96–98
Wilson, John 336
Wintgens, Luc J. 358
Wolf, Werner 75 f.
Wolf, Yvonne 193, 222, 225
Wolfe, Tom 319
Woolf, Virginia
    "Together and Apart" 120 f.
Wordsworth, William
    "The World Is Too Much With Us"
    178–180, 184 f.
Wörtche, Thomas 228 f.
Wyatt, Sir Thomas
    "They Flee from Me that Sometime
    Did Me Seek" 180–185
    "My Lute, Awake" 185

Yacobi, Tamar 52, 60, 68, 91, 109, 131,
    156, 246, 354

Zanichelli, Marta 322
Zarefsky, David 335
Zerweck, Bruno 68, 123, 148, 157, 197,
    234, 381
Zipfel, Frank 15, 133, 137, 140, 145, 156,
    175
Zunshine, Lisa 61, 99, 144, 146 f.
Zusak, Markus
    The Book Thief 124
Zymner, Rüdiger 175

www.ingramcontent.com/pod-product-compliance
Lightning Source LLC
Chambersburg PA
CBHW071808230426
43670CB00013B/2396